PEARSON

ALWAYS

Jonathan Berk • Peter DeMarzo • Jarrad Harford

Fundamentals of Corporate Finance

Custom Edition for FIN 320 California State University Fullerton

Taken from:
Fundamentals of Corporate Finance, Third Edition
by Jonathan Berk, Peter DeMarzo, and Jarrad Harford

Pearson Learning Solutions, 501 Boylston Street, Suite 900, Boston, MA 02116
A Pearson Education Company
www.pearsoned.com

Printed in the United States of America

4 5 6 7 8 9 10 v092 18 17 16 15

000200010271906526

MS

ISBN 10: 1-269-93935-1
ISBN 13: 978-1-269-93935-5

CALIFORNIA STATE UNIVERSITY, FULLERTON

Mihaylo College of Business and Economics
Department of Finance, SGMH 5113, 657–278–2217

Dear Mihaylo Student,

Welcome to **FIN 320, Financial Management I,** your first finance class here at Cal State Fullerton. All business majors are required to take this upper–division core course and for most students it is their first exposure to the fascinating area of finance. As you will soon learn in this class, the primary goal of business is a financial one – to increase the value of the firm. Regardless of your concentration, as a business major it is extremely important for your future professional life that you understand financial concepts. No company can be successful without a solid financial foundation. Should you decide to declare a finance concentration, it would be smart to take FIN 321, **Financial Management II**, next; and to do so as soon as possible, so that you have a very solid foundation for all of the other courses in finance, investments, insurance, real estate and related courses in our Department.

Please note that we have created a custom edition of the text for your class in cooperation with Pearson (http://www.pearson.com/), and with the authors of the hardcover version of our text, Professors Jonathan Berk, Peter DeMarzo and Jarrad Harford. Your custom edition comes with access to MyFinanceLab, which will be used for homework and quizzes in every section of FIN 320. Together, the cost of these instructional tools for you is about $100, less than half what it would cost should we use the hardcover edition of the text, *Fundamentals of Corporate Finance*. We made this decision intentionally to maintain a reasonable cost for your education. Please take advantage of both the custom text and the many important tools available to you in MyFinanceLab to increase your learning and retention of fundamental financial concepts.

Our department is proud that a finance major who graduated from CSUF in 1969 is the major donor for our College! Our building and the College are named after him, Steven G. Mihaylo. He and other alumni believe in passing on the benefits they received here as students to future generations of students, so that they may receive a high quality education and enrich their lives by contributing to society both personally and professionally.

We hope this text will enable you to master the financial concepts included and will be used by you as a reference book when you begin your career. Finance faculty believes that the education you receive here at CSUF will lay the foundation for a very fruitful and fulfilling life. Feel free to provide us with feedback to improve our efforts to provide you with the best finance education available. We have a web page specifically devoted to FIN 320 – please see below.

Sincerely,

Professor Amadeu DaSilva
Coordinator, Finance 320

Professor Carolyn Chang
Chair, Department of Finance

Brief Contents

Detailed Contents

About the Authors

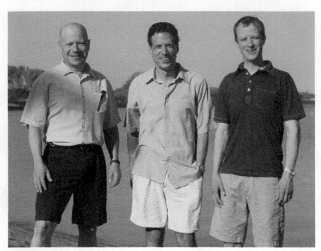

Jonathan Berk, Peter DeMarzo, and Jarrad Harford

Jonathan Berk is the A.P. Giannini Professor of Finance at the Graduate School of Business, Stanford University and is a Research Associate at the National Bureau of Economic Research. Prior to earning his Ph.D., he worked as an Associate at Goldman Sachs (where his education in finance really began).

Professor Berk's research interests in finance include corporate valuation, capital structure, mutual funds, asset pricing, experimental economics, and labor economics. His work has won a number of research awards including the TIAA-CREF Paul A. Samuelson Award, the Smith Breeden Prize, Best Paper of the Year in *The Review of Financial Studies*, and the FAME Research Prize. His paper, "A Critique of Size-Related Anomalies," was selected as one of the two best papers ever published in *The Review of Financial Studies* and one of the top 100 papers published in the history of Oxford University Press. In recognition of his influence on the practice of finance he has received the Bernstein-Fabozzi/Jacobs Levy Award, the Graham and Dodd Award of Excellence, and the Roger F. Murray Prize. He served as an Associate Editor of the *Journal of Finance* for eight years, and is currently a Director of the American Finance Association and is a member of the advisory board of the *Journal of Portfolio Management*. He has also served as an Academic Director of the Financial Management Association. Born in Johannesburg, South Africa, Professor Berk is married, with two daughters, and is an avid skier and biker.

Peter DeMarzo is the Mizuho Financial Group Professor of Finance and former Senior Associate Dean for Academic Affairs at the Stanford Graduate School of Business. He is also a Research Associate at the National Bureau of Economic Research. He currently teaches MBA and Ph.D. courses in Corporate Finance and Financial Modeling. In addition to his experience at the Stanford Graduate School of Business, Professor DeMarzo has taught at the Haas School of Business and the Kellogg Graduate School of Management, and he was a National Fellow at the Hoover Institution.

Professor DeMarzo received the Sloan Teaching Excellence Award at Stanford in 2004 and 2006, and the Earl F. Cheit Outstanding Teaching Award at U.C. Berkeley in 1998. Professor DeMarzo has served as an Associate Editor for *The Review of Financial Studies*, *Financial Management*, and the *B.E. Journals in Economic Analysis and Policy*, as well as a Director of the American Finance Association. He has served as Vice President and President of the Western Finance Association. Professor DeMarzo's research is in the area of corporate investment and financing, asset securitization, financial contracting, and market regulation. His recent work has examined issues of the optimal design of contracts and securities, the regulation of insider trading and broker-dealers bank capital regulation, and the influence of information asymmetries on corporate disclosures and investment. He has received numerous awards including the Western Finance Association Corporate Finance Award and the Barclays Global Investors/Michael Brennan best-paper award from *The Review of Financial Studies*. Professor DeMarzo was born in Whitestone, New York, and is married with three boys. He and his family enjoy hiking, biking, and skiing.

Jarrad Harford is the Marion B. Ingersoll Professor of Finance at the University of Washington. Prior to Washington, Professor Harford taught at the Lundquist College of Business at the University of Oregon. He received his PhD in Finance with a minor in Organizations and Markets from the University of Rochester. Professor Harford has taught the core undergraduate finance course, Business Finance, for over sixteen years, as well as an elective in Mergers and Acquisitions, and "Finance for Non-financial Executives" in the executive education program. He has won numerous awards for his teaching, including the UW Finance Professor of the Year (2010, 2012), Panhellenic/Interfraternity Council Business Professor of the Year Award (2011, 2013), ISMBA Excellence in Teaching Award (2006), and the Wells Fargo Faculty Award for Undergraduate Teaching (2005). Professor Harford is currently a Managing Editor of the *Journal of Financial and Quantitative Analysis*, and serves as an Associate Editor for the *Journal of Financial Economics*, *Review of Financial Studies*, and *Journal of Corporate Finance*. Professor Harford was born in Pennsylvania, is married, and has two sons. He and his family enjoy traveling, hiking, and skiing.

Bridging Theory and Practice

EXAMPLE 7.1
Stock Prices
and Returns

MyFinanceLab

PROBLEM

Suppose you expect Longs Drug Stores to pay an annual dividend of $0.56 per share in the coming year and to trade for $45.50 per share at the end of the year. If investments with equivalent risk to Longs' stock have an expected return of 6.80%, what is the most you would pay today for Longs' stock? What dividend yield and capital gain rate would you expect at this price?

SOLUTION

PLAN

We can use Eq. 7.1 to solve for the beginning price we would pay now (P_0) given our expectations about dividends $(Div_1 = \$0.56)$ and future price $(P_1 = \$45.50)$ and the return we need to expect to earn to be willing to invest $(r_E = 0.068)$. We can then use Eq. 7.2 to calculate the dividend yield and capital gain rate.

EXECUTE

Using Eq. 7.1, we have

$$P_0 = \frac{Div_1 + P_1}{1 + r_E} = \frac{\$0.56 + \$45.50}{1.0680} = \$43.13$$

Referring to Eq. 7.2, we see that at this price, Longs' dividend yield is $Div_1/P_0 = 0.56/43.13 = 1.30\%$. The expected capital gain is $\$45.50 - \$43.13 = \$2.37$ per share, for a capital gain rate of $2.37/43.13 = 5.50\%$.

EVALUATE

At a price of $43.13, Longs' expected total return is $1.30\% + 5.50\% = 6.80\%$, which is equal to its equity cost of capital (the return being paid by investments with equivalent risk to Longs'). This amount is the most we would be willing to pay for Longs' stock. If we paid more, our expected return would be less than 6.8% and we would rather invest elsewhere.

PROBLEM

Ellen is 35 years old and she has decided it is time to plan seriously for her retirement. At the end of each year until she is 65, she will save $10,000 in a retirement account. If the account earns 10% per year, how much will Ellen have in her account at age 65?

SOLUTION

PLAN

As always, we begin with a timeline. In this case, it is helpful to keep track of both the dates and Ellen's age:

35	36	37	65
0	1	2	30
	$10,000	$10,000	$10,000

Ellen's savings plan looks like an annuity of $10,000 per year for 30 years. (*Hint*: It is easy to become confused when you just look at age, rather than at both dates and age. A common error is to think there are only $65 - 36 = 29$ payments. Writing down both dates and age avoids this problem.)

To determine the amount Ellen will have in her account at age 65, we'll need to compute the future value of this annuity.

EXECUTE

$$FV = \$10,000 \times \frac{1}{0.10}(1.10^{30} - 1)$$
$$= \$10,000 \times 164.49$$
$$= \$1.645 \text{ million at age 65}$$

(Continued)

Study Aids with a Practical Focus

To be successful, students need to master the core concepts and learn to identify and solve problems that today's practitioners face.

▶ The **Valuation Principle** is presented as the foundation of all financial decision making: The central idea is that a firm should take projects or make investments that increase the *value* of the firm. The tools of finance determine the impact of a project or investment on the firm's value by comparing the costs and benefits in equivalent terms. The Valuation Principle is first introduced in Chapter 3, revisited in the part openers, and integrated throughout the text.

▶ **Guided Problem Solutions (GPS)** are Examples that accompany every important concept using a consistent problem-solving methodology that breaks the solution process into three steps: *Plan*, *Execute*, and *Evaluate*. This approach aids student comprehension, enhances their ability to model the solution process when tackling problems on their own, and demonstrates the importance of interpreting the mathematical solution.

▶ **Personal Finance GPS** Examples showcase the use of financial analysis in everyday life by setting problems in scenarios, such as purchasing a new car or house and saving for retirement.

▶ **Common Mistake** boxes alert students to frequently made mistakes stemming from misunderstanding of core concepts and calculations—in the classroom and in the field.

COMMON MISTAKE Summing Cash Flows Across Time

Once you understand the time value of money, our first rule may seem straightforward. However, it is very common, especially for those who have not studied finance, to violate this rule, simply treating all cash flows as comparable regardless of when they are received. One example is in sports contracts. In 2011, Albert Pujols signed a contract with the Los Angeles Angels that was repeatedly referred to as a "$240 million" contract. The $240 million comes from simply adding up all the payments Pujols would receive over the 10 years of the contract—treating dollars received in 10 years the same as dollars received today. The same thing occurred when Lionel Messi signed a contract extension with FC Barcelona in 2013, giving him a "$150 million" contract through 2018.

Global Financial Crisis boxes reflect the reality of the recent financial crisis and ongoing sovereign debt crisis, noting lessons learned. Boxes interspersed through the book illustrate and analyze key details.

GLOBAL FINANCIAL CRISIS

2008–2009: A Very Cold IPO Market

The drop in IPO issues during the 2008 financial crisis was both global and dramatic. The bar graph shows the total worldwide dollar volume of IPO proceeds in billions of dollars (blue bars) and number of deals (red line) by quarter, from the last quarter of 2006 to the first quarter of 2009. Comparing the fourth quarter of 2007 (a record quarter for IPO issues) to the fourth quarter of 2008, dollar volume dropped a stunning 97% from $102 billion to just $3 billion.

Things got even worse in the first quarter of 2009 with just $1.4 billion raised. The market for IPOs essentially dried up altogether.

During the 2008 financial crisis, IPO markets were not the only equity issue markets that saw a collapse in volume. Markets for seasoned equity offerings and leveraged buyouts also collapsed. The extreme market uncertainty at the time created a "flight to quality." Investors, wary of taking risk, sought to move their capital into risk-free investments like U.S. Treasury securities. The result was a crash in existing equity prices and a greatly reduced supply of new capital to risky asset classes.

Source: Shifting Landscape—Are You Ready? Global IPO Trends report 2009, Ernst & Young.

Practitioner Interviews from notable professionals featured in many chapters highlight leaders in the field and address the effects of the financial crisis.

INTERVIEW WITH KEVIN M. WARSH

Kevin M. Warsh, *a lecturer at Stanford's Graduate School of Business and a distinguished visiting fellow at the Hoover Institution*, was a Federal Reserve governor from 2006 to 2011, serving as chief liaison to the financial markets.

QUESTION: *What are the main policy instruments used by central banks to control the economy?*

ANSWER: The Federal Reserve (Fed) deploys several policy tools to achieve its goals of price stability, maximum sustainable employment, and financial stability. Lowering the federal funds short-term interest rate, the primary policy instrument, stimulates the economy. Raising the federal funds rate generally slows the economy. Buying and selling short-term U.S. Treasury securities through *open market operations* is standard practice. Prior to the 2007–2009 financial crisis, the Fed's balance sheet ranged from $700–$900 billion. But when the Fed was unable to lower interest rates further because rates were so close to zero already, it resorted to large-scale, longer-term open market operations to increase liquidity in the financial system in the hopes of stimulating the economy further, thus growing its balance sheet significantly. With *open mouth operations*, the Fed's announcements of its intent to buy or sell assets indicates its desired degree of future policy accommodation, often prompting markets to react by adjusting interest rates immediately. The Fed's Lender-of-Last-Resort authority allows it to lend money against good collateral to troubled institutions under

the financial wherewithal of each other. One effective, innovative tool, the *Term Auction Facility (TAF)*, stimulated the economy by providing cheap and readily available term funding to banks, large and small, on the front lines of the economy, thus encouraging them to extend credit to businesses and consumers. After reducing the policy rate to near zero to help revive the economy, the Fed instituted two *Quantitative Easing (QE)* programs—special purchases of government and agency securities—to increase money supply, promote lending, and according to some proponents, increase prices of riskier assets.

The Fed also addressed the global financial crisis by establishing temporary *central bank liquidity swap lines* with the European Central Bank and other major central banks. Using this facility, a foreign central bank is able to obtain dollar funding for its customers by swapping euros for dollars or another currency and agreeing to reverse the swap at a later date. The Fed does not take exchange rate risk, but it is subject to the credit risk of its central bank counterparty.

QUESTION: *What tools is the European Central Bank (ECB) using to address the sovereign debt crisis? How does its approach compare to the Fed's approach to the 2007–2009 financial crisis?*

(Continued)

General Interest boxes highlight timely material from current financial events that shed light on business problems and real company practices.

The Credit Crisis and Bond Yields

The financial crisis that engulfed the world's economies in 2008 originated as a credit crisis that first emerged in August 2007. At that time, problems in the mortgage market had led to the bankruptcy of several large mortgage lenders. The default of these firms, and the downgrading of many of the bonds backed by mortgages these firms had made, caused many investors to reassess the risk of other bonds in their portfolios. As perceptions of risk increased, and investors attempted to move into safer U.S. Treasury securities, the prices of corporate bonds fell and so their credit spreads rose relative to

Treasuries, as shown in Figure 6.7. Panel (a) shows the yield spreads for long-term corporate bonds, where we can see that spreads of even the highest-rated Aaa bonds increased dramatically, from a typical level of 0.5% to over 2% by the fall of 2008. Panel (b) shows a similar pattern for the rate banks had to pay on short-term loans compared to the yields of short-term Treasury bills. This increase in borrowing costs made it more costly for firms to raise the capital needed for new investment, slowing economic growth. The decline in these spreads in early 2009 was viewed by many as an important first step in mitigating the ongoing impact of the financial crisis on the rest of the economy.

Teaching Every Student to Think Finance

notation

C	cash flow	P	initial principal or deposit, or equivalent present value
C_n	cash flow at date n		
FV	future value	PV	present value
FV_n	future value on date n	r	interest rate or rate of return
g	growth rate		
N	date of the last cash flow in a stream of cash flows		

Simplified Presentation of Mathematics

Because one of the hardest parts of learning finance for non-majors is mastering the jargon, math, and non-standardized notation, *Fundamentals of Corporate Finance* systematically uses:

▶ **Notation Boxes.** Each chapter begins with a Notation box that defines the variables and the acronyms used in the chapter and serves as a "legend" for students' reference.

▶ **Numbered and Labeled Equations.** The first time a full equation is given in notation form it is numbered. Key equations are titled and revisited in the summary and in end papers.

▶ **Timelines.** Introduced in Chapter 3, timelines are emphasized as the important first step in solving *every* problem that involves cash flows over time.

Using a Financial Calculator

Financial calculators are programmed to perform most present and future value calculations. However, we recommend that you develop an understanding of the formulas before using the shortcuts. We provide a more extensive discussion of financial calculators on page 95 and in the appendix to Chapter 4, but we'll cover the relevant functions for this chapter here. To use financial calculator functions, you always enter the known values first and then the calculator solves for the unknown.

To answer Example 3.4 with a financial calculator, do the following:

Concept	Number of Periods	Interest Rate per Period	Recurring Payments	Future Value
Calculator Key	N	I/Y	PMT	FV
Enter	10	6	0	15000

Because you are solving for the present value (PV), press the FV key last (on an HP calculator), or press CPT then the PV key on a TI calculator. The calculator will return −8375.92. Note that the calculator balances inflows with outflows, so because the FV is positive (an inflow), it returns the PV as a negative (an outflow).

If you were solving for the future value instead, you would enter:

N	I/Y	PV	PMT
10	6	−8375.92	0

And finally, on an HP, press the FV key or on a TI, press CPT and then the FV key.

▶ **Financial Calculator** instructions, including a box in Chapter 4 on solving for future and present values, and appendices to Chapters 4, 6, and 15 with keystrokes for HP-10BII and TI BAII Plus Professional calculators, highlight this problem-solving tool.

TABLE 18.18

Pro Forma Statement of Cash Flows for KMS, 2014–2018

Year	2013	2014	2015	2016	2017	2018
Statement of Cash Flows ($000s)						
Net Income		7,600	8,807	11,141	13,739	16,627
Depreciation		7,443	7,498	7,549	7,594	7,634
Changes in Working Capital						
Accounts Receivable		−2,561	−2,827	−3,144	−3,491	−3,872
Inventory		−2,696	−2,976	−3,309	−3,675	−4,076
Accounts Payable		2,157	2,381	2,647	2,940	3,261
Cash from Operating Activities		11,942	12,884	14,884	17,107	19,574
Capital Expenditures		−25,000	−8,000	−8,000	−8,000	−8,000
Other Investment		—	—	—	—	—
Cash from Investing Activities		−25,000	−8,000	−8,000	−8,000	−8,000
Net Borrowing		20,000	—	—	—	—
Dividends		−4,786	−2,503	−4,237	−6,167	−8,313
Cash from Financing Activities		15,214	−2,503	−4,237	−6,167	−8,313
Change in Cash (9 + 12 + 15)		2,157	2,381	2,647	2,940	3,261

▶ **Spreadsheet Tables.** Select tables are available on MyFinanceLab as Excel® files, enabling students to change inputs and manipulate the underlying calculations. Icons in the text show students where spreadsheets are available in the eText.

USING EXCEL

Capital Budgeting Using a Spreadsheet Program

Capital budgeting forecasts and analysis are most easily performed in a spreadsheet program. Here, we highlight a few best practices when developing your own capital budgets.

Create a Project Dashboard

All capital budgeting analyses begin with a set of assumptions regarding future revenues and costs associated with the investment. Centralize these assumptions within your spreadsheet in a project dashboard so they are easy to locate, review, and potentially modify. Here, we show an example for the HomeNet project.

	A B	C	D	E	F	G	H	I	J
1	HomeNet Capital Budget								
2	**Key Assumptions**								
3	*Revenues & Costs*		Year 0	Year 1	Year 2	Year 3	Year 4	Year 5	
4	HomeNet Units Sold			50	50	50	50		
5	HomeNet Ave. Price/Unit			$ 260.00	$ 260.00	$ 260.00	$ 260.00		
6	HomeNet Cost/Unit			$ 110.00	$ 110.00	$ 110.00	$ 110.00		
7	*Operating Expenses*								
8	Marketing, Support & Rent			(2,800)	(2,800)	(2,800)	(2,800)		
9	*Capital Expenditures*								
10	Purchase Equipment		(7,500)						
11	*Other Assumptions*								
12	Depreciation Schedule		0.0%	20.0%	20.0%	20.0%	20.0%	20.0%	
13	Corporate Tax Rate		40.0%	40.0%	40.0%	40.0%	40.0%	40.0%	
14	Receivables (% sales)		15.0%	15.0%	15.0%	15.0%	15.0%	15.0%	
15	Payables (% expenses)		15.0%	15.0%	15.0%	15.0%	15.0%	15.0%	
16									

(Continued)

▶ **Using Excel** boxes describe Excel techniques and include screenshots to serve as a guide for students using this technology.

▶ **Excel End-of-Chapter Problems** indicated by an Excel icon have instructor solutions and student templates available in MyFinanceLab. New to this edition, select Excel questions are now available to assign in MyFinanceLab as Simulated Excel problems with algorithmically generated values. Students can solve the problem using Excel as they would in the real world.

Practice Finance
to Learn Finance

MyFinanceLab

Here is what you should know after reading this chapter. MyFinanceLab will help you identify what you know, and where to go when you need to practice.

Key Points and Equations	Key Terms	Online Practice
4.1 Valuing a Stream of Cash Flows • The present value of a cash flow stream is: $$PV = C_0 + \frac{C_1}{(1+r)} + \frac{C_2}{(1+r)^2} + \cdots + \frac{C_N}{(1+r)^N} \quad (4.3)$$	stream of cash flows, p. 92	MyFinanceLab Study Plan 4.1
4.2 Perpetuities • A perpetuity is a stream of equal cash flows C paid every period, forever. The present value of a perpetuity is: $$PV(C \text{ in Perpetuity}) = \frac{C}{r} \quad (4.4)$$	consol, p. 96 perpetuity, p. 96	MyFinanceLab Study Plan 4.2
4.3 Annuities • An annuity is a stream of equal cash flows C paid every period for N periods. The present value of an annuity is: $$C \times \frac{1}{r}\left(1 - \frac{1}{(1+r)^N}\right) \quad (4.5)$$ • The future value of an annuity at the end of the annuity is: $$C \times \frac{1}{r}\left((1+r)^N - 1\right) \quad (4.6)$$	annuity, p. 99	MyFinanceLab Study Plan 4.3 Interactive Annuity Calculator Financial Calculator Tutorials: Calculating the Present Value of an Annuity and Solving for the Future Value of an Annuity

Working problems is the proven way to cement and demonstrate an understanding of finance.

▶ **Concept Check questions** at the end of each section enable students to test their understanding and target areas in which they need further review.

▶ **End-of-chapter problems written personally by Jonathan Berk, Peter DeMarzo, and Jarrad Harford** offer instructors the opportunity to assign first-rate materials to students for homework and practice with the confidence that the problems are consistent with the chapter content. All end-of-chapter problems are available in MyFinanceLab, the fully integrated homework and tutorial system. Both the problems and solutions, which were also prepared by the authors, have been class-tested and accuracy checked to ensure quality. Excel icons indicate the availability of instructor solutions and student templates in the Textbook Resources tab of MyFinanceLab.

End-of-Chapter Materials Reinforce Learning

Testing understanding of central concepts is crucial to learning finance.

▶ **MyFinanceLab Chapter Summary** presents the key points and conclusions from each chapter, provides a list of key terms with page numbers, and indicates online practice opportunities.

▶ **Data Cases** present in-depth scenarios in a business setting with questions designed to guide students' analysis. Many questions involve the use of Internet resources.

▶ **Integrative Cases** occur at the end of most parts and present a capstone extended problem for each part with a scenario and data for students to analyze based on that subset of chapters.

DATA CASE

This is your second interview with a prestigious brokerage firm for a job as an equity analyst. You survived the morning interviews with the department manager and the vice president of equity. Everything has gone so well that they want to test your ability as an analyst. You are seated in a room with a computer and a list with the names of two companies—Caterpillar (CAT) and Microsoft (MSFT). You have 90 minutes to complete the following tasks:

1. Download the annual income statements, balance sheets, and cash flow statements for the last four fiscal years from MarketWatch (www.marketwatch.com). Enter each company's stock symbol and then go to "financials." Copy and paste the financial statements into Excel.

2. Find historical stock prices for each firm from Yahoo! Finance (finance.yahoo.com). Enter the stock symbol, click "Historical Prices" in the left column, and enter the proper date range to cover the last day of the month corresponding to the date of each financial statement. Use the closing stock prices (not the adjusted close). To calculate the firm's market capitalization at each date, multiply the number of shares outstanding (see "Basic Weighted Shares Outstanding" on the income statement) by the firm's historic stock price.

Preface

Finance professors are united by their commitment to shaping future generations of financial professionals as well as instilling financial awareness and skills in non-majors. Our goal with *Fundamentals of Corporate Finance* is to provide an accessible presentation for both finance and non-finance majors. We know from experience that countless undergraduate students have felt that corporate finance is challenging. It is tempting to make finance *seem* accessible by de-emphasizing the core principles and instead concentrating on the results. In our over 50 years of combined teaching experience, we have found that emphasizing the core concepts in finance—which are clear and intuitive at heart—is what makes the subject matter accessible. What makes the subject challenging is that it is often difficult for a novice to distinguish between these core ideas and other intuitively appealing approaches that, if used in financial decision making, will lead to incorrect decisions.

The 2007–2009 financial crisis was fueled in part by many practitioners' poor decision making when they did not understand—or chose to ignore—the core concepts that underlie finance and the pedagogy in this book. With this point in mind, we present finance as one unified whole based on two simple, powerful ideas: (1) valuation drives decision making—the firm should take projects for which the value of the benefits exceeds the value of the costs, and (2) in a competitive market, market prices (rather than individual preferences) determine values. We combine these two ideas with what we call the *Valuation Principle*, and from it we establish all of the key ideas in corporate finance.

New to This Edition

All text discussions and figures, tables, and facts have been updated to accurately reflect exciting developments in the field of finance in the last three years. Specific highlights include the following:

- **Expanded discussion of the Global Financial Crisis.** Special boxes throughout the text tie the material to aspects of the 2007–2009 financial crisis. These boxes highlight the connection between what the students are learning and the Dodd-Frank Act, Bernie Madoff's Ponzi scheme, teaser rates and subprime loans, yield spreads, hot and cold IPO markets, capital structure, bailouts, and more. We also include a new interview with Kevin Warsh, a former Federal Reserve Governor.
- **Real-world examples** have been updated to reflect data through 2013.
- **New Media-Rich Pearson eText** includes Author Solution Videos that walk through the in-text examples using math, the financial calculator, and spreadsheets. Select in-text graphs and figures have been digitally enhanced to allow students to interact with variables to affect outcomes and bring concepts to life.
- **Using Excel boxes** have been expanded and provide hands-on instruction of how to use Excel to solve financial problems and include screenshots to serve as a guide for students.
- **Time value of money chapters** have been reorganized to quickly build the fundamental concepts and then apply them to both annual and more frequent cash flows.

▷ **New centralized coverage of financial ratios** in a specific section in Chapter 2 provides students with the tools to analyze financial statements.

▷ **We added over 50 new problems** and refined many others, once again personally writing and solving each one. In addition, every single problem is available in MyFinanceLab, the groundbreaking homework and tutorial system that accompanies the book.

▷ **We replaced and added Data Cases and Integrative Cases** throughout the book, giving students a chance to apply the material with realistic data-analyzing exercises and problems that integrate material across chapters in each major part of the book.

▷ **A new algorithmic Test Bank** is now available through TestGen and in MyFinanceLab.

Emphasis on Valuation

As painful as the financial crisis was, there is a silver lining: with the increasing focus on finance in the news, today's undergraduate students arrive in the classroom with an interest in finance. We strive to use that natural interest and motivation to overcome their fear of the subject and communicate time-tested core principles. Again, we take what has worked in the classroom and apply it to the text: By providing examples involving familiar companies such as Starbucks and Apple, making consistent use of real-world data, and demonstrating personal finance applications of core concepts, we strive to keep both non-finance and finance majors engaged.

By learning to apply the Valuation Principle, students develop the skills to make the types of comparisons—among loan options, investments, projects, and so on—that turn them into knowledgeable, confident financial consumers and managers. When students see how to apply finance to their personal lives and future careers, they grasp that finance is more than abstract, mathematically based concepts.

Table of Contents Overview

Fundamentals of Corporate Finance offers coverage of the major topical areas for introductory-level undergraduate courses. Our focus is on financial decision making related to the corporation's choice of which investments to make or how to raise the capital required to fund an investment. We designed the book with the need for flexibility and with consideration of time pressures throughout the semester in mind.

Part 1	Introduction	
	Ch. 1: Corporate Finance and the Financial Manager	Introduces the corporation and its governance; Updated to include the Dodd-Frank Act
	Ch. 2: Introduction to Financial Statement Analysis	Introduces key financial statements; Coverage of financial ratios has been centralized to prepare students to analyze financial statements holistically
Part 2	Interest Rates and Valuing Cash Flows	
	Ch. 3: Time Value of Money: An Introduction	Introduces the Valuation Principle and time value of money techniques for single-period investments
	Ch. 4: Time Value of Money: Valuing Cash Flow Streams	Introduces the mechanics of discounting; New examples with non-annual interest rates provide time value of money applications in a personal loan context

Ch. 22: Mergers and Acquisitions	Considers motives and methods for mergers and acquisitions, including leveraged buyouts
Ch. 23: International Corporate Finance	Analyzes the valuation of projects with foreign currency cash flows with integrated or segregated capital markets
Online Chapters (on **MyFinanceLab** at www.myfinancelab.com)	
Leasing Insurance and Risk Management Corporate Governance	Opportunities for course customization with online-only chapter offerings

A Complete Instructor and Student Support Package

MyFinanceLab

This fully integrated online homework system gives students the hands-on practice and tutorial help they need to learn finance efficiently. Ample opportunities for online practice and assessment in **MyFinanceLab** (www.myfinancelab.com) are seamlessly integrated into each chapter and organized by section within the chapter summaries. For more details, see the inside front cover.

Videos

Video clips available in MyFinanceLab profile well-known firms such as Boeing and Intel through interviews and analysis. The videos focus on core topical areas such as capital budgeting and risk and return. New author-recorded problem videos walk through and explain problems in major chapters.

Solutions Manual

The Solutions Manual provides students with detailed, accuracy-verified solutions to the problems in the book. The solutions, like the problems, were written by the authors themselves. Spreadsheet solutions in Excel, which allow the student to see the effect of changes in the input variables on the outcome, are also available to instructors for designated problems at the Instructor Resource Center (www.pearsonhighered.com/irc).

PowerPoint Presentations

The **PowerPoint Presentation**, authored by Janet Payne and William Chittenden of Texas State University, is available in lecture form and includes art and tables from the book and additional examples. The PowerPoint presentation includes all tables and figures, examples, key terms, and spreadsheet tables from the textbook. All PowerPoint presentations are also available for download from the Instructor Resource Center at www.pearsonhighered.com/irc.

Test Bank

The **Test Bank** provides a wealth of accuracy-verified, algorithmic testing material. Each chapter offers a wide variety of true/false, short answer, and multiple-choice questions contributed by Salil Sarkar of the University of Texas at Arlington, Karan Bhanot of the University of Texas at San Antonio, and instructional designer David Stuart. Questions are verified by difficulty level and skill type, and correlated to the chapter topics. Numerical problems include step-by-step solutions and have been made algorithmic so they can be assigned for repeated practice.

Every question in the Test Bank is available in **TestGen® software** for both Windows and Macintosh® computers. This easy-to-use testing software is a valuable test preparation tool that allows professors to view, edit, and add questions. Both the Test Item File and the TestGen computerized test bank are available for download from the Instructor Resource Center at www.pearsonhighered.com/irc, and all questions can be assigned via MyFinanceLab.

Instructor's Manual

The **Instructor's Manual** was written by Mary R. Brown of the University of Illinois–Chicago, and contains annotated chapter outlines, lecture launchers, and questions for further class discussion. It also contains the solutions to the Data Cases and part-ending case problems, as well as answers to the end-of-chapter Critical Thinking questions in the book. As an additional resource to guide instructors with students who are planning to take the CFA exam, CFA learning outcomes met in each chapter are listed. A section also details how the end-of-chapter problems map to the accreditation standards set by the Association to Advance Collegiate Schools of Business (AACSB), so that instructors can track students' mastery of the AACSB standards. The **Instructor's Manual** is available for download as Microsoft Word files or as Adobe® PDF files from the Instructor Resource Center at www.pearsonhighered.com/irc.

Acknowledgments

Given the scope of this project, identifying the many people who made it happen is a tall order. This textbook was the product of the expertise and hard work of many talented colleagues. We are especially gratified with the work of those who developed the array of print supplements that accompany the book: Janet Payne and William Chittenden for the Power-Point presentations; Mary R. Brown, for the Instructor's Manual; James Linck, for serving as advisor for the videos; and our MyFinanceLab content development team, including Melissa Honig, Miguel Leonarte, Noel Lotz, Sarah Peterson, and Susan Schoenberg. We're also deeply appreciative of Susan White's contributions to the part-ending cases.

Creating a truly error-free text is a challenge we could not have lived up to without our team of expert error checkers. Robert James subjected the text and problem solutions to his exacting standards, Kathleen Cantwell provided a critical copyeditor's eye, and Holly McLean-Aldis carefully proofread the text. We are indebted to Jared Stanfield for his adept research support throughout the writing process.

At Pearson Education, we would like to single out Donna Battista, for her continued leadership and market insight; Erin McDonagh, for her expert project management; Melissa Honig and Megan Rees, for their digital media expertise; and our production team, Meredith Gertz and especially Gillian Hall, for expertly managing the transformation of our files into a beautiful bound book. They were helped by Kalpana Arumugam at Laserwords, whose team provided the fantastic composition and artwork. We are truly thankful for the indispensable help provided by these and other professionals, including Jack Lewis.

We are indebted to our colleagues for the time and expertise invested as manuscript reviewers, class testers, and focus group participants. We list all of these contributors on the following pages, but want to single out one group, our First Edition editorial board, for special notice: Tom Berry, *DePaul University*; Elizabeth Booth, *Michigan State University*; Julie Dahlquist, the *University of Texas–San Antonio*; Michaël Dewally, *Marquette University*; Robert M. Donchez, the *University of Colorado–Boulder*; Belinda Mucklow, the *University of Wisconsin–Madison*; Coleen Pantalone, *Northeastern University*; and Susan White, the *University of Maryland*. We strived to incorporate every contributor's input and are truly grateful for each comment and suggestion. The book has benefited enormously from this input.

Reviewers

Pankaj Agrrawal, *University of Maine*

Daniel Ahern, *California State University–Chico*

Paul Asabere, *Temple University*

Ajeyo Banerjee, *University of Colorado–Denver*

Tom Berry, *DePaul University*

Karan Bhanot, *University of Texas–San Antonio*

Rafiqul Bhuyan, *California State University–San Bernardino*

Eugene Bland, *Texas A&M University–Corpus Christi*

Matej Blasko, *University of Georgia*

Elizabeth Booth, *Michigan State University*

Mary Brown, *University of Illinois–Chicago*

Bill Brunsen, *Eastern New Mexico University*

David G. Cazier, *Brigham Young University–Provo*

Leo Chan, *Delaware State University*

Cindy Chen, *California State University–Long Beach*

Haiyu Chen, *Youngstown State University*

James F. Cotter, *Wake Forest University*

Vicentiu Covrig, *California State University–Northridge*

Julie Dahlquist, *University of Texas–San Antonio*

Pieter de Jong, *University of Texas–Arlington*

Andrea L. DeMaskey, *Villanova University*

Xiaohui Deng, *California State University–Fresno*

Michaël Dewally, *Marquette University*

Robert M. Donchez, *University of Colorado Boulder*

Gang Dong, *Rutgers University*

Dean Drenk, *Montana State University*

Robert Dubil, *University of Utah*

Hsing Fang, *California State University–Los Angeles*

David O. Fricke, *University of North Carolina–Pembroke*

Scott Fung, *California State University–East Bay*

Sharon Garrison, *University of Arizona*

Rakesh Gupta, *Central Queensland University*

Joseph D. Haley, *St. Cloud State University*

Thomas Hall, *Christopher Newport University*

Karen Hallows, *University of Maryland*

Karen L. Hamilton, *Georgia Southern University*

Robert Hanson, *Eastern Michigan University*

Mahfuzul Haque, *Indiana State University*

Edward C. Howell, *Northwood University*

Ping Hsiao, *San Francisco State University*

Xiaoqing Hu, *University of Illinois at Chicago*

Pankaj Jain, *University of Memphis*

Robert James, *Boston College*

Susan Ji, *Baruch College, City University of New York*

Domingo Joaquin, *Illinois State University*

Fred R. Kaen, *University of New Hampshire*

Terrill Keasler, *Appalachian State University*

Howard Keen, *Temple University*

Brett A. King, *University of North Alabama*

Daniel Klein, *Bowling Green State University*

Gregory Kuhlemeyer, *Carroll University*

Rose Neng Lai, *University of Macau*

Keith Lam, *University of Macau*

Reinhold P. Lamb, *University of North Florida*

Douglas Lamdin, *University of Maryland–Baltimore County*

Mark J. Laplante, *University of Georgia*

Sie Ting Lau, *Nanyang Technological University*

Richard LeCompte, *Wichita State University*

Adam Y.C. Lei, *Midwestern State University*

Qian Li, *Midwestern State University*

Chang Liu, *Washington State University*

Wei Liu, *Texas A&M University*

Hugh Marble III, *University of Vermont*

James Milanese, *University of North Carolina at Greensboro*

Sunil K. Mohanty, *University of St. Thomas*

Ted Moorman, *Northern Illinois University*

James Morris, *University of Colorado–Denver*

Belinda Mucklow, *University of Wisconsin–Madison*

Rick Nelson, *University of Minnesota*

Tom C. Nelson, *University of Colorado–Boulder*

Curtis Nicholls, *Bucknell University*

Anthony C. Ng, *Hong Kong Polytechnic University*

Coleen Pantalone, *Northeastern University*

Daniel Park, *Azusa Pacific University*

Janet Payne, *Texas State University*

Jay Peroni, *College of Charleston*

Lynn Pi, *Hong Kong University of Science and Technology*

J. Michael Pinegar, *Brigham Young University*

Annette Poulsen, *University of Georgia*

Eric Powers, *University of South Carolina*

Rose M. Prasad, *Central Michigan University*

Shoba Premkumar, *Iowa State University*

Mark K. Pyles, *College of Charleston*

A.A.B. Resing, *Hogeschool Van Amsterdam*

Greg Richey, *California State University, San Bernardino*

Scott Roark, *Boise State University*

David L. Robbins, *University of New Mexico*

Andrew Samwick, *Dartmouth College*

Salil K. Sarkar, *University of Texas–Arlington*

Oliver Schnusenberg, *University of North Florida*

Kenneth Scislaw, *University of Alabama–Huntsville*

Roger Severns, *Minnesota State University–Mankato*

Tatyana Sokolyk, *University of Wyoming*

Andrew C. Spieler, *Hofstra University*

Timothy G. Sullivan, *Bentley College*

Janikan Supanvanij, *St. Cloud State University*

Hugo Tang, *Purdue University*

Oranee Tawatnuntachai, *Pennsylvania State University–Harrisburg*

Robert Terpstra, *University of Macau*

Thomas Thomson, *University of Texas–San Antonio*
Olaf J. Thorp, *Babson College*
Ed Tiryakian, *Duke University*
Emery Trahan, *Northeastern University*
Joe Ueng, *University of St. Thomas*
Mo Vaziri, *California State University–San Bernardino*
Premal P. Vora, *Pennsylvania State University–Harrisburg*
Hefei Wang, *University of Illinois–Chicago*
Gwendolyn Webb, *Baruch College*
Paul M. Weinstock, *Ohio State University*
Susan White, *University of Maryland*
Annie Wong, *Western Connecticut State University*
Xiaoyan Xu, *San Jose State University*
Zhong-gou Zhou, *California State University–Northridge*
Kermit C. Zieg, Jr., *Florida Institute of Technology*

Focus Group Participants

Anne-Marie Anderson, *Lehigh University*
Sung Bae, *Bowling Green State University*
H. Kent Baker, *American University*
Steven Beach, *Radford University*
Rafiqul Bhuyan, *California State University–San Bernardino*
Deanne Butchey, *Florida International University*
Leo Chan, *Delaware State University*
George Chang, *Grand Valley State University*
Haiwei Chen, *California State University–San Bernardino*
Haiyu Chen, *Youngstown State University*
Massimiliano De Santis, *Dartmouth College*
Jocelyn Evans, *College of Charleston*
Kathleen Fuller, *University of Mississippi*
Xavier Garza Gomez, *University of Houston–Victoria*
William Gentry, *Williams College*
Axel Grossmann, *Radford University*
Pankaj Jain, *University of Memphis*
Zhenhu Jin, *Valparaiso University*
Steve Johnson, *University of Northern Iowa*
Steven Jones, *Samford University*
Yong-Cheol Kim, *University of Wisconsin–Milwaukee*
Robert Kiss, *Eastern Michigan University*
Ann Marie Klingenhagen, *DePaul University*
Thomas J. Krissek, *Northeastern Illinois University*
Olivier Maisondieu Laforge, *University of Nebraska–Omaha*
Douglas Lamdin, *University of Maryland–Baltimore County*
D. Scott Lee, *Texas A&M University*
Stanley A. Martin, *University of Colorado–Boulder*

Jamshid Mehran, *Indiana University, South Bend*
Sunil Mohanty, *University of St. Thomas*
Karyn L. Neuhauser, *State University of New York–Plattsburgh*
Thomas O'Brien, *University of Connecticut*
Hyuna Park, *Minnesota State University–Mankato*
G. Michael Phillips, *California State University–Northridge*
Wendy Pirie, *Valparaiso University*
Antonio Rodriguez, *Texas A&M International University*
Camelia S. Rotaru, *St. Edward's University*
Salil Sarkar, *University of Texas at Arlington*
Mark Sunderman, *University of Wyoming*
Chu-Sheng Tai, *Texas Southern University*
Oranee Tawatnuntachai, *Pennsylvania State University–Harrisburg*
Benedict Udemgba, *Alcorn State University*
Rahul Verma, *University of Houston–Downtown*
Angelo P. Vignola, *Loyola University–Chicago*
Premal Vora, *Pennsylvania State University–Harrisburg*
Eric Wehrly, *Seattle University*
Yan A. Xie, *University of Michigan–Dearborn*
Fang Zhao, *Siena College*
Sophie Zong, *California State University–Stanislaus*

Class Testers

Tom Berry, *DePaul University*
Eugene Bland, *Texas A&M University–Corpus Christi*
Charles Blaylock, *Murray State University*
Mary Brown, *University of Illinois–Chicago*
Bill Brunsen, *Eastern New Mexico University*
Sarah Bryant Bower, *Shippensburg University of Pennsylvania*
Alva Wright Butcher, *University of Puget Sound*
David G. Cazier, *Brigham Young University–Provo*
Asim G. Celik, *University of Nevada–Reno*
Michaël Dewally, *Marquette University*
Richard Gaddis, *Oklahoma Wesleyan University*
TeWhan Hahn, *Auburn University–Montgomery*
Matthew Hood, *University of Southern Mississippi*
Zhenhu Jin, *Valparaiso University*
Travis Jones, *Florida Gulf Coast University*
Francis E. Laatsch, *Bowling Green State University*
Diane Lander, *Saint Michael's College*
Vance Lesseig, *Texas State University*
Frances Maloy, *University of Washington*
Jamshid Mehran, *Indiana University–South Bend*
Belinda Mucklow, *University of Wisconsin–Madison*
Kuo-Chung Tseng, *California State University–Fresno*
Kermit C. Zieg, Jr., *Florida Institute of Technology*

Introduction

Valuation Principle Connection. What is *corporate finance*? No matter what your role in a corporation, an understanding of why and how financial decisions are made is essential. The focus of this book is how to make optimal corporate financial decisions. In Part 1, we lay the foundation for our study of corporate finance. In Chapter 1, we begin by introducing the corporation and related business forms. We then examine the role of financial managers and outside investors in decision making for the firm. To make optimal decisions, a decision maker needs information. As a result, in Chapter 2, we review and analyze an important source of information for corporate decision making—the firm's accounting statements. These chapters will introduce us to the role and objective of the financial manager and some of the information the financial manager uses in applying the Valuation Principle to make optimal decisions. Then, in Part 2, we will introduce and begin applying the Valuation Principle.

1

Corporate Finance and the Financial Manager

LEARNING OBJECTIVES

- Grasp the importance of financial information in both your personal and business lives

- Understand the important features of the four main types of firms and see why the advantages of the corporate form have led it to dominate economic activity

- Explain the goal of the financial manager and the reasoning behind that goal, as well as understand the three main types of decisions a financial manager makes

- Know how a corporation is managed and controlled, the financial manager's place in it, and some of the ethical issues financial managers face

- Understand the importance of financial markets, such as stock markets, to a corporation and the financial manager's role as liaison to those markets

- Recognize the role that financial institutions play in the financial cycle of the economy

This book focuses on how people in corporations make financial decisions. Despite its name, much of what we discuss in corporate finance applies to the financial decisions made within any organization, including not-for-profit entities such as charities and universities. In this chapter, we introduce the four main types of firms. We stress corporations, however, because they represent 85% of U.S. business revenue. We also highlight the financial manager's critical role inside any business enterprise. What products to launch, how to pay to develop those products, what profits to keep and how to return profits to investors—all of these decisions and many more fall within corporate finance. The financial manager makes these decisions with the goal of maximizing the value of the business, which is determined in the financial markets. In this chapter and throughout the book, we will focus on this goal, provide you with the tools to make financial management decisions, and show you how the financial markets provide funds to a corporation and produce market prices that are key inputs to any financial manager's investment analysis.

1.1   Why Study Finance?

Finance and financial thinking are everywhere in our daily lives. Consider your decision to go to college. You surely weighed alternatives, such as starting a full-time job immediately, and then decided that college provided you with the greatest net benefit. More and more, individuals are taking charge of their personal finances with decisions such as:

- When to start saving and how much to save for retirement.
- Whether a car loan or lease is more advantageous.
- Whether a particular stock is a good investment.
- How to evaluate the terms of a home mortgage.

Our career paths have become less predictable and more dynamic. In previous generations, it was common to work for one employer your entire career. Today, that would be highly unusual. Most of us will instead change jobs, and possibly even careers, many times. With each new opportunity, we must weigh all the costs and benefits, financial and otherwise.

Some financial decisions, such as whether to pay $2.00 for your morning coffee, are simple, but most are more complex. In your business career, you may face questions such as:

- Should your firm launch a new product?
- Which supplier should your firm choose?
- Should your firm produce a part of the product or outsource production?
- Should your firm issue new stock or borrow money instead?
- How can you raise money for your start-up firm?

In this book, you will learn how all of these decisions in your personal life and inside a business are tied together by one powerful concept, the *Valuation Principle*. The Valuation Principle shows how to make the costs and benefits of a decision comparable so that we can weigh them properly. Learning to apply the Valuation Principle will give you the skills to make the types of comparisons—among loan options, investments, and projects—that will turn you into a knowledgeable, confident financial consumer and manager.

From 2007 to 2009 we witnessed a credit freeze, a severe stock market decline, and the failures of well-known financial institutions. Attempts to understand these elements of the crisis, their origins, and how they affect our businesses and personal finances have highlighted the need for learning core financial principles and concepts.

Whether you plan to major in finance or simply take this one course, you will find the fundamental financial knowledge gained here to be essential in your personal and business lives.

1.2   The Four Types of Firms

We begin our study of corporate finance by examining the types of firms that financial managers run. As shown in Figure 1.1, There are four major types of firms: sole proprietorships, partnerships, limited liability companies, and corporations. We explain each organizational form in turn, but our primary focus is on the most important form—the corporation.

Sole Proprietorships

sole proprietorship A business owned and run by one person.

A **sole proprietorship** is a business owned and run by one person. Sole proprietorships are usually very small with few, if any, employees. Although they do not account for much sales revenue in the economy, they are the most common type of firm in the world. In 2007, an estimated 71% of businesses in the United States were sole proprietorships, although they generated only 5% of the revenue.[1]

We now consider the key features of a sole proprietorship.

1. Sole proprietorships have the advantage of being straightforward to set up. Consequently, many new businesses use this organizational form.

2. The principal limitation of a sole proprietorship is that there is no separation between the firm and the owner—the firm can have only one owner who runs the business. If there are other investors, they cannot hold an ownership stake in the firm.

3. The owner has unlimited personal liability for the firm's debts. That is, if the firm defaults on any debt payment, the lender can (and will) require the owner to repay the loan from personal assets. An owner who cannot afford to repay a loan for which he or she is personally liable must declare personal bankruptcy.

4. The life of a sole proprietorship is limited to the life of the owner. It is also difficult to transfer ownership of a sole proprietorship.

For most growing businesses, the disadvantages of a sole proprietorship outweigh the advantages. As soon as the firm reaches the point at which it can borrow without the owner agreeing to be personally liable, the owners typically convert the business into another form. Conversion also has other benefits that we will consider as we discuss the other forms below.

FIGURE 1.1

Types of U.S. Firms

There are four major types of firms in the United States. As (a) and (b) show, although the majority of U.S. firms are sole proprietorships, they generate only a small fraction of total revenue, in contrast to corporations.

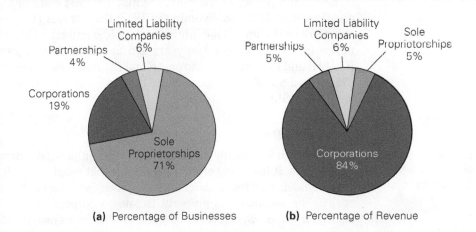

(a) Percentage of Businesses   **(b)** Percentage of Revenue

Source: www.bizstats.com.

---

[1]U.S. Census Bureau National Data Book.

Partnerships

partnership A business owned and run by more than one owner.

A **partnership** is a business owned and run by more than one owner. Key features include the following:

1. *All* partners are liable for the firm's debt. That is, a lender can require *any* partner to repay all the firm's outstanding debts.
2. The partnership ends in the event of the death or withdrawal of any single partner.
3. Partners can avoid liquidation if the partnership agreement provides for alternatives such as a buyout of a deceased or withdrawn partner.

Some old and established businesses remain as partnerships or sole proprietorships. Often these firms are the types of businesses in which the owners' personal reputations are the basis for the businesses. For example, law firms, medical practices, and accounting firms are frequently organized as partnerships. For such enterprises, the partners' personal liability increases the confidence of the firm's clients that the partners will strive to maintain the firm's reputation.

limited partnership A partnership with two kinds of owners: general partners and limited partners.

limited liability When an investor's liability is limited to her investment.

A **limited partnership** is a partnership with two kinds of owners: general partners and limited partners. In this case, the general partners have the same rights and privileges as partners in any general partnership—they are personally liable for the firm's debt obligations. Limited partners, however, have **limited liability**—that is, their liability is limited to their investment. Their private property cannot be seized to pay off the firm's outstanding debts. Furthermore, the death or withdrawal of a limited partner does not dissolve the partnership, and a limited partner's interest is transferable. However, a limited partner has no management authority and cannot legally be involved in the managerial decision making for the business.

Limited Liability Companies

limited liability company (LLC) A limited partnership without a general partner.

A **limited liability company (LLC)** is like a limited partnership but without a general partner. That is, all the owners (referred to as *members*) have limited liability, but unlike limited partners, they can also run the business (as managing members). The LLC is a relatively new entity in the United States. The first state to pass a statute allowing the creation of an LLC was Wyoming in 1977; the last was Hawaii in 1997. Internationally, companies with limited liability are much older and established. LLCs first rose to prominence in Germany over 100 years ago as a *Gesellschaft mit beschränkter Haftung* (GmbH) and then in other European and Latin American countries. An LLC is known in France as a Société à responsabilité limitée (SAR), and by similar names in Italy (SRL) and Spain (SL).

Corporations

corporation A legally defined, artificial being, separate from its owners.

A **corporation** is a legally defined, artificial being (a legal entity), separate from its owners. As such, it has many of the legal powers that people have. It can enter into contracts, acquire assets, and incur obligations, and it enjoys protection under the U.S. Constitution against the seizure of its property. Because a corporation is a legal entity separate and distinct from its owners, it is solely responsible for its own obligations. Consequently, the owners of a corporation (or its employees, customers, etc.) are not liable for any obligations the corporation enters into. Similarly, the corporation is not liable for any personal obligations of its owners.

In the same way that it is difficult to imagine modern business life without e-mail and cell phones, the corporation revolutionized the economy. On February 2, 1819, the U.S. Supreme Court established the legal precedent that the property of a corporation, similar to that of a person, is private and entitled to protection under the U.S. Constitution.[2] This decision led to dramatic growth in the number of U.S. corporations from fewer than 1000 in 1830 to 50,000 in 1890. Today, the corporate structure is ubiquitous, not only in the United States (where it is responsible for 85% of business revenue), but all over the world.

Formation of a Corporation. A corporation must be legally formed, which means that the state in which it is incorporated must formally give its consent to the incorporation by chartering it. Setting up a corporation is therefore considerably more costly than setting up a sole proprietorship. The state of Delaware has a particularly attractive legal environment for corporations, so many corporations choose to incorporate there. For jurisdictional purposes, a corporation is a citizen of the state in which it is incorporated. Most firms hire lawyers to create a corporate charter that includes formal articles of incorporation and a set of bylaws. The corporate charter specifies the initial rules that govern how the corporation is run.

Ownership of a Corporation. There is no limit to the number of owners a corporation can have. Because most corporations have many owners, each owner owns only a fraction of the corporation. The entire ownership stake of a corporation is divided into shares known as **stock**. The collection of all the outstanding shares of a corporation is known as the **equity** of the corporation. An owner of a share of stock in the corporation is known as a **shareholder, stockholder, or equity holder**. Shareholders are entitled to **dividend payments**; that is, payments made at the discretion of the corporation to its equity holders. Shareholders usually receive a share of the dividend payments that is proportional to the amount of stock they own. For example, a shareholder who owns 25% of the firm's shares would be entitled to 25% of the total dividend payment.

An important feature of a corporation is that there is no limitation on who can own its stock. That is, an owner of a corporation need not have any special expertise or qualification. This feature allows free and anonymous trade in the shares of the corporation and provides one of the most important advantages of organizing a firm as a corporation. Corporations can raise substantial amounts of capital because they can sell ownership shares to anonymous outside investors.

The availability of outside funding has enabled corporations to dominate the economy. Let's look at one of the world's largest firms, Microsoft Corporation, as an example. Microsoft reported annual revenue of $77.8 billion over the 12 months from July 2012 through June 2013. The total value of the company (the owners' collective wealth in the company) as of June 2013 was $288 billion. The company employed 99,000 people. Putting these numbers into perspective, treating the sales of $77.8 billion as gross domestic product (GDP) in 2012 would rank Microsoft (just behind Ecuador) as the 65th richest *country* (out of almost 200).[3] Ecuador has almost 14.5 million people, about 146 times as many people as employees at Microsoft. Indeed, if the number of Microsoft employees were used as the "population" of the corporation, Microsoft would rank just above Antigua and Barbuda as the 22nd least populous country on Earth!

stock The ownership or equity of a corporation divided into shares.

equity The collection of all the outstanding shares of a corporation.

shareholder (also stockholder or equity holder) An owner of a share of stock or equity in a corporation.

dividend payments Payments made at the discretion of the corporation to its equity holders.

---

[2]The case was Dartmouth v. Woodward and the full text of John Marshall's decision can be found at www.constitution.org/dwebster/dartmouth_decision.htm.

[3]World Development Indicators database, September 26, 2013. For quick reference tables on GDP, go to www.worldbank.org/data/quickreference.html.

Tax Implications for Corporate Entities

An important difference among the types of corporate organizational forms is the way they are taxed. Because a corporation is a separate legal entity, a corporation's profits are subject to taxation separate from its owners' tax obligations. In effect, shareholders of a corporation pay taxes twice. First, the corporation pays tax on its profits, and then when the remaining profits are distributed to the shareholders, the shareholders pay their own personal income tax on this income. This system is sometimes referred to as *double taxation*.

EXAMPLE 1.1

Taxation of Corporate Earnings

MyFinanceLab

PROBLEM

You are a shareholder in a corporation. The corporation earns $5.00 per share before taxes. After it has paid taxes, it will distribute the rest of its earnings to you as a dividend (we make this simplifying assumption, but should note that most corporations retain some of their earnings for reinvestment). The dividend is income to you, so you will then pay taxes on these earnings. The corporate tax rate is 40% and your tax rate on dividend income is 15%. How much of the earnings remains after all taxes are paid?

SOLUTION

PLAN

Earnings before taxes: $5.00   Corporate tax rate: 40%   Personal dividend tax rate: 15%

To calculate the corporation's earnings after taxes, first we subtract the taxes paid at the corporate level from the pretax earnings of $5.00. The taxes paid will be 40% (the corporate tax rate) of $5.00. Since all of the after-corporate tax earnings will be paid to you as a dividend, you will pay taxes of 15% on that amount. The amount leftover is what remains after all taxes are paid.

EXECUTE

$5.00 per share × 0.40 = $2.00 in taxes at the corporate level, leaving $5.00 − $2.00 = $3.00 in after-corporate tax earnings per share to distribute.

You will pay $3.00 × 0.15 = $0.45 in taxes on that dividend, leaving you with $2.55 from the original $5.00 after all taxes.

EVALUATE

As a shareholder, you keep $2.55 of the original $5.00 in earnings; the remaining $2.00 + $0.45 = $2.45 is paid as taxes. Thus, your total effective tax rate is 2.45/5 = 49%.

S corporations Those corporations that elect subchapter S tax treatment and are exempted by the U.S. Internal Revenue Service's tax code from double taxation.

S Corporations. The corporate organizational structure is the only organizational structure subject to double taxation. However, the U.S. Internal Revenue Code exempts **S corporations** from double taxation because they elect subchapter S tax treatment. Under subchapter S tax regulations, the firm's profits (and losses) are not subject to corporate taxes, but instead are allocated directly to shareholders based on their ownership share. The shareholders must include these profits as income on their individual tax returns (even if no money is distributed to them). However, after the shareholders have paid income taxes on these profits, no further tax is due.

Corporate Taxation Around the World

Most countries offer investors in corporations some relief from double taxation. Thirty countries make up the Organization for Economic Co-operation and Development (OECD), and of these countries, only Ireland offers no relief whatsoever. A few countries, including Australia, Finland, Mexico, New Zealand, and Norway, offer complete relief by effectively not taxing dividend income. The United States offers partial relief by having a lower tax rate on dividend income than on other sources of income. As of 2013, qualified dividends are taxed at 15% or 20%, depending on the investor's tax bracket, rates significantly below their personal income tax rate.

EXAMPLE 1.2

Taxation of S
Corporation Earnings

MyFinanceLab

PROBLEM
Rework Example 1.1, assuming the corporation in that example has elected subchapter S tax treatment and your tax rate on non-dividend income is 30%.

SOLUTION
PLAN

Earnings before taxes: $5.00   Corporate tax rate: 0%   Personal tax rate: 30%

In this case, the corporation pays no taxes. It earned $5.00 per share. In an S corporation, all income is treated as personal income to you, whether or not the corporation chooses to distribute or retain this cash. As a result, you must pay a 30% tax rate on those earnings.

EXECUTE

Your income taxes are $0.30 \times \$5.00 = \$1.50$, leaving you with $\$5.00 - \$1.50 = \$3.50$ in after-tax earnings.

EVALUATE

The $1.50 in taxes that you pay is substantially lower than the $2.45 you paid in Example 1.1. As a result, you are left with $3.50 per share after all taxes instead of $2.55. However, note that in a C corporation, you are only taxed when you receive the income as a dividend, whereas in an S corporation, you pay taxes on the income immediately regardless of whether the corporation distributes it as a dividend or reinvests it in the company.

C corporations
Corporations that have no restrictions on who owns their shares or the number of shareholders; they cannot qualify for subchapter S tax treatment and are subject to direct taxation.

C Corporations. The government places strict limitations on the qualifications for subchapter S tax treatment. In particular, the shareholders of such corporations must be individuals who are U.S. citizens or residents, and there can be no more than 100 of them. Because most corporations have no restrictions on who owns their shares or the number of shareholders, they cannot qualify for subchapter S tax treatment. Thus, most corporations are **C corporations**, which are corporations subject to corporate taxes.

As we have discussed, there are four main types of firms: sole proprietorships, partnerships (general and limited), limited liability companies, and corporations ("S" and "C"). To help you see the differences among them, Table 1.1 compares and contrasts the main characteristics of each.

TABLE 1.1

Characteristics of the
Different Types of Firms

	Number of Owners	Liability for Firm's Debts	Owners Manage the Firm	Ownership Change Dissolves Firm	Taxation
Sole Proprietorship	One	Yes	Yes	Yes	Personal
Partnership	Unlimited	Yes; each partner is liable for the entire amount	Yes	Yes	Personal
Limited Partnership	At least one general partner (GP), no limit on limited partners (LP)	GP-Yes LP-No	GP-Yes LP-No	GP-Yes LP-No	Personal
Limited Liability Company	Unlimited	No	Yes	No*	Personal
S Corporation	At most 100	No	No (but they legally may)	No	Personal
C Corporation	Unlimited	No	No (but they legally may)	No	Double

*However, most LLCs require the approval of the other members to transfer your ownership.

1. What is a limited liability company (LLC)? How does it differ from a limited partnership?
2. What are the advantages and disadvantages of organizing a business as a corporation?

1.3 The Financial Manager

As of January 2013, Apple, Inc. had just over 939 *million* shares of stock held by 27,450 owners.[4] Because there are many owners of a corporation, each of whom can freely trade their stock, it is often not feasible for the owners of a corporation to have direct control of the firm. It falls to the financial manager to make the financial decisions of the business for the stockholders. Within the corporation, the financial manager has three main tasks:

1. Make investment decisions.
2. Make financing decisions.
3. Manage short-term cash needs.

We will discuss each of these in turn, along with the financial manager's overarching goal.

Making Investment Decisions

The financial manager's most important job is to make the firm's investment decisions. The financial manager must weigh the costs and benefits of each investment or project and decide which ones qualify as good uses of the money stockholders have invested in the firm. These investment decisions fundamentally shape what the firm does and whether it will add value for its owners. For example, it may seem hard to imagine now, but there was a time when Apple's financial managers were evaluating whether to invest in the development of the first iPhone. They had to weigh the substantial development and production costs against uncertain future sales. Their analysis indicated that it was a good investment, and the rest is history. In this book, you will learn all the tools necessary to make these investment decisions.

GLOBAL FINANCIAL CRISIS

The Dodd-Frank Act

In response to the 2008 financial crisis, the U.S. federal government reevaluated its role in the control and management of financial institutions and private corporations. Signed into law on July 21, 2010, the **Dodd-Frank Wall Street Reform and Consumer Protection Act** brought a sweeping change to financial regulation in response to widespread calls for financial regulatory system reform after the near collapse of the world's financial system in the fall of 2008 and the ensuing global credit crisis. History indeed repeats itself: It was in the wake of the 1929 stock market crash and subsequent Great Depression that Congress passed the Glass-Steagall Act establishing the Federal Deposit Insurance Corporation (FDIC) and instituted significant bank reforms to regulate transactions between commercial banks and securities firms.

The Dodd-Frank Act aims to (1) promote U.S. financial stability by "improving accountability and transparency in the financial system," (2) put an end to the notion of "too big to fail," (3) "protect the American taxpayer by ending bailouts," and (4) "protect consumers from abusive financial services practices." Time will tell whether the Act will actually achieve these important goals.

Implementing the wide-ranging financial reforms in the Dodd-Frank Act requires the work of many federal agencies, either through rulemaking or other regulatory actions. As of mid-2012, two years since Dodd-Frank's passage, 129 of the reforms have been finalized, providing a clear picture of the Dodd-Frank regulatory framework. But another 271 rules or actions, containing many of the core Dodd-Frank reforms, await completion.

---

[4]Apple, Inc., Notice of 2013 Annual Meeting of Shareholders, January 7, 2013.

Making Financing Decisions

Once the financial manager has decided which investments to make, he or she also decides how to pay for them. Large investments may require the corporation to raise additional money. The financial manager must decide whether to raise more money from new and existing owners by selling more shares of stock (equity) or to borrow the money instead (bonds and other debt). A bond is a security sold by governments and corporations to raise money from investors today in exchange for a promised future payment. It can be viewed as a loan from those investors to the issuer. In this book, we will discuss the characteristics of each source of money and how to decide which one to use in the context of the corporation's overall mix of debt and equity.

Managing Short-Term Cash Needs

The financial manager must ensure that the firm has enough cash on hand to meet its obligations from day to day. This job, also commonly known as *managing working capital,*[5] may seem straightforward, but in a young or growing company, it can mean the difference between success and failure. Even companies with great products require a lot of money to develop and bring those products to market. Consider the costs to Starbucks of launching their VIA instant coffee, which included developing the instant coffee crystals and creating a big marketing campaign for them, or the costs to Boeing of producing the 787—billions of dollars were spent before the first 787 finally left the ground in December 2009. A company typically burns through a significant amount of cash before the sales of the product generate income. The financial manager's job is to make sure that limited access to cash does not hinder the firm's success.

The Goal of the Financial Manager

All of these decisions by the financial manager are made within the context of the overriding goal of financial management—*to maximize the wealth of the owners, the stockholders*. The stockholders have invested in the corporation, putting their money at risk to become the owners of the corporation. Thus, the financial manager is a

caretaker of the stockholders' money, making decisions in their interests. Many corporations have thousands of owners (shareholders). These shareholders vary from large institutions to small first-time investors, from retirees living off their investments to young employees just starting to save for retirement. Each owner is likely to have different interests and priorities. Whose interests and priorities determine the goals of the firm? You might be surprised to learn that the interests of shareholders are aligned for many, if not most, important decisions. Regardless of their own personal financial position and stage in life, all the shareholders will agree that they are better off if the value of their investment in the corporation is maximized. For example, suppose the decision concerns whether to develop a new product that will be a profitable investment for the corporation. All shareholders will very likely agree that developing this product is a good idea. Returning to our iPhone example, by October 2010, Apple shares were worth three times as much as they were in January 2007, when the first iPhone was introduced. All Apple shareholders at the time of the development of the first iPhone are clearly

---

[5]*Working capital* refers to things such as cash on hand, inventories, raw materials, loans to suppliers, and payments from customers—the grease that keeps the wheels of production moving. We will discuss working capital in more detail in Chapter 2 and devote all of Chapter 19 to working capital management.

much better off because of it, whether they have since sold their shares of Apple to pay for retirement, or are still holding those shares in their retirement savings account.

Even when all the owners of a corporation agree on the goals of the corporation, these goals must be implemented. In the next section, we will discuss the financial manager's place in the corporation and how owners exert control over the corporation.

Shareholder Value Versus Stakeholder Value

While the goal of a financial manager is to increase the value of the firm to its shareholders, this responsibility does not imply that the impact of the firm's decisions on other stakeholders, such as employees or customers, can be ignored. By creating additional value for customers, the firm can raise prices and increase profits.

Similarly, if the firm makes decisions that benefit employees (for example, increasing their job security), it will be able to offer lower wages or benefit from increased productivity. On the other hand, if customers or employees anticipate that the firm is likely to exploit them, they will demand lower prices or higher wages. Thus, to maximize shareholder value, the financial manager must consider the impact of her decision on all stakeholders of the firm.

Concept Check

3. What are the main types of decisions that a financial manager makes?
4. What is the goal of the financial manager?

1.4 The Financial Manager's Place in the Corporation

We've established that the stockholders own the corporation but rely on financial managers to actively manage the corporation. The *board of directors* and the management team headed by the *chief executive officer* possess direct control of the corporation. In this section, we explain how the responsibilities for the corporation are divided between these two entities and describe conflicts that arise between stockholders and the management team.

The Corporate Management Team

board of directors
A group of people elected by shareholders who have the ultimate decision-making authority in the corporation.

The shareholders of a corporation exercise their control by electing a **board of directors**, a group of people who have the ultimate decision-making authority in the corporation. In most corporations, each share of stock gives a shareholder one vote in the election of the board of directors, so investors with more shares have more influence. When one or two shareholders own a very large proportion of the outstanding stock, these shareholders might either be on the board of directors themselves, or they may have the right to appoint a number of directors.

chief executive officer (CEO) The person charged with running the corporation by instituting the rules and policies set by the board of directors.

The board of directors makes rules on how the corporation should be run (including how the top managers in the corporation are compensated), sets policy, and monitors the performance of the company. The board of directors delegates most decisions that involve the day-to-day running of the corporation to its management. The **chief executive officer (CEO)** is charged with running the corporation by instituting the rules and policies set by the board of directors. The size of the rest of the management team varies from corporation to corporation. In some corporations, the separation of powers between the board of directors and CEO is not always distinct. In fact, the CEO can also be the chairman of the board of directors. The most senior financial manager is the chief financial officer (CFO), often reporting directly to the CEO. Figure 1.2 presents part of a typical organizational chart for a corporation, highlighting the positions a financial manager may take.

FIGURE 1.2

The Financial Functions Within a Corporation

The board of directors, representing the stockholders, controls the corporation and hires the top management team. A financial manager might hold any of the green-shaded positions, including the Chief Financial Officer (CFO) role. The controller oversees accounting and tax functions. The treasurer oversees more traditional finance functions, such as capital budgeting (making investment decisions), risk management (managing the firm's exposure to movements in the financial markets), and credit management (managing the terms and policies of any credit the firm extends to its customers).

Ethics and Incentives in Corporations

A corporation is run by a management team, separate from its owners. How can the owners of a corporation ensure that the management team will implement their goals?

agency problem When managers, despite being hired as the agents of shareholders, put their self-interest ahead of the interests of those shareholders.

Agency Problems. Many people claim that because of the separation of ownership and control in a corporation, managers have little incentive to work in the interests of the shareholders when this means working against their self-interest. Economists call this an **agency problem**—when managers, despite being hired as the agents of shareholders, put their self-interest ahead of the interests of those shareholders. Managers face the ethical dilemma of whether to adhere to their responsibility to put the interests of shareholders first, or to do what is in their personal best interests. This problem is commonly addressed in practice by minimizing the number of decisions managers make that require putting their self-interest against the interests of the shareholders. For example, managers' compensation contracts are designed to ensure that most decisions in the shareholders' interest are also in the managers' interests; shareholders often tie the compensation of top managers to the corporation's profits or perhaps to its stock price. There is, however, a limitation to this strategy. By tying compensation too closely to performance, shareholders might be asking managers to take on more risk than they are comfortable taking. As a result, the managers may not make decisions that shareholders want them to, or it might be hard to find talented managers willing to accept the job. For example, biotech firms take big risks on drugs that fight cancer, AIDS, and other widespread diseases. The market for a successful drug is huge, but the risk of failure is high. Investors who put only some of their money in biotech may be comfortable with this risk, but managers who have all of their compensation tied to the success of such a drug might opt to develop a less risky drug that has a smaller market.

The Dodd-Frank Act on Corporate Compensation and Governance

Compensation is one of the most important conflicts of interest between corporate executives and shareholders. To limit senior corporate executives' influence over their own compensation and prevent excessive compensation, the Act directs the SEC to adopt new rules that:

- Mandate the independence of a firm's compensation committee and its advisers.
- Provide shareholders the opportunity to approve—in a non-binding, advisory vote—the compensation of executive officers at least once every three years (referred to as a "Say-on-Pay" vote).
- Require firm disclosure and shareholder approval of large bonus payments (so-called "golden parachutes") to ousted senior executives as the result of a takeover.
- Require disclosure of the relationship of executive pay to the company's performance, as well as the ratio between the CEO's total compensation and that of the median employee.
- Create "clawback" provisions that allow firms to recoup compensation paid based on erroneous financial results.

Further potential for conflicts of interest and ethical considerations arise when some stakeholders in the corporation benefit and others lose from a decision. Shareholders and managers are two stakeholders in the corporation, but others include the regular employees and the communities in which the company operates, for example. Managers may decide to take the interests of other stakeholders into account in their decisions, such as keeping a loss-generating factory open because it is the main provider of jobs in a small town, paying above local market wages to factory workers in a developing country, or operating a plant at a higher environmental standard than local law mandates.

In some cases, these actions that benefit other stakeholders may also benefit the firm's shareholders by creating a more dedicated workforce, generating positive publicity with customers, or other indirect effects. In other instances, when these decisions benefit other stakeholders at shareholders' expense, they represent a form of corporate charity. Indeed, many if not most corporations explicitly donate (on behalf of their shareholders) to local and global causes. Shareholders often approve of such actions, even though they are costly and so reduce their wealth. While it is the manager's job to make decisions that maximize shareholder value, shareholders—who own the firm—also want the firm's actions to reflect their moral and ethical values. Of course, shareholders may not have identical preferences in these matters, leading to potential sources of conflict.

The CEO's Performance. Another way shareholders can encourage managers to work in the interests of shareholders is to discipline them if they do not. If shareholders are unhappy with a CEO's performance, they could, in principle, pressure the board to oust the CEO. Disney's Michael Eisner, Hewlett-Packard's Carly Fiorina, and Home Depot's Robert Nardelli were all forced to resign by their boards. Despite these high-profile examples, directors and top executives are rarely replaced through a grassroots shareholder uprising.

Citizens United v. Federal Election Commission

On January 21, 2010, the U.S. Supreme Court ruled on what some scholars have argued is the most important First Amendment case in many years. In *Citizens United v. Federal Election Commission*, the Court held, in a controversial 5–4 decision, that the First Amendment allows corporations and unions to make political expenditures in support of a particular candidate. This ruling overturned existing restrictions on political campaigning by corporations. Because it is highly unlikely that all shareholders of a corporation would unanimously support a particular candidate, allowing such activities effectively guarantees a potential conflict of interest.

Instead, dissatisfied investors often choose to sell their shares. Of course, somebody must be willing to buy the shares from the dissatisfied shareholders. If enough shareholders are dissatisfied, the only way to entice investors to buy (or hold) the shares is to offer them a low price. Similarly, investors who see a well-managed corporation, will want to purchase shares, which drives the stock price up. Thus, the stock price of the corporation is a barometer for corporate leaders that continuously gives them feedback on the shareholders' opinion of their performance.

When the stock performs poorly, the board of directors might react by replacing the CEO. In some corporations, however, the senior executives might be entrenched because boards of directors do not have the independence or motivation to replace them. Often, the reluctance to fire results when the board is comprised of people who are close friends of the CEO and lack objectivity. In corporations in which the CEO is entrenched and doing a poor job, the expectation of continued poor performance will cause the stock price to be low. Low stock prices create a profit opportunity. In a **hostile takeover**, an individual or organization—sometimes known as a *corporate raider*—purchases a large fraction of a company's stock and in doing so gets enough votes to replace the board of directors and the CEO. With a new superior management team, the stock is a much more attractive investment, which would likely result in a price rise and a profit for the corporate raider and the other shareholders. Although the words "hostile" and "raider" have negative connotations, corporate raiders provide an important service to shareholders. The mere threat of being removed as a result of a hostile takeover is often enough to discipline bad managers and motivate boards of directors to make difficult decisions. Consequently, the fact that a corporation's shares can be publicly traded creates a "market for corporate control" that encourages managers and boards of directors to act in the interests of their shareholders.

hostile takeover
A situation in which an individual or organization—sometimes referred to as a *corporate raider*—purchases a large fraction of a company's stock and in doing so gets enough votes to replace the board of directors and its CEO.

Concept Check

5. How do shareholders control a corporation?

6. What types of jobs would a financial manager have in a corporation?

7. What ethical issues could confront a financial manager?

1.5 The Stock Market

In Section 1.3, we established the goal of the financial manager: to maximize the wealth of the owners, the stockholders. The value of the owners' investments in the corporation is determined by the price of a share of the corporation's stock. Corporations can be private or public. A private corporation has a limited number of owners and there is no organized market for its shares, making it hard to determine the market price of its shares at any point in time. A public corporation has many owners and its shares trade on an organized market, called a **stock market** (or **stock exchange** or **bourse**). These markets provide *liquidity* for a company's shares and determine the market price for those shares. An investment is **liquid** if it can be easily turned into cash by selling it immediately at a competitive market price. An investor in a public company values the ability to turn his investment into cash easily and quickly by simply selling his shares on one of these markets. In this section, we provide an overview of the functioning of the major stock markets. The analysis and trading by participants in these markets provides an evaluation of the financial managers' decisions that determines the stock price and provides essential feedback to the managers on their decisions.

stock market (also stock exchange or bourse) Organized market on which the shares of many corporations are traded.

liquid Describes an investment that can be easily turned into cash because it can be sold immediately at a competitive market price.

The Largest Stock Markets

The best known U.S. stock market and one of the largest stock markets in the world is the New York Stock Exchange (NYSE). Billions of dollars of stock are exchanged every day on the NYSE. Other U.S. stock markets include the American Stock Exchange (AMEX), NASDAQ (the National Association of Security Dealers Automated Quotation system), and regional exchanges such as the Midwest Stock Exchange. Most other countries have at least one stock market. Outside the United States, the biggest stock markets are the London Stock Exchange (LSE) and the Tokyo Stock Exchange (TSE). Figure 1.3 ranks the world's largest stock exchanges by trading volume.

primary market When a corporation issues new shares of stock and sells them to investors.

secondary market Markets, such as NYSE or NASDAQ, where shares of a corporation are traded between investors without the involvement of the corporation.

Primary Versus Secondary Markets

All of the markets in Figure 1.3 are *secondary markets*. The **primary market** refers to a corporation issuing new shares of stock and selling them to investors. After this initial transaction between the corporation and investors, the shares continue to trade in a **secondary market** between investors without the involvement of the corporation. For example, if you wish to buy 100 shares of Starbucks Coffee, you could place an order on the NASDAQ, where Starbucks trades under the ticker symbol SBUX. You would buy your shares from someone who already held shares of Starbucks, not from Starbucks itself.

FIGURE 1.3

Worldwide Stock Markets Ranked by Volume of Trade

The bar graph shows the 10 biggest stock markets in the world ranked by total value of shares traded on exchange in 2012.

Source: www.world-exchanges.org.

designated market makers
Individuals on the NYSE floor who who have an obligation to help maintain liquidity in their assigned stocks.

bid price The price at which a market maker or specialist is willing to buy a security.

ask price The price at which a market maker or specialist is willing to sell a security.

Physical Stock Markets

The NYSE is an example of a physical market. It is located at 11 Wall Street in New York City. The NYSE uses computers to match most buys and sells. However, it augments this process with **designated market makers (DMM)**, individuals on the floor of the exchange who are obligated to commit their own capital to maintain liquidity in their assigned stocks. These DMMs, who have replaced the market-making specialists formerly found on the NYSE, post quotes to buy the stock (at the **bid price**) and sell the stock (at the **ask price**). They are required to provide the highest bids and lowest asks a specified percentage of the time. They also manage the opening and closing of trading as well as step in to provide liquidity (sell or buy) when buy and sell orders are imbalanced or volatility is high. The exchange has rules that attempt to ensure that bid and ask prices do not get too far apart and that large price changes take place through a series of small changes, rather than in one big jump. Large investment banks and brokerages buy trading licenses that entitle

INTERVIEW WITH

JEAN-FRANÇOIS THÉODORE*

Jean-François Théodore is the Deputy CEO of NYSE Euronext, the largest stock exchange group in the world.

QUESTION: *How have technological innovations shaped financial markets?*

ANSWER: At the end of the 1980s, the electronic execution of market orders transformed the organization and operation of the financial markets, resulting in continuous securities trading. Since then, technology has become a key driver of change in the financial industry, enabling markets to become faster and increasingly more competitive, at a time when client requirements are growing and diversifying, particularly regarding the speed of execution and volumes, notably from algorithmic traders.

QUESTION: *The Paris Stock Exchange has experienced profound upheavals recently. What have the most important changes been?*

ANSWER: The Paris Stock Exchange, like other leading stock markets, has changed significantly in recent years.

With the decompartmentalization and globalization of financial activities, securities markets, which were once national, public, or cooperative institutions, have abandoned their cooperative status or listed for trading on their own market. This change is transforming securities markets into real capitalistic enterprises oriented toward innovation and the optimization of their resources. It also favors mergers among the various market operators, with the objective of creating greater homogeneity in the financial markets, capital fluidity, diversity in the service offering, and reduced costs for publicly traded companies, investors, and intermediaries.

A few months after the introduction of the euro in September 2000, the Paris Stock Exchange played a pioneering role by merging with the Amsterdam and Brussels exchanges to become the first pan-European stock exchange: Euronext. Two years later,

after its own initial public offering, Euronext acquired the British derivatives market Liffe and integrated the Lisbon exchange. In April 2007, in an unprecedented event for our business sector, Euronext merged with the New York Stock Exchange, resulting in NYSE Euronext, the largest and most liquid securities market group in the world.

QUESTION: *What benefits do companies and investors receive from the merger of NYSE and Euronext?*

ANSWER: In 2007, over 4000 companies from 55 different countries were listed for trading on NYSE Euronext, representing a total market capitalization of close to 21,000 billion euros, more than the next four exchanges combined.

Present in six countries in the world, NYSE Euronext has an unequaled listing offer, with increased visibility and liquidity and expanded financing opportunities for issuers. Backed by a globally recognized label, NYSE Euronext enables companies to be listed on a market adapted to their size and location, within a stable regulatory environment, in dollarsand/or in euros (the world's two leading currencies), and under the accounting standards of their choice (IFRS or US GAAP).

In addition, the integration of the different NYSE Euronext markets, combined with the technological excellence of its digital market information system and the diverse array of financial products and services, encourages cross-border trading and increased liquidity, benefiting all users. In fact, more than one spot trade out of every three trades in the world is made on NYSE Euronext.

*This interview was conducted by Gunther Capelle-Blancard and Nicolas Couderc.

them to access the floor and trade on the exchange. Because license holders can go to IBM's trading post, for example, and directly sell IBM shares to the highest bidder or buy IBM shares at the lowest offered price, the exchange is an **auction market**.

Ask prices exceed bid prices. This difference is called the **bid-ask spread**. Because investors buy at the ask (the higher price) and sell at the bid (the lower price), the bid-ask spread is a **transaction cost** they have to pay in order to trade. When specialists in a physical market such as the NYSE take the other side of the trade from their customers, this transaction cost accrues to them as a profit. It is the compensation they demand for providing a liquid market by standing ready to honor any quoted price. Investors also pay other forms of transactions costs such as commissions.

Over-the-Counter Stock Markets

In today's technology-driven economy, a stock market does not need to have a physical location. Stock transactions can be made over the phone or by computer network. Consequently, stock markets such as NASDAQ, which are called **over-the-counter (OTC) markets**, are a collection of dealers or market makers connected by computer networks and telephones. An important difference between the NYSE and NASDAQ is that on the NYSE, each stock has only one market maker. On NASDAQ, stocks can and do have multiple market makers who compete with each other. Each market maker must post bid and ask prices in the NASDAQ network, where they can be viewed by all participants. Because investors do not directly interact to set the prices, NASDAQ and other over-the-counter markets are **dealer markets**. The NASDAQ system posts the best prices first and fills orders accordingly. This process guarantees investors the best possible price at the moment, whether they are buying or selling.

Listing Standards

Each exchange has its own **listing standards**, outlines of the requirements a company must meet to be traded on the exchange. These standards usually require that the company has enough shares outstanding for shareholders to have a liquid market and to be of interest to a broad set of investors. The NYSE's standards are more stringent than those of NASDAQ; traditionally, there has been a certain pride in being listed on the NYSE. Many companies would start on the NASDAQ and then move to the NYSE as they grew. However, NASDAQ has retained many big, successful companies such as Starbucks, Apple, and Microsoft. The two exchanges compete actively over listings of larger companies (NASDAQ landed Facebook and the NYSE won Twitter's listing) and the decision of where to list often comes down to which exchange the company's board believes will give its stockholders the best execution and liquidity for their trades.

Other Financial Markets

Of course, stock markets are not the only financial markets. There are markets to trade practically anything—some of them are physical places like the NYSE and others are purely electronic, like the NASDAQ. Two of the largest financial markets in the world, the bond market and the foreign exchange market, are simply networks of dealers connected by phone and computer. We will discuss these markets in more detail in later chapters (Chapters 6 and 15 for bonds and Chapter 23 for foreign exchange). Commodities like oil, wheat, and soybeans are traded on physical exchanges like the New York Mercantile Exchange. *Derivative securities*, which are complicated financial products used to hedge risks, are traded in locations like the Chicago Board Options Exchange (discussed in Chapter 21).

auction market A market where share prices are set through direct interaction of buyers and sellers.

bid-ask spread The amount by which the ask price exceeds the bid price.

transaction cost In most markets, an expense such as a broker commission and the bid-ask spread investors must pay in order to trade securities.

over-the-counter (OTC) market A market without a physical location, in which dealers are connected by computers and telephones.

dealer market A market where dealers buy and sell for their own accounts.

listing standards Outlines of the requirements a company must meet to be traded on the exchange.

NYSE, AMEX, DJIA, S&P 500: Awash in Acronyms

With all of these acronyms floating around, it's easy to get confused. You may have heard of the "Dow Jones" or "Dow Jones (Industrial) Average" and the "S&P 500" on news reports about the stock markets. The NYSE, AMEX, and NASDAQ are all stock markets where the prices of stocks are determined through trading. However, when commentators talk about whether stocks are up or down in general in a given day, they often refer to the Dow Jones Industrial Average (DJIA) and the Standard and Poor's 500 (S&P 500). The DJIA and S&P 500 are simply measures of the aggregate price level of collections of preselected stocks—30 in the case of the DJIA and 500 in the case of the S&P 500. These stocks were selected by Dow Jones (the publisher of the *Wall Street Journal*) or Standard & Poor's as representative of the overall market. The S&P 500 consists of 500 of the highest-valued U.S. companies. While fewer in number, the 30 stocks in the DJIA include companies such as Microsoft, Walmart, Boeing, and 3M, and are selected to cover the important sectors in the U.S. economy. The table below shows the 30 stocks in the DJIA as of September 2013. Dow Jones editors choose these stocks to reflect the overall U.S. economy. The membership of the index has changed over time to reflect the U.S. economy's transition from being industrial-driven to being more services and technology based. For example, they added Chevron in 2008 to capture the growing importance of energy. In 2012, they added UnitedHealth, the United States' largest insurer, to reflect the importance of healthcare for an aging U.S. population. Both the DJIA and S&P 500 include stocks that are traded on the NYSE and stocks that are traded on NASDAQ and so are distinct from the exchanges themselves.

Composition of the Dow Jones Industrial Average (DJIA)

3M Co.	General Electric Co.	Nike Inc.
AT&T Inc	Goldman Sachs Group Inc.	Pfizer Inc.
American Express Co.	Home Depot Inc.	Procter & Gamble Co.
Boeing Co.	Intel Corp.	Travelers Co.
Caterpillar Inc.	International Business Machines	UnitedHealth Group Inc.
Chevron Corp.	Johnson & Johnson	United Technologies Corp.
Cisco Systems Inc.	J.P. Morgan Chase & Co.	Verizon Communications Inc.
Coca-Cola Co.	McDonald's Corp.	Visa Inc.
Du Pont	Merck & Co.	Walmart Stores Inc.
Exxon Mobil Co.	Microsoft Corp.	Walt Disney Co.

Source: djindexes.com.

Concept Check

8. What advantage does a stock market provide to corporate investors? To financial managers?

9. What are the main differences between the NYSE and NASDAQ?

1.6 Financial Institutions

The spread of the 2008 financial crisis from subprime mortgages to Wall Street to traditional banks and businesses drew everyone's attention to *financial institutions* and their role in the economy. In general, **financial institutions** are entities that provide financial services, such as taking deposits, managing investments, brokering financial transactions, or making loans. In this section, we describe the key types of financial institutions and their functions.

financial institutions
Entities that provide financial services, such as taking deposits, managing investments, brokering financial transactions, or making loans.

The Financial Cycle

Keeping the names and roles of the different types of financial institutions straight can be challenging. It is helpful to think of the basic financial cycle, depicted in Figure 1.4, as context. In the financial cycle, (1) people invest and save their money, (2) that money, through loans and stock, flows to companies who use it to fund growth through new

FIGURE 1.4

The Financial Cycle

This figure depicts the basic financial cycle, which matches funds from savers to companies that have projects requiring funds and then returns the profits from those projects back to the savers and investors.

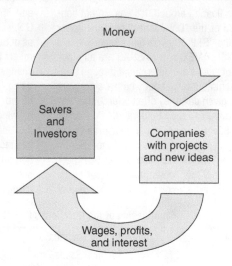

Types of Financial Institutions

products, generating profits and wages, and (3) the money then flows back to the savers and investors. All financial institutions play a role at some point in this cycle of connecting money with ideas and returning the profits back to the savers and investors.

Types of Financial Institutions

Table 1.2 lists the major categories of financial institutions, provides examples of representative firms, and summarizes the institutions' sources and uses of funds.

Financial conglomerates, sometimes referred to as *financial services firms*, combine more than one type of institution. Examples include Bank of America, JPMorgan Chase, and Deutsche Bank, all of which engage in commercial banking (like Wells Fargo) as well as investment banking. Investment banking refers to the business of advising companies in major financial transactions. Examples include buying and selling companies or divisions, and raising new capital by issuing stock or bonds. Goldman Sachs and Morgan Stanley are financial institutions that are focused on investment banking activities.

Role of Financial Institutions

Financial institutions have a role beyond moving funds from those who have extra funds (savers) to those who need funds (borrowers and firms): They also move funds through time. For example, suppose you need a $20,000 car loan. You need $20,000 now, but do not have it. However, you will have it in the future as you earn a salary. The financial institution, in this case a bank or credit union, helps transfer your future salary into funds today by issuing you a loan.

Financial institutions also help spread out risk-bearing. Insurance companies essentially pool premiums together from policyholders and pay the claims of those who have an accident, fire, medical need, or who die. This process spreads the financial risk of these events out across a large pool of policyholders and the investors in the insurance company. Similarly, mutual funds and pension funds take your savings and spread them out among the stocks and bonds of many different companies, limiting your risk exposure to any one company.

TABLE 1.2

Financial Institutions and Their Roles in the Financial Cycle

Institution	Source of Money	Use of Money
Banks and Credit Unions Examples: *Wells Fargo, SunTrust*	Deposits (savings)	Loans to people and businesses
Insurance Companies Examples: *Liberty Mutual, Allstate*	Premiums and investment earnings	Invests mostly in bonds and some stocks, using the investment income to pay claims
Mutual Funds Examples: *Vanguard, Fidelity*	People's investments (savings)	Buys stocks, bonds, and other financial instruments on behalf of its investors
Pension Funds Examples: *CalPERS, REST*	Retirement savings contributed through the workplace	Similar to mutual funds, except with the purpose of providing retirement income
Hedge Funds Examples: *Bridgewater, Soros Fund*	Investments by wealthy individuals and endowments	Invests in any kind of investment in an attempt to maximize returns
Venture Capital Funds Examples: *Kleiner Perkins, Sequoia Capital*	Investments by wealthy individuals and endowments	Invests in start-up, entrepreneurial firms
Private Equity Funds Examples: *TPG Capital, KKR*	Investments by wealthy individuals and endowments	Purchases whole companies by using a small amount of equity and borrowing the rest

While you may have seen coverage of the stock markets and discussion of financial institutions on the news, it is unlikely that you have been exposed to the finance function within a firm. In this chapter, we provided a sense of what corporate finance is all about, what a financial manager does, and the importance of stock markets and financial institutions. In upcoming chapters, you will learn how to make financial management decisions and how to use financial market information. We will explore the tools of financial analysis hand-in-hand with a clear understanding of when to apply them and why they work.

Concept Check

10. What is the basic financial cycle?

11. What are the three main roles financial institutions play?

MyFinanceLab

Here is what you should know after reading this chapter. MyFinanceLab will help you identify what you know, and where to go when you need to practice.

Key Points and Equations	Key Terms	Online Practice

1.1 Why Study Finance?

- Finance and financial decisions are everywhere in our daily lives.
- Many financial decisions are simple, but others are complex. All are tied together by the Valuation Principle—the foundation for financial decision making—which you will learn in this book.

1.2 The Four Types of Firms • There are four types of firms in the United States: sole proprietorships, partnerships, limited liability companies, and corporations. • Firms with unlimited personal liability include sole proprietorships and partnerships. • Firms with limited liability include limited partnerships, limited liability companies, and corporations. • A corporation is a legally defined artificial being (a judicial person or legal entity) that has many of the legal powers people have. It can enter into contracts, acquire assets, and incur obligations, and it enjoys protection under the U.S. Constitution against the seizure of its property. • The shareholders in a C corporation effectively must pay tax twice. The corporation pays tax once and then investors must pay personal tax on any funds that are distributed. S corporations are exempt from the corporate income tax. • The ownership of a corporation is divided into shares of stock collectively known as equity. Investors in these shares are called shareholders, stockholders, or equity holders.	C corporations, p. 9 corporation, p. 6 dividend payments, p. 7 equity, p. 7 equity holder, p. 7 limited liability, p. 6 limited liability company (LLC), p. 6 limited partnership, p. 6 partnership, p. 6 S corporations, p. 8 shareholder, p. 7 sole proprietorship, p. 5 stock, p. 7 stockholder, p. 7	MyFinanceLab Study Plan 1.2
1.3 The Financial Manager • The financial manager makes investing, financing, and cash flow management decisions. • The goal of the financial manager is to maximize the wealth of the shareholders (maximize the stock price).		MyFinanceLab Study Plan 1.3
1.4 The Financial Manager's Place in the Corporation • The ownership and control of a corporation are separate. Shareholders exercise their control indirectly through the board of directors.	agency problem, p. 13 board of directors, p. 12 chief executive officer (CEO), p. 12 hostile takeover, p. 15	MyFinanceLab Study Plan 1.4
1.5 The Stock Market • The shares of public corporations are traded on stock markets. The shares of private corporations do not trade on a stock market. • When a firm sells shares to investors, that is a primary market. The stock markets, such as NYSE and NASDAQ, are secondary markets where investors trade shares among each other. • NASDAQ is a dealer market, characterized by market makers trading for their own accounts.	ask price, p. 17 auction market, p. 18 bid-ask spread, p. 18 bid price, p. 17 bourse, p. 15 dealer market, p. 18 designated market makers, p. 17 liquid, p. 15 listing standards, p. 18 over-the-counter (OTC) market, p. 18 primary market, p. 16 secondary market, p. 16 stock exchange, p. 15 stock market, p. 15 transaction cost, p. 18	MyFinanceLab Study Plan 1.5

1.6 **Financial Institutions**
- In the basic financial cycle, money flows from savers and investors to companies and entrepreneurs with ideas, and then back to the savers and investors in the form of profits and interest.
- Financial institutions all play some role in this cycle.
- Financial institutions also help move money through time (e.g., loans against future wages) and spread risk across large investor bases.

financial institutions, MyFinanceLab
    p. 19   Study Plan 1.6

PROBLEMS

All problems are available in MyFinanceLab.

The Four Types of Firms

1. What is the most important difference between a corporation and *all* other organizational forms?

2. What does the phrase *limited liability* mean in a corporate context?

3. Which organizational forms give their owners limited liability?

4. What are the main advantages and disadvantages of organizing a firm as a corporation?

5. Explain the difference between an S and a C corporation.

6. You are a shareholder in a C corporation. The corporation earns $2.00 per share before taxes. Once it has paid taxes it will distribute the rest of its earnings to you as a dividend. Assume the corporate tax rate is 40% and the personal tax rate on (both dividend and non-dividend) income is 30%. How much is left for you after all taxes are paid?

7. Repeat Problem 6 assuming the corporation is an S corporation.

The Financial Manager

8. What is the most important type of decision that the financial manager makes?

9. Why do all shareholders agree on the same goal for the financial manager?

The Financial Manager's Place in the Corporation

10. Corporate managers work for the owners of the corporation. Consequently, they should make decisions that are in the interests of the owners, rather than in their own interests. What strategies are available to shareholders to help ensure that managers are motivated to act this way?

11. Recall the last time you ate at an expensive restaurant where you paid the bill. Now think about the last time you ate at a similar restaurant, but your parents paid the bill. Did you order more food (or more expensive food) when your parents paid? Explain how this relates to the agency problem in corporations.

12. Suppose you are considering renting an apartment. You, the renter, can be viewed as an agent while the company that owns the apartment can be viewed as the principal. What agency conflicts do you anticipate? Suppose, instead, that you work for the apartment company. What features would you put into the lease agreement that would give the renter incentives to take good care of the apartment?

13. You are the CEO of a company and you are considering entering into an agreement to have your company buy another company. You think the price might be too high, but you will be the CEO of the combined, much larger company. You know that when the company gets bigger, your pay and prestige will increase. What is the nature of the agency conflict here and how is it related to ethical considerations?

The Stock Market

14. What is the difference between a public and a private corporation?

15. What is the difference between a primary and a secondary market?

16. What are some of the differences between the NYSE and the NASDAQ?

17. Explain why the bid-ask spread is a transaction cost.

18. The following quote on Yahoo! stock appeared on July 10, 2013, on Yahoo! Finance:

If you wanted to buy Yahoo!, what price would you pay per share? How much would you receive per share if you wanted to sell Yahoo!?

Financial Institutions

19. What is the financial cycle?

20. How do financial institutions help with risk-bearing?

21. What role do investment banks play in the economy?

22. What are some of the similarities and differences among mutual funds, pension funds, and hedge funds?

Introduction to Financial Statement Analysis

LEARNING OBJECTIVES

- Know why the disclosure of financial information through financial statements is critical to investors

- Understand the function of the balance sheet

- Understand how the income statement is used

- Interpret a statement of cash flows

- Understand the management's discussion and analysis and the statement of stockholders' equity

- Analyze a firm through its financial statements, including using the DuPont Identity

- Understand the main purpose and aspects of the Sarbanes-Oxley reforms following Enron and other financial scandals

As we discussed in Chapter 1, anyone with money to invest is a potential investor who can own shares in a corporation. As a result, corporations are often widely held, with investors ranging from individuals who hold one share to large financial institutions that own millions of shares. For example, in 2012, International Business Machines Corporation (IBM) had about 1.2 billion shares outstanding held by nearly 600,000 stockholders. Although the corporate organizational structure greatly facilitates the firm's access to investment capital, it also means that stock ownership is most investors' sole tie to the company. How, then, do investors learn enough about a company to know whether or not they should invest in it? One way firms evaluate their performance and communicate this information to investors is through their *financial statements*. Financial statements also enable financial managers to assess the success of their own firm and compare it to competitors.

Firms regularly issue financial statements to communicate financial information to the investment community. A detailed description of the preparation and analysis of these statements is sufficiently complicated that to do it justice would require an entire book. In this chapter, we briefly review the subject, emphasizing only the material that investors and corporate financial managers need in order to make the corporate finance decisions we discuss in the text.

We review the four main types of financial statements, present examples of these statements for a firm, and discuss where an investor or manager might find various types of information about the company. We also discuss some of the financial ratios used to assess a firm's performance and value. We close the chapter with a look at financial reporting abuses and the Sarbanes-Oxley regulatory response.

2.1 Firms' Disclosure of Financial Information

financial statements
Accounting reports issued by a firm quarterly and/or annually that present past performance information and a snapshot of the firm's assets and the financing of those assets.

Financial statements are accounting reports issued by a firm periodically (usually quarterly and annually) that present past performance information and a snapshot of the firm's assets and the financing of those assets. Public companies in the United States are required to file their financial statements with the U.S. Securities and Exchange Commission (SEC) on a quarterly basis on form *10-Q* and annually on form *10-K*.[1] They must also send an **annual report (10-K)** with their financial statements to their shareholders each year. Often, private companies also prepare financial statements, but they usually do not have to disclose these reports to the public. Financial statements are important tools with which investors, financial analysts, and other interested outside parties (such as creditors) obtain information about a corporation. They are also useful for managers within the firm as a source of information for the corporate financial decisions we discussed in Chapter 1. In this section, we examine the guidelines for preparing financial statements and introduce the different types of financial statements.

annual report (10-K) The yearly summary of business, accompanying or including financial statements, sent by U.S. public companies to their shareholders.

Preparation of Financial Statements

Generally Accepted Accounting Principles (GAAP) A common set of rules and a standard format for public companies to use when they prepare their financial reports.

Reports about a company's performance must be understandable and accurate. In the United States, the Financial Accounting Standards Board (FASB) establishes **Generally Accepted Accounting Principles (GAAP)** to provide a common set of rules and a standard format for public companies to use when they prepare their reports. This standardization also makes it easier to compare the financial results of different firms.

International Financial Reporting Standards

Generally Accepted Accounting Principles (GAAP) differ among countries. As a result, companies face tremendous accounting complexities when they operate internationally. Investors also face difficulty interpreting financial statements of foreign companies, which discourages them from investing abroad. As companies and capital markets become more global, however, interest in harmonization of accounting standards across countries has increased.

The most important harmonization project began in 1973 when representatives of 10 countries (including the United States) established the International Accounting Standards Committee. This effort led to the creation of the International Accounting Standards Board (IASB) in 2001, with headquarters in London. Now the IASB has issued a set of International Financial Reporting Standards (IFRS).

The IFRS are taking root throughout the world. The European Union (EU) approved an accounting regulation in 2002 requiring all publicly traded EU companies to follow IFRS in their consolidated financial statements starting in 2005. As of 2012, more than 120 jurisdictions either require or permit the use of IFRS, including the EU, Australia, Brazil, Canada, Russia, Hong Kong, Taiwan, and Singapore. China, India, and Japan will soon follow suit. In fact,

currently all major stock exchanges around the world accept IFRS except the United States and Japan, which maintain their local GAAP.

The main difference between U.S. GAAP and IFRS is conceptual—U.S. GAAP are based primarily on accounting rules with specific guidance in applying them, whereas IFRS are based more on principles requiring professional judgment by accountants, and specific guidance in application is limited. Even so, some differences in rules also exist. For example, U.S. GAAP generally prohibit the upward revaluation of non-financial assets, whereas the IFRS allow the revaluation of some such assets to fair value. U.S. GAAP also rely more heavily on historical cost, as opposed to "fair value," to estimate the value of assets and liabilities.

Effort to achieve convergence between U.S. GAAP and IFRS was spurred by the Sarbanes-Oxley Act of 2002 in the United States. It included a provision that U.S. accounting standards move toward international convergence on high-quality accounting standards. Currently, SEC regulations still require public U.S. firms to report using U.S. GAAP. That said, modifications to both IFRS and U.S. GAAP have brought the two closer together, with the key remaining differences in the areas of revenue recognition, impairment charges, leasing, insurance, and the treatment of financial instruments. As of the end of 2013, the SEC is re-evaluating convergence between U.S. GAAP and IFRS, but U.S. and international standard setters work together on new accounting issues that arise.

---

[1]The Securities and Exchange Commission was established by Congress in 1934 to regulate securities (for example, stocks and bonds) issued to the public and the financial markets (exchanges) on which those securities trade.

SUE FRIEDEN

Sue Frieden is Ernst & Young's Global Managing Partner, Quality & Risk Management. A member of the Global Executive board, she is responsible for every aspect of quality and risk management—employees, services, procedures, and clients.

QUESTION: *Do today's financial statements give the investing public what they need?*

ANSWER: Globally, we are seeing an effort to provide more forward-looking information to investors. But fundamental questions remain, such as how fully do investors understand financial statements and how fully do they read them? Research shows that most individual investors don't rely on financial statements much at all. We need to determine how the financial statement and related reporting models can be improved. To do that we will need a dialogue involving investors, regulators, analysts, auditors, stock exchanges, academics, and others to ensure that financial statements and other reporting models are as relevant as they can be.

QUESTION: *Ernst & Young is a global organization. How do accounting standards in the U.S. compare to those elsewhere?*

ANSWER: In January of 2005, 100 countries outside the U.S. began the process of adopting new accounting standards (International Financial Reporting Standards) that would in large measure be based on principles rather than rules. As global markets become more complex, we all need to be playing by the same set of rules. As a first step, we need consistency from country to country. There are definite challenges to overcome in reconciling principle-based and rules-based systems, but we are optimistic that these challenges will inevitably get resolved. At the same time, there are efforts underway to ensure that auditing standards are globally consistent. Ultimately, financial statements prepared under global standards and audited under consistent global auditing standards will better serve investors.

QUESTION: *What role does the audit firm play in our financial markets, and how has that changed since the collapse of Arthur Andersen?*

ANSWER: The accounting profession has seen unprecedented change recently. The passage of Sarbanes-Oxley and other changes are helping to restore public trust. We're now engaging on a regular basis with a wider range of stakeholders—companies, boards, policymakers, opinion leaders, investors, and academia. And we've had the chance to step back and ask ourselves why we do what we do as accounting professionals, and why it matters. In terms of the services we offer, much of what we do helps companies comply with regulations, guard against undue risks, and implement sound transactions. Part of the value in what we do is providing all stakeholders the basis to understand whether companies are playing by the rules—be they accounting, financial reporting, or tax rules. We help create confidence in financial data. The public may not understand precisely what auditors do or how we do it, but they care that we exist, because it provides them the confidence they so badly need and want.

QUESTION: *Accounting standards seem to be shifting from historical cost-based methods to methods that rely on current market values of assets. During the financial crisis, however, many financial institutions complained that "mark-to-market" rules exacerbated their financial difficulties. Do you believe accounting professionals should rethink the wisdom of moving to market-based accounting methods?*

ANSWER: Fair value accounting can certainly be improved, particularly in light of the difficulty in applying fair value in illiquid markets, which the financial crisis highlighted, and because of some of the anomalies that fair value accounting can produce. But, by and large, fair value accounting provided transparency into reality for investors. It is the most transparent way to reflect the economic reality of prevailing market conditions and provide investors and companies with current financial information on which they can base investment and management decisions. Fair value accounting did not cause the economic crisis; it simply kept a fair scorecard.

---

auditor A neutral third party, which corporations are required to hire, that checks a firm's annual financial statements to ensure they are prepared according to GAAP, and provides evidence to support the reliability of the information.

Investors also need some assurance that the financial statements are prepared accurately. Publicly traded corporations are required to hire a neutral third party, known as an **auditor**, to check the annual financial statements, ensure they are prepared according to GAAP, and provide evidence to support the reliability of the information.

Types of Financial Statements

Every public company is required to produce four financial statements: the *balance sheet*, the *income statement*, the *statement of cash flows*, and the *statement of stockholders' equity*. These financial statements provide investors and creditors with an overview of the firm's financial performance. In the sections that follow, we take a close look at the content of these financial statements.

1. What is the role of an auditor?
2. What are the four financial statements that all public companies must produce?

2.2 The Balance Sheet

balance sheet A list of a firm's assets and liabilities that provides a snapshot of the firm's financial position at a given point in time.

The **balance sheet**, or **statement of financial position**,[2] lists the firm's *assets* and *liabilities*, providing a snapshot of the firm's financial position at a given point in time. Table 2.1 shows the balance sheet for a fictitious company, Global Corporation. Notice that the balance sheet is divided into two parts ("sides") with the assets on the left side and the liabilities on the right side.

assets The cash, inventory, property, plant, and equipment, and other investments a company has made.

1. The **assets** list the firm's cash, inventory, property, plant and equipment, and any other investments the company has made.
2. The **liabilities** show the firm's obligations to its creditors.

liabilities A firm's obligations to its creditors.

3. Also shown with liabilities on the right side of the balance sheet is the *stockholders' equity*. **Stockholders' equity** (also called **shareholders' equity**), the difference between the firm's assets and liabilities, is an accounting measure of the firm's net worth. For Global, the stockholders' equity has two parts: (1) **common stock and paid-in surplus**, the amount that stockholders have directly invested in the firm through purchasing stock from the company and (2) **retained earnings**, which are profits made by the firm, but retained within the firm and reinvested in assets or held as cash. We will take a more detailed look at retained earnings in our discussion of the statement of cash flows later in this chapter.

shareholders' equity, stockholders' equity An accounting measure of a firm's net worth that represents the difference between the firm's assets and its liabilities.

common stock and paid-in surplus The amount that stockholders have directly invested in the firm through purchasing stock from the company.

The assets on the left side show how the firm uses its capital (its investments), and the information on the right side summarizes the sources of capital, or how the firm raises the money it needs. Because of the way stockholders' equity is calculated, the left and right sides must balance:

The Balance Sheet Identity

$$\text{Assets} = \text{Liabilities} + \text{Stockholders' Equity} \tag{2.1}$$

In Table 2.1, total assets for 2013 ($170.1 million) are equal to total liabilities ($147.9 million) plus stockholders' equity ($22.2 million).

retained earnings Profits made by the firm, but retained within the firm and reinvested in assets or held as cash.

Let's examine Global's assets, liabilities, and stockholders' equity in more detail.

Assets

In Table 2.1, Global's assets are divided into *current* and *long-term assets*. We discuss each in turn.

---

[2]In IFRS and recent U.S. GAAP pronouncements, the balance sheet is referred to as the *statement of financial position*.

TABLE 2.1

Global Corporation Balance Sheet for 2013 and 2012 ($ millions)

Assets	2013	2012	Liabilities and Stockholders' Equity	2013	2012
Current Assets			**Current Liabilities**		
Cash	23.2	20.5	Accounts payable	29.2	26.5
Accounts receivable	18.5	13.2	Notes payable/short-term debt	5.5	3.2
Inventories	15.3	14.3			
Total current assets	57.0	48.0	Total current liabilities	34.7	29.7
Long-Term Assets			**Long-Term Liabilities**		
Net property, plant, and equipment	113.1	80.9	Long-term debt	113.2	78.0
Total long-term assets	113.1	80.9	Total long-term liabilities	113.2	78.0
			Total Liabilities	**147.9**	**107.7**
			Stockholders' Equity		
			Common stock and paid-in surplus	8.0	8.0
			Retained earnings	14.2	13.2
			Total Stockholders' Equity	**22.2**	**21.2**
Total Assets	**170.1**	**128.9**	**Total Liabilities and Stockholders' Equity**	**170.1**	**128.9**

current assets Cash or assets that can be converted into cash within one year.

marketable securities Short-term, low-risk investments that can be easily sold and converted to cash.

accounts receivable Amounts owed to a firm by customers who have purchased goods or services on credit.

inventories A firm's raw materials as well as its work-in-progress and finished goods.

long-term assets Assets that produce tangible benefits for more than one year.

depreciation A yearly deduction a firm makes from the value of its fixed assets (other than land) over time, according to a depreciation schedule that depends on an asset's life span.

book value The acquisition cost of an asset less its accumulated depreciation.

Current Assets. **Current assets** are either cash or assets that can be converted into cash within one year. This category includes:

1. Cash and other **marketable securities**, which are short-term, low-risk investments that can be easily sold and converted to cash (such as money market investments, like government debt, that mature within a year);

2. **Accounts receivable**, which are amounts owed to the firm by customers who have purchased goods or services on credit;

3. **Inventories**, which are composed of raw materials as well as work-in-progress and finished goods; and

4. Other current assets, which is a catch-all category that includes items such as prepaid expenses (such as rent or insurance).

Long-Term Assets. Assets such as real estate or machinery that produce tangible benefits for more than one year are called **long-term assets**. If Global spends $2 million on new equipment, this $2 million will be included with net property, plant, and equipment under long-term assets on the balance sheet. Because equipment tends to wear out or become obsolete over time, Global will reduce the value recorded for this equipment through a yearly deduction called **depreciation** according to a depreciation schedule that depends on an asset's life span. Depreciation is not an actual cash expense that the firm pays; it is a way of recognizing that buildings and equipment wear out and thus become less valuable the older they get. The **book value** of an asset, which is the value shown in the firm's financial statements, is equal to its acquisition cost less accumulated depreciation. The figures for net property, plant, and equipment show the total book value of these assets.

Other long-term assets can include such items as property not used in business operations, start-up costs in connection with a new business, trademarks and patents, and property held for sale. The sum of all the firms' assets is the total assets at the bottom of the left side of the balance sheet in Table 2.1.

Liabilities

We now examine the liabilities, shown on the right side of the balance sheet, which are divided into *current* and *long-term liabilities.*

current liabilities
Liabilities that will be satisfied within one year.

accounts payable The amounts owed to creditors for products or services purchased with credit.

notes payable, short-term debt Loans that must be repaid in the next year.

net working capital The difference between a firm's current assets and current liabilities that represents the capital available in the short term to run the business.

Current Liabilities. Liabilities that will be satisfied within one year are known as **current liabilities**. They include:

1. **Accounts payable**, the amounts owed to suppliers for products or services purchased with credit.
2. **Notes payable** and **short-term debt**, loans that must be repaid in the next year. Any repayment of long-term debt that will occur within the next year would also be listed here as current maturities of long-term debt.
3. Accrual items, such as salary or taxes, that are owed but have not yet been paid, and deferred or unearned revenue, which is revenue that has been received for products or services that have not yet been delivered.

The difference between current assets and current liabilities is the firm's **net working capital**, the capital available in the short term to run the business. While notes payable and short-term debt are included in current liabilities, they are different from accounts payable and accrual items. Notes payable and short-term debt are related to financing decisions of the firm, while accounts payable and accruals arise from operating decisions of the firm. This distinction is important later when we see that financial managers generally try to keep these two decisions (operating and financing) separate.

$$\text{Net Working Capital} = \text{Current Assets} - \text{Current Liabilities} \qquad (2.2)$$

For example, in 2013, Global's net working capital totaled $22.3 million ($57.0 million in current assets − $34.7 million in current liabilities). Firms with low (or negative) net working capital may face a shortage of funds. In such cases, the liabilities due in the short term exceed the company's cash and expected payments on receivables.

long-term debt Any loan or debt obligation with a maturity of more than a year.

Long-Term Liabilities. Long-term liabilities are liabilities that extend beyond one year. When a firm needs to raise funds to purchase an asset or make an investment, it may borrow those funds through a long-term loan. That loan would appear on the balance sheet as **long-term debt**, which is any loan or debt obligation with a maturity of more than a year.

Stockholders' Equity

book value of equity The difference between the book value of a firm's assets and its liabilities; also called *shareholders' equity* and *stockholders' equity*, it represents the net worth of a firm from an accounting perspective.

The sum of the current liabilities and long-term liabilities is total liabilities. The difference between the firm's assets and liabilities is the *stockholders' equity*; it is also called the **book value of equity** or *shareholders' equity*. As we stated earlier, it represents the net worth of the firm from an accounting perspective. The two main components are common stock and paid-in surplus and retained earnings. These two components form the book value of stockholders' ownership claims, stemming from their direct investment and reinvestment of profits.

Ideally, the balance sheet would provide us with an accurate assessment of the true value of the firm's equity. Unfortunately, this is unlikely to be the case. First, many of the assets listed on the balance sheet are valued based on their historical cost rather than their true value today. For example, an office building is listed on the balance sheet according to its historical cost less its accumulated depreciation. But the actual value of the office building today may be very different than this amount; in fact, if real estate prices went up it will be worth *more* than the amount the firm paid for it years ago. The same is true for other property, plant, and equipment: The true value today of an asset may be very different from, and even exceed, its book value. A second, and probably more important, problem is that *many of the firm's valuable assets are not captured on the balance sheet.* Consider, for example, the expertise of the firm's employees, the firm's reputation in the marketplace, the relationships with customers and suppliers, and the quality of the management team. All these assets add to the value of the firm but do not appear on the balance sheet. Although the book value of a firm's equity is not a good estimate of its true value as an ongoing firm, it is sometimes used as an estimate of the **liquidation value** of the firm, the value that would be left after its assets were sold and liabilities paid.

liquidation value The value of a firm after its assets are sold and liabilities paid.

Market Value Versus Book Value

For these reasons, the book value of equity is an inaccurate assessment of the actual value of the firm's equity. Thus, it is not surprising that it will often differ substantially from the amount investors are willing to pay for the equity. The total market value of a firm's equity equals the market price per share times the number of shares, referred to as the company's **market capitalization**. The market value of a stock does not depend on the historical cost of the firm's assets; instead, it depends on what investors expect those assets to produce in the future. To see the difference, think about what happens when a company like Boeing unveils a new plane. Investors' expectations about future cash flows from selling those planes increase the stock price immediately, elevating the market value of Boeing. However, the revenue from selling the planes will only be reflected in Boeing's financial statements when it actually sells them.

market capitalization The total market value of equity; equals the market price per share times the number of shares.

Finally, we note that the book value of equity can be negative (liabilities exceed assets), and that a negative book value of equity is not necessarily an indication of poor

EXAMPLE 2.1

Market Versus Book Value

MyFinanceLab

PROBLEM

If Global has 3.6 million shares outstanding, and these shares are trading for a price of $10.00 per share, what is Global's market capitalization? How does the market capitalization compare to Global's book value of equity?

SOLUTION

PLAN

Market capitalization is equal to price per share times shares outstanding. We can find Global's book value of equity at the bottom of the right side of its balance sheet.

EXECUTE

Global's market capitalization is ($10.00/share) $\times$ (3.6 million shares) = $36 million. This market capitalization is significantly higher than Global's book value of equity of $22.2 million.

EVALUATE

Global must have sources of value that do not appear on the balance sheet. These include potential opportunities for growth, the quality of the management team, relationships with suppliers and customers, etc.

performance. Successful firms are often able to borrow in excess of the book value of their assets because creditors recognize that the market value of the assets is far higher. For example, in June 2005 Amazon.com had total liabilities of $2.6 billion and a book value of equity of −$64 million. At the same time, the market value of its equity was over $15 billion. Clearly, investors recognized that Amazon's assets were worth far more than the book value reported on the balance sheet. By 2013, several years of strong growth had brought its book value of equity to over $8 billion and its market value of equity to more than $120 billion!

Market-to-Book Ratio

market-to-book ratio (price-to-book [P/B] ratio) The ratio of a firm's market (equity) capitalization to the book value of its stockholders' equity.

In Example 2.1, we compared the market and book values of Global's equity. A common way to make this comparison is to compute the **market-to-book ratio** (also called the **price-to-book [P/B] ratio**), which is the ratio of a firm's market capitalization to the book value of stockholders' equity.

$$\text{Market-to-Book Ratio} = \frac{\text{Market Value of Equity}}{\text{Book Value of Equity}} \tag{2.3}$$

It is one of many financial ratios used to evaluate a firm. The market-to-book ratio for most successful firms substantially exceeds 1, indicating that the value of the firm's assets when put to use exceeds their historical cost (or liquidation value). The ratio will vary across firms due to differences in fundamental firm characteristics as well as the value added by management. Thus, this ratio is one way a company's stock price provides feedback to its managers on the market's assessment of their decisions.

In mid-2013, AmeriServ Financial, Inc. (ASRV) had a market-to-book ratio of 0.64, a reflection of investors' assessment that many of AmeriServ's assets were unlikely to be profitable and were worth less than their book value. Citigroup's market-to-book ratio of 0.83 tells a similar story. Figure 2.1 shows that at the same time, the average market-to-book ratio for the financial services industry was about 1, and for large U.S. firms it was close to 3. In contrast, consider that Amazon.com, Inc. (AMZN) had a market-to-book ratio of over 14, and the average for technology firms was about 5. Analysts often classify firms with low market-to-book ratios as **value stocks**, and those with high market-to-book ratios as **growth stocks**.

value stocks Firms with low market-to-book ratios.

growth stocks Firms with high market-to-book ratios.

Enterprise Value

enterprise value The total market value of a firm's equity and debt, less the value of its cash and marketable securities. It measures the value of the firm's underlying business.

A firm's market capitalization measures the market value of the firm's equity, or the value that remains after the firm has paid its debts. So it includes any cash the firm holds. But what if you are interested in just the value of the business itself? The **enterprise value** of a firm assesses the value of the underlying business assets, unencumbered by debt and separate from any cash and marketable securities. We compute it as follows:

$$\text{Enterprise Value} = \text{Market Value of Equity} + \text{Debt} - \text{Cash} \tag{2.4}$$

For example, given its market capitalization from Example 2.1, Global's enterprise value in 2013 is $36 + 118.7 − 23.2 = \$131.5$ million. We can interpret the enterprise value as the cost to take over the business. That is, it would cost $36 + 118.7 = \$154.7$ million to buy all of Global's equity and pay off its debts. Because we would acquire Global's $23.2 million in cash (which can be used to pay off Global's debt), the net cost is only $154.7 − 23.2 = \$131.5$ million.

FIGURE 2.1

Market-to-Book
Ratios in 2013

This figure presents market-to-book ratios of different firms and groups of firms in 2013. Firms that might be classified as value stocks (low market-to-book ratios) are in red and those that might be classified as growth stocks (high market-to-book ratios) are in blue.

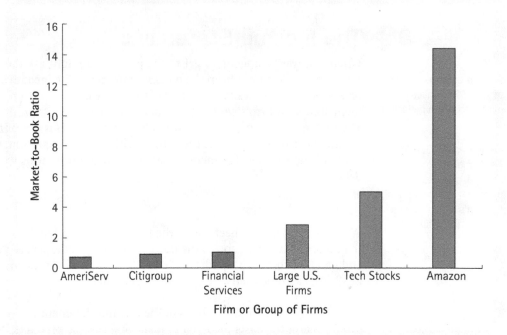

EXAMPLE 2.2

Computing
Enterprise Value

MyFinanceLab

PROBLEM

In June 2013, H. J. Heinz Co. (HNZ) had 320.7 million shares outstanding, a share price of $72.36, a book value of debt of $4.98 billion, and cash of $1.1 billion. What was Heinz's market capitalization (its market value of equity)? What was its enterprise value?

SOLUTION

PLAN

Share Price	$72.36
Shares Outstanding	320.7 million
Cash	$1.10 billion
Debt (book)	$4.98 billion

We will solve the problem using Eq. 2.4: Enterprise Value = Market Value of Equity + Debt − Cash. We can compute the market capitalization by multiplying the share price times the number of shares outstanding. We are given the amount of cash and the amount of debt.

EXECUTE

Heinz had a market capitalization of $72.36/share × 320.7 million shares = $23.21 billion. Thus, Heinz's enterprise value was 23.21 + 4.98 − 1.10 = $27.09 billion.

EVALUATE

The value of Heinz's underlying business, separate from any cash it holds, should be equal to the total value of the financial claims (equity and debt) on that business, which is its enterprise value of $27.09 billion.

3. What is depreciation designed to capture?

4. The book value of a company's assets usually does not equal the market value of those assets. What are some reasons for this difference?

2.3 The Income Statement

income statement A list of a firm's revenues and expenses over a period of time.

When you want someone to get to the point, you might ask them for the "bottom line." This expression comes from the *income statement*. The **income statement** lists the firm's revenues and expenses over a period of time. The last or "bottom" line of the income statement shows the firm's **net income**, which is a measure of its profitability during the period. The income statement is sometimes called a *profit and loss* or *P&L statement*, and the net income is also referred to as the firm's **earnings**. In this section, we examine the components of the income statement in detail and introduce ratios we can use to analyze this data.

net income or earnings
The last or "bottom" line of a firm's income statement that is a measure of the firm's income over a given period of time.

Earnings Calculations

Whereas the balance sheet shows the firm's assets and liabilities at a given point in time, the income statement shows the flow of revenues and expenses generated by those assets and liabilities between two dates. Table 2.2 shows Global's income statement for 2013 and 2012. We examine each category on the statement.

gross profit The third line of an income statement that represents the difference between a firm's sales revenues and its costs.

Gross Profit. The first two lines of the income statement list the revenues from sales of products and the costs incurred to make and sell the products. Note that in accounting, the terms *revenues* and *net sales* are equivalent. Net sales is simply gross sales minus any returns, discounts, and allowances. We will simply use the term *sales* from here forward. The third line is **gross profit**, the difference between sales revenues and the cost of sales.

TABLE 2.2

Global Corporation's
Income Statement
Sheet for 2013
and 2012

GLOBAL CORPORATION Income Statement Year ended December 31 (in $ millions)		
	2013	2012
Net sales	186.7	176.1
Cost of sales	−153.4	−147.3
Gross Profit	33.3	28.8
Selling, general, and administrative expenses	−13.5	−13
Research and development	−8.2	−7.6
Depreciation and amortization	−1.2	−1.1
Operating Income	10.4	7.1
Other income	—	—
Earnings Before Interest and Taxes (EBIT)	10.4	7.1
Interest income (expense)	−7.7	−4.6
Pretax Income	2.7	2.5
Taxes	−0.7	−0.6
Net Income	2.0	1.9
Earnings per share:	$0.56	$0.53
Diluted earnings per share:	$0.53	$0.50

Operating Expenses. The next group of items is operating expenses. These are expenses from the ordinary course of running the business that are not directly related to producing the goods or services being sold. They include administrative expenses and overhead, salaries, marketing costs, and research and development expenses. The third type of operating expense, depreciation and amortization (a charge that captures the change in value of acquired assets), represents an estimate of the costs that arise from wear and tear or obsolescence of the firm's assets.[3] It is not an actual cash expense. The firm's gross profit less its operating expenses is called **operating income**.

operating income
A firm's gross profit less its operating expenses.

Earnings Before Interest and Taxes. We next include other sources of income or expenses that arise from activities that are not the central part of a company's business. Cash flows from the firm's financial investments are one example of other income that would be listed here. After we have adjusted for other sources of income or expenses, we have the firm's earnings before interest and taxes, or **EBIT**.

EBIT A firm's earnings before interest and taxes are deducted.

Pretax and Net Income. From EBIT, we deduct the interest paid on outstanding debt to compute Global's pretax income, and then we deduct corporate taxes to determine the firm's net income.

Net income represents the total earnings of the firm's equity holders. It is often reported on a per-share basis as the firm's **earnings per share (EPS)**, which we compute by dividing net income by the total number of shares outstanding:

earnings per share (EPS) A firm's net income divided by the total number of shares outstanding.

$$\text{EPS} = \frac{\text{Net Income}}{\text{Shares Outstanding}} = \frac{\$2.0 \text{ million}}{3.6 \text{ million shares}} = \$0.56 \text{ per share} \qquad (2.5)$$

Although Global has only 3.6 million shares outstanding as of the end of 2013 (from Example 2.1), the number of shares outstanding may grow if Global has made commitments that would cause it to issue more shares. Consider these two examples:

stock options The right to buy a certain number of shares of stock by a specific date at a specific price.

1. Suppose Global compensates its employees or executives with **stock options** that give the holder the right to buy a certain number of shares by a specific date at a specific price. If employees "exercise" these options, the company issues new stock and the number of shares outstanding would grow.

convertible bonds Corporate bonds with a provision that gives the bondholder an option to convert each bond owned into a fixed number of shares of common stock.

2. The number of shares may also grow if the firm issues **convertible bonds**, a form of debt that can be converted into shares of common stock.

In the cases of stock options and convertible bonds, because there will be more total shares to divide the same earnings, this growth in the number of shares is referred to as **dilution**. Firms disclose the potential for dilution from options they have awarded by reporting **diluted EPS**, which shows the earnings per share the company would have if the stock options were exercised. For example, if Global has awarded options for 200,000 shares of stock to its key executives, its diluted EPS is $2.0 million/3.8 million shares = $0.53.

dilution An increase in the total number of shares that will divide a fixed amount of earnings.

diluted EPS The earnings per share a company would have based on the total number of shares including the effects of all stock options and convertible bonds.

EBITDA

As will become clear when we discuss the Statement of Cash Flows in the next section, neither EBIT nor net income are the same as the firm's cash flow. So, financial analysts often compute a firm's earnings before interest, taxes, depreciation, and amortization, or **EBITDA**. Because depreciation and amortization are not cash expenses for the firm,

---

[3]Only certain types of amortization are deductible as a pretax expense (e.g., amortization of the cost of an acquired patent). Amortization of goodwill is not a pretax expense and is generally included as an extraordinary item after taxes are deducted.

EBITDA A computation of a firm's earnings before interest, taxes, depreciation, and amortization are deducted.

EBITDA reflects the cash a firm has earned from its operations. If we add back Global's depreciation and amortization to its EBIT, we find that its EBITDA in 2013 was $10.4 + 1.2 = \$11.6$ million.

Concept Check

5. What do a firm's earnings measure?
6. What is dilution?

2.4   The Statement of Cash Flows

The income statement provides a measure of the firm's profit over a given time period. However, it does not indicate the amount of *cash* the firm has earned. There are two reasons that net income does not correspond to cash earned. First, there are non-cash entries on the income statement, such as depreciation and amortization. Second, certain uses, such as the purchase of a building or expenditures on inventory, and sources of cash, such as the collection of accounts receivable, are not reported on the income statement. The firm's **statement of cash flows** utilizes the information from the income statement and balance sheet to determine how much cash the firm has generated, and how that cash has been allocated, during a set period. Cash is important: It is needed to pay bills and maintain operations and is the source of any return of investment for investors. Thus, from the perspective of an investor attempting to value the firm or a financial manager concerned about cash flows (vs. earnings), the statement of cash flows provides what may be the most important information of the four financial statements.

statement of cash flows An accounting statement that shows how a firm has used the cash it earned during a set period.

The statement of cash flows is divided into three sections: operating activities, investment activities, and financing activities. These sections roughly correspond to the three major jobs of the financial manager.

1. *Operating activities* starts with net income from the income statement. It then adjusts this number by adding back all non-cash entries related to the firm's operating activities.
2. *Investment activities* lists the cash used for investment.
3. *Financing activities* shows the flow of cash between the firm and its investors.

Global's statement of cash flows is shown in Table 2.3. In this section, we take a close look at each component of the statement of cash flows.

Operating Activity

The first section of Global's statement of cash flows adjusts net income by all non-cash items related to operating activity. For instance, depreciation is deducted when computing net income, but it is not an actual cash expense. Thus, we add it back to net income when determining the amount of cash the firm has generated. Similarly, we add back any other non-cash expenses (for example, deferred taxes).

Next, we adjust for changes to net working capital that arise from changes to accounts receivable, accounts payable, or inventory. When a firm sells a product, it records the revenue as income even though it may not receive the cash from that sale immediately. Instead, it may grant the customer credit and let the customer pay in the future. The customer's obligation adds to the firm's accounts receivable. We use the following guidelines to adjust for changes in working capital:

1. Accounts receivable: When a sale is recorded as part of net income, but the cash has not yet been received from the customer, we must adjust the cash flows by *deducting* the increases in accounts receivable. This increase represents additional lending by the firm to its customers and it reduces the cash available to the firm.

2. Accounts payable: We *add* increases in accounts payable. Accounts payable represents borrowing by the firm from its suppliers. This borrowing increases the cash available to the firm.

3. Inventory: Finally, we *deduct* increases in inventory. Increases in inventory are not recorded as an expense and do not contribute to net income (the cost of the goods are only included in net income when the goods are actually sold). However, the cost of increasing inventory is a cash expense for the firm and must be deducted.

Working capital adjustments address the difference between the time when sales and costs are recorded on the income statement and when the cash actually goes in and out of the firm. For example, Table 2.3 shows that in 2013 we *subtracted* the $5.3 million increase in accounts receivable from net income as part of the operating cash flow calculation. What happened? From Table 2.2, we see that Global had $10.6 million more in sales in 2013 than

TABLE 2.3

Global Corporation's Statement of Cash Flows for 2013 and 2012

GLOBAL CORPORATION Statement of Cash Flows Year ended December 31 (in $ millions)		
	2013	2012
Operating activities		
Net income	2.0	1.9
Depreciation and amortization	1.2	1.1
Cash effect of changes in		
Accounts receivable	−5.3	−0.3
Accounts payable	2.7	−0.5
Inventory	−1.0	−1.0
Cash from operating activities	−0.4	1.2
Investment activities		
Capital expenditures	−33.4	−4.0
Acquisitions and other investing activity	—	—
Cash from investing activities	−33.4	−4.0
Financing activities		
Dividends paid	−1.0	−1.0
Sale or purchase of stock	—	—
Increase in short-term borrowing	2.3	3.0
Increase in long-term borrowing	35.2	2.5
Cash from financing activities	36.5	4.5
Change in cash and cash equivalents	2.7	1.7

in 2012. However, from Table 2.1, we also see that Global's accounts receivable increased from $13.2 million in 2012 to $18.5 million in 2013. So, even though Global's sales were up considerably, it has not yet collected all the cash flow for those sales—instead, Global's customers owe it $5.3 million more at the end of 2013 than they did at the end of 2012. Because the statement of cash flows starts with net income, which includes sales for which Global has not yet been paid, we deduct the additional $5.3 million in sales Global is still owed when computing the actual cash flows it generated.

We must make a similar adjustment for inventory. Global does not record the cost of the inventory until it is sold, when it is included in the cost of goods sold. However, when it actually pays for the inventory, cash has flowed out of Global, decreasing operating cash flow. The opposite is true for accounts payable—Global has recorded additional expenses without actually paying for them yet. Those expenses reduce net income, but do not represent cash outflows.

Finally, we add depreciation to net income before calculating operating cash flow. Depreciation is an accounting adjustment to book value that is an expense, but not a cash outflow. That is, when Global's property, plant, and equipment depreciate by $1.2 million, it does not literally cost Global $1.2 million in cash flow. Because this is an expense that reduces net income, but not an actual cash outflow, we must add it back to calculate cash flow. We will talk more about depreciation when we do capital budgeting in Chapter 9. All these adjustments mean that cash flow can be very different from net income. Although Global showed positive net income on the income statement, it actually had a negative $0.4 million cash flow from operating activity, in large part because of the increase in accounts receivable.

EXAMPLE 2.3
The Impact of Depreciation on Cash Flow

MyFinanceLab

PROBLEM

Suppose Global had an additional $1 million depreciation expense in 2013. If Global's tax rate on pretax income is 26%, what would be the impact of this expense on Global's earnings? How would it impact Global's cash at the end of the year?

SOLUTION

PLAN

Depreciation is an operating expense, so Global's operating income, EBIT, and pretax income would be affected. With a tax rate of 26%, Global's tax bill will decrease by 26 cents for every dollar that pretax income is reduced. In order to determine how Global's cash would be impacted, we have to determine the effect of the additional depreciation on cash flows. Recall that depreciation is not an actual cash outflow, even though it is treated as an expense, so the only effect on cash flow is through the reduction in taxes.

EXECUTE

Global's operating income, EBIT, and pretax income would fall by $1 million because of the $1 million in additional operating expense due to depreciation.

This $1 million decrease in pretax income would reduce Global's tax bill by 26% × $1 million = $0.26 million. Therefore, net income would fall by $1 − $0.26 = $0.74 million.

On the statement of cash flows, net income would fall by $0.74 million, but we would add back the additional depreciation of $1 million because it is not a cash expense. Thus, cash from operating activities would rise by −$0.74 + 1 = $0.26 million. Therefore, Global's cash balance at the end of the year would increase by $0.26 million, the amount of the tax savings that resulted from the additional depreciation deduction.

EVALUATE

The increase in cash balance comes completely from the reduction in taxes. Because Global pays $0.26 million less in taxes even though its cash expenses have not increased, it has $0.26 million more in cash at the end of the year.

Investment Activity

capital expenditures
Purchases of new
property, plant, and
equipment.

The next section of the statement of cash flows shows the cash required for investment activities. Purchases of new property, plant, and equipment are **capital expenditures**. Recall that capital expenditures do not appear immediately as expenses on the income statement. Instead, the firm depreciates these assets and deducts depreciation expenses over time. To determine the firm's cash flow, we already added back depreciation because it is not an actual cash expense. Now, we subtract the actual capital expenditure that the firm made. Similarly, we also deduct other assets purchased or investments made by the firm, such as acquisitions. In Table 2.3, we see that in 2013, Global spent $33.4 million in cash on investing activities. This can be confirmed by adding the depreciation amount of $1.2 from Table 2.2 to the change in net fixed assets of ($113.1–$80.9) from Table 2.1.

Financing Activity

The last section of the statement of cash flows shows the cash flows from financing activities. Dividends paid to shareholders are a cash outflow. Global paid $1 million to its shareholders as dividends in 2013.

The difference between a firm's net income and the amount it spends on dividends is referred to as the firm's retained earnings for that year:

$$\text{Retained Earnings} = \text{Net Income} - \text{Dividends} \qquad (2.6)$$

payout ratio The ratio of
a firm's dividends to its
net income.

Global retained $2 million − $1 million = $1 million, or 50% of its earnings in 2013. This makes its *payout ratio* for 2013 equal to 50%. A firm's **payout ratio** is the ratio of its dividends to its net income:

$$\text{Payout Ratio} = \frac{\text{Dividends}}{\text{Net Income}} \qquad (2.7)$$

Also listed under financing activity is any cash the company received from the sale of its own stock, or cash spent buying (repurchasing) its own stock. Global did not issue or repurchase stock during this period.

The last items to include in this section result from changes to Global's short-term and long-term borrowing. Global raised money by issuing debt, so the increases in short-term and long-term borrowing represent cash inflows. The last line of the statement of cash flows combines the cash flows from these three activities to calculate the overall change in the firm's cash balance over the period of the statement. In this case, Global had cash inflows of $2.7 million in 2013, which matches the change in cash from 2012 to 2013 shown earlier in the balance sheet. By looking at the statement in Table 2.3 as a whole, we can determine that Global chose to borrow (mainly in the form of long-term debt) to cover the cost of its investment and operating activities. Although the firm's cash balance has increased, Global's negative operating cash flows and relatively high expenditures on investment activities might give investors some reasons for concern. If this pattern continues, Global will need to raise new external capital to remain in business.

Concept Check

7. Why does a firm's net income not correspond to cash earned?
8. What are the components of the statement of cash flows?

2.5 Other Financial Statement Information

The most important elements of a firm's financial statements are the balance sheet, income statement, and the statement of cash flows, which we have already discussed. Several other pieces of information contained in the financial statements warrant brief mention: the *statement of stockholders' equity*, the *management discussion and analysis*, and *notes to the financial statements*.

Statement of Stockholders' Equity

statement of stockholders' equity An accounting statement that breaks down the stockholders' equity computed on the balance sheet into the amount that came from issuing new shares versus retained earnings.

The **statement of stockholders' equity** breaks down the stockholders' equity computed on the balance sheet into the amount that came from issuing shares (par value plus paid-in capital) versus retained earnings. Because the book value of stockholders' equity is not a useful assessment of value for financial purposes, financial managers use the statement of stockholders' equity infrequently (so we will skip the computational details here). We can, however, determine the change in stockholder's equity using information from the firm's other financial statements as follows:[4]

$$\text{Change in Stockholders' Equity} = \text{Retained Earnings} + \text{Net Sales of Stock}$$
$$= \text{Net Income} - \text{Dividends} + \text{Sales of Stock}$$
$$- \text{Repurchases of Stock} \qquad (2.8)$$

For example, because Global had no stock sales or repurchases, its stockholders' equity increased by the amount of its retained earnings, or $1.0 million, in 2013. Note that this result matches the change in stockholders' equity shown earlier on Global's balance sheet.

Management Discussion and Analysis

management discussion and analysis (MD&A) A preface to the financial statements in which a company's management discusses the recent year (or quarter), providing a background on the company and any significant events that may have occurred.

The **management discussion and analysis (MD&A)** is a preface to the financial statements in which the company's management discusses the recent year (or quarter), providing a background on the company and any significant events that may have occurred. Management may also discuss the coming year, and outline goals and new projects.

Management must also discuss any important risks that the firm faces or issues that may affect the firm's liquidity or resources. Management is also required to disclose any **off-balance sheet transactions**, which are transactions or arrangements that can have a material impact on the firm's future performance yet do not appear on the balance sheet. For example, if a firm has made guarantees that it will compensate a buyer for losses related to an asset purchased from the firm, these guarantees represent a potential future liability for the firm that must be disclosed as part of the MD&A.

off-balance sheet transactions Transactions or arrangements that can have a material impact on a firm's future performance yet do not appear on the balance sheet.

Notes to the Financial Statements

In addition to the four financial statements, companies provide extensive notes with additional details on the information provided in the statements. For example, the notes document important accounting assumptions that were used in preparing the statements. They often provide information specific to a firm's subsidiaries or its separate product lines. They show the details of the firm's stock-based compensation plans for employees and the different types of debt the firm has outstanding. Details of acquisitions, spin-offs, leases, taxes, and risk management activities are also given. The information provided in the notes is often very important to a full interpretation of the firm's financial statements.

Concept Check

9. Where do off-balance sheet transactions appear in a firm's financial statements?

10. What information do the notes to financial statements provide?

2.6 Financial Statement Analysis

Investors often use accounting statements to evaluate a firm in one of two ways:

1. Compare the firm with itself by analyzing how the firm has changed over time.
2. Compare the firm to other similar firms using a common set of financial ratios.

---

[4]Sales of stock would also include any stock-based compensation.

In this section, we will describe the most commonly used ratios—related to profitability, liquidity, asset efficiency, working capital, interest coverage, leverage, valuation, and operating returns—and explain how each one is used in practice.

Profitability Ratios

We introduce three profitability ratios: *gross margin*, *operating margin*, and *net profit margin*.

gross margin The ratio of gross profit to revenues (sales), it reflects the ability of the company to sell a product for more than the sum of the direct costs of making it.

Gross Margin. The **gross margin** of a firm is the ratio of gross profit to revenues (sales):

$$\text{Gross Margin} = \frac{\text{Gross Profit}}{\text{Sales}} \qquad (2.9)$$

The gross margin simply reflects the ability of the company to sell a product for more than the sum of the direct costs of making it. All of the firm's other expenses of doing business (those not directly related to producing the goods sold) must be covered by this margin. In 2013, Global's gross profit was $33.3 million and its sales were $186.7 million, for a gross margin of 33.3/186.7 = 17.84%.

operating margin The ratio of operating income to revenues, it reveals how much a company has earned from each dollar of sales before deducting interest and taxes.

Operating Margin. Because operating income reflects all of the expenses of doing business, another important profitability ratio is the **operating margin**, the ratio of operating income to revenues:

$$\text{Operating Margin} = \frac{\text{Operating Income}}{\text{Sales}} \qquad (2.10)$$

The operating margin reveals how much a company earns before interest and taxes from each dollar of sales. Global's operating margin in 2013 was 10.4/186.7 = 5.57%, an increase from its 2012 operating margin of 7.1/176.1 = 4.03%. By comparing operating margins across firms within an industry, we can assess the relative efficiency of firms' operations. For example, in 2012, United Continental Holdings (UAL) had an operating margin of 0.2% (i.e., they gained 0.2 cents for each dollar in revenues). However, competitor Alaska Air Group (ALK) had an operating margin of 12.02%.

Differences in operating margins can also result from differences in strategy. For example, in 2010, Walmart Stores had an operating margin of 5.97% while high-end retailer Nordstrom had an operating margin of 11.07%. In this case, Walmart's lower operating margin is not a result of its inefficiency but is part of its strategy of offering lower prices to sell common products in high volume. Indeed, Walmart's sales were more than 38 times higher than those of Nordstrom.

net profit margin The ratio of net income to revenues, it shows the fraction of each dollar in revenues that is available to equity holders after the firm pays its expenses, plus interest and taxes.

Net Profit Margin. A firm's **net profit margin** is the ratio of net income to revenues:

$$\text{Net Profit Margin} = \frac{\text{Net Income}}{\text{Sales}} \qquad (2.11)$$

The net profit margin shows the fraction of each dollar in revenues that is available to equity holders after the firm pays its expenses, interest, and taxes. Global's net profit margin in 2013 was 2.0/186.7 = 1.07%. Differences in net profit margins can be due to differences in efficiency, but they can also result from differences in leverage (the firm's reliance on debt financing), which determines the amount of interest payments.

Liquidity Ratios

current ratio The ratio of current assets to current liabilities.

quick ratio ("acid-test ratio") The ratio of current assets other than inventory to current liabilities.

Creditors often compare a firm's current assets and current liabilities to assess whether the firm has sufficient working capital to meet its short-term needs. This comparison is sometimes summarized in the firm's **current ratio**, the ratio of current assets to current liabilities. A more stringent test of the firm's liquidity is the **quick ratio ("acid-test" ratio)**, which compares only cash and "near cash" assets, such as short-term investments and accounts receivable, to current liabilities.

$$\text{Current Ratio} = \frac{\text{Current Assets}}{\text{Current Liabilities}} \tag{2.12}$$

$$\text{Quick Ratio} = \frac{\text{Current Assets} - \text{Inventory}}{\text{Current Liabilities}} \tag{2.13}$$

In 2013, Global's quick ratio was $(57.0 - 15.3)/34.7 = 1.20$. A higher current or quick ratio implies less risk of the firm experiencing a cash shortfall in the near future. A reason to exclude inventory is that an increase in the current ratio that results from an unusual increase in inventory could be an indicator that the firm is having difficulty selling its products.

cash ratio The ratio of cash to current liabilities.

Ultimately, firms need cash to pay employees and meet other obligations. Running out of cash can be very costly for a firm, so firms often gauge their cash position by calculating the **cash ratio**, which is the most stringent liquidity ratio:

$$\text{Cash Ratio} = \frac{\text{Cash}}{\text{Current Liabilities}} \tag{2.14}$$

Asset Efficiency

asset turnover The ratio of sales to total assets.

A financial manager can use the combined information in the firm's income statement and balance sheet to gauge how efficiently his or her firm is utilizing its assets. A first broad measure of efficiency is **asset turnover**, the ratio of sales to total assets:

$$\text{Asset Turnover} = \frac{\text{Sales}}{\text{Total Assets}} \tag{2.15}$$

Low values of asset turnover indicate that the firm is not generating much revenue (sales) per dollar of assets. In 2013, Global's $170.1 million in assets generated $186.7 million in sales, for an asset turnover ratio of 1.1 (=$186.7/$170.1). Since total assets includes assets, such as cash, that are not directly involved in generating sales, Global's manager might also look at Global's fixed asset turnover, which is equal to sales divided by fixed assets:

$$\text{Fixed Asset Turnover} = \frac{\text{Sales}}{\text{Fixed Assets}} \tag{2.16}$$

accounts receivable days (average collection period or days sales outstanding) An expression of a firm's accounts receivable in terms of the number of days' worth of sales that the accounts receivable represents.

Global's fixed assets in 2013 were $113.1 million worth of property, plant, and equipment, yielding a fixed asset turnover of 1.7 (= $186.7/$113.1). Low asset turnover ratios indicate that the firm is generating relatively few sales given the amount of assets it employs.

Working Capital Ratios

Global's managers might be further interested in how efficiently they are managing their net working capital. We can express the firm's accounts receivable in terms of the number of days' worth of sales that it represents, called the **accounts receivable days**, **average collection period**, or **days sales outstanding**:[5]

$$\text{Accounts Receivable Days} = \frac{\text{Accounts Receivable}}{\text{Average Daily Sales}} \qquad (2.17)$$

accounts payable days An expression of a firm's accounts payable in terms of the number of days' worth of cost of goods sold that the accounts payable represents.

inventory days An expression of a firm's inventory in terms of the number of days' worth of cost of goods sold that the inventory represents.

inventory turnover ratio The cost of goods sold divided by either the latest cost of inventory or the average inventory over the year, it shows how efficiently companies turn their inventory into sales.

Given average daily sales of $186.7 million/365 = $0.51 million in 2013, Global's receivables of $18.5 million represent 18.5/0.51 = 36 days' worth of sales. In other words, Global takes a little over one month to collect payment from its customers, on average. In 2012, Global's accounts receivable represented only 27.5 days worth of sales. Although the number of receivable days can fluctuate seasonally, a significant unexplained increase could be a cause for concern (perhaps indicating the firm is doing a poor job collecting from its customers or is trying to boost sales by offering generous credit terms). Similar ratios exist for accounts payable and inventory. Those ratios are called **accounts payable days** (accounts payable divided by average daily cost of goods sold) and **inventory days** (inventory divided by average daily cost of goods sold).

We can also compute how efficiently firms use inventory. The **inventory turnover ratio** is equal to the cost of goods sold divided by either the latest cost of inventory or the average inventory over the year. We use the cost of goods sold because that is how inventory costs are reflected on the income statement. It is also common to use sales in the numerator to make the ratio more like the asset turnover ratios.

$$\text{Inventory Turnover} = \frac{\text{Cost of Goods Sold}}{\text{Inventory}} \qquad (2.18)$$

As with the other ratios in this section, a normal level for this ratio can vary substantially for different industries, although a higher level (more dollars of sales per dollar of inventory) is generally better.

EXAMPLE 2.4

Computing Working Capital Ratios

MyFinanceLab

PROBLEM

Compute Global's accounts payable days, inventory days, and inventory turnover for 2013.

SOLUTION

PLAN AND ORGANIZE

Working capital ratios require information from both the balance sheet and the income statement. For these ratios, we need inventory and accounts payable from the balance sheet and cost of goods sold from the income statement (often listed as cost of sales).

Inventory = 15.3, Accounts payable = 29.2, Cost of goods sold (cost of sales) = 153.4

EXECUTE

$$\text{Accounts payable days} = \frac{\text{Accounts Payable}}{\text{Average Daily Cost of Goods Sold}} = \frac{29.2}{(153.4/365)} = 69.48$$

$$\text{Inventory days} = \frac{\text{Inventory}}{\text{Average Daily Cost of Goods Sold}} = \frac{15.3}{(153.4/365)} = 36.40$$

$$\text{Inventory turnover} = \frac{\text{Cost of Goods Sold}}{\text{Inventory}} = \frac{153.4}{15.3} = 10.03$$

(Continued)

[5]Accounts receivable days can also be calculated based on the average accounts receivable at the end of the current and prior years.

EVALUATE

Assuming that Global's accounts payable at year-end on its balance sheet is representative of the normal amount during the year, Global is able, on average, to take about 69.5 days to pay its suppliers. This compares well with the 27.5 days we calculated that it waits on average to be paid (its accounts receivable days). Global typically takes 36 days to sell its inventory. Note that inventory turnover and inventory days tell us the same thing in different ways—if it takes Global about 36 days to sell its inventory, then it turns over its inventory about 10 times per 365-day year. In Chapter 19 on working capital management, we'll see how a company's receivable, inventory, and payable days make up its operating cycle.

Interest Coverage Ratios

interest coverage ratio or times interest earned (TIE) ratio An assessment by lenders of a firm's leverage, it is equal to a measure of earnings divided by interest.

Lenders often assess a firm's leverage by computing an **interest coverage ratio**, also known as a **times interest earned (TIE) ratio**, which is equal to a measure of earnings divided by interest. Financial managers watch these ratios carefully because they assess how easily the firm will be able to cover its interest payments. There is no one accepted measure of earnings for these ratios; it is common to consider operating income, EBIT, or EBITDA as a multiple of the firm's interest expenses. When this ratio is high, it indicates that the firm is earning much more than is necessary to meet its required interest payments.

EXAMPLE 2.5

Computing Interest Coverage Ratios

MyFinanceLab

PROBLEM

Assess Global's ability to meet its interest obligations by calculating interest coverage ratios using both EBIT and EBITDA.

SOLUTION

PLAN AND ORGANIZE

Gather the EBIT, depreciation, and amortization and interest expense for each year from Global's income statement.

2012: EBIT = 7.1, EBITDA = 7.1 + 1.1, Interest expense = 4.6

2013: EBIT = 10.4, EBITDA = 10.4 + 1.2, Interest expense = 7.7

EXECUTE

In 2012 and 2013, Global had the following interest coverage ratios:

$$2012: \frac{\text{EBIT}}{\text{Interest}} = \frac{7.1}{4.6} = 1.54 \quad \text{and} \quad \frac{\text{EBITDA}}{\text{Interest}} = \frac{7.1 + 1.1}{4.6} = 1.78$$

$$2013: \frac{\text{EBIT}}{\text{Interest}} = \frac{10.4}{7.7} = 1.35 \quad \text{and} \quad \frac{\text{EBITDA}}{\text{Interest}} = \frac{10.4 + 1.2}{7.7} = 1.51$$

EVALUATE

The coverage ratios indicate that Global is generating enough cash to cover its interest obligations. However, Global's low—and declining—interest coverage could be a source of concern for its creditors.

Leverage Ratios

leverage A measure of the extent to which a firm relies on debt as a source of financing.

Another important piece of information that we can learn from a firm's balance sheet is the firm's **leverage**, or the extent to which it relies on debt as a source of financing. The **debt-equity ratio** is a common ratio used to assess a firm's leverage that we calculate by

debt-equity ratio The ratio of a firm's total amount of short- and long-term debt (including current maturities) to the value of its equity, which may be calculated based on market or book values.

dividing the total amount of short- and long-term debt (including current maturities) by the total stockholders' equity:

$$\text{Debt-Equity Ratio} = \frac{\text{Total Debt}}{\text{Total Equity}} \qquad (2.19)$$

We can calculate this ratio using either book or market values for equity and debt. From Table 2.1, Global's debt in 2013 includes notes payable ($5.5 million) and long-term debt ($113.2 million), for a total of $118.7 million. Therefore, using the book value of equity, its *book* debt-equity ratio is 118.7/22.2 = 5.3. Note the large increase from 2012, when the book debt-equity ratio was only (3.2 + 78)/21.2 = 3.8.

Because of the difficulty interpreting the book value of equity, the book debt-equity ratio is not especially useful. It is more informative to compare the firm's debt to the market value of its equity. Global's debt-equity ratio in 2013, using the market value of equity (from Example 2.1), is 118.7/36 = 3.3, which means Global's debt is a bit more than triple the market value of its equity.[6] As we will see later in the text, a firm's *market* debt-equity ratio has important consequences for the risk and return of its stock.

debt-to-capital ratio The ratio of total debt to total debt plus total equity.

We can also calculate the fraction of the firm financed by debt in terms of its **debt-to-capital ratio**:

$$\text{Debt-to-Capital Ratio} = \frac{\text{Total Debt}}{\text{Total Equity} + \text{Total Debt}} \qquad (2.20)$$

Again, this ratio can be computed using book or market values.

While leverage increases the risk to the firm's equity holders, firms may also hold cash reserves in order to reduce risk. Thus, another useful measure to consider is the firm's

net debt Debt in excess of a firm's cash reserves.

net debt, or debt in excess of its cash reserves:

$$\text{Net Debt} = \text{Total Debt} - \text{Excess Cash \& Short-Term Investments} \qquad (2.21)$$

To understand why net debt may be a more relevant measure of leverage, consider a firm with more cash than debt outstanding: Because such a firm could pay off its debts immediately using its available cash, it has not increased its risk and has no effective leverage.

debt-to-enterprise value ratio The ratio of a firm's net debt to its enterprise value.

Analogous to the debt-to-capital ratio, we can use the concept of net debt to compute the firm's **debt-to-enterprise value ratio**:

$$\text{Debt-to-Enterprise Value Ratio} = \frac{\text{Net Debt}}{\text{Market Value of Equity} + \text{Net Debt}}$$

$$= \frac{\text{Net Debt}}{\text{Enterprise Value}} \qquad (2.22)$$

Given Global's 2013 cash balance of $23.2 million, and total long- and short-term debt of $118.7 million, its net debt is 118.7 − 23.2 = $95.5 million.[7] Given its market value of equity of $36.0 million, Global's enterprise value in 2013 is 36.0 + 95.5 = $131.5 million, and thus its debt-to-enterprise value ratio is 95.5/131.5 = 72.6%. That is, 72.6% of Global's underlying business activity is financed via debt.

---

[6]In this calculation, we have compared the market value of equity to the book value of debt. Strictly speaking, it would be best to use the market value of debt. But because the market value of debt is generally not very different from its book value, this distinction is often ignored in practice.

[7]While net debt should ideally be calculated by deducting cash in excess of the firm's operating needs, absent additional information, it is typical in practice to deduct all cash on the balance sheet.

equity multiplier A measure of leverage equal to total assets divided by total equity.

A final measure of leverage is a firm's **equity multiplier**, measured in book value terms as Total Assets/Book Value of Equity. As we will see shortly, this measure captures the amplification of the firm's accounting returns that results from leverage. The market value equity multiplier, which is generally measured as Enterprise Value/Market Value of Equity, indicates the amplification of shareholders' financial risk that results from leverage.

Valuation Ratios

Analysts and investors use a number of ratios to gauge the market value of a firm. The most important is the firm's **price-earnings ratio (P/E)**:

price-earnings ratio (P/E) The ratio of the market value of equity to the firm's earnings, or its share price to its earnings per share.

$$\text{P/E Ratio} = \frac{\text{Market Capitalization}}{\text{Net Income}} = \frac{\text{Share Price}}{\text{Earnings per Share}} \tag{2.23}$$

That is, the P/E ratio is the ratio of the value of equity to the firm's earnings, either on a total basis or on a per-share basis. Following Eq. 2.23, Global's P/E ratio in 2013 was $36/2.0 = 10/0.56 = 18$. The P/E ratio is a simple measure that is often used to assess whether a stock is over- or under-valued, based on the idea that the value of a stock should be proportional to the level of earnings it can generate for its shareholders. P/E ratios can vary widely across industries and tend to be higher for industries with high growth rates. For example, in 2010, the average large U.S. firm had a P/E ratio of about 19. But software firms, which tend to have above-average growth rates, had an average P/E ratio of 28. One way to capture the idea that a higher P/E ratio can be justified by a higher growth rate is to compare it to the company's expected earnings growth rate. For example, if Global's expected growth rate is 18%, then it would have a P/E to Growth, or **PEG ratio**, of 1. Some investors consider PEG ratios of 1 or below as indicating the stock is fairly priced, but would question whether the company is potentially overvalued if the PEG is higher than 1.

PEG ratio The ratio of a firm's P/E to its expected earnings growth rate.

The P/E ratio considers the value of the firm's equity and so depends on its leverage. Recall that the amount of assets controlled by the equity holders can be increased through the use of leverage. To assess the market value of the underlying business, it is common to consider valuation ratios based on the firm's enterprise value. Typical ratios include the ratio of enterprise value to revenue, or enterprise value to operating income, or EBITDA. These ratios compare the value of the business to its sales, operating profits, or cash flow. Similar to the P/E ratio, managers use these ratios to make intra-industry comparisons of how firms are priced in the market.

COMMON MISTAKE   Mismatched Ratios

When considering valuation (and other) ratios, be sure that the items you are comparing both represent amounts related to the entire firm or that both represent amounts related solely to equity holders. For example, a firm's share price and market capitalization are values associated with the firm's equity. Thus, it makes sense to compare them to the firm's earnings per share or net income, which are amounts to equity holders after interest has been paid to debt holders. We must be careful, however, if we compare a firm's market capitalization to its revenues, operating income, or EBITDA. These amounts are related to the whole firm, and both debt and equity holders have a claim to them. Therefore, it is better to compare revenues, operating income, or EBITDA to the enterprise value of the firm, which includes both debt and equity.

The P/E ratio is not useful when the firm's earnings are negative. In this case, it is common to look at the firm's enterprise value relative to sales. The risk in doing so, however, is that earnings might be negative because the firm's underlying business model is fundamentally flawed, as was the case for many Internet firms in the late 1990s.

EXAMPLE 2.6

Computing Profitability and Valuation Ratios

MyFinanceLab

PROBLEM

Consider the following data from 2012 for Walmart Stores and Target Corporation ($ billions):

	Walmart Stores (WMT)	Target Corporation (TGT)
Sales	469	73
Operating Income	28	5
Net Income	17	3
Market Capitalization	222	38
Cash	8	1
Debt	54	18

Compare Walmart's and Target's operating margin, net profit margin, P/E ratio, and the ratio of enterprise value to operating income and sales.

SOLUTION

PLAN

The table contains all of the raw data, but we need to compute the ratios using the inputs in the table.

Operating Margin = Operating Income/Sales
Net Profit Margin = Net Income/Sales
P/E Ratio = Price/Earnings = Market Capitalization/Net Income
Enterprise Value to Operating Income = Enterprise Value/Operating Income
Enterprise Value to Sales = Enterprise Value/Sales

EXECUTE

Walmart had an operating margin of 28/469 = 6.0%, a net profit margin of 17/469 = 3.6%, and a P/E ratio of 222/17 = 13.1. Its enterprise value was 222 + 54 − 8 = $268 billion. Its ratio to operating income is 268/28 = 9.6, and its ratio to sales is 268/469 = 0.57.

Target had an operating margin of 5/73 = 6.8%, a net profit margin of 3/73 = 4.1%, and a P/E ratio of 38/3 = 12.7. Its enterprise value was 38 + 18 − 1 = $55 billion. Its ratio to operating income is 55/5 = 11, and its ratio to sales is 55/73 = 0.75.

EVALUATE

Target has a slightly higher operating margin, net profit margin, and enterprise value ratio, but a slightly lower P/E ratio. This suggests that the market expects similar growth rates from Target and Walmart, despite large differences in size.

Operating Returns

return on equity (ROE) The ratio of a firm's net income to the book value of its equity.

Analysts and financial managers often evaluate the firm's return on investment by comparing its income to its investment using ratios such as the firm's **return on equity (ROE)**:[8]

$$\text{Return on Equity} = \frac{\text{Net Income}}{\text{Book Value of Equity}} \qquad (2.24)$$

Global's ROE in 2013 was 2.0/22.2 = 9.0%. The ROE provides a measure of the return that the firm has earned on its past investments. A high ROE may indicate the firm is able to find investment opportunities that are very profitable. Of course, one weakness of this measure is the difficulty in interpreting the book value of equity.

---

[8]Because net income is measured over the year, the ROE can also be calculated based on the average book value of equity at the end of the current and prior years.

return on assets (ROA) The ratio of net income plus interest expense to the total book value of the firm's assets.

Another common measure is the **return on assets (ROA)**, which is net income plus interest expense divided by the total assets. The ROA calculation includes interest expense in the numerator because the assets in the denominator have been funded by both debt and equity investors. A firm must earn both a positive ROE and ROA to grow.

As a performance measure, ROA has the benefit that it is less sensitive to leverage than ROE. However, it is sensitive to working capital—for example, an equal increase in the firm's receivables and payables will increase total assets and thus lower ROA. To avoid this problem, we can consider the firm's **return on invested capital (ROIC)**:

return on invested capital (ROIC) The ratio of the after-tax profit before interest to the book value of invested capital not being held as cash (book equity plus net debt)

$$\text{Return on Invested Capital} = \frac{\text{EBIT} (1 - \text{Tax Rate})}{\text{Book Value of Equity} + \text{Net Debt}} \tag{2.25}$$

The return on invested capital measures the after-tax profit generated by the business itself, excluding any interest expenses (or interest income), and compares it to the capital raised from equity and debt holders that has already been deployed (i.e., is not held as cash). Of the three measures of operating returns, ROIC is the most useful in assessing the performance of the underlying business.

EXAMPLE 2.7
Computing Operating Returns

MyFinanceLab

PROBLEM

Assess how Global's ability to use its assets effectively has changed in the last year by computing the change in its return on assets.

SOLUTION

PLAN AND ORGANIZE

In order to compute ROA, we need net income, interest expense, and total assets.

	2012	2013
Net Income	1.9	2.0
Interest Expense	4.6	7.7
Total Assets	128.9	170.1

EXECUTE

In 2013, Global's ROA was $(2.0 + 7.7)/170.1 = 5.7\%$, compared to an ROA in 2012 of $(1.9 + 4.6)/128.9 = 5.0\%$.

EVALUATE

The improvement in Global's ROA from 2012 to 2013 suggests that Global was able to use its assets more effectively and increase its return over this period.

The DuPont Identity

DuPont Identity Expresses return on equity as the product of profit margin, asset turnover, and a measure of leverage.

Global's financial manager will need to know that its ROE is 9%, but that financial manager would also need to understand the drivers of his or her firm's return on equity. High margins, efficient use of assets, or even simply high leverage could all lead to a higher return on equity. By delving deeper into the sources of return on equity, the financial manager can gain a clear sense of the firm's financial picture. One common tool for doing so is the **DuPont Identity**, named for the company that popularized it, which expresses return on equity as the product of profit margin, asset turnover, and a measure of leverage.

To understand the DuPont Identity, we start with ROE and decompose it in steps into the drivers identified in the identity. First, we simply multiply ROE by (sales/sales), which is just 1, and rearrange terms:

$$\text{ROE} = \left(\frac{\text{Net Income}}{\text{Total Equity}}\right)\left(\frac{\text{Sales}}{\text{Sales}}\right) = \left(\frac{\text{Net Income}}{\text{Sales}}\right)\left(\frac{\text{Sales}}{\text{Total Equity}}\right) \qquad (2.26)$$

This expression says that ROE can be thought of as net income per dollar of sales (profit margin) times the amount of sales per dollar of equity. For example, Global's ROE comes from its profit margin of 1.07% multiplied by its sales per dollar of equity ($186.7/22.2 = 8.41$): $1.07\% \times 8.41 = 9\%$. We can take the decomposition further by multiplying Eq. 2.26 by (total assets/total assets), which again is just 1, and rearranging the terms:

DuPont Identity

$$\text{ROE} = \left(\frac{\text{Net Income}}{\text{Sales}}\right)\left(\frac{\text{Sales}}{\text{Total Equity}}\right)\left(\frac{\text{Total Assets}}{\text{Total Assets}}\right)$$

$$= \left(\frac{\text{Net Income}}{\text{Sales}}\right)\left(\frac{\text{Sales}}{\text{Total Assets}}\right)\left(\frac{\text{Total Assets}}{\text{Total Equity}}\right) \qquad (2.27)$$

This final expression says that ROE is equal to net income per dollar of sales (profit margin) times sales per dollar of assets (asset turnover) times assets per dollar of equity (equity multiplier). Equation 2.27 is the DuPont Identity, expressing return on equity as the product of profit margin, asset turnover, and the equity multiplier. Turning to Global, its equity multiplier is $7.7 (=170.1/22.2)$. A financial manager at Global looking for ways to increase ROE could assess the drivers behind its current ROE with the DuPont Identity. With a profit margin of 1.07%, asset turnover of 1.1, and an equity multiplier of 7.7, we have:

$$\text{ROE} = 9\% = (1.07\%)(1.1)(7.7)$$

This decomposition of ROE shows that leverage is already high (confirmed by the fact that the book debt-to-equity ratio shows that Global's debt is more than five times its equity). However, Global is operating with only 1% profit margins and relatively low asset turnover. Thus, Global's managers should focus on utilizing the firm's existing assets more efficiently and lowering costs to increase the profit margin.[9]

EXAMPLE 2.8

DuPont Analysis

MyFinanceLab

PROBLEM

The following table contains information about Walmart (WMT) and Nordstrom (JWN). Compute their respective ROEs and then determine how much Walmart would need to increase its profit margin in order to match Nordstrom's ROE.

	Profit Margin	Asset Turnover	Equity Multiplier
Walmart	3.6%	2.3	2.7
Nordstrom	6.1%	1.5	4.2

(Continued)

---

[9]Although the DuPont Identity makes it look like you can increase ROE just by increasing leverage, it is not quite that simple. An increase in leverage will increase your interest expense, decreasing your profit margin.

SOLUTION

PLAN AND ORGANIZE

The table contains all the relevant information to use the DuPont Identity to compute the ROE. We can compute the ROE of each company by multiplying together its profit margin, asset turnover, and equity multiplier. In order to determine how much Walmart would need to increase its profit margin to match Nordstrom's ROE, we can set Walmart's ROE equal to Nordstrom's, keep its turnover and equity multiplier fixed, and solve for the profit margin.

EXECUTE

Using the DuPont Identity, we have:

$$\text{ROE}_{\text{WMT}} = 3.6\% \times 2.3 \times 2.7 = 22.4\%$$

$$\text{ROE}_{\text{JWN}} = 6.1\% \times 1.5 \times 4.2 = 38.4\%$$

Now, using Nordstrom's ROE, but Walmart's asset turnover and equity multiplier, we can solve for the profit margin that Walmart needs to achieve Nordstrom's ROE:

$$38.4\% = \text{Margin} \times 2.3 \times 2.7$$

$$\text{Margin} = 38.4\%/6.21 = 6.2\%$$

EVALUATE

Walmart would have to increase its profit margin from 3.6% to 6.2% in order to match Nordstrom's ROE. It would be able to achieve Nordstrom's ROE with much lower leverage and around the same profit margin as Nordstrom (6.2% vs. 6.1%) because of its higher turnover.

Table 2.4 summarizes financial ratios and provides typical values of those ratios for the manufacturing, retail, and service sectors along with the 500 firms in the S&P 500 index.

TABLE 2.4

A Summary of Key Financial Ratios

Ratio	Formula	Manufacturing	Retail	Service	S&P 500
Profitability Ratios					
Gross Margin	Gross Profit / Sales	45.3%	33.9%	56.4%	43.3%
Operating Margin	Operating Income / Sales	21.2%	12.6%	28.2%	24.3%
Net Profit Margin	Net Income / Sales	10.1%	5.5%	12.3%	9.6%
Liquidity Ratios					
Current Ratio	Current Assets / Current Liabilities	2.17	1.74	1.75	1.82
Quick Ratio	Current Assets − Inventory / Current Liabilities	1.67	0.84	1.70	1.43
Cash Ratio	Cash / Current Liabilities	0.88	0.49	0.89	0.70
Efficiency and Working Capital Ratios					
Accounts Receivable Days	Accounts Receivable / Average Daily Sales	57.66	11.52	61.54	64.36
Fixed Asset Turnover	Sales / Fixed Assets	6.37	5.94	10.17	8.38

Ratio	Formula	Manufacturing	Retail	Service	S&P 500
Total Asset Turnover	$\dfrac{\text{Sales}}{\text{Total Assets}}$	0.91	1.91	0.71	0.84
Inventory Turnover	$\dfrac{\text{Cost of Goods Sold}}{\text{Inventory}}$	6.75	10.80	29.78	11.58
Interest Coverage Ratios					
EBIT/Interest Coverage	$\dfrac{\text{EBIT}}{\text{Interest Expense}}$	16.35	20.46	15.73	14.25
EBITDA/Interest Coverage	$\dfrac{\text{EBITDA}}{\text{Interest Expense}}$	20.56	26.79	19.99	18.41
Leverage Ratios					
Book Debt-to-Equity Ratio	$\dfrac{\text{Total Debt}}{\text{Book Value of Total Equity}}$	83.5%	65.7%	90.9%	90.1%
Market Debt-to-Equity Ratio	$\dfrac{\text{Total Debt}}{\text{Market Value of Total Equity}}$	27.1%	24.4%	35.7%	40.2%
Debt-to-Capital Ratio	$\dfrac{\text{Total Debt}}{\text{Total Equity} + \text{Total Debt}}$	37.4%	31.7%	37.2%	39.1%
Debt-to-Enterprise Value	$\dfrac{\text{Net Debt}}{\text{Enterprise Value}}$	7.9%	10.5%	9.7%	13.1%
Equity Multiplier	$\dfrac{\text{Total Assets}}{\text{Total Equity}}$	3.98	2.74	3.28	4.18
Operating Returns					
Return on Equity	$\dfrac{\text{Net Income}}{\text{Book Value of Equity}}$	17.1%	18.8%	16.8%	11.6%
Return on Assets	$\dfrac{\text{Net Income} + \text{Interest Expense}}{\text{Total Assets}}$	8.4%	9.4%	8.5%	6.9%
Return on Invested Capital (ROIC)	$\dfrac{\text{EBIT}(1 - \text{Tax Rate})}{\text{Book Value of Equity} + \text{Net Debt}}$	13.0%	15.0%	13.3%	11.5%
Valuation Ratios					
Market-to-Book Ratio	$\dfrac{\text{Market Value of Equity}}{\text{Book Value of Equity}}$	4.0	4.4	4.2	3.4
Price-to-Earnings Ratio	$\dfrac{\text{Share Price}}{\text{Earnings per Share}}$	17.2	17.9	20.1	17.5
Enterprise Value Ratios (typical values shown are based on EV/EBITDA)	$\dfrac{\text{Enterprise Value}}{\text{EBIT or EBITDA or Sales}}$	9.2	9.6	9.5	9.1

Source: Standard and Poors' Compustat.

Concept Check

11. What does a high debt-to-equity ratio tell you?
12. What is a firm's enterprise value?
13. How can a financial manager use the DuPont Identity to assess the firm's ROE?
14. How do you use the price-earnings (P/E) ratio to gauge the market value of a firm?

Financial Reporting in Practice

The various financial statements we have examined are of critical importance to investors and financial managers alike. Even with safeguards such as GAAP and auditors, financial reporting abuses unfortunately do take place. We now review one of the most infamous recent examples and offer some concluding thoughts to guide financial managers through the complexities of financial statements.

Enron

Enron is the most well-known of the accounting scandals of the early 2000s. Enron started as an operator of natural gas pipelines but evolved into a global trader dealing in a range of products including gas, oil, electricity, and even broadband Internet capacity. A series of events unfolded that led Enron to file what was at the time the largest bankruptcy filing in U.S. history in December 2001. By the end of 2001, the market value of Enron's shares had fallen by over $60 billion.

Interestingly, throughout the 1990s and up to late 2001, Enron was touted as one of the most successful and profitable companies in America. *Fortune* rated Enron "The Most Innovative Company in America" for six straight years, from 1995 to 2000. But while many aspects of Enron's business were successful, subsequent investigations suggest that Enron executives had been manipulating Enron's financial statements to mislead investors and artificially inflate the price of Enron's stock and to maintain its credit rating. In 2000, for example, 96% of Enron's reported earnings were the result of accounting manipulation.[10]

Although the accounting manipulation that Enron used was quite sophisticated, the essence of most of the deceptive transactions was surprisingly simple. Enron sold assets at inflated prices to other firms (or, in many cases, business entities that Enron's CFO Andrew Fastow had created), together with a promise to buy back those assets at an even higher future price. Thus, Enron was effectively borrowing money, receiving cash today in exchange for a promise to pay more cash in the future. But Enron recorded the incoming cash as revenue and then hid the promises to buy the assets back in a variety of ways.[11] In the end, much of their revenue growth and profits in the late 1990s were the result of this type of manipulation.

The Sarbanes-Oxley Act

Sarbanes-Oxley Act (SOX) Legislation passed by Congress in 2002, intended to improve the accuracy of financial information given to both boards and shareholders.

Accurate and up-to-date financial statements are essential to investors evaluating investment opportunities. In 2002, Congress passed the **Sarbanes-Oxley Act (SOX)**. While SOX contains many provisions, the overall intent of the legislation was to improve the accuracy of information given to both boards and shareholders. SOX attempted to achieve this goal in three ways: (1) by overhauling incentives and independence in the auditing process, (2) by stiffening penalties for providing false information, and (3) by forcing companies to validate their internal financial control processes.

Many of the problems at Enron and elsewhere were kept hidden from boards and shareholders until it was too late. In the wake of these scandals, many people felt that the

---

[10]John R. Kroger, "Enron, Fraud and Securities Reform: An Enron Prosecutor's Perspective," *University of Colorado Law Review*, December 2005, pp. 57–138.

[11]In some cases, these promises were called "price risk management liabilities" and hidden with other trading activities; in other cases they were off-balance sheet transactions that were not fully disclosed.

accounting statements of these companies, while often remaining true to the letter of GAAP, did not present an accurate picture of the financial health of the companies.

Auditing firms are supposed to ensure that a company's financial statements accurately reflect the financial state of the firm. In reality, most auditors have a long-standing relationship with their audit clients; this extended relationship and the auditors' desire to keep the lucrative auditing fees make auditors less willing to challenge management. More importantly, perhaps, most accounting firms have developed large and extremely profitable consulting divisions. Obviously, if an audit team refuses to accommodate a request by a client's management, that client will be less likely to choose the accounting firm's consulting division for its next consulting contract. SOX addressed this concern by putting strict limits on the amount of non-audit fees (consulting or otherwise) that an accounting firm can earn from the same firm that it audits. It also required that audit partners rotate every five years to limit the likelihood that auditing relationships become too cozy over time. Finally, SOX called on the SEC to force companies to have audit committees that are dominated by outside directors, and required that at least one outside director has a financial background.

SOX also stiffened the criminal penalties for providing false information to shareholders. It required both the CEO and the CFO to personally attest to the accuracy of the financial statements presented to shareholders and to sign a statement to that effect. Penalties for providing false or misleading financial statements were increased under SOX—fines of as much as $5 million and imprisonment of a maximum of 20 years are permitted. Further, CEOs and CFOs must return bonuses or profits from the sale of stock or the exercise of options during any period covered by statements that are later restated.

Finally, Section 404 of SOX requires senior management and the boards of public companies to attest to the effectiveness and validity of the process through which funds are allocated and controlled, and outcomes monitored throughout the firm. Section 404 has arguably garnered more attention than any other section in SOX because of the potentially enormous burden it places on every firm to validate its entire financial control system. When the SEC estimated the cost of implementing Section 404, its staff economists put the total cost at $1.24 billion. In 2005, surveys by Financial Executives International and the American Electronics Association predicted that the actual cost would be between $20 billion and $35 billion.[12] The burden of complying with this provision is greater, as a fraction of revenue, for smaller companies. The surveys cited earlier found that multibillion-dollar companies would pay less than 0.05% of their revenues to comply, whereas small companies with less than $20 million in revenues would pay more than 3% of their revenues to comply.

Dodd-Frank Act

To mitigate the compliance burden on small firms, the Dodd-Frank Wall Street Reform and Consumer Protection Act passed in 2010 exempts firms with less than $75 million in publicly held shares from the SOX Section 404 requirements. It also requires the SEC to study how it might reduce cost for medium-sized firms with a public float of less than $250 million, and to assess whether such measures would encourage more firms to list on U.S. exchanges.

Dodd-Frank also broadened the whistleblower provisions of SOX, so that an individual who provides "information related to a possible violation of the federal securities laws (including any rules or regulations thereunder)" that results in penalties or recoveries by the SEC or agencies is eligible to receive from 10 to 30% of that penalty or recovery.

---

[12]American Electronics Association, "Sarbanes-Oxley Section 404: The 'Section' of Unintended Consequences and Its Impact on Small Business" (2005).

Bernard Madoff's Ponzi Scheme

"It's only when the tide goes out that you learn who's been swimming naked." — *Warren Buffett*

On December 11, 2008, federal agents arrested Bernie Madoff, one of the largest and most successful hedge fund managers. It turned out that the $65 billion[13] fund he ran was in fact a fraud. His spectacular performance of the last 17 years, generating consistent annual returns between 10% and 15%, was actually a complete fabrication. Madoff had been running the world's largest Ponzi scheme: That is, he used the capital contributed by new investors to pay off old investors. His strategy was so successful that for more than a decade investors ranging from Steven Spielberg to New York University, as well as a number of large banks and investment advisors, lined up to invest with him. Indeed, Madoff quite likely would have been able to hide the fraud until his deathbed had not the global financial crisis spurred many investors to seek to withdraw funds from their Madoff accounts in order to raise cash and cover losses elsewhere in their portfolios. In addition, the financial crisis meant there were fewer new investors with both the cash and the willingness to invest. As a result, Madoff did not have enough new capital to pay off the investors who wanted to withdraw their capital, and the scheme finally collapsed.

How was Madoff able to hide perhaps the largest fraud of all time for so long? Rather than simply manipulate his accounting statements, Madoff *made them up* with the assistance of a virtually unknown accounting firm with only one active accountant. Although many investors may have questioned why such a large fund, with $65 billion in assets, would choose an unknown and tiny audit firm, not enough of them recognized this choice as a potential red flag. In addition, because Madoff's firm was private, it was not subject to the strict regulatory requirements for public companies (such as the Sarbanes-Oxley Act) and so had weak reporting requirements. As this case makes clear, when making an investment decision, it is important not only to review the firm's financial statements, but also to consider the reliability and reputation of the auditors who prepared them.

The Financial Statements: A Useful Starting Point

In this chapter, we have highlighted the role of the financial statements in informing outside analysts, investors, and the financial managers themselves about the performance, position, and financial condition of the firm. However, especially from the financial manager's perspective, financial statements are only a starting point. For example, we have emphasized the importance of market values over book values. We have also shown that while much can be learned through ratio analysis, these ratios are only markers that point the financial manager toward areas where the firm is doing well or where he or she needs to focus an effort toward improvement. No single ratio tells the whole story. However, by studying all of the financial statements and considering ratios that assess profitability, leverage, and efficiency, you should be able to develop a clear sense of the health and performance of the firm. Finally, the usefulness of the financial statements to investors relies on the ethics of those constructing them. However, even in cases of deception, an informed reader of the financial statements could have spotted the warning signs by focusing on the statement of cash flows and carefully reading the notes to the financial statements.

Concept Check

15. Describe the transactions Enron used to increase its reported earnings.
16. What is the Sarbanes-Oxley Act?

---

[13]$65 billion is the total amount Madoff had reported to his investors, including (fictitious) returns; investigators are still trying to determine the exact amount that investors had actually contributed to the fund, but it appears to be in excess of $17 billion (see www.madoff.com).

MyFinanceLab	Here is what you should know after reading this chapter. MyFinanceLab will help you identify what you know, and where to go when you need to practice.

Key Points and Equations	Key Terms	Online Practice
2.1 Firms' Disclosure of Financial Information • Financial statements are accounting reports that a firm issues periodically to describe its past performance. • Investors, financial analysts, managers, and other interested parties, such as creditors, rely on financial statements to obtain reliable information about a corporation. • The main types of financial statements are the balance sheet, the income statement, the statement of cash flows, and the statement of stockholders' equity. • While the U.S. maintains its own GAAP, most countries in the world are standardizing their accounting systems around International Financial Reporting Standards.	annual report (10-K), p. 26 auditor, p. 27 financial statements, p. 26 Generally Accepted Accounting Principles (GAAP), p. 26	MyFinanceLab Study Plan 2.1
2.2 The Balance Sheet • The balance sheet shows the current financial position (assets, liabilities, and stockholders' equity) of the firm at a single point in time. • The two sides of the balance sheet must balance: $$\text{Assets} = \text{Liabilities} + \text{Stockholders' Equity} (2.1)$$ • Stockholders' equity is the book value of the firm's equity. It differs from the market value of the firm's equity, its market capitalization, because of the way assets and liabilities are recorded for accounting purposes. • A successful firm's market-to-book ratio typically exceeds 1. • The enterprise value of a firm is the total value of its underlying business operations: $$\text{Enterprise Value} = \text{Market Value of Equity} + \text{Debt} - \text{Cash} (2.4)$$	accounts payable, p. 30 accounts receivable, p. 29 assets, p. 28 balance sheet, p. 28 book value, p. 29 book value of equity, p. 30 common stock and paid-in surplus, p. 28 current assets, p. 29 current liabilities, p. 30 depreciation, p. 29 enterprise value, p. 32 growth stocks, p. 32 inventories, p. 29 liabilities, p. 28 liquidation value, p. 31 long-term assets, p. 29 long-term debt, p. 30 market capitalization, p. 31 marketable securities, p. 29 market-to-book ratio (price-to-book [P/B] ratio), p. 32 net working capital, p. 30 notes payable, p. 30 retained earnings, p. 28 shareholders' equity, p. 28 short-term debt, p. 30 statement of financial position, p. 28 stockholders' equity, p. 28 value stocks, p. 32	MyFinanceLab Study Plan 2.2

2.3 The Income Statement

- The income statement reports the firm's revenues and expenses, and it computes the firm's bottom line of net income, or earnings.
- Net income is often reported on a per-share basis as the firm's earnings per share:

$$\text{Earnings per Share (EPS)} = \text{Net Income/Shares Outstanding} \quad (2.5)$$

- We compute diluted EPS by adding to the number of shares outstanding the possible increase in the number of shares from the exercise of stock options the firm has awarded.

MyFinanceLab
Study Plan 2.3

2.4 The Statement of Cash Flows

- The statement of cash flows reports the sources and uses of the firm's cash. It shows the adjustments to net income for non-cash expenses and changes to net working capital, as well as the cash used (or provided) from investing and financing activities.

MyFinanceLab
Study Plan 2.4

2.5 Other Financial Statement Information

- The management discussion and analysis section of the financial statement contains management's overview of the firm's performance, as well as disclosure of risks the firm faces, including those from off-balance sheet transactions.
- The statement of stockholders' equity breaks down the stockholders' equity computed on the balance sheet into the amount that came from issuing new shares versus retained earnings. It is not particularly useful for financial valuation purposes.
- The notes to a firm's financial statements generally contain important details regarding the numbers used in the main statements.

MyFinanceLab
Study Plan 2.5

2.6 Financial Statement Analysis

- Profitability ratios show the firm's operating or net income as a fraction of sales, and they are an indication of a firm's efficiency and its pricing strategy.
- Liquidity ratios help creditors assess whether the firm has enough cash to meet its short-term needs.
- Asset efficiency ratios assess how efficiently the firm is using its assets by showing how many dollars of revenues the firm produces per dollar of assets.
- Working capital ratios express the firm's working capital as a number of days of sales (for receivables) or cost of sales (for inventory or payables).

MyFinanceLab
Study Plan 2.6

- Interest coverage ratios indicate the ratio of the firm's income or cash flows to its interest expenses, and they are a measure of financial strength.
- A common ratio used to assess a firm's leverage is:

$$\text{Debt-Equity Ratio} = \frac{\text{Total Debt}}{\text{Total Equity}} \quad (2.19)$$

- This ratio is most informative when computed using the market value of equity. It indicates the degree of leverage of the firm.
- Valuation ratios compute market capitalization or enterprise value of the firm relative to its earnings or operating income.
- The P/E ratio computes the value of a share of stock relative to the firm's EPS. P/E ratios tend to be high for fast-growing firms.
- When comparing valuation ratios, it is important to be sure both the numerator and denominator match in terms of whether they include debt.
- ROE and ROA are typical operating return ratios. ROE expresses the firm's net income as a return on the book value of its equity. ROA expresses net income plus interest as a return on total assets.
- The DuPont Identity says that

$$\text{ROE} = \left(\frac{\text{Net Income}}{\text{Sales}} \right) \times \left(\frac{\text{Sales}}{\text{Total Assets}} \right)$$

$$\times \left(\frac{\text{Total Assets}}{\text{Total Equity}} \right) \quad (2.27)$$

inventory days, p. 43
inventory turnover ratio, p. 43
leverage, p. 44
net debt, p. 45
net profit margin, p. 41
operating margin, p. 41
PEG ratio, p. 46
price-earnings ratio (P/E), p. 46
quick ratio ("acid-test ratio"),
    p. 42
return on assets (ROA), p. 48
return on invested capital
    (ROIC), p. 48
return on equity (ROE), p. 47
times interest earned (TIE) ratio,
    p. 44

2.7 Financial Reporting in Practice

- Recent accounting scandals have drawn attention to the importance of financial statements. New legislation has increased the penalties for fraud, and tightened the procedures firms must use to ensure that statements are accurate.

Sarbanes-Oxley Act (SOX), p. 52

MyFinanceLab
Study Plan 2.7

CRITICAL
THINKING

1. Why do firms disclose financial information?

2. Who reads financial statements? List at least three different categories of people. For each category, provide an example of the type of information they might be interested in and discuss why.

3. What is the purpose of the balance sheet?

4. What is the purpose of the income statement?

5. How does the statement of cash flows differ from the income statement?

6. Can a firm with positive net income run out of cash? Explain.

7. How can you use the balance sheet to assess the health of a firm?

8. How are the balance sheet and the income statement related?

9. What is the DuPont Identity and how can a financial manager use it?

10. What can you learn from the management's discussion in the financial statements or the notes to the financial statements?

11. How did accounting fraud contribute to the collapse of Enron?

PROBLEMS

All problems are available in MyFinanceLab. An asterisk * indicates problems with a higher level of difficulty.

Firms' Disclosure of Financial Information

1. What four financial statements can be found in a firm's 10-K filing? What checks are there on the accuracy of these statements?

2. What is GAAP and who oversees it?

3. Confirm that you can find the most recent financial statements for Starbucks Corporation (SBUX) using the following sources:
   a. From the company's Web page. (*Hint*: Search their Web site for "investor relations.")
   b. From the SEC Web site (www.sec.gov). (*Hint*: Search for company filings in the EDGAR database.)
   c. From the Yahoo! Finance Web site (finance.yahoo.com).
   d. From at least one other source. (*Hint*: Enter "SBUX 10K" at www.bing.com.)

The Balance Sheet

4. Consider the following potential events that might have occurred to Global on December 30, 2013. For each one, indicate which line items in Global's balance sheet would be affected and by how much. Also indicate the change to Global's book value of equity.
   a. Global used $20 million of its available cash to repay $20 million of its long-term debt.
   b. A warehouse fire destroyed $5 million worth of uninsured inventory.
   c. Global used $5 million in cash and $5 million in new long-term debt to purchase a $10 million building.
   d. A large customer owing $3 million for products it already received declared bankruptcy, leaving no possibility that Global would ever receive payment.
   e. Global's engineers discover a new manufacturing process that will cut the cost of its flagship product by more than 50%.
   f. A key competitor announces a radical new pricing policy that will drastically undercut Global's prices.

5. What was the change in Global's book value of equity from 2012 to 2013 according to Table 2.1? Does this imply that the market price of Global's shares increased in 2013? Explain.

6. Use Google Finance (www.google.com/finance) to find the balance sheet data for Qualcomm (QCOM) as of the end of September 2012.
   a. How much did Qualcomm have in cash and short-term investments?
   b. What were Qualcomm's total accounts receivable?
   c. What were Qualcomm's total assets?
   d. What were Qualcomm's total liabilities? How much of this was long-term debt?
   e. What was the book value of Qualcomm's equity?

7. Find the annual 10-K report for Green Mountain Coffee Roasters (GMCR) online for 2012 (filed in September 2012). Answer the following questions from its balance sheet:
   a. How much cash did Green Mountain have?
   b. What were Green Mountain total assets?
   c. What were Green Mountain total liabilities? How much debt did Green Mountain have?
   d. What was the book value of Green Mountain's equity?

Income Statement

8. Find online the annual 10-K report for Green Mountain Coffee Roasters (GMCR) for its 2012 fiscal year, filed in September 2012. Answer the following questions from the income statement:
   a. What were Green Mountain's revenues for 2012? By what percentage did revenues grow from 2011?
   b. What were Green Mountain's operating and net profit margins in 2012? How do they compare with its margins in 2011?
   c. What were Green Mountain's diluted earnings per share in 2012? What number of shares is this EPS based on?

TABLE 2.5

2009–2013 Financial Statement Data and Stock Price Data for Mydeco Corp.

Mydeco Corp. 2009–2013	(All data as of fiscal year end; $ in millions)				
Income Statement	**2009**	**2010**	**2011**	**2012**	**2013**
Revenue	404.3	363.8	424.6	510.7	604.1
Cost of Goods Sold	(188.3)	(173.8)	(206.2)	(246.8)	(293.4)
Gross Profit	215.9	190.0	218.3	263.9	310.7
Sales and Marketing	(66.7)	(66.4)	(82.8)	(102.1)	(120.8)
Administration	(60.6)	(59.1)	(59.4)	(66.4)	(78.5)
Depreciation & Amortization	(27.3)	(27.0)	(34.3)	(38.4)	(38.6)
EBIT	61.3	37.4	41.8	57.0	72.8
Interest Income (Expense)	(33.7)	(32.9)	(32.2)	(37.4)	(39.4)
Pretax Income	27.7	4.5	9.6	19.6	33.4
Income Tax	(9.7)	(1.6)	(3.4)	(6.9)	(11.7)
Net Income	18.0	2.9	6.2	12.7	21.7
Shares Outstanding (millions)	55.0	55.0	55.0	55.0	55.0
Earnings per Share	$0.33	$0.05	$0.11	$0.23	$0.39
Balance Sheet	**2009**	**2010**	**2011**	**2012**	**2013**
Assets					
Cash	48.8	68.8	86.2	77.4	84.9
Accounts Receivable	88.6	69.8	69.8	76.9	86.1
Inventory	33.7	30.9	28.4	31.7	35.3
Total Current Assets	171.1	169.4	184.4	186.1	206.3
Net Property, Plant, & Equipment	245.3	243.2	308.9	345.5	347.0
Goodwill & Intangibles	361.7	361.7	361.7	361.7	361.7
Total Assets	778.1	774.3	855.0	893.3	914.9

(Continued)

Mydeco Corp. 2009–2013		(All data as of fiscal year end; $ in millions)			
Balance Sheet (continued)	**2009**	**2010**	**2011**	**2012**	**2013**
Liabilities & Stockholders' Equity					
Accounts Payable	18.7	17.9	22.0	26.8	31.7
Accrued Compensation	6.7	6.4	7.0	8.1	9.7
Total Current Liabilities	25.5	24.2	29.0	34.9	41.4
Long-Term Debt	500.0	500.0	575.0	600.0	600.0
Total Liabilities	525.5	524.2	604.0	634.9	641.4
Stockholders' Equity	252.6	250.1	251.0	258.3	273.5
Total Liabilities & Stock-holders' Equity	778.1	774.3	855.0	893.3	914.9
Statement of Cash Flows	**2009**	**2010**	**2011**	**2012**	**2013**
Net Income	18.0	2.9	6.2	12.7	21.7
Depreciation & Amortization	27.3	27.0	34.3	38.4	38.6
Change in Accounts Receivable	3.9	18.8	(0.0)	(7.2)	(9.1)
Change in Inventory	(2.9)	2.9	2.5	(3.3)	(3.6)
Change in Payables & Accrued Compensation	2.2	(1.3)	4.8	5.9	6.5
Cash from Operations	48.4	50.4	47.8	46.6	54.0
Capital Expenditures	(25.0)	(25.0)	(100.0)	(75.0)	(40.0)
Cash from Investing Activities	(25.0)	(25.0)	(100.0)	(75.0)	(40.0)
Dividends Paid	(5.4)	(5.4)	(5.4)	(5.4)	(6.5)
Sale (or Purchase) of Stock	—	—	—	—	-
Debt Issuance (Pay Down)	—	—	75.0	25.0	-
Cash from Financing Activities	(5.4)	(5.4)	69.6	19.6	(6.5)
Change in Cash	18.0	20.0	17.4	(8.8)	7.5
Mydeco Stock Price	*$7.90*	*$3.29*	*$5.23*	*$8.70*	*$10.87*

9. See Table 2.5 showing financial statement data and stock price data for Mydeco Corp.
   a. By what percentage did Mydeco's revenues grow each year from 2010 to 2013?
   b. By what percentage did net income grow each year?
   c. Why might the growth rates of revenues and net income differ?

10. See Table 2.5 showing financial statement data and stock price data for Mydeco Corp. Suppose Mydeco repurchases 2 million shares each year from 2010 to 2013. What would its earnings per share be in 2013?

11. See Table 2.5 showing financial statement data and stock price data for Mydeco Corp. Suppose Mydeco had purchased additional equipment for $12 million at the end of 2010, and this equipment was depreciated by $4 million per year in 2011, 2012, and 2013. Given Mydeco's tax rate of 35%, what impact would this additional purchase have had on Mydeco's net income in years 2010–2013?

12. See Table 2.5 showing financial statement data and stock price data for Mydeco Corp. Suppose Mydeco's costs and expenses had been the same fraction of revenues in 2010–2013 as they were in 2009. What would Mydeco's EPS have been each year in this case?

13. Suppose a firm's tax rate is 35%.
    a. What effect would a $10 million operating expense have on this year's earnings? What effect would it have on next year's earnings?
    b. What effect would a $10 million capital expense have on this year's earnings if the capital is depreciated at a rate of $2 million per year for five years? What effect would it have on next year's earnings?

*14. Quisco Systems has 6.5 billion shares outstanding and a share price of $18. Quisco is considering developing a new networking product in house at a cost of $500 million. Alternatively, Quisco can acquire a firm that already has the technology for $900 million worth (at the current price) of Quisco stock. Suppose that absent the expense of the new technology, Quisco will have EPS of $0.80.
    a. Suppose Quisco develops the product in house. What impact would the development cost have on Quisco's EPS? Assume all costs are incurred this year and are treated as an R&D expense, Quisco's tax rate is 35%, and the number of shares outstanding is unchanged.
    b. Suppose Quisco does not develop the product in house but instead acquires the technology. What effect would the acquisition have on Quisco's EPS this year? (Note that acquisition expenses do not appear directly on the income statement. Assume the firm was acquired at the start of the year and has no revenues or expenses of its own, so that the only effect on EPS is due to the change in the number of shares outstanding.)
    c. Which method of acquiring the technology has a smaller impact on earnings? Is this method cheaper? Explain.

The Statement of Cash Flows

15. Find online the 2012 annual 10-K report Green Mountain Coffee Roasters (GMCR), filed in September 2012. Answer the following questions from its cash flow statement:
    a. How much cash did Green Mountain generate from operating activities in 2012?
    b. What was Green Mountain's depreciation expense in 2012?
    c. How much cash was invested in new property and equipment (net of any sales) in 2012?
    d. How much did Green Mountain raise from the sale of shares of its stock (net of any purchases) in 2012?

16. See the cash flow statement below (all values in thousands of dollars) (*see MyFinanceLab for the data in Excel format*):
    a. What were the company's cumulative earnings over these four quarters? What were its cumulative cash flows from operating activities?

Quarter	4	3	2	1
Net income	276,710	228,964	194,062	218,532
Operating Activities, Cash Flows Provided by or Used in				
Depreciation	69,997	75,733	74,570	73,173
Adjustments to net income	14,359	(13,142)	48,826	(47,993)
Changes in accounts receivable	(38,869)	(53,218)	100,732	(84,711)
Changes in liabilities	82,816	(111,577)	201,725	39,949
Changes in inventories	(195,186)	(114,121)	85,028	57,681
Changes in other operating activities	17,675	(26,574)	12,692	(2,097)

(*Continued*)

Quarter	4	3	2	1
Total Cash Flow from Operating Activities	227,502	(13,935)	717,635	254,534
Investing Activities, Cash Flows Provided by or Used in				
Capital expenditures	(82,584)	(41,634)	(100,109)	(69,170)
Investments	(5,465)	5,465	(93,153)	(48,330)
Other cash flows from investing activities	(108,903)	732	(58,069)	20,652
Total Cash Flows from Investing Activities	(196,952)	(35,437)	(251,331)	(96,848)
Financing Activities, Cash Flows Provided by or Used in				
Dividends paid	(131,483)	(131,333)	(119,452)	(121,404)
Sale purchase of stock	78,774	1,210	(76,807)	(79,288)
Net borrowings	515,709	114,766	(283,696)	64,885
Other cash flows from financing activities	(282)	2,000	(46,234)	39,763
Total Cash Flows from Financing Activities	462,718	(13,357)	(526,189)	(96,044)
Effect of exchange rate changes	(119,960)	(610)	32,807	6,890
Change in Cash and Cash Equivalents	$373,308	(63,339)	(27,078)	$68,532

b. What fraction of the cash from operating activities was used for investment over the four quarters?

c. What fraction of the cash from operating activities was used for financing activities over the four quarters?

17. Suppose your firm receives a $5 million order on the last day of the year. You fill the order with $2 million worth of inventory. The customer picks up the entire order the same day and pays $1 million up front in cash; you also issue a bill for the customer to pay the remaining balance of $4 million within 40 days. Suppose your firm's tax rate is 0% (i.e., ignore taxes). Determine the consequences of this transaction for each of the following:
   a. Revenues
   b. Earnings
   c. Receivables
   d. Inventory
   e. Cash

18. Nokela Industries purchases a $40 million cyclo-converter. The cyclo-converter will be depreciated by $10 million per year over four years, starting this year. Suppose Nokela's tax rate is 40%.
   a. What impact will the cost of the purchase have on earnings for each of the next four years?
   b. What impact will the cost of the purchase have on the firm's cash flow for the next four years?

Financial Statement Analysis

19. In April 2013, General Electric (GE) had a book value of equity of $123 billion, 10.3 billion shares outstanding, and a market price of $23 per share. GE also had cash of $90 billion, and total debt of $397 billion.
    a. What was GE's market capitalization? What was GE's market-to-book ratio?
    b. What was GE's book debt-equity ratio? What was GE's market debt-equity ratio?
    c. What was GE's enterprise value?

20. In April 2013, Apple had cash of $39.14 billion, current assets of $63.34 billion, and current liabilities of $35.51 billion. It also had inventories of $1.25 billion.
    a. What was Apple's current ratio?
    b. What was Apple's quick ratio?
    c. In April 2013, Dell had a quick ratio of 1.13 and a current ratio of 1.19. What can you say about the asset liquidity of Apple relative to Dell?

21. In mid-2012, the following information was true about Abercrombie and Fitch (ANF) and The Gap (GPS), both clothing retailers. Values (except price per share) are in millions of dollars.

	Book Equity	Price per Share	Number of Shares (millions)
ANF	1,693	35.48	82.55
GPS	3,017	27.90	489.22

   a. What is the market-to-book ratio of each company?
   b. What conclusions do you draw from comparing the two ratios?

22. In fiscal year 2011, Starbucks Corporation (SBUX) had revenue of $11.70 billion, gross profit of $6.75 billion, and net income of $1.25 billion. Peet's Coffee and Tea (PEET) had revenue of $372 million, gross profit of $72.7 million, and net income of $17.8 million.
    a. Compare the gross margins for Starbucks and Peet's.
    b. Compare the net profit margins for Starbucks and Peet's.
    c. Which firm was more profitable in 2011?

23. Local Co. has sales of $10 million and cost of sales of $6 million. Its selling, general, and administrative expenses are $500,000 and its research and development is $1 million. It has annual depreciation charges of $1 million and a tax rate of 35%.
    a. What is Local's gross margin?
    b. What is Local's operating margin?
    c. What is Local's net profit margin?

24. If Local Co., the company in Problem 23, had an increase in selling expenses of $300,000, how would that affect each of its margins?

25. If Local Co., the company in Problem 23, had interest expense of $800,000, how would that affect each of its margins?

26. Chutes & Co. has interest expense of $1 million and an operating margin of 10% on total sales of $30 million. What is Chutes' interest coverage ratio?

27. Ladders, Inc. has a net profit margin of 5% on sales of $50 million. It has book value of equity of $40 million and total liabilities with a book value of $30 million. What is Ladders' ROE? ROA?

28. JPJ Corp has sales of $1 million, accounts receivable of $50,000, total assets of $5 million (of which $3 million are fixed assets), inventory of $150,000, and cost of goods sold of $600,000. What is JPJ's accounts receivable days? Fixed asset turnover? Total asset turnover? Inventory turnover?

29. If JPJ Corp (the company in Problem 28) is able to increase sales by 10% but keep its total and fixed asset growth to only 5%, what will its new asset turnover ratios be?

*30. Suppose that in 2013, Global launched an aggressive marketing campaign that boosted sales by 15%. However, their operating margin fell from 5.57% to 4.50%. Suppose that they had no other income, interest expenses were unchanged, and taxes were the same percentage of pretax income as in 2012.
    a. What was Global's EBIT in 2013?
    b. What was Global's income in 2013?
    c. If Global's P/E ratio and number of shares outstanding remained unchanged, what was Global's share price in 2013?

31. You are analyzing the leverage of two firms and you note the following (all values in millions of dollars):

	Debt	Book Equity	Market Equity	Operating Income	Interest Expense
Firm A	500	300	400	100	50
Firm B	80	35	40	8	7

    a. What is the market debt-to-equity ratio of each firm?
    b. What is the book debt-to-equity ratio of each firm?
    c. What is the interest coverage ratio of each firm?
    d. Which firm will have more difficulty meeting its debt obligations?

32. For 2012, Walmart and Target had the following information (all values are in millions of dollars):

	Sales (Income Statement)	Cost of Goods Sold (Income Statement)	Accounts Receivable (Balance Sheet)	Inventory (Balance Sheet)
Walmart	469,162	352,488	6,768	43,803
Target	73,301	50,568	6,857	7,903

    a. What is each company's accounts receivable days?
    b. What is each company's inventory turnover?
    c. Which company is managing its accounts receivable and inventory more efficiently?

33. In January 2013, United Airlines (UAL) had a market capitalization of $8.0 billion, debt of $13.2 billion, and cash of $4.8 billion. United Airlines had revenues of $37.2 billion. Southwest Airlines (LUV) had a market capitalization of $7.6 billion, debt of $3.2 billion, cash of $3.0 billion, and revenues of $17.1 billion.
    a. Compare the market capitalization-to-revenue ratio (also called the price-to-sales ratio) for United Airlines and Southwest Airlines.
    b. Compare the enterprise value-to-revenue ratio for United Airlines and Southwest Airlines.
    c. Which of these comparisons is more meaningful? Explain.

34. Consider a retail firm with a net profit margin of 3.5%, a total asset turnover of 1.8, total assets of $44 million, and a book value of equity of $18 million.
    a. What is the firm's current ROE?
    b. If the firm increased its net profit margin to 4%, what would its ROE be?
    c. If, in addition, the firm increased its revenues by 20% (while maintaining this higher profit margin and without changing its assets or liabilities), what would its ROE be?

*35. Find online the annual 10-K report for Green Mountain Coffee Roasters (GMCR) for its 2012 fiscal year, filed in September 2012.
    a. Compute Green Mountain's net profit margin, total asset turnover, and equity multiplier.
    b. Verify the DuPont Identity for Green Mountain's ROE.
    c. If Green Mountain's managers wanted to increase its ROE by 1 percentage point, how much higher would their asset turnover need to be?

36. Repeat the analysis from parts a and b in Problem 35 using Starbucks Corporation (SBUX) instead. Specifically, use Starbucks' 2012 fiscal data, filed in September 2012. Based on the DuPont Identity, what explains the difference between the two firms' ROEs?

Other Financial Statement Information

37. Some balance sheet information is shown here (all values in millions of dollars) (*see* MyFinanceLab *for the data in Excel format*):

Balance Sheet: Assets	31-Mar-13	31-Dec-12	30-Sep-12	30-Jun-12
Assets				
Current Assets				
Cash and cash equivalents	293	300	255	232
Net receivables	401	362	385	460
Inventory	374	342	437	306
Other current assets	60	43	53	45
Total Current Assets	1,128	1,047	1,130	1,043
Long-term investments	128	97	—	200
Property, plant, and equipment	979	991	995	1,052
Goodwill	744	748	736	742
Other assets	777	827	911	797
Total Assets	3,756	3,710	3,772	3,834
Liabilities				
Current Liabilities				
Accounts payable	876	1,467	922	980
Short/current long-term debt	410	2	173	288
Other current liabilities	—	—	—	—
Total Current Liabilities	1,286	1,469	1,095	1,268
Long-term debt	2,381	2,124	474	475
Other liabilities	435	574	559	551
Total Liabilities	4,102	4,167	2,128	2,294
Total Stockholder Equity	−346	−457	1,644	1,540
Total Liabilities and Stockholder Equity	$3,756	$3,710	$3,772	$3,834

a. What change in the book value of the company's equity took place at the end of 2012?

b. Is the company's market-to-book ratio meaningful? Is its book debt-equity ratio meaningful? Explain.

c. Find the company's other financial statements from that time online. What was the cause of the change to its book value of equity at the end of 2012?

d. Does the company's book value of equity in 2013 imply that it is unprofitable? Explain.

Financial Reporting in Practice

38. Find online the annual 10-K report for Green Mountain Coffee Roasters (GMCR) for 2012, filed in September 2012.

    a. Which auditing firm certified the financial statements?

    b. Which officers of Green Mountain certified the financial statements?

DATA CASE

This is your second interview with a prestigious brokerage firm for a job as an equity analyst. You survived the morning interviews with the department manager and the vice president of equity. Everything has gone so well that they want to test your ability as an analyst. You are seated in a room with a computer and a list with the names of two companies—Caterpillar (CAT) and Microsoft (MSFT). You have 90 minutes to complete the following tasks:

1. Download the annual income statements, balance sheets, and cash flow statements for the last four fiscal years from MarketWatch (www.marketwatch.com). Enter each company's stock symbol and then go to "financials." Copy and paste the financial statements into Excel.

2. Find historical stock prices for each firm from Yahoo! Finance (finance.yahoo.com). Enter the stock symbol, click "Historical Prices" in the left column, and enter the proper date range to cover the last day of the month corresponding to the date of each financial statement. Use the closing stock prices (not the adjusted close). To calculate the firm's market capitalization at each date, multiply the number of shares outstanding (see "Basic Weighted Shares Outstanding" on the income statement) by the firm's historic stock price.

3. For each of the four years of statements, compute the following ratios for each firm:

   Valuation Ratios
   Price-earnings ratio (for EPS use diluted EPS total)
   Market-to-book ratio
   Enterprise value-to-EBITDA
   (For debt, include long-term and short-term debt; for cash, include marketable securities.)

   Profitability Ratios
   Operating margin (use operating income after depreciation)
   Net profit margin
   Return on equity

   Financial Strength Ratios
   Current ratio
   Book debt–equity ratio
   Market debt–equity ratio
   Interest coverage ratio (EBIT ÷ interest expense)

4. Obtain industry averages for each firm from Reuters.com (www.reuters.com/finance/stocks). Enter the stock symbol at the top of the page in the "Symbol lookup" and then click the "Financials" button, and then click "Search".

   a. Scroll down to "Valuation Ratios," and compare each firm's ratios to the available industry ratios for the most recent year. (Ignore the "Company" column as your calculations will be different.)

   b. Analyze the performance of each firm versus the industry and comment on any trends in each individual firm's performance. Identify any strengths or weaknesses you find in each firm.

5. Examine the market-to-book ratios you calculated for each firm. Which, if either, of the two firms can be considered "growth firms" and which, if either, can be considered "value firms"?

6. Compare the valuation ratios across the two firms. How do you interpret the difference between them?

7. Consider the enterprise value of both firms for each of the four years. How have the values of both firms changed over the time period?

Interest Rates and Valuing Cash Flows

Valuation Principle Connection. In this part of the text, we introduce the basic tools for making financial decisions. Chapter 3 presents the most important idea in this book, the *Valuation Principle*. The Valuation Principle states that we can use market prices to determine the value of an investment opportunity to the firm. As we progress through our study of corporate finance, we will demonstrate that the Valuation Principle is the one unifying principle that underlies all of finance and links all the ideas throughout this book.

Every day, managers in companies all over the world make financial decisions. These range from relatively minor decisions such as a local hardware store owner's determination of when to restock inventory, to major decisions such as Starbucks' 2008 closing of more than 600 stores, Apple's 2010 launch of the iPad, and Microsoft's 2012 software overhaul launching Windows 8. What do these diverse decisions have in common? They all were made by comparing the costs of the action against the value to the firm of the benefits. Specifically, a company's managers must determine what it is worth to the company today to receive the project's future cash inflows while paying its cash outflows.

In Chapter 3, we start to build the tools to undertake this analysis with a central concept in financial economics—the *time value of money.* In Chapter 4, we explain how to value any series of future cash flows and derive a few useful shortcuts for valuing various types of cash flow patterns. Chapter 5 discusses how interest rates are quoted in the market and how to handle interest rates that compound more frequently than once per year. In Chapter 6, we will apply what we have learned about interest rates and the present value of cash flows to the task of valuing bonds. In the last chapter of Part 2, Chapter 7, we discuss the features of common stocks and learn how to calculate an estimate of their value.

Time Value of Money: An Introduction

LEARNING OBJECTIVES

- Identify the roles of financial managers and competitive markets in decision making

- Understand the Valuation Principle, and how it can be used to identify decisions that increase the value of the firm

- Assess the effect of interest rates on today's value of future cash flows

- Calculate the value of distant cash flows in the present and of current cash flows in the future

notation

r	interest rate	C	cash flow
PV	present value	n	number of periods
FV	future value		

In 2011, Amazon.com managers decided to more directly compete in the tablet market with the launch of the Kindle Fire, and they priced it at $199, which by some estimates was either at or below the cost to build it. How did Amazon's managers decide this was the right decision for the company?

Every decision has future consequences that will affect the value of the firm. These consequences will generally include both benefits and costs. For example, in addition to the up-front cost of developing its own mobile phone and software, Amazon will also incur ongoing costs associated with future software and hardware development for the Fire, marketing efforts, and customer support. The benefits to Amazon include the revenues from the sales as well as additional content purchased through the device. This decision will increase Amazon's value if these benefits outweigh the costs.

More generally, a decision is good for the firm's investors if it increases the firm's value by providing benefits whose value exceeds the costs. But how do we compare costs and benefits that occur at different points in time, or are in different currencies, or have different risks associated with them? To make a valid comparison, we must use the tools of finance to express all costs and benefits in common terms. We convert all costs and benefits into a common currency and common point of time, such as dollars today. In this chapter, we learn (1) how to use market information to evaluate costs and benefits and (2) why market prices are so important. Then, we will start to build the critical tools relating to the time value of money. These tools will allow you to correctly compare the costs and benefits of a decision no matter when they occur.

3.1 Cost-Benefit Analysis

The first step in decision making is to identify the costs and benefits of a decision. In this section, we look at the role of financial managers in evaluating costs and benefits and the tools they use to quantify them.

Role of the Financial Manager

A financial manager's job is to make decisions on behalf of the firm's investors. Our objective in this book is to explain how to make decisions that increase the value of the firm to its investors. In principle, the idea is simple and intuitive: For good decisions, the benefits exceed the costs. Of course, real-world opportunities are usually complex and the costs and benefits are often difficult to quantify. Quantifying them often means using skills from other management disciplines, as in the following examples:

Marketing: to determine the increase in revenues resulting from an advertising campaign

Economics: to determine the increase in demand from lowering the price of a product

Organizational Behavior: to determine the effect of changes in management structure on productivity

Strategy: to determine a competitor's response to a price increase

Operations: to determine production costs after the modernization of a manufacturing plant

For the remainder of this text, we will assume we can rely on experts in these areas to provide this information so the costs and benefits associated with a decision have already been identified. With that task done, the financial manager's job is to compare the costs and benefits and determine the best decision for the value of the firm.

Quantifying Costs and Benefits

Any decision in which the value of the benefits exceeds the costs will increase the value of the firm. To evaluate the costs and benefits of a decision, we must value the options in the same terms—cash today. Let's make this concrete with a simple example.

Suppose a jewelry manufacturer has the opportunity to trade 200 ounces of silver for 10 ounces of gold today. An ounce of silver differs in value from an ounce of gold. Consequently, it is incorrect to compare 200 ounces to 10 ounces and conclude that the larger quantity is better. Instead, to compare the cost of the silver and the benefit of the gold, we first need to quantify their values in equivalent terms—cash today.

Consider the silver. What is its cash value today? Suppose silver can be bought and sold for a current market price of $20 per ounce. Then the 200 ounces of silver we would give up has a cash value of:[1]

$$(200 \text{ ounces of silver}) \times (\$20/\text{ounce of silver}) = \$4000$$

If the current market price for gold is $1000 per ounce, then the 10 ounces of gold we would receive has a cash value of

$$(10 \text{ ounces of gold}) \times (\$1000/\text{ounce of gold}) = \$10{,}000$$

We have now quantified the decision. The jeweler's opportunity has a benefit of $10,000 and a cost of $4000. The net benefit of the decision is $10,000 − $4000 = $6000 today.

---

[1]You might wonder whether commissions and other transactions costs need to be included in this calculation. For now, we will ignore transactions costs, but we will discuss their effect in later chapters.

The net value of the decision is positive, so by accepting the trade, the jewelry firm will be richer by $6000.

Role of Competitive Market Prices. Suppose the jeweler works exclusively on silver jewelry or thinks the price of silver should be higher. Should his decision change? The answer is no—he can always make the trade and then buy silver at the current market price. Even if he has no use for the gold, he can immediately sell it for $10,000, buy back the 200 ounces of silver at the current market price of $4000, and pocket the remaining $6000. Thus, independent of his own views or preferences, the value of the silver to the jeweler is $4000.

competitive market A market in which a good can be bought *and* sold at the same price.

Because the jeweler can both buy and sell silver at its current market price, his personal preferences or use for silver and his opinion of the fair price are irrelevant in evaluating the value of this opportunity. This observation highlights an important general principle related to goods trading in a **competitive market**, a market in which a good can be bought *and* sold at the same price. Whenever a good trades in a competitive market, that price determines the value of the good. This point is one of the central and most powerful ideas in finance. It will underlie almost every concept we develop throughout the text.

EXAMPLE 3.1

Competitive Market Prices Determine Value

MyFinanceLab

PROBLEM

You have just won a radio contest and are disappointed to learn that the prize is four tickets to the Def Leppard reunion tour (face value $40 each). Not being a fan of 1980s power rock, you have no intention of going to the show. However, the radio station offers you another option: two tickets to your favorite band's sold-out show (face value $45 each). You notice that, on eBay, tickets to the Def Leppard show are being bought and sold for $30 apiece and tickets to your favorite band's show are being bought and sold at $50 each. What should you do?

SOLUTION

PLAN

Market prices, not your personal preferences (or the face value of the tickets), are relevant here:

> 4 Def Leppard tickets at $30 apiece
>
> 2 of your favorite band's tickets at $50 apiece

You need to compare the market value of each option and choose the one with the highest market value.

EXECUTE

The Def Leppard tickets have a total value of $120 ($4 \times \$30$) versus the $100 total value of the other 2 tickets ($2 \times \$50$). Instead of taking the tickets to your favorite band, you should accept the Def Leppard tickets, sell them on eBay, and use the proceeds to buy 2 tickets to your favorite band's show. You'll even have $20 left over to buy a T-shirt.

EVALUATE

Even though you prefer your favorite band, you should still take the opportunity to get the Def Leppard tickets instead. As we emphasized earlier, whether this opportunity is attractive depends on its net value using market prices. Because the value of Def Leppard tickets is $20 more than the value of your favorite band's tickets, the opportunity is appealing.

Concept Check

1. When costs and benefits are in different units or goods, how can we compare them?

2. If crude oil trades in a competitive market, would an oil refiner that has a use for the oil value it differently than another investor would?

3.2 Market Prices and the Valuation Principle

In the previous examples, the right decisions for the firms were clear because the costs and benefits were easy to evaluate and compare. They were easy to evaluate because we were able to use current market prices to convert them into equivalent cash values. Once we can express costs and benefits in terms of cash today, it is a straightforward process to compare them and determine whether the decision will increase the firm's value.

The Valuation Principle

Our discussion so far establishes competitive market prices as the way to evaluate the costs and benefits of a decision in terms of cash today. Once we do this, it is a simple matter to determine the best decision for the firm. The best decision makes the firm and its investors wealthier, because the value of its benefits exceeds the value of its costs. We call this idea the Valuation Principle:

The Valuation Principle:

The value of a commodity or an asset to the firm or its investors is determined by its competitive market price. The benefits and costs of a decision should be evaluated using those market prices. When the value of the benefits exceeds the value of the costs, the decision will increase the market value of the firm.

The Valuation Principle provides the basis for decision making throughout this text. In the remainder of this chapter, we apply it to decisions whose costs and benefits occur at different points in time.

EXAMPLE 3.2

Applying the
Valuation Principle

MyFinanceLab

PROBLEM

You are the operations manager at your firm. Due to a pre-existing contract, you have the opportunity to acquire 200 barrels of oil and 3000 pounds of copper for a total of $25,000. The current market price of oil is $90 per barrel and for copper is $3.50 per pound. You are not sure that you need all the oil and copper, so you are wondering whether you should take this opportunity. How valuable is it? Would your decision change if you believed the value of oil or copper would plummet over the next month?

SOLUTION

PLAN

We need to quantify the costs and benefits using market prices. We are comparing $25,000 with:

　200 barrels of oil at $90 per barrel

　3000 pounds of copper at $3.50 per pound

EXECUTE

Using the competitive market prices we have:

$$(200 \text{ barrels of oil}) \times (\$90/\text{barrel today}) = \$18,000 \text{ today}$$
$$(3000 \text{ pounds of copper}) \times (\$3.50/\text{pound today}) = \$10,500 \text{ today}$$

The value of the opportunity is the value of the oil plus the value of the copper less the cost of the opportunity, or $18,000 + $10,500 − $25,000 = $3500 today. Because the value is positive, we should take it. This value depends only on the *current* market prices for oil and copper. If we do not need all of the oil and copper, we can sell the excess at current market prices. Even if we thought the value of oil or copper was about to plummet, the value of this investment would be unchanged. (We can always exchange them for dollars immediately at the current market prices.)

EVALUATE

Since we are transacting today, only the current prices in a competitive market matter. Our own use for or opinion about the future prospects of oil or copper do not alter the value of the decision today. This decision is good for the firm and will increase its value by $3500.

Why There Can Be Only One Competitive Price for a Good

The Valuation Principle and finance in general rely on using a competitive market price to value a cost or benefit. We cannot have two different competitive market prices for the same good—otherwise we would arrive at two different values. Fortunately, powerful market forces keep competitive prices the same. To illustrate, imagine what you would do if you saw gold simultaneously trading for two different prices. You and everyone else who noticed the difference would buy at the low price and sell at the high price for as many ounces of gold as possible, making instant risk-free profits. The flood of buy and sell orders would push the two prices together until the profit was eliminated. These forces establish the **Law of One Price**, which states that in competitive markets, the same good or securities must have the same price. More generally, securities that produce exactly the same cash flows must have the same price.

In general, the practice of buying and selling equivalent goods in different markets to take advantage of a price difference is known as **arbitrage**. We refer to any situation in which it is possible to make a profit without taking any risk or making any investment as an **arbitrage opportunity**. Because an arbitrage opportunity's benefits are more valuable than its costs, whenever an arbitrage opportunity appears in financial markets, investors will race to take advantage of it and their trades will eliminate the opportunity.

Retail stores often quote different prices for the same item in different countries. *The Economist* magazine has long compared prices for a McDonald's Big Mac around the world. Here, we compare Big Mac prices from January 2013. The price in the local currency and converted to U.S. dollars is listed. Of course, these prices are not examples of competitive market prices, because you can only buy a Big Mac at these prices. Hence, they do not present an arbitrage opportunity. Even if shipping were free, you could buy as many Big Macs as you could get your hands on in India but you would not be able to sell those rotten Big Macs in Venezuela for a profit!

Law of One Price In competitive markets, securities with the same cash flows must have the same price.

arbitrage The practice of buying and selling equivalent goods to take advantage of a price difference.

arbitrage opportunity Any situation in which it is possible to make a profit without taking any risk or making any investment.

Country	Local Cost	U.S. Dollar Cost
India	89.00 rupees	$1.67
Hong Kong	17.00 HK dollars	$2.19
Russia	72.88 rubles	$2.43
China	16.00 yuan	$2.57
Mexico	37.00 pesos	$2.90
UAE	12.00 dirhams	$3.27
Japan	320.00 yen	$3.51
United States	4.37 US dollars	$4.37
France	3.60 euros	$4.89
Australia	4.70 Australian dollars	$4.90
Germany	3.64 euros	$4.94
Canada	5.41 Canadian dollars	$5.39
Brazil	11.25 reais	$5.64
Switzerland	6.50 Swiss francs	$7.12
Sweden	48.40 Swedish krona	$7.62
Venezuela	39.00 bolivares fuertes	$9.08

Source: Economist.com.

> **Your Personal Financial Decisions**
>
> While the focus of this text is on the decisions a finan-
> cial manager makes in a business setting, you will soon see that
> concepts and skills you will learn here apply to personal decisions
> as well. As a normal part of life we all make decisions that trade
> off benefits and costs across time. Going to college, purchasing
> this book, saving for a new car or house down payment, taking
> out a car loan or home loan, buying shares of stock, and deciding
> between jobs are just a few examples of decisions you have
> faced or could face in the near future. As you read through this
> book, you will see that the Valuation Principle is the foundation
> of *all* financial decision making—whether in a business or in a
> personal context.

**Concept
Check**

3. How do investors' profit motives keep competitive market prices correct?

4. How do we determine whether a decision increases the value of the firm?

3.3   The Time Value of Money and Interest Rates

Unlike the examples presented so far, most financial decisions have costs and benefits that occur at different points in time. For example, typical investment projects incur costs up front and provide benefits in the future. In this section, we show how to account for this time difference when using the Valuation Principle to make a decision.

The Time Value of Money

Your company has an investment opportunity with the following cash flows:

> Cost: $100,000 today
> Benefit: $105,000 in one year

Both are expressed in dollar terms, but are the cost and benefit directly comparable? No. Calculating the project's net value as $105,000 − $100,000 = 5000 is incorrect because it ignores the *timing* of the costs and benefits. That is, it treats money today as equivalent to money in one year. In general, a dollar received today is worth *more* than a dollar received in one year: If you have $1 today, you can invest it now and have more money in the future. For example, if you deposit it in a bank account paying 10% interest, you will have $1.10 at the end of one year. We call the difference in value between money today and money in the future the **time value of money**.

time value of money The difference in value between money received today and money received in the future; also, the observation that two cash flows at two different points in time have different values.

Figure 3.1 illustrates how we use competitive market prices and interest rates to convert between dollars today and other goods, or dollars in the future. Just like silver and gold, money today and money tomorrow are not the same thing. We compare them just like we did with silver and gold—using competitive market prices. But in the case of money, what is the price? It is the interest rate, the price for exchanging money today for money in a year. We can use the interest rate to determine values in the same way we used competitive market prices. Once we quantify all the costs and benefits of an investment

FIGURE 3.1

Converting Between Dollars Today and Gold or Dollars in the Future

We can convert dollars today to different goods or points in time by using the competitive market price or interest rate. Once values are in equivalent terms, we can use the Valuation Principle to make a decision.

in terms of dollars today, we can rely on the Valuation Principle to determine whether the investment will increase the firm's value.

The Interest Rate: Converting Cash Across Time

We now develop the tools needed to value our $100,000 investment opportunity correctly. By depositing money into a savings account, we can convert money today into money in the future with no risk. Similarly, by borrowing money from the bank, we can exchange money in the future for money today. Suppose the current annual interest rate is 10%. By investing $1 today we can convert this $1 into $1.10 in one year. Similarly, by borrowing at this rate, we can exchange $1.10 in one year for $1 today. More generally, we define the **interest rate**, r, for a given period as the interest rate at which money can be borrowed or lent over that period. In our example, the interest rate is 10% and we can exchange 1 dollar today for $(1 + .10)$ dollars in one year. In general, we can exchange 1 dollar today for $(1 + r)$ dollars in one year, and vice versa. We refer to $(1 + r)$ as the **interest rate factor** for cash flows; it defines how we convert cash flows across time, and has units of "$ in one year/$ today."

Like other market prices, the interest rate ultimately depends on supply and demand. In particular, the interest rate equates the supply of savings to the demand for borrowing. But regardless of how it is determined, once we know the interest rate, we can apply the Valuation Principle and use it to evaluate other decisions in which costs and benefits are separated in time.

interest rate The rate at which money can be borrowed or lent over a given period.

interest rate factor One plus the interest rate, it is the rate of exchange between dollars today and dollars in the future. It has units of "$ in the future/$ today."

Value of $100,000 Investment in One Year. Let's reevaluate the investment we considered earlier, this time taking into account the time value of money. If the interest rate is 10%, then your company faces a choice: use $1 today, or deposit it and have $1.10 in one year. That means we can think of $1.10 as the cost of every dollar used today. So, we can express the cost of the investment as:

$$\text{Cost} = (\$100,000 \text{ today}) \times \left(\frac{\$1.10 \text{ in one year}}{\$1 \text{ today}} \right)$$

$$= \$110,000 \text{ in one year}$$

Think of this amount as the opportunity cost of spending $100,000 today: The firm gives up the $110,000 it would have had in one year if it had left the money in the bank. Alternatively, by borrowing the $100,000 from the same bank, the firm would owe $110,000 in one year.

	Today	One Year
Investment	−$100,000	+$105,000
Bank	−$100,000	+$110,000

We have used a market price, the interest rate, to put both the costs and benefits in terms of "dollars in one year," so now we can use the Valuation Principle to compare them and compute the investment's net value by subtracting the cost of the investment from the benefit in one year:

$$\$105,000 - \$110,000 = -\$5000 \text{ in one year}$$

In other words, the firm could earn $5000 more in one year by putting the $100,000 in the bank rather than making this investment. Because the net value is negative, we should reject the investment: If we took it, the firm would be $5000 poorer in one year than if we didn't.

Value of $100,000 Investment Today. The preceding calculation expressed the value of the costs and benefits in terms of dollars in one year. Alternatively, we can use the interest rate factor to convert to dollars today. Consider the benefit of $105,000 in one year. What is the equivalent amount in terms of dollars today? That is, how much would we need to have in the bank today so we end up with $105,000 in the bank in one year? We find this amount by dividing $105,000 by the interest rate factor:

$$\text{Benefit} = (\$105,000 \text{ in one year}) \div \left(\frac{\$1.10 \text{ in one year}}{\$1 \text{ today}} \right)$$
$$= \$95,454.55 \text{ today}$$

This is also the amount the bank would lend to us today if we promised to repay $105,000 in one year.[2] Thus, it is the competitive market price at which we can "buy" or "sell" today an amount of $105,000 in one year.

	Today	One Year
Value of Cost Today	−$100,000	+$105,000
Value of Benefit Today	+$95,454.55 ⟵ $\dfrac{105,000}{1.10}$ ⟵	

Now we are ready to compute the net value of the investment today (as opposed to its net value in one year) by subtracting the cost from the benefit:

$$\$95,454.55 - \$100,000 = -\$4545.45 \text{ today}$$

Because this net value is calculated in terms of dollars today (in the present), it is typically called the *net present value*. We will formally introduce this concept in Chapter 8. Once again, the negative result indicates that we should reject the investment. Taking the investment would make the firm $4,545.45 poorer today because it gave up $100,000 for something worth only $95,454.55.

---

[2]We are assuming the bank is willing to lend at the same 10% interest rate, which would be the case if there were no risk associated with the cash flow.

Present Versus Future Value. This calculation demonstrates that our decision is the same whether we express the value of the investment in terms of dollars in one year or dollars today: We should reject the investment. Indeed, if we convert from dollars today to dollars in one year,

$$(-\$4545.45 \text{ today}) \times (\$1.10 \text{ in one year}/\$1 \text{ today}) = -\$5000 \text{ in one year}$$

we see that the two results are equivalent, but expressed as values at different points in time. When we express the value in terms of dollars today, we call it the **present value (PV)** of the investment. If we express it in terms of dollars in the future, we call it the **future value (FV)** of the investment.

present value (PV) The value of a cost or benefit computed in terms of cash today.

future value (FV) The value of a cash flow that is moved forward in time.

discount factor The value today of a dollar received in the future.

discount rate The appropriate rate to discount a cash flow to determine its value at an earlier time.

Discount Factors and Rates. In the preceding calculation, we can interpret

$$\frac{1}{1+r} = \frac{1}{1.10} = 0.90909$$

as the *price* today of $1 in one year. In other words, for just under 91 cents, you can "buy" $1 to be delivered in one year. Note that the value is less than $1—money in the future is worth less today, so its price reflects a discount. Because it provides the discount at which we can purchase money in the future, the amount $1/(1+r)$ is called the one-year **discount factor**. The interest rate is also referred to as the **discount rate** for an investment.

EXAMPLE 3.3

Comparing Revenues at Different Points in Time

MyFinanceLab

PROBLEM

The launch of Sony's PlayStation 3 was delayed until November 2006, giving Microsoft's Xbox 360 a full year on the market without competition. Sony did not repeat this mistake in 2013 when PS4 launched at the same time as Xbox One. Imagine that it is November 2005 and you are the marketing manager for the PlayStation. You estimate that if PlayStation 3 were ready to be launched immediately, you could sell $2 billion worth of the console in its first year. However, if your launch is delayed a year, you believe that Microsoft's head start will reduce your first-year sales by 20% to $1.6 billion. If the interest rate is 8%, what is the cost of a delay of the first year's revenues in terms of dollars in 2005?

SOLUTION

PLAN

Revenues if released today: $2 billion   Revenue if delayed: $1.6 billion   Interest rate: 8%

We need to compute the revenues if the launch is delayed and compare them to the revenues from launching today. However, in order to make a fair comparison, we need to convert the future revenues of the PlayStation if they are delayed into an equivalent present value of those revenues today.

EXECUTE

If the launch is delayed to 2006, revenues will drop by 20% of $2 billion, or $400 million, to $1.6 billion. To compare this amount to revenues of $2 billion if launched in 2005, we must convert it using the interest rate of 8%:

$$\$1.6 \text{ billion in 2006} \div (\$1.08 \text{ in 2006}/\$1 \text{ in 2005}) = \frac{\$1.6 \text{ billion}}{(1.08)} = \$1.481 \text{ billion in 2005}$$

Therefore, the cost of a delay of one year is

$$\$2 \text{ billion} - \$1.481 \text{ billion} = \$0.519 \text{ billion (\$519 million)}.$$

(Continued)

Timelines

timeline A linear representation of the timing of (potential) cash flows.

Our visual representation of the cost and benefit of the $100,000 investment in this section is an example of a **timeline**, a linear representation of the timing of the expected cash flows. Timelines are an important first step in organizing and then solving a financial problem. We use them throughout this text.

Constructing a Timeline. To understand how to construct a timeline, assume a friend owes you money. He has agreed to repay the loan by making two payments of $10,000 at the end of each of the next two years. We represent this information on a timeline as follows:

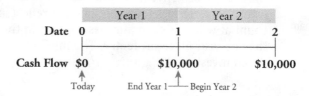

Identifying Dates on a Timeline. To track cash flows, we interpret each point on the timeline as a specific date. The space between date 0 and date 1 represents the first year of the loan. Date 0 is today, the beginning of the first year, and date 1 is the end of the first year. The $10,000 cash flow below date 1 is the payment you will receive at the end of the first year. Similarly, date 1 is the beginning of the second year, date 2 is the end of the second year, and the $10,000 cash flow below date 2 is the payment you will receive at the end of the second year. Note that date 1 signifies *both* the end of year 1 *and* the beginning of year 2, which makes sense since those dates are effectively the same point in time.[3]

Distinguishing Cash Inflows from Outflows. In this example, both cash flows are inflows. In many cases, however, a financial decision will include inflows and outflows. To differentiate between the two types of cash flows, we assign a different sign to each: Inflows (cash flows received) are positive cash flows, whereas outflows (cash flows paid out) are negative cash flows.

To illustrate, suppose you have agreed to lend your brother $10,000 today. Your brother has agreed to repay this loan with interest by making payments of $6000 at the end of each of the next two years. The timeline is:

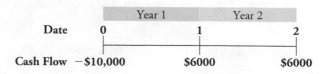

---

[3] That is, there is no real time difference between a cash flow paid at 11:59 P.M. on December 31 and one paid at 12:01 A.M. on January 1, although there may be some other differences such as taxation, which we will overlook for now.

Notice that the first cash flow at date 0 (today) is represented as −$10,000 because it is an outflow. The subsequent cash flows of $6000 are positive because they are inflows.

Representing Various Time Periods. So far, we have used timelines to show the cash flows that occur at the end of each year. Actually, timelines can represent cash flows that take place at any point in time. For example, if you pay rent each month, you could use a timeline such as the one in our first example to represent two rental payments, but you would replace the "year" label with "month."

Many of the timelines included in this chapter are simple. Consequently, you may feel that it is not worth the time or trouble to construct them. As you progress to more difficult problems, however, you will find that timelines identify events in a transaction or investment that are easy to overlook. If you fail to recognize these cash flows, you will make flawed financial decisions. Therefore, approach *every* problem by drawing the timeline as we do in this chapter and the next.

Concept Check

5. How is an interest rate like a price?

6. Is the value today of money to be received in one year higher when interest rates are high or when interest rates are low?

3.4   Valuing Cash Flows at Different Points in Time

The example of the $100,000 investment in the previous section laid the groundwork for how we will compare cash flows that happen at different points in time. In this section, we will generalize from the example by introducing three important rules central to financial decision making that allow us to compare or combine values across time.

Rule 1: Comparing and Combining Values

Our first rule is that it is only possible to compare or combine values at the same point in time. This rule restates a conclusion from the last section: Only cash flows in the same units can be compared or combined. A dollar today and a dollar in one year are not equivalent. Having money now is more valuable than having money in the future; if you have the money today you can invest it and earn interest.

To compare or combine cash flows that occur at different points in time, you first need to convert the cash flows into the same units by moving them to the same point in time. The next two rules show how to move the cash flows on the timeline.

COMMON MISTAKE   **Summing Cash Flows Across Time**

Once you understand the time value of money, our first rule may seem straightforward. However, it is very common, especially for those who have not studied finance, to violate this rule, simply treating all cash flows as comparable regardless of when they are received. One example is in sports contracts. In 2011, Albert Pujols signed a contract with the Los Angeles Angels that was repeatedly referred to as a "$240 million" contract. The $240 million comes from simply adding up all the payments Pujols would receive over the 10 years of the contract—treating dollars received in 10 years the same as dollars received today. The same thing occurred when Lionel Messi signed a contract extension with FC Barcelona in 2013, giving him a "$150 million" contract through 2018.

Rule 2: Compounding

Suppose we have $1000 today, and we wish to determine the equivalent amount in one year's time. If the current market interest rate is 10%, we saw in the last section that we can use that rate as an exchange rate, meaning the rate at which we exchange money today for money in one year, to move the cash flow forward in time. That is:

$$(\$1000 \text{ today}) \times (\$1.10 \text{ in one year}/\$1 \text{ today}) = \$1100 \text{ in one year}$$

compounding Computing the return on an investment over a long horizon by multiplying the return factors associated with each intervening period.

In general, if the market interest rate for the year is r, then we multiply by the interest rate factor, $(1 + r)$ to move the cash flow from the beginning to the end of the year. We multiply by $(1 + r)$ because at the end of the year you will have $(1 \times$ your original investment$)$ plus interest in the amount of $(r \times$ your original investment$)$. This process of moving forward along the timeline to determine a cash flow's value in the future (its future value) is known as **compounding**. *Our second rule stipulates that to calculate a cash flow's future value, you must compound it.*

We can apply this rule repeatedly. Suppose we want to know how much the $1000 is worth in two years' time. If the interest rate for year 2 is also 10%, then we convert as we just did:

$$(\$1100 \text{ in one year}) \times (\$1.10 \text{ in two years}/\$1 \text{ in one year}) = \$1210 \text{ in two years}$$

Let's represent this calculation on a timeline:

```
        0                1                2
        |                |                |
     $1000 ────────▶  $1100 ────────▶  $1210
            × 1.10            × 1.10
```

Given a 10% interest rate, all of the cash flows—$1000 at date 0, $1100 at date 1, and $1210 at date 2—are equivalent. They have the same value but are expressed in different units (different points in time). An arrow that points to the right indicates that the value is being moved forward in time—that is, compounded.

In the preceding example, $1210 is the future value of $1000 two years from today. Note that the value grows as we move the cash flow further in the future. In the last section, we defined the time value of money as the difference in value between money today and money in the future. Here, we can say that $1210 in two years is equivalent to $1000 today. The reason money is more valuable to you today is that you have opportunities to invest it. As in this example, by having money sooner, you can invest it (here at a 10% return) so that it will grow to a larger amount in the future. Note also that the equivalent amount grows by $100 the first year, but by $110 the second year. In the second year, we earn interest on our original $1000, plus we earn interest on the $100 interest we received in the first year. This effect of earning interest on both the original principal plus the accumulated interest, so that you are earning "interest on interest," is known as **compound interest**. Figure 3.2 shows how over time the amount of money you earn from interest on interest grows so that it will eventually exceed the amount of money that you earn as interest on your original deposit.

compound interest The effect of earning "interest on interest."

How does the future value change in the third year? Continuing to use the same approach, we compound the cash flow a third time. Assuming the competitive market interest rate is fixed at 10%, we get:

$$\$1000 \times (1.10) \times (1.10) \times (1.10) = \$1000 \times (1.10)^3 = \$1331$$

FIGURE 3.2

The Composition of Interest over Time

This bar graph shows how the account balance and the composition of the interest changes over time when an investor starts with an original deposit of $1000, represented by the red area, in an account earning 10% interest over a 20-year period. Note that the turquoise area representing interest on interest grows, and by year 15 has become larger than the interest on the original deposit, shown in green. By year 20, the interest on interest the investor earned is $3727.50, while the interest earned on the original $1000 is $2000.

In general, to compute a cash flow C's value n periods into the future, we must compound it by the n intervening interest rate factors. If the interest rate r is constant, this calculation yields:

Future Value of a Cash Flow

$$FV_n = C \times \underbrace{(1 + r) \times (1 + r) \times \cdots \times (1 + r)}_{n \text{ times}} = C \times (1 + r)^n \tag{3.1}$$

Rule of 72

Another way to think about the effect of compounding is to consider how long it will take your money to double given different interest rates. Suppose you want to know how many years it will take for $1 to grow to a future value of $2. You want the number of years, n, to solve:

$$FV_n = \$1 \times (1 + r)^n = \$2$$

If you solve this formula for different interest rates, you will find the following approximation:

Years to double $\approx 72 \div$ (interest rate in percent)

This simple "Rule of 72" is fairly accurate (that is, within one year of the exact doubling time) for interest rates higher than 2%. For example, if the interest rate is 9%, the doubling time should be about $72 \div 9 = 8$ years. Indeed, $1.09^8 = 1.99$! So, given a 9% interest rate, your money will approximately double every 8 years.

Rule 3: Discounting

The third rule describes how to put a value today on a cash flow that comes in the future. Suppose you would like to compute the value today of $1000 that you anticipate receiving in one year. If the current market interest rate is 10%, you can compute this value by converting units as we did in the last section:

($1000 in one year) ÷ ($1.10 in one year/$1 today) = $909.09 today

That is, to move the cash flow back along the timeline, we divide it by the interest rate factor, $(1 + r)$, where r is the interest rate. This process of finding the equivalent value today of a future cash flow is known as **discounting**. *Our third rule stipulates that to calculate the value of a future cash flow at an earlier point in time, we must discount it.*

discounting Finding the equivalent value today of a future cash flow by multiplying by a discount factor, or equivalently, dividing by 1 plus the discount rate.

Suppose that you anticipate receiving the $1000 two years from today rather than in one year. If the interest rate for both years is 10%, you can prepare the following timeline:

When the interest rate is 10%, all of the cash flows—$826.45 at date 0, $909.09 at date 1, and $1000 at date 2—are equivalent. They represent the same value in different units (different points in time). The arrow points to the left to indicate that the value is being moved backward in time or discounted. Note that the value decreases the further in the future is the original cash flow.

The value of a future cash flow at an earlier point on the timeline is its present value at the earlier point in time. That is, $826.45 is the present value at date 0 of $1000 in two years. Recall that the present value is the "do-it-yourself" price to produce a future cash flow. Thus, if we invested $826.45 today for two years at 10% interest, we would have a future value of $1000, using the second rule of valuing cash flows:

Suppose the $1000 were three years away and you wanted to compute the present value. Again, if the interest rate is 10%, we have:

That is, the present value today of a cash flow of $1000 in three years is given by:

$1000 ÷ (1.10) ÷ (1.10) ÷ (1.10) = $1000 ÷ (1.10)^3 = $751.31

In general, to compute the present value of a cash flow C that comes n periods from now, we must discount it by the n intervening interest rate factors. If the interest rate r is constant, this yields:

Present Value of a Cash Flow

$$PV = C \div (1 + r)^n = \frac{C}{(1 + r)^n} \tag{3.2}$$

EXAMPLE 3.4

Present Value
of a Single Future
Cash Flow

MyFinanceLab

PROBLEM

You are considering investing in a savings bond that will pay $15,000 in 10 years. If the competitive market interest rate is fixed at 6% per year, what is the bond worth today?

SOLUTION

PLAN

First, set up your timeline. The cash flows for this bond are represented by the following timeline:

Thus, the bond is worth $15,000 in 10 years. To determine the value today, we compute the present value using Equation 3.2 and our interest rate of 6%.

EXECUTE

$$PV = \frac{15,000}{1.06^{10}} = \$8375.92 \text{ today}$$

EVALUATE

The bond is worth much less today than its final payoff because of the time value of money.

As we've seen in this section, we can compare cash flows at different points in time as long as we follow the Three Rules of Valuing Cash Flows, summarized in Table 3.1. Armed with these three rules, a financial manager can compare an investment's costs and benefits that are spread out over time and apply the Valuation Principle to make the right decision. In Chapter 4, we will show you how to apply these rules to situations involving multiple cash flows at different points in time.

TABLE 3.1

The Three Rules of
Valuing Cash Flows

Rule	Formula
1: Only values at the same point in time can be compared or combined.	None
2: To calculate a cash flow's future value, we must compound it.	Future value of a cash flow: $FV_n = C \times (1 + r)^n$
3: To calculate the present value of a future cash flow, we must discount it.	Present value of a cash flow: $PV = C \div (1 + r)^n = \dfrac{C}{(1 + r)^n}$

Concept
Check

7. Can you compare or combine cash flows at different times?

8. What do you need to know to compute a cash flow's present or future value?

Using a Financial Calculator

Financial calculators are programmed to perform most present and future value calculations. However, we recommend that you develop an understanding of the formulas before using the shortcuts. We provide a more extensive discussion of financial calculators on page 95 and in the appendix to Chapter 4, but we'll cover the relevant functions for this chapter here. To use financial calculator functions, you always enter the known values first and then the calculator solves for the unknown.

To answer Example 3.4 with a financial calculator, do the following:

Concept	Number of Periods	Interest Rate per Period	Recurring Payments	Future Value
Calculator Key	N	I/Y	PMT	FV
Enter	10	6	0	15000

Because you are solving for the present value (PV), press the PV key last (on an HP calculator), or press CPT then the PV key on a TI calculator. The calculator will return −8375.92. Note that the calculator balances inflows with outflows, so because the FV is positive (an inflow), it returns the PV as a negative (an outflow).

If you were solving for the future value instead, you would enter:

N	I/Y	PV	PMT
10	6	−8375.92	0

And finally, on an HP, press the FV key or on a TI, press CPT and then the FV key.

MyFinanceLab

Here is what you should know after reading this chapter. MyFinanceLab will help you identify what you know, and where to go when you need to practice.

Key Points and Equations	Key Terms	Online Practice
3.1 Cost-Benefit Analysis • To evaluate a decision, we must value the incremental costs and benefits associated with that decision. A good decision is one for which the value of the benefits exceeds the value of the costs. • To compare costs and benefits that occur at different points in time we must put all costs and benefits in common terms. Typically, we convert costs and benefits into cash today. • A competitive market is one in which a good can be bought and sold at the same price. We use prices from competitive markets to determine the cash value of a good.	competitive market, p. 73	MyFinanceLab Study Plan 3.1

3.2 Market Prices and the Valuation Principle
- Arbitrage is the process of trading to take advantage of equivalent goods that have different prices in different competitive markets.
- If equivalent goods or securities trade simultaneously in different competitive markets, they will trade for the same price in each market. This is equivalent to saying that no arbitrage opportunities should exist.
- The Valuation Principle states that the value of a commodity or an asset to the firm or its investors is determined by its competitive market price. The benefits and costs of a decision should be evaluated using those market prices. When the value of the benefits exceeds the value of the costs, the decision will increase the market value of the firm.

arbitrage, p. 75
arbitrage opportunity, p. 75
Law of One Price, p. 75

MyFinanceLab
Study Plan 3.2

3.3 The Time Value of Money and Interest Rates
- The time value of money is the difference in value between money today and money in the future.
- The rate at which we can exchange money today for money in the future by borrowing or investing is the current market interest rate.
- The present value (PV) of a cash flow is its value in terms of cash today.
- Timelines are a critical first step in organizing the cash flows in a financial problem.

discount factor, p. 79
discount rate, p. 79
future value (FV), p. 79
interest rate, p. 77
interest rate factor, p. 77
present value (PV), p. 79
time value of money, p. 76
timeline, p. 80

MyFinanceLab
Study Plan 3.3

3.4 Valuing Cash Flows at Different Points in Time
- There are three rules of valuing cash flows:
  a. Only cash flows that occur at the same point in time can be compared or combined.
  b. To calculate a cash flow's future value, you must compound it.
  c. To calculate a cash flow's present value, you must discount it.
- The future value in n years of a cash flow C today is:
$$C \times (1 + r)^n \qquad (3.1)$$
- The present value today of a cash flow C received in n years is:
$$C \div (1 + r)^n \qquad (3.2)$$

compounding, p. 82
compound interest, p. 82
discounting, p. 84

MyFinanceLab
Study Plan 3.4

Financial Calculator Tutorials: Calculating the Future Value of a Lump Sum and Solving for the Present Value of a Single Future Cash Flow

CRITICAL THINKING

1. What makes an investment decision a good one?
2. How important are our personal preferences in valuing an investment decision?
3. Why are market prices useful to a financial manager?
4. Why is arbitrage important to competitive market prices?
5. How does the Valuation Principle help a financial manager make decisions?
6. Can we directly compare dollar amounts received at different points in time?

7. Why is a cash flow in the future worth less than the same amount today?

8. What is a discount rate?

9. What is compound interest?

10. What is the intuition behind the geometric growth in interest?

PROBLEMS

*All problems are available in MyFinanceLab. An asterisk * indicates problems with a higher level of difficulty.*

Cost-Benefit Analysis

1. Honda Motor Company is considering offering a $2000 rebate on its minivan, low-ering the vehicle's price from $30,000 to $28,000. The marketing group estimates that this rebate will increase sales over the next year from 40,000 to 55,000 vehicles. Suppose Honda's profit margin with the rebate is $6000 per vehicle. If the change in sales is the only consequence of this decision, what are its costs and benefits? Is it a good idea?

2. You are an international shrimp trader. A food producer in the Czech Republic offers to pay you 2 million Czech koruna today in exchange for a year's supply of frozen shrimp. Your Thai supplier will provide you with the same supply for 3 million Thai baht today. If the current competitive market exchange rates are 25.50 koruna per dollar and 41.25 baht per dollar, what is the value of this exchange to you?

3. Suppose your employer offers you a choice between a $5000 bonus and 100 shares of the company's stock. Whichever one you choose will be awarded today. The stock is currently trading at $63 per share.
   a. Suppose that if you receive the stock bonus, you are free to trade it. Which form of the bonus should you choose? What is its value?
   b. Suppose that if you receive the stock bonus, you are required to hold it for at least one year. What can you say about the value of the stock bonus now? What will your decision depend on?

4. Suppose Big Bank offers an interest rate of 5.5% on both savings and loans, and Bank Enn offers an interest rate of 6% on both savings and loans.
   a. What profit opportunity is available?
   b. Which bank would experience a surge in the demand for loans? Which bank would receive a surge in deposits?
   c. What would you expect to happen to the interest rates the two banks are offering?

5. If the cost of buying a CD and ripping the tracks to your iPod (including your time) is $25, what is the most Apple could charge on iTunes for a whole 15-track CD?

6. Some companies cross-list their shares, meaning that their stock trades on more than one stock exchange. For example, Research In Motion, the maker of BlackBerry mobile devices, trades on both the Toronto Stock Exchange and NASDAQ. If its price in Toronto is 50 Canadian dollars per share and anyone can exchange Canadian dol-lars for U.S. dollars at the rate of US$0.95 per C$1.00, what must RIM's price be on NASDAQ?

Market Prices and the Valuation Principle

7. Bubba is a shrimp farmer. In an ironic twist, Bubba is allergic to shellfish, so he can-not eat any shrimp. Each day he has a one-ton supply of shrimp. The market price of shrimp is $10,000 per ton.

    a. What is the value of a ton of shrimp to him?

    b. Would this value change if he were not allergic to shrimp? Why or why not?

8. Brett has almond orchards, but he is sick of almonds and prefers to eat walnuts instead. The owner of the walnut orchard next door has offered to swap this year's crop with him. Assume he produces 1000 tons of almonds and his neighbor produces 800 tons of walnuts. If the market price of almonds is $100 per ton and the market price of walnuts is $110 per ton:

    a. Should he make the exchange?

    b. Does it matter whether he prefers almonds or walnuts? Why or why not?

The Time Value of Money and Interest Rates

9. You have $100 and a bank is offering 5% interest on deposits. If you deposit the money in the bank, how much will you have in one year?

10. You expect to have $1000 in one year. A bank is offering loans at 6% interest per year. How much can you borrow today?

11. A friend asks to borrow $55 from you and in return will pay you $58 in one year. If your bank is offering a 6% interest rate on deposits and loans:

    a. How much would you have in one year if you deposited the $55 instead?

    b. How much money could you borrow today if you pay the bank $58 in one year?

    c. Should you loan the money to your friend or deposit it in the bank?

12. You plan to borrow $1000 from a bank. In exchange for $1000 today, you promise to pay $1080 in one year. What does the cash flow timeline look like from your perspective? What does it look like from the bank's perspective?

13. The local electronics store is offering a promotion "1-year: same as cash," meaning that you can buy a TV now, and wait a year to pay (with no interest). So, if you take home a $1000 TV today, you will owe them $1000 in one year. If your bank is offering 4% interest, what is the true cost of the TV to you today?

Valuing Cash Flows at Different Points in Time

14. Suppose the interest rate is 4%.

    a. Having $200 today is equivalent to having what amount in one year?

    b. Having $200 in one year is equivalent to having what amount today?

    c. Which would you prefer, $200 today or $200 in one year? Does your answer depend on when you need the money? Why or why not?

15. You are considering a savings bond that will pay $100 in 10 years. If the interest rate is 2%, what should you pay today for the bond?

16. If your bank pays you 1.5% interest and you deposit $500 today, what will your balance be in 5 years?

17. Consider the following alternatives:

    i. $100 received in one year

    ii. $200 received in 5 years

    iii. $300 received in 10 years

    a. Rank the alternatives from most valuable to least valuable if the interest rate is 10% per year.

    b. What is your ranking if the interest rate is only 5% per year?

    c. What is your ranking if the interest rate is 20% per year?

*18. Suppose you invest $1000 in an account paying 8% interest per year.
   a. What is the balance in the account after 3 years? How much of this balance corresponds to "interest on interest"?
   b. What is the balance in the account after 25 years? How much of this balance corresponds to "interest on interest"?

19. Calculate the future value of $2000 in
   a. 5 years at an interest rate of 5% per year.
   b. 10 years at an interest rate of 5% per year.
   c. 5 years at an interest rate of 10% per year.
   *d. Why is the amount of interest earned in part (a) less than half the amount of interest earned in part (b)?

20. What is the present value of $10,000 received
   a. 12 years from today when the interest rate is 4% per year?
   b. 20 years from today when the interest rate is 8% per year?
   c. 6 years from today when the interest rate is 2% per year?

21. Your brother has offered to give you either $5000 today or $10,000 in 10 years. If the interest rate is 7% per year, which option is preferable?

22. Your bank pays 2.5% interest per year. You put $1000 in the bank today and $500 more in the bank in one year. How much will you have in the bank in 2 years?

23. Your cousin is currently 12 years old. She will be going to college in 6 years. Your aunt and uncle would like to have $100,000 in a savings account to fund her education at that time. If the account promises to pay a fixed interest rate of 4% per year, how much money do they need to put into the account today to ensure that they will have $100,000 in 6 years?

24. Your mom is thinking of retiring. Her retirement plan will pay her either $250,000 immediately on retirement or $350,000 five years after the date of her retirement. Which alternative should she choose if the interest rate is
   a. 0% per year?
   b. 8% per year?
   c. 20% per year?

25. You are planning to invest $5000 in an account earning 9% per year for retirement.
   a. If you put the $5000 in an account at age 23, and withdraw it 42 years later, how much will you have?
   b. If you wait 10 years before making the deposit, so that it stays in the account for only 32 years, how much will you have at the end?

*26. Your grandfather put some money in an account for you on the day you were born. You are now 18 years old and are allowed to withdraw the money for the first time. The account currently has $3996 in it and pays an 8% interest rate.
   a. How much money would be in the account if you left the money there until your 25th birthday?
   b. What if you left the money until your 65th birthday?
   c. How much money did your grandfather originally put in the account?

4

Time Value of Money: Valuing Cash Flow Streams

LEARNING OBJECTIVES

- Value a series of many cash flows

- Value a perpetual series of regular cash flows called a *perpetuity*

- Value a common set of regular cash flows called an *annuity*

- Value both perpetuities and annuities when the cash flows grow at a constant rate

- Compute the number of periods, cash flow, or rate of return of a loan or investment

- Value cash flow streams with non-annual payments

notation

C	cash flow	P	initial principal or deposit, or equivalent present value
C_n	cash flow at date n		
FV	future value	PV	present value
FV_n	future value on date n	r	interest rate or rate of return
g	growth rate		
N	date of the last cash flow in a stream of cash flows		

As we have discussed, to evaluate a project a financial manager must compare its costs and benefits. In most cases, the cash flows in financial investments involve more than one future period. Thus, the financial manager is faced with the task of trading off a known up-front cost against a series of uncertain future benefits. We learned to value those costs and benefits by computing their cash values today—their present values.

In financial management, as well as your personal finances, you will need to evaluate series of cash flows occurring across time. In this chapter, we build on the tools we developed in Chapter 3 to value any series of cash flows. We will develop shortcuts for valuing *annuities*, *perpetuities*, and other special cases of assets with cash flows that follow regular patterns.

In Chapter 5, we will learn how interest rates are quoted and determined. Once we understand how interest rates are quoted, it will be straightforward to extend the tools of this chapter to cash flows that occur more frequently than once per year.

Valuing a Stream of Cash Flows

stream of cash flows
A series of cash flows lasting several periods.

We refer to a series of cash flows lasting several periods as a **stream of cash flows**. As with single cash flows, we can represent a stream of cash flows on a timeline. In this chapter, we will continue to use timelines and the rules of cash flow valuation introduced in Chapter 3 to organize and then solve financial problems.

Applying the Rules of Valuing Cash Flows to a Cash Flow Stream

Most investment opportunities have multiple cash flows that occur at different points in time. In Chapter 3, we learned the rules to value such cash flows:

Rule 1: Only values at the same point in time can be compared or combined.

Rule 2: To calculate a cash flow's future value, we must compound it using Eq. 3.1 from Chapter 3.

$$FV_n = C \times (1 + r)^n \tag{4.1}$$

Rule 3: To calculate the present value of a future cash flow, we must discount it using Eq. 3.2 from Chapter 3.

$$PV = C \div (1 + r)^n = \frac{C}{(1 + r)^n} \tag{4.2}$$

The rules of cash flow valuation allow us to compare and combine cash flows that occur at different points in time. Suppose we plan to save $1000 today and $1000 at the end of each of the next two years. If we earn a fixed 10% interest rate on our savings, how much will we have three years from today?

Again, we start with a timeline:

The timeline shows the three deposits we plan to make. We need to compute their value at the end of three years.

We can use the cash flow valuation rules in a number of ways to solve this problem. First, we can take the deposit at date 0 and move it forward to date 1. Because it is then in the same time period as the date 1 deposit, we can combine the two amounts to find out the total in the bank on date 1:

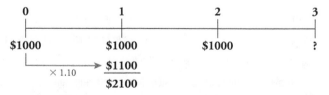

Using the first two rules, we find that our total savings on date 1 will be $2100. Continuing in this fashion, we can solve the problem as follows:

The total amount we will have in the bank at the end of three years is $3641. This amount is the future value of our $1000 savings deposits.

Another approach to the problem is to compute the future value in year 3 of each cash flow separately. Once all three amounts are in year 3 dollars, we can then combine them.

Both calculations give the same future value of $3641. As long as we follow the rules, we get the same result. The order in which we apply the rules does not matter. The calculation we choose depends on which is more convenient for the problem at hand.

Now we formalize this approach by deriving a general formula for valuing a stream of cash flows.

Consider a stream of cash flows: C_0 at date 0, C_1 at date 1, and so on, up to C_N at date N. We represent this cash flow stream on a timeline as follows:

Using the rules of cash flow valuation, we compute the present value of this cash flow stream in two steps. First, we compute the present value of each individual cash flow. Then, once the cash flows are in common units of dollars today, we can combine them.

For a given interest rate r, we represent this process on the timeline as follows:

$$C_0 + \frac{C_1}{(1+r)} + \frac{C_2}{(1+r)^2} + \ldots + \frac{C_N}{(1+r)^N}$$

This timeline provides the general formula for the present value of a cash flow stream:

$$PV = C_0 + \frac{C_1}{(1+r)} + \frac{C_2}{(1+r)^2} + \cdots + \frac{C_N}{(1+r)^N} \tag{4.3}$$

That is, the present value of the cash flow stream is the sum of the present values of each cash flow. Recall from Chapter 3 that we defined the present value as the dollar amount you would need to invest today to produce the single cash flow in the future. The same idea holds in this context. The present value is the amount you need to invest today to generate the cash flows stream $C_0, C_1, \ldots, C_N$. That is, receiving those cash flows is equivalent to having their present value in the bank today.

PERSONAL FINANCE

EXAMPLE 4.1

Present Value of a
Stream of Cash Flows

MyFinanceLab

PROBLEM

You have just graduated and need money to buy a new car. Your rich Uncle Henry will lend you the money as long as you agree to pay him back within four years, and you offer to pay him the rate of interest that he would otherwise get by putting his money in a savings account. Based on your earnings and living expenses, you think you will be able to pay him $5000 in one year, and then $8000 each year for the next three years. If Uncle Henry would otherwise earn 6% per year on his savings, how much can you borrow from him?

SOLUTION

PLAN

The cash flows you can promise Uncle Henry are as follows:

How much money should Uncle Henry be willing to give you today in return for your promise of these payments? He should be willing to give you an amount that is equivalent to these payments in present value terms. This is the amount of money that it would take him to produce these same cash flows. We will (1) solve the problem using Eq. 4.3 and then (2) verify our answer by calculating the future value of this amount.

EXECUTE

1. We can calculate the PV as follows:

$$PV = \frac{5000}{1.06} + \frac{8000}{1.06^2} + \frac{8000}{1.06^3} + \frac{8000}{1.06^4}$$
$$= 4716.98 + 7119.97 + 6716.95 + 6336.75$$
$$= \$24{,}890.65$$

Now suppose that Uncle Henry gives you the money, and then deposits your payments to him in the bank each year. How much will he have four years from now?

We need to compute the future value of the annual deposits. One way to do this is to compute the bank balance each year:

2. To verify our answer, suppose your uncle kept his $24,890.65 in the bank today earning 6% interest. In four years he would have:

$$FV = \$24{,}890.65 \times (1.06)^4 = \$31{,}423.87 \text{ in 4 years}$$

We get the same answer both ways (within a penny, which is due to rounding).

EVALUATE

Thus, Uncle Henry should be willing to lend you $24,890.65 in exchange for your promised payments. This amount is less than the total you will pay him ($5000 + $8000 + $8000 + $8000 = $29,000) due to the time value of money.

Example 4.1 illustrates that if you want to compute the future value of a stream of cash flows, you can do it directly (the first approach), or you can first compute the present value and then move it to the future (the second approach). As always, we use Eq. 4.1 to calculate the future value of any present value. Because we obey the rules of valuing cash flows in both cases, we get the same result.

Using a Financial Calculator: Solving for Present and Future Values of Cash Flow Streams

So far, we have used formulas to compute present values and future values of cash flow streams. As we discussed at the end of Chapter 3, both financial calculators and spreadsheets have these formulas preprogrammed to quicken the process. In this box, we focus on financial calculators, but spreadsheets such as Excel have very similar shortcut functions.

Financial calculators have a set of functions that perform the calculations that finance professionals do most often. These functions are all based on the following timeline, which among other things can handle most types of loans:

$$
\begin{array}{ccccc}
0 & 1 & 2 & & NPER \\
\mid & \mid & \mid & \cdots & \mid \\
PV & PMT & PMT & & PMT + FV
\end{array}
$$

There are a total of five variables: number of periods (N or $NPER$), present value (PV), cash flow or "payment" (PMT), future value (FV), and the interest rate, denoted I/Y. Each function takes four of these variables as inputs and returns the value of the fifth one that ensures that the sum of the present value of the cash flows is zero.

By setting the recurring payments equal to 0, you could compute present and future values of single cash flows such as we have done above using Eqs. 4.2 and 4.1. In the examples shown in Sections 4.2 through 4.4, we will calculate cash flows using the **PMT** button. The best way to learn to use a financial calculator is by practicing. We present one example below. We will also show the calculator buttons for any additional examples in this chapter that can be solved with financial calculator functions. Finally, the appendix to this chapter contains step-by-step instructions for using the two most popular financial calculators.

Example
Suppose you plan to invest $20,000 in an account paying 8% interest. You will invest an additional $1000 at the end of each year for 15 years. How much will you have in the account in 15 years? We represent this problem with the following timeline:

$$
\begin{array}{ccccc}
0 & 1 & 2 & & NPER = 15 \\
\mid & \mid & \mid & \cdots & \mid \\
PV = -\$20{,}000 & PMT = -\$1000 & -\$1000 & & FV = ?
\end{array}
$$

To compute the solution, we enter the four variables we know, $N = 15$, $I/Y = 8$, $PV = -20{,}000$, $PMT = -\$1000$, and solve for the one we want to determine: FV. Specifically, for the HP-10BII or TI-BAII Plus calculators:

1. Enter 15 and press the **N** button.
2. Enter 8 and press the **I/Y** button (**I/YR** for the HP calculator).
3. Enter −20,000 and press the **PV** button.
4. Enter −$1000 and press the **PMT** button.
5. Press the **FV** button (for the Texas Instruments calculator, press **CPT** and then **FV**).

	N	I/Y	PV	PMT	FV
Given:	15	8	−20,000	−1000	
Solve for:					90,595.50
	Excel Formula: =FV(0.08,15,−1000,−20000)				

The calculator then shows a future value of $90,595.50.

Note that we entered *PV* and *PMT* as negative numbers (the amounts we are putting *into* the bank), and *FV* is shown as a positive number (the amount we can take *out* of the bank). It is important to use signs correctly to indicate the direction in which the money is flowing when using the calculator functions. You will see more examples of getting the sign of the cash flows correct throughout the chapter.

Excel has the same functions, but it calls "N," "NPER" and "I/Y," "RATE." *Also, it is important to note that you enter an interest rate of 8% as "8" in a financial calculator, but as "0.08" in Excel.*

EXAMPLE 4.2

Computing the
Future Value

MyFinanceLab

PROBLEM

Let's revisit the savings plan we considered earlier: We plan to save $1000 today and at the end of each of the next two years. At a fixed 10% interest rate, how much will we have in the bank three years from today?

SOLUTION

PLAN

We'll start with the timeline for this savings plan:

Let's solve this problem in a different way than we did in the text, while still following the rules we established. First, we'll compute the present value of the cash flows. Then, we'll compute its value three years later (its future value).

EXECUTE

There are several ways to calculate the present value of the cash flows. Here, we treat each cash flow separately and then combine the present values.

Saving $2735.54 today is equivalent to saving $1000 per year for three years. Now let's compute future value in year 3 of that $2735.54:

EVALUATE

This answer of $3641 is precisely the same result we found earlier. As long as we apply the three rules of valuing cash flows, we will always get the correct answer.

Concept
Check

1. How do you calculate the present value of a cash flow stream?

2. How do you calculate the future value of a cash flow stream?

4.2　Perpetuities

The formulas we have developed so far allow us to compute the present or future value of any cash flow stream. In this section and the next one, we consider two types of cash flow streams, *perpetuities* and *annuities*, and learn shortcuts for valuing them. These shortcuts are possible because the cash flows follow a regular pattern.

Perpetuities

perpetuity A stream of equal cash flows that occurs at regular intervals and lasts forever.

consol A bond that promises its owner a fixed cash flow every year, forever.

A **perpetuity** is a stream of equal cash flows that occur at regular intervals and last forever. One example is the British government bond called a **consol** (or *perpetual bond*). Consol bonds promise the owner a fixed cash flow every year, forever.

Here is the timeline for a perpetuity:

Note from the timeline that the first cash flow does not occur immediately; *it arrives at the end of the first period*. This timing is sometimes referred to as *payment in arrears* and is a standard convention in loan payment calculations and elsewhere, so we adopt it throughout this text.

Using the formula for the present value, the present value of a perpetuity with payment C and interest rate r is given by:

$$PV = \frac{C}{(1+r)} + \frac{C}{(1+r)^2} + \frac{C}{(1+r)^3} + \cdots$$

Notice that all the cash flows (C in the formula) are the same because the cash flow for a perpetuity is constant. Also, because the first cash flow is in one period, there is no cash flow at time 0 $(C_0 = 0)$.

To find the value of a perpetuity by discounting one cash flow at a time would take forever—literally! You might wonder how, even with a shortcut, the sum of an infinite number of positive terms could be finite. The answer is that the cash flows in the future are discounted for an ever-increasing number of periods, so their contribution to the sum eventually becomes negligible.

To derive the shortcut, we calculate the value of a perpetuity by creating our own perpetuity. The Valuation Principle tells us that the value of a perpetuity must be the same as the cost we incurred to create our own identical perpetuity. To illustrate, suppose you could invest $100 in a bank account paying 5% interest per year, forever. At the end of one year, you will have $105 in the bank—your original $100 plus $5 in interest. Suppose you withdraw the $5 interest and reinvest the $100 for a second year. Again, you will have $105 after one year, and you can withdraw $5 and reinvest $100 for another year. By doing this year after year, you can withdraw $5 every year in perpetuity:

By investing $100 in the bank today, you can, in effect, create a perpetuity paying $5 per year. Because the bank will "sell" us (allow us to create) the perpetuity for $100, the present value of the $5 per year in perpetuity is this "do-it-yourself" cost of $100.

Now let's generalize this argument. Suppose we invest an amount P in a bank account with an interest rate r. Every year we can withdraw the interest we have earned, $C = r \times P$, leaving the principal, P, in the bank. Because our cost for creating the perpetuity is only the initial investment of principal (P), the value of receiving C in perpetuity is therefore the upfront cost P. Rearranging $C = r \times P$ to solve for P we have $P = C/r$. Therefore:

Present Value of a Perpetuity

$$PV(C \text{ in Perpetuity}) = \frac{C}{r} \tag{4.4}$$

By depositing the amount $\dfrac{C}{r}$ today, we can withdraw interest of $\dfrac{C}{r} \times r = C$ each period in perpetuity.

Note the logic of our argument. To determine the present value of a cash flow stream, we computed the "do-it-yourself" cost of creating those same cash flows at the bank. This is an extremely useful and powerful approach—and is much simpler and faster than summing those infinite terms![1]

Historical Examples of Perpetuities

Companies sometimes issue bonds that they call perpetuities, but in fact are not really perpetuities. For example, in mid-2010, Europe's largest bank, HSBC, sold $3.4 billion of "perpetual" bonds that promise investors a fixed amount each year with no maturity date. But while the bonds have no fixed maturity, they are not exactly true perpetuities as HSBC has the right to pay off the bonds after 5½ years. Thus, the bond's payments might not last forever. Perpetual bonds were some of the first bonds ever issued. The oldest perpetuities that are still making interest payments were issued in 1624 by the *Hoogheemraadschap Lekdijk Bovendams*, a seventeenth-century Dutch water board responsible for upkeep of the local dikes. To verify that these bonds continue to pay interest, two finance professors at Yale University,

William Goetzmann and Geert Rouwenhorst, purchased one of these bonds on July 1, 2003, and collected 26 years of back interest. On its issue date in 1648, this bond originally paid interest in Carolus guilders. Over the next 355 years, the currency of payment changed to Flemish pounds, Dutch guilders, and most recently euros. Recently, the bond was paying interest of €11.34 annually.

Although the Dutch bonds are the oldest perpetuities still in existence, the first perpetuities date from much earlier times. For example, *cencus agreements* and *rentes*, which were forms of perpetuities and annuities, were issued in the twelfth century in Italy, France, and Spain. They were initially designed to circumvent the usury laws of the Catholic Church: Because they did not require the repayment of principal, in the eyes of the church they were not considered loans.

PERSONAL FINANCE

EXAMPLE 4.3

Endowing a Perpetuity

MyFinanceLab

PROBLEM

You want to endow an annual graduation party at your alma mater. You want the event to be memorable, so you budget $30,000 per year forever for the party. If the university earns 8% per year on its investments, and if the first party is in one year's time, how much will you need to donate to endow the party?

SOLUTION

PLAN

The timeline of the cash flows you want to provide is:

This is a standard perpetuity of $30,000 per year. The funding you would need to give the university in perpetuity is the present value of this cash flow stream.

EXECUTE

Use the formula for a perpetuity:

$$PV = C/r = \$30,000/0.08 = \$375,000 \text{ today}$$

EVALUATE

If you donate $375,000 today, and if the university invests it at 8% per year forever, then the graduates will have $30,000 every year to fund their graduation party.

---

[1]Another mathematical derivation of this result exists (see the online appendix), but it is less intuitive.

Discounting One Too Many Times

The perpetuity formula assumes that the first payment occurs at the end of the first period (at date 1). Sometimes perpetuities have cash flows that start later. In this case, we can adapt the perpetuity formula to compute the present value, but we need to do so carefully to avoid a common mistake.

To illustrate, consider the graduation party described in Example 4.3. Rather than starting in one year, suppose the first party will be held two years from today. How would this delay change the amount of the donation required?

Now the timeline looks like this:

We need to determine the present value of these cash flows, as it tells us the amount of money needed in the bank today to finance the future parties. We cannot apply the perpetuity formula directly, however, because these cash flows are not *exactly* a perpetuity as we defined it. Specifically, the cash flow in the first period is "missing." But consider the situation on date 1—at that point, the first

party is one period away and then the cash flows occur regularly. From the perspective of date 1, this *is* a perpetuity, and we can apply the formula. From the preceding calculation, we know we need $375,000 on date 1 to have enough to start the parties on date 2. We rewrite the timeline as follows:

Our goal can now be restated more simply: How much do we need to invest today to have $375,000 in one year? This is a simple present value calculation:

$$PV = \$375,000/1.08 = \$347,222 \text{ today}$$

A common mistake is to discount the $375,000 twice because the first party is in two periods. *Remember—the present value formula for the perpetuity already discounts the cash flows to one period prior to the first cash flow.* Keep in mind that this common mistake may be made with perpetuities, annuities, and all the other special cases discussed in this chapter. All these formulas discount the cash flows to one period prior to the first cash flow.

3. What are some examples of perpetuities?
4. What is the intuition behind the fact that an infinite stream of cash flows has a finite present value?

4.3 Annuities

annuity A stream of equal cash flows arriving at a regular interval and ending after a specified time period.

An **annuity** is a stream consisting of a fixed number of equal cash flows paid at regular intervals. So the difference between an annuity and a perpetuity is that an annuity ends after some fixed number of payments whereas a perpetuity continues forever. Most car loans, mortgages, and some bonds are annuities. We represent the cash flows of an annuity on a timeline as follows:

Note that just as with the perpetuity, we adopt the convention that the first payment takes place at date 1, one period from today. The present value of an N-period annuity with payment C and interest rate r is:

$$PV = \frac{C}{(1+r)} + \frac{C}{(1+r)^2} + \frac{C}{(1+r)^3} + \cdots + \frac{C}{(1+r)^N}$$

Present Value of an Annuity

To find a simpler formula, we use the same approach we followed with the perpetuity: Find a way to create your own annuity. To illustrate, suppose you invest $100 in a bank account paying 5% interest. At the end of one year, you will have $105 in the bank—your original

$100 plus $5 in interest. Using the same strategy as you did for calculating the value of a perpetuity, suppose you withdraw the $5 interest and reinvest the $100 for a second year. Once again you will have $105 after one year. You can repeat the process, withdrawing $5 and reinvesting $100, every year. For a perpetuity, you left the principal in the bank forever. Alternatively, you might decide after 20 years to close the account and withdraw the principal. In that case, your cash flows will look like this:

With your initial $100 investment, you have created a 20-year annuity of $5 per year, plus you will receive an extra $100 at the end of 20 years. The Valuation Principle's Law of One Price tells us that things that produce exactly the same cash flows must have the same value. Because it only took an initial investment of $100 to create the cash flows on the timeline, the present value of these cash flows is $100, or:

$$\$100 = PV(\text{20-year annuity of \$5 per year}) + PV(\$100 \text{ in 20 years})$$

So if we invest $100 now, we can receive $5 per year for 20 years as well as $100 in the 20th year, representing the following cash flows:

0	1	2		20
−$100	$5	$5	...	$5 + $100

Rearranging the equation above shows that the cost of a 20-year annuity of $5 per year is $100 minus the present value of $100 in 20 years.

$$PV(\text{20-year annuity of \$5 per year}) = \$100 - PV(\$100 \text{ in 20 years})$$

$$= 100 - \frac{100}{(1.05)^{20}} = \$100 - \$37.69 = \$62.31$$

0	1	2		20
−$100	$5	$5	...	$5 + $100

Removing the $100 in 20 years and its present value ($37.69) leaves the following cash flows:

−$62.31	$5	$5	...	$5

So the present value of $5 for 20 years is $62.31. Intuitively, the value of the annuity is the initial investment in the bank account minus the present value of the principal that will be left in the account after 20 years.

The $5 we receive every year is the interest on the $100 and can be written as $100(.05) = $5. Rearranging this equation, we have $100 = $5/.05. If we substitute $5/.05 into our formula above, we can represent the PV of the annuity as a function of its cash flow ($5), the discount rate (5%) and the number of years (20):

$$PV(\text{20-year annuity of \$5 per year}) = \frac{\$5}{.05} - \frac{\dfrac{\$5}{.05}}{(1.05)^{20}} = \overset{\displaystyle C}{\underset{}{\frac{\$5}{.05}}}\left(1 - \frac{1}{(1.05)^{\overset{N}{\downarrow}20}}\right)$$

$$= \$5 \times \frac{1}{.05}\left(1 - \frac{1}{(1.05)^{20}}\right)$$

$$\underset{r}{\underset{\longleftarrow\!\!\longrightarrow}{}}$$

This method is very useful because we will most often want to know the PV of the annuity given its cash flow, discount rate, and number of years. We can write this as a general formula for the present value of an annuity of C for N periods:

Present Value of an Annuity

$$PV(\text{Annuity of } C \text{ for } N \text{ Periods with Interest Rate } r) = C \times \frac{1}{r}\left(1 - \frac{1}{(1+r)^{N}}\right) \quad (4.5)$$

PROBLEM

You are the lucky winner of a $30 million state lottery. You can take your prize money either as (a) 30 payments of $1 million per year (starting today), or (b) $15 million paid today. If the interest rate is 8%, which option should you choose?

SOLUTION

PLAN

Option (a) provides $30 million in prize money but paid over time. To evaluate it correctly, we must convert it to a present value. Here is the timeline:

0	1	2	29
$1 million	$1 million	$1 million	$1 million

Because the first payment starts today, the last payment will occur in 29 years (for a total of 30 payments).[2] The $1 million at date 0 is already stated in present value terms, but we need to compute the present value of the remaining payments. Fortunately, this case looks like a 29-year annuity of $1 million per year, so we can use the annuity formula.

EXECUTE

We use the annuity formula:

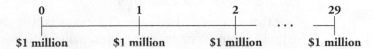

$$PV(\text{29-year annuity of \$1 million at 8\% annual interest}) = \$1 \text{ million} \times \frac{1}{0.08}\left(1 - \frac{1}{1.08^{29}}\right)$$

$$= \$1 \text{ million} \times 11.16$$

$$= \$11.16 \text{ million today}$$

(Continued)

---

[2]An annuity in which the first payment occurs immediately is sometimes called an *annuity due*. Throughout this text, we always use the term "annuity" to mean one that is paid in arrears.

Thus, the total present value of the cash flows is $1 million + $11.16 million = $12.16 million. In timeline form:

0	1	2		29
$1 million	$1 million	$1 million	...	$1 million

$11.16 million
$12.16 million

Option (b), $15 million upfront, is more valuable—even though the total amount of money paid is half that of option (a).

Financial calculators or Excel can handle annuities easily—just enter the cash flow in the annuity as the *PMT*:

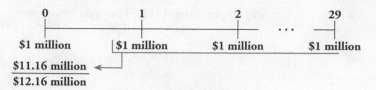

	N	I/Y	PV	PMT	FV
Given:	29	8		1,000,000	0
Solve for:			−11,158,406		
Excel Formula:			=PV(RATE,NPER,PMT,FV)=PV(0.08,29,1000000,0)		

Both the financial calculator and Excel will give you the PV of the 29 payments ($11,158,406, or 11.16 million), to which you must add the first payment of $1 million just as shown.

EVALUATE

The reason for the difference is the time value of money. If you have the $15 million today, you can use $1 million immediately and invest the remaining $14 million at an 8% interest rate. This strategy will give you $14 million × 8% = $1.12 million per year in perpetuity! Alternatively, you can spend $15 million − $11.16 million = $3.84 million today, and invest the remaining $11.16 million, which will still allow you to withdraw $1 million each year for the next 29 years before your account is depleted.

Future Value of an Annuity

Now that we have derived a simple formula for the present value of an annuity, it is easy to find a simple formula for the future value. If we want to know the value N years in the future, we move the present value N periods forward on the timeline.

0	1	2		20
	C	C	...	C

$$PV = \frac{C}{r}\left(1 - \frac{1}{(1+r)^N}\right) \longrightarrow FV = \frac{C}{r}\left(1 - \frac{1}{(1+r)^N}\right) \times (1+r)^N$$

As the timeline shows, we compound the present value for N periods at interest rate r:

Future Value of an Annuity

$$FV(\text{Annuity}) = PV \times (1+r)^N$$

$$= \frac{C}{r}\left(1 - \frac{1}{(1+r)^N}\right) \times (1+r)^N$$

$$= C \times \frac{1}{r}\left((1+r)^N - 1\right) \tag{4.6}$$

This formula is useful if we want to know how a savings account will grow over time if the investor deposits the same amount every period.

PERSONAL FINANCE

EXAMPLE 4.5

Retirement Savings
Plan Annuity

MyFinanceLab

PROBLEM

Ellen is 35 years old and she has decided it is time to plan seriously for her retirement. At the end of each year until she is 65, she will save $10,000 in a retirement account. If the account earns 10% per year, how much will Ellen have in her account at age 65?

SOLUTION

PLAN

As always, we begin with a timeline. In this case, it is helpful to keep track of both the dates and Ellen's age:

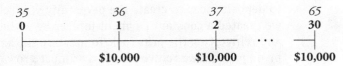

Ellen's savings plan looks like an annuity of $10,000 per year for 30 years. (*Hint:* It is easy to become confused when you just look at age, rather than at both dates and age. A common error is to think there are only $65 - 36 = 29$ payments. Writing down both dates and age avoids this problem.)

To determine the amount Ellen will have in her account at age 65, we'll need to compute the future value of this annuity.

EXECUTE

$$FV = \$10,000 \times \frac{1}{0.10}(1.10^{30} - 1)$$

$$= \$10,000 \times 164.49$$

$$= \$1.645 \text{ million at age 65}$$

Using a financial calculator or Excel:

	N	I/Y	PV	PMT	FV
Given:	30	10	0	−10,000	
Solve for:					1,644,940
	Excel Formula: =FV(RATE,NPER, PMT, PV)=FV(0.10,30,−10000,0)				

EVALUATE

By investing $10,000 per year for 30 years (a total of $300,000) and earning interest on those investments, the compounding will allow Ellen to retire with $1.645 million.

Concept
Check

5. What are some examples of annuities?

6. What is the difference between an annuity and a perpetuity?

4.4 Growing Cash Flows

So far, we have considered only cash flow streams that have the same cash flow every period. If, instead, the cash flows are expected to grow at a constant rate in each period, we can also derive a simple formula for the present value of the future stream.

Growing Perpetuity

growing perpetuity
A stream of cash flows that occurs at regular intervals and grows at a constant rate forever.

A **growing perpetuity** is a stream of cash flows that occur at regular intervals and grow at a constant rate forever. For example, a growing perpetuity with a first payment of $100 that grows at a rate of 3% has the following timeline:

To derive the formula for the present value of a growing perpetuity, we follow the same logic used for a regular perpetuity: Compute the amount you would need to deposit today to create the perpetuity yourself. In the case of a regular perpetuity, we created a constant payment forever by withdrawing the interest earned each year and reinvesting the principal. To increase the amount we can withdraw each year, the principal that we reinvest each year must grow. Therefore, we withdraw less than the full amount of interest earned each period, using the remaining interest to increase our principal.

Let's consider a specific case. Suppose you want to create a perpetuity growing at 2%, so you invest $100 in a bank account that pays 5% interest. At the end of one year, you will have $105 in the bank—your original $100 plus $5 in interest. If you withdraw only $3, you will have $102 to reinvest—2% more than the amount you had initially. This amount will then grow to $102 × 1.05 = $107.10 in the following year, and you can withdraw $3 × 1.02 = $3.06, which will leave you with principal of $107.10 − $3.06 = $104.04. Note that $102 × 1.02 = $104.04. That is, both the amount you withdraw and the principal you reinvest grow by 2% each year. On a timeline, these cash flows look like this:

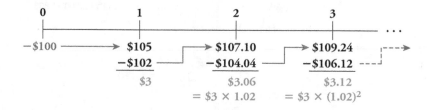

By following this strategy, you have created a growing perpetuity that starts at $3 and grows 2% per year. This growing perpetuity must have a present value equal to the cost of $100.

We can generalize this argument. If we want to increase the amount we withdraw from the bank each year by g, then the principal in the bank will have to grow by the same factor g. That is, instead of reinvesting P in the second year, we should reinvest $P(1 + g) = P + gP$. In order to increase our principal by gP, we need to leave gP of the interest in the account, so of the total interest of rP, we can only withdraw $rP - gP = P(r - g)$. We demonstrate this for the first year of our example:

Initial amount deposited	$100	P
Interest earned	(.05)($100)	rP
Amount needed to increase principal	(.02)($100)	gP
Amount withdrawn	(.05)($100) − (.02)($100)	$rP - gP$
	= $100(.05 − .02)	= $P(r - g)$

Denoting our withdrawal as C, we have $C = P(r - g)$. Solving this equation for P, the initial amount deposited in the bank account, gives the present value of a growing perpetuity with initial cash flow C:[3]

Present Value of a Growing Perpetuity

$$PV(\text{Growing Perpetuity}) = \frac{C}{r - g} \tag{4.7}$$

To understand intuitively the formula for a growing perpetuity, start with the formula for a perpetuity. In the earlier case, you had to put enough money in the bank to ensure that the interest earned matched the cash flows of the regular perpetuity. In the case of a growing perpetuity, you need to put more than that amount in the bank because you have to finance the growth in the cash flows. How much more? If the bank pays interest at a rate of 5%, then all that is left to take out, if you want to make sure the principal grows 2% per year, is the difference: $5\% - 2\% = 3\%$. So instead of the present value of the perpetuity being the first cash flow divided by the interest rate, it is now the first cash flow divided by the *difference* between the interest rate and the growth rate.

PERSONAL FINANCE

EXAMPLE 4.6

Endowing a Growing Perpetuity

MyFinanceLab

PROBLEM

In Example 4.3, you planned to donate money to your alma mater to fund an annual $30,000 graduation party. Given an interest rate of 8% per year, the required donation was the present value of:

$$PV = \$30{,}000/0.08 = \$375{,}000 \text{ today}$$

Before accepting the money, however, the student association has asked that you increase the donation to account for the effect of inflation on the cost of the party in future years. Although $30,000 is adequate for next year's party, the students estimate that the party's cost will rise by 4% per year thereafter. To satisfy their request, how much do you need to donate now?

SOLUTION

PLAN

The cost of the party next year is $30,000, and the cost then increases 4% per year forever. From the timeline, we recognize the form of a growing perpetuity and can value it that way.

EXECUTE

To finance the growing cost, you need to provide the present value today of:

$$PV = \$30{,}000/(0.08 - 0.04) = \$750{,}000 \text{ today}$$

EVALUATE

You need to double the size of your gift!

---

[3]Suppose $g \geq r$. Then the cash flows grow even faster than they are discounted; each term in the sum of discounted cash flows gets larger, rather than smaller. In this case, the sum is infinite! What does an infinite present value mean? Remember that the present value is the "do-it-yourself" cost of creating the cash flows. An infinite present value means that no matter how much money you start with, it is *impossible* to sustain a growth rate of g forever and reproduce those cash flows on your own. Growing perpetuities of this sort cannot exist in practice because no one would be willing to offer one at any finite price. A promise to pay an amount that forever grew faster than the interest rate is also unlikely to be kept (or believed by any savvy buyer). The only viable growing perpetuities are those where the perpetual growth rate is less than the interest rate, so we assume that $g < r$ for a growing perpetuity.

Growing Annuity

growing annuity A stream of cash flows, growing at a constant rate and paid at regular intervals, that end after a specified number of periods.

A **growing annuity** is a stream of N growing cash flows, paid at regular intervals. It is a growing perpetuity that eventually comes to an end. The following timeline shows a growing annuity with initial cash flow C, growing at rate g every period until period N:

The conventions used earlier still apply: (1) The first cash flow arrives at the end of the first period and (2) the first cash flow is before growth. The last cash flow therefore reflects only $N - 1$ periods of growth.

    The present value of an N-period growing annuity with initial cash flow C, growth rate g, and interest rate r is given by

Present Value of a Growing Annuity

$$PV = C \times \frac{1}{r-g}\left(1 - \left(\frac{1+g}{1+r}\right)^{N}\right) \tag{4.8}$$

Because the annuity has a finite number of terms, Eq. 4.8 also works when $g > r$.[4] The process of deriving this simple expression for the present value of a growing annuity is the same as for a regular annuity. Interested readers may consult the online appendix for details.

EXAMPLE 4.7

Retirement Savings with a Growing Annuity

MyFinanceLab

PROBLEM

In Example 4.5, Ellen considered saving $10,000 per year for her retirement. Although $10,000 is the most she can save in the first year, she expects her salary to increase each year so that she will be able to increase her savings by 5% per year. With this plan, if she earns 10% per year on her savings, how much will Ellen have in her account at age 65?

SOLUTION

PLAN

Her new savings plan is represented by the following timeline:

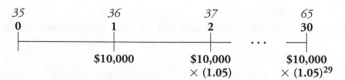

This example involves a 30-year growing annuity, with a growth rate of 5%, and an initial cash flow of $10,000. We can use Eq. 4.8 to solve for the present value of this growing annuity. Then we can use Eq. 4.1 to calculate the future value.

---

[4]Equation 4.8 does not work for $g = r$. But in that case, growth and discounting cancel out, and the present value is equivalent to receiving all the cash flows at date 1: $PV = C \times N/(1+r)$.

EXECUTE

The present value of Ellen's growing annuity is given by

$$PV = \$10,000 \times \frac{1}{0.10 - 0.05}\left(1 - \left(\frac{1.05}{1.10}\right)^{30}\right)$$

$$= \$10,000 \times 15.0463$$

$$= \$150,463 \text{ today}$$

Ellen's proposed savings plan is equivalent to having $150,463 in the bank *today*. To determine the amount she will have at age 65, we need to move this amount forward 30 years:

$$FV = \$150,463 \times 1.10^{30}$$

$$= \$2.625 \text{ million in 30 years}$$

EVALUATE

Ellen will have $2.625 million at age 65 using the new savings plan. This sum is almost $1 million more than she had without the additional annual increases in savings. Because she is increasing her savings amount each year and the interest on the cumulative increases continues to compound, her final savings is much greater.

Concept Check

7. How can an infinitely growing stream of cash flows have a finite value?

8. What is an example of a growing perpetuity?

4.5 Solving for Variables Other Than Present Value or Future Value

So far, we have calculated the present value or future value of a stream of cash flows. Sometimes, however, we know the present value or future value, but do not know one of the variables that so far we have been given as an input. For example, when you take out a loan, you may know the amount you would like to borrow, but may not know the loan payments that will be required to repay it. Or, if you make a deposit into a bank account, you may want to calculate how long it will take before your balance reaches a certain level. In such situations, we use the present and/or future values as inputs, and solve for the variable we are interested in. We examine several special cases in this section.

Solving for the Cash Flows

Let's consider an example where we know the present value of an investment, but do not know the cash flows. The best example is a loan—you know how much you want to borrow (the present value) and you know the interest rate, but you do not know how much you need to repay each year. Suppose you are opening a business that requires an initial investment of $100,000. Your bank manager has agreed to lend you this money. The terms of the loan state that you will make equal annual payments for the next 10 years and will pay an interest rate of 8% with the first payment due one year from today. What is your annual payment?

From the bank's perspective, the timeline looks like this:

The bank will give you $100,000 today in exchange for 10 equal payments over the next decade. You need to determine the size of the payment C that the bank will require. For the bank to be willing to lend you $100,000, the loan cash flows must have a present value of $100,000 when evaluated at the bank's interest rate of 8%. That is:

$$100,000 = PV(\text{10-year annuity of } C \text{ per year, evaluated at the loan rate})$$

Using the formula for the present value of an annuity (Eq. 4.5),

$$100,000 = C \times \frac{1}{0.08}\left(1 - \frac{1}{1.08^{10}}\right) = C \times 6.71$$

Solving this equation for C gives:

$$C = \frac{100,000}{6.71} = 14,903$$

You will be required to make 10 annual payments of $14,903 in exchange for $100,000 today.

We can also solve this problem with a financial calculator or Excel (from your standpoint the $100,000 is positive and the payments are negative):

	N	I/Y	PV	PMT	FV
Given:	10	8	100,000		0
Solve for:				−14,903	
Excel Formula:	=PMT(RATE,NPER,PV,FV)=PMT(0.08,10,100000,0)				

In general, when solving for a loan payment, think of the amount borrowed (the loan principal) as the present value of the payments. If the payments of the loan are an annuity, we can solve for the payment of the loan by inverting the annuity formula. Writing the equation for the payments formally for a loan with principal P, requiring N periodic payments of C and interest rate r, we have:

Cash Flow in an Annuity (Loan Payment)

$$C = \frac{P}{\frac{1}{r}\left(1 - \frac{1}{(1+r)^N}\right)} \tag{4.9}$$

PROBLEM

Your firm plans to buy a warehouse for $100,000. The bank offers you a 30-year loan with equal annual payments and an interest rate of 8% per year. The bank requires that your firm pays 20% of the purchase price as a down payment, so you can borrow only $80,000. What is the annual loan payment?

SOLUTION

PLAN

We start with the timeline (from the bank's perspective):

Using Eq. 4.9, we can solve for the loan payment, C, given $N = 30$, $r = 0.08$, and $P = \$80,000$.

EXECUTE

Equation 4.9 gives the following payment (cash flow):

$$C = \frac{P}{\frac{1}{r}\left(1 - \frac{1}{(1+r)^N}\right)} = \frac{80,000}{\frac{1}{0.08}\left(1 - \frac{1}{(1.08)^{30}}\right)}$$

$$= \$7106.19$$

Using a financial calculator or Excel:

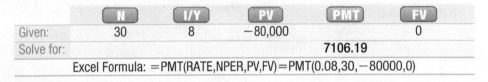

	N	I/Y	PV	PMT	FV
Given:	30	8	−80,000		0
Solve for:				7106.19	
Excel Formula: =PMT(RATE,NPER,PV,FV)=PMT(0.08,30,−80000,0)					

EVALUATE

Your firm will need to pay $7106.19 each year to repay the loan. The bank is willing to accept these payments because the PV of 30 annual payments of $7106.19 at 8% interest rate per year is exactly equal to the $80,000 it is giving you today.

We can use this same idea to solve for the cash flows when we know the future value rather than the present value. As an example, suppose you have just graduated from college and you decide to be prudent and start saving for a down payment on a house. You would like to have $60,000 saved in 10 years. If you can earn 7% per year on your savings, how much do you need to save each year to meet your goal?

The timeline for this example is:

```
0           1           2              10
|-----------|-----------|------ ... ---|
          -$C         -$C            -$C
                                   +$60,000
```

That is, you plan to save some amount C per year, and then withdraw $60,000 from the bank in 10 years. Therefore, we need to find the annuity payment that has a future value of $60,000 in 10 years. Use the formula for the future value of an annuity from Eq. 4.6:

$$60,000 = FV(\text{annuity}) = C \times \frac{1}{0.07}(1.07^{10} - 1) = C \times 13.816$$

Therefore, $C = \dfrac{60,000}{13.816} = \$4343$. Thus, you need to save $4343 per year. If you do, then at a 7% interest rate your savings will grow to $60,000 in 10 years when you are ready to buy a house.

Now let's solve this problem using a financial calculator or Excel:

	N	I/Y	PV	PMT	FV
Given:	10	7	0		60,000
Solve for:				−4343	
Excel Formula: =PMT(RATE,NPER,PV,FV)=PMT(0.07,10,0,60000)					

Once again, we find that you need to save $4343 per year for 10 years to accumulate $60,000.

Rate of Return

In some situations, you know the cost of an investment opportunity and the expected cash flows from it, but you do not know the rate of return. The rate of return on the investment opportunity is the rate at which the present value of the benefits exactly offsets the cost.

For example, suppose you have an investment opportunity that requires a $1000 investment today and will have a $2000 payoff in six years. This would appear on a timeline as:

$$
\begin{array}{ccccc}
0 & 1 & 2 & & 6 \\
\vert & \vert & \vert & \cdots & \vert \\
-\$1000 & & & & \$2000
\end{array}
$$

One way to analyze this investment is to ask the question: What interest rate, r, would you need so that the present value of what you get is exactly equal to the present value of what you give up?

$$1000 = \frac{2000}{(1+r)^6}$$

Rearranging this calculation gives the following:

$$1000 \times (1+r)^6 = 2000$$

That is, r is the interest rate you would need to earn on your $1000 to have a future value of $2000 in six years. We can solve for r as follows:

$$1 + r = \left(\frac{2000}{1000}\right)^{\frac{1}{6}} = 1.1225$$

Or, $r = 0.1225$. This rate is the rate of return of this investment opportunity. Making this investment is like earning 12.25% per year on your money for six years.

When there are just two cash flows, as in the preceding example, it is straightforward to compute the rate of return. Consider the general case in which you invest an amount P today, and receive FV in N years:

$$P \times (1+r)^N = FV$$
$$1 + r = (FV/P)^{1/N}$$

That is, we take the total return of the investment over N years, FV/P, and convert it to an equivalent one-year rate by raising it to the power $1/N$.

Now let's consider a more sophisticated example. Suppose your firm needs to purchase a new forklift. The dealer gives you two options: (1) a price for the forklift if you pay cash and (2) the annual payments if you take out a loan from the dealer. To evaluate the loan that the dealer is offering, you will want to compare the rate on the loan with the rate that your bank is willing to offer you. Given the loan payment that the dealer quotes, how do you compute the interest rate charged by the dealer?

In this case, we need to compute the rate of return of the dealer's loan. Suppose the cash price of the forklift is $40,000, and the dealer offers financing with no down payment and four annual payments of $15,000. This loan has the following timeline:

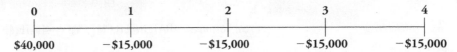

From the timeline, it is clear that the loan is a four-year annuity with a payment of $15,000 per year and a present value of $40,000. Setting the present value of the cash flows equal to zero requires that the present value of the payments equals the purchase price:

$$40,000 = 15,000 \times \frac{1}{r}\left(1 - \frac{1}{(1+r)^4}\right)$$

The value of r that solves this equation is the interest rate charged on the loan. Unfortunately, in this case, there is no simple way to solve for the interest rate r.[5] The only way to solve this equation is to guess at values of r until you find the right one.

Start by guessing $r = 10\%$. In this case, the value of the annuity is:

$$15,000 \times \frac{1}{0.10}\left(1 - \frac{1}{(1.10)^4}\right) = 47,548$$

The present value of the payments is too large. To lower it, we need to use a higher interest rate. This time we guess 20%:

$$15,000 \times \frac{1}{0.20}\left(1 - \frac{1}{(1.20)^4}\right) = 38,831$$

Now the present value of the payments is too low, so we must pick a rate between 10% and 20%. We continue to guess until we find the right rate. Let's try 18.45%:

$$15,000 \times \frac{1}{0.1845}\left(1 - \frac{1}{(1.1845)^4}\right) = 40,000$$

The interest rate charged by the dealer is 18.45%.

An easier solution than guessing the rate of return and manually calculating values is to use a spreadsheet or calculator to automate the guessing process. When the cash flows are an annuity, as in this example, we can use a financial calculator or Excel to compute the rate of return. Both solve (with slightly varying notation—recall that I/Y is the discount rate and PMT is the cash flow or payment) the following equation:

$$0 = PV + PMT \times \frac{1}{I/Y}\left(1 - \frac{1}{(1+I/Y)^N}\right) + \frac{FV}{(1+I/Y)^N}$$

The equation ensures that the value of investing in the annuity is zero in that the present value of the costs and benefits exactly offset each other. When the unknown variable is the

---

[5] With five or more periods and general cash flows, there is *no* general formula to solve for r; trial and error (by hand or computer) is the *only* way to compute it.

interest rate, it will solve for the interest rate that sets the equation equal to zero. For this case, you could use a financial calculator or Excel, as follows:

	N	I/Y	PV	PMT	FV
Given:	4		40,000	−15,000	0
Solve for:		18.45			
Excel Formula: =RATE(NPER,PMT,PV,FV)=RATE(4,−15000,40000,0)					

Both the financial calculator and Excel correctly compute a rate of return of 18.45%.

PERSONAL FINANCE

EXAMPLE 4.9

Computing the
Rate of Return
with a Financial
Calculator

MyFinanceLab

PROBLEM

Let's return to the lottery prize in Example 4.4. How high of a rate of return do you need to earn by investing on your own in order to prefer the $15 million payout?

SOLUTION

PLAN

Recall that the lottery offers you the following deal: take either (a) 30 payments of $1 million per year starting immediately, or (b) a $15 million lump sum payment immediately. The first option is an annuity of 29 payments of $1 million plus an initial $1 million payment.

0	1	2		29
$1 million	$1 million	$1 million	...	$1 million

We need to solve for the rate of return that makes the two offers equivalent. Anything above that rate of return would make the present value of the annuity lower than the $15 million lump sum payment, and anything below that rate of return would make it greater than the $15 million payment.

EXECUTE

We set the present value of option (a) equal to option (b), which is already in present value since it is an immediate payment of $15 million:

$$\$15 \text{ million} = \$1 \text{ million} + \$1 \text{ million} \times \frac{1}{r}\left(1 - \frac{1}{(1+r)^{29}}\right)$$

$$\$14 \text{ million} = \$1 \text{ million} \times \frac{1}{r}\left(1 - \frac{1}{(1+r)^{29}}\right)$$

Using a financial calculator to solve for r:

	N	I/Y	PV	PMT	FV
Given:	29		−14,000,000	1,000,000	0
Solve for:		5.72			
Excel Formula: =RATE(NPER,PMT,PV,FV)=RATE(29,1000000,−14000000,0)					

The rate of return equating the two options is 5.72%.

EVALUATE

5.72% is the rate of return that makes giving up the $15 million payment and taking the 30 installments of $1 million an even trade in terms of present value. If you could earn more than 5.72% investing on your own, then you could take the $15 million, invest it and generate 30 installments that are each more than $1 million. If you could not earn at least 5.72% on your investments, you would be unable to replicate the $1 million installments on your own and would be better off choosing the installment plan.

Solving for the Number of Periods

In addition to solving for cash flows or the interest rate, we can solve for the amount of time it will take a sum of money to grow to a known value. In this case, the interest rate, present value, and future value are all known. We need to compute how long it will take for the present value to grow to the future value.

Suppose we invest $10,000 in an account paying 10% interest, and we want to know how long it will take for the amount to grow to $20,000. We want to determine N.

In terms of our formulas, we need to find N so that the future value of our investment equals $20,000:

$$FV = \$10,000 \times 1.10^N = \$20,000 \tag{4.10}$$

One approach is to use trial and error to find N, as with the rate of return we calculated earlier. For example, with $N = 7$ years, $FV = \$19,487$, so it will take longer than 7 years. With $N = 8$ years, $FV = \$21,436$, so it will take between 7 and 8 years.

Alternatively, this problem can be solved on a financial calculator or Excel. In this case, we solve for N:

	N	I/Y	PV	PMT	FV
Given:		10	−10,000	0	20,000
Solve for:	7.27				
Excel Formula:	=NPER(RATE,PMT,PV,FV)=NPER(0.10,0,−10000,20000)				

It will take about 7.3 years for our savings to grow to $20,000. The problem of solving for the number of periods can also be solved mathematically using logarithms.

PERSONAL FINANCE

EXAMPLE 4.10

Solving for the
Number of Periods
in a Savings Plan

MyFinanceLab

PROBLEM

Let's return to your savings for a down payment on a house. Imagine that some time has passed and you have $10,050 saved already, and you can now afford to save $5000 per year at the end of each year. Also, interest rates have increased so that you now earn 7.25% per year on your savings. How long will it take to reach your goal of $60,000?

SOLUTION

PLAN

The timeline for this problem is:

We need to find N so that the future value of your current savings plus the future value of your planned additional savings (which is an annuity) equals your desired amount. There are two contributors to the future value: the initial lump sum of $10,050 that will continue to earn interest, and the annuity contributions of $5000 per year that will earn interest as they are contributed. Thus, we need to find the future value of the lump sum plus the future value of the annuity.

(Continued)

EXECUTE

We can solve this problem using a financial calculator or Excel:

	N	I/Y	PV	PMT	FV
Given:		7.25	−10,050	−5000	60,000
Solve for:	7.00				

Excel Formula: =NPER(RATE,PMT,PV,FV)=NPER(0.0725,−5000,−10050,60000)

There is also a mathematical solution. We can calculate the future value of the initial cash flow by using Eq. 4.1 and the future value of the annuity using Eq. 4.6:

$$10{,}050 \times 1.0725^N + 5000 \times \frac{1}{0.0725}(1.0725^N - 1) = 60{,}000$$

Rearranging the equation to solve for N,

$$1.0725^N = \frac{60{,}000 \times 0.0725 + 5000}{10{,}050 \times 0.0725 + 5000} = 1.632$$

we can then solve for N:

$$N = \frac{\ln(1.632)}{\ln(1.0725)} = 7 \text{ years}$$

EVALUATE

It will take seven years to save the down payment.

Concept Check

9. What are examples of times you would need to solve for the cash flow in an annuity?

10. When you are solving for the interest rate, if you keep PV and FV constant, but extend the time period, will the interest rate be higher or lower?

4.6 Non-Annual Cash Flows

Until now, we have only considered cash flow streams that occur at annual intervals. Do the same tools apply if the cash flows occur at another interval, say monthly? The answer is yes: Everything we have learned about annual cash flow streams applies to monthly cash flow streams as long as:

1. The interest rate is specified as a monthly rate.
2. The number of periods is expressed in months.

For example, suppose you have a credit card that charges 2% interest per month. If you have a $1000 balance on the card today, and make no payments for six months, your future balance in one year's time will be

$$FV = C \times (1 + r)^n = \$1000 \times (1.02)^6 = \$1126.16$$

We apply the future value formula exactly as before, but with r equal to the *monthly* interest rate and n equal to the number of *months*.

The same logic applies to annuities, as shown in Example 4.11.

EXAMPLE 4.11

Evaluating an
Annuity with Monthly
Cash Flows

MyFinanceLab

PROBLEM

You are about to purchase a new car and have two payment options. You can pay $20,000 in cash immediately, or you can get a loan that requires you to pay $500 each month for the next 48 months (four years). If the monthly interest rate you earn on your cash is 0.5%, which option should you choose?

SOLUTION

Let's start by writing down the timeline of the loan payments:

The timeline shows that the loan is a 48-period annuity. Using the annuity formula, the present value is

$$PV(\text{48-period annuity of \$500}) = \$500 \times \frac{1}{0.005}\left(1 - \frac{1}{1.005^{48}}\right)$$

$$= \$21,290$$

Alternatively, we may use the annuity spreadsheet to solve the problem:

	NPER	RATE	PV	PMT	FV
Given:	48	0.50%		500	0
Solve for:			(21,290)		
		Excel Formula: =PV(0.005,48,500,0)			

EVALUATE

Thus, taking the loan is equivalent to paying $21,290 today, which is costlier than paying cash. You should pay cash for the car.

What should you do if you aren't given a monthly rate? In Chapter 5, we will discuss how interest rates are quoted and you will learn how to convert between annual and monthly (or quarterly) rates.

Summing It Up

We began this chapter with the goal of further developing the tools a financial manager needs to be able to apply the Valuation Principle by valuing the costs and benefits of a decision. Starting from Chapter 3's fundamental concept of the time value of money—a dollar today is worth more than a dollar tomorrow—we learned how to calculate the equivalent value of a stream of future cash flows today and today's cash flows in the future. We then learned some shortcuts for handling common sets of regular cash flows such as those found in perpetuities and loans. As we have seen, the discount rate is a critical input to any of our present value or future value calculations. Throughout this chapter, we have taken the discount rate as given.

What determines these discount rates? The Valuation Principle shows us that we must rely on market information to assess the value of cash flows across time. In Chapter 5, we will learn the drivers of market interest rates as well as how they are quoted. Understanding interest rate quoting conventions will also allow us to extend the tools we developed in this chapter to situations where the interest rate is compounded more frequently than once per year.

Concept
Check

11. Do the present and future value formulas depend upon the cash flows occurring at annual intervals?

12. When cash flows occur at a non-annual interval, what interest rate must you use? What number of periods must you use?

MyFinanceLab Here is what you should know after reading this chapter. MyFinanceLab will help you identify what you know, and where to go when you need to practice.

Key Points and Equations	Key Terms	Online Practice
4.1 Valuing a Stream of Cash Flows • The present value of a cash flow stream is: $$PV = C_0 + \frac{C_1}{(1 + r)} + \frac{C_2}{(1 + r)^2} + \cdots + \frac{C_N}{(1 + r)^N} \quad (4.3)$$	stream of cash flows, p. 92	MyFinanceLab Study Plan 4.1
4.2 Perpetuities • A perpetuity is a stream of equal cash flows C paid every period, forever. The present value of a perpetuity is: $$PV(C \text{ in Perpetuity}) = \frac{C}{r} \quad (4.4)$$	consol, p. 96 perpetuity, p. 96	MyFinanceLab Study Plan 4.2
4.3 Annuities • An annuity is a stream of equal cash flows C paid every period for N periods. The present value of an annuity is: $$C \times \frac{1}{r}\left(1 - \frac{1}{(1 + r)^N}\right) \quad (4.5)$$ • The future value of an annuity at the end of the annuity is: $$C \times \frac{1}{r}\left((1 + r)^N - 1\right) \quad (4.6)$$	annuity, p. 99	MyFinanceLab Study Plan 4.3 Interactive Annuity Calculator Financial Calculator Tutorials: Calculating the Present Value of an Annuity and Solving for the Future Value of an Annuity
4.4 Growing Cash Flows • In a growing perpetuity, the cash flows grow at a constant rate g each period. The present value of a growing perpetuity is: $$\frac{C}{r - g} \quad (4.7)$$ • A growing annuity is like a growing perpetuity, but with an ending point. The present value of a growing annuity is: $$PV = C \times \frac{1}{r - g}\left(1 - \left(\frac{1 + g}{1 + r}\right)^N\right) \quad (4.8)$$	growing annuity, p. 106 growing perpetuity, p. 104	MyFinanceLab Study Plan 4.4
4.5 Solving for Variables Other Than Present Value or Future Value • The annuity and perpetuity formulas can be used to solve for the annuity payments when either the present value or the future value is known.		MyFinanceLab Study Plan 4.5

- The periodic payment on an N-period loan with principal P and interest rate r is:

$$C = \frac{P}{\frac{1}{r}\left(1 - \frac{1}{(1+r)^N}\right)} \qquad (4.9)$$

- The rate of return of an investment opportunity is the interest rate at which the PV of the benefits of the investment opportunity exactly offset the PV of the costs.
- The annuity formulas can be used to solve for the number of periods it takes to save a fixed amount of money.

4.6 Non-Annual Cash Flows	MyFinanceLab Study Plan 4.6

- Monthly cash flow streams (or any other period length) can be evaluated in exactly the same way as annual cash flow streams as long as the interest rate and number of periods are expressed in monthly terms.

CRITICAL THINKING

1. What is the intuition behind the fact that the present value of a stream of cash flows is just the sum of the present values of each individual cash flow?

2. What must be true about a cash flow stream in order for us to be able to use the shortcut formulas?

3. What is the difference between an annuity and a perpetuity?

4. What are some examples of perpetuities?

5. How can a perpetuity have a finite value?

6. What are some examples of annuities?

7. What must be true about the growth rate in order for a growing perpetuity to have a finite value?

8. In what types of situations would it be useful to solve for the number of periods or the rate of return?

PROBLEMS

*All problems are available in MyFinanceLab. An asterisk * indicates problems with a higher level of difficulty.*

Valuing a Stream of Cash Flows

1. a. What is the present value of the following set of cash flows, discounted at 10% per year?

Year	1	2	3	4	5
CF	10	20	30	40	50

b. What is the present value of the following set of cash flows, discounted at 10% per year?

Year	1	2	3	4	5
CF	50	40	30	20	10

c. Each set contains the same cash flows (10, 20, 30, 40, 50), so why is the present value different?

2. What is the present value of the following set of cash flows, discounted at 15% per year?

Year	1	2	3	4
CF	100	−100	200	−200

3. You want to borrow $10,000. You figure that you can make the following payments. If the interest rate on the loan is 8.5% per year, will your payments be enough to pay off the $10,000 loan?

Year	1	2	3	4
Payment	2000	3000	3500	3975

4. You have a balance of $5000 on your credit card, which charges an interest rate of 1.5% per month. Looking at your budget, you figure you can make the following payments. Will they be enough to pay off your credit card?

Month	1	2	3	4	5	6	7	8
Payment	500	550	600	650	700	750	800	850

5. You have just taken out a five-year loan from a bank to buy an engagement ring. The ring costs $5000. You plan to put down $1000 and borrow $4000. You will need to make annual payments of $1000 at the end of each year. Show the timeline of the loan from your perspective. How would the timeline differ if you created it from the bank's perspective?

6. You currently have a one-year-old loan outstanding on your car. You make monthly payments of $300. You have just made a payment. The loan has four years to go (i.e., it had an original term of five years). Show the timeline from your perspective. How would the timeline differ if you created it from the bank's perspective?

7. You plan to deposit $500 in a bank account now and $300 at the end of one year. If the account earns 3% interest per year, what will the balance be in the account right after you make the second deposit?

8. You have just received a windfall from an investment you made in a friend's business. She will be paying you $10,000 at the end of this year, $20,000 at the end of next year, and $30,000 at the end of the year after that (three years from today). The interest rate is 3.5% per year.
   a. What is the present value of your windfall?
   b. What is the future value of your windfall in three years (on the date of the last payment)?

9. Suppose you receive $100 at the end of each year for the next three years.
   a. If the interest rate is 8%, what is the present value of these cash flows?

b. What is the future value in three years of the present value you computed in (a)?

c. Suppose you deposit the cash flows in a bank account that pays 8% interest per year. What is the balance in the account at the end of each of the next three years (after your deposit is made)? How does the final bank balance compare with your answer in (b)?

10. You have a loan outstanding. It requires making three annual payments of $1000 each at the end of the next three years. Your bank has offered to allow you to skip making the next two payments in lieu of making one large payment at the end of the loan's term in three years. If the interest rate on the loan is 5%, what final payment will the bank require you to make so that it is indifferent to the two forms of payment?

11. Assume you can earn 9% per year on your investments.

a. If you invest $100,000 for retirement at age 30, how much will you have 35 years later for retirement?

b. If you wait until age 40 to invest the $100,000, how much will you have 25 years later for retirement?

c. Why is the difference so large?

Perpetuities

12. You want to endow a scholarship that will pay $10,000 per year forever, starting one year from now. If the school's endowment discount rate is 7%, what amount must you donate to endow the scholarship?

13. How would your answer to Problem 8 change if you endow it now, but it makes the first award to a student 10 years from today?

14. The British government has a consol bond outstanding paying £100 per year forever. Assume the current interest rate is 4% per year.

a. What is the value of the bond immediately after a payment is made?

b. What is the value of the bond immediately before a payment is made?

Annuities

15. What is the present value of $1000 paid at the end of each of the next 100 years if the interest rate is 7% per year?

16. Your grandmother has been putting $1000 into a savings account on every birthday since your first (that is, when you turned one). The account pays an interest rate of 3%. How much money will be in the account immediately after your grandmother makes the deposit on your 18th birthday?

17. Assume that your parents wanted to have $160,000 saved for college by your 18th birthday and they started saving on your first birthday. They saved the same amount each year on your birthday and earned 8% per year on their investments.

a. How much would they have to save each year to reach their goal?

b. If they think you will take five years instead of four to graduate and decide to have $200,000 saved just in case, how much more would they have to save each year to reach their new goal?

*18. When you purchased your car, you took out a five-year annual-payment loan with an interest rate of 6% per year. The annual payment on the car is $5000. You have just made a payment and have now decided to pay off the loan by repaying the outstanding balance. What is the payoff amount for the following scenarios?

a. You have owned the car for one year (so there are four years left on the loan)?

b. You have owned the car for four years (so there is one year left on the loan)?

19. You figure that the total cost of college will be $100,000 per year 18 years from today. If your discount rate is 8% compounded annually, what is the present value today of four years of college costs starting 18 years from today?

20. Assume that Social Security promises you $40,000 per year starting when you retire 45 years from today (the first $40,000 will be paid 45 years from now). If your discount rate is 7%, compounded annually, and you plan to live for 15 years after retiring (so that you will receive a total of 16 payments including the first one), what is the value today of Social Security's promise? (*See MyFinanceLab for the data in Excel Format.*)

*21. When Alex Rodriguez moved to the Texas Rangers in 2001, he received a lot of attention for his "$252 million" contract (the total of the payments promised was $252 million). He later moved to the Yankees, but assume the following in order to determine the value of his contract when he signed it:

Rodriguez earns $16 million in the first year, $17 million in years 2 through 4, $19 million in years 5 and 6, $23 million in year 7, and $27 million in years 8 through 10. He also receives his $10 million signing bonus spread equally over the first 5 years ($2 million per year). His deferred payments begin in 2011. The deferred payment amounts total $33 million and are $5 million, then $4 million, then eight amounts of $3 million (ending in 2020). However, the actual payouts will be different. All of the deferred payments will earn 3% per year until they are paid. For example, the $5 million is deferred from 2001 to 2011, or 10 years, meaning that it will actually be $6.7196 million when paid. Assume that the $4 million payment deferred to 2012 is deferred from 2002 (each payment is deferred 10 years).

The contract is a 10-year contract, but each year has a deferred component so that cash flows are paid out over a total of 20 years. The contractual payments, signing bonus, and deferred components are given below. Note that, by contract, the deferred components are not paid in the year they are earned, but instead are paid (plus interest) 10 years later.

2001	2002	2003	2004	2005	2006	2007	2008	2009	2010
$16M	$17M	$17M	$17M	$19M	$19M	$23M	$27M	$27M	$27M
$2M	$2M	$2M	$2M	$2M					
Deferred									
$5M	$4M	$3M	$3M	$3M	$3M	$3M	$3M	$3M	$3M

Assume that an appropriate discount rate for A-Rod to apply to the contract payments is 7% per year.
a. Calculate the true promised payments under this contract, including the deferred payments with interest.
b. Draw a timeline of all of the payments.
c. Calculate the present value of the contract.
d. Compare the present value of the contract to the quoted value of $252 million. What explains the difference?

*22. You are trying to decide how much to save for retirement. Assume you plan to save $5000 per year with the first investment made one year from now. You think you can earn 10% per year on your investments and you plan to retire in 43 years, immediately after making your last $5000 investment.
a. How much will you have in your retirement account on the day you retire?
b. If, instead of investing $5000 per year, you wanted to make one lump-sum investment today for your retirement that will result in the same retirement saving, how much would that lump sum need to be?

c. If you hope to live for 20 years in retirement, how much can you withdraw every year in retirement (starting one year after retirement) so that you will just exhaust your savings with the 20th withdrawal (assume your savings will continue to earn 10% in retirement)?

d. If, instead, you decide to withdraw $300,000 per year in retirement (again with the first withdrawal one year after retiring), how many years will it take until you exhaust your savings? (Use trial-and-error, a financial calculator: solve for "N", or Excel: function NPER)

e. Assuming the most you can afford to save is $1000 per year, but you want to retire with $1 million in your investment account, how high of a return do you need to earn on your investments? (Use trial-and-error, a financial calculator: solve for the interest rate, or Excel: function RATE)

Growing Cash Flows

23. A rich relative has bequeathed you a growing perpetuity. The first payment will occur in a year and will be $1000. Each year after that, you will receive a payment on the anniversary of the last payment that is 8% larger than the last payment. This pattern of payments will go on forever. Assume that the interest rate is 12% per year.
   a. What is today's value of the bequest?
   b. What is the value of the bequest immediately after the first payment is made?

*24. You are thinking of building a new machine that will save you $1000 in the first year. The machine will then begin to wear out so that the savings decline at a rate of 2% per year forever. What is the present value of the savings if the interest rate is 5% per year?

25. When Alfred Nobel died, he left the majority of his estate to fund five prizes, each to be awarded annually in perpetuity starting one year after he died (the sixth one, in economics, was added later).
   a. If he wanted the cash award of each of the five prizes to be $45,000 and his estate could earn 7% per year, how much would he need to fund his prizes?
   b. If he wanted the value of each prize to grow by 4% per year (perhaps to keep up with inflation), how much would he need to leave? Assume that the first amount was still $45,000.
   c. His heirs were surprised by his will and fought it. If they had been able to keep the amount of money you calculated in (b), and had invested it at 7% per year, how much would they have in 2014, 118 years after his death?

26. You work for a pharmaceutical company that has developed a new drug. The patent on the drug will last 17 years. You expect that the drug's profits will be $2 million in its first year and that this amount will grow at a rate of 5% per year for the next 17 years. Once the patent expires, other pharmaceutical companies will be able to produce the same drug and competition will likely drive profits to zero. What is the present value of the new drug if the interest rate is 10% per year?

27. A rich aunt has promised you $5000 one year from today. In addition, each year after that, she has promised you a payment (on the anniversary of the last payment) that is 3% larger than the last payment. She will continue to show this generosity for 20 years, giving a total of 20 payments. If the interest rate is 5%, what is her promise worth today?

Solving for Variables Other Than Present Value or Future Value

28. You are thinking about buying a savings bond. The bond costs $50 today and will mature in 10 years with a value of $100. What annual interest rate will the bond earn?

29. You have an investment account that started with $1000 10 years ago and which now has grown to $5000.
   a. What annual rate of return have you earned (you have made no additional contributions to the account)?
   b. If the savings bond earns 15% per year from now on, what will the account's value be 10 years from now?

30. You have an investment opportunity that requires an initial investment of $5000 today and will pay $6000 in one year. What is the rate of return of this opportunity?

31. You have decided to buy a perpetual bond. The bond makes one payment at the end of every year forever and has an interest rate of 5%. If the bond initially costs $1000, what is the payment every year?

32. You are thinking of purchasing a house. The house costs $350,000. You have $50,000 in cash that you can use as a down payment on the house, but you need to borrow the rest of the purchase price. The bank is offering a 30-year mortgage that requires annual payments and has an interest rate of 7% per year. What will your annual payment be if you sign this mortgage?

*33. You are thinking about buying a piece of art that costs $50,000. The art dealer is proposing the following deal: He will lend you the money, and you will repay the loan by making the same payment every two years for the next 20 years (i.e., a total of 10 payments). If the interest rate is 4% per year, how much will you have to pay every two years?

*34. You would like to buy the house and take the mortgage described in Problem 28. You can afford to pay only $23,500 per year. The bank agrees to allow you to pay this amount each year, yet still borrow $300,000. At the end of the mortgage (in 30 years), you must make a balloon payment; that is, you must repay the remaining balance on the mortgage. How much will this balloon payment be?

*35. You are saving for retirement. To live comfortably, you decide you will need to save $2 million by the time you are 65. Today is your 22nd birthday, and you decide, starting today and continuing on every birthday up to and including your 65th birthday, that you will put the same amount into a savings account. If the interest rate is 5%, how much must you set aside each year to ensure that you will have $2 million in the account on your 65th birthday?

36. You receive a $10,000 check from your grandparents for graduation. You decide to save it toward a down payment on a house. You invest it earning 10% per year and you think you will need to have $20,000 saved for the down payment. How long will it be before the $10,000 has grown to $20,000?

37. A local bank is running the following advertisement: "For just $1000 we will pay you $100 forever!" The fine print says that for a $1000 deposit, the bank will pay $100 every year in perpetuity, starting one year after the deposit is made. What interest rate is the bank advertising (what is the rate of return of this investment)?

*38. You are thinking of making an investment in a new factory. The factory will generate revenues of $1 million per year for as long as you maintain it. You expect that the maintenance costs will start at $50,000 per year and will increase 5% per year thereafter. Assume that all revenue and maintenance costs occur at the end of the year. You intend to run the factory as long as it continues to make a positive cash flow (as long as the cash generated by the plant exceeds the maintenance costs). The factory can be built and become operational immediately and the interest rate is 6% per year.

a. What is the present value of the revenues?
b. What is the present value of the maintenance costs?
c. If the plant costs $10 million to build, should you invest in the factory?

*39. You have just turned 22 years old, received your bachelor's degree, and accepted your first job. Now you must decide how much money to put into your retirement plan. The plan works as follows: Every dollar in the plan earns 7% per year. You cannot make withdrawals until you retire on your 65th birthday. After that, you can make withdrawals as you see fit. You decide that you will plan to live to 100 and work until you turn 65. You estimate that to live comfortably in retirement, you will need $100,000 per year, starting at the end of the first year of retirement and ending on your 100th birthday. You will contribute the same amount to the plan at the end of every year that you work. How much do you need to contribute each year to fund your retirement?

Non-Annual Cash Flows

40. Suppose you currently have $5000 in your savings account, and your bank pays interest at a rate of 0.5% per month. If you make no further deposits or withdrawals, how much will you have in the account in five years?

41. Your firm spends $5000 every month on printing and mailing costs, sending statements to customers. If the interest rate is 0.5% per month, what is the present value of eliminating this cost by sending the statements electronically?

42. You are looking to buy a car and can afford to pay $200 per month. If the interest rate on a car loan is 0.75% per month for a 60-month loan, what is the most expensive car you can afford to buy?

43. You have just entered college and have decided to pay for your living expenses using a credit card that has no minimum monthly payment. You intend to charge $1000 per month on the card for the next 45 months. The card carries a monthly interest rate of 1%. How much money will you owe on the card 46 months from now, when you receive your first statement post-graduation?

DATA CASE

Assume that today is August 1, 2012. Natasha Kingery is 30 years old and has a Bachelor of Science degree in computer science. She is currently employed as a Tier 2 field service representative for a telephony corporation located in Seattle, Washington, and earns $38,000 a year that she anticipates will grow at 3% per year. Natasha hopes to retire at age 65 and has just begun to think about the future.

Natasha has $75,000 that she recently inherited from her aunt. She invested this money in 10-year Treasury bonds. She is considering whether she should further her education and would use her inheritance to pay for it.

She has investigated a couple of options and is asking for your help as a financial planning intern to determine the financial consequences associated with each option. Natasha has already been accepted to two programs and could start either one soon.

One alternative that Natasha is considering is attaining a certification in network design. This certification would automatically promote her to a Tier 3 field service representative in her company. The base salary for a Tier 3 representative is $10,000 more than the salary of a Tier 2 representative, and she anticipates that this salary differential will grow at a rate of 3% a year for as long as she remains employed. The certification program requires the completion of 20 Web-based courses and a score of 80% or better on the final exam. She has learned that the average amount of time necessary to finish the program is one year. The total cost of the program is $5000, due when she enrolls in the program. Because she will do all the work for the certification on her own time, Natasha does not expect to lose any income during the certification process.

Another option is going back to school for an MBA degree. With an MBA degree, Natasha expects to be promoted to a managerial position in her current firm. The managerial position pays $20,000 a year more than her current position. She expects that this salary differential will also grow at a rate of 3% per year for as long as she keeps working. The evening program, which will take three years to complete, costs $25,000 per year, due at the beginning of each of her three years in school. Because she will attend classes in the evening, Natasha doesn't expect to lose any income while she is earning her MBA if she chooses to undertake it.

1. Determine the interest rate Natasha is currently earning on her inheritance by going to Yahoo! Finance (http://finance.yahoo.com) and clicking the 10 Yr Bond link in the Market Summary section. Then go to the Historical Prices link and enter the appropriate date, August 1, 2012, to obtain the closing yield or interest rate that she is earning. Use this interest rate as the discount rate for the remainder of this problem.

2. Create a timeline in Excel for Natasha's current situation, as well as the certification program and MBA degree options, using the following assumptions:
   a. Salaries for the year are paid only once, at the end of the year.
   b. The salary increase becomes effective immediately upon graduating from the MBA program or being certified. That is, because the increases become effective immediately but salaries are paid at the end of the year, the first salary increase will be paid exactly one year after graduation or certification.

3. Calculate the present value of the salary differential for completing the certification program. Subtract the cost of the program to get the value of undertaking the certification program.

4. Calculate the present value of the salary differential for completing the MBA degree. Calculate the present value of the cost of the MBA program. Based on your calculations, determine the value of undertaking the MBA.

5. Based on your answers to Questions 3 and 4, what advice would you give to Natasha? What if the two programs are mutually exclusive? If Natasha undertakes one of the programs, there is no further benefit to undertaking the other program. Would your advice change?

Chapter 4
APPENDIX

Using a Financial Calculator

Specifying Decimal Places

Make sure you have plenty of decimal places displayed!

HP-10BII

TI BAII Plus Professional

Toggling Between the Beginning and End of a Period

You should always make sure that your calculator is in *end-of-period* mode.

HP-10BII

TI BAII Plus Professional

[2ND] [PMT]

Set the Number of Periods per Year

To avoid a lot of confusion later, always set your periods per year (P/Y) to 1:

HP-10BII

[ ] [PMT] [1]

TI BAII Plus Professional

[2ND] [I/Y] [1] [ENTER]

General TVM Buttons

HP-10BII

[N] [I/YR] [PV] [PMT] [FV]

TI BAII Plus Professional

[N] [I/Y] [PV] [PMT] [FV]

Solving for the Future Value of an Annuity (Example 4.5)

Ellen is 35 years old, and she has decided it is time to plan seriously for her retirement. At the end of each year until she is 65, she will save $10,000 in a retirement account. If the account earns 10% per year, how much will Ellen have in her account at age 65? [*Answer*: $1,644,940]

HP-10BII

[ ] [C]						Press [Orange Shift] and then the [C] button to clear all previous entries.
[3] [0] [N]						Enter the Number of periods.
[1] [0] [I/YR]						Enter the market annual interest rate.
[1] [0] [0] [0] [0] [PMT]						Enter the Payment amount per period.
[0] [PV]						Indicate that there is no initial amount in the retirement account.
[FV]						Solve for the Future Value.

TI-BAII Plus Professional

Press [2ND] and then the [FV] button to clear all previous entries.

Enter the Number of periods.

Enter the market annual interest rate.

Enter the payment amount per period.
Indicate that there is no initial amount in the retirement account.

Solve for the Future Value.

Solving for the Rate of Return

If you have an initial cash outflow of $2000 and one cash inflow per year for the following four years of $1000, $400, $400, and $800, what is the rate of return on the project per year (sometimes called the *Internal Rate of Return* or *IRR* on the calculators)? [*Answer*: 12.12%]

HP-10BII

Press [Orange Shift] and then the [C] button to clear all previous entries.

Enter the initial cash outflow.

Enter the first cash inflow.

Enter the second cash inflow.

Enter the number of consecutive periods the second cash inflow occurs.

Enter the fourth cash inflow.

Press [Orange Shift] and then the [CST] button to calculate the IRR/year.

TI-BAII Plus Professional

Access Cash Flow Worksheet.

Press [2ND] and then the [CE|C] button to clear all previous entries.

Enter the initial cash outflow.

Enter the first cash inflow.

Leave the frequency of the initial cash inflow at 1 (Default Setting).

Enter the second cash inflow.

Enter the frequency of the second cash inflow as 2.

Enter the fourth cash inflow.

Leave the frequency of the fourth cash inflow at 1 (Default Setting).

Solve for the IRR.

5

Interest Rates

LEARNING OBJECTIVES

- Understand the different ways interest rates are quoted

- Use quoted rates to calculate loan payments and balances

- Know how inflation, expectations, and risk combine to determine interest rates

- See the link between interest rates in the market and a firm's opportunity cost of capital

notation

APR	annual percentage rate	n	number of periods
APY	annual percentage yield	N	date of the last cash flow in a stream of cash flows
C	cash flow		
C_n	cash flow that arrives in period n	PV	present value
EAR	effective annual rate	r	interest rate or discount rate
FV	future value	r_n	interest rate or discount rate for an n-year term
m	number of compounding periods per year		

In Chapters 3 and 4, we explored the mechanics of computing present values and future values given a market interest rate. Recall that an interest rate allows us to convert money at one point in time to another. But how do we determine that interest rate? In this chapter, we consider the factors that affect interest rates and discuss how to determine the appropriate discount rate for a set of cash flows. We begin by looking at the way interest is paid and interest rates are quoted, and we show how to calculate the effective interest paid in one year given different quoting conventions. We then consider some of the main determinants of interest rates—namely, inflation and economic growth. Because interest rates tend to change over time, investors will demand different interest rates for different investment horizons, based on their expectations and the risk involved in longer time horizons.

5.1   Interest Rate Quotes and Adjustments

If you spend some time looking through a newspaper, you will find literally dozens of interest rates discussed and advertised, from savings deposit rates to auto loan rates to interest rates being paid on the government's debt. Interest rates are clearly central to the functioning of any financial system. To understand interest rates, it's important to think of interest rates as a price—the price of using money. When you borrow money to buy a car, you are using the bank's money now to get the car and paying the money back over time. The interest rate on your loan is the price you pay to be able to convert your future loan payments into a car today. Similarly, when you deposit money into a savings account, you are letting the bank use your money until you withdraw it later. The interest the bank pays you on your deposit is the price it pays to use your money (for things like making car loans).

Just like any other price, interest rates are set by market forces, in particular the supply of and demand for funds. When the supply (savings) is high and the demand (borrowing) is low, interest rates are low, other things being equal. Additionally, as we discuss later in the chapter, interest rates are also influenced by expected inflation and risk.

In order to be able to study and use interest rates, we have to understand how they are quoted. In practice, interest is paid, and interest rates are quoted, in different ways. For example, in mid-2012, Metropolitan National Bank offered savings accounts with an interest rate of 1.65% paid at the end of each year, while AIG Bank offered an annual interest rate of only 1.60%, but paid on a daily basis. Interest rates can also differ depending on the investment horizon. In July 2012, investors earned less than 0.25% on one-year risk-free U.S. Treasury Bills, but could earn more than 2.3% on 20-year Treasuries. Interest rates can also vary due to risk or tax consequences: The U.S. government is able to borrow at a lower interest rate than Johnson & Johnson, which in turn can borrow at a lower rate than American Airlines.

Because interest rates may be quoted for different time intervals, such as monthly, semiannually, or annually, it is often necessary to adjust the interest rate to a time period that matches that of our cash flows. We explore these mechanics of interest rates in this section.

The Effective Annual Rate

effective annual rate (EAR) or annual percentage yield (APY) The total amount of interest that will be earned at the end of one year.

Interest rates are often reported as an **effective annual rate (EAR)** or **annual percentage yield (APY)**, which indicates the total amount of interest that will be earned at the end of one year.[1] We have used this method of quoting the interest rate thus far in this book, and in Chapters 3 and 4 we used the EAR as the discount rate r in our time value of money calculations. For example, with an EAR of 5%, a $100 investment grows to

$$\$100 \times (1 + r) = \$100 \times (1.05) = \$105$$

in one year. After two years it will grow to:

$$\$100 \times (1 + r)^2 = \$100 \times (1.05)^2 = \$110.25$$

Month:	0		1		2
Cash flow:	$100	$\times (1.05)$	= $105	$\times (1.05)$	= $110.25
	$100	$\times$	$(1.05)^2$	=	$110.25
	$100	$\times$	(1.1025)	=	$110.25

---

[1]The effective annual rate is also referred to as the *effective annual yield* (EAY).

Adjusting the Discount Rate to Different Time Periods

The preceding example shows that earning an effective annual rate of 5% for two years is equivalent to earning 10.25% in total interest over the entire period:

$$\$100 \times (1.05)^2 = \$100 \times 1.1025 = \$110.25$$

In general, by raising the interest rate factor $(1 + r)$ to the appropriate power, we can compute an equivalent interest rate for a longer time period.

We can use the same method to find the equivalent interest rate for periods shorter than one year. In this case, we raise the interest rate factor $(1 + r)$ to the appropriate fractional power. For example, earning 5% interest in one year is equivalent to receiving

$$(1 + r)^{0.5} = (1.05)^{0.5} = \$1.0247$$

for each $1 invested every six months (0.5 years). That is, a 5% effective annual rate is equivalent to an interest rate of approximately 2.47% earned every six months. We can verify this result by computing the interest we would earn in one year by investing for two six-month periods at this rate:

$$(1 + r)^2 = (1.0247)^2 = \$1.05$$

Month:	0		$\frac{1}{2}$		1
Cash flow:	$1	$\times (1.0247)$	$= \$1.0247$	$\times (1.0247)$	$= \$1.05$
	$1	$\times$	$(1.0247)^2$	$=$	$\$1.05$
	$1	$\times$	(1.05)	$=$	$\$1.05$

In general, we can convert a discount rate of r for one period to an equivalent discount rate for n periods using the following formula:

$$\text{Equivalent } n\text{-period Discount Rate} = (1 + r)^n - 1 \qquad (5.1)$$

In this formula, n can be larger than 1 (to compute a rate over more than one period) or smaller than 1 (to compute a rate over a fraction of a period).

When computing present or future values, you should adjust the discount rate to match the time period of the cash flows.

This adjustment is necessary to apply the perpetuity or annuity formulas to non-annual cash flows, as shown in Example 5.1.

PERSONAL FINANCE

EXAMPLE 5.1

Valuing Monthly
Cash Flows

MyFinanceLab

PROBLEM

Suppose your bank account pays interest monthly with an effective annual rate of 6%. What amount of interest will you earn each month?

If you have no money in the bank today, how much will you need to save at the end of each month to accumulate $100,000 in 10 years?

SOLUTION

PLAN

We can use Eq. 5.1 to convert the EAR to a monthly rate, answering the first question. The second question is a future value of an annuity question. It is asking how big a monthly annuity we would have to deposit in order to end up with $100,000 in 10 years. However, in order to solve this problem, we need to write the timeline in terms of *monthly* periods because our cash flows (deposits) will be monthly:

(Continued)

That is, we can view the savings plan as a monthly annuity with $10 \times 12 = 120$ monthly payments. We have the future value of the annuity ($100,000), the length of time (120 months), and we will have the monthly interest rate from the answer to the first part of the question. We can then use the future value of an annuity formula (Eq. 4.6) to solve for the monthly deposit.

EXECUTE

From Eq. 5.1, a 6% EAR is equivalent to earning $(1.06)^{1/12} - 1 = 0.4868\%$ per month. The exponent in this equation is $1/12$ because the period is $1/12$ th of a year (a month).

To determine the amount to save each month to reach the goal of $100,000 in 120 months, we must determine the amount C of the monthly payment that will have a future value of $100,000 in 120 months, given an interest rate of 0.4868% per month. Now that we have all of the inputs in terms of months (monthly payment, monthly interest rate, and total number of months), we use the future value of annuity formula from Chapter 4 to solve this problem:

$$FV\,(\text{annuity}) = C \times \frac{1}{r}\left[\,(1+r)^{\,n} - 1\,\right]$$

We solve for the payment C using the equivalent monthly interest rate $r = 0.4868\%$, and $n = 120$ months:

$$C = \frac{FV\,(\text{Annuity})}{\dfrac{1}{r}\left[\,(1+r)^{\,n} - 1\,\right]} = \frac{\$100{,}000}{\dfrac{1}{0.004868}\left[\,(1.004868)^{120} - 1\,\right]} = \$615.47 \text{ per month}$$

We can also compute this result using a financial calculator or spreadsheet:

	N	I/Y	PV	PMT	FV
Given:	120	0.4868	0		100,000
Solve for:				−615.47	
Excel Formula:	= PMT(RATE,NPER,PV,FV)=PMT(0.004868,120,0,100000)				

EVALUATE

Thus, if we save $615.47 per month and we earn interest monthly at an effective annual rate of 6%, we will have $100,000 in 10 years. Notice that the timing in the annuity formula must be consistent for all of the inputs. In this case, we had a monthly deposit, so we needed to convert our interest rate to a monthly interest rate and then use total number of months (120) instead of years.

Annual Percentage Rates

annual percentage rate (APR) Indicates the amount of interest earned in one year without the effect of compounding.

simple interest Interest earned without the effect of compounding.

The most common way to quote interest rates is in terms of an **annual percentage rate (APR)**, which indicates the amount of **simple interest** earned in one year, that is, the amount of interest earned *without* the effect of compounding. Because it does not include the effect of compounding, the APR quote is typically less than the actual amount of interest that you will earn. To compute the actual amount that you will earn in one year, you must first convert the APR to an effective annual rate.

For example, suppose Granite Bank advertises savings accounts with an interest rate of "6% APR with monthly compounding." When it quotes a rate this way, Granite Bank really means that you will earn $6\%/12 = 0.5\%$ every month. That is, an APR with monthly compounding is actually a way of quoting a *monthly* interest rate, rather than an annual interest rate. In this case, the actual rate being quoted is 0.5% *per month,* and by convention,

Using the EAR in the Annuity Formula

At this point, many students make the mistake of trying to use the EAR in the annuity formula. The interest rate in the annuity formula must match the frequency of the cash flows. That's why in Example 5.1, we first converted the EAR into a monthly rate and then used the annuity formula to compute the monthly loan payments. The common mistake in this case would be to use the EAR in the annuity formula to obtain annual cash flows, and then divide those cash flows by 12 to obtain the monthly payments.

This process will produce the wrong answer. To see why, consider the timing of the first deposit in Example 5.1. With a monthly rate and monthly payments, the annuity formula assumes that the first payment will be made one month from now. It then assumes that you will be making 11 more monthly deposits before the end of the first year. Each of those deposits will start earning interest as soon as you make it. In contrast, if you use an EAR and calculate an annual cash flow, the formula assumes that you will make your first deposit one *year* from now, so that you will forgo a whole year of interest before you start earning anything. Thus, you can see that the EAR approach misses the fact that you are making deposits earlier and more often than annually, so you are adding to your interest-earning principal more frequently than once per year.

the bank states it as an APR by multiplying by 12 months. Because the interest compounds each month, you will actually have

$$\$1 \times (1.005)^{12} = \$1.061678$$

at the end of one year, for an effective annual rate of 6.1678%. The 6.1678% that you earn on your deposit is higher than the quoted 6% APR due to compounding: In later months, you earn interest on the interest paid in earlier months. To summarize, an actual rate of 0.5% *per month* can be stated in either of the following ways:

- 6% APR, compounded monthly
- EAR of 6.1678%, which is the actual rate earned *per year*

It is important to remember that because the APR does not reflect the true amount you will earn over one year, *the APR itself cannot be used as a discount rate.* Instead, the APR is a way of quoting the actual interest earned each compounding period:

$$\text{Interest Rate per Compounding Period} = \frac{APR}{m}$$

$$(m = \text{number of compounding periods per year}) \tag{5.2}$$

Once we have computed the interest earned per compounding period from Eq. 5.2, we can compute the equivalent interest rate for any other time interval using Eq. 5.1. Thus, the effective annual rate corresponding to an APR is given by the following conversion formula:

Converting an APR to an EAR

$$1 + EAR = \left(1 + \frac{APR}{m}\right)^m$$

$$(m = \text{number of compounding periods per year}) \tag{5.3}$$

Table 5.1 shows the effective annual rates that correspond to an APR of 6% with different compounding intervals. The EAR increases with the frequency of compounding because of the ability to earn interest on interest sooner. Investments can compound even more frequently than daily. In principle, the compounding interval could be hourly or every second. As a practical matter, compounding more frequently than daily has a negligible impact on the effective annual rate and is rarely observed.

When working with APRs, we must first convert the APR to a discount rate per compounding interval using Eq. 5.2, or to an EAR using Eq. 5.3, before evaluating the present or future value of a set of cash flows.

TABLE 5.1

Effective Annual Rates
for a 6% APR
with Different
Compounding Periods

Compounding Interval	Effective Annual Rate
Annual	$\left(1 + \dfrac{0.06}{1}\right)^1 - 1 = 6\%$
Semiannual	$\left(1 + \dfrac{0.06}{2}\right)^2 - 1 = 6.09\%$
Monthly	$\left(1 + \dfrac{0.06}{12}\right)^{12} - 1 = 6.1678\%$
Daily	$\left(1 + \dfrac{0.06}{365}\right)^{365} - 1 = 6.1831\%$

EXAMPLE 5.2

Converting the APR
to a Discount Rate

MyFinanceLab

PROBLEM

Your firm is purchasing a new telephone system that will last for four years. You can purchase the system for an up-front cost of $150,000, or you can lease the system from the manufacturer for $4000 paid at the end of each month. The lease price is offered for a 48-month lease with no early termination—you cannot end the lease early. Your firm can borrow at an interest rate of 6% APR with monthly compounding. Should you purchase the system outright or pay $4000 per month?

SOLUTION

PLAN

The cost of leasing the system is a 48-month annuity of $4000 per month:

Month:	0	1	2		48
Payment:		$4000	$4000	...	$4000

We can compute the present value of the lease cash flows using the annuity formula, but first we need to compute the discount rate that corresponds to a period length of one month. To do so, we convert the borrowing cost of 6% APR with monthly compounding to a monthly discount rate using Eq. 5.2. Once we have a monthly rate, we can use the present value of annuity formula Eq. 4.5 to compute the present value of the monthly payments and compare it to the cost of buying the system.

EXECUTE

As Eq. 5.2 shows, the 6% APR with monthly compounding really means 6%/12 = 0.5% every month. The 12 comes from the fact that there are 12 monthly compounding periods per year. Now that we have the true rate corresponding to the stated APR, we can use that discount rate in the annuity formula Eq. 4.5 to compute the present value of the monthly payments:

$$PV = 4000 \times \frac{1}{0.005}\left(1 - \frac{1}{1.005^{48}}\right) = \$170{,}321.27$$

Using a financial calculator or spreadsheet:

	N	I/Y	PV	PMT	FV
Given:	48	0.5		−4000	0
Solve for:			170,321.27		
	Excel Formula: =PV(RATE,NPER,PMT,FV)=PV(0.005,48,−4000,0)				

EVALUATE

Thus, paying $4000 per month for 48 months is equivalent to paying a present value of $170,321.27 today. This cost is $170,321.27 − $150,000 = $20,321.27 higher than the cost of purchasing the system, so it is better to pay $150,000 for the system rather than lease it. One way to interpret this result is as follows: At a 6% APR with monthly compounding, by promising to repay $4000 per month your firm can borrow $170,321 today. With this loan it could purchase the phone system and have an additional $20,321 to use for other purposes.

1. What is the difference between an EAR and an APR quote?
2. Why can't the APR be used as a discount rate?

5.2 Application: Discount Rates and Loans

Now that we have explained how to compute the discount rate from an interest rate quote, let's apply the concept to solve two common financial problems: calculating a loan payment and calculating the remaining balance on a loan.

Computing Loan Payments

amortizing loan A loan on which the borrower makes monthly payments that include interest on the loan plus some part of the loan balance.

Many loans, such as mortgages and car loans, have monthly payments and are quoted in terms of an APR with monthly compounding. These types of loans are **amortizing loans**, which means that each month you pay interest on the loan plus some part of the loan balance. Each monthly payment is the same, and the loan is fully repaid with the final payment. Typical terms for a new car loan might be "6.75% APR for 60 months." When the compounding interval for the APR is not stated explicitly, it is equal to the interval between the payments, or one month in this case. Thus, this quote means that the loan will be repaid with 60 equal monthly payments, computed using a 6.75% APR with monthly compounding. It sometimes helps to look at the loan from the bank's point of view: The bank will give you $30,000 in cash today to use to buy the car. In return, you will give the bank 60 equal payments each month for 60 months, starting one month from now. In order for the bank to be willing to accept this exchange, it must be true that the present value of what you will give the bank, discounted at the loan's interest rate, is equal to the amount of cash the bank is giving you now. Consider the timeline for a $30,000 car loan with these terms:

The payment, C, is set so that the present value of the cash flows, evaluated using the loan interest rate, equals the original principal amount of $30,000. In this case, the 6.75% APR with monthly compounding corresponds to a one-month discount rate of $6.75\%/12 = 0.5625\%$. It is important that the discount rate matches the frequency of the cash flows—here we have a monthly discount rate and a monthly loan payment, so we can proceed. Because the loan payments are an annuity, we can use Eq. 4.9 to find C:

$$C = \frac{P}{\frac{1}{r}\left(1 - \frac{1}{(1+r)^N}\right)} = \frac{30{,}000}{\frac{1}{0.005625}\left(1 - \frac{1}{(1+0.005625)^{60}}\right)} = \$590.50$$

Alternatively, we can solve for the payment C using a financial calculator or spreadsheet:

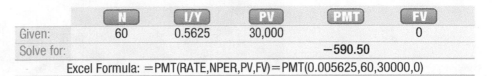

	N	I/Y	PV	PMT	FV
Given:	60	0.5625	30,000		0
Solve for:				−590.50	
Excel Formula:	=PMT(RATE,NPER,PV,FV)=PMT(0.005625,60,30000,0)				

Your loan payment each month includes interest and repayment of part of the principal, reducing the amount you still owe. Because the loan balance (the amount you still owe) is decreasing each month, the interest that accrues on that balance is decreasing. As a result, even though your payment stays the same over the entire 60-month life of the loan, the part of that payment needed to cover interest each month is constantly decreasing and the part left over to reduce the principal further is constantly increasing. We illustrate this effect in Panel (a) of Figure 5.1, where we show the proportion of each

FIGURE 5.1

Amortizing Loan

Panel (a) shows how the interest (red) and principal portions (blue) of the monthly payment on the $30,000 car loan change over the life of the loan. Panel (b) illustrates the effect on the outstanding balance (principal) of the loan. Note that as the balance decreases, the amount of the payment needed to cover interest on that balance decreases, allowing more of the payment to be used to reduce the principal.

Panel (a)

Panel (b)

Teaser Rates and Subprime Loans

Some loans, such as adjustable rate mortgages (ARMs), have interest rates that are not constant over the life of the loan. When the interest rate on such a loan changes, the loan payments are recalculated based on the loan's current outstanding balance, the new interest rate, and the remaining life of the loan.

Adjustable rate mortgages were the most common type of so-called "subprime" loans made to homebuyers with poor credit histories. These loans often featured low initial rates, aptly named *teaser rates*. After a short period (often 2 to 5 years) the interest rate would jump to a higher rate, implying that the monthly payment would also jump. For example, a $500,000 30-year mortgage with a teaser rate of 4.8% would have monthly payments of $2623.33 initially. If, after 2 years, the rate increased to 7.2%, the new monthly interest rate would be 7.2%/12 = 0.6% per month. With the higher rate, the monthly payment would jump to $3355.62!

While the loan might have been affordable at the initial teaser rate, many subprime borrowers could not afford the higher payments that were required after the loan rate adjusted. Prior to 2007, while interest rates remained low and home prices were high (and increasing), such borrowers were able to avoid default simply by refinancing their loans into new loans that also featured low initial teaser rates. In this way, they were able to keep their payments low. But as mortgage rates increased and housing prices began to decline in 2007, this strategy for keeping their loan payments low was no longer possible. In many cases, the outstanding loan balance exceeded the market value of the home, making lenders unwilling to refinance the loans. Stuck with a loan at a now unaffordable interest rate, many homeowners defaulted, and the rate of foreclosure on subprime loans skyrocketed.

To prevent future lenders from using teaser rates to get borrowers into loans they might not ultimately be able to afford, the Dodd-Frank Act requires lenders to verify that borrowers have sufficient income to repay their loans even after the teaser rate expires.

monthly loan payment that covers interest (red) and the portion left over to reduce the principal (blue). As you can see, $168.75 of your first $590.50 payment is needed just to cover interest accrued over the first month ($30,000 × 0.005625 = $168.75). However, this amount steadily decreases so that by the end of the loan, nearly all of your payment is going toward principal.

Panel (b) of Figure 5.1 shows the effect of your payments on the loan balance. When you make your first payment of $590.50, $168.75 covers interest on the loan, leaving $421.75 to reduce the principal to $30,000 − $421.75 = $29,578.25. The next month, you owe interest only on the $29,578.25 loan balance, which is $166.38, leaving more of your $590.50 payment to reduce the principal further. This effect continues so that each month more of your payment is available to reduce the principal, causing the principal to decrease rapidly toward the end of the loan as you are taking bigger and bigger chunks out of the balance.

Computing the Outstanding Loan Balance

As Figure 5.1 shows, the outstanding balance on an amortizing loan is different each month. The amount you owe at any point can be calculated as the present value of your future obligations on the loan. So, the outstanding balance, also called the *outstanding principal,* is equal to the present value of the remaining future loan payments, again evaluated using the loan interest rate. We calculate the outstanding loan balance by determining the present value of the remaining loan payments using the loan rate as the discount rate.

PERSONAL FINANCE

EXAMPLE 5.3

Computing the
Outstanding Loan
Balance

MyFinanceLab

PROBLEM

Let's say that you are now three years into your $30,000 car loan from the previous section and you decide to sell the car. When you sell the car, you will need to pay whatever the remaining balance is on your car loan. After 36 months of payments, how much do you still owe on your car loan?

SOLUTION

PLAN

We have already determined that the monthly payments on the loan are $590.50. The remaining balance on the loan is the present value of the remaining two years, or 24 months, of payments. Thus, we can just use the annuity formula with the monthly rate of 0.5625%, a monthly payment of $590.50, and 24 months remaining.

EXECUTE

$$\text{Balance with 24 months remaining} = \$590.50 \times \frac{1}{0.005625}\left(1 - \frac{1}{1.005625^{24}}\right) = \$13{,}222.32$$

Thus, after three years, you owe $13,222.32 on the loan.
Using a financial calculator or spreadsheet:

	N	I/Y	PV	PMT	FV
Given:	24	0.5625		−590.50	0
Solve for:			13,222.32		
Excel Formula: =PV(RATE,NPER,PMT,FV)=PV(0.005625,24,−590.50,0)					

You could also compute this as the FV of the original loan amount after deducting payments:

	N	I/Y	PV	PMT	FV
Given:	36	0.5625	30,000	−590.50	
Solve for:					13,222.56
Excel Formula: =FV(RATE,NPER,PMT,PV)=FV(0.005625,36,−590.50,30000)					

The 24 cent difference is due to rounding on the payment amount.

EVALUATE

At any point in time, including when you first take out the loan, you can calculate the balance of the loan as the present value of your remaining payments. Recall that when the bank gave you the $30,000 in the first place, it was willing to take 60 monthly payments of $590.50 in return only because the present value of those payments was equivalent to the cash it was giving you. Any time that you want to end the loan, the bank will charge you a lump sum equal to the present value of what it would receive if you continued making your payments as planned. As the second approach shows, the amount you owe can also be thought of as the future value of the original amount borrowed after deducting payments made along the way.

Concept
Check

3. How is the principal repaid in an amortizing loan?

4. Why does the part of your loan payment covering interest change over time?

5.3 The Determinants of Interest Rates

Now that we understand how interest rates are quoted and used in loans, we turn to a broader question: How are interest rates determined? Fundamentally, interest rates are determined by market forces based on the relative supply and demand of funds. This supply and demand is in turn determined by the willingness of individuals, banks, and firms to borrow, save, and lend. Changes in interest rates affect consumer decisions, such as how much you can borrow for a car loan or mortgage. Because they change the present value of future cash flows, changes in interest rates also have a broad impact on capital budgeting decisions within the firm. In this section, we look at some of the factors that may influence interest rates, such as inflation, current economic activity, and expectations of future growth.

Inflation and Real Versus Nominal Rates

nominal interest rates Interest rates quoted by banks and other financial institutions that indicate the rate at which money will grow if invested for a certain period of time.

Inflation measures how the purchasing power of a given amount of currency declines due to increasing prices. How many times have you heard the expression, "A dollar just doesn't buy what it used to"? We've all witnessed the steady upward climb of prices—for example, your morning coffee probably costs a little more today than it did five years ago. Inflation affects how we evaluate the interest rates being quoted by banks and other financial institutions. Those interest rates, and the ones we have used for discounting cash flows in this book, are **nominal interest rates**, which indicate the rate at which your money will grow if invested for a certain period. Of course, if prices in the economy are also increasing due to inflation, the nominal interest rate does not represent the true increase in purchasing power that will result from investing.

For example, let's say that a cup of coffee costs $1 this year. If you have $100, you could buy 100 coffees. Instead, if you put that $100 in a bank account earning 5.06% per year, you will have $105.06 at the end of the year. But how much better off will you really be? That depends on how much prices have increased over the same year. If inflation was 3% over the year, then that cup of coffee would cost 3% more, or $1.03 at the end of the year. Thus, you could take your $105.06 and buy $105.06/$1.03 = 102 coffees, so you're really only 2% better off.

real interest rate The rate of growth of purchasing power, after adjusting for inflation.

That 2% is your **real interest rate**: the rate of growth of your purchasing power, after adjusting for inflation. Just as in the example, we can calculate the rate of growth of purchasing power as follows:

$$\text{Growth in Purchasing Power} = 1 + \text{Real Rate} = \frac{1 + \text{Nominal Rate}}{1 + \text{Inflation Rate}}$$

$$= \frac{\text{Growth of Money}}{\text{Growth of Prices}} \quad (5.4)$$

We can rearrange Eq. 5.4 to find the following formula for the real interest rate, together with a convenient approximation for the real interest rate when inflation rates are low:

The Real Interest Rate

$$\text{Real Rate} = \frac{\text{Nominal Rate} - \text{Inflation Rate}}{1 + \text{Inflation Rate}} \approx \text{Nominal Rate} - \text{Inflation Rate} \quad (5.5)$$

That is, the real interest rate is approximately equal to the nominal interest rate less the rate of inflation.[2]

---

[2]The real interest rate should not be used as a discount rate for future cash flows. It can be used as a discount rate only if the cash flows are not the expected cash flows that will be paid, but are the equivalent cash flows before adjusting them for growth due to inflation (in that case, we say the cash flows are in *real terms*). This approach is error prone, however, so throughout this book we will always forecast cash flows including any growth due to inflation, and discount using nominal interest rates.

EXAMPLE 5.4

Calculating the Real
Interest Rate

MyFinanceLab

PROBLEM

At the start of 2008, one-year U.S. government bond rates were about 3.3%, while the inflation rate that year was 0.1%. At the start of 2011, one-year interest rates were about 0.3%, and the inflation rate that year was about 3.0%. What were the real interest rates in 2008 and in 2011?

SOLUTION

Using Eq. 5.5, the real interest rate in 2008 was $(3.3\% - 0.1\%)/(1.001) = 3.20\%$. In 2011, the real interest rate was $(0.3\% - 3.0\%)/(1.03) = -2.62\%$.

EVALUATE

Note that the real interest rate was negative in 2011, indicating that interest rates were insufficient to keep up with inflation: Investors in U.S. government bonds were able to buy less at the end of the year than they could have purchased at the start of the year. On the other hand, there was hardly any inflation.

Figure 5.2 shows the history of nominal interest rates and inflation rates in the United States since 1955. Note that the nominal interest rate tends to move with inflation. Intuitively, individuals' willingness to save will depend on the growth in purchasing power they can expect (given by the real interest rate). Thus, when the inflation rate is high, a higher nominal interest rate is needed to induce individuals to save. This was evident in the late 1970s and early 1980s when inflation reached double-digits in the United States, and nominal rates increased in response.

Investment and Interest Rate Policy

Interest rates affect not only individuals' propensity to save, but also firms' incentive to raise capital and invest. Consider an opportunity that requires an up-front investment of

FIGURE 5.2

U.S. Interest Rates
and Inflation Rates,
1962–2013

The graph shows U.S. nominal interest rates (in blue) and inflation rates (in red) from 1962–2013. Note that interest rates tend to be high when inflation is high. Interest rates are one-year Treasury rates, and inflation rates are the increase in the U.S. Bureau of Labor Statistics' consumer price index over the coming year, with both series computed on a monthly basis. The difference between them thus reflects the approximate real interest rate earned by holding Treasuries.

Source: St. Louis Federal Reserve Economic Data (FRED).

$10 million and generates a cash flow of $3 million per year for four years. If the interest rate is 5%, this investment's benefits have a PV of:

$$PV = \frac{3}{1.05} + \frac{3}{1.05^2} + \frac{3}{1.05^3} + \frac{3}{1.05^4} = \$10.638 \text{ million}$$

If the interest rate is 9%, the PV falls to

$$PV = \frac{3}{1.09} + \frac{3}{1.09^2} + \frac{3}{1.09^3} + \frac{3}{1.09^4} = \$9.719 \text{ million}$$

and the investment is no longer profitable given its $10 million cost. The reason, of course, is that we are discounting the positive cash flows at a higher rate, which reduces their present value. The cost of $10 million occurs today, however, so its present value is independent of the discount rate.

More generally, when the costs of an investment precede the benefits, an increase in the interest rate will make the investment less attractive. All else being equal, higher interest rates will therefore tend to shrink the set of good investments available to firms. The Federal Reserve in the United States and central banks in other countries attempt to use this relationship between interest rates and investment incentives when trying to guide the economy. They will often lower interest rates in an attempt to stimulate investment if the economy is slowing, and they will raise interest rates to reduce investment if the economy is "overheating" and inflation is on the rise.

Monetary Policy, Deflation, and the 2008 Financial Crisis. When the 2008 financial crisis struck the economy, the U.S. Federal Reserve responded quickly to mitigate its impact on the broader economy by cutting its short-term interest rate target to 0% by year's end. But while this use of monetary policy is generally quite effective, because consumer prices were falling in late 2008, the inflation rate was negative, and so even with a 0% nominal interest rate the real interest rate remained positive initially. The consequence of this deflation, and the risk that it might continue, meant that the Federal Reserve was "out of

---

How Is Inflation Actually Calculated?

Inflation is calculated as the rate of change in the *Consumer Price Index* (CPI). The CPI measures what it costs each month to purchase a standard set of goods that the average consumer would buy. How controversial can price data be?

To gather the price information, data collectors visit stores and gather 80,000 retail price quotes and 5000 housing rent quotes. The data is sent daily to Washington, DC, where analysts at the Bureau of Labor Statistics seek to determine if part of a price change captures a change in quality or inflation. Because this adjustment can be subjective, herein lies the controversy in the CPI calculation. The *Wall Street Journal*, covering the controversy, reported the following examples:

- A 57-inch television in which the price dropped from $2238.99 to $1909.97. Going over the checklist, the data gatherer in the field discovered the old version had a built-in high-definition tuner. The new one did not. The analyst estimated that the tuner was valued at $513.69. This turned what appeared to be a 14.7% price decrease into a 10.7% increase.

- A 27-inch television where the price appeared to stay the same, but an analyst determined that the price had declined. The latest model had a flat screen, something that consumers value more than the curved screen in the old model. The newer TV also had a 10-watt stereo, compared with the weaker 6-watt stereo in the older model.

Critics argue that this quality adjustment most often ends up making a price increase look smaller or even turning it into a decline. Thus, they conclude that the government underestimates the true rate of inflation. Supporters argue that these adjustments are necessary because paying more for a better product is not equivalent to paying more for the same product. This debate is important because many union contracts, for example, have wages linked to inflation, and investors need good inflation data to determine what interest rate to demand.

WSJ Source: Aeppel, T., "New and Improved: An Inflation Debate Brews Over Intangibles at the Mall—Critics Say U.S. Plays Down CPI Through Adjustments For Quality, Not Just Price—Value of a TV's Flat Screen," 9 May 2005, A1.

ammunition" with regard to its usual weapon against an economic slowdown—it could not lower rates further.[3] This problem was one of the reasons the United States and other governments began to consider other measures, such as increased government spending and investment, to stimulate their economies. Former Federal Reserve Governor Kevin Warsh further discusses monetary policy responses to the economic crisis in both the United States and Europe in the interview box on page 142.

The Yield Curve and Discount Rates

term structure The relationship between the investment term and the interest rate.

yield curve A plot of bond yields as a function of the bonds' maturity date.

The interest rates that banks offer on investments or charge on loans depend on the horizon, or *term,* of the investment or loan. For example, suppose you are willing to put your money in a CD (certificate of deposit)[4] that matures in two years (meaning that you cannot get the money back before then without a penalty). The bank will offer you a higher rate of interest for this CD than if you put your money in a statement savings account, where you can withdraw your funds at any time. The relationship between the investment term and the interest rate is called the **term structure** of interest rates. We can plot this relationship on a graph called the **yield curve**. Figure 5.3 shows the term

FIGURE 5.3

Term Structure of Risk-Free U.S. Interest Rates, November 2006, 2007, and 2008

The figure shows the interest rate available from investing in risk-free U.S. Treasury securities with different investment terms. In each case, the interest rates differ depending on the horizon. For example, in 2008, the interest rate on a 10-year loan (3.41%) was more than three times the rate on a 1-year loan (0.91%).

Term (years)	Date		
	Nov-06	Nov-07	Nov-08
0.5	5.23%	3.32%	0.47%
1	4.99%	3.16%	0.91%
2	4.80%	3.16%	0.98%
3	4.72%	3.12%	1.26%
4	4.63%	3.34%	1.69%
5	4.64%	3.48%	2.01%
6	4.65%	3.63%	2.49%
7	4.66%	3.79%	2.90%
8	4.69%	3.96%	3.21%
9	4.70%	4.00%	3.38%
10	4.73%	4.18%	3.41%
15	4.89%	4.44%	3.86%
20	4.87%	4.45%	3.87%

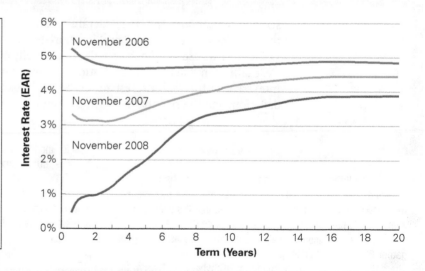

(Data from U.S. Treasury securities.)

---

[3]Why couldn't the Federal Reserve go further and make nominal interest rates negative? Since individuals can always hold cash (or put their money in a savings account) and earn at least a zero return, the nominal interest rate can never be *significantly* negative. But because storing cash is costly, and because investors viewed many banks as unsafe, short-term U.S. Treasury interest rates were actually slightly negative (down to −0.05%) at several points throughout this period! (See Chapter 6 for further discussion.)

[4]A certificate of deposit is a short- or medium-term debt instrument offered by banks. You deposit money in the bank for a stated period of time and normally receive a fixed rate of interest. The rate is higher than it would be on a savings account because you cannot withdraw your money early without paying a penalty.

structure and corresponding yield curve of U.S. interest rates that were available to investors in November 2006, 2007, and 2008. In each case, note that the interest rate depends on the horizon, and that the difference between short-term and long-term interest rates was especially pronounced in 2008. The rates plotted are interest rates for U.S. Treasury securities, which are considered to be free of any risk of default (the U.S. government will not default on its loans). Thus, each of these rates is a **risk-free interest rate**, which is the interest rate at which money can be borrowed or lent without risk over a given period.

risk-free interest rate The interest rate at which money can be borrowed or lent without risk over a given period.

We can use the term structure to compute the present and future values of a risk-free cash flow over different investment horizons. For example, $100 invested for one year at the one-year interest rate in November 2008 would grow to a future value of

$$\$100 \times 1.0091 = \$100.91$$

at the end of one year, and $100 invested for 10 years at the 10-year interest rate in November 2008 would grow to:[5]

$$\$100 \times (1.0341)^{10} = \$139.84$$

We can apply the same logic when computing the present value of cash flows with different maturities. A risk-free cash flow received in two years should be discounted at the two-year interest rate, and a cash flow received in 10 years should be discounted at the 10-year interest rate. In general, a risk-free cash flow of C_n received in n years has the present value

$$PV = \frac{C_n}{(1 + r_n)^n} \tag{5.6}$$

where r_n is the risk-free interest rate for an n-year term. In other words, when computing a present value we must match the term of the cash flow and term of the discount rate.

Combining Eq. 5.6 for cash flows in different years leads to the general formula for the present value of a cash flow stream:

Present Value of a Cash Flow Stream Using a Term Structure of Discount Rates

$$PV = \frac{C_1}{1 + r_1} + \frac{C_2}{(1 + r_2)^2} + \cdots + \frac{C_N}{(1 + r_N)^N} \tag{5.7}$$

Note the difference between Eq. 5.7 and Eq. 4.3. Here, we use a different discount rate for each cash flow, based on the rate from the yield curve with the same term. When interest rates are very similar across maturities, we say that the yield curve is flat, because it is close to a flat line. When the yield curve is relatively flat, as it was in November 2006, the distinction of using different rates for each cash flow is relatively minor and is often ignored by discounting using a single "average" interest rate r. But when short-term and long-term interest rates vary widely, as they did in November 2008, Eq. 5.7 should be used.

---

[5]We could also invest for 10 years by investing at the one-year interest rate for 10 years in a row. However, because we do not know what future interest rates will be, our ultimate payoff would not be risk free.

Warning: All of our shortcuts for computing present values (annuity and perpetuity formulas, and financial calculators) are based on discounting all of the cash flows *at the same rate*. They *cannot* be used in situations in which cash flows need to be discounted at different rates.

KEVIN M. WARSH

Kevin M. Warsh, *a lecturer at Stanford's Graduate School of Business and a distinguished visiting fellow at the Hoover Institution*, was a Federal Reserve governor from 2006 to 2011, serving as chief liaison to the financial markets.

QUESTION: *What are the main policy instruments used by central banks to control the economy?*

ANSWER: The Federal Reserve (Fed) deploys several policy tools to achieve its goals of price stability, maximum sustainable employment, and financial stability. Lowering the federal funds short-term interest rate, the primary policy instrument, stimulates the economy. Raising the federal funds rate generally slows the economy. Buying and selling short-term U.S. Treasury securities through *open market operations* is standard practice. Prior to the 2007–2009 financial crisis, the Fed's balance sheet ranged from $700–$900 billion. But when the Fed was unable to lower interest rates further because rates were so close to zero already, it resorted to large-scale, longer-term open market operations to increase liquidity in the financial system in the hopes of stimulating the economy further, thus growing its balance sheet significantly. With *open mouth operations*, the Fed's announcements of its intent to buy or sell assets indicates its desired degree of future policy accommodation, often prompting markets to react by adjusting interest rates immediately. The Fed's Lender-of-Last-Resort authority allows it to lend money against good collateral to troubled institutions under certain conditions.

QUESTION: *What factors limit the effectiveness of Fed policy?*

ANSWER: Monetary policy does not act in isolation. Fiscal (taxing and spending), trade, and regulatory policies have huge consequence on the state of economic and financial conditions. In the short term, monetary policy can help buy time for an economy to improve, but it cannot cure structural failings of an economy in isolation or compensate for the country's growing indebtedness.

QUESTION: *What tools did the Fed create to address the 2007–2009 financial crisis?*

ANSWER: During the darkest days of the crisis, markets did not operate effectively, prices for securities did not clear, and banks and other financial institutions lacked clarity and confidence in the financial wherewithal of each other. One effective, innovative tool, the *Term Auction Facility (TAF)*, stimulated the economy by providing cheap and readily available term funding to banks, large and small, on the front lines of the economy, thus encouraging them to extend credit to businesses and consumers. After reducing the policy rate to near zero to help revive the economy, the Fed instituted two *Quantitative Easing (QE)* programs—special purchases of government and agency securities—to increase money supply, promote lending, and according to some proponents, increase prices of riskier assets.

The Fed also addressed the global financial crisis by establishing temporary *central bank liquidity swap lines* with the European Central Bank and other major central banks. Using this facility, a foreign central bank is able to obtain dollar funding for its customers by swapping euros for dollars or another currency and agreeing to reverse the swap at a later date. The Fed does not take exchange rate risk, but it is subject to the credit risk of its central bank counterparty.

QUESTION: *What tools is the European Central Bank (ECB) using to address the sovereign debt crisis? How does its approach compare to the Fed's approach to the 2007–2009 financial crisis?*

ANSWER: As a novel economic federation, the ECB finds itself in a more difficult position than the Fed. The underlying economies and competitiveness are markedly different across the Eurozone—in Germany versus Greece, for example. From 2007 until mid-2010, many European financiers and policymakers believed that global financial crisis was largely American-made, with some strains exported to the continent. By mid-2010, however, they recognized that it was indeed a global crisis. The ECB is formally charged with a single mandate of ensuring price stability, rather than the broader mandate of the Fed. Still, its actions ultimately mirrored many of those undertaken by the Fed: lowering the effective policy rate to record lows, providing direct liquidity to the Eurozone's financial institutions to avoid a potential run on the banking system, and instituting the Security Market Purchase program (buying sovereign credit of some of its distressed countries).

EXAMPLE 5.5

Using the Term
Structure to Compute
Present Values

MyFinanceLab

PROBLEM

Compute the present value of a risk-free five-year annuity of $1000 per year, given the yield curve for November 2008 in Figure 5.3.

SOLUTION

PLAN

The timeline of the cash flows of the annuity is:

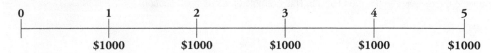

We can use the table next to the yield curve to identify the interest rate corresponding to each length of time: 1, 2, 3, 4, and 5 years. With the cash flows and those interest rates, we can compute the PV.

EXECUTE

From Figure 5.3, we see that the interest rates are: 0.91%, 0.98%, 1.26%, 1.69%, and 2.01%, for terms of 1, 2, 3, 4, and 5 years, respectively.

To compute the present value, we discount each cash flow by the corresponding interest rate:

$$PV = \frac{1000}{1.0091} + \frac{1000}{1.0098^2} + \frac{1000}{1.0126^3} + \frac{1000}{1.0169^4} + \frac{1000}{1.0201^5} = \$4775$$

EVALUATE

The yield curve tells us the market interest rate per year for each different maturity. In order to correctly calculate the PV of cash flows from five different maturities, we need to use the five different interest rates corresponding to those maturities. Note that we cannot use the annuity formula here because the discount rates differ for each cash flow.

COMMON MISTAKE Using the Annuity Formula When Discount Rates Vary

When computing the present value of an annuity, a common mistake is to use the annuity formula with a single interest rate even though interest rates vary with the investment horizon. For example, we *cannot* compute the present value of the five-year annuity in Example 5.5 using the five-year interest rate from November 2008:

$$PV \neq \$1000 \times \frac{1}{0.0201}\left(1 - \frac{1}{1.0201^5}\right) = \$4712$$

If we want to find the single interest rate that we could use to value the annuity, we must first compute the present value of the annuity using Eq. 5.7 and then solve for its rate of return. For the annuity in Example 5.5, we use a financial calculator or spreadsheet to find its rate of return of 1.55%. The rate of return of the annuity is always between the highest and lowest discount rates used to calculate its present value, as is the case in this example.

	N	I/Y	PV	PMT	FV
Given:	5		−4775	1000	0
Solve for:		1.55			
	Excel Formula: =RATE(NPER,PMT,PV,FV)=RATE(5,1000,−4775,0)				

The Yield Curve and the Economy

As Figure 5.4 illustrates, the yield curve changes over time. Sometimes, short-term rates are close to long-term rates, and at other times they may be very different. What accounts for the changing shape of the yield curve?

FIGURE 5.4

Yield Curve Shapes

The figure shows three different yield curve shapes. The blue line represents a "normal" yield curve. Most of the time the yield curve has this shape—moderately upward sloping. The red line depicts a steep yield curve—note the larger than normal difference between short-term rates (2%) and long-term rates (7%), making the yield curve look steeper than normal. This example of a steep yield curve is from October 1991. Finally, the green line depicts an inverted yield curve, so called because it slopes downward instead of upward. This happens when short-term rates are higher than long-term rates as they were in January 1981. We discuss why the shape of the yield curve changes over time in the rest of this section.

(a) Normal Yield Curve   (b) Steep Yield Curve   (c) Inverted Yield Curve

federal funds rate The overnight loan rate charged by banks with excess reserves at a Federal Reserve bank (called *federal funds*) to banks that need additional funds to meet reserve requirements.

Interest Rate Determination. The Federal Reserve determines very short-term interest rates through its influence on the **federal funds rate**, which is the rate at which banks can borrow cash reserves on an overnight basis. All other interest rates on the yield curve are set in the market and are adjusted until the supply of lending matches the demand for borrowing at each loan term. As we shall see, expectations of future interest rate changes have a major effect on investors' willingness to lend or borrow for longer terms and, therefore, on the shape of the yield curve.

Suppose short-term interest rates are equal to long-term interest rates. If interest rates are expected to rise in the future, investors would not want to make long-term investments. Instead, they could do better by investing on a short-term basis and then reinvesting after interest rates rise. Thus, if interest rates are expected to rise, long-term interest rates will tend to be higher than short-term rates to attract investors.

Similarly, if interest rates are expected to fall in the future, then borrowers would not wish to borrow at long-term rates that are equal to short-term rates. They would do better by borrowing on a short-term basis, and then taking out a new loan after rates fall. So, if interest rates are expected to fall, long-term rates will tend to be lower than short-term rates to attract borrowers.

Yield Curve Shape. These arguments indicate that the shape of the yield curve will be strongly influenced by interest rate expectations. A sharply increasing (*steep*) yield curve, with long-term rates much higher than short-term rates, generally indicates that interest rates are expected to rise in the future. A decreasing (*inverted*) yield curve, with long-term rates lower than short-term rates, generally signals an expected decline in future interest rates. Because interest rates tend to drop in response to a slowdown in the economy, an inverted yield curve is often interpreted as a negative forecast for economic growth. Indeed, as Figure 5.5 illustrates, each of the last seven recessions in the United States was preceded by a period in which the yield curve was inverted (note the red shaded areas before the gray

FIGURE 5.5

Short-Term Versus Long-Term U.S. Interest Rates and Recessions

One-year and 10-year U.S. Treasury rates are plotted, with the spread between them shaded in green if the shape of the yield curve is increasing (the one-year rate is below the 10-year rate) and in red if the yield curve is inverted (the one-year rate exceeds the 10-year rate). Gray bars show the dates of U.S. recessions as determined by the National Bureau of Economic Research. Note that inverted yield curves tend to precede recessions as determined by the National Bureau of Economic Research. In recessions, interest rates tend to fall, with short-term rates dropping further. As a result, the yield curve tends to be steep coming out of a recession.

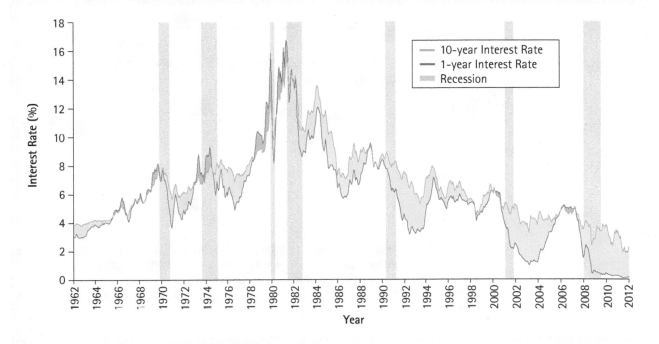

bars indicating a recession). Conversely, the yield curve tends to be steep (and therefore shaded blue) as the economy comes out of a recession and interest rates are expected to rise.

The normal shape of the yield curve is moderately upward sloping. This would be the case if investors almost always believed that interest rates were going to rise in the future. But that is unlikely, so there have to be other forces at work to cause long-term interest rates normally to be higher than short-term rates. The most commonly cited reason is that long-term loans are riskier than short-term loans. If you make a 30-year loan today and lock in the interest rate, the present value of the payments you receive on the loan is very sensitive to even small changes in market interest rates. This sensitivity is due to the effect of compounding a change in interest rates over a 30-year period. To see this effect, consider Example 5.6.

EXAMPLE 5.6

Long-Term Versus
Short-Term Loans

MyFinanceLab

PROBLEM

You work for a bank that has just made two loans. In one, you lent $909.09 today in return for $1000 in one year. In the other, you lent $909.09 today in return for $15,863.08 in 30 years. The difference between the loan amount and repayment amount is based on an interest rate of 10% per year. Imagine that immediately after you make the loans, news about economic growth is announced that increases inflation expectations, so that the market interest rate for loans like these jumps to 11%. Loans make up a major part of a bank's assets, so you are naturally concerned about the value of these loans. What is the effect of the interest rate change on the value to the bank of the promised repayment of these loans?

SOLUTION

PLAN

Each of these loans has only one repayment cash flow at the end of the loan. They differ only by the time to repayment:

The effect on the value of the future repayment to the bank today is just the PV of the loan repayment, calculated at the new market interest rate.

EXECUTE

For the one-year loan:

$$PV = \frac{\$1000}{(1.11)^1} = \$900.90$$

For the 30-year loan:

$$PV = \frac{\$15,863.08}{(1.11)^{30}} = \$692.94$$

EVALUATE

The value of the one-year loan decreased by $909.09 − $900.90 = $8.19, or 0.9%, but the value of the 30-year loan decreased by $909.09 − $692.94 = $216.15, or almost 24%! The small change in market interest rates, compounded over a longer period, resulted in a much larger change in the present value of the loan repayment. You can see why investors and banks view longer-term loans as being riskier than short-term loans.

In addition to specifying the discount rates for risk-free cash flows that occur at different horizons, it is also a potential leading indicator of future economic growth. Due to these qualities, the yield curve provides extremely important information for a business manager.

Concept
Check

5. What is the difference between a nominal and real interest rate?

6. How are interest rates and the level of investment made by businesses related?

5.4   The Opportunity Cost of Capital

opportunity cost of capital or cost of capital The best available expected return offered in the market on an investment of comparable risk and term to the cash flow being discounted; the return the investor forgoes on an alternative investment of equivalent risk and term when the investor takes on a new investment.

As we have seen in this chapter, the interest rates we observe in the market will vary based on quoting conventions, the term of the investment, and risk. In this chapter, we have developed the tools to account for these differences and gained insights into how interest rates are determined. This knowledge will provide the foundation for our study of bonds in Chapter 6.

In Chapter 3, we argued that the Valuation Principle tells us to use the "market interest rate" to compute present values and evaluate an investment opportunity. But with so many interest rates to choose from, the term "market interest rate" is inherently ambiguous. Therefore, going forward in the book, we will base the discount rate that we use to evaluate cash flows on the investor's **opportunity cost of capital** (or more simply, the **cost of capital**), which is *the best available expected return offered in the market on an investment of comparable risk and term to the cash flow being discounted.*

In order to understand the definition of opportunity cost of capital, it helps to think of yourself as a financial manager competing with financial managers at other firms to attract investors' funds (capital). In order to attract investors to invest in your firm or creditors to lend to your firm, you have to be able to offer them an expected return at least as good as what they could get elsewhere in the market for the same risk and length of investment. Now it is easier to see where the term (opportunity) cost of capital comes from—investors in your firm are giving up the opportunity to invest their funds elsewhere. This is an opportunity cost to them and to overcome it you must offer them a return equal to or better than their opportunity cost of capital. Even if you already have the funds internally in the firm to invest, the logic still applies. You could either return the funds to your shareholders to invest elsewhere, or reinvest them in a new project; however, you should only reinvest them if doing so provides a better return than the shareholders' other opportunities.

The opportunity cost of capital is the return the investor forgoes when the investor takes on a new investment. For a risk-free project, it will typically correspond to the interest rate on U.S. Treasury securities with a similar term. But the cost of capital is a much more general concept that can be applied to risky investments as well.

EXAMPLE 5.7

The Opportunity Cost of Capital

MyFinanceLab

PROBLEM

Suppose a friend offers to borrow $100 from you today and in return pay you $110 one year from today. Looking in the market for other options for investing the $100, you find your best alternative option that you view as equally risky as lending it to your friend. That option has an expected return of 8%. What should you do?

SOLUTION

PLAN

Your decision depends on what the opportunity cost is of lending your money to your friend. If you lend her the $100, then you cannot invest it in the alternative with an 8% expected return. Thus, by making the loan, you are giving up the opportunity to invest for an 8% expected return. You can make your decision by using your 8% opportunity cost of capital to value the $110 in one year.

EXECUTE

The value of the $110 in one year is its present value, discounted at 8%:

$$PV = \frac{\$110}{(1.08)^1} = \$101.85$$

The $100 loan is worth $101.85 to you today, so you make the loan.

EVALUATE

The Valuation Principle tells us that we can determine the value of an investment by using market prices to value the benefits net of the costs. As this example shows, market prices determine what our best alternative opportunities are, so that we can decide whether an investment is worth the cost.

Chapter 3 introduced the Valuation Principle as a unifying theme in finance. In this and the preceding chapters, we have developed the fundamental tools a financial manager needs to value cash flows at different points in time. In this last section, we reiterated the importance of using market information to determine the opportunity cost of capital, which is your discount rate in valuation calculations. In Chapter 6, we will study bonds and how they are priced, which provides us with an immediate application of the knowledge we have built so far.

| Concept | 7. | What is the opportunity cost of capital? |
| Check | 8. | Can you ignore the cost of capital if you already have the funds inside the firm? |

MyFinanceLab

Here is what you should know after reading this chapter. MyFinanceLab will help you identify what you know, and where to go when you need to practice.

Key Points and Equations	Key Terms	Online Practice
5.1 Interest Rate Quotes and Adjustments • Just like any other price, interest rates are set by market forces, in particular the supply and demand of funds. • The effective annual rate (EAR) (or annual percentage yield—APY) indicates the actual amount of interest earned in one year. The EAR can be used as a discount rate for annual cash flows. • Given an EAR r, the equivalent discount rate for an n-year time interval, where n may be more than one year or less than or equal to one year (a fraction), is: $$\text{Equivalent } n\text{-period Discount Rate}$$ $$= (1 + r)^n - 1 \qquad (5.1)$$ • An annual percentage rate (APR) is a common way of quoting interest rates. The actual interest rate per period is the APR/number of compounding periods per year. APRs cannot be used as discount rates. • We need to know the compounding interval of an APR to determine the EAR: $$1 + EAR = \left(1 + \frac{APR}{m}\right)^m \qquad (5.3)$$ m = number of compounding periods per year. • For a given APR, the EAR increases with the compounding frequency.	annual percentage rate (APR), p. 130 annual percentage yield (APY), 128 effective annual rate (EAR), p. 128 simple interest, p. 130	MyFinanceLab Study Plan 5.1
5.2 Application: Discount Rates and Loans • Loan rates are typically stated as APRs. The outstanding balance of a loan is equal to the present value of the loan cash flows, when evaluated using the actual interest rate per payment interval based on the loan rate. • In each loan payment on an amortizing loan, you pay interest on the loan plus some part of the loan balance.	amortizing loan, p. 133	MyFinanceLab Study Plan 5.2

5.3 The Determinants of Interest Rates

- Quoted interest rates are nominal interest rates, which indicate the rate of growth of the money invested. The real interest rate indicates the rate of growth of one's purchasing power after adjusting for inflation.
- Given a nominal interest rate and an inflation rate, the real interest rate is:

$$\text{Real Rate} = \frac{\text{Nominal Rate} - \text{Inflation Rate}}{1 + \text{Inflation Rate}}$$

$$\approx \text{Nominal} - \text{Inflation Rate} \qquad (5.5)$$

- Nominal interest rates tend to be high when inflation is high and low when inflation is low.
- Higher interest rates tend to reduce the attractiveness of typical investment projects. The U.S. Federal Reserve raises interest rates to moderate investment and combat inflation and lowers interest rates to stimulate investment and economic growth.
- Interest rates differ with the investment horizon according to the term structure of interest rates. The graph plotting interest rates as a function of the horizon is called the yield curve.
- Cash flows should be discounted using the discount rate that is appropriate for their horizon. Thus, the *PV* of a cash flow stream is:

$$PV = \frac{C_1}{1 + r_1} + \frac{C_2}{(1 + r_2)^2} + \cdots + \frac{C_N}{(1 + r_N)^N} \qquad (5.7)$$

- Annuity and perpetuity formulas cannot be applied when discount rates vary with the horizon.
- The shape of the yield curve tends to vary with investors' expectations of future economic growth and interest rates. It tends to be inverted prior to recessions and to be steep coming out of a recession. Because investors view long-term loans as riskier, long-term rates are generally higher than short-term rates.

federal funds rate, p. 144
nominal interest rates, p. 137
real interest rate, p. 137
risk-free interest rate, p. 141
term structure, p. 140
yield curve, p. 140

MyFinanceLab Study Plan 5.3

Interactive Yield Curve

5.4 The Opportunity Cost of Capital

- An investor's opportunity cost of capital (or simply, the cost of capital) is the best available expected return offered in the market on an investment of comparable risk and term to the cash flow being discounted.

(opportunity) cost of capital, p. 146

MyFinanceLab Study Plan 5.4

CRITICAL THINKING

1. Explain how an interest rate is just a price.

2. Why is the EAR for 6% APR, with semiannual compounding, higher than 6%?

3. Why is it so important to match the frequency of the interest rate to the frequency of the cash flows?

4. Why aren't the payments for a 15-year mortgage twice the payments for a 30-year mortgage at the same rate?

5. What mistake do you make when you discount real cash flows with nominal discount rates?

6. How do changes in inflation expectations impact interest rates?

7. Can the nominal interest rate available to an investor be negative? (*Hint*: Consider the interest rate earned from saving cash "under the mattress.") Can the real interest rate be negative?

8. In the early 1980s, inflation was in the double-digits and the yield curve sloped sharply downward. What did the yield curve say about investors' expectations about future inflation rates?

9. What do we mean when we refer to the "opportunity cost" of capital?

PROBLEMS

All problems in this chapter are available in MyFinanceLab. An asterisk * indicates problems with a higher level of difficulty.

Interest Rate Quotes and Adjustments

1. Your bank is offering you an account that will pay 20% interest in total for a two-year deposit. Determine the equivalent discount rate for a period length of
   a. six months.
   b. one year.
   c. one month.

2. You are looking to buy a car and you have been offered a loan with an APR of 6%, compounded monthly.
   a. What is the true monthly rate of interest?
   b. What is the EAR?

3. You are considering two ways of financing a spring break vacation. You could put it on your credit card, at 15% APR, compounded monthly, or borrow the money from your parents, who want an 8% interest payment every six months. Which is the lower rate?

4. Which do you prefer: a bank account that pays 5% per year (EAR) for three years or
   a. an account that pays 2.5% every six months for three years?
   b. an account that pays 7.5% every 18 months for three years?
   c. an account that pays 0.5% per month for three years?

*5. You have been offered a job with an unusual bonus structure. As long as you stay with the firm, you will get an extra $70,000 every seven years, starting seven years from now. What is the present value of this incentive if you plan to work for the company for 42 years and the interest rate is 6% (EAR)?

6. You have found three investment choices for a one-year deposit: 10% APR compounded monthly, 10% APR compounded annually, and 9% APR compounded daily. Compute the EAR for each investment choice. (Assume that there are 365 days in the year.)

7. Your bank account pays interest with an EAR of 5%. What is the APR quote for this account based on semiannual compounding? What is the APR with monthly compounding?

8. Suppose the interest rate is 8% APR with monthly compounding. What is the present value of an annuity that pays $100 every six months for five years?

9. A payday loan is structured to obscure the true interest rate you are paying. For example, in Washington, you pay a $30 "fee" for a two-week $200 payday loan (when you repay the loan, you pay $230). What is the effective annual interest rate for this loan?

10. You have been accepted into college. The college guarantees that your tuition will not increase for the four years you attend. The first $10,000 tuition payment is due in six months. After that, the same payment is due every six months until you have made a total of eight payments. The college offers a bank account that allows you to withdraw money every six months and has a fixed APR of 4% (semiannual) guaranteed to remain the same over the next four years. How much money must you deposit today if you intend to make no further deposits and would like to make all the tuition payments from this account, leaving the account empty when the last payment is made?

Application: Discount Rates and Loans

11. You make monthly payments on your car loan. It has a quoted APR of 5% (monthly compounding). What percentage of the outstanding principal do you pay in interest each month?

12. Suppose Capital One is advertising a 60-month, 5.99% APR motorcycle loan. If you need to borrow $8000 to purchase your dream Harley-Davidson, what will your monthly payment be?

13. Suppose Oppenheimer Bank is offering a 30-year mortgage with an EAR of 6.80%. If you plan to borrow $150,000, what will your monthly payment be?

14. You have just taken out a $20,000 car loan with a 6% APR, compounded monthly. The loan is for five years. When you make your first payment in one month, how much of the payment will go toward the principal of the loan and how much will go toward interest?

 *15. You are buying a house and the mortgage company offers to let you pay a "point" (1% of the total amount of the loan) to reduce your APR from 6.5% to 6.25% on your $400,000, 30-year mortgage with monthly payments. If you plan to be in the house for at least five years, should you do it?

16. You have decided to refinance your mortgage. You plan to borrow whatever is outstanding on your current mortgage. The current monthly payment is $2356 and you have made every payment on time. The original term of the mortgage was 30 years, and the mortgage is exactly four years and eight months old. You have just made your monthly payment. The mortgage interest rate is 6.375% (APR). How much do you owe on the mortgage today?

*17. You have just sold your house for $1,000,000 in cash. Your mortgage was originally a 30-year mortgage with monthly payments and an initial balance of $800,000. The mortgage is currently exactly 18½ years old, and you have just made a payment. If the interest rate on the mortgage is 5.25% (APR), how much cash will you have from the sale once you pay off the mortgage?

18. You have just purchased a car and taken out a $50,000 loan. The loan has a five-year term with monthly payments and an APR of 6%.

a. How much will you pay in interest, and how much will you pay in principal, during the first month, second month, and first year? (*Hint*: Compute the loan balance after one month, two months, and one year.)

b. How much will you pay in interest, and how much will you pay in principal, during the fourth year (i.e., between three and four years from now)?

19. You are thinking about leasing a car. The purchase price of the car is $30,000. The residual value (the amount you could pay to keep the car at the end of the lease) is $15,000 at the end of 36 months. Assume the first lease payment is due one month after you get the car. The interest rate implicit in the lease is 6% APR, compounded monthly. What will your lease payments be for a 36-month lease?

*20. You have some extra cash this month and you are considering putting it toward your car loan. Your interest rate is 7%, your loan payments are $600 per month, and you have 36 months left on your loan. If you pay an additional $1000 with your next regular $600 payment (due in one month), how much will it reduce the amount of time left to pay off your loan?

*21. You have an outstanding student loan with required payments of $500 per month for the next four years. The interest rate on the loan is 9% APR (monthly). You are considering making an extra payment of $100 today (i.e., you will pay an extra $100 that you are not required to pay). If you are required to continue to make payments of $500 per month until the loan is paid off, what is the amount of your final payment? What effective rate of return (expressed as an APR with monthly compounding) have you earned on the $100?

*22. Consider again the setting of Problem 21. Now that you realize your best investment is to prepay your student loan, you decide to prepay as much as you can each month. Looking at your budget, you can afford to pay an extra $250 per month in addition to your required monthly payments of $500, or $750 in total each month. How long will it take you to pay off the loan?

*23. If you decide to take the mortgage in Problem 13, Oppenheimer Bank will offer you the following deal: Instead of making the monthly payment you computed in that problem every month, you can make half the payment every two weeks (so that you will make 52/2 = 26 payments per year). How long will it take to pay off the mortgage if the EAR remains the same at 6.80%.

*24. Your friend tells you he has a very simple trick for taking one-third off the time it takes to repay your mortgage: Use your Christmas bonus to make an extra payment on January 1 of each year (that is, pay your monthly payment due on that day twice). If you take out your mortgage on July 1, so your first monthly payment is due August 1, and you make an extra payment every January 1, how long will it take to pay off the mortgage? Assume that the mortgage has an original term of 30 years and an APR of 12%.

25. The mortgage on your house is five years old. It required monthly payments of $1402, had an original term of 30 years, and had an interest rate of 10% (APR). In the intervening five years, interest rates have fallen and so you have decided to refinance—that is, you will roll over the outstanding balance into a new mortgage. The new mortgage has a 30-year term, requires monthly payments, and has an interest rate of 6 5/8% (APR).

a. What monthly repayments will be required with the new loan?

b. If you still want to pay off the mortgage in 25 years, what monthly payment should you make after you refinance?

c. Suppose you are willing to continue making monthly payments of $1402. How long will it take you to pay off the mortgage after refinancing?

d. Suppose you are willing to continue making monthly payments of $1402, and want to pay off the mortgage in 25 years. How much additional cash can you borrow today as part of the refinancing?

26. You have credit card debt of $25,000 that has an APR (monthly compounding) of 15%. Each month you pay the minimum monthly payment. You are required to pay only the outstanding interest. You have received an offer in the mail for an otherwise identical credit card with an APR of 12%. After considering all your alternatives, you decide to switch cards, roll over the outstanding balance on the old card into the new card, and borrow additional money as well. How much can you borrow today on the new card without changing the minimum monthly payment you will be required to pay?

27. Your firm has taken out a $500,000 loan with 9% APR (compounded monthly) for some commercial property. As is common in commercial real estate, the loan is a five-year loan based on a 15-year amortization. This means that your loan payments will be calculated as if you will take 15 years to pay off the loan, but you actually must do so in five years. To do this, you will make 59 equal payments based on the 15-year amortization schedule and then make a final 60th payment to pay the remaining balance.

a. What will your monthly payments be?

b. What will your final payment be?

*28. Five years ago you took out a 5/1 adjustable rate mortgage and the five-year fixed rate period has just expired. The loan was originally for $300,000 with 360 payments at 4.2% APR, compounded monthly.

a. Now that you have made 60 payments, what is the remaining balance on the loan?

b. If the interest rate increases by 1%, to 5.2% APR, compounded monthly, what will your new payments be?

The Determinants of Interest Rates

29. In 1975, interest rates were 7.85% and the rate of inflation was 12.3% in the United States. What was the real interest rate in 1975? How would the purchasing power of your savings have changed over the year?

30. If the rate of inflation is 5%, what nominal interest rate is necessary for you to earn a 3% real interest rate on your investment?

31. Assume the inflation rate is 3% APR, compounded annually. Would you rather earn a nominal return of 5% APR, compounded semiannually, or a real return of 2% APR, compounded quarterly?

32. Assume inflation is 0.2% per month. Would you rather earn a nominal return of 0.75% per month, or a real return of 6.5% APR, compounded annually?

33. You are pleased to see that you have been given a 5% raise this year. However, you read on the *Wall Street Journal* Web site that inflation over the past year has been 2%. How much better off are you in terms of real purchasing power?

34. What is the shape of the yield curve given in the following term structure? What expectations are investors likely to have about future interest rates?

Term	1 year	2 years	3 years	5 years	7 years	10 years	20 years
Rate (EAR, %)	1.99	2.41	2.74	3.32	3.76	4.13	4.93

35. See the Treasury Yield Curve from June 2013 below. At the time, some were concerned about whether the Federal Reserve's stimulus activities would lead to high inflation. Based on the Yield Curve, can you tell whether the bond market was concerned about inflation? Explain.

Term	1	2	3	5	7	10	30
Rate (EAR %)	0.13	0.32	0.53	1.12	1.62	2.21	3.36

The Opportunity Cost of Capital

36. You are thinking about investing $5000 in your friend's landscaping business. Even though you know the investment is risky and you can't be sure, you expect your investment to be worth $5750 next year. You notice that the rate for one-year Treasury bills is 1%. However, you feel that other investments of equal risk to your friend's landscape business offer a 10% expected return for the year. What should you do?

37. You have invested in a business that proudly reports that it is profitable. Your investment of $5000 has produced a profit of $300. The managers think that if you leave your $5000 invested with them, they should be able to generate $300 per year in profits for you in perpetuity. Evaluating other investment opportunities, you note that other long-term investments of similar risk offer an expected return of 8%. Should you remain invested in this firm?

6

Bonds

LEARNING OBJECTIVES

- Understand bond terminology

- Compute the price and yield to maturity of a zero-coupon bond

- Compute the price and yield to maturity of a coupon bond

- Analyze why bond prices change over time

- Know how credit risk affects the expected return from holding a corporate bond

notation

CPN	coupon payment on a bond	*y*	yield to maturity
FV	face value of a bond	*YTM*	yield to maturity
n	number of periods	YTM_n	yield to maturity on a zero-coupon bond with *n* periods to maturity
P	initial price of a bond		
PV	present value		

In this chapter, we introduce bonds and apply our tools for valuing cash flows to them. Bonds are simply loans. When an investor buys a bond from an issuer, the investor is lending money to the bond issuer. Who are the issuers of bonds? Federal and local governments issue bonds to finance long-term projects, and many companies issue bonds as part of their debt financing.

Understanding bonds and their pricing is useful for several reasons. First, we can use the prices of risk-free government bonds to determine the risk-free interest rates that produce the yield curves discussed in Chapter 5. As we saw there, the yield curve provides important information for valuing risk-free cash flows and assessing expectations of inflation and economic growth. Second, firms often issue bonds to fund their own investments. The return investors receive on those bonds is one factor that determines a firm's cost of capital. Finally, bonds provide an opportunity to begin our study of how securities are priced in a competitive market. The bond markets are very large and very liquid; there are more than $34 *trillion* of bonds outstanding in the U.S. markets alone.[1] Further, the ideas we develop in this chapter will be helpful when we turn to the topic of valuing stocks in Chapter 7.

Pricing bonds gives us an opportunity to apply what we've learned in the last three chapters about valuing cash flows using competitive market prices. As we explained in Chapter 3, the Valuation Principle implies that the price of a security in a competitive market should be the present value of the cash flows an investor will receive from owning it. Thus, we begin the chapter by evaluating the promised cash flows for different types of bonds. If a bond is risk-free, so that the promised cash flows will be paid with certainty, we can use the Law of One Price to directly relate the return of a bond and its price. We then discuss how and why bond prices change over time. Once we have a firm understanding of the pricing of bonds in the absence of risk, we add the risk of default, where cash flows are not known with certainty. The risk of default and its implications are important considerations for a financial manager who is considering issuing corporate bonds. (In Chapter 15, we will discuss the details of issuing debt financing and cover some additional corporate bond features.)

6.1 Bond Terminology

bond certificate States the terms of a bond as well as the amounts and dates of all payments to be made.

maturity date The final repayment date of a bond.

term The time remaining until the final repayment date of a bond.

face value, par value, principal amount The notional amount of a bond used to compute its interest payments. The face value of the bond is generally due at the bond's maturity.

coupons The promised interest payments of a bond, paid periodically until the maturity date of the bond.

coupon rate Determines the amount of each coupon payment of a bond. The coupon rate, expressed as an APR, is set by the issuer and stated on the bond certificate.

Recall from Chapter 1 that a bond is a security sold by governments and corporations to raise money from investors today in exchange for a promised future payment. The terms of the bond are described as part of the **bond certificate**, which indicates the amounts and dates of all payments to be made. A bond certificate is shown in Figure 6.1. Payments on the bond are made until a final repayment date called the **maturity date** of the bond. The time remaining until the repayment date is known as the **term** of the bond.

Bonds typically make two types of payments to their holders. The principal or **face value** (also known as **par value** or **principal amount**) of a bond is the notional amount we use to compute the interest payments. Typically, the face value is repaid at maturity. It is generally denominated in standard increments such as $1000. A bond with a $1000 face value, for example, is often referred to as a "$1000 bond."

In addition to the face value, some bonds also promise additional payments called **coupons**. The bond certificate typically specifies that the coupons will be paid periodically (for example, semiannually) until the maturity date of the bond. As you can see from Figure 6.1, historically, on a payment date, the holder of the bond would clip off the next coupon for the next payment and present it for payment. It follows that the interest payments on the bond are called *coupon payments*. Today, the majority of bonds are registered electronically but the term remains.

The amount of each coupon payment is determined by the **coupon rate** of the bond. This coupon rate is set by the issuer and stated on the bond certificate. By convention, the coupon rate is expressed as an APR, so the amount of each coupon payment, *CPN*, is:

Coupon Payment

$$CPN = \frac{\text{Coupon Rate} \times \text{Face Value}}{\text{Number of Coupon Payments per Year}} \tag{6.1}$$

For example, a "$1000 bond with a 10% coupon rate and semiannual payments" will pay coupon payments of $(10\% \times \$1000)/2 = \$50$ every six months.

Table 6.1 summarizes the bond terminology we have presented thus far.

---

[1]Outstanding U.S. Bond Market Debt, www.sifma.org. December 2009.

FIGURE 6.1

A Bearer Bond and Its Unclipped Coupons Issued by the Elmira and Williamsport Railroad Company for $500

Source: Courtesy Heritage Auctions, Inc. © 1999–2006.

TABLE 6.1

Review of Bond Terminology

Bond Certificate	States the terms of a bond as well as the amounts and dates of all payments to be made.
Coupons	The promised interest payments of a bond. Usually paid semiannually, but the frequency is specified in the bond certificate. They are determined by the coupon rate, which is stated on the bond certificate. The amount paid is equal to: $$\frac{\text{Coupon Rate} \times \text{Face Value}}{\text{Number of Coupon Payments per Year}}$$
Maturity Date	Final repayment date of the bond. Payments continue until this date.
Principal or Face Value	The notional amount used to compute the interest payment. It is usually repaid on the maturity date. Also called *par value*.
Term	The time remaining until the repayment date.

Concept Check

1. What types of cash flows does a bond buyer receive?
2. How are the periodic coupon payments on a bond determined?

6.2　Zero-Coupon Bonds

zero-coupon bond A bond that makes only one payment at maturity.

Treasury bills Zero-coupon bonds, issued by the U.S. government, with a maturity of up to one year.

Not all bonds have coupon payments. Bonds without coupons are called **zero-coupon bonds.** As these are the simplest type of bond, we shall analyze them first. The only cash payment an investor in a zero-coupon bond receives is the face value of the bond on the maturity date. **Treasury bills**, which are U.S. government bonds with a maturity of up to one year, are zero-coupon bonds. The general name for risk-free zero coupon bonds is "STRIPS," which is an abbreviation of Separately Tradable Registered Interest and Principal Securities.

Zero-Coupon Bond Cash Flows

There are only two cash flows if we purchase and hold a zero-coupon bond. First, we pay the bond's current market price at the time we make the purchase. Then, at the maturity date, we receive the bond's face value. For example, suppose that a one-year, risk-free, zero-coupon bond with a $100,000 face value has an initial price of $96,618.36. If you purchased this bond and held it to maturity, you would have the following cash flows:

```
        0                    1
        |————————————————————|
    −$96,618.36          $100,000
```

discount A price at which bonds trade that is less than their face value.

pure discount bonds Zero-coupon bonds.

Note that although the bond pays no "interest" directly, as an investor you are compensated for the time value of your money by purchasing the bond at a discount to its face value. Recall from Chapter 3 that the present value of a future cash flow is less than the cash flow itself. As a result, prior to its maturity date, the price of a zero-coupon bond is always less than its face value. That is, zero-coupon bonds always trade at a **discount** (a price lower than the face value), so they are also called **pure discount bonds**.

Yield to Maturity of a Zero-Coupon Bond

Now that we understand the cash flows associated with a zero-coupon bond, we can calculate the rate of return of buying a bond and holding it until maturity. Recall from Chapter 4 that we can always find the rate of return of an investment opportunity as the discount rate that equates the present value of the investment to its costs. With a zero-coupon bond, the price is the cost of the bond. So, the rate of return on the zero-coupon bond is the discount rate that makes the present value of the future cash flow received (that is, the bond principal) equal to the cost of the bond. We can extend this concept to a coupon bond: the rate of return is the discount rate at which the present value of all future cash flows from the bond equals the price of the bond. The rate of return of an investment in a bond is given a special name, the **yield to maturity (YTM)** or just the *yield*:

yield to maturity (YTM) The rate of return of an investment in a bond that is held to its maturity date, or the discount rate that sets the present value of the promised bond payments equal to the current market price of the bond.

> *The yield to maturity of a bond is the discount rate that sets the present value of the promised bond payments equal to the current market price of the bond.*

Intuitively, the yield to maturity for a zero-coupon bond is the return you will earn as an investor by buying the bond at its current market price, holding the bond to maturity, and receiving the promised face value payment.

Let's determine the yield to maturity of the one-year zero-coupon bond discussed earlier. According to the definition, the yield to maturity of the one-year bond solves the following equation:

$$96,618.36 = \frac{100,000}{1 + YTM_1}$$

In this case:

$$1 + YTM_1 = \frac{100,000}{96,618.36} = 1.035$$

That is, the yield to maturity for this bond is 3.5%. Because the bond is risk free, investing in this bond and holding it to maturity is like earning 3.5% interest on your initial investment:

$$\$96,618.36 \times 1.035 = \$100,000$$

Pure Discount Bonds Trading at a Premium

On December 9, 2008, in the midst of one of the worst financial crises in history, the unthinkable happened: For the first time since the Great Depression, U.S. Treasury Bills traded at a negative yield. That is, these risk-free pure discount bonds traded at premium. As Bloomberg.com reported: "If you invested $1 million in three-month bills at today's negative discount rate of 0.01%, for a price of 100.002556, at maturity you would receive the par value for a loss of $25.56."

A negative yield on a Treasury bill implies that investors have an arbitrage opportunity: By *selling* the bill, and holding the proceeds in cash, they would have a risk-free *profit* of $25.56. Why did investors not rush to take advantage of the arbitrage opportunity and thereby eliminate it?

Well, first, the negative yields did not last very long, suggesting that, in fact, investors did rush to take advantage of this opportunity. But second, after closer consideration, the opportunity might not have been a sure risk-free arbitrage. When selling a Treasury

security, the investor must choose where to invest, or at least hold, the proceeds. In normal times, investors would be happy to deposit the proceeds with a bank, and consider this deposit to be risk free. But these were not normal times—many investors had great concerns about the financial stability of banks and other financial intermediaries. Perhaps investors shied away from this "arbitrage" opportunity because they were worried that the cash they would receive could not be held safely *anywhere* (even putting it "under the mattress" has a risk of theft!). Thus, we can view the $25.56 as the price investors were willing to pay to have the U.S. Treasury hold their money safely for them at a time when no other investments seemed truly safe.

In July 2012, the same phenomenon repeated itself in Europe when investors purchased newly issued German bonds at a negative yield of −0.06% The negative yields reflected concern about the safety of European banks. In addition, investors were worried that should the common currency zone break up, countries such as Germany might redenominate their debts into a stronger currency. Investors might therefore be willing to accept a negative yield as a hedge against the Eurozone unraveling.

We can use a similar method to find the yield to maturity for any maturity zero-coupon bond:

Yield to Maturity of an *n*-Year Zero-Coupon Bond

$$1 + YTM_n = \left(\frac{\text{Face Value}}{\text{Price}}\right)^{1/n} \tag{6.2}$$

The yield to maturity (YTM_n) in Eq. 6.2 is the per-period rate of return for holding the bond from today until maturity on date n.

EXAMPLE 6.1
Yields for Different Maturities

MyFinanceLab

PROBLEM

Suppose the following zero-coupon bonds are trading at the prices shown below per $100 face value. Determine the corresponding yield to maturity for each bond.

Maturity	1 year	2 years	3 years	4 years
Price	$96.62	$92.45	$87.63	$83.06

SOLUTION

PLAN

We can use Eq. 6.2 to solve for the YTM of the bonds. The table gives the prices and number of years to maturity and the face value is $100 per bond.

EXECUTE

Using Eq. 6.2, we have

$$YTM_1 = (100/96.62)^{1/1} - 1 = 3.50\%$$
$$YTM_2 = (100/92.45)^{1/2} - 1 = 4.00\%$$

(Continued)

$$YTM_3 = (100/87.63)^{1/3} - 1 = 4.50\%$$
$$YTM_4 = (100/83.06)^{1/4} - 1 = 4.75\%$$

EVALUATE

Solving for the YTM of a zero-coupon bond is the same process we used to solve for the rate of return in Chapter 4. Indeed, the YTM is the rate of return of buying the bond.

Risk-Free Interest Rates

Above, we calculated the yield to maturity of the one-year risk-free bond as 3.5%. But recall that the Valuation Principle's Law of One Price implies that all one-year risk-free investments must earn this same return of 3.5%. That is, 3.5% must be *the* competitive-market risk-free interest rate.

More generally, in Chapter 5, we discussed the competitive market interest rate r_n available from today until date n for risk-free cash flows. Recall that we used this interest rate as the cost of capital for a risk-free cash flow that occurs on date n. A default-free zero-coupon bond that matures on date n provides a risk-free return over the same period. So the Law of One Price guarantees that the risk-free interest rate equals the yield to maturity on such a bond. Consequently, we will often refer to the yield to maturity of the appropriate maturity, zero-coupon risk-free bond as *the* risk-free interest rate. Some financial professionals also use the term **spot interest rates** to refer to these default-free, zero-coupon yields because these rates are offered "on the spot" at that point in time.

In Chapter 5, we introduced the yield curve, which plots the risk-free interest rate for different maturities. These risk-free interest rates correspond to the yields of risk-free zero-coupon bonds. Thus, the yield curve we introduced in Chapter 5 is also referred to as the **zero-coupon yield curve**. Figure 6.2 illustrates the yield curve consistent with the zero-coupon bond prices in Example 6.1.

spot interest rates Default-free, zero-coupon yields.

zero-coupon yield curve A plot of the yield of risk-free zero-coupon bonds (STRIPS) as a function of the bond's maturity date.

FIGURE 6.2

Zero-Coupon Yield Curve Consistent with the Bond Prices in Example 6.1

Recall from Chapter 5 that a yield curve simply plots the yield to maturity of investments of different maturities. In this figure, we show the yield curve that would be produced by plotting the yield to maturities determined by the bond prices in Example 6.1. Note that as in this figure, the longer maturities generally have higher yields.

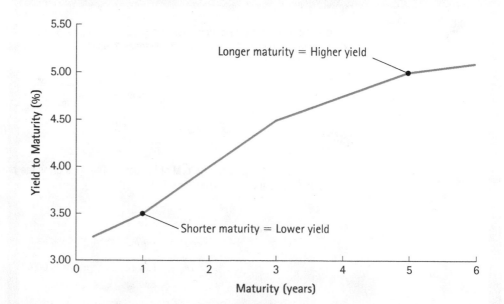

In Example 6.1, we used the bond's price to compute its yield to maturity. But from the definition of the yield to maturity, we can also use a bond's yield to compute its price. In the case of a zero-coupon bond, the price is simply equal to the present value of the bond's face value, discounted at the bond's yield to maturity.

EXAMPLE 6.2

Computing the Price of a Zero-Coupon Bond

MyFinanceLab

PROBLEM

Given the yield curve shown in Figure 6.2, what is the price of a five-year risk-free zero-coupon bond with a face value of $100?

SOLUTION

PLAN

We can compute the bond's price as the present value of its face amount, where the discount rate is the bond's yield to maturity. From the yield curve, the yield to maturity for five-year risk-free zero-coupon bonds is 5.0%.

EXECUTE

$$P = 100/(1.05)^5 = 78.35$$

EVALUATE

We can compute the price of a zero-coupon bond simply by computing the present value of the face amount using the bond's yield to maturity. Note that the price of the five-year zero-coupon bond is even lower than the price of the other zero-coupon bonds in Example 6.1, because the face amount is the same but we must wait longer to receive it.

Concept
Check

3. Why would you want to know the yield to maturity of a bond?

4. What is the relationship between a bond's price and its yield to maturity?

6.3   Coupon Bonds

coupon bonds Bonds that pay regular coupon interest payments up to maturity, when the face value is also paid.

Treasury notes A type of U.S. Treasury coupon security, currently traded in financial markets, with original maturities from one to ten years.

Treasury bonds A type of U.S. Treasury coupon security, currently traded in financial markets, with original maturities of more than ten years.

Similar to zero-coupon bonds, **coupon bonds** pay investors their face value at maturity. In addition, these bonds make regular coupon interest payments. As Table 6.2 indicates, two types of U.S. Treasury coupon securities are currently traded in financial markets: **Treasury notes**, which have original maturities from one to ten years, and **Treasury bonds**, which have original maturities of more than ten years. The original maturity is the term of the bond at the time it was originally issued.

TABLE 6.2

Existing U.S. Treasury Securities

Treasury Security	Type	Original Maturity
Bills	Discount	4, 13, 26, and 52 weeks
Notes	Coupon	2, 3, 5, and 10 year
Bonds	Coupon	20 and 30 year

Coupon Bond Cash Flows

While an investor's return on a zero-coupon bond comes from buying it at a discount to its principal value, the return on a coupon bond comes from two sources: (1) any difference between the purchase price and the principal value, and (2) its periodic coupon payments. Before we can compute the yield to maturity of a coupon bond, we need to know all of its cash flows, including the coupon interest payments and when they are paid. In Example 6.3, we take a bond description and translate it into the bond's cash flows.

EXAMPLE 6.3

The Cash Flows of a
Coupon Bond or Note

MyFinanceLab

PROBLEM

Assume that it is May 15, 2010 and the U.S. Treasury has just issued securities with a May 2015 maturity, $1000 par value, and a 2.2% coupon rate with semiannual coupons. Since the original maturity is only five years, these would be called "notes" as opposed to "bonds." The first coupon payment will be paid on November 15, 2010. What cash flows will you receive if you hold this note until maturity?

SOLUTION

PLAN

The description of the note should be sufficient to determine all of its cash flows. The phrase "May 2015 maturity, $1000 par value" tells us that this is a note with a face value of $1000 and five years to maturity. The phrase "2.2% coupon rate with semiannual coupons" tells us that the note pays a total of 2.2% of its face value each year in two equal semiannual installments. Finally, we know that the first coupon is paid on November 15, 2010.

EXECUTE

The face value of this note is $1000. Because this note pays coupons semiannually, using Eq. 6.1 you can compute that you will receive a coupon payment every six months of $CPN = (2.2\% \times \$1000)/2 = \$11$. Here is the timeline based on a six-month period and there are a total of 10 cash flows:

May 2010	Nov. 2010	May 2011	Nov. 2011	May 2015
	$11	$11	$11	$11 + $1000

Note that the last payment occurs five years (10 six-month periods) from now and is composed of both a coupon payment of $11 and the face value payment of $1000.

EVALUATE

Since a note is just a package of cash flows, we need to know those cash flows in order to value the note. That's why the description of the note contains all of the information we would need to construct its cash flow timeline.

The U.S. Treasury Market

In most years, the U.S. Federal Government spends more than it takes in through taxes and other revenue sources. To finance this deficit, the U.S. Department of the Treasury issues debt instruments, commonly known as "Treasuries." The market for Treasury securities is huge and extremely liquid. At the beginning of 2013, the total amount of public debt outstanding was over $16.77 *trillion*. Treasury securities are held by institutional investors such as insurance companies, pension funds and bond mutual funds, individual investors, and even other governmental agencies (such as the Federal Reserve) as shown in the pie chart below. The figures are in *billions* of dollars (6524 billion is 6.524 trillion).

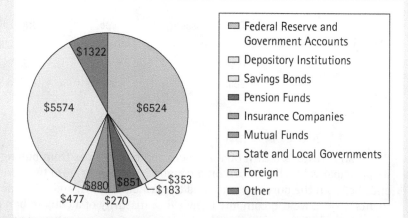

Legend:
- Federal Reserve and Government Accounts
- Depository Institutions
- Savings Bonds
- Pension Funds
- Insurance Companies
- Mutual Funds
- State and Local Governments
- Foreign
- Other

Values: $1322, $5574, $6524, $880, $851, $353, $183, $477, $270

Source: Treasury Bulletin Ownership of Federal Securities, www.fms.treas.gov/bulletin/index.html, December 2012.

Yield to Maturity of a Coupon Bond

Once we have determined the coupon bond's cash flows, given its market price we can determine its yield to maturity. Recall that the yield to maturity for a bond is the rate of return of investing in the bond and holding it to maturity. This investment has the cash flows shown in the timeline below:

The yield to maturity of the bond is the *single* discount rate that equates the present value of the bond's remaining cash flows to its current price. For zero-coupon bonds, there were only two cash flows. But coupon bonds have many cash flows, complicating the yield to maturity calculation. From the timeline, we see that the coupon payments represent an annuity, so the yield to maturity is the interest rate y that solves the following equation:

Yield to Maturity of a Coupon Bond

$$P = \underbrace{CPN \times \overbrace{\frac{1}{y}\left(1 - \frac{1}{(1+y)^N}\right)}^{\text{Annuity Factor using the YTM } (y)}}_{\substack{\text{Present Value of all of the periodic coupon} \\ \text{payments}}} + \underbrace{\frac{FV}{(1+y)^N}}_{\substack{\text{Present Value of the} \\ \text{Face Value repayment} \\ \text{using the YTM } (y)}} \tag{6.3}$$

Unfortunately, unlike zero-coupon bonds, there is no simple formula to solve for the yield to maturity directly. Instead, we need to use either trial and error or, more commonly, a financial calculator or a spreadsheet (both of which we demonstrate in Example 6.4).

When we calculate a bond's yield to maturity by solving Eq. 6.3, the yield we compute will be a rate *per coupon interval*. However, yields are typically quoted as APRs, so we multiply by the number of coupons per year, thereby converting the answer into an APR quote with the same compounding interval as the coupon rate.

EXAMPLE 6.4

Computing the Yield to Maturity of a Coupon Bond

MyFinanceLab

PROBLEM

Consider the five-year, $1000 bond with a 2.2% coupon rate and semiannual coupons described in Example 6.3. If this bond is currently trading for a price of $963.11, what is the bond's yield to maturity?

SOLUTION

PLAN

We worked out the bond's cash flows in Example 6.3. From the cash flow timeline, we can see that the bond consists of an annuity of 10 payments of $11, paid every six months, and one lump-sum payment of $1000 in five years (in 10 six-month periods). We can use Eq. 6.3 to solve for the yield to maturity. However, we must use six-month intervals consistently throughout the equation.

EXECUTE

Because the bond has 10 remaining coupon payments, we compute its yield y by solving Eq. 6.3 for this bond:

$$963.11 = 11 \times \frac{1}{y}\left(1 - \frac{1}{(1+y)^{10}}\right) + \frac{1000}{(1+y)^{10}}$$

(Continued)

We can solve it by trial and error, a financial calculator, or a spreadsheet. To use a financial calculator, we enter the price we pay as a negative number for the PV (it is a cash outflow), the coupon payments as the PMT, and the bond's par value as its FV. Finally, we enter the number of coupon payments remaining (10) as N.

	N	I/Y	PV	PMT	FV
Given:	10		−963.11	11	1000
Solve for:		1.50			
Excel Formula: =RATE(NPER,PMT,PV,FV)=RATE(10,11,−963.11,1000)					

Therefore, $y = 1.5\%$. Because the bond pays coupons semiannually, this yield is for a six-month period. We convert it to an APR by multiplying by the number of coupon payments per year. Thus, the bond has a yield to maturity equal to a 3% APR with semiannual compounding.

EVALUATE

As the equation shows, the yield to maturity is the discount rate that equates the present value of the bond's cash flows with its price. Note that the YTM is higher than the coupon rate and the price is lower than the par value. We will discuss why in the next section.

We can also use Eq. 6.3 to compute a bond's price based on its yield to maturity. We simply discount the cash flows using the yield, as in Example 6.5.

EXAMPLE 6.5

Computing a Bond
Price from Its Yield
to Maturity

MyFinanceLab

PROBLEM

Consider again the five-year, $1000 bond with a 2.2% coupon rate and semiannual coupons in Example 6.4. Suppose interest rates drop and the bond's yield to maturity decreases to 2% (expressed as an APR with semiannual compounding). What price is the bond trading for now? And what is the effective annual yield on this bond?

SOLUTION

PLAN

Given the yield, we can compute the price using Eq. 6.3. First, note that a 2% APR is equivalent to a semiannual rate of 1%. Also, recall that the cash flows of this bond are an annuity of 10 payments of $11, paid every six months, and one lump-sum cash flow of $1000 (the face value), paid in five years (10 six-month periods). In Chapter 5, we learned how to compute an effective annual rate from an APR using Eq. 5.3. We do the same here to compute the effective annual yield from the bond's yield to maturity expressed as an APR.

EXECUTE

Using Eq. 6.3 and the six-month yield of 1%, the bond price must be:

$$P = 11 \times \frac{1}{0.01}\left(1 - \frac{1}{1.01^{10}}\right) + \frac{1000}{1.01^{10}} = \$1009.47$$

We can also use a financial calculator or spreadsheet:

	N	I/Y	PV	PMT	FV
Given:	10	1		11	1000
Solve for:			−1009.47		
Excel Formula: =PV(RATE,NPER,PMT,FV)=PV(.01,10,11,1000)					

The effective annual yield corresponding to 1% every six months is:

$$(1 + .01)^2 - 1 = .0201, \text{ or } 2.01\%$$

EVALUATE

The bond's price has risen to $1009.47, lowering the return from investing in it from 1.5% to 1% per six-month period. Interest rates have dropped, so the lower return brings the bond's yield into line with the lower competitive rates being offered for similar risk and maturity elsewhere in the market.

Finding Bond Prices on the Web

Unlike the NYSE where many stocks are traded, there is no particular physical location where bonds are traded. Instead, they are traded electronically. Recently, the Financial Industry Regulatory Authority (FINRA) has made an effort to make bond prices more widely available. Their Web site, www.finra.org/marketdata, allows anyone to search for the most recent trades and quotes for bonds. Here, we show a screenshot from the Web site displaying the pricing information for one of Procter and Gamble's (PG) bonds.

The bond pays coupons of 8.000%, and they are fixed at this rate, as shown near the bottom of the screen.

The last trade was $139.96 per $100 face value, implying a yield to maturity of 3.606%.

Coupons are paid semiannually in March and September.

Coupon rate is fixed.

Source: www.finra.org/marketdata, July 19, 2013.

Coupon Bond Price Quotes

Because we can convert any price into a yield, and vice versa, prices and yields are often used interchangeably. For example, the bond in Example 6.5 could be quoted as having a yield of 2% or a price of $1009.47 per $1000 face value. Indeed, bond traders generally quote bond yields rather than bond prices. One advantage of quoting the yield to maturity rather than the price is that the yield is independent of the face value of the bond. When prices are quoted in the bond market, they are conventionally quoted per $100 face value. Thus, the bond in Example 6.5 would be quoted as having a price of $100.947 (per $100 face value), which would imply an actual price of $1009.47 given the $1000 face value of the bond.

Concept
Check

5. What cash flows does a company pay to investors holding its coupon bonds?

6. What do we need in order to value a coupon bond?

6.4 Why Bond Prices Change

premium A price at which coupon bonds trade that is greater than their face value.

As we mentioned earlier, zero-coupon bonds always trade for a discount—that is, prior to maturity, their price is less than their face value. But as shown in Examples 6.4 and 6.5, coupon bonds may trade at a discount, or at a **premium** (a price greater than their face value). In this section, we identify when a bond will trade at a discount or premium, as well as how the bond's price will change due to the passage of time and fluctuations in interest rates.

par A price at which coupon bonds trade that is equal to their face value.

Most issuers of coupon bonds choose a coupon rate so that the bonds will *initially* trade at, or very close to, **par** (that is, at the bond's face value). For example, the U.S. Treasury sets the coupon rates on its notes and bonds in this way. After the issue date, the market price of a bond generally changes over time for two reasons. First, as time passes, the bond gets closer to its maturity date. Holding fixed the bond's yield to maturity, the present value of the bond's remaining cash flows changes as the time to maturity decreases. Second, at any point in time, changes in market interest rates affect the bond's yield to maturity and its price (the present value of the remaining cash flows). We explore these two effects in the remainder of this section.

Interest Rate Changes and Bond Prices

If a bond sells at par (at its face value), the only return investors will earn is from the coupons that the bond pays. Therefore, the bond's coupon rate will exactly equal its yield to maturity. As interest rates in the economy fluctuate, the yields that investors demand to invest in bonds will also change. Imagine that your company issues a bond when market interest rates imply a YTM of 8%, setting the coupon rate to be 8%. Suppose interest rates then rise so that new bonds have a YTM of 9%. These new bonds would have a coupon rate of 9% and sell for $1000. So, for $1000, the investor would get $90 per year until the bond matured. Your existing bond was issued when rates were lower such that its coupon is fixed at 8%, so it offers payments of $80 per year until maturity. Because its cash flows are lower, the 8% bond must have a lower price than the 9% bond.[2] Thus, the price of the 8% bond will fall until the investor is indifferent between buying the 8% bond and buying the 9% bond. Figure 6.3 illustrates the relationship between the bond's price and its yield to maturity.

---

[2]Otherwise, if the 8% bond had the same or higher price, there would be an arbitrage opportunity: One could sell the 8% bond and buy the 9% bond, receiving cash today and higher coupons going forward.

In our example, the price of the 8% bond will drop to below face value ($1000), so it will be trading at a discount (also called trading *below par*). If the bond trades at a discount, an investor who buys the bond will earn a return both from receiving the coupons *and* from receiving a face value that exceeds the price paid for the bond. As a result, if a bond trades at a discount, its yield to maturity will exceed its coupon rate.

A bond that pays a coupon can also trade at a premium to its face value (trading *above par*). Imagine what would have happened in our example if interest rates had gone down to 7% instead of up to 9%. Then, the holder of the existing 8% bond would not part with it for $1000. Instead, its price would have to rise until the yield to maturity from buying it at that price would be 7%. In this case, an investor's return from the coupons is diminished by receiving a face value less than the price paid for the bond. *Thus, a bond trades at a premium whenever its yield to maturity is less than its coupon rate.*[3]

FIGURE 6.3

A Bond's Price Versus Its Yield to Maturity

At a price of $1000, the 8% semiannual coupon bond offers an 8% YTM. In order for the 8% coupon bond to offer a competitive yield to maturity, its price must fall until its yield to maturity rises to the 9% yield being offered by otherwise similar bonds. In the example depicted here, for a bond with five years left to maturity, its price must fall to $960.44 before investors will be indifferent between buying it and the 9% coupon bond priced at $1000. The curve depicts this bond's price at yields to maturity between 6% and 10%.

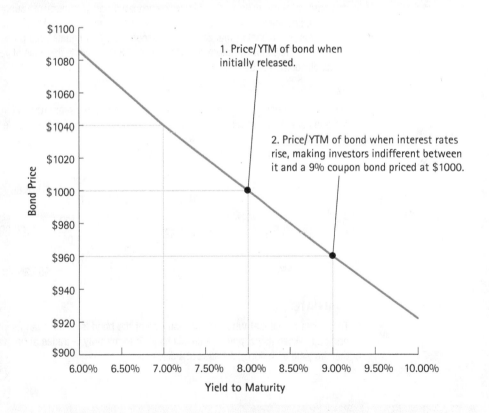

---

[3]The terms "discount" and "premium" are simply descriptive and are not meant to imply that you should try to buy bonds at a discount and avoid buying bonds at a premium. In a competitive market, the Law of One Price ensures that all similar bonds are priced to earn the same return. When you buy a bond, the price exactly equals the present value of the bond's cash flows, so that you earn a fair return, but not an abnormally good (or bad) return.

This example illustrates a general phenomenon. A higher yield to maturity means that investors demand a higher return for investing. They apply a higher discount rate to the bond's remaining cash flows, reducing their present value and hence the bond's price. The reverse holds when interest rates fall. Investors then demand a lower yield to maturity, reducing the discount rate applied to the bond's cash flows and raising the price. Therefore, *as interest rates and bond yields rise, bond prices will fall, and vice versa, so that interest rates and bond prices always move in the opposite direction.*

Table 6.3 summarizes the relationship between interest rates and bond prices.

EXAMPLE 6.6

Determining the Discount or Premium of a Coupon Bond

MyFinanceLab

PROBLEM

Consider three 30-year bonds with annual coupon payments. One bond has a 10% coupon rate, one has a 5% coupon rate, and one has a 3% coupon rate. If the yield to maturity of each bond is 5%, what is the price of each bond per $100 face value? Which bond trades at a premium, which trades at a discount, and which trades at par?

SOLUTION

PLAN

From the description of the bonds, we can determine their cash flows. Each bond has 30 years to maturity and pays its coupons annually. Therefore, each bond has an annuity of coupon payments, paid annually for 30 years, and then the face value paid as a lump sum in 30 years. They are all priced so that their yield to maturity is 5%, meaning that 5% is the discount rate that equates the present value of the cash flows to the price of the bond. Therefore, we can use Eq. 6.3 to compute the price of each bond as the PV of its cash flows, discounted at 5%.

EXECUTE

For the 10% coupon bond, the annuity cash flows are $10 per year (10% of each $100 face value). Similarly, the annuity cash flows for the 5% and 3% bonds are $5 and $3 per year. We use a $100 face value for all of the bonds.

Using Eq. 6.3 and these cash flows, the bond prices are:

$$P(10\% \text{ coupon}) = 10 \times \frac{1}{0.05}\left(1 - \frac{1}{1.05^{30}}\right) + \frac{100}{1.05^{30}} = \$176.86 \text{ (trades at a premium)}$$

$$P(5\% \text{ coupon}) = 5 \times \frac{1}{0.05}\left(1 - \frac{1}{1.05^{30}}\right) + \frac{100}{1.05^{30}} = \$100.00 \text{ (trades at par)}$$

$$P(3\% \text{ coupon}) = 3 \times \frac{1}{0.05}\left(1 - \frac{1}{1.05^{30}}\right) + \frac{100}{1.05^{30}} = \$69.26 \text{ (trades at a discount)}$$

EVALUATE

The prices reveal that when the coupon rate of the bond is higher than its yield to maturity, it trades at a premium. When its coupon rate equals its yield to maturity, it trades at par. When its coupon rate is lower than its yield to maturity, it trades at a discount.

TABLE 6.3

Bond Prices Immediately After a Coupon Payment

When the bond price is . . .	greater than the face value	equal to the face value	less than the face value
We say the bond trades . . .	"above par" or "at a premium"	"at par"	"below par" or "at a discount"
This occurs when . . .	Coupon Rate > Yield to Maturity	Coupon Rate = Yield to Maturity	Coupon Rate < Yield to Maturity

Time and Bond Prices

Let's consider the effect of time on the price of a bond. As the next payment from a bond grows nearer, the price of the bond increases to reflect the increasing present value of that cash flow. Take a bond paying semiannual coupons of $50 and imagine tracking the price of the bond starting on the day after the last coupon payment was made. The price would slowly rise over the following six months as the next $50 coupon payment grows closer and closer. It will peak right before the coupon payment is made, when buying the bond still entitles you to receive the $50 payment immediately. If you buy the bond right after the coupon payment is made, you do not have the right to receive that $50 coupon. The price you are willing to pay for the bond will therefore be $50 less than it was right before the coupon was paid. This pattern—the price slowly rising as a coupon payment nears and then dropping abruptly after the payment is made—continues for the life of the bond. Figure 6.4 illustrates this phenomenon.

FIGURE 6.4

The Effect of Time on Bond Prices

The graph illustrates the effects of the passage of time on bond prices when the yield remains constant, in this case 5%. The price of a zero-coupon bond rises smoothly. The prices of the coupon bonds are indicated by the zigzag lines. Notice that the prices rise between coupon payments, but tumble on the coupon date, reflecting the amount of the coupon payment. For each coupon bond, the gray line shows the trend of the bond price just after each coupon is paid.

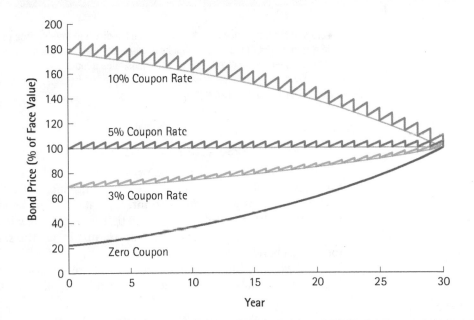

EXAMPLE 6.7

The Effect of Time on the Price of a Bond

MyFinanceLab

PROBLEM

Suppose you purchase a 30-year, zero-coupon bond with a yield to maturity of 5%. For a face value of $100, the bond will initially trade for:

$$P(\,30 \text{ years to maturity}\,) = \frac{100}{1.05^{30}} = \$23.14$$

If the bond's yield to maturity remains at 5%, what will its price be five years later? If you purchased the bond at $23.14 and sold it five years later, what would the rate of return of your investment be?

(Continued)

SOLUTION

PLAN

If the bond was originally a 30-year bond and five years have passed, then it has 25 years left to maturity. If the yield to maturity does not change, then you can compute the price of the bond with 25 years left exactly as we did for 30 years, but using 25 years of discounting instead of 30.

Once you have the price in five years, you can compute the rate of return of your investment just as we did in Chapter 4. The FV is the price in five years, the PV is the initial price ($23.14), and the number of years is five.

EXECUTE

$$P\,(\,25\text{ years to maturity}\,) = \frac{100}{1.05^{25}} = \$29.53$$

If you purchased the bond for $23.14 and then sold it after five years for $29.53, the rate of return of your investment would be

$$\left(\frac{29.53}{23.14}\right)^{1/5} - 1 = 5.0\%$$

That is, your return is the same as the yield to maturity of the bond.

EVALUATE

Note that the bond price is higher, and hence the discount from its face value is smaller, when there is less time to maturity. The discount shrinks because the yield has not changed, but there is less time until the face value will be received. This example illustrates a more general property for bonds: *If a bond's yield to maturity does not change, then the rate of return of an investment in the bond equals its yield to maturity even if you sell the bond early.*

Interest Rate Risk and Bond Prices

While the effect of time on bond prices is predictable, unpredictable changes in interest rates will also affect bond prices. Further, bonds with different characteristics will respond differently to changes in interest rates—some bonds will react more strongly than others. We showed in Chapter 5 that investors view long-term loans to be riskier than short-term loans. Because bonds are just loans, the same is true of short- versus long-term bonds.

The example illustrates how bonds of different maturity will have different sensitivities to interest rate changes. However, even bonds with the same maturity will differ in

EXAMPLE 6.8

The Interest Rate
Sensitivity of Bonds

MyFinanceLab

PROBLEM

Consider a 10-year coupon bond and a 30-year coupon bond, both with 10% annual coupons. By what percentage will the price of each bond change if its yield to maturity increases from 5% to 6%?

SOLUTION

PLAN

We need to compute the price of each bond for each yield to maturity and then calculate the percentage change in the prices. For both bonds, the cash flows are $10 per year for $100 in face value and then the $100 face value repaid at maturity. The only difference is the maturity: 10 years and 30 years. With those cash flows, we can use Eq. 6.3 to compute the prices.

EXECUTE

YTM	10-Year, 10% Annual Coupon Bond	30-Year, 10% Annual Coupon Bond
5%	$10 \times \dfrac{1}{0.05}\left(1 - \dfrac{1}{1.05^{10}}\right) + \dfrac{100}{1.05^{10}} = \$138.61$	$10 \times \dfrac{1}{0.05}\left(1 - \dfrac{1}{1.05^{30}}\right) + \dfrac{100}{1.05^{30}} = \$176.86$
6%	$10 \times \dfrac{1}{0.06}\left(1 - \dfrac{1}{1.06^{10}}\right) + \dfrac{100}{1.06^{10}} = \$129.44$	$10 \times \dfrac{1}{0.06}\left(1 - \dfrac{1}{1.06^{30}}\right) + \dfrac{100}{1.06^{30}} = \$155.06$

The price of the 10-year bond changes by $(129.44 - 138.61)/138.61 = -6.6\%$ if its yield to maturity increases from 5% to 6%.

For the 30-year bond, the price change is $(155.06 - 176.86)/176.86 = -12.3\%$.

EVALUATE

The 30-year bond is almost twice as sensitive to a change in the yield than is the 10-year bond. In fact, if we graph the price and yields of the two bonds, we can see that the line for the 30-year bond, shown in blue, is steeper throughout than the green line for the 10-year bond, reflecting its heightened sensitivity to interest rate changes.

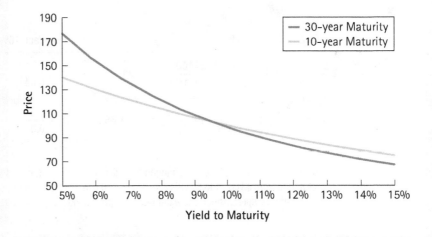

interest rate sensitivity if their coupon rates are different. Bonds with higher coupon rates—because they pay higher cash flows up-front—are less sensitive to interest rate changes than otherwise identical bonds with lower coupon rates.[4] Table 6.4 summarizes this conclusion.

TABLE 6.4

Bond Prices and Interest Rates

Bond Characteristic	Effect on Interest Rate Risk
Longer term to maturity	Increase
Higher coupon payments	Decrease

---

[4]The *duration* of a bond measures its sensitivity to interest rate changes. A full discussion of the concept of duration is beyond the scope of this book.

EXAMPLE 6.9
Coupons and Interest Rate Sensitivity

MyFinanceLab

PROBLEM

Consider two bonds, each of which pays semiannual coupons and has five years left until maturity. One has a coupon rate of 5% and the other has a coupon rate of 10%, but both currently have a yield to maturity of 8%. By what percentage will the price of each bond change if its yield to maturity decreases from 8% to 7%?

SOLUTION

PLAN

As in Example 6.8, we need to compute the price of each bond at 8% and 7% yield to maturities and then compute the percentage change in price. Each bond has 10 semiannual coupon payments remaining along with the repayment of par value at maturity. The cash flows per $100 of face value for the first bond are $2.50 every six months and then $100 at maturity. The cash flows per $100 of face value for the second bond are $5 every six months and then $100 at maturity. Since the cash flows are semiannual, the yield to maturity is quoted as a semiannually compounded APR, so we convert the yields to match the frequency of the cash flows by dividing by two. With semiannual rates of 4% and 3.5%, we can use Eq. 6.3 to compute the prices.

EXECUTE

YTM	Five-Year, 5% Coupon Bond	Five-Year, 10% Coupon Bond
8%	$2.50 \times \dfrac{1}{0.04}\left(1 - \dfrac{1}{1.04^{10}}\right) + \dfrac{100}{1.04^{10}} = \$87.83$	$5 \times \dfrac{1}{0.04}\left(1 - \dfrac{1}{1.04^{10}}\right) + \dfrac{100}{1.04^{10}} = \$108.11$
7%	$2.50 \times \dfrac{1}{0.035}\left(1 - \dfrac{1}{1.035^{10}}\right) + \dfrac{100}{1.035^{10}} = \$91.68$	$5 \times \dfrac{1}{0.035}\left(1 - \dfrac{1}{1.035^{10}}\right) + \dfrac{100}{1.035^{10}} = \$112.47$

The 5% coupon bond's price changed from $87.83 to $91.68, or 4.4%, but the 10% coupon bond's price changed from $108.11 to $112.47, or 4.0%. You can calculate the price change very quickly with a financial calculator or spreadsheet. For example, take the 5% coupon bond at 8% YTM (4% per 6 months):

	N	I/Y	PV	PMT	FV
Given:	10	4		2.50	100
Solve for:			−87.83		
	Excel Formula: =PV(RATE,NPER,PMT,FV)=PV(.04,10,2.5,100)				

With all of the basic bond information entered, you can simply change the I/Y by entering 3.5 and pressing I/Y and then solve for PV again. So, with just a few keystrokes, you will have the new price of $91.68.

EVALUATE

The bond with the smaller coupon payments is more sensitive to changes in interest rates. Because its coupons are smaller relative to its par value, a larger fraction of its cash flows are received later. As we learned in Example 6.8, later cash flows are affected more greatly by changes in interest rates, so compared to the 10% coupon bond, the effect of the interest change is greater for the cash flows of the 5% coupon bond.

Clean and Dirty Prices for Coupon Bonds

As Figure 6.4 illustrates, coupon bond prices fluctuate around the time of each coupon payment in a sawtooth pattern: The value of the coupon bond rises as the next coupon payment gets closer and then drops after it has been paid. This fluctuation occurs even if there is no change in the bond's yield to maturity.

Bond traders are more concerned about changes in the bond's price that arise due to changes in the bond's yield, rather than these predictable patterns around coupon payments. As a result, they often do not quote the price of a bond in terms of its actual cash price, which is also called the **dirty price** or **invoice price** of the bond. Instead, bonds are often quoted in terms of a **clean price**, which is the bond's cash price less an adjustment for accrued interest, the amount of the next coupon payment that has already accrued:

$$\text{Clean Price} = \text{Cash (Dirty) Price} - \text{Accrued Interest}$$

$$\text{Accrued Interest} = \text{Coupon Amount} \times \left(\frac{\text{Days Since Last Coupon Payment}}{\text{Days in Current Coupon Period}} \right)$$

Note that immediately before a coupon payment is made, the accrued interest will equal the full amount of the coupon. Immediately after the coupon payment is made, the accrued interest will be zero. Thus, accrued interest will rise and fall in a sawtooth pattern as each coupon payment passes.

If we subtract accrued interest from the bond's cash price and compute the clean price, the sawtooth pattern is eliminated.

dirty price or invoice price A bond's actual cash price.

clean price A bond's cash price less an adjustment for accrued interest, the amount of the next coupon payment that has already accrued.

Bond Prices in Practice

In actuality, bond prices are subject to the effects of both the passage of time and changes in interest rates. Bond prices converge to the bond's face value due to the time effect, but simultaneously move up and down due to unpredictable changes in bond yields. Figure 6.5 illustrates this behavior by demonstrating how the price of the 30-year, zero-coupon bond might change over its life. Note that the bond price tends to converge to the face value as the bond approaches the maturity date, but also moves higher when its yield falls and lower when its yield rises.

As the fluctuating price in Figure 6.5 demonstrates, prior to maturity the bond is exposed to interest rate risk. If an investor chooses to sell and the bond's yield to maturity has decreased, then the investor will receive a high price and earn a high return. If the yield to maturity has increased, the bond price is low at the time of sale and the investor will earn a low return.

Concept Check

7. Why do interest rates and bond prices move in opposite directions?

8. If a bond's yield to maturity does not change, how does its cash price change between coupon payments?

FIGURE 6.5

Yield to Maturity
and Bond Price
Fluctuations
over Time

The graphs illustrate changes in price and yield for a 30-year zero-coupon bond over its life. Panel (a) illustrates the changes in the bond's yield to maturity (YTM) over its life. In Panel (b), the actual bond price is shown in blue. Because the YTM does not remain constant over the bond's life, the bond's price fluctuates as it converges to the face value over time. Also shown is the price if the YTM remained fixed at 4%, 5%, or 6%. Panel (a) shows that the bond's YTM mostly remained between 4% and 6%. The broken lines in Panel (b) show the price of the bond if its YTM had remained constant at those levels. Note that in all cases, the bond's price must eventually converge to $100 on its maturity date.

Panel (a) The Bond's Yield to Maturity over Time

Panel (b) The Bond's Price over Time (Price = $100 on Maturity Date)

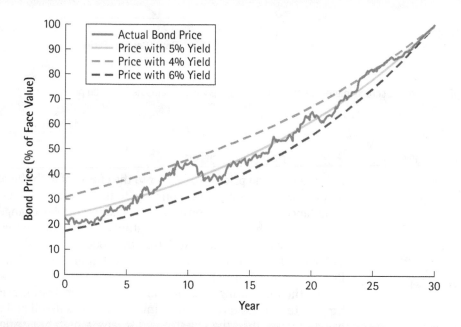

6.5 Corporate Bonds

corporate bonds Bonds
issued by corporations.

In the previous sections, we developed the basics of bond pricing in the context of U.S. Treasury bonds, which have no risk of default. In this section, our focus is on **corporate bonds**, which are bonds issued by corporations. We will examine the role of default risk in the price and yield to maturity of corporate bonds. As we will see, corporations with higher default risk will need to pay higher coupons to attract buyers to their bonds.

TABLE 6.5

Interest Rates on Five-Year Bonds for Various Borrowers, July 2013

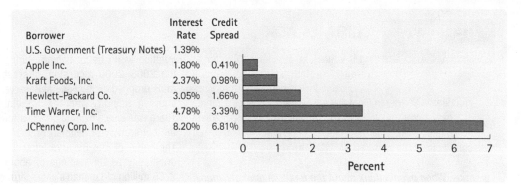

Borrower	Interest Rate	Credit Spread
U.S. Government (Treasury Notes)	1.39%	
Apple Inc.	1.80%	0.41%
Kraft Foods, Inc.	2.37%	0.98%
Hewlett-Packard Co.	3.05%	1.66%
Time Warner, Inc.	4.78%	3.39%
JCPenney Corp. Inc.	8.20%	6.81%

Credit Risk

Table 6.5 lists the interest rates paid by a number of different borrowers in mid-2013 for a five-year bond. Why do these interest rates vary so widely? The lowest interest rate is the 1.39% rate paid on U.S. Treasury notes. United States Treasury securities are widely regarded to be risk-free because there is virtually no chance the government will fail to pay the interest and default on these bonds. Thus, as we noted in Section 6.2, when we refer to the "risk-free interest rate," we mean the rate on U.S. Treasuries.

The remaining bonds are all corporate bonds. With corporate bonds, the bond issuer may default—that is, it might not pay back the full amount promised in the bond prospectus. For example, a company with financial difficulties may be unable to fully repay the loan. This risk of default, which is known as the **credit risk** of the bond, means that the bond's cash flows are not known with certainty. To compensate for the risk that the firm may default, investors demand a higher interest rate than the rate on U.S. Treasuries.[5] The difference between the interest rate of the loan and the Treasury rate will depend on investors' assessment of the likelihood that the firm will default. For example, investors place a higher probability of default on JCPenney than on Apple, forcing JCPenney to pay a larger credit spread, which is reflected in a higher interest rate.

credit risk The risk of default by the issuer of any bond that is not default free; it is an indication that the bond's cash flows are not known with certainty.

Are Treasuries Really Default-Free Securities?

Most investors treat U.S. Treasury securities as risk free, meaning that they believe there is no chance of default (a convention we follow in this book). But are Treasuries really risk free? The answer depends on what you mean by "risk free."

No one can be certain that the U.S. government will never default on its bonds—but most people believe the probability of such an event is very small. More importantly, the default probability is smaller than for any other bond. So saying that the yield on a U.S. Treasury security is risk free really means that the Treasury security is the lowest-risk investment denominated in U.S. dollars in the world.

That said, there have been occasions in the past where Treasury holders did not receive exactly what they were promised: In 1790, Treasury Secretary Alexander Hamilton lowered the interest rate on outstanding debt and in 1933 President Franklin Roosevelt suspended bondholders' right to be paid in gold rather than currency.

A new risk emerged in mid-2011 when a series of large budget deficits brought the United States up against the debt ceiling, a constraint imposed by Congress limiting the overall amount of debt the government can incur. An act of Congress was required by August 2011 for the Treasury to meet its obligations and avoid a default. In response to the political uncertainty about whether Congress would raise the ceiling in time, Standard & Poor's downgraded its rating of U.S. Government bonds. Congress ultimately raised the debt ceiling and no default occurred. The incident did, however, serve as a reminder that perhaps no investment is truly "risk free."

---

[5]Because trading in corporate bonds is much less liquid than trading in Treasuries, part of the increased interest rate is to compensate investors for this lack of liquidity.

LISA BLACK

Lisa Black is Managing Director at Teachers Insurance and Annuity Association, a major financial services company. A Chartered Financial Analyst, she oversees a variety of fixed income funds, including money market, intermediate bond, high-yield, emerging market debt, and inflation-linked bond funds.

QUESTION: *When people think about the financial markets, many of them picture the equity markets. How big and how active are the bond markets compared to the equity markets?*

ANSWER: The dollar volume of bonds traded daily is about 10 times that of equity markets. For example, a single $15 billion issue of 10-year Treasury bonds will sell in one day. The market value of the Barclays Capital U.S. Universal Bond Index of dollar-denominated debt as of June 30, 2009, was $13.8 trillion, with the U.S. Aggregate Index (investment-grade debt) accounting for almost 90%. It includes Treasuries, agencies, corporate bonds, and mortgage-backed securities. Other major sectors of the Universal Index include corporate high-yield bonds, Eurodollar bonds, emerging markets, and private placements.

QUESTION: *How do the bond markets operate?*

ANSWER: Firms and governments turn to bond markets when they need to borrow money to fund new construction projects, finance acquisitions, and for general corporate purposes. On the other side, institutions like TIAA-CREF, endowments, and foundations have funds to invest. Wall Street investment bankers serve as intermediaries, matching up borrowers with creditors in terms of maturity needs and risk appetite. Because we provide annuities for college professors, for example, we invest money for longer periods of time than an insurance company that needs funds to pay claims. In the institutional world, bond funds typically trade in blocks of bonds ranging from $5 million to $50 million at a time.

QUESTION: *What drives changes in the values of Treasury bonds?*

ANSWER: The simple answer is that when interest rates rise, bond prices fall. The key is to dig below that reality to see *why* interest rates rise and fall. A major factor is investors' expectations for inflation and economic growth. Interest rates generally rise when the expectation is that growth will accelerate, because

inflation won't be far behind. During the 2008–2009 recession, interest rates dropped as the Federal Reserve injected liquidity into the system. There was also a flight to quality after the bankruptcy of Lehman Brothers. The value of The Reserve Fund fell drastically as its holdings of about $785 million of Lehman's short-term debt securities became all but worthless. Worried retail and institutional investors sold their money market funds and purchased U.S. Treasury bills and notes to protect their principal. With increased demand, interest rates on risk-free Treasury securities fell sharply. At one point, T-bills even had a negative yield.

QUESTION: *What impact did the 2008–2009 financial crisis have on the bond market? What changes do you anticipate going forward as a result?*

ANSWER: While the effects of the crisis on equity markets have been widely discussed, the effects on the bond market have been just as profound. Particularly noteworthy is the role governments and central bankers have played—and likely will continue to play—to stabilize financial institutions deemed too big or important to fail. The Fed introduced an unprecedented number of stimulus programs to unfreeze credit markets, including programs to guarantee money funds. The challenge will be how and when the various support programs and financial infusions will end and/or be paid back. In addition, the rating agencies' role and ratings methodologies will likely be subject to greater scrutiny, both from regulators and investors.

In the corporate sector, many borrowers—the automotive industries, for example—could not raise debt financing during the crisis. Credit spreads widened dramatically as investors shunned even AAA- and AA-rated credits. Major institutional investors sat on the sidelines for several months, and the corporate bond new-issue market was essentially nonexistent. Not until the federal government announced programs to increase liquidity did institutional investors reenter the market, first buying only the highest credit-quality instruments, such as first mortgage bonds issued by utilities and government-guaranteed mortgage-backed securities. Investors then began to move down the credit-quality chain, selectively focusing on issuers that could weather an economic downturn.

Corporate Bond Yields

How does the credit risk of default affect bond prices and yields? The cash flows promised by the bond are the most that bondholders can hope to receive. Due to credit risk, the cash flows that a purchaser of a corporate bond actually *expects* to receive may be less than that amount. For example, GM struggled financially in 2006 and 2007, substantially increasing the chance that they would default on their bonds, and GM subsequently did in 2009. Realizing this risk, investors in GM bonds incorporated an increased probability that the bond payments would not be made as promised and prices of the bonds fell. Because the yield to maturity of GM's bonds is computed by comparing the price to the *promised* cash flows, the yield to maturity *increased* as the probability of being paid as promised decreased. This example highlights the following general truths:

1. Investors pay less for bonds with credit risk than they would for an otherwise identical default-free bond.

2. Because the yield to maturity for a bond is calculated using the promised cash flows instead of the *expected* cash flows, the yield of bonds with credit risk will be higher than that of otherwise identical default-free bonds.

These two points lead us to an important conclusion: *the yield to maturity of a default-able bond is not equal to the expected return of investing in the bond.* The promised cash flows used to determine the yield to maturity are always higher than the expected cash flows investors use to calculate the expected return. As a result, the yield to maturity will always be higher than the expected return of investing in the bond. *Moreover, a higher yield to maturity does not necessarily imply that a bond's expected return is higher.*

Bond Ratings

investment-grade bonds Bonds in the top four categories of credit-worthiness with a low risk of default.

The probability of default is clearly important to the price you are willing to pay for a corporate bond. How do you assess a firm's likelihood of default? Several companies rate the creditworthiness of bonds and make this information available to investors. By consulting these ratings, investors can assess the creditworthiness of a particular bond issue. The ratings therefore encourage widespread investor participation and relatively liquid markets. The two best-known bond-rating companies are Standard & Poor's and Moody's. Table 6.6 summarizes the rating classes each company uses. Bonds with the highest rating (Aaa or AAA) are judged to be least likely to default.

speculative bonds, junk bonds, or high-yield bonds Bonds in one of the bottom five categories of creditworthiness (below investment grade) that have a high risk of default.

Bonds in the top four categories are often referred to as **investment-grade bonds** because of their low default risk. Bonds in the bottom five categories are often called **speculative bonds**, **junk bonds**, **or high-yield bonds** because their likelihood of default is high and so they promise higher yields. The rating depends on the risk of bankruptcy as well as the bondholders' ability to lay claim to the firm's assets in the event of such a bankruptcy. Thus, debt issues with a low-priority claim in bankruptcy will have a lower rating than issues from the same company that have a high priority in bankruptcy or that are backed by a specific asset such as a building or a plant.

Corporate Yield Curves

default spread or credit spread The difference between the risk-free interest rate on U.S. Treasury notes and the interest rates on all other loans. The magnitude of the credit spread will depend on investors' assessment of the likelihood that a particular firm will default.

Just as we can construct a yield curve from risk-free Treasury securities, we can plot a similar yield curve for corporate bonds. Figure 6.6 shows the average yields of U.S. corporate coupon bonds with three different Standard & Poor's bond ratings: two curves are for investment-grade bonds (AAA and BBB) and one is for junk bonds (B). Figure 6.6 also includes the U.S. (coupon-paying) Treasury yield curve. We refer to the difference between the yields of the corporate bonds and the Treasury yields as the **default spread** or **credit spread**. This difference can be seen in Figure 6.6 as the distance between the bottom blue line for Treasuries and each of the red, green, and purple lines as default probability increases. Credit spreads fluctuate as perceptions regarding the probability of default change. Note that the credit spread is high for bonds with low ratings and therefore a greater likelihood of default.

TABLE 6.6

Bond Ratings and the Number of U.S. Public Firms with Those Ratings for Fiscal Year 2011

Moody's	Standard & Poor's	Number of Public Firms	Description (Moody's)
Investment Grade Debt			
Aaa	AAA	6	Judged to be of the best quality. They carry the smallest degree of investment risk and are generally referred to as "gilt edged."
Aa	AA	19	Judged to be of high quality by all standards. Together with the Aaa group, they constitute what are generally known as high-grade bonds.
A	A	177	Possess many favorable investment attributes and are considered as upper-medium-grade obligations. Factors giving security to principal and interest are considered adequate at present, but may not remain that way.
Baa	BBB	431	Are considered as medium-grade obligations (i.e., they are neither highly protected nor poorly secured).
Speculative Bonds ("Junk Bonds")			
Ba	BB	331	Judged to have speculative elements; their future cannot be considered as well assured.
B	B	321	Generally lack characteristics of the desirable investment. Assurance of interest and principal payments over any long period may be small.
Caa	CCC	12	Are of poor standing. Such issues may be in default or there may be present elements of danger with respect to principal or interest.
Ca	CC	1	Are speculative to a high degree. Such issues are often in default or have other marked shortcomings.
C	C, D	5	Lowest-rated class of bonds, and issues so rated can be regarded as having extremely poor prospects of ever attaining any real investment standing.

Source: www.moodys.com and S&P Compustat.

FIGURE 6.6

Corporate Yield Curves for Various Ratings, July 2013

This figure shows the yield curve for U.S. Treasury securities and yield curves for corporate securities with ratings AA (in green), and BBB (in orange). Note how the yield to maturity is higher for the corporate bonds, which have a higher probability of default than the U.S. Treasury securities.

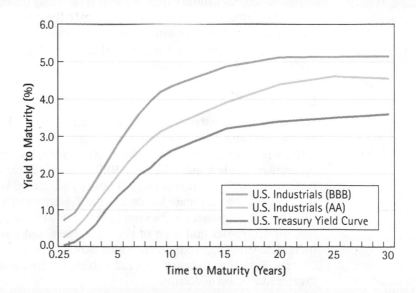

Source: Bloomberg.

EXAMPLE 6.10

Credit Spreads and
Bond Prices

PROBLEM

Your firm has a credit rating of AA. You notice that the credit spread for 10-year maturity AA debt is 90 basis points (0.90%). Your firm's 10-year debt has a coupon rate of 5%. You see that new 10-year Treasury notes are being issued at par with a coupon rate of 4.5%. What should be the price of your outstanding 10-year bonds?

SOLUTION

PLAN

If the credit spread is 90 basis points, then the yield to maturity (YTM) on your debt should be the YTM on similar Treasuries plus 0.9%. The fact that new 10-year Treasuries are being issued at par with coupons of 4.5% means that with a coupon rate of 4.5%, these notes are selling for $100 per $100 face value. Thus, their YTM is 4.5% and your debt's YTM should be 4.5% + 0.9% = 5.4%. The cash flows on your bonds are $5 per year for every $100 face value, paid as $2.50 every six months. The six-month rate corresponding to a 5.4% yield is 5.4%/2 = 2.7%. Armed with this information, you can use Eq. 6.3 to compute the price of your bonds.

EXECUTE

$$2.50 \times \frac{1}{0.027}\left(1 - \frac{1}{1.027^{20}}\right) + \frac{100}{1.027^{20}} = \$96.94$$

EVALUATE

Your bonds offer a higher coupon (5% vs. 4.5%) than Treasuries of the same maturity, but sell for a lower price ($96.94 vs. $100). The reason is the credit spread. Your firm's higher probability of default leads investors to demand a higher YTM on your debt. To provide a higher YTM, the purchase price for the debt must be lower. If your debt paid 5.4% coupons, it would sell at $100, the same as the Treasuries. But to get that price, you would have to offer coupons that are 90 basis points higher than those on the Treasuries—exactly enough to offset the credit spread.

The Credit Crisis and Bond Yields

The financial crisis that engulfed the world's economies in 2008 originated as a credit crisis that first emerged in August 2007. At that time, problems in the mortgage market had led to the bankruptcy of several large mortgage lenders. The default of these firms, and the downgrading of many of the bonds backed by mortgages these firms had made, caused many investors to reassess the risk of other bonds in their portfolios. As perceptions of risk increased, and investors attempted to move into safer U.S. Treasury securities, the prices of corporate bonds fell and so their credit spreads rose relative to Treasuries, as shown in Figure 6.7. Panel (a) shows the yield spreads for long-term corporate bonds, where we can see that spreads of even the highest-rated Aaa bonds increased dramatically, from a typical level of 0.5% to over 2% by the fall of 2008. Panel (b) shows a similar pattern for the rate banks had to pay on short-term loans compared to the yields of short-term Treasury bills. This increase in borrowing costs made it more costly for firms to raise the capital needed for new investment, slowing economic growth. The decline in these spreads in early 2009 was viewed by many as an important first step in mitigating the ongoing impact of the financial crisis on the rest of the economy.

As we indicated at the beginning of this chapter, the bond market, while less well-known than the stock markets, is large and important. Because debt is a substantial part of the financing of most corporations, a financial manager needs to understand bonds and how investors price the company's bonds. In this chapter, we have introduced the major types of bonds, how bonds repay investors, and how they are priced. In Chapter 15, we will discuss the bond markets further, including the process a firm goes through to issue debt.

FIGURE 6.7

Yield Spreads and the
Financial Crisis

Panel (a) shows the yield spread between long-term (30-year) U.S. corporate and Treasury bonds. Panel (b) shows the yield spread of short-term loans to major international banks (called LIBOR) and U.S. Treasury bills (also referred to as the *Treasury-Eurodollar* or *"TED" spread*). Note the dramatic increase in these spreads beginning in August 2007 and again in September 2008, before beginning to decline in late 2008 and early 2009.

Panel (a): Yield Spread of Long-Term Corporate
Bonds Versus U.S. Treasury Bonds

Panel (b): Yield Spread of Short-Term Loans to Major
International Banks (LIBOR) Versus U.S. Treasury Bonds

Source: Bloomberg.com.

9. What is a junk bond?

10. How will the yield to maturity of a bond vary with the bond's risk of default?

<table>
<tr><td>**MyFinanceLab**</td><td>Here is what you should know after reading this chapter. MyFinanceLab will help you identify what you know, and where to go when you need to practice.</td></tr>
</table>

Key Points and Equations	Key Terms	Online Practice
6.1 Bond Terminology • Bonds pay both coupon and principal or face value payments to investors. By convention, the coupon rate of a bond is expressed as an APR, so the amount of each coupon payment, CPN, is: $$CPN = \frac{\text{Coupon Rate} \times \text{Face Value}}{\text{Number of Coupon Payments per Year}} \quad (6.1)$$	bond certificate, p. 156 coupon rate, p. 156 coupons, p. 156 face value, p. 156 maturity date, p. 156 par value, p. 156 principal amount, p. 156 term, p. 156	MyFinanceLab Study Plan 6.1
6.2 Zero-Coupon Bonds • Zero-coupon bonds make no coupon payments, so investors receive only the bond's face value. • The rate of return of a bond is called its yield to maturity (or yield). The yield to maturity of a bond is the discount rate that sets the present value of the promised bond payments equal to the current market price of the bond. • The yield to maturity for a zero-coupon bond is given by: $$1 + YTM_n = \left(\frac{\text{Face Value}}{\text{Price}}\right)^{1/n} \quad (6.2)$$ • The risk-free interest rate for an investment until date n equals the yield to maturity of a risk-free zero-coupon bond that matures on date n. A plot of these rates against maturity is called the zero-coupon yield curve.	discount, p. 158 pure discount bond, p. 158 spot interest rates, p. 160 Treasury bills, p. 157 yield to maturity (YTM), p. 158 zero-coupon bond, p. 157 zero-coupon yield curve, p. 160	MyFinanceLab Study Plan 6.2 Financial Calculator Tutorial: Solving for the Yield to Maturity of a Bond
6.3 Coupon Bonds • The yield to maturity for a coupon bond is the discount rate, y, that equates the present value of the bond's future cash flows with its price: $$P = CPN \times \frac{1}{y}\left(1 - \frac{1}{(1+y)^N}\right) + \frac{FV}{(1+y)^N} \quad (6.3)$$	coupon bonds, p. 161 Treasury bonds, p. 161 Treasury notes, p. 161	MyFinanceLab Study Plan 6.3 Financial Calculator Tutorial: Bond Valuation with Interest Compounded Semiannually

6.4 Why Bond Prices Change

- A bond will trade at a premium if its coupon rate exceeds its yield to maturity. It will trade at a discount if its coupon rate is less than its yield to maturity. If a bond's coupon rate equals its yield to maturity, it trades at par.
- As a bond approaches maturity, the price of the bond approaches its face value.
- Bond prices change as interest rates change. When interest rates rise, bond prices fall, and vice versa.
- Long-term zero-coupon bonds are more sensitive to changes in interest rates than are short-term zero-coupon bonds.
- Bonds with low coupon rates are more sensitive to changes in interest rates than are similar maturity bonds with high coupon rates.

clean price, p. 172
dirty price, p. 172
invoice price, p. 172
par, p. 166
premium, p. 166

MyFinanceLab
Study Plan 6.4

Interactive
Interest Rate
Sensitivity
Analysis

6.5 Corporate Bonds

- When a bond issuer does not make a bond payment in full, the issuer has defaulted.
- The risk that default can occur is called default or credit risk. United States Treasury securities are free of default risk.
- The expected return of a corporate bond, which is the firm's debt cost of capital, equals the risk-free rate of interest plus a risk premium. The expected return is less than the bond's yield to maturity because the yield to maturity of a bond is calculated using the promised cash flows, not the expected cash flows.
- Bond ratings summarize the creditworthiness of bonds for investors.
- The difference between yields on Treasury securities and yields on corporate bonds is called the credit spread or default spread. The credit spread compensates investors for the difference between promised and expected cash flows and for the risk of default.

corporate bonds, p. 174
credit risk, p. 175
default (credit) spread,
   p. 177
high-yield bonds,
   p. 177
investment-grade
   bonds, p. 177
junk bonds, p. 177
speculative bonds,
   p. 177

MyFinanceLab
Study Plan 6.5

CRITICAL
THINKING

1. How is a bond like a loan?

2. How does an investor receive a return from buying a bond?

3. How is yield to maturity related to the concept of rate of return?

4. Does a bond's yield to maturity determine its price or does the price determine the yield to maturity?

5. Explain why the yield of a bond that trades at a discount exceeds the bond's coupon rate.

6. Explain the relationship between interest rates and bond prices.

7. Why are longer-term bonds more sensitive to changes in interest rates than shorter-term bonds?

8. Explain why the expected return of a corporate bond does not equal its yield to maturity.

PROBLEMS

All problems in this chapter are available in MyFinanceLab.

Bond Terminology

1. Consider a 10-year bond with a face value of $1000 that has a coupon rate of 5.5%, with semiannual payments.
   a. What is the coupon payment for this bond?
   b. Draw the cash flows for the bond on a timeline.

2. Assume that a bond will make payments every six months as shown on the following timeline (using six-month periods):

   a. What is the maturity of the bond (in years)?
   b. What is the coupon rate (in percent)?
   c. What is the face value?

3. Your company wants to raise $10 million by issuing 20-year zero-coupon bonds. If the yield to maturity on the bonds will be 6% (annually compounded APR), what total principal amount of bonds must you issue?

Zero-Coupon Bonds

4. The following table summarizes prices of various default-free zero-coupon bonds (expressed as a percentage of face value):

Maturity (years)	1	2	3	4	5
Price (per $100 face value)	$95.51	$91.05	$86.38	$81.65	$76.51

   a. Compute the yield to maturity for each bond.
   b. Plot the zero-coupon yield curve (for the first five years).
   c. Is the yield curve upward sloping, downward sloping, or flat?

Use the following information for Problems 5–7. The current zero-coupon yield curve for risk-free bonds is as follows:

Maturity (years)	1	2	3	4	5
YTM	5.00%	5.50%	5.75%	5.95%	6.05%

5. What is the price per $100 face value of a two-year, zero-coupon, risk-free bond?

6. What is the price per $100 face value of a four-year, zero-coupon, risk-free bond?

7. What is the risk-free interest rate for a five-year maturity?

8. In the Global Financial Crisis box in Section 6.2, Bloomberg.com reported that the three-month Treasury bill sold for $100.002556 per $100 face value. What is the yield to maturity of this bond, expressed as an EAR?

Coupon Bonds

9. For each of the following pairs of Treasury securities (each with $1000 par value), identify which will have the higher price:
   a. A three-year zero-coupon bond or a five-year zero coupon bond?
   b. A three-year zero-coupon bond or a three-year 4% coupon bond?
   c. A two-year 5% coupon bond or a two-year 6% coupon bond?

10. The yield to maturity of a $1000 bond with a 7% coupon rate, semiannual coupons, and two years to maturity is 7.6% APR, compounded semiannually. What must its price be?

11. Assume the current Treasury yield curve shows that the spot rates for six months, one year, and 1½ years are 1%, 1.1%, and 1.3%, all quoted as semiannually compounded APRs. What is the price of a $1000 par, 4% coupon bond maturing in 1½ years (the next coupon is exactly six months from now)?

12. Suppose a 10-year, $1000 bond with an 8% coupon rate and semiannual coupons is trading for $1034.74.
   a. What is the bond's yield to maturity (expressed as an APR with semiannual compounding)?
   b. If the bond's yield to maturity changes to 9% APR, what will the bond's price be?

13. Suppose a five-year, $1000 bond with annual coupons has a price of $900 and a yield to maturity of 6%. What is the bond's coupon rate?

14. Assume that the six-month Treasury spot rate is 1.6% APR, and the one-year rate is 2% APR, both compounded semiannually. What is the price of a one-year $1000 par Treasury bond with 2% coupons?

Why Bond Prices Change

15. The prices of several bonds with face values of $1000 are summarized in the following table:

Bond	A	B	C	D
Price	$972.50	$1040.75	$1150.00	$1000.00

For each bond, state whether it trades at a discount, at par, or at a premium.

16. You have purchased a 10% coupon bond for $1040. What will happen to the bond's price if market interest rates rise?

17. Suppose a seven-year, $1000 bond with an 8% coupon rate and semiannual coupons is trading with a yield to maturity of 6.75%.
   a. Is this bond currently trading at a discount, at par, or at a premium? Explain.
   b. If the yield to maturity of the bond rises to 7.00% (APR with semiannual compounding), what price will the bond trade for?

Suppose that General Motors Acceptance Corporation issued a bond with 10 years until maturity, a face value of $1000, and a coupon rate of 7% (annual payments). The yield to maturity on this bond when it was issued was 6%. Use this information to solve Problems 18–20.

18. What was the price of this bond when it was issued?

19. Assuming the yield to maturity remains constant, what is the price of the bond immediately before it makes its first coupon payment?

20. Assuming the yield to maturity remains constant, what is the price of the bond immediately after it makes its first coupon payment?

21. Your company currently has $1000 par, 6% coupon bonds with 10 years to maturity and a price of $1078. If you want to issue new 10-year coupon bonds at par, what coupon rate do you need to set? Assume that for both bonds, the next coupon payment is due in exactly six months.

22. Suppose you purchase a 10-year bond with 6% annual coupons. You hold the bond for four years, and sell it immediately after receiving the fourth coupon. If the bond's yield to maturity was 5% when you purchased and sold the bond, what cash flows will you pay and receive from your investment in the bond per $100 face value?

Consider the following bonds for Problems 23 and 24:

Bond	Coupon Rate (annual payments)	Maturity (years)
A	0%	15
B	0%	10
C	4%	15
D	8%	10

23. What is the percentage change in the price of each bond if its yield to maturity falls from 6% to 5%?

24. Which of the bonds A–D is most sensitive to a 1% drop in interest rates from 6% to 5% and why? Which bond is least sensitive? Provide an intuition explanation for your answer.

25. Suppose you purchase a 30-year, zero-coupon bond with a yield to maturity of 6%. You hold the bond for five years before selling it.
    a. If the bond's yield to maturity is 6% when you sell it, what is the annualized rate of return of your investment?
    b. If the bond's yield to maturity is 7% when you sell it, what is the annualized rate of return of your investment?
    c. If the bond's yield to maturity is 5% when you sell it, what is the annualized rate of return of your investment?
    d. Even if a bond has no chance of default, is your investment risk free if you plan to sell it before it matures? Explain.

Corporate Bonds

26. The following table summarizes the yields to maturity on several one-year, zero-coupon securities:

Security	Yield (%)
Treasury	3.1
AAA corporate	3.2
BBB corporate	4.2
B corporate	4.9

a. What is the price (expressed as a percentage of the face value) of a one-year, zero-coupon corporate bond with an AAA rating?

b. What is the credit spread on AAA-rated corporate bonds?

c. What is the credit spread on B-rated corporate bonds?

d. How does the credit spread change with the bond rating? Why?

27. Andrew Industries is contemplating issuing a 30-year bond with a coupon rate of 7% (annual coupon payments) and a face value of $1000. Andrew believes it can get a rating of A from Standard & Poor's. However, due to recent financial difficulties at the company, Standard & Poor's is warning that it may downgrade Andrew Industries bonds to BBB. Yields on A-rated, long-term bonds are currently 6.5%, and yields on BBB-rated bonds are 6.9%.

a. What is the price of the bond if Andrew Industries maintains the A rating for the bond issue?

b. What will the price of the bond be if it is downgraded?

28. Your firm has a credit rating of A. You notice that the credit spread for five-year maturity A debt is 85 basis points (0.85%). Your firm's five-year debt has a coupon rate of 6%. You see that new five-year Treasury notes are being issued at par with a coupon rate of 2.0%. What should the price of your outstanding five-year bonds be per $100 of face value?

29. HMK Enterprises would like to raise $10 million to invest in capital expenditures. The company plans to issue five-year bonds with a face value of $1000 and a coupon rate of 6.5% (annual payments). The following table summarizes the yield to maturity for five-year (annual-pay) coupon corporate bonds of various ratings:

Rating	AAA	AA	A	BBB	BB
YTM	6.20%	6.30%	6.50%	6.90%	7.50%

a. Assuming the bonds will be rated AA, what will the price of the bonds be?

b. How much of the total principal amount of these bonds must HMK issue to raise $10 million today, assuming the bonds are AA rated? (Because HMK cannot issue a fraction of a bond, assume that all fractions are rounded to the nearest whole number.)

c. What must the rating of the bonds be for them to sell at par?

d. Suppose that when the bonds are issued, the price of each bond is $959.54. What is the likely rating of the bonds? Are they junk bonds?

30. A BBB-rated corporate bond has a yield to maturity of 8.2%. A U.S. Treasury security has a yield to maturity of 6.5%. These yields are quoted as APRs with semiannual compounding. Both bonds pay semiannual coupons at a rate of 7% and have five years to maturity.

a. What is the price (expressed as a percentage of the face value) of the Treasury bond?

b. What is the price (expressed as a percentage of the face value) of the BBB-rated corporate bond?

c. What is the credit spread on the BBB bonds?

DATA CASE

You are an intern with Ford Motor Company in its corporate finance division. The firm is planning to issue $50 million of 12% annual coupon bonds with a 10-year maturity. The firm anticipates an increase in its bond rating. Your boss wants you to determine the gain in the proceeds of the new issue if it is rated above the firm's current bond rating. To prepare this information, you will have to determine Ford's current debt rating and the yield curve for its particular rating.

1. Begin by finding the current U.S. Treasury yield curve. At the Treasury Web site (www.treas.gov), search using the term "yield curve" and select "US Treasury—Daily Treasury Yield Curve." *Beware*: There will likely be two links with the same title. Look at the description below the link and select the one that does NOT say "Real Yield . . ." You want the nominal rates. Copy the table into Excel.

2. Find the current yield spreads for the various bond ratings. Unfortunately, the current spreads are available only for a fee, so you will use old ones. Go to BondsOnline (www.bondsonline.com) and click "Today's Market." Next, click "US Corporate Bond Spreads." Copy this table to the same Excel file as the Treasury yields.

3. Find the current bond rating for Ford Motor Co. Go to Standard & Poor's Web site. Select your country. Look for the "Find a Rating" box under "Ratings" and enter Ford Motor Co. and select Ford Motor Co. from the list it returns. At this point you will have to register (it's free) or enter the username and password provided by your instructor. Use the issuer credit rating for "local long term."

4. Return to Excel and create a timeline with the cash flows and discount rates you will need to value the new bond issue.
   a. To create the required spot rates for Ford's issue, add the appropriate spread to the Treasury yield of the same maturity.
   b. The yield curve and spread rates you have found do not cover every year that you will need for the new bonds. Specifically, you do not have yields or spreads for four-, six-, eight-, and nine-year maturities. Fill these in by linearly interpolating the given yields and spreads. For example, the four-year spot rate and spread will be the average of the three- and five-year rates. The six-year rate and spread will be the average of the five- and seven-year rates. For years eight and nine you will have to spread the difference between years seven and ten across the two years.
   c. To compute the spot rates for Ford's current debt rating, add the yield spread to the Treasury rate for each maturity. However, note that the spread is in basis points, which are 1/100th of a percentage point.
   d. Compute the cash flows that would be paid to bondholders each year and add them to the timeline.

5. Use the spot rates to calculate the present value of each cash flow paid to the bondholders.

6. Compute the issue price of the bond and its initial yield to maturity.

7. Repeat steps 4–6 based on the assumption that Ford is able to raise its bond rating by one level. Compute the new yield based on the higher rating and the new bond price that would result.

8. Compute the additional cash proceeds that could be raised from the issue if the rating were improved.

Solving for the Yield to Maturity of a Bond Using a Financial Calculator

You are looking to purchase a three-year, $1000 par, 10% annual coupon bond. Payments begin one year from now. The price of the bond is $1074.51 per $1000 par value. What is the yield to maturity of the bond? [answer: 7.15%]

HP-10BII

[Orange Shift] [C]	Press [Orange Shift] and then the [C] button to clear all previous entries.
[3] [N]	Enter the number of periods.
[1] [0] [0] [PMT]	Enter the payment amount per period.
[1] [0] [0] [0] [FV]	Enter the par value of the bond you will receive in year 3.
[1] [0] [7] [4] [•] [5] [1] [+/−] [PV]	Enter present value or price of the bond you solved for earlier.
[I/YR]	Solves for the yield to maturity.

TI-BAII Plus Professional

[2ND] [FV]	Press [2ND] and then the [FV] button to clear all previous entries.
[3] [N]	Enter the number of periods.
[1] [0] [0] [PMT]	Enter the payment amount per period.
[1] [0] [0] [0] [FV]	Enter the par value of the bond you will receive in year 3.
[1] [0] [7] [4] [•] [5] [1] [+/−] [PV]	Enter present value or price of the bond you solved for earlier.
[CPT] [I/Y]	Solves for the yield to maturity.

The Yield Curve and the Law of One Price

Thus far, we have focused on the relationship between the price of an individual bond and its yield to maturity. In this section, we explore the relationship between the prices and yields of different bonds. In Chapter 3, we saw how market forces keep the same asset from having two prices at the same time—we call this the Valuation Principle's *Law of One Price*. Using the Law of One Price, we show that given the spot interest rates, which are the yields of default-free zero-coupon bonds, we can determine the price and yield of any other default-free bond. As a result, the yield curve provides sufficient information to evaluate all such bonds.

Valuing a Coupon Bond with Zero-Coupon Prices

We begin with the observation that it is possible to replicate the cash flows of a coupon bond using zero-coupon bonds. Therefore, we can use the Law of One Price to compute the price of a coupon bond from the prices of zero-coupon bonds. For example, we can replicate a three-year, $1000 bond that pays 10% annual coupons using three zero-coupon bonds as follows:

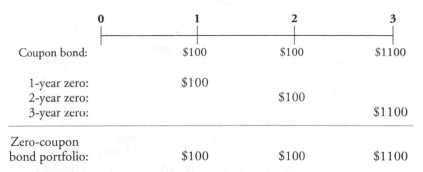

We match each coupon payment to a zero-coupon bond with a face value equal to the coupon payment and a term equal to the time remaining to the coupon date. Similarly, we match the final bond payment (final coupon plus return of face value) in three years to a three-year zero-coupon bond with a corresponding face value of $1100. Because the coupon bond cash flows are identical to the cash flows of the portfolio of zero-coupon bonds, the Law of One Price states that the price of the portfolio of zero-coupon bonds must be the same as the price of the coupon bond.

To illustrate, assume that current zero-coupon bond yields and prices are as shown in Table 6.7 (they are the same as in Example 6.1).

We can calculate the cost of the zero-coupon bond portfolio that replicates the three-year coupon bond as follows:

Zero-Coupon Bond	Face Value Required	Cost
1 Year	100	96.62
2 Years	100	92.45
3 Years	1100	$11 \times 87.63 = 963.93$
		Total Cost: $1153.00

TABLE 6.7

Yields and Prices (per $100 Face Value) for Zero-Coupon Bonds

Maturity	1 Year	2 Years	3 Years	4 Years
YTM	3.50%	4.00%	4.50%	4.75%
Price	$96.62	$92.45	$87.63	$83.06

By the Law of One Price, the three-year coupon bond must trade for a price of $1153. If the price of the coupon bond were higher, you could earn an arbitrage profit by selling the coupon bond and buying the zero-coupon bond portfolio. If the price of the coupon bond were lower, you could earn an arbitrage profit by buying the coupon bond and selling the zero-coupon bonds.

Valuing a Coupon Bond Using Zero-Coupon Yields

To this point, we have used the zero-coupon bond *prices* to derive the price of the coupon bond. Alternatively, we can use the zero-coupon bond *yields*. Recall that the yield to maturity of a zero-coupon bond is the competitive market interest rate for a risk-free investment with a term equal to the term of the zero-coupon bond. Since the cash flows of the bond are its coupon payments and face value repayment, the price of a coupon bond must equal the present value of its coupon payments and face value discounted at the competitive market interest rates (see Eq. 5.7 in Chapter 5):

Price of a Coupon Bond

$$P = PV(\text{Bond Cash Flows})$$

$$= \frac{CPN}{1 + YTM_1} + \frac{CPN}{(1 + YTM_2)^2} + \cdots + \frac{CPN + FV}{(1 + YTM_n)^n} \tag{6.4}$$

where CPN is the bond coupon payment, YTM_n is the yield to maturity of a *zero-coupon* bond that matures at the same time as the nth coupon payment, and FV is the face value of the bond. For the three-year, $1000 bond with 10% annual coupons considered earlier, we can use Eq. 6.4 to calculate its price using the zero-coupon yields in Table 6.7:

$$P = \frac{100}{1.035} + \frac{100}{1.04^2} + \frac{100 + 1000}{1.045^3} = \$1153$$

This price is identical to the price we computed earlier by replicating the bond. Thus, we can determine the no-arbitrage price of a coupon bond by discounting its cash flows using the zero-coupon yields. In other words, the information in the zero-coupon yield curve is sufficient to price all other risk-free bonds.

Coupon Bond Yields

Given the yields for zero-coupon bonds, we can use Eq. 6.4 to price a coupon bond. In Section 6.3, we saw how to compute the yield to maturity of a coupon bond from its price. Combining these results, we can determine the relationship between the yields of zero-coupon bonds and coupon-paying bonds.

Consider again the three-year, $1000 bond with 10% annual coupons. Given the zero-coupon yields in Table 6.7, we calculate a price for this bond of $1153. From Eq. 6.3, the yield to maturity of this bond is the rate y that satisfies:

$$P = 1153 = \frac{100}{(1+y)} + \frac{100}{(1+y)^2} + \frac{100 + 1000}{(1+y)^3}$$

We can solve for the yield by using a financial calculator or spreadsheet:

	N	I/Y	PV	PMT	FV
Given:	3		−1153	100	1000
Solve for:		4.44			

Excel Formula: =RATE(NPER,PMT,PV,FV)=RATE(3,100,−1153,1000)

Therefore, the yield to maturity of the bond is 4.44%. We can check this result directly as follows:

$$P = \frac{100}{1.0444} + \frac{100}{1.0444^2} + \frac{100 + 1000}{1.0444^3} = \$1153$$

Because the coupon bond provides cash flows at different points in time, the yield to maturity of a coupon bond is a weighted average of the yields of the zero-coupon bonds of equal and shorter maturities. The weights depend (in a complex way) on the magnitude of the cash flows each period. In this example, the zero-coupon bonds yields were 3.5%, 4.0%, and 4.5%. For this coupon bond, most of the value in the present value calculation comes from the present value of the third cash flow because it includes the principal, so the yield is closest to the three-year zero-coupon yield of 4.5%.

EXAMPLE 6.11

Yields on Bonds with the Same Maturity

MyFinanceLab

PROBLEM

Given the following zero-coupon yields, compare the yield to maturity for a three-year zero-coupon bond, a three-year coupon bond with 4% annual coupons, and a three-year coupon bond with 10% annual coupons. All of these bonds are default free.

Maturity	1 Year	2 Years	3 Years	4 Years
Zero-Coupon YTM	3.50%	4.00%	4.50%	4.75%

SOLUTION

PLAN

From the information provided, the yield to maturity of the three-year zero-coupon bond is 4.50%. Also, because the yields match those in Table 6.7, we already calculated the yield to maturity for the 10% coupon bond as 4.44%. To compute the yield for the 4% coupon bond, we first need to calculate its price, which we can do using Eq. 6.4. Since the coupons are 4%, paid annually, they are $40 per year for three years. The $1000 face value will be repaid at that time. Once we have the price, we can use Eq. 6.3 to compute the yield to maturity.

EXECUTE

Using Eq. 6.4, we have:

$$P = \frac{40}{1.035} + \frac{40}{1.04^2} + \frac{40 + 1000}{1.045^3} = \$986.98$$

The price of the bond with a 4% coupon is $986.98. From Eq. 6.4:

$$\$986.98 = \frac{40}{(1 + y)} + \frac{40}{(1 + y)^2} + \frac{40 + 1000}{(1 + y)^3}$$

We can calculate the yield to maturity using a financial calculator or spreadsheet:

	N	I/Y	PV	PMT	FV
Given:	3		−986.98	40	1000
Solve for:		4.47			

Excel Formula: =RATE(NPER,PMT,PV,FV)=RATE(3,40,−986.98,1000)

(Continued)

To summarize, for the three-year bonds considered:

Coupon Rate	0%	4%	10%
YTM	4.50%	4.47%	4.44%

EVALUATE

Note that even though the bonds all have the same maturity, they have different yields. In fact, holding constant the maturity, the yield decreases as the coupon rate increases. We discuss why below.

Example 6.11 shows that coupon bonds with the same maturity can have different yields depending on their coupon rates. The yield to maturity of a coupon bond is a weighted average of the yields on the zero-coupon bonds. As the coupon increases, earlier cash flows become relatively more important than later cash flows in the calculation of the present value. The shape of the yield curve keys us in on trends with the yield to maturity:

1. If the yield curve is upward sloping (as it is for the yields in Example 6.11), the resulting yield to maturity decreases with the coupon rate of the bond.
2. When the zero-coupon yield curve is downward sloping, the yield to maturity will increase with the coupon rate.
3. With a flat yield curve, all zero-coupon and coupon-paying bonds will have the same yield, independent of their maturities and coupon rates.

Treasury Yield Curves

As we have shown in this section, we can use the zero-coupon yield curve to determine the price and yield to maturity of other risk-free bonds. The plot of the yields of coupon bonds of different maturities is called the *coupon-paying yield curve*. When U.S. bond traders refer to "the yield curve," they are often referring to the coupon-paying Treasury yield curve. As we showed in Example 6.11, two coupon-paying bonds with the same maturity may have different yields. By convention, practitioners always plot the yield of the most recently issued bonds, termed the *on-the-run bonds*. Using similar methods to those employed in this section, we can apply the Law of One Price to determine the zero-coupon bond yields using the coupon-paying yield curve. Thus, either type of yield curve provides enough information to value all other risk-free bonds.

7

Stock Valuation

LEARNING OBJECTIVES

- Describe the basics of common stock, preferred stock, and stock quotes

- Compare how trades are executed on the NYSE and NASDAQ

- Value a stock as the present value of its expected future dividends

- Understand the tradeoff between dividends and growth in stock valuation

- Appreciate the limitations of valuing a stock based on expected dividends

- Value a stock as the present value of the company's total payout

notation

Div_t	dividends paid in year t	P_t	stock price at the end of year t
EPS_t	earnings per share on date t	PV	present value
g	expected dividend growth rate	r_E	equity cost of capital
N	terminal date or forecast horizon		

At 5:00 P.M. on March 21, 2013, footwear and apparel maker Nike, Inc., announced that its quarterly earnings would be higher than expected and that orders for the following year would be strong as well. The next day, Nike's stock price increased by 11% on the New York Stock Exchange to $59.53, with more than 19 million shares being traded—more than four times its average daily volume.

How might an investor decide whether to buy or sell a stock such as Nike at this price? Why would the stock suddenly be worth 11% more after the announcement of this news? What actions can Nike's managers take to further increase the stock price?

To answer these questions, we turn to the Valuation Principle. The Valuation Principle indicates that the price of a security should equal the present value of the expected cash flows an investor will receive from owning it. In this chapter, we apply this idea to stocks. Thus, to value a stock, we need to know the expected cash flows an investor will receive and the appropriate cost of capital with which to discount those cash flows. Both these quantities can be challenging to estimate, and we will develop many of the details needed to do so throughout the remainder of this text.

We begin our study of stock valuation by contrasting the different types of stocks, interpreting a stock quote, and explaining how specialists execute stock trades. We then turn to our first model of stock valuation, the *dividend-discount model*, which considers the dividends and capital gains received by investors who hold the stock for different periods.

7.1 Stock Basics

As discussed in Chapter 1, the ownership of a corporation is divided into shares of stock. A public corporation has many owners and its shares trade on a stock market that provides liquidity for a company's shares and determines the market price for those shares. In this section, we explain what a stock market quote is and introduce the two types of stocks, *common* and *preferred*.

Stock Market Reporting: Stock Quotes

Figure 7.1 shows a stock quote with basic information about Nike's stock from Google Finance (www.google.com/finance) for June 25, 2013.[1] Nike's stock is **common stock**, which means a share of ownership in the corporation gives its owner rights to any common dividends as well as rights to vote on the election of directors, mergers, and other major events. The Web page notes that the company is a public corporation (its shares are widely held and traded in a market) and that its shares trade on the NYSE (New York Stock Exchange) under the *ticker symbol* NKE. A **ticker symbol** is a unique abbreviation assigned to a publicly traded company used when its trades are reported on the ticker (a real-time electronic display of trading activity). Traditionally, shares on the NYSE have ticker symbols consisting of three or fewer characters, while shares on the NASDAQ generally have four or more characters in their ticker symbols. However, for recent listings, such as Facebook, which goes by FB on the NASDAQ and Twitter (TWTR on the NYSE), this convention no longer applies.

During the period mid-February through late June 2013, Nike paid two quarterly dividends to its common shareholders, on February 28, and May 30. The dividends are marked by a "D" and the amount of the dividend. In this case, the dividend was 21 cents per share. Thus, if you owned 1000 shares of NKE, you would have received $0.21 \times 1000 = \$210$ when Nike paid each dividend. The chart also clearly shows the jump in the price of NKE shares in March 2013 that we discussed in the chapter introduction.

Finally, the Web page displays some basic information about the performance of NKE stock. Notice the price of the last trade of NKE shares in the market ($60.39), the price that shares started at when the market opened that day ($60.42), the range of low to high prices reached during trading that day ($59.95 to $60.99), and the volume of trading for the day (5.45 million shares). The total value of all the equity of NKE is its market capitalization, equal to the price per share multiplied by the number of shares outstanding: on June 25, 2013, it was 60.39×893.61 million = \$53.97 billion. Over the preceding 52 weeks, NKE achieved a high price of $66.07 and a low price of $42.55 and had an average daily volume of shares traded of 3.54 million shares. Also, note some basic information about the company: the price-earnings ratio (P/E) and earnings per share (EPS), both of which we discussed in Chapter 2. The Web page also notes that NKE's *beta* is 0.88.[2]

common stock A share of ownership in the corporation, which confers rights to any common dividends as well as rights to vote on election of directors, mergers, and other major events.

ticker symbol A unique abbreviation assigned to a publicly traded company.

---

[1]There are many places on the Internet to get free stock information, such as Yahoo! Finance (http://finance.yahoo.com/), MSN Money (http://moneycentral.msn.com/), the *Wall Street Journal*'s Web site (www.wsj.com), and the exchange sites www.nyse.com and www.nasdaq.com.

[2]*Beta* is a measure of risk that we will discuss in Chapter 12.

FIGURE 7.1

Stock Price Quote
for Nike (NKE)

This screenshot from Google Finance shows the basic stock price information and price history charting for the common stock of Nike. The historical price chart covers the period mid-February through late June 2013. The price of $60.39 is for June 25, 2013.

Source: www.google.com/finance?q=nke.

In preceding chapters, we have learned how financial managers make decisions that affect the value of their company. Although the current price of NKE is $60.39, the stock's price has varied over time, reflecting the expected effects of new decisions and the results of past decisions.

Common Stock

We now examine the rights of common stockholders, including their voice in the running of the corporation. All rights accruing to the shareholders are in proportion to the number of shares they hold.

straight voting Voting for directors where shareholders must vote for each director separately, with each shareholder having as many votes as shares held.

Shareholder Voting. To illustrate the shareholder voting process, consider an election of 10 directors at a company with only two shareholders: Donna and Jonathan. Donna has 600 shares and Jonathan has 400, but they have very different views of how the company should be run. If the company has **straight voting**, each shareholder has as many votes for each director as shares held. That is, for each director, Donna will have 600 votes and

cumulative voting Voting for directors where each shareholder is allocated votes equal to the number of open spots multiplied by his or her number of shares.

Jonathan 400, so Jonathan will lose every vote and have no representation on the board. If the company has **cumulative voting**, each shareholder's total vote allocation for all directors is equal to the number of open spots multiplied by his or her number of shares. With 10 directors up for election, Jonathan is allocated a total of 10×400 votes (4000 votes) and Donna is allocated 10×600 votes (6000 votes) to use across the 10 director spots. Jonathan could allocate all his votes to four directors, ensuring that he has four directors representing his views on the board. Donna would do the same for six directors, ensuring her representation. With cumulative voting, even shareholders with minority blocks (less than 50%) have a chance at representation on the board.

classes Different types of common stock for the same company, often carrying different voting rights.

This example is based on the concept of one share, one vote. Some companies have different types of common stock, called **classes**, which carry different voting rights. This is typical in companies that are family run, or where the founder is still active. For example, Nike has Class A and Class B stock. Phil Knight, Nike's founder, owns almost all the Class A stock, which carries the rights to elect 9 of the company's 12 directors. Google also has Class A and Class B stock. Class A stock has been sold to the public, while Google's founders and managers hold all the Class B stock, each share of which carries 10 times the voting power of a share of Class A stock.

annual meeting Meeting held once per year where shareholders vote on directors and other proposals as well as ask managers questions.

proxy A written authorization for someone else to vote your shares.

proxy contest When two or more groups are competing to collect proxies to prevail in a matter up for shareholder vote (such as election of directors).

Shareholder Rights. Each year, companies hold an **annual meeting** at which managers and directors answer questions from shareholders, and shareholders vote on the election of directors and other proposals. All shareholders have the right to attend the annual meeting and cast their votes directly. In practice, though, most either allow the board to vote for them or direct that their shares be voted for them via **proxy**, or explicit instructions on how they should be voted. Typically, matters at the annual meeting are uncontested, but occasionally a dissident shareholder group will propose an alternative slate of directors or oppose a management proposal. In that case, each side will actively solicit the proxies of all the shareholders so they may win the vote in a **proxy contest**.

As an ownership claim, common stock carries the right to share in the profits of the corporation through dividend payments. Recall from Chapter 1 that dividends are periodic payments, usually in the form of cash, that firms make to shareholders as a partial return on their investment in the corporation. The board of directors decides the timing and amount of each dividend. Shareholders are paid dividends in proportion to the number of shares they own. If the company is liquidated through bankruptcy and there are assets left over after satisfying the claims of the creditors, shareholders divide the remaining assets proportionally based on each shareholder's number of shares.

preferred stock Stock with preference over common shares in payment of dividends and in liquidation.

Preferred Stock

Some companies have an additional issue of stock called **preferred stock**, which has preference over common shares in the distribution of dividends or cash during liquidation. While the directors can, at their discretion, choose not to pay the preferred shareholders a dividend, they cannot pay a dividend to common stockholders unless they pay the promised dividend to preferred shareholders first. For example, Nike has preferred shares that pay a $0.10 dividend per share each year. The firm must pay this dividend before common shareholders can receive a dividend.

cumulative preferred stock Preferred stock where all missed preferred dividends must be paid before any common dividends can be paid.

Cumulative Versus Non-Cumulative Preferred Stock. There are two types of preferred stock: *cumulative* and *non-cumulative*. With **cumulative preferred stock**, any unpaid dividends are carried forward. For example, if DuPont fails to pay its preferred dividend for several years, its obligation to its cumulative preferred shareholders accumulates, and it cannot pay any dividends to common shareholders until it has paid all the unpaid preferred dividends. With **non-cumulative preferred stock**, missed dividends do not accumulate, and

non-cumulative preferred stock Preferred stock where missed dividends do not accumulate. Only the current dividend is owed before common dividends can be paid.

the firm can pay current dividend payments first to preferred and then to common stock shareholders. Almost all preferred stock is cumulative. Some preferred stock also gives preferred shareholders the right to elect one or more directors to the board if the firm is substantially in arrears on preferred dividends.

Preferred Stock: Equity or Debt? You may be wondering how to think about preferred stock—is it equity or is it debt? Economically, it is like a perpetual bond because it has a promised cash flow to holders and there are consequences if those cash flows are not paid. However, unlike debtholders, preferred shareholders cannot force the firm into bankruptcy. Preferred shareholders stand in line in front of common shareholders for annual dividends, but behind regular bondholders, because interest is paid before dividends. If the firm is bankrupt, the same priority is followed in settling claims: bondholders, preferred shareholders, and then common shareholders. Finally, as long as the firm is meeting its preferred dividend obligations, the preferred shareholders have none of the control rights of owners, such as voting on directors or other important matters. However, despite all these similarities to debt, preferred shares are, for all tax and legal purposes, treated as equity.

Concept Check

1. What is a share of stock and what are dividends?
2. What are some key differences between preferred and common stock?

7.2 The Mechanics of Stock Trades

Suppose you decide to invest in Nike (NKE), and so you place a market order to buy 100 shares of its stock. A *market order* means you do not specify a price, rather you want the order to execute immediately at the most favorable price available. If instead you wanted to specify a maximum price you were willing to pay, and you were willing to wait until the shares were available at that price, you would place a *limit order*.

What actually happens when you place this market order to buy Nike stock? In market parlance, 100 shares is a "round lot" and would be considered a small order. Small orders such as this would typically be transmitted electronically to the stock exchange via a system called the *Super Display Book system* (which replaced the old SuperDOT system in 2009). Upon reaching the exchange, it would go directly to the workstation of the specialist who oversees trading in Nike stock. Recall from Chapter 1 that a specialist holds a trading license at the NYSE and acts as a market maker for a particular stock, maintaining orderly trading and stepping in to provide liquidity when needed. The small order would automatically execute against the specialist's inventory in an average time of five *milliseconds*.

If you were making a large trade, say, to buy 15,000 shares, the process would be more complex. At a physical stock market such as the NYSE, your trade would still be transmitted electronically to the exchange, but it would be sent to the wireless handheld terminal of a *floor broker*. A **floor broker** holds a trading license at the NYSE and works to get the best execution possible for investors. In this case, the floor broker would find the best way to execute the trade, which may be electronically, or may mean going to the physical location where the NKE's designated market maker is. The floor broker would take note of the bid and ask and then negotiate with any selling brokers to buy 15,000 shares at as low a price as possible. Depending on how many shares are offered for sale at the best (lowest) ask price, the trade may need to execute above the ask price in order to clear the full order. So, depending on the size of your order and the current market conditions, an order on the NYSE may be executed very quickly through electronic algorithms or through traditional interaction between floor brokers.

floor broker A person at the NYSE with a trading license who represents orders on the floor, balancing speed and price to get the best execution.

If you were buying a stock on an electronic exchange such as NASDAQ, the trade would proceed slightly differently. Recall from Chapter 1 that NASDAQ is a computer network with no physical location. Also, each stock listed on NASDAQ has an average of 24 dealers making a market in the stock. Each dealer posts bid and ask quotes and trades at those prices for its own account and for customer accounts. If you place an order through your broker or online brokerage account to buy 100 shares of Google (GOOG), the order will be transmitted electronically to the NASDAQ network where it automatically executes against the best (lowest) ask quote for Google. If you are trying to buy a bigger block, like 15,000 shares, then your stockbroker may need to negotiate with one or more of the dealers posting quotes to sell Google. Because there is no physical location for this type of negotiation, it would take place over the phone or by electronic messaging.

But how do you decide whether to buy or sell a stock in the first place? You must estimate the value of the stock and compare it to the current market price. In the rest of this chapter, we discuss one traditional approach to valuing a stock, the *dividend-discount model*.[3]

Concept Check

3. What is the role of a floor broker at the NYSE?

4. What is the role of a dealer at the NASDAQ?

7.3 The Dividend-Discount Model

The Valuation Principle implies that to value any security, we must determine the expected cash flows that an investor will receive from owning it. We begin our analysis of stock valuation by considering the cash flows for an investor with a one-year investment horizon. We will show how the stock's price and the investor's return from the investment are related. We then consider the perspective of investors with a long investment horizon. Finally, we will reach our goal of establishing the first stock valuation method: the *dividend-discount model*.

A One-Year Investor

There are two potential sources of cash flows from owning a stock:

1. The firm might pay out cash to its shareholders in the form of a dividend.
2. The investor might generate cash by selling the shares at some future date.

The total amount received in dividends and from selling the stock will depend on the investor's investment horizon. Let's begin by considering the perspective of a one-year investor.

When an investor buys a stock, she will pay the current market price for a share, P_0. While she continues to hold the stock, she will be entitled to any dividends the stock pays. Let Div_1 be the total dividends the investor expects to be paid per share during the year. At the end of the year, the investor will sell her share at the new market price. Let P_1 be the price the investor expects to sell her share at at the end of the year. Assuming for simplicity that all dividends are paid at the end of the year, we have the following timeline for this investment:

$$
\begin{array}{ccc}
0 & & 1 \\
\vdash & \! & \!\!\!\!\dashv \\
-P_0 & & Div_1 + P_1
\end{array}
$$

---

[3] In Chapter 10, we return to the question of stock valuation with a discussion of additional approaches. As you will see, when estimating the value of a stock, it is best to try several different approaches to increase the confidence in your estimate.

Of course, the future dividend payment and stock price in this timeline are not known with certainty. Rather, these values are based on the investor's expectations at the time the stock is purchased. Given these expectations, the investor will be willing to pay a price today up to the point at which the benefits equal the cost—that is, up to the point at which the current price equals the present value of the expected future dividend and sale price.

Because these cash flows are risky, we cannot discount them using the risk-free interest rate, but instead must use the cost of capital for the firm's equity. We have previously defined the cost of capital of any investment to be the expected return that investors could earn on their best alternative investment with similar risk and maturity. Thus, we must discount the equity cash flows based on the **equity cost of capital**, r_E, for the stock, which is the expected return of other investments available in the market with equivalent risk to the firm's shares. Doing so leads to the following equation for the stock price:

equity cost of capital The expected rate of return available in the market on other investments that have equivalent risk to the risk associated with the firm's shares.

$$P_0 = \frac{Div_1 + P_1}{1 + r_E} \tag{7.1}$$

If the current stock price were less than this amount, the cost would be less than the PV of the benefits, so investors would rush in and buy it, driving up the stock's price. If the stock price exceeded this amount, selling would be attractive and the stock price would quickly fall.

Dividend Yields, Capital Gains, and Total Returns

A critical part of Eq. 7.1 for determining the stock price is the firm's equity cost of capital, r_E. At the beginning of this section, we pointed out that an investor's return from holding a stock comes from dividends and cash generated from selling the stock. We can rewrite Eq. 7.1 to show these two return components. If we multiply by $(1 + r_E)$, divide by P_0, and subtract 1 from both sides, we have

Total Return

$$r_E = \frac{Div_1 + P_1}{P_0} - 1 = \underbrace{\frac{Div_1}{P_0}}_{\text{Dividend Yield}} + \underbrace{\frac{P_1 - P_0}{P_0}}_{\text{Capital Gain Rate}} \tag{7.2}$$

dividend yield The expected annual dividend of a stock divided by its current price; the percentage return an investor expects to earn from the dividend paid by the stock.

The first term on the right side of Eq. 7.2 is the stock's **dividend yield**, which is the expected annual dividend of the stock divided by its current price. The dividend yield is the percentage return the investor expects to earn from the dividend paid by the stock. The second term on the right side of Eq. 7.2 reflects the **capital gain** the investor will earn on the stock, which is the difference between the expected sale price and the original purchase price for the stock, $P_1 - P_0$. We divide the capital gain by the current stock price to express the capital gain as a percentage return, called the **capital gain rate**.

capital gain The amount by which the selling price of an asset exceeds its initial purchase price.

The sum of the dividend yield and the capital gain rate is called the **total return** of the stock. The total return is the expected return the investor will earn for a one-year investment in the stock. Equation 7.2 states that the stock's total return should equal the equity cost of capital. In other words, *the expected total return of the stock should equal the expected return of other investments available in the market with equivalent risk.*

capital gain rate An expression of capital gain as a percentage of the initial price of the asset.

This result is exactly what we would expect: The firm must pay its shareholders a return commensurate with the return they can earn elsewhere while taking the same risk. If the stock offered a higher return than other securities with the same risk, investors would sell those other investments and buy the stock instead. This activity would then drive up the stock's current price, lowering its dividend yield and capital gain rate until Eq. 7.2 holds true. If the stock offered a lower expected return, investors would sell the stock and drive down its price until Eq. 7.2 was again satisfied.

total return The sum of a stock's dividend yield and its capital gain rate.

EXAMPLE 7.1

Stock Prices
and Returns

MyFinanceLab

PROBLEM

Suppose you expect Longs Drug Stores to pay an annual dividend of $0.56 per share in the coming year and to trade for $45.50 per share at the end of the year. If investments with equivalent risk to Longs' stock have an expected return of 6.80%, what is the most you would pay today for Longs' stock? What dividend yield and capital gain rate would you expect at this price?

SOLUTION

PLAN

We can use Eq. 7.1 to solve for the beginning price we would pay now (P_0) given our expectations about dividends ($Div_1 = \$0.56$) and future price ($P_1 = \$45.50$) and the return we need to expect to earn to be willing to invest ($r_E = 0.068$). We can then use Eq. 7.2 to calculate the dividend yield and capital gain rate.

EXECUTE

Using Eq. 7.1, we have

$$P_0 = \frac{Div_1 + P_1}{1 + r_E} = \frac{\$0.56 + \$45.50}{1.0680} = \$43.13$$

Referring to Eq. 7.2, we see that at this price, Longs' dividend yield is $Div_1/P_0 = 0.56/43.13 = 1.30\%$. The expected capital gain is $\$45.50 - \$43.13 = \$2.37$ per share, for a capital gain rate of $2.37/43.13 = 5.50\%$.

EVALUATE

At a price of $43.13, Longs' expected total return is $1.30\% + 5.50\% = 6.80\%$, which is equal to its equity cost of capital (the return being paid by investments with equivalent risk to Longs'). This amount is the most we would be willing to pay for Longs' stock. If we paid more, our expected return would be less than 6.8% and we would rather invest elsewhere.

A Multiyear Investor

We now extend the intuition we developed for the one-year investor's return to a multiyear investor. Equation 7.1 depends upon the expected stock price in one year, P_1. But suppose we planned to hold the stock for two years. Then we would receive dividends in both year 1 and year 2 before selling the stock, as shown in the following timeline:

```
     0              1              2
     |              |              |
   -P_0           Div_1        Div_2 + P_2
```

Setting the stock price equal to the present value of the future cash flows in this case implies:[4]

$$P_0 = \frac{Div_1}{1 + r_E} + \frac{Div_2 + P_2}{(1 + r_E)^2} \tag{7.3}$$

Equations 7.1 and 7.3 are different: As a two-year investor we care about the dividend and stock price in year 2, but these terms do not appear in Eq. 7.1. Does this difference imply that a two-year investor will value the stock differently than a one-year investor?

---

[4]In using the same equity cost of capital for both periods, we are assuming that the equity cost of capital does not depend on the term of the cash flows; that is, r_E is not different for year 2 (or any other year). Otherwise, we would need to adjust for the term structure of the equity cost of capital (as we did with the yield curve for risk-free cash flows in Chapter 5). This step would complicate the analysis but would not change its results.

The answer to this question is no. A one-year investor does not care about the dividend and stock price in year 2 directly. She will care about them indirectly, however, because they will affect the price for which she can sell the stock at the end of year 1. For example, suppose the investor sells the stock to another one-year investor with the same expectations. The new investor will expect to receive the dividend and stock price at the end of year 2, so he will be willing to pay

$$P_1 = \frac{Div_2 + P_2}{1 + r_E}$$

for the stock. Substituting this expression for P_1 into Eq. 7.1, we get the same result as in Eq. 7.3:

$$P_0 = \frac{Div_1 + P_1}{1 + r_E} = \frac{Div_1}{1 + r_E} + \frac{1}{1 + r_E} \overbrace{\left(\frac{Div_2 + P_2}{1 + r_E} \right)}^{P_1}$$

$$= \frac{Div_1}{1 + r_E} + \frac{Div_2 + P_2}{(1 + r_E)^2}$$

Thus, the formula for the stock price for a two-year investor is the same as that for a sequence of two one-year investors.

Dividend-Discount Model Equation

dividend-discount model A model that values shares of a firm according to the present value of the future dividends the firm will pay.

We can continue this process for any number of years by replacing the final stock price with the value that the next holder of the stock would be willing to pay. Doing so leads to the general **dividend-discount model** for the stock price, where the horizon N is arbitrary:

Dividend-Discount Model

$$P_0 = \frac{Div_1}{1 + r_E} + \frac{Div_2}{(1 + r_E)^2} + \cdots + \frac{Div_N}{(1 + r_E)^N} + \frac{P_N}{(1 + r_E)^N} \qquad (7.4)$$

Equation 7.4 applies to a single N-year investor, who will collect dividends for N years and then sell the stock, or to a series of investors who hold the stock for shorter periods and then resell it. Note that Eq. 7.4 holds for *any* horizon N. As a consequence, all investors (with the same expectations) will attach the same value to the stock, independent of their investment horizons. How long they intend to hold the stock and whether they collect their return in the form of dividends or capital gains is irrelevant. For the special case in which the firm eventually pays dividends and is never acquired or liquidated, it is possible to hold the shares forever. In this scenario, rather than having a stopping point where we sell the shares, we rewrite Eq. 7.4 to show that the dividends go on into the future:

$$P_0 = \frac{Div_1}{1 + r_E} + \frac{Div_2}{(1 + r_E)^2} + \frac{Div_3}{(1 + r_E)^3} + \cdots \qquad (7.5)$$

That is, *the price of the stock is equal to the present value of all of the expected future dividends it will pay.*

Concept Check

5. How do you calculate the total return of a stock?

6. What discount rate do you use to discount the future cash flows of a stock?

7.4 Estimating Dividends in the Dividend-Discount Model

Equation 7.5 expresses the value of a stock in terms of the expected future dividends the firm will pay. Of course, estimating these dividends—especially for the distant future—is difficult. A commonly used approximation is to assume that in the long run, dividends will grow at a constant rate. In this section, we consider the implications of this assumption for stock prices and explore the tradeoff between dividends and growth.

Constant Dividend Growth

The simplest forecast for the firm's future dividends states that they will grow at a constant rate, g, forever. That case yields the following timeline for the cash flows for an investor who buys the stock today and holds it:

Because the expected dividends are a constant growth perpetuity, we can use Eq. 4.7 to calculate their present value. We then obtain the following simple formula for the stock price:[5]

Constant Dividend Growth Model

$$P_0 = \frac{Div_1}{r_E - g} \tag{7.6}$$

According to the **constant dividend growth model**, the value of the firm depends on the dividend level next year, divided by the equity cost of capital adjusted by the growth rate.

constant dividend growth model A model for valuing a stock by viewing its dividends as a constant growth perpetuity.

EXAMPLE 7.2
Valuing a Firm with Constant Dividend Growth

MyFinanceLab

PROBLEM

Consolidated Edison, Inc. (Con Ed) is a regulated utility company that services the New York City area. Suppose Con Ed plans to pay $2.30 per share in dividends in the coming year. If its equity cost of capital is 7% and dividends are expected to grow by 2% per year in the future, estimate the value of Con Ed's stock.

SOLUTION

PLAN

Because the dividends are expected to grow perpetually at a constant rate, we can use Eq. 7.6 to value Con Ed. The next dividend (Div_1) is expected to be $2.30, the growth rate ($g$) is 2%, and the equity cost of capital (r_E) is 7%.

EXECUTE

$$P_0 = \frac{Div_1}{r_E - g} = \frac{\$2.30}{0.07 - 0.02} = \$46.00$$

EVALUATE

You would be willing to pay 20 times this year's dividend of $2.30 to own Con Ed stock because you are buying a claim to this year's dividend *and* to an infinite growing series of future dividends.

---

[5]As discussed in Chapter 4, this formula requires that $g < r_E$. Otherwise, the present value of the growing perpetuity is infinite. The implication here is that it is impossible for a stock's dividends to grow at a rate $g > r_E$ forever. If the growth rate does exceed r_E, the situation must be temporary, and the constant growth model cannot be applied in such a case.

For another interpretation of Eq. 7.6, note that we can rearrange it as follows:

$$r_E = \frac{Div_1}{P_0} + g \tag{7.7}$$

Comparing Eq. 7.7 with Eq. 7.2, we see that g equals the expected capital gain rate. In other words, with constant expected dividend growth, the expected growth rate of the share price matches the growth rate of the dividends.

Dividends Versus Investment and Growth

In Eq. 7.6, the firm's share price increases with the current dividend level, Div_1, and the expected growth rate, g. To maximize its share price, a firm would like to increase both these quantities. Often, however, the firm faces a tradeoff: Increasing growth may require investment, and money spent on investment cannot be used to pay dividends. The constant dividend growth model provides insight into this tradeoff.

dividend payout rate
The fraction of a firm's earnings that the firm pays out as dividends each year.

A Simple Model of Growth. What determines the rate of growth of a firm's dividends? If we define a firm's **dividend payout rate** as the fraction of its earnings that the firm pays as dividends each year, then we can write the firm's dividend per share at date t as follows:

$$Div_t = \underbrace{\frac{\text{Earnings}_t}{\text{Shares Outstanding}_t}}_{EPS_t} \times \text{Dividend Payout Rate}_t \tag{7.8}$$

That is, the dividend each year is equal to the firm's earnings per share (EPS) multiplied by its dividend payout rate. The firm can, therefore, increase its dividend in three ways:

1. It can increase its earnings (net income).
2. It can increase its dividend payout rate.
3. It can decrease its number of shares outstanding.

Suppose for now that the firm does not issue new shares (or buy back its existing shares), so that the number of shares outstanding remains fixed. We can then explore the tradeoff between options 1 and 2.

A firm can do one of two things with its earnings: It can pay them out to investors, or it can retain and reinvest them. By investing cash today, a firm can increase its future dividends. For simplicity, let's assume that absent reinvesting its retained earnings, the firm does not grow, so the current level of earnings generated by the firm remains constant. If all increases in future earnings result exclusively from new investment made with retained earnings, then

$$\text{Change in Earnings} = \text{New Investment} \times \text{Return on New Investment} \tag{7.9}$$

retention rate The fraction of a firm's current earnings that the firm retains.

New investment equals the firm's earnings multiplied by its **retention rate**, or the fraction of current earnings that the firm retains:

$$\text{New Investment} = \text{Earnings} \times \text{Retention Rate} \tag{7.10}$$

Substituting Eq. 7.10 into Eq. 7.9 and dividing by earnings gives an expression for the growth rate of earnings:

$$\text{Earnings Growth Rate} = \frac{\text{Change in Earnings}}{\text{Earnings}}$$

$$= \text{Retention Rate} \times \text{Return on New Investment} \tag{7.11}$$

If the firm chooses to keep its dividend payout rate constant, then the growth in its dividends will equal the growth in its earnings:

$$g = \text{Retention Rate} \times \text{Return on New Investment} \qquad (7.12)$$

Profitable Growth. Equation 7.12 shows that a firm can increase its growth rate by retaining more of its earnings. But if the firm retains more earnings, and as a result pays out a smaller fraction of those earnings as dividends, then according to Eq. 7.8 the firm may have to cut its dividend in the short run. If a firm wants to increase its share price, should it cut its dividend and invest more, or should it cut its investments and increase its dividend? Not surprisingly, the answer to this question will depend on the profitability of the firm's investments. Let's consider an example.

EXAMPLE 7.3

Cutting Dividends for Profitable Growth

MyFinanceLab

PROBLEM

Crane Sporting Goods expects to have earnings per share of $6 in the coming year. Rather than reinvest these earnings and grow, the firm plans to pay out all of its earnings as a dividend. With these expectations of no growth, Crane's current share price is $60.

Suppose Crane could cut its dividend payout rate to 75% for the foreseeable future and use the retained earnings to open new stores. The return on its investment in these stores is expected to be 12%. If we assume that the risk of these new investments is the same as the risk of its existing investments, then the firm's equity cost of capital is unchanged. What effect would this new policy have on Crane's stock price?

SOLUTION

PLAN

To figure out the effect of this policy on Crane's stock price, we need to know several things. First, we need to compute its equity cost of capital. Next, we must determine Crane's dividend and growth rate under the new policy.

Because we know that Crane currently has a growth rate of 0 ($g = 0$), a dividend of $6, and a price of $60, we can use Eq. 7.7 to estimate r_E. Next, the new dividend will simply be 75% of the old dividend of $6. Finally, given a retention rate of 25% and a return on new investment of 12%, we can use Eq. 7.12 to compute the new growth rate (g). Finally, armed with the new dividend, Crane's equity cost of capital, and its new growth rate, we can use Eq. 7.6 to compute the price of Crane's shares if it institutes the new policy.

EXECUTE

Using Eq. 7.7 to estimate r_E, we have

$$r_E = \frac{Div_1}{P_0} + g = \frac{\$6}{\$60} + 0\% = 0.10 + 0$$

In other words, to justify Crane's stock price under its current policy, the expected return of other stocks in the market with equivalent risk must be 10%.

Next, we consider the consequences of the new policy. If Crane reduces its dividend payout rate to 75%, then from Eq. 7.8 its dividend this coming year will fall to $Div_1 = EPS_1 \times 75\% = \$6 \times 75\% = \$4.50$.

At the same time, because the firm will now retain 25% of its earnings to invest in new stores, from Eq. 7.12 its growth rate will increase to

$$g = \text{Retention Rate} \times \text{Return on New Investment} = 0.25 \times 0.12 = 0.03 = 3\%$$

Assuming Crane can continue to grow at this rate, we can compute its share price under the new policy using the constant dividend growth model of Eq. 7.6:

$$P_0 = \frac{Div_1}{r_E - g} = \frac{\$4.50}{0.10 - 0.03} = \$64.29$$

EVALUATE

Crane's share price should rise from $60 to $64.29 if the company cuts its dividend in order to increase its investment and growth. By using its earnings to invest in projects that offer a rate of return (12%) greater than its equity cost of capital (10%), Crane has created value for its shareholders.

In Example 7.3, cutting the firm's dividend in favor of growth raised the firm's stock price. This is not always the case, however, as Example 7.4 demonstrates.

EXAMPLE 7.4

Unprofitable Growth

MyFinanceLab

PROBLEM

Suppose Crane Sporting Goods decides to cut its dividend payout rate to 75% to invest in new stores, as in Example 7.3. But now suppose that the return on these new investments is 8%, rather than 12%. Given its expected earnings per share this year of $6 and its equity cost of capital of 10% (we again assume that the risk of the new investments is the same as its existing investments), what will happen to Crane's current share price in this case?

SOLUTION

PLAN

We will follow the steps in Example 7.3, except that in this case, we assume a return on new investments of 8% when computing the new growth rate (g) instead of 12% as in Example 7.3.

EXECUTE

Just as in Example 7.3, Crane's dividend will fall to $6 \times 0.75 = $4.50. Its growth rate under the new policy, given the lower return on new investment, will now be $g = 0.25 \times 0.08 = 0.02 = 2\%$. The new share price is therefore

$$P_0 = \frac{Div_1}{r_E - g} = \frac{\$4.50}{0.10 - 0.02} = \$56.25$$

EVALUATE

Even though Crane will grow under the new policy, the return on its new investments is too low. The company's share price will fall if it cuts its dividend to make new investments with a return of only 8%. By reinvesting its earnings at a rate (8%) that is lower than its equity cost of capital (10%), Crane has reduced shareholder value.

Comparing Example 7.3 with Example 7.4, we see that the effect of cutting the firm's dividend to grow crucially depends on the value of the new investments the firm plans to make. In Example 7.3, the return on new investment of 12% exceeds the firm's equity cost of capital of 10%, so the investment is a good one. In Example 7.4, however, the return on new investment is only 8%, so the new investment's return is below the firm's cost of capital. In that case, the new investment is not worthwhile even though it will lead to earnings growth. In this example, we can check that cutting the firm's dividend to increase investment will create value and raise the stock price if, and only if, the new investments generate a return greater than their cost of capital. In Chapter 8, we will consider more generally how to identify projects that create value and thus increase the stock price.

Changing Growth Rates

Successful young firms often have very high initial earnings growth rates. During this period of high growth, firms often retain 100% of their earnings to exploit profitable investment opportunities. As they mature, their growth slows to rates more typical of established companies. At that point, their earnings exceed their investment needs and they begin to pay dividends.

We cannot use the constant dividend growth model to value the stock of such a firm for two reasons:

1. These firms often pay *no* dividends when they are young.
2. Their growth rate continues to change over time until they mature.

However, we can use the general form of the dividend-discount model to value such a firm by applying the constant growth model to calculate the future share price of the stock P_N once the firm matures and its expected growth rate stabilizes:

Specifically, if the firm is expected to grow at a long-term rate g after year $N + 1$, then from the constant dividend growth model:

$$P_N = \frac{Div_{N+1}}{r_E - g} \tag{7.13}$$

We can then use this estimate of P_N as a final cash flow in the dividend-discount model. Intuitively, we value the stock as the present value of the dividends we will receive plus the present value of the price we expect to be able to sell the stock for in the future. For example, consider a company with expected dividends of $2.00, $2.50, and $3.00 in each of the next three years. After that point, its dividends are expected to grow at a constant rate of 5%. If its equity cost of capital is 12%, we can find the current price. Using Eq. 7.13, we can compute the price in year 3:

$$P_N = \frac{Div_{N+1}}{r_E - g} = \left(\frac{\$3.00\,(1.05)}{0.12 - 0.05} \right) = 45.00$$

Now, using Eq. 7.4, we calculate the current price as the PV of the first 3 years' dividends and then the price at the end of year 3:

$$P_0 = \frac{\$2.00}{1.12} + \frac{\$2.50}{(1.12)^2} + \frac{\$3.00}{(1.12)^3} + \frac{\$45.00}{(1.12)^3} = \$37.94$$

This example also reinforces an important point: The constant dividend growth model (Eq. 7.13) is just a special case of the general dividend-discount formula (Eq. 7.4). We can always value all the stream of dividends using Eq. 7.4. However, if we assume constant growth, we can apply the growing perpetuity shortcut to all or part of the dividend stream, depending on whether the constant growth starts now or at some point in the future.

COMMON MISTAKE Forgetting to "Grow" This Year's Dividend

The most common mistake in handling growing dividends is to use the current period's dividend in the numerator of the growing perpetuity formula. In the example just discussed in the text above, the dividends reached $3 in year 3, and then grew by 5% per year thereafter. A common mistake is to calculate the growing stream of dividends as

$$\frac{3.00}{0.12 - 0.05},$$

forgetting that next year's dividend (the numerator) has already grown by 5%! As we show in the example, the correct calculation is

$$\frac{3.00 \times (1.05)}{0.12 - 0.05} = \$45.$$

Also, remember to avoid the common mistake from Chapter 4: The growing perpetuity formula gives the value in year N for dividends starting in year $N + 1$. In the example above, the formula gives the value in year 3 of the growing dividend stream starting in year 4. That is why we discount the $45 back only three years.

EXAMPLE 7.5

Valuing a Firm
with Two Different
Growth Rates

MyFinanceLab

PROBLEM

Small Fry, Inc., has just invented a potato chip that looks and tastes like a french fry. Given the phenomenal market response to this product, Small Fry is reinvesting all of its earnings to expand its operations. Earnings were $2 per share this past year and are expected to grow at a rate of 20% per year until the end of year 4. At that point, other companies are likely to bring out competing products. Analysts project that at the end of year 4, Small Fry will cut its investment and begin paying 60% of its earnings as dividends. Its growth will also slow to a long-run rate of 4%. If Small Fry's equity cost of capital is 8%, what is the value of a share today?

SOLUTION

PLAN

We can use Small Fry's projected earnings growth rate and payout rate to forecast its future earnings and dividends. After year 4, Small Fry's dividends will grow at a constant 4%, so we can use the constant dividend growth model (Eq. 7.13) to value all dividends after that point. Finally, we can pull everything together with the dividend-discount model (Eq. 7.4).

EXECUTE

The following spreadsheet projects Small Fry's earnings and dividends:

Year	0	1	2	3	4	5	6
Earnings							
1 EPS Growth Rate (versus prior year)		20%	20%	20%	20%	4%	4%
2 EPS	$2.00	$2.40	$2.88	$3.46	$4.15	$4.31	$4.49
Dividends							
3 Dividend Payout Rate		0%	0%	0%	60%	60%	60%
4 Div		$ —	$ —	$ —	$2.49	$2.59	$2.69

Starting from $2.00 in year 0, EPS grows by 20% per year until year 4, after which growth slows to 4%. Small Fry's dividend payout rate is zero until year 4, when competition reduces its investment opportunities and its payout rate rises to 60%. Multiplying EPS by the dividend payout ratio, we project Small Fry's future dividends in line 4.

After year 4, Small Fry's dividends will grow at the constant expected long-run rate of 4% per year. Thus, we can use the constant dividend growth model to project Small Fry's share price at the end of year 3. Given its equity cost of capital of 8%,

$$P_3 = \frac{Div_4}{r_E - g} = \frac{\$2.49}{0.08 - 0.04} = \$62.25$$

We then apply the dividend-discount model (Eq. 7.4) with this terminal value:

$$P_0 = \frac{Div_1}{1 + r_E} + \frac{Div_2}{(1 + r_E)^2} + \frac{Div_3}{(1 + r_E)^3} + \frac{P_3}{(1 + r_E)^3} = \frac{\$62.25}{(1.08)^3} = \$49.42$$

EVALUATE

The dividend-discount model is flexible enough to handle any forecasted pattern of dividends. Here, the dividends were zero for several years and then settled into a constant growth rate, allowing us to use the constant dividend growth model as a shortcut.

TABLE 7.1

The Dividend-Discount Model

General formula	$$P_0 = \frac{Div_1}{1+r_E} + \frac{Div_2}{(1+r_E)^2} + \cdots + \frac{Div_N}{(1+r_E)^N} + \frac{P_N}{(1+r_E)^N}$$
If dividend growth is constant	$$P_0 = \frac{Div_1}{r_E - g}$$
If early growth is variable followed by constant growth	$$P_0 = \frac{Div_1}{1+r_E} + \frac{Div_2}{(1+r_E)^2} + \cdots + \frac{Div_N}{(1+r_E)^N} + \left(\frac{1}{(1+r_E)^N}\right)\left(\frac{Div_{N+1}}{r_E - g}\right)$$

Table 7.1 summarizes the dividend-discount model, including how to apply the shortcut for constant growth.

Value Drivers and the Dividend-Discount Model

Now that we have fully developed the dividend-discount model, it is worth assessing how well it does capturing the intuitive drivers of stock value. When we think about how valuable a company is, we usually focus on how profitable it is now and how that profitability will grow or decline in the future, along with the risk of investing in the company. Where are these measures captured in the dividend-discount model? Profitability determines the company's ability to pay dividends, so, implicitly in the forecasted dividend stream, we are forecasting the company's profitability. As for the risk, that is captured in the equity cost of capital we use to discount those forecasted dividends. Riskier investments require higher expected returns, which enter the dividend-discount model as higher equity cost of capital.

Concept Check

7. What are three ways that a firm can increase the amount of its future dividends per share?

8. Under what circumstances can a firm increase its share price by cutting its dividend and investing more?

7.5 Limitations of the Dividend-Discount Model

The dividend-discount model has two fundamental limitations that we will now address: its reliance on dividend forecasts and lack of applicability to non-dividend-paying stocks.

Uncertain Dividend Forecasts

The dividend-discount model values a stock based on a forecast of the future dividends paid to shareholders. But unlike a Treasury bond, whose cash flows are known with virtual certainty, a firm's future dividends carry a tremendous amount of uncertainty.

Let's reconsider the example of Nike (NKE). In 2013, NKE paid annual dividends of $0.84 (by paying four quarterly dividends of $0.21 each). If we assume an equity cost of capital of 10% and expected dividend growth of 8.5%, the constant dividend growth model implies a share price for NKE of

$$P_0 = \frac{Div_1}{r_E - g} = \frac{\$0.84\,(1 + 0.085)}{0.10 - 0.085} = \$60.76$$

which is quite close to the $60.39 share price that the stock had at the time. With a 9% dividend growth rate, however, this estimate would rise to more than $91 per share; with a 6% dividend growth rate, the estimate falls to less than $23 per share. As we see in Figure 7.2, even small changes in the assumed dividend growth rate can lead to large changes in the estimated stock price.

FIGURE 7.2

NKE Stock Prices
for Different
Expected Growth
Rates

Stock prices are based on the constant dividend growth model. We assume a dividend this year of $0.84 and an equity cost of capital of 10%. The expected dividend growth rate varies from 0% to 9%. Note how even a small change in the expected growth rate produces a large change in the stock price, especially at higher growth rates.

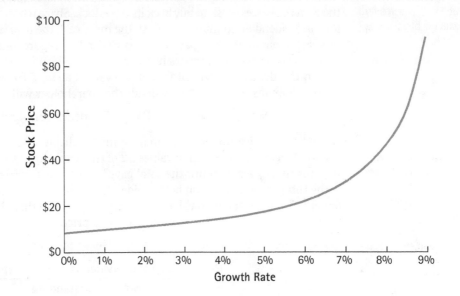

Furthermore, it is difficult to know which estimate of the dividend growth rate is more reasonable. NKE more than doubled its dividend between 2005 and 2010, but its earnings growth then moderated. Consequently, this rate of increase is not sustainable. From Eq. 7.8, forecasting dividends requires forecasting the firm's earnings, dividend payout rate, and future share count. Future earnings, however, will depend on interest expenses (which, in turn, depend on how much the firm borrows), and the firm's share count and dividend payout rate will depend on whether NKE uses a portion of its earnings to repurchase shares. Because borrowing and repurchase decisions are at management's discretion, they are more difficult to forecast reliably than other fundamental aspects of the firm's cash flows.[6]

Non-Dividend-Paying Stocks

Many companies do not pay dividends—Facebook, Amazon.com, and Google are just a few examples. How then do we value those stocks? In the next section, we discuss a small modification to the dividend-discount model to capture total payouts to shareholders, whether the payouts are dividends or not. In Chapter 10, we will discuss other valuation approaches that do not rely on payouts. Those approaches will be more meaningful once we have covered how financial managers create value within the firm through decisions about which projects to approve. So, in Chapters 8 and 9, we will cover investment decision rules and project evaluation.

Concept
Check

9. What are the main limitations of the dividend-discount model?

10. What pieces of information are needed to forecast dividends?

---

[6]We discuss management's decision to borrow funds or repurchase shares in Part 6 of the text.

7.6 # Share Repurchases and the Total Payout Model

share repurchase A transaction in which a firm uses cash to buy back its own stock.

In our discussion of the dividend-discount model, we implicitly assumed that any cash paid out by the firm to shareholders takes the form of a dividend. In recent years, an increasing number of firms have replaced dividend payouts with *share repurchases*. In a **share repurchase**, the firm uses excess cash to buy back its own stock. Share repurchases have two consequences for the dividend-discount model. First, the more cash the firm uses to repurchase shares, the less cash it has available to pay dividends. Second, by repurchasing shares, the firm decreases its share count, which increases its earnings and dividends on a per-share basis.

In the dividend-discount model, we valued a share from the perspective of a single shareholder, discounting the dividends the shareholder will receive:

$$P_0 = PV(\text{Future Dividends per Share}) \tag{7.14}$$

total payout model A method that values shares of a firm by discounting the firm's total payouts to equity holders (that is, all the cash distributed as dividends and stock repurchases) and then dividing by the current number of shares outstanding.

An alternative method that may be more reliable when a firm repurchases shares is the **total payout model**, which values *all* of the firm's equity, rather than a single share. To use this model, we discount the total payouts that the firm makes to shareholders, which is the total amount spent on both dividends *and* share repurchases (net of new share issuance).[7] This gives the total value of the firm's equity. We then divide by the current number of shares outstanding to determine the share price:

Total Payout Model

$$P_0 = \frac{PV(\text{Future Total Dividends and Net Repurchases})}{\text{Shares Outstanding}_0} \tag{7.15}$$

We can apply the same simplifications to the total payout method that we obtained by assuming constant growth in Section 7.3. The only change is that *we discount total dividends and share repurchases and use the growth rate of earnings (rather than earnings per share) when forecasting the growth of the firm's total payouts.* When the firm uses share repurchases, this method can be more reliable and easier to apply than the dividend-discount model.

EXAMPLE 7.6
Valuation with Share Repurchases

MyFinanceLab

PROBLEM

Titan Industries has 217 million shares outstanding and expects earnings at the end of this year of $860 million. Titan plans to pay out 50% of its earnings in total, paying 30% as a dividend and using 20% to repurchase shares. If Titan's earnings are expected to grow by 7.5% per year and these payout rates remain constant, determine Titan's share price assuming an equity cost of capital of 10%.

SOLUTION

PLAN

Based on the equity cost of capital of 10% and an expected earnings growth rate of 7.5%, we can compute the present value of Titan's future payouts as a constant growth perpetuity. The only input missing here is Titan's total payouts this year, which we can calculate as 50% of its earnings. The present value of all of Titan's future payouts is the value of its total equity. To obtain the price of a share, we divide the total value by the number of shares outstanding (217 million).

EXECUTE

Titan will have total payouts this year of 50% × $860 million = $430 million. Using the constant growth perpetuity formula, we have

---

[7]You can think of the total payouts as the amount you would receive if you owned 100% of the firm's shares: You would receive all the dividends, plus the proceeds from selling shares back to the firm in the share repurchase.

$$PV(\text{Future Total Dividends and Repurchases}) = \frac{\$430 \text{ million}}{0.10 - 0.075} = \$17.2 \text{ billion}$$

This present value represents the total value of Titan's equity (i.e., its market capitalization). To compute the share price, we divide by the current number of shares outstanding:

$$P_0 = \frac{\$17.2 \text{ billion}}{217 \text{ million shares}} = \$79.26 \text{ per share}$$

EVALUATE

Using the total payout method, we did not need to know the firm's split between dividends and share repurchases. To compare this method with the dividend-discount model, note that Titan will pay a dividend of 30% × ($860 million/217 million shares) = $1.19 per share, for a dividend yield of 1.19/79.26 = 1.50%. From Eq. 7.7, we can solve for Titan's expected growth rates of EPS, dividend, and share price:

$$g = r_E - \frac{Div_1}{P_0} = .10 - \frac{1.19}{79.26} = 0.085 = 8.5\%.$$

This growth rate exceeds the 7.50% growth rate of earnings because Titan's share count will decline over time owing to its share repurchases.[8]

Concept
Check

11. How does the total payout model address part of the dividend-discount model's limitations?

12. How does the growth rate used in the total payout model differ from the growth rate used in the dividend-discount model?

7.7 Putting It All Together

We now return to the questions posed at the beginning of the chapter. First, how would an investor decide whether to buy or sell Nike stock? She would value the stock using her own expectations. We showed one set of expectations about dividend growth that would be consistent with the price. If her expectations were substantially different, she might conclude that the stock was over- or under-priced at $60.39. Based on that conclusion, she would sell or buy the stock, and time would reveal whether her expectations were better than the market's.

Second, how could Nike stock suddenly be worth 11% more after Nike's announcement? As investors digested the news in Nike's announcement and updated their expectations, they would have determined that the previous day's closing price was too low based on the new information about future earnings growth. Buying pressure would then drive the stock price up until the buys and sells came into balance.

Third, what should Nike's managers do to raise the stock price further? The only way to raise the stock price is to make value-increasing decisions. We turn to this task in the next section of the book. As shown in Chapters 8 and 9, through capital budgeting analysis, managers can identify projects that add value to the company. By increasing the value of the company through good investment decisions, Nike's managers can increase the stock price. Chapter 10 returns to the question of stock valuation and extends the techniques developed here to incorporate the lessons of the next two chapters on project selection.

---

[8]We can check that an 8.5% EPS growth rate is consistent with 7.5% earnings growth and Titan's repurchase plans as follows: Given an expected share price of $79.26 × 1.085 = $86.00 next year, Titan will repurchase 20% × $860 million ÷ ($86.00 per share) = 2 million shares next year. With the decline in the number of shares from 217 million to 215 million, EPS grows by a factor of 1.075 × (217/215) = 1.085 or by 8.5%.

Key Points and Equations	Key Terms	Online Practice
7.1 Stock Basics • Ownership in a corporation is divided into shares of stock. These shares carry rights to share in the profits of the firm through future dividend payments. • The shares also come with rights to vote to elect directors and decide on other important matters. • Some firms issue preferred stock, which has preference over common stock in the payment of dividends and in liquidation, but typically carries no voting rights.	annual meeting, p. 196 classes, p. 196 common stock, p. 194 cumulative preferred stock, p. 196 cumulative voting, p. 196 non-cumulative preferred stock, p. 196 preferred stock, p. 196 proxy, p. 196 proxy contest, p. 196 straight voting, p. 195 ticker symbol, p. 194	MyFinanceLab Study Plan 7.1
7.2 The Mechanics of Stock Trades • The NYSE has a physical trading location, but many small trades execute electronically. • NASDAQ is a computer network without a specific trading location. Many trades execute automatically, while larger trades must be negotiated with one or more of the stock's dealers.	floor broker, p. 197	MyFinanceLab Study Plan 7.2
7.3 The Dividend-Discount Model • The Valuation Principle states that the value of a stock is equal to the present value of the dividends and future sale price the investor will receive. Because these cash flows are risky, they must be discounted at the equity cost of capital, which is the expected return of other securities available in the market with equivalent risk to the firm's equity. The total return of a stock is equal to the dividend yield plus the capital gain rate. The expected total return of a stock should equal its equity cost of capital: $$r_E = \frac{Div_1 + P_1}{P_0} - 1 = \underbrace{\frac{Div_1}{P_0}}_{\text{Dividend Yield}} + \underbrace{\frac{P_1 - P_0}{P_0}}_{\text{Capital Gain Rate}} \quad (7.2)$$ • When investors have the same beliefs, the dividend-discount model states that, for any horizon N, the stock price satisfies the following equation: $$P_0 = \frac{Div_1}{1 + r_E} + \frac{Div_2}{(1 + r_E)^2} + \cdots + \frac{Div_N}{(1 + r_E)^N} + \frac{P_N}{(1 + r_E)^N} \quad (7.4)$$ • If the stock eventually pays dividends and is never acquired, the dividend-discount model implies that the stock price equals the present value of all future dividends.	capital gain, p. 199 capital gain rate, p. 199 dividend-discount model, p. 201 dividend yield, p. 199 equity cost of capital, p. 199 total return, p. 199	MyFinanceLab Study Plan 7.3 Using Excel: Building a Dividend-Discount Model

7.4 Estimating Dividends in the Dividend-Discount Model

- The constant dividend growth model assumes that dividends grow at a constant expected rate, g. In that case, g is also the expected capital gain rate, and

$$P_0 = \frac{Div_1}{r_E - g} \qquad (7.6)$$

- Future dividends depend on earnings, shares outstanding, and the dividend payout rate:

$$Div_t = \underbrace{\frac{Earnings_t}{Shares\ Outstanding_t}}_{EPS_t} \times \text{Dividend Payout Rate}_t \qquad (7.8)$$

- If all increases in future earnings result exclusively from new investments made with retained earnings, then earnings growth can be found as:

$$\text{Earnings Growth Rate} = \frac{\text{Change in Earnings}}{\text{Earnings}} \qquad (7.11)$$

$$= \text{Retention Rate} \times \text{Return on New Investment}$$

  (where Retention Rate $= 1 -$ Payout Rate)
- If the dividend payout rate and the number of shares outstanding is constant, and if earnings change only as a result of new investment from retained earnings, then the growth rate of the firm's earnings, dividends, and share price is calculated as follows:

  $g = $ Retention Rate $\times$ Return on New Investment (7.12)
- Cutting the firm's dividend to increase investment will raise the stock price if, and only if, the new investments generate a return greater than their cost of capital.
- If the firm has a long-term growth rate of g after the period $N + 1$, then we can apply the dividend-discount model and use the constant dividend growth formula to estimate the terminal stock value P_N.

7.5 Limitations of the Dividend-Discount Model

- The dividend-discount model is sensitive to the dividend growth rate, which is difficult to estimate accurately.
- The dividend-discount model is not practical for valuing the majority of stocks not paying dividends. In Chapter 10, we discuss alternative approaches.

7.6 Share Repurchases and the Total Payout Model

- If the firm undertakes share repurchases, it is more reliable to use the total payout model to value the firm. In this model, the value of equity equals the present value of future total dividends and repurchases. To determine the stock price, we divide the equity value by the initial number of shares outstanding of the firm:

$$P_0 = \frac{PV(\text{Future Total Dividends and Repurchases})}{\text{Shares Outstanding}_0} \qquad (7.15)$$

- The growth rate of the firm's total payout is governed by the growth rate of earnings, not earnings per share.

CRITICAL THINKING

1. What rights come with a share of stock?

2. Which two components make up the total return to an investor in a share of stock?

3. What does the dividend-discount model say about valuing shares of stock?

4. What is the relationship between the return from reinvesting cash flows and the change in the price of the stock?

5. How can the dividend-discount model be used with changing growth rates in future dividends?

6. What are some of the drawbacks of the dividend-discount model?

7. What are share repurchases, and how can they be incorporated into the valuation of a stock?

PROBLEMS

*All problems in this chapter are available in MyFinanceLab. An asterisk * indicates problems with a higher level of difficulty.*

Stock Basics

1. If you own 15,000 shares of stock of Nike and it pays a dividend of $0.21 per share, then what is the total dividend you will receive?

2. You own 20% of the stock of a company that has 10 directors on its board. How much representation can you get on the board if the company has cumulative voting? How much representation can you ensure if the company has straight voting?

3. Anzio, Inc., has two classes of shares. Class B has 10 times the voting rights as Class A. If you own 10% of the class A shares and 20% of the Class B shares, what percentage of the total voting rights do you hold?

The Dividend-Discount Model

4. Assume Evco, Inc., has a current stock price of $50 and will pay a $2 dividend in one year; its equity cost of capital is 15%. What price must you expect Evco stock to sell for immediately after the firm pays the dividend in one year to justify its current price?

5. Assume Coleco pays an annual dividend of $1.50 and has a share price of $37.50. It announces that its annual dividend will increase to $1.75. If its dividend yield is to stay the same, what should its new share price be?

6. Anle Corporation has a current stock price of $20 and is expected to pay a dividend of $1 in one year. Its expected stock price right after paying that dividend is $22.
   a. What is Anle's equity cost of capital?
   b. How much of Anle's equity cost of capital is expected to be satisfied by dividend yield and how much by capital gain?

7. Achi Corp. has preferred stock with an annual dividend of $3. If the required return on Achi's preferred stock is 8%, what is its price? (*Hint:* For a preferred stock, the dividend growth rate is zero.)

8. Ovit, Inc., has preferred stock with a price of $20 and a dividend of $1.50 per year. What is its dividend yield?

9. Suppose Acap Corporation will pay a dividend of $2.80 per share at the end of this year and a dividend of $3 per share next year. You expect Acap's stock price to be $52 in two years. Assume that Acap's equity cost of capital is 10%.
   a. What price would you be willing to pay for a share of Acap stock today, if you planned to hold the stock for two years?
   b. Suppose instead you plan to hold the stock for one year. For what price would you expect to be able to sell a share of Acap stock in one year?
   c. Given your answer to (b), what price would you be willing to pay for a share of Acap stock today, if you planned to hold the stock for one year? How does this price compare to your answer in (a)?

10. Krell Industries has a share price of $22.00 today. If Krell is expected to pay a dividend of $0.88 this year and its stock price is expected to grow to $23.54 at the end of the year, what is Krell's dividend yield and equity cost of capital?

Estimating Dividends in the Dividend-Discount Model

11. NoGrowth Corporation currently pays a dividend of $0.50 per quarter, and it will continue to pay this dividend forever. What is the price per share of NoGrowth stock if the firm's equity cost of capital is 15%?

12. Summit Systems will pay a dividend of $1.50 this year. If you expect Summit's dividend to grow by 6% per year, what is its price per share if the firm's equity cost of capital is 11%?

13. Dorpac Corporation has a dividend yield of 1.5%. Its equity cost of capital is 8%, and its dividends are expected to grow at a constant rate.
   a. What is the expected growth rate of Dorpac's dividends?
   b. What is the expected growth rate of Dorpac's share price?

14. Laurel Enterprises expects earnings next year of $4 per share and has a 40% retention rate, which it plans to keep constant. Its equity cost of capital is 10%, which is also its expected return on new investment. Its earnings are expected to grow forever at a rate of 4% per year. If its next dividend is due in one year, what do you estimate the firm's current stock price to be?

*15. DFB, Inc., expects earnings this year of $5 per share, and it plans to pay a $3 dividend to shareholders. DFB will retain $2 per share of its earnings to reinvest in new projects that have an expected return of 15% per year. Suppose DFB will maintain the same dividend payout rate, retention rate, and return on new investments in the future and will not change its number of outstanding shares.
   a. What growth rate of earnings would you forecast for DFB?
   b. If DFB's equity cost of capital is 12%, what price would you estimate for DFB stock?
   c. Suppose instead that DFB paid a dividend of $4 per share this year and retained only $1 per share in earnings. That is, it chose to pay a higher dividend instead of reinvesting in as many new projects. If DFB maintains this higher payout rate in the future, what stock price would you estimate for the firm now? Should DFB follow this new policy?

16. Cooperton Mining just announced it will cut its dividend from $4 to $2.50 per share and use the extra funds to expand. Prior to the announcement, Cooperton's dividends were expected to grow at a 3% rate, and its share price was $50. With the planned expansion, Cooperton's dividends are expected to grow at a 5% rate. What share price

would you expect after the announcement? (Assume that the new expansion does not change Cooperton's risk.) Is the expansion a good investment?

17. Assume Gillette Corporation will pay an annual dividend of $0.65 one year from now. Analysts expect this dividend to grow at 12% per year thereafter until the fifth year. After then, growth will level off at 2% per year. According to the dividend-discount model, what is the value of a share of Gillette stock if the firm's equity cost of capital is 8%?

18. CX Enterprises has the following expected dividends: $1 in one year, $1.15 in two years, and $1.25 in three years. After that, its dividends are expected to grow at 4% per year forever (so that year 4's dividend will be 4% more than $1.25 and so on). If CX's equity cost of capital is 12%, what is the current price of its stock?

19. Assume Colgate-Palmolive Company has just paid an annual dividend of $0.96. Analysts are predicting an 11% per year growth rate in earnings over the next five years. After then, Colgate's earnings are expected to grow at the current industry average of 5.2% per year. If Colgate's equity cost of capital is 8.5% per year and its dividend payout ratio remains constant, for what price does the dividend-discount model predict Colgate stock should sell?

*20. Halliford Corporation expects to have earnings this coming year of $3 per share. Halliford plans to retain all of its earnings for the next two years. Then, for the subsequent two years, the firm will retain 50% of its earnings. It will retain 20% of its earnings from that point onward. Each year, retained earnings will be invested in new projects with an expected return of 25% per year. Any earnings that are not retained will be paid out as dividends. Assume Halliford's share count remains constant and all earnings growth comes from the investment of retained earnings. If Halliford's equity cost of capital is 10%, what price would you estimate for Halliford stock?

Share Repurchases and the Total Payout Model

21. Shatin Intl. has 10 million shares, an equity cost of capital of 13% and is expected to pay a total dividend of $20 million each year forever. It announces that it will increase its payout to shareholders. Instead of increasing its dividend, it will keep it constant and will start repurchasing $10 million of stock each year as well. How much will its stock price increase?

22. Zoom Enterprises expects that one year from now it will pay a total dividend of $5 million and repurchase $5 million worth of shares. It plans to spend $10 million on dividends and repurchases every year after that forever, although it may not always be an even split between dividends and repurchases. If Zoom's equity cost of capital is 13% and it has 5 million shares outstanding, what is its share price today?

23. Tolo Co. plans the following repurchases: $10 million in one year, nothing in two years, and $20 million in three years. After that, it will stop repurchasing and will issue dividends totaling $25 million in four years. The total paid in dividends is expected to increase by 3% per year thereafter. If Tolo has 2 million shares outstanding and an equity cost of capital of 11%, what is its price per share today?

24. AFW Industries has 200 million shares outstanding and expects earnings at the end of this year of $700 million. AFW plans to pay out 60% of its earnings in total, paying 40% as a dividend and using 20% to repurchase shares. If AFW's earnings are expected to grow by 8% per year and these payout rates remain constant, determine AFW's share price assuming an equity cost of capital of 12%.

25. Suppose Cisco Systems pays no dividends but spent $5 billion on share repurchases last year. If Cisco's equity cost of capital is 12%, and if the amount spent on repurchases

is expected to grow by 8% per year, estimate Cisco's market capitalization. If Cisco has 6 billion shares outstanding, to what stock price does this correspond?

*26. Maynard Steel plans to pay a dividend of $3 this year. The company has an expected earnings growth rate of 4% per year and an equity cost of capital of 10%.

    a. Assuming that Maynard's dividend payout rate and expected growth rate remain constant, and that the firm does not issue or repurchase shares, estimate Maynard's share price.

    b. Suppose Maynard decides to pay a dividend of $1 this year and to use the remaining $2 per share to repurchase shares. If Maynard's total payout rate remains constant, estimate Maynard's share price.

    c. If Maynard maintains the dividend and total payout rate given in (b), at what rates are Maynard's dividends and earnings per share expected to grow?

2

Integrative Case

This case draws on material from Chapters 3–7.

Adam Rust looked at his mechanic and sighed. The mechanic had just pronounced a death sentence on his road-weary car. The car had served him well—at a cost of $500 it had lasted through four years of college with minimal repairs. Now, he desperately needs wheels. He has just graduated, and has a good job at a decent starting salary. He hopes to purchase his first new car. The car dealer seems very optimistic about his ability to afford the car payments, another first for him.

The car Adam is considering is $35,000. The dealer has given him three payment options:

1. *Zero percent financing.* Make a $4000 down payment from his savings and finance the remainder with a 0% APR loan for 48 months. Adam has more than enough cash for the down payment, thanks to generous graduation gifts.

2. *Rebate with no money down.* Receive a $4000 rebate, which he would use for the down payment (and leave his savings intact), and finance the rest with a standard 48-month loan, with an 8% APR. He likes this option, as he could think of many other uses for the $4000.

3. *Pay cash.* Get the $4000 rebate and pay the rest with cash. While Adam doesn't have $35,000, he wants to evaluate this option. His parents always paid cash when they bought a family car; Adam wonders if this really was a good idea.

Adam's fellow graduate, Jenna Hawthorne, was lucky. Her parents gave her a car for graduation. Okay, it was a little Hyundai, and definitely not her dream car, but it was serviceable, and Jenna didn't have to worry about buying a new car. In fact, Jenna has been trying to decide how much of her new salary she could save. Adam knows that with a hefty car payment, saving for retirement would be very low on his priority list. Jenna believes she could easily set aside $3000 of her $45,000 salary. She is considering putting her savings in a stock fund. She just turned 22 and has a long way to go until retirement at age 65, and she considers this risk level reasonable. The fund she is looking at has earned an average of 9% over the past 15 years and could be expected to continue earning this amount, on average. While she has no current retirement savings, five years ago Jenna's grandparents gave her a new 30-year U.S. Treasury bond with a $10,000 face value.

Jenna wants to know her retirement income if she both (1) sells her Treasury bond at its current market value and invests the proceeds in the stock fund and (2) saves an additional $3000 at the end of each year in the stock fund from now until she turns 65. Once she retires, Jenna wants those savings to last for 25 years until she is 90.

Both Adam and Jenna need to determine their best options.

Case Questions

1. What are the cash flows associated with each of Adam's three car financing options?

2. Suppose that, similar to his parents, Adam had plenty of cash in the bank so that he could easily afford to pay cash for the car without running into debt now or in the foreseeable future. If his cash earns interest at a 5.4% APR (based on monthly compounding) at the bank, what would be his best purchase option for the car?

3. In fact, Adam doesn't have sufficient cash to cover all his debts including his (substantial) student loans. The loans have a 10% APR, and any money spent on the car could not be used to pay down the loans. What is the best option for Adam now? (*Hint*: Note that having an extra $1 today saves Adam roughly $1.10 next year because he can pay down the student loans. So, 10% is Adam's time value of money in this case.)

4. Suppose instead Adam has a lot of credit card debt, with an 18% APR, and he doubts he will pay off this debt completely before he pays off the car. What is Adam's best option now?

5. Suppose Jenna's Treasury bond has a coupon interest rate of 6.5%, paid semi-annually, while current Treasury bonds with the same maturity date have a yield to maturity of 5.4435% (expressed as an APR with semiannual compounding). If she has just received the bond's 10th coupon, for how much can Jenna sell her treasury bond?

6. Suppose Jenna sells the bond, reinvests the proceeds, and then saves as she planned. If, indeed, Jenna earns a 9% annual return on her savings, how much could she withdraw each year in retirement? (Assume she begins withdrawing the money from the account in equal amounts at the end of each year once her retirement begins.)

7. Jenna expects her salary to grow regularly. While there are no guarantees, she believes an increase of 4% a year is reasonable. She plans to save $3000 the first year, and then increase the amount she saves by 4% each year as her salary grows. Unfortunately, prices will also grow due to inflation. Suppose Jenna assumes there will be 3% inflation every year. In retirement, she will need to increase her withdrawals each year to keep up with inflation. In this case, how much can she withdraw at the end of the first year of her retirement? What amount does this correspond to in today's dollars? (*Hint*: Build a spreadsheet in which you track the amount in her retirement account each year.)

8. Should Jenna sell her Treasury bond and invest the proceeds in the stock fund? Give at least one reason for and against this plan.

9. At the last minute, Jenna considers investing in Coca-Cola stock at a price of $55.55 per share instead. The stock just paid an annual dividend of $1.76 and she expects the dividend to grow at 4% annually. If the next dividend is due in one year, what expected return is Coca-Cola stock offering?

Valuation and the Firm

3

Valuation Principle Connection. One of the most important decisions facing a financial manager is choosing which investments the corporation should make. These decisions fundamentally drive value in the corporation. In Chapter 8 we learn how the Valuation Principle allows us to apply the concept of *net present value (NPV)* to compare the costs and benefits of a project in terms of a common unit—namely, dollars today. We will then be able to evaluate a decision by answering this question: *Does the cash value today of its benefits exceed the cash value today of its costs?* In addition, we will see that the difference between the cash values of the benefits and costs indicates the net amount by which the decision will increase the value of the firm and therefore the wealth of its investors.

After establishing the usefulness of the NPV decision rule for making investment decisions, we discuss alternative rules found in practice and their drawbacks. The process of allocating the firm's capital for investment is known as *capital budgeting.* In Chapter 9, we outline how to estimate a project's incremental cash flows, which then become the inputs to the NPV decision rule. Chapter 9 also provides a practical demonstration of the power of the discounting tools that were introduced in Chapters 3 and 4. Capital budgeting drives value in the firm, so in Chapter 10, Stock Valuation: A Second Look, we return to valuing the ownership claim in the firm—its stock. In Chapter 7, we valued a stock by discounting its future dividends or total payments. In Chapter 10, we consider alternative methods such as discounting free cash flows or comparing its value to that of similar, publicly traded companies.

8
Investment Decision Rules

LEARNING OBJECTIVES

- Calculate Net Present Value
- Use the NPV rule to make investment decisions
- Understand alternative decision rules and their drawbacks

- Choose between mutually exclusive alternatives
- Evaluate projects with different lives
- Rank projects when a company's resources are limited so that it cannot take all positive-NPV projects

notation

CF_n	cash flow that arrives at date n	NPV	net present value
		PV	present value
g	growth rate	r	discount rate
IRR	internal rate of return		
MIRR	modified internal rate of return		

In 2000, Toshiba and Sony began experimenting with new DVD technology, leading to Sony's decision to develop and produce Blu-ray high-definition DVD players and Toshiba's decision to develop and produce the HD-DVD player and format. So began an eight-year format war that ended in February 2008 when Toshiba decided to stop producing HD-DVD players and abandon the format. How did Toshiba and Sony managers arrive at the decision to invest in new DVD formats? How did Toshiba managers conclude that the best decision was to stop producing HD-DVD? In this chapter, we focus on the decision-making tools managers use to evaluate investment decisions. Examples of these decisions include new products, equipment purchases, and marketing campaigns.

We begin by introducing the *net present value (NPV) rule*. Although the NPV investment rule maximizes the value of the firm, some firms nevertheless use other techniques to evaluate investments and decide which projects to pursue. As a result, it is important to understand those techniques, so we will explain some commonly used alternative techniques—namely, the *payback rule* and the *internal rate of return (IRR) rule*. In each case, we define the decision rule and compare decisions based on this rule to decisions based on the NPV rule. We also illustrate the circumstances in which each of the alternative rules is likely to lead to bad investment decisions.

After establishing these rules in the context of a single, stand-alone project, we broaden our perspective to include evaluating multiple opportunities to select the best one. We conclude with a look at project selection when the firm faces limits on capital or managers' time.

8.1 The NPV Decision Rule

In the previous chapters, we learned how to convert between cash today and cash in the future using the discount rate. As long as we convert costs and benefits to the same point in time, we can use the Valuation Principle to make a decision. In practice, most corporations prefer to measure values in terms of their present value—that is, in terms of cash today. In this section, we apply the Valuation Principle to derive the concept of the *net present value* or *NPV*, which we can use to define the "golden rule" of financial decision making, the *NPV rule*.

Net Present Value

net present value (NPV)
The difference between the present value of a project's or investment's benefits and the present value of its costs.

When the value of a cost or benefit is computed in terms of cash today, we refer to it as the present value (PV). Similarly, we define the **net present value (NPV)** of a project or investment as the difference between the present value of its benefits and the present value of its costs:

Net Present Value

$$NPV = PV(\text{Benefits}) - PV(\text{Costs}) \tag{8.1}$$

Let's consider a simple example. Suppose your firm is offered the following investment opportunity: In exchange for $500 today, you will receive $550 in one year. If the interest rate is 8% per year, then:

$$PV(\text{Benefit}) = (\$550 \text{ in one year}) \div (\$1.08 \text{ in one year}/\$1 \text{ today})$$
$$= \$509.26 \text{ today}$$

This PV is the amount you would need to put in the bank today to generate $550 in one year ($509.26 \times 1.08 = \$550$). In other words, *the present value is the amount you need to invest at the current interest rate to recreate the cash flow*. We can think of this as the cash cost today of generating the cash flow ourselves.

Once the costs and benefits are in present value terms, we can compare them by computing the investment's NPV:

$$NPV = \$509.26 - \$500 = \$9.26 \text{ today}$$

The NPV is positive, so the benefits outweigh the costs, which means the firm should undertake this investment opportunity.

But what if you don't have the $500 needed to cover the initial cost of the project? Does the project still have the same value? Because we computed the value using competitive market prices, it should not depend on your tastes or the amount of cash you have in the bank. If you don't have the $500, suppose you borrow $509.26 from the bank at the 8% interest rate and then take the project. What are your cash flows in this case?

Today: $509.26 (loan) − $500 (invested in the project) = $9.26

In one year: $550 (from project) − $509.26 × 1.08 (loan balance) = $0

This transaction leaves you with exactly $9.26 extra cash in your pocket today and no future net obligations. So taking the project is similar to having an extra $9.26 in cash up front. Thus, the NPV expresses the value of an investment decision as an amount of cash received today. *As long as the NPV is positive, the decision increases the value of the firm and is a good decision regardless of your current cash needs or preferences regarding when to spend the money.*

<table>
<tr><td>

EXAMPLE 8.1

The NPV Is Equivalent to Cash Today

MyFinanceLab

</td><td>

PROBLEM

After saving $1500 by waiting tables, you are about to buy a 50-inch LCD TV. You notice that the store is offering a "one year same as cash" deal. You can take the TV home today and pay nothing until one year from now, when you will owe the store the $1500 purchase price. If your savings account earns 5% per year, what is the NPV of this offer? Show that its NPV represents cash in your pocket.

SOLUTION

PLAN

You are getting something worth $1500 today (the TV) and in exchange will need to pay $1500 in one year. Think of it as getting back the $1500 you thought you would have to spend today to get the TV. We treat it as a positive cash flow.
Cash flows:

Today	In one year
+$1500	−$1500

The discount rate for calculating the present value of the payment in one year is your interest rate of 5%. You need to compare the present value of the cost ($1500 in one year) to the benefit today (a $1500 TV).

EXECUTE

$$NPV = +1500 - \frac{1500}{(1.05)} = 1500 - 1428.57 = \$71.43$$

You could take $1428.57 of the $1500 you had saved for the TV and put it in your savings account. With interest, in one year it would grow to $1428.57 \times (1.05) = \$1500$, enough to pay the store. The extra $71.43 is money in your pocket to spend as you like (or put toward the speaker system for your new media room).

EVALUATE

By taking the delayed payment offer, we have extra net cash flows of $71.43 today. If we put $1428.57 in the bank, it will be just enough to offset our $1500 obligation in the future. Therefore, this offer is equivalent to receiving $71.43 today, without any future net obligations.

</td></tr>
</table>

The NPV Decision Rule

As shown in Example 8.1, the Valuation Principle implies that we should undertake projects with a positive NPV because undertaking those projects increases wealth. That is, good projects are those for which the present value of the benefits exceeds the present value of the costs. As a result, the value of the firm increases and investors are wealthier. Projects with negative NPVs have costs that exceed their benefits. Accepting them is equivalent to losing money today.

NPV decision rule When choosing among investment alternatives, take the alternative with the highest NPV. Choosing this alternative is equivalent to receiving its NPV in cash today.

We capture this logic in the **NPV Decision Rule**:

When making an investment decision, take the alternative with the highest NPV. Choosing this alternative is equivalent to receiving its NPV in cash today.

Because NPV is expressed in terms of cash today, using the NPV decision rule is a simple way to apply the Valuation Principle. Decisions that increase wealth are superior to those that decrease wealth. We don't need to know anything about the investor's preferences to reach this conclusion. As long as we have correctly captured all the cash flows of a project and applied the appropriate discount rate, we can determine whether the project makes us wealthier. Being wealthier increases our options and makes us better off, whatever our preferences are.

A common way companies apply the NPV rule in financial practices is when deciding whether to accept or reject a project. Because rejecting the project generally has $NPV = 0$ (there are no new costs or benefits from not doing the project), the NPV decision rule implies that we should

- Accept positive-NPV projects; accepting them is equivalent to receiving their NPV in cash today, and
- Reject negative-NPV projects; accepting them would reduce the value of the firm, whereas rejecting them has no cost ($NPV = 0$).

If the NPV is exactly zero, then you will neither gain nor lose by accepting the project instead of rejecting it, which also has an NPV of zero. It is not a bad project because it does not reduce the firm's value, but it does not add value to the firm either.

Concept Check

1. What is the NPV decision rule? How is it related to the Valuation Principle?
2. Why doesn't the NPV decision rule depend on the investor's preferences?

8.2   Using the NPV Rule

We continue our discussion of investment decision rules by considering a take-it-or-leave-it decision about a single, stand-alone project. By undertaking this project, the firm does not constrain its ability to take other projects. In the case of a stand-alone project, the alternatives we are considering are to accept or reject a project. The NPV rule then implies that we should compare the project's NPV to zero (the NPV of rejecting the project and doing nothing). Thus, we should accept the project if its NPV is positive.[1]

Organizing the Cash Flows and Computing the NPV

Researchers at Fredrick's Feed and Farm have made a breakthrough. They believe they can produce a new, environmentally friendly fertilizer at a substantial cost saving over the company's existing line of fertilizer. The fertilizer will require a new plant that can be built immediately at a cost of $81.6 million. Financial managers estimate that the benefits of the new fertilizer will be $28 million per year, starting at the end of the first year and lasting for four years, as shown by the following timeline:

Year:	0	1	2	3	4
Cash flow (in millions):	−$81.60	+$28	+$28	+$28	+$28

Thus, the cash flows are an immediate $81.6 million outflow followed by an annuity inflow of $28 million per year for four years. Therefore, given a discount rate r, the NPV of this project is:

---

[1]Some prefer to state the rule that the project should be accepted if its NPV is non-negative. Since the firm should be indifferent at an NPV of exactly zero (you will neither gain nor lose by accepting the project instead of rejecting it), we prefer to state it this way. A zero NPV project is not a bad project because it does not reduce the firm's value, but it does not add value to the firm either.

$$NPV = -81.6 + \frac{28}{1+r} + \frac{28}{(1+r)^2} + \frac{28}{(1+r)^3} + \frac{28}{(1+r)^4} \qquad (8.2)$$

We can also use the annuity formula from Chapter 4 to write the NPV as:

$$NPV = -81.6 + \frac{28}{r}\left(1 - \frac{1}{(1+r)^4}\right) \qquad (8.3)$$

To apply the NPV rule, we need to know the cost of capital. The financial managers responsible for this project estimate a cost of capital of 10% per year. If we replace r in Eq. 8.2 or 8.3 with the project's cost of capital of 10%, we get an NPV of $7.2 million, which is positive. Recall that a net present value tells us the present value of the benefits (positive cash flows) net of the costs (negative cash flows) of the project. By putting everything into present values, it puts all the costs and benefits on an equal footing for comparison. In this case, the benefits outweigh the costs by $7.2 million in present value. The NPV investment rule indicates that by making the investment, Fredrick's will increase the value of the firm today by $7.2 million, so Fredrick's should undertake this project.

The NPV Profile

NPV profile A graph of a project's NPV over a range of discount rates.

The NPV of the project depends on its appropriate cost of capital. Often, there may be some uncertainty regarding the project's cost of capital. In that case, it is helpful to compute an **NPV profile**, which graphs the project's NPV over a range of discount rates. It is easiest to prepare the NPV profile using a spreadsheet such as Excel. We simply repeat our calculation of the NPV above using a range of different discount rates instead of only 10%. Figure 8.1 presents the NPV profile for Fredrick's project by plotting the NPV as a function of the discount rate, r.[2]

FIGURE 8.1

NPV of Fredrick's New Project

The graph in Panel (b) shows the NPV as a function of the discount rate based on the data in Panel (a). The NPV is positive, represented by the green-shaded area, only for discount rates that are less than 14%, the *internal rate of return (IRR)*. Given the cost of capital of 10%, the project has a positive NPV of $7.2 million. The red-shaded area indicates discount rates above the 14% IRR with negative NPVs.

Panel (a)

Discount Rate	NPV ($ millions)
0%	$30.4
2%	$25.0
4%	$20.0
6%	$15.4
8%	$11.1
10%	$7.2
12%	$3.4
14%	$0.0
16%	−$3.3
18%	−$6.3
20%	−$9.1
22%	−$11.8
24%	−$14.3

Panel (b)

Cost of Capital

IRR = 14%

Discount Rate

---

[2]In the online appendix to this chapter, we show you how to create an NPV profile in Excel. You can find this in the chapter resources section of MyFinanceLab.

Notice that the NPV is positive only for discount rates that are less than 14% (the green shaded area in Figure 8.1). Referring to the graph and the accompanying data table, we see that at 14% the NPV is zero. The discount rate that sets the net present value of the cash flows equal to zero is an investment's **internal rate of return (IRR)**. Thus, by constructing the NPV profile, we have determined that Fredrick's project has an IRR of 14%. We can also compute the IRR without graphing the NPV by using a financial calculator or a spreadsheet's IRR function (see the appendix to Chapter 4. The calculator instructions for solving for the rate of return can be used to solve for the IRR).

internal rate of return (IRR) The interest rate that sets the net present value of the cash flows equal to zero.

	N	I/Y	PV	PMT	FV
Given:	4		−81.6	28	0
Solve for:		14			
Excel Formula: =RATE(NPER,PMT,PV,FV)=RATE(4,28,−81.6,0)					

Measuring Sensitivity with IRR

In our Fredrick's example, the firm's managers provided the cost of capital. If you are unsure of your cost of capital estimate, it is important to determine how sensitive your analysis is to errors in this estimate. The IRR can provide this information. For Fredrick's, if the cost of capital estimate is more than the 14% IRR, the NPV will be negative (see the red shaded area in Figure 8.1). Therefore, as long as our estimate of the cost of capital of 10% is within 4% of the true cost of capital, our decision to accept the project is correct. In general, the difference between the cost of capital and the IRR tells us the amount of estimation error in the cost of capital estimate that can exist without altering the original decision.

Alternative Rules Versus the NPV Rule

The NPV rule indicates that Fredrick's should undertake the investment in fertilizer technology. As we evaluate alternative rules for project selection in the subsequent sections, keep in mind that sometimes other investment rules may give the same answer as the NPV rule, but at other times they may disagree. When the rules conflict, always base your decision on the NPV rule, which is the most accurate and reliable decision rule.

Concept Check

3. Explain the NPV rule for stand-alone projects.

4. How can you interpret the difference between the cost of capital and the IRR?

8.3   Alternative Decision Rules

Even though the NPV rule is the most accurate and reliable rule, in practice a wide variety of rules are applied, often in tandem with the NPV rule. In a 2001 study, John Graham and Campbell Harvey[3] found that 75% of the firms they surveyed used the NPV rule for making investment decisions. This result is substantially different from that found in a similar study in 1977 by L. J. Gitman and J. R. Forrester,[4] who found that only 10% of firms used

---

[3]John Graham and Campbell Harvey, "The Theory and Practice of Corporate Finance: Evidence from the Field," *Journal of Financial Economics* 60 (2001): 187–243.

[4]L. J. Gitman and J. R. Forrester, Jr., "A Survey of Capital Budgeting Techniques Used by Major U.S. Firms," *Financial Management* 6 (1977): 66–71.

Here we discuss how to use Microsoft Excel to solve for NPV and IRR. We also identify some pitfalls to avoid when using Excel.

NPV Function: Leaving Out Date 0

Excel's NPV function has the format *NPV (rate, value1, value2, . . .*), where "rate" is the interest rate per period used to discount the cash flows, and "value1", "value2", etc., are the cash flows (or ranges of cash flows). The NPV function computes the present value of the cash flows *assuming the first cash flow occurs at date 1.* Therefore, if a project's first cash flow occurs at date 0, we cannot use the NPV function by itself to compute the NPV. We can use the NPV function to compute the present value of the cash flows from date 1 onward, and then we must add the date 0 cash flow to that result to calculate the NPV. The screenshot below shows the difference. The first NPV calculation (outlined in blue) is correct: we used the NPV function for all of the cash flows occurring at time 1 and later and then added on the first cash flow occurring at time 0 since it is already in present value. The second calculation (outlined in green) is incorrect: we used the NPV function for all of the cash flows, but the function assumed that the first cash flow occurs in period 1 instead of immediately.

NPV Function: Ignoring Blank Cells

Another pitfall with the NPV function is that cash flows that are left blank are treated differently from cash flows that are equal to zero. If the cash flow is left blank, *both the cash flow and the period are ignored.* For example, the second set of cash flows below is equivalent to the first—we have simply left the cash flow for date 2 blank instead of entering a "0." However, the NPV function ignores the blank cell at date 2 and assumes the cash flow is 10 at date 1 and 110 at date 2, which is clearly not what is intended and produces an incorrect answer (outlined in red).

Because of these idiosyncrasies, we avoid using Excel's NPV function. It is more reliable to compute the present value of each cash flow separately in Excel, and then sum them to determine the NPV.

IRR FUNCTION

Excel's IRR function has the format *IRR (values, guess),* where "values" is the range containing the cash flows, and "guess" is an optional starting guess where Excel begins its search for an IRR. Two things to note about the IRR function:

1. The values given to the IRR function should include all of the cash flows of the project, including the one at date 0. In this sense, the IRR and NPV functions in Excel are inconsistent.

2. Like the NPV function, the IRR ignores the period associated with any blank cells.

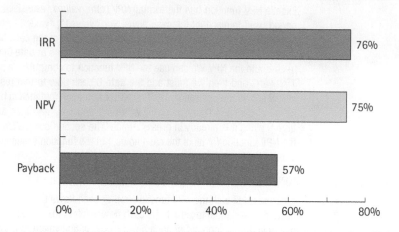

FIGURE 8.2

The Most Popular
Decision Rules
Used by CFOs

The bar graph shows the most popular decision rules used by CFOs in Professors Graham and Harvey's 2001 survey. Many CFOs used more than one method, but no other methods were mentioned by more than half of CFOs.

IRR — 76%
NPV — 75%
Payback — 57%

the NPV rule. Business students in recent years have been listening to their finance professors! Even so, Graham and Harvey's study indicates that one-fourth of U.S. corporations do not use the NPV rule. Exactly why other capital budgeting techniques are used in practice is not always clear. Figure 8.2 summarizes the top three decision rules given in the survey. Because you may encounter these techniques in the business world, you should know what they are, how they are used, and how they compare to NPV. In this section, we examine alternative decision rules for single, stand-alone projects within the firm. The focus here is on *the payback rule* and *the IRR rule*.

The Payback Rule

payback investment rule Only projects that pay back their initial investment within a prespecified period are undertaken.

The simplest investment rule is the **payback investment rule**, which states that you should only accept a project if its cash flows pay back its initial investment within a prespecified period. The rule is based on the notion that an opportunity that pays back its initial investment quickly is a good idea. To apply the payback rule,

payback period The amount of time until the cash flows from a project offset the initial investment. The time it takes to pay back the initial investment.

1. Calculate the amount of time it takes to pay back the initial investment, called the **payback period.**

2. Accept the project if the payback period is less than a prespecified length of time— usually a few years.

3. Reject the project if the payback period is greater than that prespecified length of time.

For example, a firm might adopt any project with a payback period of less than two years.

EXAMPLE 8.2

Using the
Payback Rule

MyFinanceLab

PROBLEM

Assume Fredrick's requires all projects to have a payback period of two years or less. Would the firm undertake the fertilizer project under this rule?

SOLUTION

PLAN

In order to implement the payback rule, we need to know whether the sum of the inflows from the project will exceed the initial investment before the end of two years. The project has inflows of $28 million per year and an initial investment of $81.6 million.

EXECUTE

The sum of the cash flows for years 1 and 2 is $28 \times 2 = $56 million, which will not cover the initial investment of $81.6 million. In fact, it will not be until year 3 that the cash inflows exceed the initial investment ($28 \times 3 = $84 million). Because the payback period for this project exceeds two years, Fredrick's will reject the project.

EVALUATE

While simple to compute, the payback rule requires us to use an arbitrary cutoff period in summing the cash flows. Furthermore, note that the payback rule does not discount future cash flows. Instead, it simply sums the cash flows and compares them to a cash outflow in the present. In this case, Fredrick's would have rejected a project that would have increased the value of the firm.

Relying on the payback rule analysis in Example 8.2, Fredrick's will reject the project. However, as we saw earlier, with a cost of capital of 10%, the NPV is $7.2 million. Following the payback rule would be a mistake because Fredrick's will pass up a project worth $7.2 million.

The payback rule is not as reliable as the NPV rule because it (1) ignores the time value of money, (2) ignores cash flows after the payback period, and (3) lacks a decision criterion grounded in economics (what is the right number of years to require for a payback period?). Some companies have addressed the first failing by computing the payback period using discounted cash flows, called the **discounted payback rule**. However, this does not solve the fundamental problem because the other two failings remain. Despite these failings, Graham and Harvey found that about 57% of the firms they surveyed reported using the payback rule as part of the decision-making process.

discounted payback rule Only accept projects where the sum of the discounted cash flows within the payback period is greater than or equal to the initial investment.

Why do some companies consider the payback rule? The answer probably relates to its simplicity. This rule is typically used for small investment decisions—for example, whether to purchase a new copy machine or to service the old one. In such cases, the cost of making an incorrect decision might not be large enough to justify the time required to calculate the NPV. The appeal of the payback rule is that it favors short-term projects. Some firms are unwilling to commit capital to long-term investments. Also, if the required payback period is short (one to two years), then most projects that satisfy the payback rule will have a positive NPV.

The Internal Rate of Return Rule

internal rate of return (IRR) investment rule A decision rule that accepts any investment opportunity where the IRR exceeds the opportunity cost of capital and otherwise rejects the opportunity.

Similar to NPV, the **internal rate of return (IRR) investment rule** is based on the concept that if the return on the investment opportunity you are considering is greater than the return on other alternatives in the market with equivalent risk and maturity (i.e., the project's cost of capital), you should undertake the investment opportunity. We state the rule formally as follows:

IRR investment rule: Take any investment opportunity whose IRR exceeds the opportunity cost of capital. Turn down any opportunity whose IRR is less than the opportunity cost of capital.

The IRR investment rule will give the correct answer (that is, the same answer as the NPV rule) in many—but not all—situations. For instance, it gives the correct answer for Fredrick's fertilizer opportunity. From Figure 8.1, whenever the cost of capital is in the green area below the IRR (14%), the project has a positive NPV and you should undertake the investment. Table 8.1 summarizes our analysis of Fredrick's new project. The NPV and IRR rules agree, but using the payback rule with a required payback period of two years or less would cause Fredrick's to reject the project.

TABLE 8.1

Summary of NPV, IRR, and Payback for Fredrick's New Project

NPV at 10%	$7.2 million	Accept ($7.2 million > 0)
Payback Period	3 years	Reject (3 years $>$ 2 year required payback)
IRR	14%	Accept (14% $>$ 10% cost of capital)

In general, the IRR rule works for a stand-alone project if all of the project's negative cash flows precede its positive cash flows. But in other cases, the IRR rule may disagree with the NPV rule and thus be incorrect. Let's examine several situations in which the IRR fails.

Delayed Investments. Star basketball player Evan Cole is graduating from college with a degree in finance and preparing for the NBA draft. Several companies have already approached him with endorsement contracts. Two competing sports drink companies are pursuing him. QuenchIt offers him a single up-front payment of $1 million to exclusively endorse their sports drink for three years. PowerUp offers $500,000 per year, payable at the end of each of the next three years, to endorse their product exclusively. Which offer is better? One direct way to compare the two contracts is to realize that signing with QuenchIt causes Evan to forgo the PowerUp contract, or $500,000 per year. Considering the risk of his alternative income sources and available investment opportunities, Evan estimates his opportunity cost of capital to be 10%. The timeline of Evan's investment opportunity is:

0	1	2	3
$1,000,000	$-$500,000	$-$500,000	$-$500,000

The NPV of Evan's investment opportunity is:

$$NPV = 1,000,000 - \frac{500,000}{1+r} - \frac{500,000}{(1+r)^2} - \frac{500,000}{(1+r)^3}$$

By setting the NPV equal to zero and solving for r, we find the IRR. We can use either a financial calculator or a spreadsheet to find the IRR:

	N	I/Y	PV	PMT	FV
Given:	3		1,000,000	$-$500,000	0
Solve for:		23.38			
Excel Formula: =RATE(NPER,PMT,PV,FV)=RATE(3,−500000,1000000,0)

The 23.38% IRR is larger than the 10% opportunity cost of capital. According to the IRR rule, Evan should sign the deal. But what does the NPV rule say?

$$NPV = 1,000,000 - \frac{500,000}{1.1} - \frac{500,000}{1.1^2} - \frac{500,000}{1.1^3} = -\$243,426$$

At a 10% discount rate, the NPV is negative, so signing the deal would reduce Evan's wealth. He should not sign the endorsement deal with QuenchIt, and should sign with PowerUp instead.

To resolve this conflict, we can prepare an NPV profile for the QuenchIt contract. Figure 8.3 plots the NPV of the investment opportunity for a range of discount rates. It shows that, no matter what the cost of capital is, the IRR rule and the NPV rule will give exactly opposite recommendations. That is, the NPV is positive only when the opportunity cost of capital is *above* 23.38% (the IRR). Evan should accept the investment only when the opportunity cost of capital is greater than the IRR, the opposite of what the IRR rule recommends.

Figure 8.3 also illustrates the problem with using the IRR rule in this case. For most investment opportunities, expenses occur initially and cash is received later. In this case, Evan receives cash *up front* from QuenchIt but the forgone cash flows from PowerUp occurred later. It is as if Evan borrowed money, and when you borrow money you prefer as *low* a rate as possible. Evan's optimal rule is to borrow money as long as the rate at which he borrows is *less* than the cost of capital.

Even though the IRR rule fails to give the correct answer in this case, the IRR itself still provides useful information *in conjunction* with the NPV rule. As mentioned earlier, the IRR provides information on how sensitive the investment decision is to uncertainty in the cost of capital estimate. In this case, the difference between the cost of capital and the IRR is large—10% versus 23.38%. Evan would have to have underestimated the cost of capital by 13.38% to make the NPV positive.

Multiple IRRs. Evan has informed QuenchIt that it needs to sweeten the deal before he will accept it. In response, the company has agreed to make an additional payment of $600,000 in 10 years as deferred compensation for the long-term increase in sales that

FIGURE 8.3

NPV of Evan Cole's $1 Million QuenchIt Deal

When all the benefits of an investment occur at time zero and before the costs, the NPV is an *increasing* function of the discount rate. The NPV is positive in the green-shaded areas and negative in the red-shaded areas. Notice that the NPV is positive when the cost of capital is above 23.38%, the IRR, so the NPV and IRR rules conflict.

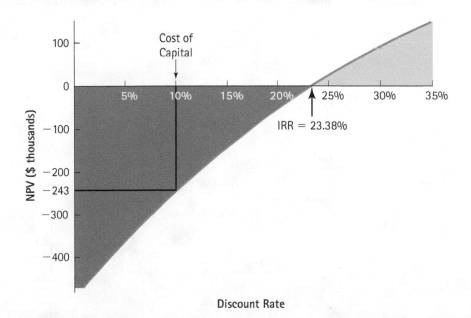

even a short-term endorsement by Evan would bring. Should he accept or reject the new offer?

We begin with the new timeline:

0	1	2	3	4	...	9	10
+$1,000,000	−$500,000	−$500,000	−$500,000	0		0	+$600,000

The NPV of Evan's new investment opportunity is:

$$NPV = 1,000,000 - \frac{500,000}{1+r} - \frac{500,000}{(1+r)^2} - \frac{500,000}{(1+r)^3} + \frac{600,000}{(1+r)^{10}}$$

We can find the IRR for this investment opportunity by creating an NPV profile and noting where it crosses zero. Figure 8.4 plots the NPV of the opportunity at different discount rates. In this case, there are *two* IRRs—that is, there are two values of r that set the NPV equal to zero. You can verify this fact by substituting IRRs of 5.79% and 13.80% for r into the equation. Because there is more than one IRR, we cannot apply the IRR rule. It is also worth noting that you should take special care when using a spreadsheet or financial calculator to determine the IRR. Both solve for the IRR through trial and error because you cannot calculate the IRR directly. In cases where there is more than one IRR, the spreadsheet or calculator will simply produce the first one that it finds, with no indication that there could be others! Some financial calculators will return an error message if there are multiple IRRs. Thus, it always pays to create the NPV profile.

For guidance, let's turn to the NPV rule. If the cost of capital were *either* below 5.79% or above 13.80%, Evan should undertake the opportunity. But given his cost of capital of 10%, he should still turn it down. Notice that even though the IRR rule fails in this case,

FIGURE 8.4

NPV of Evan's Sports Drink Deal with Additional Deferred Payments

The graph in Panel (b) shows the NPV of Evan's deal with additional deferred payment based on the data in Panel (a). In this case, there are two IRRs, invalidating the IRR rule. If the opportunity cost of capital is *either* below 5.79% or above 13.80%, Evan should accept the deal because the NPV is then positive, as indicated by the green-shaded areas. At any point between the two IRRs, the NPV is negative (see the red-shaded area).

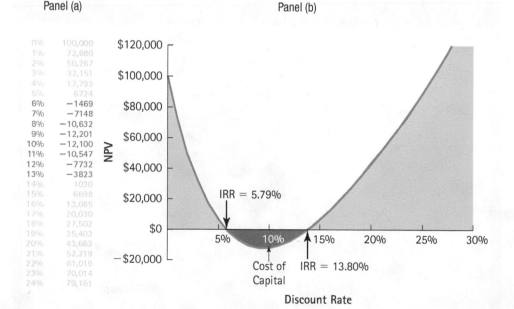

Panel (a)	
0%	100,000
1%	72,680
2%	50,267
3%	32,151
4%	17,793
5%	6724
6%	−1469
7%	−7148
8%	−10,632
9%	−12,201
10%	−12,100
11%	−10,547
12%	−7732
13%	−3823
14%	1030
15%	6698
16%	13,065
17%	20,030
18%	27,502
19%	35,403
20%	43,663
21%	52,219
22%	61,019
23%	70,014
24%	79,161

IRR Versus the IRR Rule

Throughout this subsection, we have distinguished between the IRR itself and the IRR rule. While we have pointed out the shortcomings of using the IRR rule to make investment decisions, *the IRR itself remains a very useful tool.* The IRR measures the average return of the investment and indicates the sensitivity of the NPV to estimation error in the cost of capital. Thus, knowing the IRR can be very useful, but relying on it to make investment decisions can be hazardous.

the two IRRs are still useful as bounds on the cost of capital estimate. If the cost of capital estimate is wrong, and it is actually smaller than 5.79% or larger than 13.80%, the decision not to pursue the project will change because it will have a positive NPV.

There is no easy fix for the IRR rule when there are multiple IRRs. Although the NPV is negative between the IRRs in this example, the reverse is also possible (see Figure 8.5). In that case, the project would have a positive NPV for discount rates between the IRRs rather than for discount rates lower or higher than the IRRs. Furthermore, there are situations in which more than two IRRs exist.[5] In such situations, our only choice is to rely on the NPV rule.

Modified Internal Rate of Return

modified internal rate of return (MIRR) The discount rate that sets the NPV of modified cash flows of a project equal to zero. Cash flows are modified so there is only one negative cash flow (and one sign change) to ensure that only one IRR exists.

The fact that there can be multiple IRRs for the cash flows from a project is a clear disadvantage for the IRR. To overcome this, some have proposed various ways of modifying the cash flows before computing the IRR. All these modifications have the common feature that they group the cash flows so that there is only one negative cash flow, occurring at either the beginning or the end. In that case, there is only one sign change for the cash flows as a whole and hence only one IRR. This new IRR, computed as the discount rate that sets the NPV of the modified cash flows of the project equal to zero, is called the **modified internal rate of return (MIRR)**.

FIGURE 8.5

NPV Profile for a Project with Multiple IRRs

The graph shows the NPV profile for a multiple-IRR project with cash flows of −$1000, $2500, and −$1540 in years 0, 1, and 2, respectively. As the NPV profile shows, the project has two IRRs: 10% and 40%.

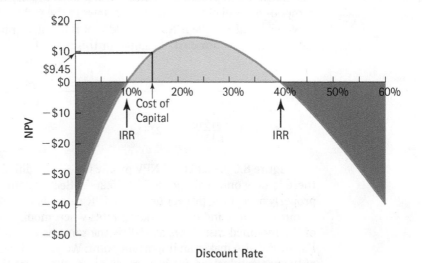

[5]In general, there can be as many IRRs as the number of times the project's cash flows change sign over time.

Why Do Rules Other Than the NPV Rule Persist?

Professors Graham and Harvey found that a sizable minority of firms (25%) in their study do not use the NPV rule at all. In addition, about 50% of firms surveyed used the payback rule. Furthermore, it appears that most firms use *both* the NPV rule and the IRR rule. Why do firms use rules other than NPV if they can lead to erroneous decisions?

One possible explanation for this phenomenon is that Graham and Harvey's survey results might be misleading. CFOs who were using the IRR as a sensitivity measure in conjunction with the NPV rule might have checked both the IRR box and the NPV box on the survey. The question they were asked was, "How frequently does your firm use the following techniques when deciding which projects or acquisitions to pursue?" By computing the IRR and using it in conjunction with the NPV rule to estimate the sensitivity of their results, they might have felt they were using *both* techniques. Nevertheless, a significant minority of managers surveyed replied

that they used only the IRR rule, so this explanation cannot be the whole story.

One common reason that managers give for using the IRR rule exclusively is that you do not need to know the opportunity cost of capital to calculate the IRR. On a superficial level, this is true: The IRR does not depend on the cost of capital. You may not need to know the cost of capital to *calculate* the IRR, but you certainly need to know the cost of capital when you *apply* the IRR rule. Consequently, the opportunity cost is as important to the IRR rule as it is to the NPV rule.

In our opinion, some firms use the IRR rule exclusively because the IRR sums up the attractiveness of investment opportunity in a single number without requiring the person running the numbers to make an assumption about the cost of capital. However, if a CFO wants a brief summary of an investment opportunity but does not want her employee to make a cost of capital assumption, she can also request a plot of the NPV as a function of the discount rate. Neither this request nor a request for the IRR requires knowing the cost of capital, but the NPV profile has the distinct advantage of being much more informative and reliable.

MIRR Technique. Let's clarify this with an example. You are considering a project that has the following three cash flows:

The NPV profile for this project, shown in Figure 8.5, identifies the two IRRs for this project as 10% and 40%.

Assume that your discount rate for this project is 15%. As Figure 8.5 shows, the NPV of the project at 15% is $9.45. We could modify the cash flows of the project to eliminate the multiple IRR problem. By discounting all of the negative cash flows to the present and compounding all of the positive cash flows to the end of the project, we have only two cash flows, yielding a single IRR. What discount rate and compounding rate should we use? One natural choice is our cost of capital for this project, which is 15%.

Figure 8.6 presents the NPV profile for our modified cash flows. As Figure 8.6 shows, there is now only a single IRR, at 15.25%. Because our cost of capital is 15%, we would properly accept the project using the IRR rule. Also note that the advantage of using 15% as our discount and compounding rates when modifying the cash flows is that the NPV of the modified cash flows at 15% is the same as the NPV of the true cash flows at 15%. Figure 8.6 also makes an important point: We are no longer evaluating the true cash flows of the project. Instead, we have modified them to force them to produce a single IRR. The NPV profile of the true cash flows of the project is given earlier in Figure 8.5 and is clearly different from the one produced by the modified cash flows in Figure 8.6.

FIGURE 8.6

NPV Profile of Modified Cash Flows for the Multiple-IRR Project from Figure 8.5

The graph presents the NPV profile for the modified project cash flows of −2164.46 in year 0 and 2875 in year 2. The modified cash flows have only one IRR: 15.25%. Given the 15% cost of capital, the IRR rule confirms that we should accept the project.

There is no set way to modify project cash flows to produce an MIRR. Two other approaches that each solve the multiple IRR problem are:

1. Discount all the negative cash flows to time 0 and leave the positive cash flows alone.

2. Leave the initial cash flow alone and compound all the remaining cash flows to the final period of the project. In this approach, you are implicitly reinvesting all the cash flows from the project at your compound rate until the project is complete.

Again, in either case, if you use the project's cost of capital as your discount and compounding rate, you will not alter the NPV of the project at that discount rate. Furthermore, a decision to accept or reject the project based on the modified IRR will be the same as the one based on the NPV decision rule.

MIRR: A Final Word. There is considerable debate about whether MIRR is actually better than IRR. Most of the argument centers on whether it is advisable to modify the cash flows of the project. The IRR is truly an internal rate of return based solely on the actual cash flows of the project. However, the IRR implicitly assumes that all cash flows generated by the project are reinvested at the project's IRR rather than at the firm's cost of capital until the project ends. For a project with a high IRR, this may be an unrealistic assumption. Furthermore, there may be more than one IRR, which complicates its use. The MIRR avoids these problems, but is based on a set of cash flows modified through the use of a chosen discount and compounding rate. Thus, it is not really an internal rate of return and is no longer based solely on the actual cash flows of the project. Finally, MIRR still does not solve some of the other problems associated with using IRR when choosing among projects.

Concept Check

5. How do you apply the payback rule?

6. Under what conditions will the IRR rule lead to the same decision as the NPV rule?

8.4 Choosing Between Projects

Thus far, we have considered only decisions where the choice is either to accept or to reject a single, stand-alone project. Sometimes, however, a firm must choose just one project from among several possible projects. For example, a manager may be evaluating alternative package designs for a new product. The manager must choose only one of the designs. When choosing any one project excludes us from taking the other projects, we are facing **mutually exclusive projects**.

mutually exclusive projects Projects that compete with one another; by accepting one, you exclude the others.

When projects, such as the package designs, are mutually exclusive, it is not enough to determine which projects have positive NPVs. With mutually exclusive projects, the manager's goal is to rank the projects and choose the best one. In this situation, the NPV rule provides a straightforward answer: *Pick the project with the highest NPV.*

EXAMPLE 8.3
NPV and Mutually Exclusive Projects

MyFinanceLab

PROBLEM

You own a small piece of commercial land near a university. You are considering what to do with it. You have been approached with an offer to buy it for $220,000. You are also considering three alternative uses yourself: a bar, a coffee shop, and an apparel store. You assume that you would operate your choice indefinitely, eventually leaving the business to your children. You have collected the following information about the uses. What should you do?

	Initial Investment	Cash Flow in the First Year (CF_1)	Growth Rate (g)	Cost of Capital (r)
Bar	$400,000	$60,000	3.5%	12%
Coffee Shop	$200,000	$40,000	3%	10%
Apparel Store	$500,000	$75,000	3%	13%

SOLUTION

PLAN

Since you can develop only one project (you only have one piece of land), these are mutually exclusive projects. In order to decide which project is most valuable, you need to rank them by NPV. Each of these projects (except for selling the land) has cash flows that can be valued as a growing perpetuity, so from Chapter 4, the present value of the inflows is $CF_1/(r-g)$. The NPV of each investment will be:

$$\frac{CF_1}{r-g} - \text{Initial Investment}$$

EXECUTE

The NPVs are:

$$\text{Bar: } \frac{\$60,000}{0.12 - 0.035} - \$400,000 = \$305,882$$

$$\text{Coffee Shop: } \frac{\$40,000}{0.10 - 0.03} - \$200,000 = \$371,429$$

$$\text{Apparel Store: } \frac{\$75,000}{0.13 - 0.03} - \$500,000 = \$250,000$$

So, the ranking is

Alternative	NPV
Coffee Shop	$371,429
Bar	$305,882
Apparel Store	$250,000
Sell the Land	$220,000

You should choose the coffee shop.

EVALUATE

All the alternatives have positive NPVs, but you can take only one of them, so you should choose the one that creates the most value. Even though the coffee shop has the lowest cash flows, its lower start-up cost coupled with its lower cost of capital (it is less risky) make it the best choice.

Because the IRR is a measure of the expected return of investing in the project, you might be tempted to extend the IRR investment rule to the case of mutually exclusive projects by picking the project with the highest IRR. Unfortunately, picking one project over another simply because it has a larger IRR can lead to mistakes. Problems arise when the mutually exclusive investments have differences in scale (require different initial investments) and when they have different cash flow patterns. We discuss each of these situations in turn.

Differences in Scale

Would you prefer a 200% return on $1 or a 10% return on $1 million? The former return certainly sounds impressive and gives you great bragging rights, but at the end of the day you make only $2. The latter opportunity may sound much more mundane, but you make $100,000. This comparison illustrates an important shortcoming of IRR: Because it is a return, you cannot tell how much value has actually been created without knowing the basis for the return—a 10% IRR can have very different value implications for an initial investment of $1 million versus an initial investment of $100 million.

If a project has a positive NPV, then if we can double its size, its NPV will double: By the Valuation Principle, doubling the cash flows of an investment opportunity must make it worth twice as much. However, the IRR rule does not have this property—it is unaffected by the scale of the investment opportunity because the IRR measures the average return of the investment. Thus, the IRR rule cannot be used to compare projects of different scales. Let's illustrate this concept in the context of an example.

Identical Scale. We begin by considering two mutually exclusive projects with the same scale. Javier is evaluating two investment opportunities. If he goes into business with his girlfriend, he would need to invest $10,000 and the business would generate incremental cash flows of $6000 per year for three years. Alternatively, he could start a two-computer Internet café. The computer setup will cost $10,000 and will generate $5000 for three years. The opportunity cost of capital for both opportunities is 12% and both will require all his time, so Javier must choose between them. How valuable is each opportunity, and which one should Javier choose?

Let's consider both the NPV and IRR of each project. The timeline for the investment with Javier's girlfriend is:

The NPV of the investment opportunity when $r = 0.12$ is:

$$NPV = -10,000 + \frac{6000}{1.12} + \frac{6000}{1.12^2} + \frac{6000}{1.12^3} = \$4411$$

We can determine the IRR of this investment by using a financial calculator or spreadsheet:

	N	**I/Y**	**PV**	**PMT**	**FV**
Given:	3		−10,000	6000	0
Solve for:		36.3			
Excel Formula: =RATE(NPER,PMT,PV,FV)=RATE(3,6000,−10000,0)					

Thus, the IRR for Javier's investment in his girlfriend's business is 36.3%.
The timeline for his investment in the Internet café is:

```
      0           1           2           3
      |-----------|-----------|-----------|
   -10,000      +5000       +5000       +5000
```

The NPV of the investment opportunity when $r = 0.12$ is:

$$NPV = -10,000 + \frac{5000}{1.12} + \frac{5000}{1.12^2} + \frac{5000}{1.12^3} = \$2009$$

The \$2009 NPV of the Internet café is lower than the \$4411 NPV for his girlfriend's business, so Javier should join his girlfriend in business. Luckily, it appears that Javier does not need to choose between his checkbook and his relationship!

We could also compare IRRs. For the Internet café, we would find that the IRR is 23.4%. The Internet café has a lower IRR than the investment in his girlfriend's business. As Figure 8.7 shows, in this case the project with the higher IRR has the higher NPV.

Change in Scale. What happens if we change the scale of one of the projects? Javier's finance professor points out that, given the space available in the facility, five times as many

FIGURE 8.7

NPV of Javier's Investment Opportunities with the Two-Computer Internet Café

The NPV of his girlfriend's business is always larger than the NPV of the computer Internet café. The same is true for the IRR; the IRR of his girlfriend's business is 36.3%, while the IRR for the Internet café is 23.4%.

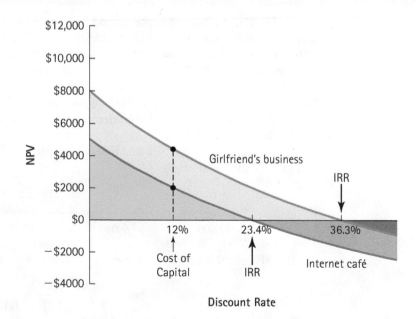

computers could be installed in the Internet café. His setup cost would now be $50,000 and his annual cash flows would be $25,000. What should Javier do now?

Note that the IRR is unaffected by the scale. Because we are scaling all the cash flows

	N	I/Y	PV	PMT	FV
Given:	3		−50,000	25,000	0
Solve for:		23.4			
Excel Formula: =RATE(NPER,PMT,PV,FV)=RATE(3,25000,−50000,0)					

up by a factor of 5, a 10-machine Internet café has exactly the same IRR as a 2-machine Internet café, so his girlfriend's business still has a higher IRR than the Internet café:

However, the NPV of the Internet café does grow by the scale—it is five times larger:

$$NPV = -50{,}000 + \frac{25{,}000}{1.12} + \frac{25{,}000}{1.12^2} + \frac{25{,}000}{1.12^3} = \$10{,}046$$

Now Javier should invest in the 10-computer Internet café. As Figure 8.8 shows, the NPV of the 10-computer Internet café exceeds the NPV of going into business with his girlfriend whenever the cost of capital is less than 20%. In this case, even though the IRR of going into business with his girlfriend exceeds the IRR of the Internet café, picking the investment opportunity with the higher IRR does not result in taking the opportunity with the higher NPV.

Percentage Return Versus Dollar Impact on Value. This result might seem counterintuitive and you can imagine Javier having a difficult time explaining to his girlfriend why he

FIGURE 8.8

NPV of Javier's Investment Opportunities with the Ten-Computer Internet Café

As in Figure 8.7, the IRR of his girlfriend's business is 36.3%, while the IRR for the Internet café is 23.4%. But in this case, the NPV of his girlfriend's business is larger than the NPV of the 10-computer Internet café only for discount rates over 20%.

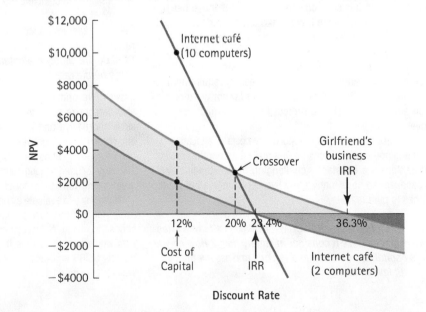

is choosing a lower return over going into business with her. Why would anyone turn down an investment opportunity with a 36.3% return (IRR) in favor of one with only a 23.4% return? The answer is that the latter opportunity, the Internet café, makes more money. Recall the comparison at the beginning of this section: a 200% return on $1 versus a 10% return on $1 million. We agreed that ranking the returns was not the same as ranking the value created. The IRR is a measure of the average return, which can be valuable information. When you are comparing mutually exclusive projects of different scale, however, you need to know the dollar impact on value—the NPV.

INTERVIEW WITH

DICK GRANNIS

Dick Grannis is Senior Vice President and Treasurer of QUALCOMM Incorporated, a world leader in digital wireless communications technology and semiconductors, headquartered in San Diego. He joined the company in 1991 and oversees the company's $10 billion cash investment portfolio. He works primarily on investment banking, capital structure, and international finance.

QUESTION: *QUALCOMM has a wide variety of products in different business lines. How does your capital budgeting process for new products work?*

ANSWER: QUALCOMM evaluates new projects (such as new products, equipment, technologies, research and development, acquisitions, and strategic investments) by using traditional financial measurements including DCF models, IRR levels, peak funding requirements, the time needed to reach cumulative positive cash flows, and the short-term impact of the investment on our reported net earnings. For strategic investments, we consider the possible value of financial, competitive, technology and/or market value enhancements to our core businesses—even if those benefits cannot be quantified. Overall, we make capital budgeting decisions based on a combination of objective analyses and our own business judgment.

We do not engage in capital budgeting and analysis if the project represents an immediate and necessary requirement for our business operations. One example is new software or production equipment to start a project that has already received approval.

We are also mindful of the opportunity costs of allocating our internal engineering resources on one project vs. another project. We view this as a constantly challenging but worthwhile exercise, because we have many attractive opportunities but limited resources to pursue them.

QUESTION: *How often does QUALCOMM evaluate its hurdle rates and what factors does it consider in setting them? How do you allocate capital across areas and regions and assess the risk of non-U.S. investments?*

ANSWER: QUALCOMM encourages its financial planners to utilize hurdle (or discount) rates that vary according to the risk of the particular project. We expect a rate of return commensurate with the project's risk. Our finance staff considers a wide range of discount rates and chooses one that fits the project's expected risk profile and time horizon. The range can be from 6.00% to 8.00% for relatively safe investments in the domestic market to 50% or more for equity investments in foreign markets that may be illiquid and difficult to predict. We re-evaluate our hurdle rates at least every year.

We analyze key factors including: (i) market adoption risk (whether or not customers will buy the new product or service at the price and volume we expect), (ii) technology development risk (whether or not we can develop and patent the new product or service as expected), (iii) execution risk (whether we can launch the new product or service cost effectively and on time), and (iv) dedicated asset risk (the amount of resources that must be consumed to complete the work).

QUESTION: *How are projects categorized and how are the hurdle rates for new projects determined? What would happen if QUALCOMM simply evaluated all new projects against the same hurdle rate?*

ANSWER: We primarily categorize projects by risk level, but we also categorize projects by the expected time horizon. We consider short-term and long-term projects to balance our needs and achieve our objectives. For example, immediate projects and opportunities may demand a great amount of attention, but we also stay focused on long-term projects because they often create greater long-term value for stockholders.

If we were to evaluate all new projects against the same hurdle rate, then our business planners would, by default, consistently choose to invest in the highest risk projects because those projects would appear to have the greatest expected returns in DCF models or IRR analyses. That approach would probably not work well for very long.

EXAMPLE 8.4

Computing the
Crossover Point

MyFinanceLab

PROBLEM

Solve for the crossover point for Javier from Figure 8.8.

SOLUTION

PLAN

The *crossover point* is the discount rate that makes the NPV of the two alternatives equal. We can find the discount rate by setting the equations for the NPV of each project equal to each other and solving for the discount rate. In general, we can always compute the effect of choosing the Internet café over his girlfriend's business as the difference of the NPVs. At the crossover point the difference is 0.

EXECUTE

Setting the difference equal to 0:

$$NPV = -50,000 + \frac{25,000}{1+r} + \frac{25,000}{(1+r)^2} + \frac{25,000}{(1+r)^3}$$

$$-\left(-10,000 + \frac{6000}{(1+r)} + \frac{6000}{(1+r)^2} + \frac{6000}{(1+r)^3}\right) = 0$$

combining terms, we have

$$-40,000 + \frac{19,000}{(1+r)} + \frac{19,000}{(1+r)^2} + \frac{19,000}{(1+r)^3} = 0$$

As you can see, solving for the crossover point is just like solving for the IRR, so we will need to use a financial calculator or spreadsheet:

	N	I/Y	PV	PMT	FV
Given:	3		−40,000	19,000	0
Solve for:		20.04			
	Excel Formula: =RATE(NPER,PMT,PV,FV)=RATE(3,19000,−40000,0)				

We find that the crossover occurs at a discount rate of 20.04%.

EVALUATE

Just as the NPV of a project tells us the value impact of taking the project, so the difference of the NPVs of two alternatives tells us the *incremental* impact of choosing one project over another. The crossover point is the discount rate at which we would be indifferent between the two projects because the incremental value of choosing one over the other would be zero.

Timing of the Cash Flows

Even when projects have the same scale, the IRR may lead you to rank them incorrectly due to differences in the timing of the cash flows. The reason for this is that the IRR is expressed as a return, but the dollar value of earning a given return—and therefore the NPV—depends on how long the return is earned. Consider a high-IRR project with cash flows paid back quickly. It may have a lower NPV than a project with a lower IRR whose cash flows are paid back over a longer period. This sensitivity to timing is another reason why you cannot use the IRR to choose between mutually exclusive investments. To see this in the context of an example, let's return to Javier's Internet café.

Javier believes that after starting the Internet café, he may be able to sell his stake in the business at the end of the first year for $40,000 (he will stay on and manage the business after he sells). Thus, counting his first-year profit of $25,000, he would earn a total of $65,000 after one year. In that case, the timeline is:

```
        0              1
        ├──────────────┤
    −$50,000       +$65,000
```

FIGURE 8.9

NPV with and
without Selling

The IRR from selling after one year (30%) is larger than the IRR without selling (23.4%). However, the
NPV from selling after one year exceeds the NPV without selling only for discount rates that are in
excess of 16.3% (see the yellow-shaded area versus the blue-shaded area). Thus, given a cost of capital
of 12%, it is better not to sell the Internet café after one year, despite the higher IRR.

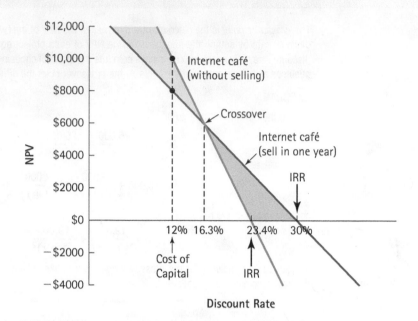

Figure 8.9 plots the NPV profile for the café with and without selling it after one year. If Javier sells, the NPV profile crosses the *x*-axis at 30%, which is its IRR. The IRR for the café if he does not sell is still 23.4%. Therefore, if Javier picks the alternative with the higher IRR, he will sell. However, since the height of each line indicates the NPV of that decision, we can see that his NPV given a 12% cost of capital is higher if he chooses not to sell. (In fact, the NPV is higher as long as the cost of capital is less than 16.3%.) The intuition is as follows: While the 30% IRR from selling is high, this return is only earned in the first year. While the 23.4% IRR from not selling is not as high, it is still attractive relative to the cost of capital, and it is earned over a longer period. Again, only by comparing the NPV can we determine which option is truly more valuable.

The Bottom Line on IRR.   As these examples make clear, picking the investment opportunity with the largest IRR can lead to mistakes. In general, it is dangerous to use the IRR in cases where you are choosing between projects, or anytime when your decision to accept or reject one project would affect your decision on another project. In such a situation, always rely on NPV.

Concept
Check

7.   What is the most reliable way to choose between mutually exclusive projects?

8.   For mutually exclusive projects, explain why picking one project over another because it has a larger IRR can lead to mistakes.

8.5   Evaluating Projects with Different Lives

Often, a company will need to choose between two solutions to the same problem. A complication arises when those solutions last for different periods of time. For example, a firm could be considering two vendors for its internal network servers. Each vendor offers the same level of service, but they use different equipment. Vendor A offers a more expensive server with lower per-year operating costs that it guarantees for three years. Vendor B offers a less expensive server with higher per-year operating costs that it guarantees for two years. The costs are shown in Table 8.2 along with the present value of the costs of each option, discounted at the 10% cost of capital for this project.

TABLE 8.2

Cash Flows ($ thousands) for Network Server Options

Year	PV at 10%	0	1	2	3
A	−12.49	−10	−1	−1	−1
B	−10.47	−7	−2	−2	

Note that all of the cash flows are negative, and so is the present value. This is a choice of an internal server, where the project must be taken and the benefits are diffuse (the company could not function effectively without an internal network). Thus, we are trying to minimize the cost of providing this service for the company. Table 8.2 shows that option A is more expensive on a present value basis ($-\$12{,}487$ versus $-\$10{,}471$). However, the comparison is not that simple: Option A lasts for three years while option B lasts for two. The decision comes down to whether it is worth paying $2000 more for option A to get the extra year. One method that is used to evaluate alternatives such as these that have different lives is to compute the **equivalent annual annuity (EAA)** for each project, which is the level annual cash flow with the same present value as the cash flows of the project. The intuition is that we can think of the cost of each solution as the constant annual cost that gives us the same present value of the lumpy cash flows of buying and operating the server. On a timeline, equivalent annual annuity cash flows would appear as follows:

equivalent annual annuity (EAA) The level annual cash flow that has the same present value as the cash flows of a project. Used to evaluate alternative projects with different lives.

When you have a level cash flow at a constant interval, you are dealing with an annuity and that is exactly how to approach this problem. We know the present value ($-\$12.49$) the number of years (3), and the discount rate (10%). We need to solve for the cash flow, of an equivalent annuity. Recall from Chapter 4 that the formula (Eq. 4.9) for solving for the cash flow in an annuity is:

$$\text{Cash Flow} = \frac{\text{Present Value}}{\frac{1}{r}\left(1 - \frac{1}{(1+r)^N}\right)} = \frac{-12.49}{\frac{1}{0.10}\left(1 - \frac{1}{(1.10)^3}\right)} = -5.02$$

So, buying and operating server A is equivalent to spending $5020 per year to have a network server. We can repeat the calculation for server B, but for a two-year annuity because server B has only a two-year life (the change in exponent is highlighted):

$$\text{Cash Flow} = \frac{\text{Present Value}}{\frac{1}{r}\left(1 - \frac{1}{(1+r)^N}\right)} = \frac{-10.47}{\frac{1}{0.10}\left(1 - \frac{1}{(1.10)^2}\right)} = -6.03$$

Therefore, we can reinterpret the cost of each alternative as shown in Table 8.3:

Now we are ready to choose between the two servers. Server A is equivalent to spending $5020 per year and server B is equivalent to spending $6030 per year to have a network server. Seen in this light, server A appears to be the less expensive solution.

TABLE 8.3

Cash Flows ($ thousands) for
Network Server Options, Expressed
as Equivalent Annual Annuities

Year	PV at 10%	0	1	2	3
A	−12.49	0	−5.02	−5.02	−5.02
B	−10.47	0	−6.03	−6.03	

EXAMPLE 8.5

Computing
an Equivalent
Annual Annuity

MyFinanceLab

PROBLEM

You are about to sign the contract for server A from Table 8.2 when a third vendor approaches you with another option that lasts for four years. The cash flows for server C are given below. Should you choose the new option or stick with server A?

Server C
($ thousands)

SOLUTION

PLAN

In order to compare this new option to server A, we need to put server C on an equal footing by computing its annual cost. We can do this by:

1. Computing its NPV at the 10% discount rate we used above.
2. Computing the equivalent four-year annuity with the same present value.

EXECUTE

$$PV = -14 - 1.2\left(\frac{1}{0.10}\right)\left[1 - \frac{1}{(1.10)^4}\right] = -17.80$$

$$\text{Cash Flow} = \frac{PV}{\frac{1}{r}\left[1 - \frac{1}{(1+r)^N}\right]} = \frac{-17.80}{\frac{1}{0.10}\left[1 - \frac{1}{(1.10)^4}\right]} = -5.62$$

Server C's annual cost of $5620 is greater than the annual cost of server A ($5020), so we should still choose server A.

EVALUATE

In this case, the additional cost associated with purchasing and maintaining server C is not worth the extra year we get from choosing it. By putting all of these costs into an equivalent annuity, the EAA tool allows us to see that.

Important Considerations When Using the Equivalent Annual Annuity

Although server A appears to be the lowest-cost alternative, there are several factors to consider before making our decision.

Required Life. We computed the equivalent annual cost of server A assuming we would use it for three years. But suppose it is likely that we will not need the server in the third year. Then we would be paying for something that we would not use. In that case, it may be cheaper to purchase server B, which provides coverage for the years we will need it at a lower total cost.[6]

---

[6]In this scenario, we should also consider any salvage value that server A might have if we sold it after two years.

Replacement Cost. When we compare servers A and B based on their equivalent annual cost, we are assuming that the cost of servers will not change over time. But suppose we believe a dramatic change in technology will reduce the cost of servers by the third year to an annual cost of $2000 per year. Then server B has the advantage that we can upgrade to the new technology sooner. The cost of three years of service from either server in this case can be represented as follows:

Year	PV at 10%	0	1	2	3
A	−12.49	0	−5.02	−5.02	−5.02
B	−11.97	0	−6.03	−6.03	−2.00

Therefore, when cost or performance is expected to change significantly over time, it may be cheaper to purchase server B despite its higher equivalent annual cost because it gives us the option to switch to the new technology sooner.

Concept
Check

9. Explain why choosing the option with the highest NPV is not always correct when the options have different lives.

10. What issues should you keep in mind when choosing among projects with different lives?

8.6 Choosing Among Projects When Resources Are Limited

In the previous sections, we compared projects that had *identical* resource needs. For example, in Javier's case, we assumed that both the Internet café and his girlfriend's business demanded all of his time. In this section, we develop an approach for situations where the choices have differing resource needs.

Evaluating Projects with Different Resource Requirements

In some situations, different investment opportunities demand different amounts of a particular resource. If there is a fixed supply of the resource so that you cannot undertake all possible opportunities, simply picking the highest NPV opportunity might not lead to the best decision.

We usually assume that you will be able to finance all positive NPV projects that you have. In reality, managers work within the constraint of a budget that restricts the amount of capital they may invest in a given period. Such a constraint would force a manager to choose among positive NPV projects to maximize the total NPV while staying within her budget. For example, assume you are considering the three projects in Table 8.4, and that you have a budget of $200 million. Table 8.4 shows the NPV of each project and the initial investment that each project requires. Project A has the highest NPV but it uses up the entire budget. Projects B and C can *both* be undertaken (together they use the entire budget), and their combined NPV exceeds the NPV of project A; thus, you should initiate them both. Together, their NPV is $145 million compared to $100 million for project A alone.

TABLE 8.4

Possible Projects for $200 Million Budget

Project	NPV ($ millions)	Initial Investment ($ millions)	NPV/Initial Investment
A	100	200	0.500
B	75	120	0.625
C	70	80	0.875

Profitability Index. Note that in the last column of Table 8.4 we included the ratio of the project's NPV to its initial investment. We can interpret this as telling us that for every dollar invested in project A, we will generate 50 cents in value (over and above the dollar investment).[7] Both projects B and C generate higher NPVs per dollar invested than project A, consistent with the fact that given our budget of $200 million, the two of them together created a higher NPV than project A alone.

In this simple example, identifying the optimal combination of projects to undertake is straightforward. In actual situations replete with many projects and resources, finding the optimal combination can be difficult. Practitioners often use the **profitability index (PI)** to help identify the optimal combination of projects to undertake in such situations:

profitability index (PI) Measures the NPV per unit of resource consumed.

Profitability Index

$$\text{Profitability Index} = \frac{\text{Value Created}}{\text{Resource Consumed}} = \frac{\text{NPV}}{\text{Resource Consumed}} \tag{8.4}$$

The profitability index measures the "bang for your buck"—that is, the value created in terms of NPV per unit of resource consumed. After computing the profitability index, we can rank projects based on it. Starting with the project with the highest index, we move down the ranking, taking all projects until the resource is consumed. In Table 8.4, the ratio in the last column is the profitability index. Note how the profitability index rule would correctly select projects B and C.

EXAMPLE 8.6

Profitability Index with a Human Resource Constraint

MyFinanceLab

PROBLEM

Your division at NetIt, a large networking company, has put together a project proposal to develop a new home networking router. The expected NPV of the project is $17.7 million, and the project will require 50 software engineers. NetIt has 190 engineers available, and is unable to hire additional qualified engineers in the short run. Therefore, the router project must compete with the following other projects for these engineers:

Project	NPV ($ millions)	Engineering Headcount (EHC)
Router	17.7	50
Project A	22.7	47
Project B	8.1	44
Project C	14.0	40
Project D	11.5	61
Project E	20.6	58
Project F	12.9	32
Total	107.5	332

How should NetIt prioritize these projects?

SOLUTION

PLAN

The goal is to maximize the total NPV that we can create with 190 engineers (at most). We can use Eq. 8.4 to determine the profitability index for each project. In this case, since engineers are our limited resource, we will use Engineering Headcount in the denominator. Once we have the profitability index for each project, we can sort them based on the index.

---

[7]Sometimes, practitioners add 1 to this ratio such that the interpretation would be that every dollar invested returned $1.50. Leaving off the additional 1 allows the ratio to be applied to resources other than budgets as we show in Example 8.6.

EXECUTE

Project	NPV ($ millions)	Engineering Headcount (EHC)	Profitability Index (NPV per EHC)	Cumulative EHC Required
Project A	22.7	47	0.483	47
Project F	12.9	32	0.403	79 (47 + 32)
Project E	20.6	58	0.355	137 (79 + 58)
Router	17.7	50	0.354	187 (137 + 50)
Project C	14.0	40	0.350	
Project D	11.5	61	0.189	
Project B	8.1	44	0.184	

As shown in the table above, we assigned the resource to the projects in descending order according to the profitability index. The final column shows the cumulative use of the resource as each project is taken on until the resource is used up. To maximize NPV within the constraint of 190 engineers, NetIt should choose the first four projects on the list.

EVALUATE

By ranking projects in terms of their NPV per engineer, we find the most value we can create, given our 190 engineers. There is no other combination of projects that will create more value without using more engineers than we have. This ranking also shows us exactly what the engineering constraint costs us—this resource constraint forces NetIt to forgo three otherwise valuable projects (C, D, and B) with a total NPV of $33.6 million.

Shortcomings of the Profitability Index. Although the profitability index is simple to compute and use, in some situations it does not give an accurate answer. For example, suppose in Example 8.6 that NetIt has an additional small project with an NPV of only $100,000 that requires three engineers. The profitability index in this case is $0.1/3 = 0.03$, so this project would appear at the bottom of the ranking. However, notice that three of the 190 employees are not being used after the first four projects are selected. As a result, it would make sense to take on this project even though it would be ranked last because it would exactly use up our constraint.

In general, because the profitability index already includes the cost of capital (in computing the NPV), it would be better if the firm could raise additional funding to relieve the constraint. If the constraint is something else (such as engineers or physical capacity), there may be no way to relieve the constraint quickly enough to avoid having to choose among projects. Nonetheless, because all of the projects being ranked are value-increasing positive NPV projects, it is still better to focus on relieving the constraint.

A more serious problem occurs when multiple resource constraints apply. In this case, the profitability index can break down completely. The only surefire way to find the best combination of projects is to search through all of them. Although this process may sound exceedingly time-consuming, there are more advanced techniques that can tackle this specific kind of problem.[8] By using these techniques on a computer, the solution can usually be obtained almost instantaneously.

Concept Check

11. Explain why picking the project with the highest NPV might not be optimal when you evaluate projects with different resource requirements.

12. What does the profitability index tell you?

---

[8]Specifically, there are techniques called *integer and linear programming* that can be used to find the combination with the highest NPV when there are multiple constraints that must be satisfied. These methods are available, for example, in many spreadsheet programs.

8.7   Putting It All Together

In Table 8.5, we summarize the decision rules outlined in this chapter. As a financial manager, you are likely to run into many different types of investment decision rules in your career. In fact, in the interview in this chapter, the Treasurer of QUALCOMM mentions five

TABLE 8.5

Summary of
Decision Rules

NPV

Definition	• The difference between the present value of an investment's benefits and the present value of its costs
Rule	• Take any investment opportunity where the NPV is positive; turn down any opportunity where it is negative
Advantages	• Corresponds directly to the impact of the project on the firm's value • Direct application of the Valuation Principle
Disadvantages	• Relies on an accurate estimate of the discount rate • Can be time-consuming to compute

IRR

Definition	• The interest rate that sets the net present value of the cash flows equal to zero; the average return of the investment
Rule	• Take any investment opportunity where its IRR exceeds the opportunity cost of capital; turn down any opportunity where its IRR is less than the opportunity cost of capital
Advantages	• Related to the NPV rule and usually yields the same (correct) decision
Disadvantages	• Hard to compute • Multiple IRRs lead to ambiguity • Cannot be used to choose among projects • Can be misleading if inflows come before outflows

Payback Period

Definition	• The amount of time it takes to pay back the initial investment
Rule	• Accept the project if the payback period is less than a prespecified length of time—usually a few years; otherwise, turn it down
Advantages	• Simple to compute • Favors liquidity
Disadvantages	• No guidance as to correct payback cutoff • Ignores cash flows after the cutoff completely • Not necessarily consistent with maximizing shareholder wealth

Profitability Index

Definition	• NPV/Resource Consumed
Rule	• Rank projects according to their PI based on the constrained resource and move down the list accepting value-creating projects until the resource is exhausted
Advantages	• Uses the NPV to measure the benefit • Allows projects to be ranked on value created per unit of resource consumed
Disadvantages	• Breaks down when there is more than one constraint • Requires careful attention to make sure the constrained resource is completely utilized

different decision rules used by his company when evaluating investments. We have demonstrated that while alternative decision rules may sometimes (or even often) agree with the NPV decision rule, only the NPV decision rule is always correct. This is because the NPV provides you with a dollar-value measure of the impact of the project on shareholder wealth. Thus, it is the only rule that is directly tied to your goal of maximizing shareholder wealth. Computing the IRR can be a useful supplement to the NPV because knowing the IRR allows you to gauge how sensitive your decision is to errors in your discount rate. And some decision metrics are much simpler to calculate, such as the payback period. However, you should never rely on an alternative rule to make investment decisions.

If you are employed by a firm that uses the IRR rule (or another rule) exclusively, our advice is to always calculate the NPV. If the two rules agree, you can feel comfortable reporting the IRR rule recommendation. If they do not agree, you should investigate why the IRR rule failed by using the concepts in this chapter. Once you have identified the problem, you can alert your superiors to it and perhaps persuade them to adopt the NPV rule.

MyFinanceLab

Here is what you should know after reading this chapter. MyFinanceLab will help you identify what you know, and where to go when you need to practice.

Key Points and Equations	Key Terms	Online Practice
8.1 The NPV Decision Rule • The net present value (NPV) of a project is $$PV(\text{Benefits}) - PV(\text{Costs}) \qquad (8.1)$$ • A good project is one with a positive net present value. • The NPV decision rule states that when choosing from among a set of alternatives, choose the one with the highest NPV. The NPV of a project is equivalent to the cash value today of the project. • Regardless of our preferences for cash today versus cash in the future, we should always first maximize NPV. We can then borrow or lend to shift cash flows through time and find our most preferred pattern of cash flows.	net present value (NPV), p. 224 NPV decision rule, p. 225	MyFinanceLab Study Plan 8.1 Financial Calculator Tutorial: Calculating the Net Present Value of a Series of Uneven Cash Flows
8.2 Using the NPV Rule • If your objective is to maximize wealth, the NPV rule always gives the correct answer. • The difference between the cost of capital and the IRR is the maximum amount of estimation error that can exist in the cost of capital estimate without altering the original decision.	internal rate of return (IRR), p. 228 NPV profile, p. 227	MyFinanceLab Study Plan 8.2 Using Excel: Making an NPV Profile

8.3 Alternative Decision Rules

- Payback investment rule: Calculate the amount of time it takes to pay back the initial investment (the payback period). If the payback period is less than a prespecified length of time, accept the project. Otherwise, turn it down.
- IRR investment rule: Take any investment opportunity whose IRR exceeds the opportunity cost of capital. Turn down any opportunity whose IRR is less than the opportunity cost of capital.
- The IRR rule may give the wrong answer if the cash flows have an up-front payment (negative investment). When there are multiple IRRs or the IRR does not exist, the IRR rule cannot be used.
- Project cash flows can be modified to eliminate the multiple IRR problem. The modified IRR is calculated based on these modified cash flows.

discounted payback rule, p. 231
internal rate of return (IRR) investment rule, p. 231
modified internal rate of return (MIRR), p. 235
payback investment rule, p. 230
payback period, p. 230

8.4 Choosing Between Projects

- When choosing among mutually exclusive investment opportunities, pick the opportunity with the highest NPV. Do not use IRR to choose among mutually exclusive investment opportunities.

mutually exclusive projects, p. 238

8.5 Evaluating Projects with Different Lives

- When choosing among projects with different lives, you need a standard basis of comparison. First, compute an annuity with an equivalent present value to the NPV of each project. Then the projects can be compared on their cost or value created *per year*.

equivalent annual annuity (EAA), p. 245

8.6 Choosing Among Projects When Resources Are Limited

- When choosing among projects competing for the same resource, rank the projects by their profitability indices and pick the set of projects with the highest profitability indices that can still be undertaken given the limited resource.

$$\text{Profitability Index} = \frac{\text{Value Created}}{\text{Resource Consumed}}$$
$$= \frac{NPV}{\text{Resource Consumed}} \quad (8.4)$$

profitability index (PI), p. 248

CRITICAL THINKING

1. What is the NPV rule?

2. How is the NPV rule related to the goal of maximizing shareholder wealth?

3. What is the intuition behind the payback rule? What are some of its drawbacks?

4. What is the intuition behind the IRR rule? What are some of its drawbacks?

5. Under what conditions will the IRR rule and the NPV rule give the same accept/reject decision?

6. When is it possible to have multiple IRRs?

7. How does the MIRR solve the problem of multiple IRRs?

8. Why is it generally a bad idea to use IRR to choose between mutually exclusive projects?

9. When should you use the equivalent annual annuity?

10. What is the intuition behind the profitability index?

PROBLEMS

*All problems in this chapter are available in MyFinanceLab. An asterisk * indicates problems with a higher level of difficulty. If a problem requires you to calculate IRR, you should use a spreadsheet or financial calculator.*

The NPV Decision Rule

1. You have an opportunity to invest $50,000 now in return for $60,000 in one year. If your cost of capital is 8%, what is the NPV of this investment?

2. You have an opportunity to invest $100,000 now in return for $80,000 in one year and $30,000 in two years. If your cost of capital is 9%, what is the NPV of this investment?

3. Your storage firm has been offered $100,000 in one year to store some goods for one year. Assume your costs are $95,000, payable immediately, and the cost of capital is 8%. Should you take the contract?

4. You are preparing to produce some goods for sale. You will sell them in one year and you will incur costs of $80,000 immediately. If your cost of capital is 7%, what is the minimum dollar amount you need to expect to sell the goods for in order for this to be a non-negative NPV?

5. You run a construction firm. You have just won a contract to build a government office building. Building it will require an investment of $10 million today and $5 million in one year. The government will pay you $20 million in one year upon the building's completion. Assume the cost of capital is 10%.
   a. What is the NPV of this opportunity?
   b. How can your firm turn this NPV into cash today?

6. You have been offered a unique investment opportunity. If you invest $10,000 today, you will receive $500 one year from now, $1500 two years from now, and $10,000 ten years from now.
   a. What is the NPV of the opportunity if the cost of capital is 6% per year? Should you take the opportunity?
   b. What is the NPV of the opportunity if the cost of capital is 2% per year? Should you take it now?

7. Marian Plunket owns her own business and is considering an investment. If she undertakes the investment, it will pay $4000 at the end of each of the next three years. The opportunity requires an initial investment of $1000 plus an additional investment at the end of the second year of $5000. What is the NPV of this opportunity if the cost of capital is 2% per year? Should Marian take it?

Using the NPV Rule

8. Your factory has been offered a contract to produce a part for a new printer. The contract would be for three years and your cash flows from the contract would be

$5 million per year. Your up-front setup costs to be ready to produce the part would be $8 million. Your cost of capital for this contract is 8%.

a. What does the NPV rule say you should do?

b. If you take the contract, what will be the change in the value of your firm?

9. You are considering opening a new plant. The plant will cost $100 million up front and will take one year to build. After that, it is expected to produce profits of $30 million at the end of every year of production. The cash flows are expected to last forever. Calculate the NPV of this investment opportunity if your cost of capital is 8%. Should you make the investment? Calculate the IRR and use it to determine the maximum deviation allowable in the cost of capital estimate to leave the decision unchanged.

10. Bill Clinton reportedly was paid $10 million to write his book *My Life.* The book took three years to write. In the time he spent writing, Clinton could have been paid to make speeches. Given his popularity, assume that he could earn $8 million per year (paid at the end of the year) speaking instead of writing. Assume his cost of capital is 10% per year.

a. What is the NPV of agreeing to write the book (ignoring any royalty payments)?

b. Assume that, once the book was finished, it was expected to generate royalties of $5 million in the first year (paid at the end of the year) and these royalties were expected to decrease at a rate of 30% per year in perpetuity. What is the NPV of the book with the royalty payments?

*11. FastTrack Bikes, Inc., is thinking of developing a new composite road bike. Development will take six years and the cost is $200,000 per year. Once in production, the bike is expected to make $300,000 per year for 10 years. The cash inflows begin at the end of year 7.

Assuming the cost of capital is 10%:

a. Calculate the NPV of this investment opportunity. Should the company make the investment?

b. Calculate the IRR and use it to determine the maximum deviation allowable in the cost of capital estimate to leave the decision unchanged.

c. How long must development last to change the decision?

Assuming the cost of capital is 14%:

a. Calculate the NPV of this investment opportunity. Should the company make the investment?

b. How much must this cost of capital estimate deviate to change the decision?

c. How long must development last to change the decision?

12. OpenSeas, Inc., is evaluating the purchase of a new cruise ship. The ship will cost $500 million, and will operate for 20 years. OpenSeas expects annual cash flows from operating the ship to be $70 million and its cost of capital is 12%.

a. Prepare an NPV profile of the purchase.

b. Identify the IRR on the graph.

c. Should OpenSeas proceed with the purchase?

d. How far off could OpenSeas' cost of capital estimate be before your purchase decision would change?

Alternative Decision Rules

13. You are a real estate agent thinking of placing a sign advertising your services at a local bus stop. The sign will cost $5000 and will be posted for one year. You expect that it will generate additional free cash flow of $500 per month. What is the payback period?

14. Does the IRR rule agree with the NPV rule in Problem 8?

15. How many IRRs are there in part (a) of Problem 10? Does the IRR rule give the correct answer in this case?

16. How many IRRs are there in part (b) of Problem 10? Does the IRR rule work in this case?

17. Professor Wendy Smith has been offered the following deal: A law firm would like to retain her for an up-front payment of $50,000. In return, for the next year the firm would have access to eight hours of her time every month. Smith's rate is $550 per hour and her opportunity cost of capital is 15% per year. What does the IRR rule advise regarding this opportunity? What about the NPV rule?

18. Innovation Company is thinking about marketing a new software product. Up-front costs to market and develop the product are $5 million. The product is expected to generate profits of $1 million per year for 10 years. The company will have to provide product support expected to cost $100,000 per year in perpetuity. Assume all profits and expenses occur at the end of the year.
    a. What is the NPV of this investment if the cost of capital is 6%? Should the firm undertake the project? Repeat the analysis for discount rates of 2% and 11%.
    b. How many IRRs does this investment opportunity have?
    c. What does the IRR rule indicate about this investment?

19. You own a coal mining company and are considering opening a new mine. The mine will cost $120 million to open. If this money is spent immediately, the mine will generate $20 million for the next 10 years. After that, the coal will run out and the site must be cleaned and maintained at environmental standards. The cleaning and maintenance are expected to cost $2 million per year in perpetuity. What does the IRR rule say about whether you should accept this opportunity? If the cost of capital is 8%, what does the NPV rule say?

20. Your firm is considering a project that will cost $4.55 million up front, generate cash flows of $3.5 million per year for three years, and then have a cleanup and shutdown cost of $6 million in the fourth year.
    a. How many IRRs does this project have?
    b. Calculate a modified IRR for this project discounting the outflows and leaving the inflows unchanged. Assume a discount and compounding rate of 10%.
    c. Using the MIRR and a cost of capital of 10%, would you take the project?

21. You have just been offered a contract worth $1 million per year for five years. However, to take the contract, you will need to purchase some new equipment. Your discount rate for this project is 12%. You are still negotiating the purchase price of the equipment. What is the most you can pay for the equipment and not have a negative NPV?

*22. You are getting ready to start a new project that will incur some cleanup and shutdown costs when it is completed. The project costs $5.4 million up front and is expected to generate $1.1 million per year for 10 years and then have some shutdown costs in year 11. Use the MIRR approach to find the maximum shutdown costs you could incur and still meet your cost of capital of 15% on this project.

*23. You are considering investing in a new gold mine in South Africa. Gold in South Africa is buried very deep, so the mine will require an initial investment of $250 million. Once this investment is made, the mine is expected to produce revenues of $30 million per year for the next 20 years. It will cost $10 million per year to operate the mine.

After 20 years, the gold will be depleted. The mine must then be stabilized on an ongoing basis, which will cost $5 million per year in perpetuity. Calculate the IRR of this investment. (*Hint*: Plot the NPV as a function of the discount rate.)

24. You are evaluating a project that will cost $500,000, but is expected to produce cash flows of $125,000 per year for 10 years, with the first cash flow in one year. Your cost of capital is 11% and your company's preferred payback period is three years or less.
    a. What is the payback period of this project?
    b. Should you take the project if you want to increase the value of the company?

25. You are considering making a movie. The movie is expected to cost $10 million up front and take a year to produce. After that, it is expected to make $5 million in the year it is released and $2 million for the following four years. What is the payback period of this investment? If you require a payback period of two years, will you make the movie? Does the movie have positive NPV if the cost of capital is 10%?

Choosing Between Projects

26. You are choosing between two projects, but can only take one. The cash flows for the projects are given in the following table:

	0	1	2	3	4
A	−$50	25	20	20	15
B	−$100	20	40	50	60

   a. What are the IRRs of the two projects?
   b. If your discount rate is 5%, what are the NPVs of the two projects?
   c. Why do IRR and NPV rank the two projects differently?

27. You are deciding between two mutually exclusive investment opportunities. Both require the same initial investment of $10 million. Investment A will generate $2 million per year (starting at the end of the first year) in perpetuity. Investment B will generate $1.5 million at the end of the first year and its revenues will grow at 2% per year for every year after that.
   a. Which investment has the higher IRR?
   b. Which investment has the higher NPV when the cost of capital is 7%?
   c. In this case, when does picking the higher IRR give the correct answer as to which investment is the better opportunity?

28. You are considering the following projects and can take only one. Your cost of capital is 11%.

	0	1	2	3	4
A	−100	25	30	40	50
B	−100	50	40	30	20

   a. What is the NPV of each project at your cost of capital?
   b. What is the IRR of each project?
   c. At what cost of capital are you indifferent between the two projects?
   d. What should you do?

29. You need a particular piece of equipment for your production process. An equipment-leasing company has offered to lease you the equipment for $10,000 per year if you sign a guaranteed five-year lease. The company would also maintain the equipment for you as part of the lease. Alternatively, you could buy and maintain the equipment

yourself. The cash flows (in thousands) from doing so are listed below (the equipment has an economic life of five years). If your discount rate is 7%, what should you do?

0	1	2	3	4	5
−40	−2	−2	−2	−2	−2

Evaluating Projects with Different Lives

30. You are trying to decide between two mobile phone carriers. Carrier A requires you to pay $200 for the phone and monthly charges of $60 for 24 months. Carrier B wants you to pay $100 for the phone and monthly charges of $70 for 12 months. Assume you will keep replacing the phone after your contract expires. Your cost of capital is 4%. Based on cost alone, which carrier should you choose?

31. Gateway Tours is choosing between two bus models. One is more expensive to purchase and maintain, but lasts much longer than the other. Its discount rate is 11%. It plans to continue with one of the two models for the foreseeable future; which should it choose? Based on the costs of each model shown below, which should it choose?

Model	0	1	2	3	4	5 ...	7
Old Reliable	−200	−4	−4	−4	−4	−4 ...	−4
Short and Sweet	−100	−2	−2	−2	−2		

32. Hassle-Free Web is bidding to provide Web hosting services for Hotel Lisbon. Hotel Lisbon pays its current provider $10,000 per year for hosting its Web page, handling transactions, etc. Hassle-Free figures that it will need to purchase equipment worth $15,000 up front and then spend $2000 per year on monitoring, updates, and bandwidth to provide the service for three years. If Hassle-Free's cost of capital is 10%, can it bid less than $10,000 per year to provide the service and still increase its value by doing so?

33. You have to buy a new copier. The cost of the copier is $2000, plus $400 per year in maintenance costs. The copier will last for five years. Alternatively, a local company offers to lease the copier to you and do the maintenance as well. If your discount rate is 6%, what is the most you would be willing to pay per year to lease the copier (your first lease payment is due in one year)?

Choosing Among Projects When Resources Are Limited

34. Fabulous Fabricators needs to decide how to allocate space in its production facility this year. It is considering the following contracts:

	NPV	Use of Facility
A	$2 million	100%
B	$1 million	60%
C	$1.5 million	40%

   a. What are the profitability indexes of the projects?
   b. What should Fabulous Fabricators do?

35. Kartman Corporation is evaluating four real estate investments. Management plans to buy the properties today and sell them three years from today. The annual discount rate for these investments is 15%. The following table summarizes the initial cost and the sale price in three years for each property:

	Cost Today	Sale Price in Year 3
Parkside Acres	$650,000	$1,150,000
Real Property Estates	800,000	1,400,000
Lost Lake Properties	650,000	1,050,000
Overlook	150,000	350,000

Kartman has a total capital budget of $800,000 to invest in properties. Which properties should it choose?

36. Orchid Biotech Company is evaluating several development projects for experimental drugs. Although the cash flows are difficult to forecast, the company has come up with the following estimates of the initial capital requirements and NPVs for the projects. Given a wide variety of staffing needs, the company has also estimated the number of research scientists required for each development project (all cost values are given in millions of dollars).

Project Number	Initial Capital	Number of Research Scientists	NPV
I	$10	2	$10.1
II	15	3	19.0
III	15	4	22.0
IV	20	3	25.0
V	30	12	60.2

a. Suppose that Orchid has a total capital budget of $60 million. How should it prioritize these projects?

b. Suppose that Orchid currently has 12 research scientists and does not anticipate being able to hire more in the near future. How should Orchid prioritize these projects?

DATA CASE

After the close of trading on May 6, 2009, Vanda Pharmaceuticals (VNDA) announced that the Food and Drug Administration had approved its drug, Fanapt, for the treatment of schizophrenia. Imagine that you are working as a stock analyst for a large investment firm and Vanda is one of the firms you track. On May 7, 2009, Vanda's stock price increased substantially and your boss wants to you to issue a statement about the size of the cash flows necessary to support the stock price reaction. Therefore, she wants you to estimate the net cash flows the market had anticipated from sales of the new drug. She advises that you treat the value anticipated by the market as the NPV of selling the drug, then work backward from the NPV to determine the annual cash flows necessary to generate that value. Your boss advises that the best way to capture the value is to take the change in stock price from closing on May 6, 2009 to closing on May 7, 2009. You nod your head in agreement, trying to look like you understand how to proceed. You are relatively new to the job and the term NPV is somewhat familiar to you.

1. To determine the change in stock price over this period, go to Yahoo! Finance (http://finance.yahoo.com) and enter the stock symbol for Vanda (VNDA). Then click on "Historical Prices" and enter the appropriate dates. Use the adjusted closing prices for the two dates.

2. To determine the change in value, multiply the change in stock price by the number of shares outstanding. The number of shares outstanding around those dates can be found by going to the company's investor relations Web site. Start at http://www.vandapharma.com and then click "Investor Relations." Next, select the "SEC Filings" link on the left side of the screen, and locate the 10-Q from May 11, 2009. The fastest way to do this is to select "Quarterly Filings" from the drop-down menu under Groupings Filter and then click "Search." Next, click the Excel symbol in the "5/11/09 10-Q" row and open the Excel spreadsheet. In the Balance Sheet tab, under the March 31, 2009 column, you will find the number of shares of Common Stock (in thousands) as of March 31, 2009.

   Because the change in value represents the "expected" NPV of the project, you will have to find the annual net cash flows that would provide this NPV. For this analysis, you will need to estimate the cost of capital for the project. We show how to calculate the cost of capital in subsequent chapters; for now, use the New York University (NYU) cost of capital Web site (http://pages.stern.nyu.edu/~adamodar/New_Home_Page/datafile/wacc.htm). Locate the cost of capital in the far-right column for the "Biotechnology" industry.

3. Use the cost of capital from the NYU Web site and the NPV you computed to calculate the constant annual cash flow that provides this NPV. Compute cash flows for 5-, 10-, and 15-year horizons.

Fundamentals of Capital Budgeting

LEARNING OBJECTIVES

- Identify the types of cash flows needed in the capital budgeting process

- Forecast incremental earnings in a pro forma earnings statement for a project

- Convert forecasted earnings to free cash flows and compute a project's NPV

- Recognize common pitfalls that arise in identifying a project's incremental free cash flows

- Assess the sensitivity of a project's NPV to changes in your assumptions

- Identify the most common options available to managers in projects and understand why these options can be valuable

notation

CapEx	capital expenditures	*NPV*	net present value
EBIT	earnings before interest and taxes	NWC_t	net working capital in year t
FCF_t	free cash flow in year t	*PV*	present value
IRR	internal rate of return	r	projected cost of capital

An important responsibility of corporate financial managers is determining which projects or investments a firm should undertake. *Capital budgeting*, the focus of this chapter, is the process of analyzing investment opportunities and deciding which ones to accept. In doing so, we are allocating the firm's funds to various projects—we are budgeting its capital. Chapter 8 covered the various methods for evaluating projects and proved that NPV will be the most reliable and accurate method for doing so. In retrospect, this may not be surprising as it is the only rule directly tied to the Valuation Principle. To implement the NPV rule, we must compute the NPV of our projects and accept only those projects for which the NPV is positive. In the last chapter, we spoke about Sony and Toshiba each using investment decision rules to pursue competing high-definition DVD standards (and eventually for Toshiba, to decide to abandon HD-DVD). In order to implement the investment decision rules, financial managers from Toshiba, for example, first had to forecast the incremental cash flows associated with the investments and later had to forecast the incremental cash flows associated with the decision to stop investing in HD-DVD. The process of forecasting those cash flows, crucial inputs in the investment decision process, is our focus in this chapter.

We begin by estimating the project's expected cash flows by forecasting the project's revenues and costs. Using these cash flows, we can compute the project's NPV—its contribution to shareholder value. Then, because the cash flow forecasts almost always contain uncertainty, we demonstrate how to compute the sensitivity of the NPV to the uncertainty in the forecasts. Finally, we examine the relationship between a project's flexibility and its NPV.

9.1 The Capital Budgeting Process

capital budget Lists the projects and investments that a company plans to undertake during the next period.

capital budgeting The process of analyzing projects and investment opportunities and deciding which ones to accept.

The first step in analyzing various investment opportunities is compiling a list of potential projects. A **capital budget** lists the projects and investments that a company plans to undertake during the next period. To create this list, firms analyze projects and investment opportunities and decide which ones to accept through a process called **capital budgeting**. This process begins with forecasts of each project's future consequences for the firm. Some of these consequences will affect the firm's revenues; others will affect its costs. Our ultimate goal is to determine the effect of the decision to accept or reject a project on the firm's cash flows, and evaluate the NPV of these cash flows to assess the consequences of the decision for the firm's value. Figure 9.1 depicts the types of cash flows found in a typical project. We will examine each of these as we proceed through our discussion of capital budgeting.

Of course, forecasting these cash flows is frequently challenging. We will often need to rely on different experts within the firm to obtain estimates for many of them. For example, the marketing department may provide sales forecasts, the operations manager may provide information about production costs, and the firm's engineers may estimate the up-front research and development expenses that are required to launch the project. Another important source of information comes from looking at past projects of the firm, or those of other firms in the same industry. In particular, practitioners often base their assessments of a project's revenues and costs using information on revenues and costs that can be learned from the historical financial statements of the firm or its competitors.

Once we have these estimates, how do we organize them? One common starting point is to consider the consequences of the project for the firm's earnings. Thus, we will *begin*

FIGURE 9.1

Cash Flows in a Typical Project

The diagram shows some typical cash flows in project analysis and their timing.

incremental earnings
The amount by which a firm's earnings are expected to change as a result of an investment decision.

our analysis in Section 9.2 by determining the **incremental earnings** of a project—that is, the amount by which a firm's earnings are expected to change as a result of an investment decision. The incremental earnings forecast tells us how the decision will affect the firm's reported profits from an accounting perspective. However, as we emphasized in Chapter 2, *earnings are not actual cash flows.* We need to estimate the project's cash flows to determine its NPV and decide whether it is a good project for the firm. Therefore, in Section 9.3, we demonstrate how to use the incremental earnings to forecast the actual cash flows of the project. Understanding how to compute the cash flow consequences of an investment based on its earning consequences is important for a number of reasons. First, as a practical matter, financial managers often begin by forecasting earnings. Second, if we are looking at historical data, accounting information is often the only information that is readily available.

Concept Check

1. What is capital budgeting, and what is its goal?
2. Why is computing a project's effect on the firm's earnings insufficient for capital budgeting?

9.2 Forecasting Incremental Earnings

Let's begin our discussion of incremental earnings with a simple example that we will examine throughout this section. Suppose you are considering whether to upgrade your manufacturing plant to increase its capacity by purchasing a new piece of equipment. The equipment costs $1 million, plus an additional $20,000 to transport it and install it. You will also spend $50,000 on engineering costs to redesign the plant to accommodate the increased capacity. What are the initial earnings consequences of this decision?

Operating Expenses Versus Capital Expenditures

Most projects require some form of up-front investment—we may need to conduct a marketing survey, develop a prototype, or launch an ad campaign. These types of costs are accounted for as operating expenses in the year that they are incurred. However, many projects also include investments in plant, property, and/or equipment, called *capital expenditures.* Recall from Chapter 2 that while investments in plant, property, and equipment are cash expenses, they are not directly listed as expenses when calculating *earnings.* Instead, the firm deducts a fraction of the cost of these items each year as depreciation. Financial managers use several different methods to compute depreciation. The simplest method is **straight-line depreciation**, in which an asset's cost is divided equally over its depreciable life (we discuss another common method in Section 9.4).

straight-line depreciation A method of depreciation in which an asset's cost is divided equally over its life.

In our example, the up-front costs associated with the decision to increase capacity have two distinct consequences for the firm's earnings. First, the $50,000 spent on redesigning the plant is an operating expense reported in year 0. For the $1,020,000 spent to buy, ship, and install the machine, accounting principles as well as tax rules require you to depreciate the $1,020,000 over the depreciable life of the equipment. Assuming that the equipment has a five-year depreciable life and that we use the straight-line method, we would expense $1,020,000/5 = $204,000 per year for five years. (The motivation for this accounting treatment is to match the cost of acquiring the machine to the timing of the revenues it will generate.)

	Year	0	1	2	3	4	5
2	Operating Expenses (Plant Redesign)	−$50,000					
3	Depreciation (New Equipment)		−$204,000	−$204,000	−$204,000	−$204,000	−$204,000

As the timeline shows, the up-front cash outflow of $1,020,000 to purchase and set up the machine is not recognized as an expense in year 0. Instead, it appears as depreciation expenses in years 1 through 5. Remember that these *depreciation expenses do not correspond to actual cash outflows.* This accounting and tax treatment of capital expenditures is one of the key reasons why earnings are not an accurate representation of cash flows. We will return to this issue in Section 9.3.[1]

Incremental Revenue and Cost Estimates

Our next step is to estimate the ongoing revenues and costs for the project. Forecasting future revenues and costs is challenging. The most successful practitioners collect as much information as possible before tackling this task—they will talk to members of marketing and sales teams as well as company economists to develop an estimate of sales, and they will talk to engineering and production teams to refine their estimate of costs.

There are several factors to consider when estimating a project's revenues and costs, including the following:

1. A new product typically has lower sales initially, as customers gradually become aware of the product. Sales will then accelerate, plateau, and ultimately decline as the product nears obsolescence or faces increased competition.

2. The average selling price of a product and its cost of production will generally change over time. Prices and costs tend to rise with the general level of inflation in the economy. The prices of technology products, however, often fall over time as newer, superior technologies emerge and production costs decline.

3. For most industries, competition tends to reduce profit margins over time.

Our focus here is on how to get from these forecasts to incremental earnings and then to cash flows. Chapter 18 discusses forecasting methods in more detail.

All our revenue and cost estimates should be *incremental*, meaning that we only account for additional sales and costs generated by the project. For example, if we are evaluating the purchase of a faster manufacturing machine, we are only concerned with how many additional units of the product we will be able to sell (and at what price) and any additional costs created by the new machine. We do not forecast total sales and costs because those include our production using the old machine. *Remember, we are evaluating how the project will <u>change</u> the cash flows of the firm. That is why we focus on <u>incremental</u> revenues and costs.*

Let's return to our plant upgrade example. Assume that after we have bought and installed the machine and redesigned the plant, our additional capacity will allow us to generate incremental revenues of $500,000 per year for five years. Those incremental revenues will be associated with $150,000 per year in incremental costs. In that case, our revenue, cost, and depreciation estimates for the project are as shown below (in thousands of dollars):

1	Year	0	1	2	3	4	5
2	Incremental Revenues		500	500	500	500	500
3	Incremental Costs	−50	−150	−150	−150	−150	−150
4	Depreciation		−204	−204	−204	−204	−204

---

[1]Some students might note that for financial reporting, the asset should be depreciated to salvage value. For tax purposes, salvage value is always treated as zero, so this is the relevant method for capital budgeting.

Now that we have these estimates, we are ready to compute the consequences of our project for the firm's earnings. As we saw in Chapter 2, both depreciation expenses and the actual costs of producing (e.g., cost of goods sold) must be subtracted from revenues, so that:

$$\text{Incremental Earnings Before Interest and Taxes (EBIT)} = \text{Incremental Revenue} \\ - \text{Incremental Costs} - \text{Depreciation} \tag{9.1}$$

Taxes

marginal corporate tax rate The tax rate a firm will pay on an incremental dollar of pretax income.

The final expense we must account for is corporate taxes. The correct tax rate to use is the firm's **marginal corporate tax rate**, which is the tax rate it will pay on an *incremental* dollar of pretax income. The incremental income tax expense is calculated as:

$$\text{Income Tax} = \text{EBIT} \times \text{The Firm's Marginal Corporate Tax Rate} \tag{9.2}$$

Incremental Earnings Forecast

We're now ready to put the pieces together for an incremental earnings forecast. Assume our firm faces a marginal tax rate of 40% and that the firm as a whole has at least $50,000 in profits in year 0 for the incremental costs in that year to offset. Then the incremental earnings (or net income) are as follows (in thousands of dollars):[2]

	Year	0	1	2	3	4	5
1	Year	0	1	2	3	4	5
2	Incremental Revenues		500	500	500	500	500
3	Incremental Costs	−50	−150	−150	−150	−150	−150
4	Depreciation		−204	−204	−204	−204	−204
5	**EBIT**	−50	146	146	146	146	146
6	Income Tax at 40%	20	−58.4	−58.4	−58.4	−58.4	−58.4
7	**Incremental Earnings**	**−30**	**87.6**	**87.6**	**87.6**	**87.6**	**87.6**

We can combine Eqs. 9.1 and 9.2 to compute incremental earnings directly. For example, in years 1 through 5 we have:

$$\text{Incremental Earnings} = (\text{Incremental Revenues} - \text{Incremental Cost} \\ - \text{Depreciation}) \times (1 - \text{Tax Rate}) \tag{9.3}$$

$$\text{Incremental Earnings} = (500,000 - 150,000 - 204,000) \\ \times (1 - 0.4) = 87,600$$

EXAMPLE 9.1

Incremental Earnings

MyFinanceLab

PROBLEM

Suppose that Linksys is considering the development of a wireless home networking appliance, called HomeNet, that will provide both the hardware and the software necessary to run an entire home from any Internet connection. In addition to connecting PCs and printers, HomeNet will control new Internet-capable stereos, digital video recorders, heating and air-conditioning units, major appliances, telephone and security systems, office equipment, and so on. The major competitor for HomeNet is a product being developed by Brandt-Quigley Corporation.

Based on extensive marketing surveys, the sales forecast for HomeNet is 50,000 units per year. Given the pace of technological change, Linksys expects the product will have a four-year life and an expected

---

[2]While revenues and costs occur throughout the year, the standard convention, which we adopt here, is to list revenues and costs in the year in which they occur. Thus, cash flows that occur at the end of one year will be listed in a different column than those that occur at the start of the next year, even though they may occur only weeks apart. When additional precision is required, cash flows are often estimated on a quarterly or monthly basis.

wholesale price of $260 (the price Linksys will receive from stores). Actual production will be outsourced at a cost (including packaging) of $110 per unit.

To verify the compatibility of new consumer Internet-ready appliances, as they become available, with the HomeNet system, Linksys must also establish a new lab for testing purposes. It will rent the lab space, but will need to purchase $7.5 million of new equipment. The equipment will be depreciated using the straight-line method over a five-year life. Linksys's marginal tax rate is 40%.

The lab will be operational at the end of one year. At that time, HomeNet will be ready to ship. Linksys expects to spend $2.8 million per year on rental costs for the lab space, as well as marketing and support for this product. Forecast the incremental earnings from the HomeNet project.

SOLUTION

PLAN

We need four items to calculate incremental earnings: (1) incremental revenues, (2) incremental costs, (3) depreciation, and (4) the marginal tax rate:

Incremental revenues are:	Additional units sold $\times$ price = 50,000 $\times$ $260 = $13,000,000
Incremental costs are:	Additional units sold $\times$ production costs = 50,000 $\times$ $110 = $5,500,000
	Selling, general, and administrative = $2,800,000 for rent, marketing, and support
Depreciation is:	Depreciable basis/Depreciable life = $7,500,000/5 = $1,500,000
Marginal tax rate is:	40%

Note that even though the project lasts for four years, the equipment has a five-year life, so we must account for the final depreciation charge in the fifth year.

EXECUTE (IN $000S)

	Year	0	1	2	3	4	5
1							
2	Revenues		13,000	13,000	13,000	13,000	—
3	Cost of Goods Sold		−5,500	−5,500	−5,500	−5,500	—
4	**Gross Profit**		7,500	7,500	7,500	7,500	—
5	Selling, General, and Administrative		−2,800	−2,800	−2,800	−2,800	—
6	Depreciation		−1,500	−1,500	−1,500	−1,500	−1,500
7	**EBIT**		3,200	3,200	3,200	3,200	−1,500
8	Income Tax at 40%		−1,280	−1,280	−1,280	−1,280	600
9	**Incremental Earnings**		**1,920**	**1,920**	**1,920**	**1,920**	**−900**

EVALUATE

These incremental earnings are an intermediate step on the way to calculating the incremental cash flows that would form the basis of any analysis of the HomeNet project. The cost of the equipment does not affect earnings in the year it is purchased, but does so through the depreciation expense in the following five years. Note that the depreciable life, which is based on accounting rules, does not have to be the same as the economic life of the asset—the period over which it will have value. Here, the firm will use the equipment for four years, but will depreciate it over five years.

pro forma Describes a statement that is not based on actual data but rather depicts a firm's financials under a given set of hypothetical assumptions.

Pro Forma Statement. The table calculating incremental earnings that we produced for our plant upgrade, and again in Example 9.1, is often referred to as a **pro forma** statement, because it is not based on actual data but rather depicts the firm's financials under a given set of hypothetical assumptions. In the HomeNet example, the firm's forecasts of revenues and costs were assumptions that allowed Linksys to forecast incremental earnings in a pro forma statement.

Taxes and Negative EBIT. Notice that in year 0 of our plant upgrade project, and in year 5 of the HomeNet example, EBIT is negative. Why are taxes relevant in this case? Consider the HomeNet example. HomeNet will reduce Linksys's taxable income in year 5 by $1.5

million. As long as Linksys earns taxable income elsewhere in year 5 against which it can offset HomeNet's losses, Linksys will owe $1.5 million $\times$ 40% = $600,000 *less* in taxes in year 5 than if it were not undertaking the project. Because the tax savings come from the depreciation expense on equipment for the HomeNet project, the firm should credit this tax savings to the HomeNet project.

EXAMPLE 9.2

Taxing Losses for Projects in Profitable Companies

MyFinanceLab

PROBLEM

Kellogg Company plans to launch a new line of high-fiber, zero-trans-fat breakfast pastries. The heavy advertising expenses associated with the new product launch will generate operating losses of $15 million next year for the product. Kellogg expects to earn pretax income of $460 million from operations other than the new pastries next year. If Kellogg pays a 40% tax rate on its pretax income, what will it owe in taxes next year without the new pastry product? What will it owe with the new product?

SOLUTION

PLAN

We need Kellogg's pretax income with and without the new product losses and its tax rate of 40%. We can then compute the tax without the losses and compare it to the tax with the losses.

EXECUTE

Without the new product, Kellogg will owe $460 million $\times$ 40% = $184 million in corporate taxes next year. With the new product, Kellogg's pretax income next year will be only $460 million − $15 million = $445 million, and it will owe $445 million $\times$ 40% = $178 million in tax.

EVALUATE

Thus, launching the new product reduces Kellogg's taxes next year by $184 million − $178 million = $6 million. Because the losses on the new product reduce Kellogg's taxable income dollar for dollar, it is the same as if the new product had a tax bill of *negative* $6 million.

What About Interest Expenses? In Chapter 2, we saw that to compute a firm's net income, we must first deduct interest expenses from EBIT. When evaluating a capital budgeting decision, however, we generally *do not include interest expenses*. Any incremental interest expenses will be related to the firm's decision regarding how to finance the project, which is a separate decision. Here, we wish to evaluate the earnings contributions from the project on its own, separate from the financing decision. Ultimately, managers may also look at the additional earnings consequences associated with different methods of financing the project.

  Thus, we evaluate a project *as if* the company will not use any debt to finance it (whether or not that is actually the case), and we postpone the consideration of alternative financing choices until Parts 5 and 6 of the book. Because we calculate the net income assuming no debt (no leverage), we refer to the net income we compute using Eq. 9.3, as in the pro forma in Example 9.1, as the **unlevered net income** of the project, to indicate that it does not include any interest expenses associated with debt.

unlevered net income
Net income that does not include interest expenses associated with debt.

Concept Check

3. How are operating expenses and capital expenditures treated differently when calculating incremental earnings?

4. Why do we focus only on *incremental* revenues and costs, rather than all revenues and costs of the firm?

9.3   Determining Incremental Free Cash Flow

As discussed in Chapter 2, earnings are an accounting measure of the firm's performance. They do not represent real profits: The firm cannot use its earnings to buy goods, pay employees, fund new investments, or pay dividends to shareholders. To do those things,

free cash flow The incremental effect of a project on a firm's available cash.

the firm needs cash. Thus, to evaluate a capital budgeting decision, we must determine its consequences for the firm's available cash. The incremental effect of a project on the firm's available cash is the project's incremental **free cash flow**.

Converting from Earnings to Free Cash Flow

As discussed in Chapter 2, there are important differences between earnings and cash flow. Earnings include non-cash charges, such as depreciation, but do not include expenditures on capital investment. To determine a project's free cash flow from its incremental earnings, we must adjust for these differences.

Capital Expenditures and Depreciation. As we have noted, depreciation is not a cash expense that is paid by the firm. Rather, it is a method used for accounting and tax purposes to allocate the original purchase cost of the asset over its life. Because depreciation is not a cash flow, we do not include it in the cash flow forecast. However, that does not mean we can ignore depreciation. The depreciation expense reduces our taxable earnings and in doing so reduces our taxes. Taxes are cash flows, so because depreciation affects our cash flows, it still matters. Our approach for handling depreciation is to add it back to the incremental earnings to recognize the fact that we still have the cash flow associated with it.

For example, a project has incremental gross profit (revenues minus costs) of $1 million and a $200,000 depreciation expense. If the firm's tax rate is 40%, then the incremental earnings will be $($1,000,000 - $200,000) \times (1 - 0.40) = $480,000$. However, the firm will still have $680,000 because the $200,000 depreciation expense is not an actual cash outflow. Table 9.1 shows the calculation to get the incremental free cash flow in this case. Blue boxes indicate all of the actual cash flows in the column labeled "Correct." A good way to check to make sure the incremental free cash flow is correct is to sum the actual cash flows. In this case, the firm generated $1,000,000 in gross profit (a positive cash flow), paid $320,000 in taxes (a negative cash flow), and was left with $1,000,000 - $320,000 = $680,000$, which is the amount shown as the incremental free cash flow. In the last column, labeled "Incorrect," we show what would happen if you just ignored depreciation altogether. Because EBIT would be too high, the taxes would be too high as well and consequently, the incremental free cash flow would be too low. (Note that the difference of $80,000 between the two cases is entirely due to the difference in tax payments.)

TABLE 9.1

Deducting and Then Adding Back Depreciation

	Correct	Incorrect
Incremental Gross Profit	$1,000,000	$1,000,000
Depreciation	−200,000	
EBIT	$800,000	$1,000,000
Tax at 40%	−$320,000	−$400,000
Incremental Earnings	$480,000	$600,000
Add Back Depreciation	$200,000	
Incremental Free Cash Flow	$680,000	$600,000

EXAMPLE 9.3

Incremental Free Cash Flows

MyFinanceLab

PROBLEM

Let's return to the HomeNet example. In Example 9.1, we computed the incremental earnings for HomeNet, but we need the incremental free cash flows to decide whether Linksys should proceed with the project.

SOLUTION

PLAN

The difference between the incremental earnings and incremental free cash flows in the HomeNet example will be driven by the equipment purchased for the lab. We need to recognize the $7.5 million cash outflow associated with the purchase in year 0 and add back the $1.5 million depreciation expenses from year 1 to 5 as they are not actually cash outflows.

EXECUTE (IN $000S)

We recognize the outflow for the equipment in row 11 and we add back the depreciation expenses in row 10.

	Year	0	1	2	3	4	5
1	Year	0	1	2	3	4	5
2	Revenues		13,000	13,000	13,000	13,000	–
3	Cost of Goods Sold		−5,500	−5,500	−5,500	−5,500	–
4	**Gross Profit**		7,500	7,500	7,500	7,500	–
5	Selling, General, and Administrative		−2,800	−2,800	−2,800	−2,800	–
6	Depreciation		−1,500	−1,500	−1,500	−1,500	−1,500
7	**EBIT**		3,200	3,200	3,200	3,200	−1,500
8	Income Tax at 40%		−1,280	−1,280	−1,280	−1,280	600
9	**Incremental Earnings**		1,920	1,920	1,920	1,920	−900
10	Add Back Depreciation		1,500	1,500	1,500	1,500	1,500
11	Purchase of Equipment	−7,500					
12	**Incremental Free Cash Flows**	−7,500	3,420	3,420	3,420	3,420	600

EVALUATE

By recognizing the outflow from purchasing the equipment in year 0, we account for the fact that $7.5 million left the firm at that time. By adding back the $1.5 million depreciation expenses in years 1 through 5, we adjust the incremental earnings to reflect the fact that the depreciation expense is not a cash outflow.

Net Working Capital (NWC). Another way that incremental earnings and free cash flows can differ is if there are changes in net working capital. We defined net working capital in Chapter 2 as the difference between current assets and current liabilities. The main components of net working capital are cash, inventory, receivables, and payables:

$$\text{Net Working Capital} = \text{Current Assets} - \text{Current Liabilities}$$
$$= \text{Cash} + \text{Inventory} + \text{Receivables} - \text{Payables} \qquad (9.4)$$

Note that as discussed in Chapter 2, we do not include short-term financing such as notes payable or short-term debt because those represent financing decisions that we keep separate from our investment decisions. Most projects will require the firm to invest in net working capital. Firms may need to maintain a minimum cash balance[3] to meet unexpected expenditures, and inventories of raw materials and finished product to accommodate production uncertainties and demand fluctuations. Also, customers may not pay for the goods they purchase immediately. While sales are immediately counted as part of earnings, the firm does not receive any cash until the customers actually pay. In the interim, the firm includes the amount that customers owe in its receivables. Thus, the firm's receivables measure the total credit that the firm has extended to its customers. In the same way, payables measure the credit the firm has received from its suppliers. The difference between receivables and payables is the net amount of the firm's capital that is consumed as a result of these credit transactions, known as **trade credit**.

trade credit The difference between receivables and payables (the net amount of a firm's capital consumed as a result of these credit transactions); the credit that a firm extends to its customers.

---

[3] The cash included in net working capital is cash that is *not* invested to earn a market rate of return. It includes cash held in the firm's checking account, in a company safe or cash box, in cash registers (for retail stores), and other sites.

We care about net working capital because it reflects a short-term investment that ties up cash flow that could be used elsewhere. For example, when a firm holds a lot of unsold inventory or has a lot of outstanding receivables, cash flow is tied up in the form of inventory or in the form of credit extended to customers. It is costly for the firm to tie up that cash flow because it delays the time until the cash flow is available for reinvestment or distribution to shareholders. Since we know that money has time value, we cannot ignore this delay in our forecasts for the project. Thus, whenever net working capital increases, reflecting additional investment in working capital, it represents a reduction in cash flow that year.

It is important to note that only changes in net working capital impact cash flows. For example, consider a three-year project that causes the firm to build up initial inventory by $20,000 and maintain that level of inventory in years 1 and 2, before drawing it down as the project ends and the last product is sold. It is often necessary for the initial increase in inventory to occur prior to the first sale so that the higher level of inventory would be achieved by the end of year 0. The level of the incremental net working capital in each year, the associated change in net working capital, and the cash flow implications, would be:

1	Year	0	1	2	3
2	Level of Incremental NWC	20,000	20,000	20,000	0
3	*Change* in Incremental NWC	+20,000	0	0	−20,000
4	**Cash Flow from Change in NWC**	−20,000	0	0	+20,000

Note that the cash flow effect from a change in net working capital is always equal and opposite in sign to the change in net working capital. For example, an increase in inventory represents an investment or cash outflow, while a reduction in that inventory frees up that investment of capital and represents a cash inflow. Thus, in capital budgeting we subtract changes in net working capital to arrive at the cash flows. Also notice that since the level of incremental net working capital did not change in years 1 and 2, there was no new cash flow effect. Intuitively, as the firm is using up inventory and replenishing it, the net new investment in inventory is zero, so no additional cash outflow is required. Finally, note that over the life of the project, the incremental net working capital returns to zero so that the changes (+20,000 in year 0 and −20,000 in year 3) sum to zero. Accounting principles ensure this by requiring the recapture of working capital over the life of the project.

More generally, we define the change in net working capital in year t as:

$$\text{Change in } NWC \text{ in Year } t = NWC_t - NWC_{t-1} \tag{9.5}$$

When a project causes a change in NWC, that change must be subtracted from incremental earnings to arrive at incremental free cash flows.

EXAMPLE 9.4

Incorporating Changes in Net Working Capital

MyFinanceLab

PROBLEM

Suppose that HomeNet will have no incremental cash or inventory requirements (products will be shipped directly from the contract manufacturer to customers). However, receivables related to HomeNet are expected to account for 15% of annual sales, and payables are expected to be 15% of the annual cost of goods sold (COGS). Fifteen percent of $13 million in sales is $1.95 million and 15% of $5.5 million in COGS is $825,000. HomeNet's net working capital requirements are shown in the following table:

1	Year	0	1	2	3	4	5
2	**Net Working Capital Forecast ($000s)**						
3	Cash Requirements	0	0	0	0	0	0
4	Inventory	0	0	0	0	0	0
5	Receivables (15% of Sales)	0	1,950	1,950	1,950	1,950	0
6	Payables (15% of COGS)	0	−825	−825	−825	−825	0
7	**Net Working Capital**	0	1,125	1,125	1,125	1,125	0

How does this requirement affect the project's free cash flow?

SOLUTION

PLAN

Any increases in net working capital represent an investment that reduces the cash available to the firm and so reduces free cash flow. We can use our forecast of HomeNet's net working capital requirements to complete our estimate of HomeNet's free cash flow. In year 1, net working capital increases by $1.125 million. This increase represents a cost to the firm. This reduction of free cash flow corresponds to the fact that in year 1, $1.950 million of the firm's sales and $0.825 million of its costs have not yet been paid.

In years 2–4, net working capital does not change, so no further contributions are needed. In year 5, when the project is shut down, net working capital falls by $1.125 million as the payments of the last customers are received and the final bills are paid. We add this $1.125 million to free cash flow in year 5.

EXECUTE (IN $000S)

	Year	0	1	2	3	4	5
1							
2	Net Working Capital	0	1,125	1,125	1,125	1,125	0
3	Change in NWC		+1,125	0	0	0	−1,125
4	Cash Flow Effect		−1,125	0	0	0	+1,125

The incremental free cash flows would then be:

	Year	0	1	2	3	4	5
1							
2	Revenues		13,000	13,000	13,000	13,000	0
3	Costs of Goods Sold		−5,500	−5,500	−5,500	−5,500	0
4	**Gross Profit**		7,500	7,500	7,500	7,500	0
5	Selling, General, and Administrative		−2,800	−2,800	−2,800	−2,800	0
6	Depreciation		−1,500	−1,500	−1,500	−1,500	−1,500
7	**EBIT**		3,200	3,200	3,200	3,200	−1,500
8	Income Tax at 40%		−1,280	−1,280	−1,280	−1,280	600
9	**Incremental Earnings**		1,920	1,920	1,920	1,920	−900
10	Add Back Depreciation		1,500	1,500	1,500	1,500	1,500
11	Purchase of Equipment	−7,500					
12	Subtract Changes in NWC		−1,125	0	0	0	1,125
13	**Incremental Free Cash Flows**	−7,500	2,295	3,420	3,420	3,420	1,725

EVALUATE

The free cash flows differ from unlevered net income by reflecting the cash flow effects of capital expenditures on equipment, depreciation, and changes in net working capital. Note that in the first year, free cash flow is lower than unlevered net income, reflecting the up-front investment in equipment. In later years, free cash flow exceeds unlevered net income because depreciation is not a cash expense. In the last year, the firm ultimately recovers the investment in net working capital, further boosting the free cash flow.

Calculating Free Cash Flow Directly

As we noted at the outset of this chapter, because practitioners usually begin the capital budgeting process by first forecasting earnings, we have chosen to do the same. However, we can calculate a project's free cash flow directly by using the following shorthand formula:

Free Cash Flow

$$\text{Free Cash Flow} = \overbrace{(\text{Revenues} - \text{Costs} - \text{Depreciation}) \times (1 - \text{Tax Rate})}^{\text{Unlevered Net Income}} \quad (9.6)$$
$$+ \text{Depreciation} - \text{CapEx} - \text{Change in } NWC$$

Note that we first deduct depreciation when computing the project's incremental earnings and then add it back (because it is a non-cash expense) when computing free cash flow.

Thus, the only effect of depreciation is to reduce the firm's taxable income. Indeed, we can rewrite Eq. 9.6 as:

$$\text{Free Cash Flow} = (\text{Revenues} - \text{Costs}) \times (1 - \text{Tax Rate}) - \text{CapEx}$$
$$- \text{Change in } NWC + \text{Tax Rate} \times \text{Depreciation} \quad (9.7)$$

depreciation tax shield The tax savings that result from the ability to deduct depreciation.

The last term in Eq. 9.7, Tax Rate × Depreciation, is called the **depreciation tax shield**, which is the tax savings that result from the ability to deduct depreciation. As a consequence, depreciation expenses have a *positive* impact on free cash flow. Returning to our example in Table 9.1, if the firm ignored depreciation, its taxes were $400,000 instead of $320,000, leaving it with incremental free cash flow of $600,000 instead of $680,000. Notice that the $80,000 difference is exactly equal to the tax rate (40%) multiplied by the depreciation expense ($200,000). Every dollar of depreciation expense saves the firm 40 cents in taxes, so the $200,000 depreciation expense translates into an $80,000 tax savings.

Firms often report a different depreciation expense for accounting and for tax purposes. Because only the tax consequences of depreciation are relevant for free cash flow, we should use the depreciation expense that the firm will use for tax purposes in our forecast. For tax purposes, many firms use a system called *Modified Accelerated Cost Recovery System*, which we will discuss in the next section.

Calculating the NPV

The goal of forecasting the incremental free cash flows is to have the necessary inputs to calculate the project's NPV. To compute a project's NPV, we must discount its free cash flow at the appropriate cost of capital. As discussed in Chapter 5, the cost of capital for a project is the expected return that investors could earn on their best alternative investment with similar risk and maturity. We will develop the techniques needed to estimate the cost of capital in Part 4 of the text, when we discuss risk and return. For now, we take the cost of capital as given.

We compute the present value of each free cash flow in the future by discounting it at the project's cost of capital. As explained in Chapter 3, using r to represent the cost of capital, the present value of the free cash flow in year t (or FCF_t) is:

$$PV(FCF_t) = \frac{FCF_t}{(1+r)^t} = FCF_t \times \underbrace{\frac{1}{(1+r)^t}}_{t\text{-year discount factor}} \quad (9.8)$$

EXAMPLE 9.5

Calculating the Project's NPV

MyFinanceLab

PROBLEM

Assume that Linksys's managers believe that the HomeNet project has risks similar to its existing projects, for which it has a cost of capital of 12%. Compute the NPV of the HomeNet project.

SOLUTION

PLAN

From Example 9.4, the incremental free cash flows for the HomeNet project are (in $000s):

Year	0	1	2	3	4	5
Incremental Free Cash Flows	−7,500	2,295	3,420	3,420	3,420	1,725

To compute the NPV, we sum the present values of all of the cash flows, noting that the year 0 cash outflow is already a present value.

EXECUTE

Using Eq. 9.8,

$$NPV = -7500 + \frac{2295}{(1.12)^1} + \frac{3420}{(1.12)^2} + \frac{3420}{(1.12)^3} + \frac{3420}{(1.12)^4} + \frac{1725}{(1.12)^5} = 2862$$

EVALUATE

Based on our estimates, HomeNet's NPV is $2.862 million. While HomeNet's up-front cost is $7.5 million, the present value of the additional free cash flow that Linksys will receive from the project is $10.362 million. Thus, taking the HomeNet project is equivalent to Linksys having an extra $2.862 million in the bank today.

USING EXCEL

Capital Budgeting
Using a Spreadsheet
Program

Capital budgeting forecasts and analysis are most easily performed in a spreadsheet program. Here, we highlight a few best practices when developing your own capital budgets.

Create a Project Dashboard

All capital budgeting analyses begin with a set of assumptions regarding future revenues and costs associated with the investment. Centralize these assumptions within your spreadsheet in a project dashboard so they are easy to locate, review, and potentially modify. Here, we show an example for the HomeNet project.

	A	B	C	D	E	F	G	H	I	J
1	HomeNet Capital Budget									
2	Key Assumptions									
3		Revenues & Costs		Year 0	Year 1	Year 2	Year 3	Year 4	Year 5	
4		HomeNet Units Sold			50	50	50	50		
5		HomeNet Ave. Price/Unit			$ 260.00	$ 260.00	$ 260.00	$ 260.00		
6		HomeNet Cost/Unit			$ 110.00	$ 110.00	$ 110.00	$ 110.00		
7		Operating Expenses								
8		Marketing, Support & Rent			(2,800)	(2,800)	(2,800)	(2,800)		
9		Capital Expenditures								
10		Purchase Equipment		(7,500)						
11		Other Assumptions								
12		Depreciation Schedule		0.0%	20.0%	20.0%	20.0%	20.0%	20.0%	
13		Corporate Tax Rate		40.0%	40.0%	40.0%	40.0%	40.0%	40.0%	
14		Receivables (% sales)		15.0%	15.0%	15.0%	15.0%	15.0%	15.0%	
15		Payables (% expenses)		15.0%	15.0%	15.0%	15.0%	15.0%	15.0%	
16										

Color Code for Clarity

In spreadsheet models, use a blue font to distinguish numerical assumptions from formulas. For example, HomeNet's revenue and cost estimates are set to a numerical value in year 1, whereas estimates in later years are set to equal the year 1 estimates. It is therefore clear which cells contain the main assumptions, should we wish to change them later.

Maintain Flexibility

In the HomeNet dashboard, note that we state all assumptions on an annual basis even if we expect them to remain constant. For example, we specify HomeNet's unit volume and average sale price for each year. We can then calculate HomeNet revenues each year based on the corresponding annual assumptions. Doing so provides flexibility if we later determine that HomeNet's adoption rate might vary over time or if we expect prices to follow a trend.

Never Hardcode

So that your assumptions are clear and easy to modify, reference any numerical values you need to develop your projections in the project dashboard. Never "hardcode," or enter numerical values directly into formulas. For example, in the computation of taxes in cell E24 below, we use the formula "= −E23*E13" rather than "= −E23*0.40". While the latter formula would compute the same answer, because the tax rate is hardcoded it would be difficult to update the model if the forecast for the tax rate were to change.

	A	B	C	D	E	F	G	H	I	J
22		Incremental Earnings Forecast		Year 0	Year 1	Year 2	Year 3	Year 4	Year 5	
23		EBIT			$3,200	$3,200	$3,200	$3,200	($1,500)	
24		Income Tax			=-E23*E13	($1,280)	($1,280)	($1,280)	$600	
25		Net Income			$1,920	$1,920	$1,920	$1,920	($900)	

Concept
Check

5. If depreciation expense is not a cash flow, why do we have to subtract it and add it back? Why not just ignore it?

6. Why does an increase in net working capital represent a cash outflow?

9.4   Other Effects on Incremental Free Cash Flows

When computing the incremental free cash flows of an investment decision, we should include *all* changes between the firm's free cash flows with the project versus without the project. These include opportunities forgone due to the project and effects of the project on other parts of the firm. In this section, we discuss these other effects, some of the pitfalls and common mistakes to avoid, and the complications that can arise when forecasting incremental free cash flows.

Opportunity Costs

opportunity cost The value a resource could have provided in its best alternative use.

Many projects use a resource that the company already owns. Because the firm does not need to pay cash to acquire this resource for a new project, it is tempting to assume that the resource is available for free. However, in many cases, the resource could provide value for the firm in another opportunity or project. The **opportunity cost** of using a resource is the value it could have provided in its best alternative use.[4] Because this value is lost when the resource is used by another project, we should include the opportunity cost as an incremental cost of the project. For example, your company may be considering building a retail store on land that it owns. Even though it already owns the land, it is not free to the store project. If it does not put its store on the land, the company could sell the land, for example. This forgone market price for the land is an opportunity cost of the retail store project.

The Opportunity Cost of an Idle Asset

A common mistake is to conclude that if an asset is currently idle, its opportunity cost is zero. For example, the firm might have a warehouse that is currently empty or a machine that is not being used. Often, the asset may have been idled in anticipation of taking on the new project, and would have otherwise been put to use by the firm. Even if the firm has no alternative use for the asset, the firm could choose to sell or rent the asset. The value obtained from the asset's alternative use, sale, or rental represents an opportunity cost that must be included as part of the incremental cash flows.

Project Externalities

project externalities Indirect effects of a project that may increase or decrease the profits of other business activities of a firm.

Project externalities are indirect effects of a project that may increase or decrease the profits of other business activities of the firm. For instance, some purchasers of Apple's iPad mini would otherwise have bought Apple's full size iPad. When sales of a new product displace sales of an existing product, the situation is often referred

---

[4]In Chapter 5, we defined the opportunity cost of capital as the rate you could earn on an alternative investment with equivalent risk. We similarly define the opportunity cost of using an existing asset in a project as the cash flow generated by the next-best alternative use for the asset.

cannibalization When
sales of a firm's new product displace sales of one
of its existing products.

sunk cost Any unrecoverable cost for which a firm
is already liable.

overhead expenses
Expenses associated with
activities that are not
directly attributable to a
single business activity but
instead affect many different areas of a corporation.

to as **cannibalization.** The lost sales of the existing product are an incremental cost to the
company of going forward with the new product.

Sunk Costs

A **sunk cost** is any unrecoverable cost for which the firm is already liable. Sunk costs have
been or will be paid regardless of the decision whether or not to proceed with the project.
Therefore, they are not incremental with respect to the current decision and should not
be included in its analysis. You may hire a market research firm to determine whether
there is demand for a new product you are considering and the analysis may show that
there is not enough demand, so you decide not to go forward with the project. Does that
mean you do not have to pay the research firm's bill? Of course you still have to pay the
bill, emphasizing that the cost is sunk and incurred whether you move forward with the
project or not.

A good rule to remember is that *if your decision does not affect a cash flow, then the
cash flow should not affect your decision.* If the cash flow is the same regardless of the
decision, then it is not relevant to your decision. The following are some common examples
of sunk costs you may encounter.

Fixed Overhead Expenses. **Overhead expenses** are associated with activities that are not
directly attributable to a single business activity but instead affect many different areas of
a corporation. Examples include the cost of maintaining the company's headquarters and
the salary of the CEO. These expenses are often allocated to the different business activities for accounting purposes. To the extent that these overhead costs are fixed and will be
incurred in any case, they are not incremental to the project and should not be included.
Only include as incremental expenses the *additional* overhead expenses that arise because
of the decision to take on the project.

COMMON MISTAKE **The Sunk Cost Fallacy**

Being influenced by sunk costs is such a widespread mistake that it has a special name: *sunk
cost fallacy.* The most common problem is that people "throw good
money after bad." That is, people sometimes continue to invest in a
project that has a negative NPV because they have already invested a
large amount in the project and feel that by not continuing it, the prior
investment will be wasted. The sunk cost fallacy is also sometimes

called the "Concorde effect," which refers to the British and French
governments' decision to continue funding the joint development of
the Concorde aircraft even after it was clear that sales of the plane
would fall far short of what was necessary to justify its continued
development. The project was viewed by the British government as
a commercial and financial disaster. However, the political implications of halting the project—and thereby publicly admitting that all
past expenses on the project would result in nothing—ultimately
prevented either government from abandoning the project.

Past Research and Development Expenditures. A pharmaceutical company may spend
tens of millions of dollars developing a new drug, but if it fails to produce an effect in
trials (or worse, has only negative effects), should it proceed? The company cannot get its
development costs back and the amount of those costs should have no bearing on whether
to continue developing a failed drug.

When a firm has already devoted significant resources to develop a new product, there
may be a tendency to continue investing in the product even if market conditions have
changed and the product is unlikely to be viable. The rationale that is sometimes given is
that if the product is abandoned, the money that has already been invested will be "wasted."
In other cases, a decision is made to abandon a project because it cannot possibly be successful enough to recoup the investment that has already been made. In fact, neither

argument is correct: Any money that has already been spent is a sunk cost and therefore irrelevant. The decision to continue or abandon should be based only on the incremental costs and benefits of the product going forward.

Adjusting Free Cash Flow

Here, we describe a number of complications that can arise when estimating a project's free cash flow.

Timing of Cash Flows. For simplicity, we have treated the cash flows in our examples as if they occur at annual intervals. In reality, cash flows are spread throughout the year. While it is common to forecast at the annual level, we can forecast free cash flow on a quarterly or monthly basis when greater accuracy is required. In practice, firms often choose shorter intervals for riskier projects so that they might forecast cash flows at the monthly level for projects that carry considerable risk. For example, cash flows for a new facility in Europe may be forecasted at the quarterly or annual level, but if that same facility were located in a politically unstable country, the forecasts would likely be at the monthly level.

Accelerated Depreciation. Because depreciation contributes positively to the firm's cash flow through the depreciation tax shield, it is in the firm's best interest to use the most accelerated method of depreciation that is allowable for tax purposes. By doing so, the firm will accelerate its tax savings and increase their present value. In the United States, the most accelerated depreciation method allowed by the IRS is *MACRS (Modified Accelerated Cost Recovery System) depreciation*. With **MACRS depreciation**, the firm first categorizes assets according to their recovery period. Based on the recovery period, MACRS depreciation tables assign a fraction of the purchase price that the firm can recover each year. We provide MACRS tables and recovery periods for common assets in the appendix to this chapter. As we explain in the appendix, MACRS allows for partial depreciation in year 0, when the asset is purchased and put into service.

MACRS depreciation The most accelerated cost recovery system allowed by the IRS. Based on the recovery period, MACRS depreciation tables assign a fraction of the purchase price that the firm can depreciate each year.

EXAMPLE 9.6
Computing Accelerated Depreciation

MyFinanceLab

PROBLEM

What depreciation deduction would be allowed for HomeNet's $7.5 million lab equipment using the MACRS method, assuming the lab equipment is designated to have a five-year recovery period? (See the appendix to this chapter for information on MACRS depreciation schedules.)

SOLUTION

PLAN

Table 9.4 (in the appendix) provides the percentage of the cost that can be depreciated each year. Under MACRS, we take the percentage in the table for each year and multiply it by the original purchase price of the equipment to calculate the depreciation for that year.

EXECUTE

Based on the table, the allowable depreciation expense for the lab equipment is shown below (in thousands of dollars):

	Year	0	1	2	3	4	5
1							
2	**MACRS Depreciation**						
3	Lab Equipment Cost	−7,500					
4	MACRS Depreciation Rate	20.00%	32.00%	19.20%	11.52%	11.52%	5.76%
5	Depreciation Expense	−1,500	−2,400	−1,440	−864	−864	−432

EVALUATE

Compared with straight-line depreciation, the MACRS method allows for larger depreciation deductions earlier in the asset's life, which increases the present value of the depreciation tax shield and thus raises the project's NPV. In the case of HomeNet, computing the NPV using MACRS depreciation leads to an NPV of $3.179 million.

Liquidation or Salvage Value. Assets that are no longer needed often have a resale value, or some salvage value if the parts are sold for scrap. Some assets may have a negative liquidation value. For example, it may cost money to remove and dispose of the used equipment.

In the calculation of free cash flow, we include the liquidation value of any assets that are no longer needed and may be disposed of. When an asset is liquidated, any capital gain is taxed as income. We calculate the capital gain as the difference between the sale price and the book value of the asset:

$$\text{Capital Gain} = \text{Sale Price} - \text{Book Value} \tag{9.9}$$

The book value is equal to the asset's original cost less the amount it has already been depreciated for tax purposes:

$$\text{Book Value} = \text{Purchase Price} - \text{Accumulated Depreciation} \tag{9.10}$$

We must adjust the project's free cash flow to account for the after-tax cash flow that would result from an asset sale:

$$\text{After-Tax Cash Flow from Asset Sale} = \text{Sale Price} - (\text{Tax Rate} \times \text{Capital Gain}) \tag{9.11}$$

EXAMPLE 9.7

Computing After-Tax Cash Flows from an Asset Sale

MyFinanceLab

PROBLEM

As production manager, you are overseeing the shutdown of a production line for a discontinued product. Some of the equipment can be sold for $50,000. The equipment was originally purchased four years ago for $500,000 and is being depreciated according to the five-year MACRS schedule. If your marginal tax rate is 35%, what is the after-tax cash flow you can expect from selling the equipment?

SOLUTION

PLAN

In order to compute the after-tax cash flow, you will need to compute the capital gain, which, as Eq. 9.9 shows, requires you to know the book value of the equipment. The book value is given in Eq. 9.10 as the original purchase price of the equipment less accumulated depreciation. Thus, you need to follow these steps:

1. Use the MACRS schedule to determine the accumulated depreciation.
2. Determine the book value as purchase price minus accumulated depreciation.
3. Determine the capital gain as the sale price less the book value.
4. Compute the tax owed on the capital gain and subtract it from the sale price, following Eq. 9.11, and then subtract the tax owed from the sale price.

EXECUTE

From the appendix, we see that the first five rates of the five-year MACRS schedule (including year 0) are:

Year	0	1	2	3	4
Depreciation Rate	20.00%	32.00%	19.20%	11.52%	11.52%
Depreciation Amount	100,000	160,000	96,000	57,600	57,600

Thus, the accumulated depreciation is 100,000 + 160,000 + 96,000 + 57,600 + 57,600 = 471,200, such that the remaining book value is $500,000 − $471,200 = $28,800. (Note we could have also calculated this by summing the rates for years remaining on the MACRS schedule: Year 5 is 5.76%, so .0576 × 500,000 = 28,800).

The capital gain is then $50,000 − $28,800 = $21,200 and the tax owed is 0.35 × $21,200 = $7,420.

Your after-tax cash flow is then found as the sale price minus the tax owed: $50,000 − $7,420 = $42,580.

EVALUATE

Because you are only taxed on the capital gain portion of the sale price, figuring the after-tax cash flow is not as simple as subtracting the tax rate multiplied by the sale price. Instead, you have to determine the portion of the sale price that represents a gain and compute the tax from there. The same procedure holds for selling equipment at a loss relative to book value—the loss creates a deduction for taxable income elsewhere in the company.

Tax Loss Carryforwards and Carrybacks. A firm generally identifies its marginal tax rate by determining the tax bracket that it falls into based on its overall level of pretax income. Two features of the tax code, called **tax loss carryforwards** and **carrybacks**, allow corporations to take losses during a current year and offset them against gains in nearby years. Since 1997, companies can "carry back" losses for two years and "carry forward" losses for 20 years. This tax rule means that a firm can offset losses during one year against income for the last two years, or save the losses to be offset against income during the next 20 years. When a firm can carry back losses, it receives a refund for back taxes in the current year. Otherwise, the firm must carry forward the loss and use it to offset future taxable income. When a firm has tax loss carryforwards well in excess of its current pretax income, then additional income it earns today will simply increase the taxes it owes after it exhausts its carryforwards.

tax loss carryforwards and carrybacks Two features of the U.S. tax code that allow corporations to take losses during a current year and offset them against gains in nearby years. Since 1997, companies can "carry back" losses for two years and "carry forward" losses for 20 years.

Replacement Decisions

Often, the financial manager must decide whether to replace an existing piece of equipment. The new equipment may allow increased production, resulting in incremental revenue, or it may simply be more efficient, lowering costs. The typical incremental effects associated with such a decision are salvage value from the old machine, purchase of the new machine, cost savings and revenue increases, and depreciation effects.

EXAMPLE 9.8

Replacing an Existing Machine

MyFinanceLab

PROBLEM

You are trying to decide whether to replace a machine on your production line. The new machine will cost $1 million, but will be more efficient than the old machine, reducing costs by $500,000 per year. Your old machine is fully depreciated, but you could sell it for $50,000. You would depreciate the new machine over a five-year life using MACRS. The new machine will not change your working capital needs. Your tax rate is 35%, and your cost of capital is 9%. Should you replace the machine?

SOLUTION

PLAN

Incremental revenues: 0
Incremental costs: −500,000 (a reduction in costs will appear as a positive number in the costs line of our analysis)
Depreciation schedule (from the appendix):

Year	0	1	2	3	4	5
Depreciation Rate	20.00%	32.00%	19.20%	11.52%	11.52%	5.76%
Depreciation Amount	200,000	320,000	192,000	115,200	115,200	57,600

Capital gain on salvage = $50,000 − $0 = $50,000

Cash flow from salvage value: +50,000 − (50,000)(.35) = 32,500

EXECUTE

(values in thousands)

	Year	0	1	2	3	4	5
1							
2	Incremental Revenues						
3	Incremental Costs of Goods Sold		500	500	500	500	500
4	**Incremental Gross Profit**		500	500	500	500	500
5	Depreciation	−200	−320	−192	−115.2	−115.2	−57.6
6	**EBIT**	−200	180	308	384.8	384.8	442.4
7	Income Tax at 35%	70	−63	−107.8	−134.68	−134.68	−154.84
8	**Incremental Earnings**	−130	117	200.2	250.12	250.12	287.56
9	Add Back Depreciation	200	320	192	115.2	115.2	57.6
10	Purchase of Equipment	−1,000					
11	Salvage Cash Flow	32.5					
12	**Incremental Free Cash Flows**	−897.5	437	392.2	365.32	365.32	345.16

$$NPV = -897.50 + \frac{437.00}{1.09} + \frac{392.20}{1.09^2} + \frac{365.32}{1.09^3} + \frac{365.32}{1.09^4} + \frac{345.16}{1.09^5} = 598.75$$

EVALUATE

Even though the decision has no impact on revenues, it still matters for cash flows because it reduces costs. Furthermore, both selling the old machine and buying the new machine involve cash flows with tax implications. The NPV analysis shows that replacing the machine will increase the value of the firm by almost $599,000.

Concept Check

7. Should we include sunk costs in the cash flows of a project? Why or why not?

8. Explain why it is advantageous for a firm to use the most accelerated depreciation schedule possible for tax purposes.

9.5 Analyzing the Project

When evaluating a capital budgeting project, financial managers should make the decision that maximizes NPV. As we have discussed, to compute the NPV for a project you need to estimate the incremental free cash flows and choose a discount rate. Given these inputs, the NPV calculation is relatively straightforward. The most difficult part of capital budgeting is deciding how to estimate the cash flows and cost of capital. These estimates are often subject to significant uncertainty. In this section, we look at methods that assess the importance of this uncertainty and identify the drivers of value in the project.

Sensitivity Analysis

sensitivity analysis An important capital budgeting tool that determines how the NPV varies as underlying assumptions change one at a time.

An important capital budgeting tool for assessing the effect of uncertainty in forecasts is *sensitivity analysis*. **Sensitivity analysis** breaks the NPV calculation into its component assumptions and shows how the NPV varies as underlying assumptions change. In this way, sensitivity analysis allows us to explore the effects of errors in our NPV estimates for a project. By conducting a sensitivity analysis, we learn which assumptions are the most important; we can then invest further resources and effort to refine these assumptions. Such an analysis also reveals which aspects of a project are most critical when we are actually managing the project.

In fact, we have already performed a type of sensitivity analysis in Chapter 8 when we constructed an NPV profile. By graphing the NPV of a project as a function of the discount rate, we are assessing the sensitivity of our NPV calculation to uncertainty about the correct cost of capital to use as a discount rate. In practice, financial managers explore the sensitivity of their NPV calculation to many more factors than just the discount rate.

To illustrate, consider the assumptions underlying the calculation of HomeNet's NPV in Example 9.5. There is likely to be significant uncertainty surrounding each revenue and cost assumption. In addition to the base case assumptions about units sold, sale price, cost of goods sold, net working capital, and cost of capital, Linksys's managers would also identify best- and worst-case scenarios for each. For example, assume that they identified the best- and worst-case assumptions listed in Table 9.2. Note that these are best- and worst-case scenarios for each parameter rather than representing one worst-case scenario and one best-case scenario.

To determine the importance of this uncertainty, we recalculate the NPV of the HomeNet project under the best- and worst-case assumptions for each parameter. For example, if the number of units sold is only 35,000 per year, the NPV of the project falls to −$1.13 million. We repeat this calculation for each parameter. The result is shown in Figure 9.2, which reveals that the parameter assumptions with the largest effect on NPV are the number of units sold and the sale price per unit. As a result, these assumptions deserve the greatest scrutiny during the estimation process. In addition, as the most important drivers of the project's value, these factors deserve close attention when managing the project after it starts.

TABLE 9.2

Best- and Worst-Case Assumptions for Each Parameter in the HomeNet Project

Parameter	Initial Assumption	Worst Case	Best Case
Units Sold (thousands)	50	35	65
Sale Price ($/unit)	260	240	280
Cost of Goods ($/unit)	110	120	100
NWC ($ thousands)	1125	1525	725
Cost of Capital	12%	15%	10%

FIGURE 9.2

HomeNet's NPV Under Best- and Worst-Case Parameter Assumptions

Bars show the change in NPV going from the best-case assumption to the worst-case assumption for each parameter. For example, the NPV of the project ranges from −$1.13 million if only 35,000 units are sold to $6.85 million if 65,000 units are sold. Under the initial assumptions, HomeNet's NPV is $2.862 million.

Break-Even Analysis

break-even The level of a parameter for which an investment has an NPV of zero.

A natural extension of the sensitivity analysis is to ask at what level of each parameter would the project have an NPV of zero. For each parameter, this level is its **break-even**. One example that we have already considered is the calculation of the internal rate of return (IRR). Recall from Chapter 8 that the difference between the IRR of a project and the cost of capital tells you how much error in the cost of capital it would take to change the investment decision. By either graphing the NPV profile or using the Excel IRR function, we would find that the incremental cash flows of HomeNet given in Example 9.5 imply an IRR of 26.6%. Thus, the true cost of capital can be as high as 26.6% and the project will still have a positive NPV.

break-even analysis A calculation of the value of each parameter for which the NPV of the project is zero.

We can determine the uncertainty of other parameters as well. In a **break-even analysis**, for each parameter we calculate the value at which the NPV of the project is zero. This would be tedious to do by hand, so in practice it is always done with a spreadsheet. As with the NPV profile for the discount rate, we can graph the NPV as a function of each of the critical assumptions. In each case, we keep all of the other parameters fixed at their initially assumed values and vary only the parameter in question. Figure 9.3 does this for HomeNet.

Accounting Break-Even. We have examined the break-even levels in terms of the project's NPV, which is the most useful perspective for decision making. Other accounting notions of break-even are sometimes considered, however. For example, we could compute the

EBIT break-even The level of a particular parameter for which a project's EBIT is zero.

EBIT break-even for sales, which is the level of sales for which a project's EBIT is zero.

Recall from Eq. 9.1 that the project's EBIT is Revenues − Costs − Depreciation. Costs include cost of goods sold, and selling, general, and administrative expense (SG&A). Revenues equal Units Sold × Sale Price, and cost of goods sold equals Units Sold × Cost per Unit, so we have EBIT = (Units Sold × Sale Price) − (Units Sold × Cost per Unit) − SG&A − Depreciation. Setting this equal to zero and solving for units sold:

$$\text{Units Sold} \times (\text{Sale Price} - \text{Cost per Unit}) - \text{SG\&A} - \text{Depreciation} = 0$$

$$\text{Units Sold} = \frac{\text{SG\&A} + \text{Depreciation}}{\text{Sales Price} - \text{Cost per Unit}} = \frac{2{,}800{,}000 + 1{,}500{,}000}{260 - 110} = 28{,}667$$

FIGURE 9.3

Break-Even Analysis Graphs

The graphs in Panels (a) and (b) relate two of the key parameters to the project's NPV to identify the parameters' break-even points. For example, based on the initial assumptions, the HomeNet project will break even with a sales level of 39,242 units per year. Similarly, holding sales and the other parameters constant at their initial assumed values, the project will break even at a cost of goods sold of just over $142 per unit.

Panel (a) Break-Even Point Based on Units Sold

Panel (b) Break-Even Point Based on Costs of Goods Sold

However, this EBIT break-even number is misleading. While HomeNet's EBIT break-even level of sales is only 28,667 units per year, given the large up-front investment required in HomeNet, its NPV is −$2.81 million at that sales level.

INTERVIEW WITH
DAVID HOLLAND

David Holland is currently Senior Vice President of Sports and Entertainment Solutions where he is responsible for accelerating development and adoption of Cisco solutions in that market. He was previously Senior Vice President and Treasurer of Cisco, and was responsible for managing all funding, risk, and capital market activities related to the firm's $50 billion balance sheet.

QUESTION: *What is the importance of considering free cash flow, as opposed to just the earnings implications of a financial decision?*

ANSWER: There is an adage saying, "Cash flow is a fact and earnings are an opinion." Earnings use an accounting framework and are governed by many rules, making it hard to know what earnings tell the investor. The economics of cash flow are clear: We can't dispute whether cash has come in or gone out. Cisco's investment decisions are based primarily on cash flow models because they take project risk into account and show the impact on value creation for owners of the business.

QUESTION: *What key financial metrics does Cisco use to make investment decisions?*

ANSWER: Cisco focuses primarily on net present value (NPV) for investment decisions. Robust NPV analysis goes beyond simply accepting projects with positive NPVs and rejecting those with negative NPVs. It identifies the key drivers that affect project success and demonstrates the interplay between factors that affect cash flow. For example, running a model using a lower margin approach shows us the impact on revenue growth and on operating cost structures. We can compare that to a higher margin (premium pricing) approach. The business unit manager learns how to control aspects of the business model to alleviate risk or accelerate the upside potential.

We prefer NPV to internal rate of return (IRR), which may return multiple answers or give false signals as to an investment's profitability, depending on the organization of cash flows. An attraction of IRR analysis is the ease of comparing percentage returns. However, this method hides the scope of a project. A project with a 25% return may generate $1 million in shareholder value, while another with a 13% IRR might produce $1 billion. NPV captures the size of the return in dollar terms and shows a project's impact on share price. NPV also creates an ownership framework for employees whose compensation package includes some form of stock ownership, directly tying the decision-making criteria to stock price.

QUESTION: *When developing a model to analyze a new investment, how do you deal with the uncertainty surrounding estimates, especially for new technologies?*

ANSWER: Cisco relies on strong financial modeling for the thousands of investment decisions we make every year. Our 2500 finance people worldwide work with the internal client—the business lead—to understand the assumptions in the model and to check the model's result against alternative assumptions. Evaluating the cash flows for technology projects, especially new technology, is difficult. When you buy an oil refinery, you can see the throughput and the cash flows. Identifying the relevant savings from a component technology for a larger router or switch product or a strategic move into a new area is more complex and intangible. Scenario and sensitivity analyses and game theory help us control risk by adjusting our strategy. We also look at the qualitative aspects, such as how the strategy fits into the customer sector and the directions customers are moving with their tech platforms.

QUESTION: *How does Cisco adjust for risk?*

ANSWER: To stay competitive in the technology space, we must be prepared to take some level of risk, even in down markets. We apply the same discount rate to all projects in a category, based on their market risk (i.e., sensitivity to market conditions). We do not adjust the discount rate to account for project-specific risks, because our required return has not changed and that would distort the true value of the company. To assess a project's unique risks, we model the upside or downside of cash flows with scenario and sensitivity analysis. We might analyze the sensitivity of a project's NPV to a 1% change in both revenue growth and operating costs. Then we run the model with other assumptions, developing base, optimistic, and bearish cases. We discuss these models with the business lead and rerun the models based on their input. This process improves our potential outcome and project profitability.

Scenario Analysis

scenario analysis
An important capital budgeting tool that determines how the NPV varies as multiple project parameters are changed simultaneously.

In the analysis thus far, we have considered the consequences of varying only one parameter at a time. In reality, certain factors may affect more than one parameter. **Scenario analysis** considers the effect on NPV of changing multiple project parameters simultaneously. For example, lowering HomeNet's price may increase the number of units sold. We can use scenario analysis to evaluate alternative pricing strategies for the HomeNet product in Table 9.3. In this case, the current strategy is optimal. Figure 9.4 shows the combinations of price and volume that lead to the same NPV of $2.862 million for HomeNet as the current strategy. Only strategies with price and volume combinations above the curve will lead to a higher NPV.

TABLE 9.3

Scenario Analysis of Alternative Pricing Strategies

Strategy	Sale Price ($/unit)	Expected Units Sold (thousands)	NPV ($ thousands)
Current Strategy	260	50	2862
Price Reduction	245	55	2729
Price Increase	275	45	2729

FIGURE 9.4

Price and Volume Combinations for HomeNet with Equivalent NPV

The graph shows alternative price per unit and annual volume combinations that lead to an NPV of $2.862 million. Pricing strategies with combinations above the curve will lead to a higher NPV and are superior. For example, if Linksys managers think they will be able to sell 48,000 units at a price of $275, this strategy would yield a higher NPV ($3,607 million).

48,000 units at a price of $275 each produces an NPV > $2.862 million

52,000 units at a price of $250 each produces an NPV < $2.862 million

Project Analysis
Using Excel

Here, we describe several useful Excel tools that assist with project analysis.

Goal Seek for Break-Even Analysis

Excel's goal seek function determines the break-even point for key assumptions in our model. For example, to determine the break-even level of units for annual sales, use the Goal Seek window (see the Data > What-If Analysis menu, or keyboard shortcut Alt-A-W-G). The set cell is the cell in which we calculated NPV (in this case, cell D31). To set its value to 0 (break-even), we change the average sale price (cell E5). Excel will then use trial and error to find the sale price at which the project's NPV is zero—in this case $227.73.

	A	B	C	D	E	F	G	H	I
1	**HomeNet Capital Budget**								
2	*Key Assumptions*			Year 0	Year 1	Year 2	Year 3	Year 4	Year 5
5		HomeNet Ave. Price/Unit			$ 260.00	$ 260.00	$ 260.00	$ 260.00	
30									
31		NPV		2,862					

Data Tables for Sensitivity Analysis

Data tables, which we introduced in the online appendix to Chapter 7 to construct the NPV profile, allow us to compute the sensitivity of NPV to any other input variable in our financial model. Excel can also compute a two-dimensional data table showing the sensitivity of NPV to two inputs simultaneously. For example, the data table below shows NPVs for different combinations of testing equipment cost and HomeNet's manufacturing costs.

	C	D	E	F	G	H
39	NPV			HomeNet Cost/Unit		
40		2,862	$110	$105	$100	$95
41		-7500	2,862	3,305	3,749	4,192
42		-7750	2,684	3,128	3,571	4,014
43		-8000	2,506	2,950	3,393	3,836
44	Equipment Cost	-8250	2,328	2,772	3,215	3,659
45		-8500	2,150	2,594	3,037	3,481
46		-8750	1,973	2,416	2,859	3,303
47		-9000	1,795	2,238	2,681	3,125
48		-9250	1,617	2,060	2,504	2,947
49		-9500	1,439	1,882	2,326	2,769
50		-9750	1,261	1,704	2,148	2,591
51		-10000	1,083	1,526	1,970	2,413

To construct this data table, we put the values of each input along the sides of the table (shown in blue), and a formula for the value we want to compute in the upper-left corner (cell D36, which in this case is just a link to the cell in which we computed the NPV). We select the entire table (D36:H47), bring up the Data Table window (see the Data > What-If Analysis menu or keyboard shortcut Alt-D-T), and input the locations in our project dashboard (see page 273) of the cost assumption (row input cell E6) and equipment cost (column input cell D10). The data table shows, for example, that NPV increases if we lower our manufacturing cost to $100 per unit by spending an additional $1 million on equipment to test the design.

Scenarios in the Project Dashboard

The project dashboard on page 273 shows only our base-case assumptions. We can build multiple scenarios into our project dashboard by adding additional rows with alternative assumptions, and then using Excel's index function to select the scenario we would like to use in our analysis. For example, rows 5–7 below show alternative annual sales assumptions for HomeNet. We then select the scenario to analyze by entering the appropriate number (in this case 1, 2, or 3) in the highlighted cell (C4), and use the index function to pull the appropriate data into row 4.

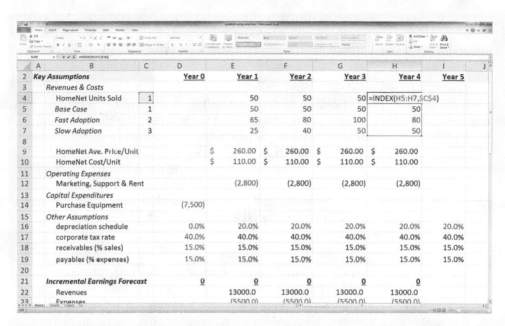

	A	B	C	D	E	F	G	H	I	J
2	**Key Assumptions**			**Year 0**	**Year 1**	**Year 2**	**Year 3**	**Year 4**	**Year 5**	
3	Revenues & Costs									
4	HomeNet Units Sold		1		50	50	50	=INDEX(H5:H7,C4)		
5	Base Case		1		50	50	50	50		
6	Fast Adoption		2		65	80	100	80		
7	Slow Adoption		3		25	40	50	50		
8										
9	HomeNet Ave. Price/Unit			$	260.00	$ 260.00	$ 260.00	$ 260.00		
10	HomeNet Cost/Unit			$	110.00	$ 110.00	$ 110.00	$ 110.00		
11	Operating Expenses									
12	Marketing, Support & Rent				(2,800)	(2,800)	(2,800)	(2,800)		
13	Capital Expenditures									
14	Purchase Equipment			(7,500)						
15	Other Assumptions									
16	depreciation schedule			0.0%	20.0%	20.0%	20.0%	20.0%	20.0%	
17	corporate tax rate			40.0%	40.0%	40.0%	40.0%	40.0%	40.0%	
18	receivables (% sales)			15.0%	15.0%	15.0%	15.0%	15.0%	15.0%	
19	payables (% expenses)			15.0%	15.0%	15.0%	15.0%	15.0%	15.0%	
20										
21	**Incremental Earnings Forecast**			0	0	0	0	0		
22	Revenues				13000.0	13000.0	13000.0	13000.0		
23	Expenses				(5500.0)	(5500.0)	(5500.0)	(5500.0)		

We can then analyze the consequences for each scenario using the one-dimensional data table in C54:D57 below, with column input cell C4.

	A	B	C	D
53				**NPV**
54		**HomeNet Units Sold**		2,862
55		Base Case	1	2,862
56		Fast Adoption	2	11,029
57		Slow Adoption	3	319

Concept Check

9. What is sensitivity analysis?

10. How does scenario analysis differ from sensitivity analysis?

9.6 Real Options in Capital Budgeting

Our approach to capital budgeting thus far has focused on the initial investment decision without explicitly considering future decisions that may need to be made over the life of a project. Rather, we assumed that our forecast of a project's expected future cash flows already incorporated the effect of future decisions that would be made. In truth, most projects contain *real options*. A **real option** is the right, but not the obligation, to make a particular business decision. Because you are not obligated to take the action, you will do so only if it increases the NPV of the project. In particular, because real options allow a decision maker to choose the most attractive alternative after new information has been learned, the presence of real options adds value to an investment opportunity. The tools to estimate the actual value created by real options are beyond the scope of this chapter and are contained later in the book. However, we introduce the concept here to give you a

real option The right to make a particular business decision, such as a capital investment.

sense of the types of real options you may encounter and establish the intuition that flexibility (more options) is valuable. Let's look at some of the most common real options in the context of Linksys's HomeNet project.

Option to Delay

option to delay commitment The option to time a particular investment

The **option to delay commitment** (the option to time an investment) is almost always present. Linksys could wait to commit to the HomeNet project. Waiting could be valuable if Linksys expects prices of the components to decrease substantially, soon-to-be-released new technology that will make the existing components obsolete, or increased sales of Web-ready appliances (heightening the demand for HomeNet). In addition, Linksys may simply want more time to gather information about the potential market for HomeNet. As with any other capital budgeting decision, Linksys would only choose to delay if doing so would increase the NPV of the project.

Option to Expand

option to expand The option to start with limited production and expand only if the product is successful.

In the section on sensitivity analysis, we looked at changes in our assumptions about units sold. All of the analysis was performed, however, under the assumption that Linksys would fully commit to and roll out the HomeNet product worldwide. We did not consider the **option to expand**, which is the option to start with limited production and expand only if the product is successful. Linksys could, instead, test market the product in limited release before committing to it fully. Doing so would create an option to expand worldwide only if HomeNet were successful in limited release. It is possible that, by reducing its up-front commitment and choosing to expand only if the product is successful, Linksys will increase the NPV of the HomeNet product. However, in this particular case, there are large costs of development that would be paid whether Linksys sells one or one million units, so limiting the initial market does not reduce the financial commitment substantially. Thus, in the case of HomeNet, it is unlikely that Linksys would choose a limited release with an option to expand.

Option to Abandon

abandonment option The option for an investor to cease investing in a project. Abandonment options can add value to a project because a firm can drop a project if it turns out to be unsuccessful.

An **abandonment option** is the option to walk away. Abandonment options can add value to a project because a firm can drop a project if it turns out to be unsuccessful. Imagine that a competitor developed new technology that allowed it to introduce a successful competing product priced at $170. At that price, HomeNet would produce negative cash flows every year. But would Linksys continue to sell HomeNet if it had to do so at a loss? Probably not. Linksys has an option to abandon the project. It could stop producing HomeNet and sell the equipment. Depending on how much Linksys believes the equipment would sell for if it abandoned the project, the abandonment option could make HomeNet attractive even if there was a substantial risk of a competing product.

All these options point to the same conclusion: *If you can build greater flexibility into your project, you will increase its NPV.* In Chapter 21, we will discuss how to value options so that you can estimate just how much more valuable the project is with greater flexibility. Many industries regularly make use of real options. For example, most movie producers build in an option for a sequel if the first movie does well. Pharmaceutical developers like Merck develop new drugs in stages, allowing them to abandon development if tests do not go well.

Concept Check

11. What are real options?

12. Why do real options increase the NPV of a project?

MyFinanceLab

Here is what you should know after reading this chapter. MyFinanceLab will help you identify what you know, and where to go when you need to practice.

Key Points and Equations	Key Terms	Online Practice
9.1 The Capital Budgeting Process • Capital budgeting is the process of analyzing investment opportunities and deciding which ones to accept. A capital budget is a list of all projects that a company plans to undertake during the next period. • We use the NPV rule to evaluate capital budgeting decisions, making decisions that maximize NPV. When deciding to accept or reject a project, we accept projects with a positive NPV.	capital budget, p. 262 capital budgeting, p. 262 incremental earnings, p. 263	MyFinanceLab Study Plan 9.1
9.2 Forecasting Incremental Earnings • The incremental earnings of a project comprise the amount by which the project is expected to change the firm's earnings. • Incremental earnings should include all incremental revenues and costs associated with the project. $$\begin{aligned}\text{Incremental Earnings} = (&\text{Incremental Revenues}\\ &- \text{Incremental Cost} - \text{Depreciation})\\ &\times (1 - \text{Tax Rate})\end{aligned} \quad (9.3)$$ • Interest and other financing-related expenses are excluded to determine the project's unlevered net income.	marginal corporate tax rate, p. 265 pro forma, p. 266 straight-line depreciation, p. 263 unlevered net income, p. 267	MyFinanceLab Study Plan 9.2
9.3 Determining Incremental Free Cash Flow • We compute free cash flow from incremental earnings by eliminating all non-cash expenses and including all capital investment. • Depreciation is not a cash expense, so it is added back. • Actual capital expenditures are deducted. • Increases in net working capital are deducted and decreases are added. Net working capital is defined as: $$\text{Cash} + \text{Inventory} + \text{Receivables} - \text{Payables} \quad (9.4)$$ • The basic calculation for free cash flow is: $$\begin{aligned}\text{Free Cash Flow} = (&\text{Revenues} - \text{Costs} - \text{Depreciation})\\ &\times (1 - \text{Tax Rate}) + \text{Depreciation}\\ &- \text{CapEx} - \text{Change in } NWC\end{aligned} \quad (9.6)$$	depreciation tax shield, p. 272 free cash flow, p. 268 trade credit, p. 269	MyFinanceLab Study Plan 9.3

9.4 Other Effects on Incremental Free Cash Flows
- An opportunity cost is the cost of using an existing asset.
- Project externalities are cash flows that occur when a project affects other areas of the company's business.
- A sunk cost is an unrecoverable cost that has already been incurred.
- Depreciation expenses affect free cash flow only through the depreciation tax shield. The firm should use the most accelerated depreciation schedule possible.
- The discount rate for a project is its cost of capital: the expected return of securities with comparable risk and horizon.
- When you sell an asset, the portion of the proceeds above its book value is taxed:

$$\text{After-Tax Cash Flow from Asset Sale} = \text{Sale Price} - (\text{Tax Rate} \times \text{Capital Gain}) \quad (9.11)$$

cannibalization, p. 275
MACRS depreciation, p. 276
opportunity cost, p. 274
overhead expenses, p. 275
project externalities, p. 274
sunk cost, p. 275
tax loss carryforwards and carrybacks, p. 278

MyFinance Lab Study Plan 9.4

HomeNet Example Spreadsheet

9.5 Analyzing the Project
- Sensitivity analysis breaks the NPV calculation into its component assumptions, showing how the NPV varies as the values of the underlying assumptions change.
- Break-even analysis computes the level of a parameter that makes the project's NPV equal zero.
- Scenario analysis considers the effect of changing multiple parameters simultaneously.

break-even, p. 281
break-even analysis, p. 281
EBIT break-even, p. 281
scenario analysis, p. 283
sensitivity analysis, p. 279

MyFinanceLab Study Plan 9.5

Interactive Sensitivity Analysis, Using Excel: Performing Sensitivity Analysis

9.6 Real Options in Capital Budgeting
- Real options are options to make a business decision, often after gathering more information. The presence of real options in a project increases the project's NPV.

abandonment option, p. 285
option to delay commitment, p. 285
option to expand, p. 285
real option, p. 285

MyFinanceLab Study Plan 9.6

CRITICAL THINKING

1. What are pro forma incremental earnings?

2. What is the difference between pro forma incremental earnings and pro forma free cash flow?

3. Why do we convert from incremental earnings to free cash flow when performing capital budgeting?

4. What is the role of net working capital in projects?

5. How does net working capital affect the cash flows of a project?

6. Why is it important to adjust project sales and costs for externalities?

7. Does accelerated depreciation generally increase or decrease NPV relative to straight-line depreciation?

8. How is sensitivity analysis performed and what is its purpose?

PROBLEMS

All problems in this chapter are available in MyFinanceLab. An asterisk * indicates problems with a higher level of difficulty.

Forecasting Incremental Earnings

1. Daily Enterprises is purchasing a $10 million machine. It will cost $50,000 to transport and install the machine. The machine has a depreciable life of five years and will have no salvage value. If Daily uses straight-line depreciation, what are the depreciation expenses associated with this machine?

2. The machine in Problem 1 will generate incremental revenues of $4 million per year along with incremental costs of $1.2 million per year. If Daily's marginal tax rate is 35%, what are the incremental earnings associated with the new machine?

3. You are upgrading to better production equipment for your firm's only product. The new equipment will allow you to make more of your product in the same amount of time. Thus, you forecast that total sales will increase next year by 20% over the current amount of 100,000 units. If your sales price is $20 per unit, what are the incremental revenues next year from the upgrade?

4. Pisa Pizza, a seller of frozen pizza, is considering introducing a healthier version of its pizza that will be low in cholesterol and contain no trans fats. The firm expects that sales of the new pizza will be $20 million per year. While many of these sales will be to new customers, Pisa Pizza estimates that 40% will come from customers who switch to the new, healthier pizza instead of buying the original version.
   a. Assume customers will spend the same amount on either version. What level of incremental sales is associated with introducing the new pizza?
   b. Suppose that 50% of the customers who would switch from Pisa Pizza's original pizza to its healthier pizza will switch to another brand if Pisa Pizza does not introduce a healthier pizza. What level of incremental sales is associated with introducing the new pizza in this case?

5. Kokomochi is considering the launch of an advertising campaign for its latest dessert product, the Mini Mochi Munch. Kokomochi plans to spend $5 million on TV, radio, and print advertising this year for the campaign. The ads are expected to boost sales of the Mini Mochi Munch by $9 million this year and by $7 million next year. In addition, the company expects that new consumers who try the Mini Mochi Munch will be more likely to try Kokomochi's other products. As a result, sales of other products are expected to rise by $2 million each year.

   Kokomochi's gross profit margin for the Mini Mochi Munch is 35%, and its gross profit margin averages 25% for all other products. The company's marginal corporate tax rate is 35% both this year and next year. What are the incremental earnings associated with the advertising campaign?

6. Hyperion, Inc., currently sells its latest high-speed color printer, the Hyper 500, for $350. It plans to lower the price to $300 next year. Its cost of goods sold for the Hyper 500 is $200 per unit, and this year's sales are expected to be 20,000 units.
   a. Suppose that if Hyperion drops the price to $300 immediately, it can increase this year's sales by 25% to 25,000 units. What would be the incremental impact on this year's EBIT of such a price drop?
   b. Suppose that for each printer sold, Hyperion expects additional sales of $75 per year on ink cartridges for the next three years, and Hyperion has a gross profit margin of 70% on ink cartridges. What is the incremental impact on EBIT for the next three years of a price drop this year?

Determining Incremental Free Cash Flow

7. You have a depreciation expense of $500,000 and a tax rate of 35%. What is your depreciation tax shield?

8. You have forecast pro forma earnings of $1,000,000. This includes the effect of $200,000 in depreciation. You also forecast a decrease in working capital of $100,000 that year. What is your forecast of free cash flows for that year?

9. Your pro forma income statement shows sales of $1,000,000, cost of goods sold as $500,000, depreciation expense of $100,000, and taxes of $160,000 due to a tax rate of 40%. What are your pro forma earnings? What is your pro forma free cash flow?

10. You are forecasting incremental free cash flows for Daily Enterprises. Based on the information in Problems 1 and 2, what are the incremental free cash flows associated with the new machine?

11. Castle View Games would like to invest in a division to develop software for video games. To evaluate this decision, the firm first attempts to project the working capital needs for this operation. Its chief financial officer has developed the following estimates (in millions of dollars) (*see MyFinanceLab for the data in Excel format*):

1	Year	1	2	3	4	5
2	Cash	6	12	15	15	15
3	Accounts Receivable	21	22	24	24	24
4	Inventory	5	7	10	12	13
5	Accounts Payable	18	22	24	25	30

Assuming that Castle View currently does not have any working capital invested in this division, calculate the cash flows associated with changes in working capital for the first five years of this investment.

12. In the HomeNet example from the chapter, its receivables are 15% of sales and its payables are 15% of COGS. Forecast the required investment in net working capital for HomeNet assuming that sales and cost of goods sold (COGS) will be as follows (*see MyFinanceLab for the data in Excel format*):

1	Year	0	1	2	3	4
2	Sales		23,500	26,438	23,794	8,566
3	COGS		9,500	10,688	9,619	3,483

13. Elmdale Enterprises is deciding whether to expand its production facilities. Although long-term cash flows are difficult to estimate, management has projected the following cash flows for the first two years (in millions of dollars) (*see MyFinanceLab for the data in Excel format*):

1	Year	1	2
2	Revenues	125	160
3	Operating Expenses (other than depreciation)	40	60
4	Depreciation	25	36
5	Increase in Net Working Capital	2	8
6	Capital Expenditures	30	40
7	Marginal Corporate Tax Rate	35%	35%

a. What are the incremental earnings for this project for years 1 and 2?
b. What are the free cash flows for this project for years 1 and 2?

14. Cellular Access, Inc., a cellular telephone service provider, reported net income of $250 million for the most recent fiscal year. The firm had depreciation expenses of $100 million, capital expenditures of $200 million, and no interest expenses. Net working capital increased by $10 million. Calculate the free cash flow for Cellular Access for the most recent fiscal year.

15. Recall the HomeNet example from the chapter. Suppose HomeNet's lab will be housed in warehouse space that the company could have otherwise rented out for $200,000 per year during years 1 through 4. How does this opportunity cost affect HomeNet's incremental earnings?

*16. One year ago, your company purchased a machine used in manufacturing for $110,000. You have learned that a new machine is available that offers many advantages and you can purchase it for $150,000 today. It will be depreciated on a straight-line basis over 10 years and has no salvage value. You expect that the new machine will produce a gross margin (revenues minus operating expenses other than depreciation) of $40,000 per year for the next 10 years. The current machine is expected to produce a gross margin of $20,000 per year. The current machine is being depreciated on a straight-line basis over a useful life of 11 years, and has no salvage value, so depreciation expense for the current machine is $10,000 per year. The market value today of the current machine is $50,000. Your company's tax rate is 45%, and the opportunity cost of capital for this type of equipment is 10%. Should your company replace its year-old machine?

*17. Beryl's Iced Tea currently rents a bottling machine for $50,000 per year, including all maintenance expenses. It is considering purchasing a machine instead and is comparing two options:
   a. Purchase the machine it is currently renting for $150,000. This machine will require $20,000 per year in ongoing maintenance expenses.
   b. Purchase a new, more advanced machine for $250,000. This machine will require $15,000 per year in ongoing maintenance expenses and will lower bottling costs by $10,000 per year. Also, $35,000 will be spent up front to train the new operators of the machine.

   Suppose the appropriate discount rate is 8% per year and the machine is purchased today. Maintenance and bottling costs are paid at the end of each year, as is the rental cost of the machine. Assume also that the machines will be depreciated via the straight-line method over seven years and that they have a 10 year life with a negligible salvage value. The marginal corporate tax rate is 35%. Should Beryl's Iced Tea continue to rent, purchase its current machine, or purchase the advanced machine?

Other Effects on Incremental Free Cash Flows

18. You have just completed a $20,000 feasibility study for a new coffee shop in some retail space you own. You bought the space two years ago for $100,000, and if you sold it today, you would net $115,000 after taxes. Outfitting the space for a coffee shop would require a capital expenditure of $30,000 plus an initial investment of $5,000 in inventory. What is the correct initial cash flow for your analysis of the coffee shop opportunity?

19. You purchased a machine for $1 million three years ago and have been applying straight-line depreciation to zero for a seven-year life. Your tax rate is 35%. If you sell the machine today (after three years of depreciation) for $700,000, what is your incremental cash flow from selling the machine?

20. The Jones Company has just completed the third year of a five-year MACRS recovery period for a piece of equipment it originally purchased for $300,000.
    a. What is the book value of the equipment?
    b. If Jones sells the equipment today for $180,000 and its tax rate is 35%, what is the after-tax cash flow from selling it?

21. Just before it is about to sell the equipment from Problem 20, Jones receives a new order. It can take the new order if it keeps the old equipment. Is there a cost to taking the order and if so, what is it? Explain.

22. Home Builder Supply, a retailer in the home improvement industry, currently operates seven retail outlets in Georgia and South Carolina. Management is contemplating building an eighth retail store across town from its most successful retail outlet. The company already owns the land for this store, which currently has an abandoned warehouse located on it. Last month, the marketing department spent $10,000 on market research to determine the extent of customer demand for the new store. Now Home Builder Supply must decide whether to build and open the new store.

    Which of the following should be included as part of the incremental earnings for the proposed new retail store?
    a. The original purchase price of the land where the store will be located.
    b. The cost of demolishing the abandoned warehouse and clearing the lot.
    c. The loss of sales in the existing retail outlet, if customers who previously drove across town to shop at the existing outlet become customers of the new store instead.
    d. The $10,000 in market research spent to evaluate customer demand.
    e. Construction costs for the new store.
    f. The value of the land if sold.
    g. Interest expense on the debt borrowed to pay the construction costs.

23. If Daily Enterprises uses MACRS instead of straight-line depreciation, which incremental free cash flows from Problem 10 would increase and which would decrease?

24. Markov Manufacturing recently spent $15 million to purchase some equipment used in the manufacture of disk drives. The firm expects that this equipment will have a useful life of five years, and its marginal corporate tax rate is 35%. The company plans to use straight-line depreciation.
    a. What is the annual depreciation expense associated with this equipment?
    b. What is the annual depreciation tax shield?
    c. Rather than straight-line depreciation, suppose Markov will use the MACRS depreciation method for the five-year life of the property. Calculate the depreciation tax shield each year for this equipment under this accelerated depreciation schedule.
    d. If Markov has a choice between straight-line and MACRS depreciation schedules, and its marginal corporate tax rate is expected to remain constant, which schedule should it choose? Why?
    e. How might your answer to part (d) change if Markov anticipates that its marginal corporate tax rate will increase substantially over the next five years?

25. Your company has been doing well, reaching $1 million in earnings, and is considering launching a new product. Designing the new product has already cost $500,000. The company estimates that it will sell 800,000 units per year for $3 per unit and variable non-labor costs will be $1 per unit. Production will end after year 3. New equipment costing $1 million will be required. The equipment will be depreciated to zero using the 7-year MACRS schedule. You plan to sell the equipment for book value at

the end of year 3. Your current level of working capital is $300,000. The new product will require the working capital to increase to a level of $380,000 immediately, then to $400,000 in year 1, in year 2 the level will be $350,000, and finally in year 3 the level will return to $300,000. Your tax rate is 35%. The discount rate for this project is 10%. Do the capital budgeting analysis for this project and calculate its NPV.

26. You work for Apple. After toiling away on $10 million worth of prototypes, you have finally produced your answer to Google Glasses: iGlasses (the name alone is genius). iGlasses will instantly transport the wearer into the world as Apple wants you to experience it: iTunes with the wink of an eye and apps that can be activated just by looking at them. You think that these will sell for 5 years until the next big thing comes along (or until users are unable to interact with actual human beings). Revenues are projected to be $450 million per year along with expenses of $350 million. You will need to spend $60 million immediately on additional equipment that will be depreciated using the 5-year MACRS schedule. Additionally, you will use some fully depreciated existing equipment that has a market value of $10 million. As iGlasses are an outcome of the R&D center, Apple plans to charge $5 million of the annual costs of the center to the iGlasses product for 5 years. Finally, Apple's working capital levels will increase from their current level of $120 million to $140 million immediately. They will remain at the elevated level until year 5, when they will return to $120 million. Apple's discount rate for this project is 15% and its tax rate is 35%. Calculate the free cash flows and determine the NPV of this project.

27. After spending $10,000 on client development, you have just been offered a big production contract by a new client. The contract will add $200,000 to your revenues for each of the next 5 years and it will cost you $100,000 per year to make the additional product. You will have to use some existing equipment and buy new equipment as well. The existing equipment is fully depreciated, but could be sold for $50,000 now. If you use it in the project, it will be worthless at the end of the project. You will buy new equipment valued at $30,000 and use the 5-year MACRS schedule to depreciate it. It will be worthless at the end of the project. Your current production manager earns $80,000 per year. Since she is busy with ongoing projects, you are planning to hire an assistant at $40,000 per year to help with the expansion. You will have to increase your inventory immediately from $20,000 to $30,000. It will return to $20,000 at the end of the project. Your company's tax rate is 35% and your discount rate is 15%. What is the NPV of the contract?

28. You are a manager at Percolated Fiber, which is considering expanding its operations in synthetic fiber manufacturing. Your boss comes into your office, drops a consultant's report on your desk, and complains, "We owe these consultants $1 million for this report, and I am not sure their analysis makes sense. Before we spend the $25 million on new equipment needed for this project, look it over and give me your opinion." You open the report and find the following estimates (in thousands of dollars) (*see MyFinanceLab for the data in Excel format*):

Year		1	2	...	9	10
1	Year	1	2	...	9	10
2	Sales Revenue	30,000	30,000		30,000	30,000
3	Costs of Goods Sold	18,000	18,000		18,000	18,000
4	**Gross Profit**	12,000	12,000		12,000	12,000
5	Selling, General, and Administrative Expenses	2,000	2,000		2,000	2,000
6	Depreciation	2,500	2,500		2,500	2,500
7	**EBIT**	7,500	7,500		7,500	7,500
8	Income Tax	2,625	2,625		2,625	2,625
9	**Net Income**	4,875	4,875		4,875	4,875

All of the estimates in the report seem correct. You note that the consultants used straight-line depreciation for the new equipment that will be purchased today (year 0), which is what the accounting department recommended. They also calculated the depreciation assuming no salvage value for the equipment, which is the company's assumption in this case. The report concludes that because the project will increase earnings by $4.875 million per year for 10 years, the project is worth $48.75 million. You think back to your glory days in finance class and realize there is more work to be done!

First, you note that the consultants have not included the fact that the project will require $10 million in working capital up front (year 0), which will be fully recovered in year 10. Next, you see they have attributed $2 million of selling, general, and administrative expenses to the project, but you know that $1 million of this amount is overhead that will be incurred even if the project is not accepted. Finally, you know that accounting earnings are not the right thing to focus on!

a. Given the available information, what are the free cash flows in years 0 through 10 that should be used to evaluate the proposed project?

b. If the cost of capital for this project is 14%, what is your estimate of the value of the new project?

Analyzing the Project

29. Bauer Industries is an automobile manufacturer. Management is currently evaluating a proposal to build a plant that will manufacture lightweight trucks. Bauer plans to use a cost of capital of 12% to evaluate this project. Based on extensive research, it has prepared the incremental free cash flow projections shown below (in millions of dollars) (*see MyFinanceLab for the data in Excel format*).

a. For this base-case scenario, what is the NPV of the plant to manufacture lightweight trucks?

	Year	0	1–9	10
1	Revenues		100.0	100.0
2	Manufacturing Expenses (other than depreciation)		−35.0	−35.0
3	Marketing Expenses		−10.0	−10.0
4	Depreciation		−15.0	−15.0
5	**EBIT**		40.0	40.0
6	Taxes at 35%		−14.0	−14.0
7	**Unlevered Net Income**		26.0	26.0
8	Depreciation		+15.0	+15.0
9	Additions to Net Working Capital		−5.0	−5.0
10	Capital Expenditures	−150.0		
11	Continuation Value			+12.0
12	**Free Cash Flow**	−150.0	36.0	48.0

b. Based on input from the marketing department, Bauer is uncertain about its revenue forecast. In particular, management would like to examine the sensitivity of the NPV to the revenue assumptions. What is the NPV of this project if revenues are 10% higher than forecast? What is the NPV if revenues are 10% lower than forecast?

c. Rather than assuming that cash flows for this project are constant, management would like to explore the sensitivity of its analysis to possible growth in revenues and operating expenses. Specifically, management would like to assume that revenues, manufacturing expenses, and marketing expenses are as given in the table for year 1 and grow by 2% per year every year starting in year 2. Management also plans to assume that the initial capital expenditures (and therefore depreciation), additions to working capital, and continuation value remain as initially specified in the table. What is the NPV of this project under these alternative assumptions? How does the NPV change if the revenues and operating expenses grow by 5% per year rather than by 2%?

    d. To examine the sensitivity of this project to the discount rate, management would like to compute the NPV for different discount rates. Create a graph, with the discount rate on the x-axis and the NPV on the y-axis, for discount rates ranging from 5% to 30%. For what ranges of discount rates does the project have a positive NPV?

 *30. Billingham Packaging is considering expanding its production capacity by purchasing a new machine, the XC-750. The cost of the XC-750 is $2.75 million. Unfortunately, installing this machine will take several months and will partially disrupt production. The firm has just completed a $50,000 feasibility study to analyze the decision to buy the XC-750, resulting in the following estimates:

- *Marketing*: Once the XC-750 is operational next year, the extra capacity is expected to generate $10 million per year in additional sales, which will continue for the 10 year life of the machine.
- *Operations*: The disruption caused by the installation will decrease sales by $5 million this year. As with Billingham's existing products, the cost of goods for the products produced by the XC-750 is expected to be 70% of their sale price. The increased production will also require increased inventory on hand of $1 million during the life of the project, including year 0.
- *Human Resources*: The expansion will require additional sales and administrative personnel at a cost of $2 million per year.
- *Accounting*: The XC-750 will be depreciated via the straight-line method over the 10 year life of the machine. The firm expects receivables from the new sales to be 15% of revenues and payables to be 10% of the cost of goods sold. Billingham's marginal corporate tax rate is 35%.

    a. Determine the incremental earnings from the purchase of the XC-750.

    b. Determine the free cash flow from the purchase of the XC-750.

    c. If the appropriate cost of capital for the expansion is 10%, compute the NPV of the purchase.

    d. While the expected new sales will be $10 million per year from the expansion, estimates range from $8 million to $12 million. What is the NPV in the worst case? In the best case?

    e. What is the break-even level of new sales from the expansion? What is the break-even level for the cost of goods sold?

    f. Billingham could instead purchase the XC-900, which offers even greater capacity. The cost of the XC-900 is $4 million. The extra capacity would not be useful in the first two years of operation, but would allow for additional sales in years 3 through 10. What level of additional sales (above the $10 million expected for the XC-750) per year in those years would justify purchasing the larger machine?

Real Options in Captial Budgeting

31. Why must real options have positive value?

32. What kind of real option does the XC-900 machine provide to Billingham in Problem 30?

33. If Billingham knows that it can sell the XC-750 to another firm for $2 million in two years, what kind of real option would that provide?

DATA CASE

You have just been hired by Hewlett-Packard (HP) in its capital budgeting division. Your first assignment is to determine the net cash flows and NPV of a proposed new type of portable computer system similar in size to an iPhone, but which has the operating power of a high-end desktop system.

Development of the new system will initially require an investment equal to 10% of net property, plant, and equipment (PPE) for the fiscal year ended October 31, 2012. The project will then require an additional investment equal to 10% of the initial investment after the first year of the project, 5% of the initial investment after the second year, and 1% of the initial investment after the third, fourth, and fifth years. The product is expected to have a life of five years. First-year revenues for the new product are expected to be 3% of total revenue for HP's fiscal year ended October 31, 2012. The new product's revenues are expected to grow at 15% for the second year, then 10% for the third, and 5% annually for the final two years of the expected life of the project. Your job is to determine the rest of the cash flows associated with this project. Your boss has indicated that the operating costs and net working capital requirements are similar to the rest of the company's products and that depreciation is straight-line for capital budgeting purposes. Welcome to the "real world." Since your boss hasn't been much help, here are some tips to guide your analysis:

1. Obtain Hewlett-Packard's financial statements. (If you really worked for Hewlett-Packard you would already have this data, but at least here you won't get fired if your analysis is off target.) Download the annual income statements, balance sheets, and cash flow statements for the last four fiscal years from Google finance (finance.google.com). Enter Hewlett-Packard's ticker symbol (HPQ) and then go to "Financials." Click "Annual," to ensure you're getting annual, instead of quarterly, data. Next, copy and paste the income statements and balance sheets into Excel.

2. You are now ready to determine the free cash flow. Compute the free cash flow for each year using Eq. 9.6 from this chapter:

$$\overbrace{(\text{Revenues} - \text{Costs} - \text{Depreciation}) \times (1 - \text{Tax Rate})}^{\text{Unlevered Net Income}}$$

$$\text{Free Cash Flow} = (\text{Revenues} - \text{Costs} - \text{Depreciation}) \times (1 - \text{Tax Rate})$$
$$+ \text{Depreciation} - \text{CapEx} - \text{Change in } NWC$$

Set up the timeline and computation of the free cash flow in separate, contiguous columns for each year of the project life. Be sure to make outflows negative and inflows positive.

a. Assume that the project's profitability will be similar to HP's existing projects in 2012 and estimate (Revenues − Costs) each year by using the 2012 EBITDA/Sales profit margin.

b. Determine the annual depreciation by assuming HP depreciates these assets by the straight-line method over a 10 year life.

c. Determine HP's tax rate by dividing HP's income taxes by its income before tax in 2012.

d. Calculate the net working capital required each year by assuming that the level of NWC will be a constant percentage of the project's sales. Use HP's 2012 NWC/Sales to estimate the required percentage. (Use only accounts receivable, accounts payable, and inventory to measure working capital. Other components of current assets and liabilities are harder to interpret and are not necessarily reflective of the project's required NWC—e.g., HP's cash holdings.)

e. To determine the free cash flow, calculate the *additional* capital investment and the *change* in net working capital each year.

3. Determine the IRR of the project and the NPV of the project at a cost of capital of 12% using the Excel functions. For the calculation of NPV, include cash flows 1 through 5 in the NPV function and then subtract the initial cost (i.e., $= NPV(\text{rate}, CF_1 : CF_5) + CF_0$). For IRR, include cash flows 0 through 5 in the cash flow range.

Chapter 9
APPENDIX

MACRS Depreciation

The U.S. tax code allows for accelerated depreciation of most assets. The depreciation method that you use for any particular asset is determined by the tax rules in effect at the time you place the asset into service. (Congress has changed the depreciation rules many times over the years, so many firms that have held property for a long time may have to use several depreciation methods simultaneously.)

For most business property placed in service after 1986, the IRS allows firms to depreciate the asset using the MACRS (Modified Accelerated Cost Recovery System) method. Under this method, you categorize each business asset into a recovery class that determines the time period over which you can write off the cost of the asset. The most commonly used items are classified as shown below:

- *3-year property*: Tractor units, race horses over 2 years old, and horses over 12 years old.
- *5-year property*: Automobiles, buses, trucks, computers and peripheral equipment, office machinery, and any property used in research and experimentation. Also includes breeding and dairy cattle.
- *7-year property*: Office furniture and fixtures, and any property that has not been designated as belonging to another class.
- *10-year property*: Water transportation equipment, single-purpose agricultural or horticultural structures, and trees or vines bearing fruit or nuts.
- *15-year property*: Depreciable improvements to land such as fences, roads, and bridges.
- *20-year property*: Farm buildings that are not agricultural or horticultural structures.
- *27.5-year property*: Residential rental property.
- *39-year property*: Nonresidential real estate, including home offices. (Note that the value of land may not be depreciated.)

Generally speaking, residential and nonresidential real estate is depreciated via the straight-line method, but other classes can be depreciated more rapidly in early years. Table 9.4 shows the standard depreciation rates for assets in the other recovery classes; refinements of this table can be applied depending on the month that the asset was placed into service (consult IRS guidelines). The table indicates the percentage of the asset's cost that may be depreciated each year, with year 1 indicating the year the asset was first put into use (typically year 0 in your spreadsheet as in Example 9.8).

The lower amount in year 1 reflects a "half-year convention" in which the asset is presumed to be in use (and thus depreciated) for half of the first year, no matter when it was actually put into use. After year 1, it is assumed that the asset depreciates more rapidly in earlier years.

TABLE 9.4

MACRS Depreciation Table Showing the Percentage of the Asset's Cost That May Be Depreciated Each Year Based on Its Recovery Period

	Depreciation Rate for Recovery Period					
Year	3 Years	5 Years	7 Years	10 Years	15 Years	20 Years
1	33.33	20.00	14.29	10.00	5.00	3.750
2	44.45	32.00	24.49	18.00	9.50	7.219
3	14.81	19.20	17.49	14.40	8.55	6.677
4	7.41	11.52	12.49	11.52	7.70	6.177
5		11.52	8.93	9.22	6.93	5.713
6		5.76	8.92	7.37	6.23	5.285
7			8.93	6.55	5.90	4.888
8			4.46	6.55	5.90	4.522
9				6.56	5.91	4.462
10				6.55	5.90	4.461
11				3.28	5.91	4.462
12					5.90	4.461
13					5.91	4.462
14					5.90	4.461
15					5.91	4.462
16					2.95	4.461
17						4.462
18						4.461
19						4.462
20						4.461
21						2.231

Stock Valuation: A Second Look

LEARNING OBJECTIVES

- Value a stock as the present value of the company's free cash flows

- Value a stock by applying common multiples based on the values of comparable firms

- Understand how information is incorporated into stock prices through competition in efficient markets

- Describe some of the behavioral biases that influence the way individual investors trade

notation

Div_t	dividends paid in year t	N	terminal date or forecast horizon
$EBIT$	earnings before interest and taxes	P_t	stock price at the end of year t
$EBITDA$	earnings before interest, taxes, depreciation, and amortization	PV	present value
EPS_t	earnings per share on date t	r_E	equity cost of capital
FCF_t	free cash flow on date t	r_{wacc}	weighted average cost of capital
g	expected dividend growth rate	V_t	enterprise value on date t
g_{FCF}	expected free cash flow growth rate		

In mid-2013, the three most valuable U.S. companies were ExxonMobil, Apple, and Google. Google does not pay a dividend, and until 2012, neither did Apple (yet in 2011 it was the most valuable company in the world). In Chapter 7, we discussed the basics of stocks and valued them using the dividend-discount model. As we pointed out at the end of that chapter, the dividend-discount model is not a practical approach for valuing the stock of the thousands of companies like Google and Facebook that do not pay dividends. We then modified the dividend-discount model to include other forms of payout such as repurchases.

Some companies, especially young ones, neither repurchase shares nor pay dividends. In this chapter, we develop a more broadly applicable method to value companies—it can even be used to value companies that currently make no cash payouts to investors. Termed the *Discounted Free Cash Flow* model, it is very closely linked to the concepts we just learned for capital budgeting. In fact, you will see that just as the discounted cash flows of a project determine the value of a project to the firm, the discounted cash flows of the firm as a whole determine its value to its investors.

The final valuation method we discuss in this chapter, the method of comparables, or "comps," is also broadly applicable to all types of companies. This method, in which we compare the firm to others in the same line of business, is based on the intuitive idea that similar companies should be valued similarly. We will learn how to use the market's valuation of one company to estimate a value of a similar company.

We close the chapter with a discussion of the role of competition in markets. We explain how information is reflected in stock prices through investor competition and discuss the implication for investors and corporate managers. Finally, we describe some common trading biases of individual investors.

10.1 The Discounted Free Cash Flow Model

In Chapter 7, we developed the dividend-discount model to value the stock of a dividend-paying firm. In this section, we outline an alternative approach to valuing the firm's shares that avoids some of the difficulties of the dividend-discount model. Specifically, we consider the *discounted free cash flow model*, which focuses on the cash flows to all of the firm's investors, both debt and equity holders. This model allows us to avoid the difficulties associated with estimating the impact of the firm's borrowing decisions on earnings. It also demonstrates the important connection between the capital budgeting analysis we did in Chapter 9 and its implications for the firm's stock price.

The dividend-discount model values a single share of stock. In the total payout model, we first value the firm's equity, rather than just a single share. The **discounted free cash flow model** goes one step further and begins by determining the total value of the firm to all investors—both equity holders *and* debt holders. We begin by estimating the firm's enterprise value, which we defined in Chapter 2 as follows:[1]

$$\text{Enterprise Value} = \text{Market Value of Equity} + \text{Debt} - \text{Cash} \tag{10.1}$$

Because the enterprise value is the value of the firm's underlying business, unencumbered by debt and separate from any cash or marketable securities, it is also the value of the underlying business to all investors. We can interpret the enterprise value as the net cost of acquiring the firm's equity, paying off all debt, and taking its cash; in essence, it is equivalent to owning the unlevered business. The advantage of the discounted free cash flow model is that it allows us to value a firm without explicitly forecasting its dividends, share repurchases, or use of debt.

discounted free cash flow model A method for estimating a firm's enterprise value by discounting its future free cash flow.

Valuing the Enterprise

How can we estimate a firm's enterprise value? To estimate the value of the firm's equity, we compute the present value of the firm's total payouts to equity holders. Likewise, to estimate a firm's enterprise value, we compute the present value of the *free cash flow* (FCF) that the firm has available to pay all investors, both debt and equity holders. We saw how to compute the free cash flow for a project in Chapter 9; we now perform the same calculation for the entire firm:

$$\text{Free Cash Flow} = EBIT \times (1 - \text{Tax Rate}) + \text{Depreciation}$$
$$- \text{Capital Expenditures} - \text{Increases in Net Working Capital} \tag{10.2}$$

Free cash flow measures the cash generated by the firm before any payments to debt or equity holders are considered.

---

[1]To be precise, when we say "cash," we are referring to the firm's cash in excess of its working capital needs, which is the amount of cash it has invested at a competitive market interest rate.

Thus, just as we determine the value of a project by calculating the NPV of the project's free cash flow, we estimate a firm's current enterprise value, V_0, by computing the present value of the firm's free cash flow:

Discounted Free Cash Flow Model

$$V_0 = PV(\text{Future Free Cash Flow of Firm}) \tag{10.3}$$

Given the enterprise value, we can estimate the share price by using Eq. 10.1 to solve for the value of equity and then divide by the total number of shares outstanding:

$$P_0 = \frac{V_0 + \text{Cash}_0 - \text{Debt}_0}{\text{Shares Outstanding}_0} \tag{10.4}$$

In the dividend-discount model, the firm's cash and debt are included indirectly through the effect of interest income and expenses on earnings. By contrast, in the discounted free cash flow model, we ignore interest income and expenses because free cash flow is based on EBIT (Earnings *Before* Interest and Taxes), but we then adjust for cash and debt directly (in Eq. 10.4).

Implementing the Model

weighted average cost of capital (WACC) The cost of capital that reflects the risk of the overall business, which is the combined risk of the firm's equity and debt.

A key difference between the discounted free cash flow model and the earlier models we have considered is the discount rate. In previous calculations, we used the firm's equity cost of capital, r_E, because we were discounting the cash flows to equity holders. Here, we are discounting the free cash flow that will be paid to both debt and equity holders. Thus, we should use the firm's **weighted average cost of capital (WACC)**, denoted by r_{wacc}. It is the cost of capital that reflects the risk of the overall business, which is the combined risk of the firm's equity *and* debt. We interpret r_{wacc} as the expected return the firm must pay to investors to compensate them for the risk of holding the firm's debt and equity together. If the firm has no debt, then $r_{wacc} = r_E$. We will develop methods to calculate the WACC explicitly in Part 4 of the text.

Given the firm's weighted average cost of capital, we implement the discounted free cash flow model in much the same way as we did the dividend-discount model. That is, we forecast the firm's free cash flow up to some horizon, together with a terminal (continuation) value of the enterprise:

$$V_0 = \frac{FCF_1}{1 + r_{wacc}} + \frac{FCF_2}{(1 + r_{wacc})^2} + \cdots + \frac{FCF_N}{(1 + r_{wacc})^N} + \frac{V_N}{(1 + r_{wacc})^N} \tag{10.5}$$

Often, we estimate the terminal value by assuming a constant long-run growth rate g_{FCF} for free cash flows beyond year N, so that

$$V_N = \frac{FCF_{N+1}}{r_{wacc} - g_{FCF}} = \left(\frac{1 + g_{FCF}}{r_{wacc} - g_{FCF}}\right) \times FCF_N \tag{10.6}$$

The long-run growth rate g_{FCF} is typically based on the expected long-run growth rate of the firm's revenues.

EXAMPLE 10.1

Valuing Nike, Inc., Stock Using Free Cash Flow

MyFinanceLab

PROBLEM

Recall our example of Nike, Inc., from Chapter 7. Nike had sales of $25.3 billion in 2012. Suppose you expect its sales to grow at a rate of 10% in 2013, but then slow by 1% per year to the long-run growth rate that is characteristic of the apparel industry—5%—by 2018. Based on Nike's past profitability and investment needs, you expect EBIT to be 10% of sales, increases in net working capital requirements to be 10% of any increase in sales, and capital expenditures to equal depreciation expenses. If Nike has $3.3 billion in cash, $1.2 billion in debt, 893.6 million shares outstanding, a tax rate of 24%, and a weighted average cost of capital of 10%, what is your estimate of the value of Nike stock in early 2013?

(Continued)

SOLUTION

PLAN

We can estimate Nike's future free cash flow by constructing a pro forma statement as we did for HomeNet in Chapter 9. The only difference is that the pro forma statement is for the whole company, rather than just one project. Furthermore, we need to calculate a terminal (or continuation) value for Nike at the end of our explicit projections. Because we expect Nike's free cash flow to grow at a constant rate after 2018, we can use Eq.10.6 to compute a terminal enterprise value. The present value of the free cash flows during the years 2013–2018 and the terminal value will be the total enterprise value for Nike. From that value, we can subtract the debt, add the cash, and divide by the number of shares outstanding to compute the price per share (Eq. 10.4).

EXECUTE

The following spreadsheet presents a simplified pro forma for Nike based on the information we have:

	Year	2012	2013	2014	2015	2016	2017	2018
1	**FCF Forecast ($ million)**							
2								
3	Sales	25,300.0	27,830.0	30,334.7	32,761.5	35,054.8	37,158.1	39,016.0
4	*Growth Versus Prior Year*		*10.0%*	*9.0%*	*8.0%*	*7.0%*	*6.0%*	*5.0%*
5	**EBIT** (10% of sales)		2,783.0	3,033.5	3,276.1	3,505.5	3,715.8	3,901.6
6	Less: Income Tax (24%)		667.9	728.0	786.3	841.3	891.8	936.4
7	Plus: Depreciation		—	—	—	—	—	—
8	Less: Capital Expenditures		—	—	—	—	—	—
9	Less: Increase in NWC (10% ΔSales)		253.0	250.5	242.7	229.3	210.3	185.8
10	**Free Cash Flow**		1,862.1	2,055.0	2,247.2	2,434.8	2,613.7	2,779.4

Because capital expenditures are expected to equal depreciation, lines 7 and 8 in the spreadsheet cancel out. We can set them both to zero rather than explicitly forecast them.

Given our assumption of constant 5% growth in free cash flows after 2018 and a weighted average cost of capital of 10%, we can use Eq. 10.6 to compute a terminal enterprise value:

$$V_{2018} = \left(\frac{1 + g_{FCF}}{r_{wacc} - g_{FCF}}\right) \times FCF_{2018} = \left(\frac{1.05}{0.10 - 0.05}\right) \times 2,779.4 = \$58,367.9 \text{ million}$$

From Eq. 10.5, Nike's current enterprise value is the present value of its free cash flows plus the present value of the firm's terminal value:

$$V_0 = \frac{1,862.1}{1.10} + \frac{2,055.0}{1.10^2} + \frac{2,247.2}{1.10^3} + \frac{2,434.8}{1.10^4} + \frac{2,613.7}{1.10^5} + \frac{2,779.4}{1.10^6} + \frac{58,367.9}{1.10^6} = \$42,881.5 \text{ million}$$

We can now estimate the value of a share of Nike stock using Eq. 10.4:

$$P_0 = \frac{\$42,881.5 + \$3,300 - \$1,200}{893.6} = \$50.34$$

EVALUATE

The total value of all of the claims, both debt and equity, on the firm must equal the total present value of all cash flows generated by the firm, in addition to any cash it currently has. The total present value of all cash flows to be generated by Nike is $42,881.5 million and it has $3,300 million in cash. Subtracting off the value of the debt claims ($1,200 million), leaves us with the total value of the equity claims and dividing by the number of shares produces the value per share.

Connection to Capital Budgeting

There is an important connection between the discounted free cash flow model and the NPV rule for capital budgeting we developed in Chapter 9. Because the firm's free cash flow is equal to the sum of the free cash flows from the firm's current and future investments, we can interpret the firm's enterprise value as the sum of the present value of its existing projects and the NPV of future ones. Hence, the NPV of any investment decision represents its contribution to the firm's enterprise value. To maximize the firm's share price, we should therefore accept those projects that have a positive NPV.

Recall also from Chapter 9 that many forecasts and estimates were necessary to estimate the free cash flows of a project. The same is true for the firm: We must forecast its future sales, operating expenses, taxes, capital requirements, and other factors to obtain its free cash flow. On the one hand, estimating free cash flow in this way gives us flexibility to incorporate many specific details about the future prospects of the firm. On the other hand, some uncertainty inevitably surrounds each assumption. Given this fact, it is important to conduct a sensitivity analysis, as described in Chapter 9, to translate this uncertainty into a range of potential values for the stock.

EXAMPLE 10.2

Sensitivity Analysis for Stock Valuation

MyFinanceLab

PROBLEM

In Example 10.1, Nike's EBIT was assumed to be 10% of sales. If Nike can reduce its operating expenses and raise its EBIT to 11% of sales, how would the estimate of the stock's value change?

SOLUTION

PLAN

In this scenario, EBIT will increase by 1% of sales compared to Example 10.1. From there, we can use the tax rate (24%) to compute the effect on the free cash flow for each year. Once we have the new free cash flows, we repeat the approach in Example 10.1 to arrive at a new stock price.

EXECUTE

In year 1, EBIT will be 1% × $27,830 million = $278.3 million higher. After taxes, this increase will raise the firm's free cash flow in year 1 by $(1 - 0.24) \times \$278.3 = \$211.5$ million, to $2,073.6 million. Doing the same calculation for each year, we get the following revised FCF estimates:

Year	2013	2014	2015	2016	2017	2018
FCF	2,073.6	2,285.5	2,496.2	2,701.2	2,896.1	3,075.9

We can now reestimate the stock price as in Example 10.1. The terminal value is $V_{2018} = [1.05/(0.10 - 0.05)] \times 3,075.9 = \$65,594.8$ million, so

$$V_0 = \frac{2,073.6}{1.10} + \frac{2,285.5}{1.10^2} + \frac{2,496.2}{1.10^3} + \frac{2,701.2}{1.10^4} + \frac{2,896.1}{1.10^5} + \frac{3,075.9}{1.10^6} + \frac{64,594.8}{1.10^6} = \$47,491 \text{ million}$$

The new estimate for the value of the stock is $P_0 = (47,491 + 3,300 - 1,200)/893.6 = \$55.50$ per share, a difference of about 10% compared to the result found in Example 10.1.

EVALUATE

Nike's stock price is fairly sensitive to changes in the assumptions about its profitability. A 1% permanent change in its margins affects the firm's stock price by 10%.

Figure 10.1 summarizes the different valuation methods we have discussed so far. We use the present value of a stock's future dividends to determine its value. We can estimate the total market capitalization of the firm's equity from the present value of the firm's total payouts, which includes dividends and share repurchases. Finally, the present value of the firm's free cash flow, which is the amount of cash the firm has available to make payments to equity or debt holders, determines the firm's enterprise value.

By computing the present value of the firm's dividends, total payouts, or free cash flows, we can estimate the value of the stock, the total value of the firm's equity, or the firm's enterprise value. The final column details what adjustment is necessary to obtain the stock price.

Present Value of...	Determines the...	To Get Stock Price Estimate...
Dividend Payments	Stock Price	No adjustment necessary
Total Payouts (all dividends and repurchases)	Equity Value	Divide by shares oustanding
Free Cash Flow (cash available to pay all security holders)	Enterprise Value	Subtract what does not belong to equity holders (debt and preferred stock), add back cash and marketable securities, and divide by shares outstanding

1. What is the relation between capital budgeting and the discounted free cash flow model?
2. Why do we ignore interest payments on the firm's debt in the discounted free cash flow model?

10.2   Valuation Based on Comparable Firms

So far, we have valued a firm or its stock by considering the expected future cash flows it will provide to its owner. The Valuation Principle then tells us that its value is the present value of its future cash flows, because the present value is the amount we would need to invest elsewhere in the market to replicate the cash flows with the same risk.

method of comparables
An estimate of the value of a firm based on the value of other, comparable firms or other investments that are expected to generate very similar cash flows in the future.

Another application of the Valuation Principle is the *method of comparables*. In the **method of comparables** (or "comps"), rather than value the firm's cash flows directly, we estimate the value of the firm based on the value of other, comparable firms or investments that we expect will generate very similar cash flows in the future. For example, consider the case of a new firm that is *identical* to an existing publicly traded company. Recall that from competitive market prices, the Valuation Principle implies that two securities with identical cash flows must have the same price. Thus, if these firms will generate identical cash flows, we can use the market value of the existing company to determine the value of the new firm.

Of course, identical companies do not really exist. Even two firms in the same industry selling the same types of products, while similar in many respects, are likely to be of a different size or scale. For example, Hewlett-Packard and Dell both sell personal computers directly to consumers using the Internet. In 2009, Hewlett-Packard had sales of $115 billion, whereas Dell had sales of approximately $53 billion. In this section, we consider ways to adjust for scale differences to use comparables to value firms with similar businesses and then discuss the strengths and weaknesses of this approach.

Valuation Multiples

valuation multiple A
ratio of a firm's value
to some measure of the
firm's scale or cash flow.

We can adjust for differences in scale between firms by expressing their value in terms of a **valuation multiple**, which is a ratio of the value to some measure of the firm's scale.

As an analogy, consider valuing an office building. A natural measure to consider would be the price per square foot for other buildings recently sold in the area. Multiplying the size of the office building under consideration by the average price per square foot would typically provide a reasonable estimate of the building's value. We can apply this same idea to stocks, replacing square footage with some more appropriate measure of the firm's scale.

The Price-Earnings Ratio. The most common valuation multiple is the price-earnings ratio, which we introduced in Chapter 2. The P/E ratio is so common that it is almost always part of the basic statistics computed for a stock (as shown in Figure 10.2, the screen-shot from Google Finance for Nike). A firm's P/E ratio is equal to the share price divided by its earnings per share. The intuition behind its use is that, when you buy a stock, you are in a sense buying the rights to the firm's future earnings. If differences in the scale of firms' earnings are likely to persist, you should be willing to pay proportionally more for a stock with higher current earnings. Using this idea, we can estimate the value of a share of stock of a firm by using the P/E ratios of other firms. For example, we can estimate the stock price of a private firm by multiplying its current earnings per share (EPS) by the average P/E ratio of comparable public firms.

FIGURE 10.2

Stock Price Quote for Nike (NKE)

This screenshot from Google Finance shows the basic stock price information and price history charting for the common stock of Nike. The historical price chart covers the period March through late June 2013. Notice that the price-earnings (P/E) ratio is listed as part of the basic information.

EXAMPLE 10.3

Valuation Using
the Price-Earnings
Ratio

PROBLEM

Suppose furniture manufacturer Herman Miller, Inc., has earnings per share of $1.38. If the average P/E of comparable furniture stocks is 21.3, estimate a value for a share of Herman Miller stock using the P/E as a valuation multiple. What are the assumptions underlying this estimate?

SOLUTION

PLAN

We estimate a share price for Herman Miller by multiplying its EPS by the P/E of comparable firms:

EPS × P/E = Earnings per Share × (Price per Share ÷ Earnings per Share) = Price per Share

EXECUTE

$P_0 = \$1.38 \times 21.3 = \$29.39$. This estimate assumes that Herman Miller will have similar future risk, payout rates, and growth rates to comparable firms in the industry.

EVALUATE

Although valuation multiples are simple to use, they rely on some very strong assumptions about the similarity of the comparable firms to the firm you are valuing. It is important to consider whether these assumptions are likely to be reasonable—and thus to hold—in each case.

---

trailing earnings A firm's earnings over the prior 12 months.

forward earnings A firm's expected earnings over the coming 12 months.

trailing P/E A firm's price-earnings (P/E) ratio calculated using trailing (past) earnings.

forward P/E A firm's price-earnings (P/E) ratio calculated using forward (expected) earnings.

We can compute a firm's P/E ratio by using either **trailing earnings**—earnings over the prior 12 months—or **forward earnings**—expected earnings over the coming 12 months—with the resulting ratio being called the **trailing P/E** or the **forward P/E**, respectively. For valuation purposes, the forward P/E is generally preferred, as we are most concerned about future earnings.

To understand how P/E ratios relate to the other valuation techniques we have discussed, consider the dividend discount model introduced in Chapter 7.[2] For example, in the case of constant dividend growth (see Eq. 7.6), we had

$$P_0 = \frac{Div_1}{r_E - g}$$

Dividing through by EPS_1, we find that

$$\text{Forward P/E} = \frac{P_0}{EPS_1} = \frac{Div_1/EPS_1}{r_E - g} = \frac{\text{Dividend Payout Rate}}{r_E - g} \tag{10.7}$$

In Chapter 7, we showed that Nike's current price is consistent with an equity cost of capital of 10% and an expected dividend growth rate of 8.5%. From the Nike quote, we can also see that Nike has earnings per share (EPS) of $2.52 and a dividend of $0.21 per quarter, or $0.84 per year which gives a dividend payout rate of $0.84/2.52 = 0.333$. Assuming that earnings growth and payout rates remain at this level for the foreseeable future, then we could compute the forward P/E as:

$$\text{Forward P/E} = \frac{0.84/2.52}{.10 - 0.085} = 22.22, \text{ which is not far off its reported P/E of 24.00.}$$

Equation 10.7 suggests that firms and industries that have high growth rates, and that generate cash well in excess of their investment needs so that they can maintain high payout rates, should have high P/E multiples. Taking the example of Nike we showed that at

---

[2]We use the dividend discount model rather than discounted cash flows because price and earnings are variables associated exclusively with equity.

FIGURE 10.3

Relating the P/E Ratio
to Expected Future
Growth

The graph shows the expected growth in earnings under two growth scenarios for Nike: 8.5% and 5%.
Current earnings per share is $2.52. Higher growth increases the PV of the earnings stream, which means
that the price increases. The result is that the higher price divided by current earnings yields a higher P/E
ratio. We found that a growth rate of 8.5% implied a P/E ratio of 22.22 while a growth rate of 5% implied
a P/E ratio of 6.67. The graph shows how higher expected growth translates into a higher P/E.

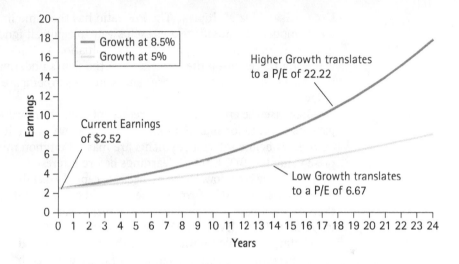

an expected growth rate of 8.5%, it would have a P/E ratio of 22.22. If our growth expectations were lower, its P/E would drop. Holding current earnings, dividends, and equity cost
of capital constant, but decreasing the growth rate to 5%, we would have:

$$\text{Forward P/E} = \frac{0.84/2.52}{.10 - 0.05} = 6.67$$

This result is much lower than its current P/E of 24.00 making it clear that simply
comparing P/E ratios without taking into account growth prospects can be highly
misleading.

Figure 10.3 shows the relationship between expected earnings growth and P/E ratios.

EXAMPLE 10.4

Growth Prospects and
the Price-Earnings
Ratio

MyFinanceLab

PROBLEM

Amazon.com and Macy's are retailers. In 2013, Amazon had a price of $306.87 and forward earnings per
share of $3.18. Macy's had a price of $49.75 and forward earnings per share of $4.47. Calculate their forward
P/E ratios and explain the difference.

SOLUTION

PLAN

We can calculate their P/E ratios by dividing each company's price per share by its forward earnings per
share. The difference we find is most likely due to different growth expectations.

EXECUTE

Forward P/E for Amazon = $306.87/$3.18 = 96.5. Forward P/E for Macy's = $49.75/$4.47 = 11.13.
Amazon's P/E ratio is higher because investors expect its earnings to grow more than Macy's.

(Continued)

EVALUATE

Although both companies are retailers, they have very different growth prospects, as reflected in their P/E ratios. Investors in Amazon.com are willing to pay 96.5 times this year's expected earnings because they are also buying the present value of high future earnings created by expected growth.

Enterprise Value Multiples. The P/E ratio has the same limitations as the dividend discount model—because it relates exclusively to equity, it ignores the effect of debt. Consequently, it is also common practice to use valuation multiples based on the firm's enterprise value. By representing the total value of the firm's underlying business rather than just the value of equity, the enterprise value allows us to compare firms with different amounts of leverage.

Because the enterprise value represents the entire value of the firm before the firm pays its debt, to form an appropriate multiple, we divide it by a measure of earnings or cash flows before interest payments are made. Common multiples to consider are enterprise value to EBIT, EBITDA (earnings before interest, taxes, depreciation, and amortization), and free cash flow. However, because capital expenditures can vary substantially from period to period (e.g., a firm may need to add capacity and build a new plant one year, but then may not need to expand further for many years), most practitioners rely on enterprise value to EBITDA (EV/EBITDA) multiples.

Enterprise value multiples value the entire firm, and so they are most closely related to the discount cash flow model. When expected free cash flow growth is constant, we can use Eq. 10.6 to write enterprise value to EBITDA as

$$\frac{V_0}{EBITDA_1} = \frac{\frac{FCF_1}{r_{wacc} - g_{FCF}}}{EBITDA_1} = \frac{FCF_1/EBITDA_1}{r_{wacc} - g_{FCF}} \tag{10.8}$$

As with the P/E multiple, this valuation multiple is higher for firms with high growth rates and low capital requirements (which means that free cash flow is high in proportion to EBITDA).

EXAMPLE 10.5
Valuation Using the Enterprise Value Multiple

MyFinanceLab

PROBLEM

Fairview, Inc., is an ocean transport company with EBITDA of $50 million, cash of $20 million, debt of $100 million, and 10 million shares outstanding. The ocean transport industry as a whole has an average EV/EBITDA ratio of 8.5. What is one estimate of Fairview's enterprise value? What is a corresponding estimate of its stock price?

SOLUTION
PLAN

To estimate Fairview's enterprise value, we multiply its EBITDA by the average EV/EBITDA ratio of its industry. From there, we can subtract Fairview's debt and add its cash to calculate its equity value. Finally, we can divide by the number of shares outstanding to arrive at its stock price.

EXECUTE

Fairview's enterprise value estimate is $50 million × 8.5 = $425 million.

Next, subtract the debt from its enterprise value and add in its cash:

$425 million − $100 million + $20 million = $345 million, which is an estimate of the equity value.

Its stock price estimate is equal to its equity value estimate divided by the number of shares outstanding:

$345 million ÷ 10 million = $34.50.

EVALUATE

If we assume that Fairview should be valued similarly to the rest of the industry, then $425 million is a reasonable estimate of its enterprise value and $34.50 is a reasonable estimate of its stock price. However, we are relying on the assumption that Fairview's expected free cash flow growth is similar to the industry average. If that assumption is wrong, so is our valuation.

Other Multiples.   Many other valuation multiples are used. Looking at the enterprise value as a multiple of sales can be useful if it is reasonable to assume the firm will maintain a similar margin in the future. For firms with substantial tangible assets, the ratio of price-to-book value of equity per share is sometimes used as a valuation multiple. Some multiples are specific to an industry. In the cable TV industry, for example, analysts compare enterprise value per subscriber.

Limitations of Multiples

If comparable firms were identical to the firm being valued, the firms' multiples would match precisely. Of course, firms are not identical, so the usefulness of a valuation multiple will inevitably depend on the nature of the differences between firms and the sensitivity of the multiples to these differences.

Table 10.1 lists several valuation multiples, as of July 2013, for firms in the footwear industry that could be used as comparables for Nike. Also shown in the table is the average for each multiple, together with the range around the average (in percentage terms). The bottom rows showing the range make it clear that the footwear industry has a lot of dispersion for all the multiples (for example, Wolverine has a price-to-book (P/B) of 4.13,

TABLE 10.1

Stock Prices and Multiples for the Footwear Industry (excluding Nike), July 2013

Name	Market Capitalization ($ million)	Enterprise Value ($ million)	P/E	Price/Book	Enterprise Value/Sales	Enterprise Value/EBITDA
Nike, Inc.	55,970	54,023	23.29	5.07	2.03	15.71
Adidas AG	23,105	23,317	32.33	3.06	1.20	11.88
Puma AG	4,330	4,085	70.56	1.96	0.96	9.34
Wolverine World Wide	2,910	3,981	37.6	4.13	1.22	9.28
Steve Madden, Ltd.	2,320	2,140	18.4	3.68	1.74	10.70
Deckers Outdoor Corp.	1,990	1,923	16.74	2.67	1.36	8.73
Crocs, Inc.	1,470	1,240	11.46	2.4	1.10	6.74
Skechers U.S.A.	1,340	1,213	67.41	1.54	0.78	18.16
Weyco Group, Inc.	301	325	16.53	1.71	1.11	9.69
R. G. Barry Corp.	197	174	14.92	2.31	1.19	6.44
Rocky Brands, Inc.	113	132	12.46	0.89	0.58	6.61
		Average	29.84	2.44	1.12	9.76
		Maximum	+136%	+70%	+55%	+86%
		Minimum	−62%	−63%	−48%	−34%

while Rocky Brands, Inc. has a P/B of only 0.89). While the Enterprise Value/Sales multiple shows the smallest variation, even with it we cannot expect to obtain a precise estimate of a firm's value.

The differences in these multiples most likely reflect differences in expected future growth rates, risk (and therefore costs of capital), and, in the case of Puma and Adidas, differences in accounting conventions between the United States and Germany. Investors in the market understand that these differences exist, so the stocks are priced accordingly. When valuing a firm using multiples, however, there is no clear guidance about how to adjust for these differences other than by narrowing the set of comparables used.

Another limitation of comparables is that they provide only information regarding the value of the firm *relative to* the other firms in the comparison set. Using multiples will not help us determine whether an entire industry is overvalued, for example. This issue became especially important during the Internet boom of the late 1990s. Because many of these firms did not have positive cash flows or earnings, new multiples were created to value them (for instance, price to "page views"). While these multiples could justify the value of these firms in relationship to one another, it was much more difficult to justify the stock prices of many of these firms using a realistic estimate of cash flows and the discounted free cash flow approach.

Comparison with Discounted Cash Flow Methods

The use of a valuation multiple based on comparables is best viewed as a shortcut. Rather than separately estimate the firm's cost of capital and future earnings or free cash flows, we rely on the market's assessment of the value of other firms with similar future prospects. In addition to its simplicity, the multiples approach has the advantage of being based on actual stock prices of real firms, rather than on what may be unrealistic forecasts of future cash flows.

The most important shortcoming of the comparables approach is that it does not take into account materially important differences among firms. For example, the approach ignores the fact that some firms have exceptionally talented managers, others have developed more efficient manufacturing processes, and still others might hold a patent on a new technology. Discounted cash flow methods have an advantage because they allow us to incorporate specific information about the firm's cost of capital or future growth. Thus, because the true driver of value for any firm is its ability to generate cash flows for its investors, the discounted cash flow methods have the potential to be more accurate than the use of a valuation multiple.

Concept
Check

3. What are some common valuation multiples?

4. What implicit assumptions do we make when valuing a firm using multiples based on comparable firms?

10.3 Stock Valuation Techniques: The Final Word

In the end, no single technique provides a final answer regarding a stock's true value. Indeed, all approaches inevitably require assumptions or forecasts that are too uncertain to provide a definitive assessment of the firm's value. Most real-world practitioners use a combination of these approaches and gain confidence in the outcome if the results are consistent across a variety of methods.

Figure 10.4 compares the ranges of values for Nike stock using the different valuation methods discussed in this chapter and in Chapter 7. The firm's stock price of $60.39 on June 25, 2013 was within the range of some methods, but higher than the range suggested by some of the multiples. Hence, based on this evidence alone, we would not conclude that the stock is obviously under- or over-priced. But if this were not the case—what if these valuation techniques produce valuations markedly different to what the stock is trading at in the market? In the next section, we tackle this question.

FIGURE 10.4

Range of Valuations
for Nike Stock Using
Various Valuation
Methods

Valuations from multiples are based on the low, high, and average values of the comparable firms from Table 10.1 (see Problems 16 and 17 at the end of this chapter). The constant dividend growth model is based on a 10% equity cost of capital and dividend growth rates of 6% to 9%, as discussed at the beginning of Section 7.5. The discounted free cash flow model is based on Example 10.1 with the range of parameters in Problem 8 at the end of this chapter. Midpoints are based on average multiples or base-case assumptions. Red and blue regions show the variation between the lowest-multiple/worst-case scenario and the highest-multiple/best-case scenario. Nike's actual share price of $60.39 is indicated by the gray line.

INTERVIEW WITH

MARILYN FEDAK

Marilyn G. Fedak is the Vice Chair, Investment Services, and was formerly head of Global Value Equities, at AllianceBernstein, a publicly traded global asset management firm with approximately $450 billion in assets.

QUESTION: *What valuation methods do you use to identify buying opportunities for value stocks?*

ANSWER: We use both a dividend-discount model (DDM) and a proprietary quantitative return model called the Global Edge Model (GEM). For our non-U.S. portfolios, we use the GEM model; in the U.S., we use a combination of GEM and the DDM.

At its most basic level, the DDM provides a way to evaluate how much we need to pay today for a company's future earnings and cash flow.* All things being equal, we are looking to buy as much earnings power as cheaply as we can. It is a very reliable methodology, *if* you have the right forecasts for companies' future earnings. Our GEM model encompasses a variety of valuation measures, such as P/E and price-to-book ratios and selected success factors—for example, ROE and price momentum.

In both the U.S. and non-U.S. portfolios, we use these valuation tools to rank companies from the most undervalued to the most expensive. We focus on the stocks that rank the highest. Our decision-making bodies, the Investment policy groups, meet with analysts to quality-control the forecasts for the highest ranked group of stocks. Once the forecasts are approved, we add risk tools to construct optimal portfolios.

QUESTION: *Are there drawbacks to these models?*

ANSWER: Both models have advantages and drawbacks. The DDM is a very reliable valuation methodology. However, its focus on forecasts of cash flow or earnings over some future period requires a large, highly skilled body of research analysts. And, it is oriented to the long term, so the timing of purchases and sales can be too early.

The Global Edge Model is very useful to efficiently evaluate investments within large universes. However, it is very oriented to

(Continued)

current profitability and valuation metrics—not the future. As such, judgment has to be applied to determine if a company is likely to sustain similar characteristics going forward.

QUESTION: *Did the precipitous decline in stock prices in late 2008 and early 2009 cause you to retool your valuation methodology?*

ANSWER: In 2006, we began studying the interaction of the DDM and GEM models and determined that combining the two models gives us superior results to a single methodology when evaluating U.S. securities. The DDM focuses on forecasts of a company's future, whereas the quant [quantitative] return model captures a

company's history and current status. This new methodology was very helpful to us in 2008, when the GEM model signaled caution for certain sectors that looked inexpensive based on the DDM.

We have also broadened our research to incorporate more external inputs and have assigned a higher probability to unlikely events such as the government intervention in the financial and auto industries. On the risk side, we have added a refinancing risk tool and are tracking short interest in various equities.

*Because of historical usage, many practitioners use the term "dividend-discount model" to refer to the entire class of cash flow discount models.

10.4 Information, Competition, and Stock Prices

As shown in Figure 10.5, the models described in this chapter and in Chapter 7 link the firm's expected future cash flows, its cost of capital (determined by its risk), and the value of its shares. But what conclusions should we draw if the actual market price of a stock does not appear to be consistent with our estimate of its value? Is it more likely that the stock is mispriced or that we are mistaken about its risk and future cash flows?

Information in Stock Prices

Suppose you are a new junior analyst assigned to research Nike stock and assess its value. You scrutinize the company's recent financial statements, look at the trends in the industry, and forecast the firm's future earnings, dividends, and free cash flows. After you carefully crunch the numbers, you estimate the stock's value to be $85 per share. On your way to present your analysis to your boss, you run into a slightly more experienced colleague in the elevator. It turns out that your colleague has been researching the same stock. But according to her analysis, the value of Nike stock is only $65 per share. What would you do?

Although you could just assume your colleague is wrong, most of us would reconsider our own analysis. The fact that someone else who has carefully studied the same stock has come to a very different conclusion is powerful evidence that you might be mistaken. In the face of this information from our colleague, you would probably adjust your assessment

FIGURE 10.5

The Valuation Triad

Valuation models determine the relationship among the firm's future cash flows, its cost of capital, and the value of its shares. We can use the stock's expected cash flows and cost of capital to assess its market price (share value). Conversely, we can use the market price to assess the firm's future cash flows or cost of capital.

of the stock's value downward. Of course, your colleague might also revise her opinion upward based on your assessment. After sharing the analyses, we would likely end up with a consensus estimate somewhere between $65 and $85 per share.

This type of encounter happens millions of times every day in the stock market. When a buyer seeks to buy a stock, the willingness of other parties to sell the same stock suggests that they value the stock differently. This information should lead both buyers and sellers to revise their valuations. Ultimately, investors trade until they reach a consensus regarding the value (market price) of the stock. In this way, stock markets aggregate the information and views of many different investors.

Thus, if your valuation model suggests a stock is worth $30 per share when it is trading for $20 per share in the market, the discrepancy is equivalent to knowing that thousands of investors—many of them professionals who have access to the best information about the stock available—disagree with your assessment. This knowledge should make you reconsider your original analysis. You would need a very compelling reason to trust your own estimate in the face of such contrary opinions.

What conclusion can we draw from this discussion? Recall Figure 10.5, in which a valuation model links the firm's future cash flows, its cost of capital, and its share price. In other words, given accurate information about any two of these variables, a valuation model allows us to make inferences about the third variable. Thus, the way we use a valuation model will depend on the quality of our information: The model will tell us the most about the variable for which our prior information is the least reliable.

For a publicly traded firm, its market price should already provide very accurate information, aggregated from a multitude of investors, regarding the true value of its shares. In these situations, the best use of a valuation model is to inform us about the things we cannot observe directly—the firm's future cash flows or cost of capital. Only in the relatively rare case in which we have some superior information that other investors lack regarding the firm's cash flows and cost of capital would it make sense to second-guess the stock price.

EXAMPLE 10.6

Using the Information in Market Prices

MyFinanceLab

PROBLEM

Suppose Tecnor Industries will have free cash flows next year of $40 million. Its weighted average cost of capital is 11%, and you expect its free cash flows to grow at a rate of approximately 4% per year, though you are somewhat unsure of the precise growth rate. Tecnor has 10 million shares outstanding, no debt, and $20 million in cash. If Tecnor stock is currently trading for $55.33 per share, how would you update your beliefs about its dividend growth rate?

SOLUTION

PLAN

If we apply the growing perpetuity formula for the growing FCF based on a 4% growth rate, we can estimate a stock price using Eqs.10.3 and 10.4. If the market price is higher than our estimate, it implies that the market expects higher growth in FCF than 4%. Conversely, if the market price is lower than our estimate, the market expects FCF growth to be less than 4%.

EXECUTE

Applying the growing perpetuity formula, we have $PV(FCF) = 40 \div (0.11 - 0.04) = \$571.43$ million. Applying Eq. 10.4, the price per share would be ($571.43 million − 0 + $20 million) ÷ 10 million shares = $59.14 per share. The market price of $55.33, however, implies that most investors expect FCF to grow at a somewhat slower rate.

EVALUATE

Given the $55.33 market price for the stock, we should lower our expectations for the FCF growth rate from 4% unless we have very strong reasons to trust our own estimate.

Competition and Efficient Markets

The notion that market prices reflect the information of many investors is a natural consequence of investor competition. If information were available that indicated buying a stock had a positive NPV, investors with that information would choose to buy the stock; their attempts to purchase it would then drive up the stock's price. By a similar logic, investors with information that selling a stock had a positive NPV would sell it, so the stock's price would fall.

The idea that competition among investors works to eliminate *all* positive-NPV trading opportunities is the **efficient markets hypothesis**. It implies that securities will be fairly priced, based on their future cash flows, given all information that is available to investors.

Forms of Market Efficiency

The type of market efficiency we describe here, where all publicly available information is incorporated very quickly into stock prices, is often called *semistrong form market efficiency*. The term "semistrong" indicates that it is not as complete as *strong form market efficiency*, where prices immediately incorporate *all* information, including private information known, for example, only to managers. Finally, the term *weak form market efficiency* means that only the history of past prices is already reflected in the stock price. It helps to think of the different forms of market efficiency as meaning that prices incorporate a steadily increasing set of information, each of which encompasses all the lower forms. For example, since the history of past prices is public information, semistrong form efficiency encompasses weak form. The diagram illustrates the idea. In the diagram, the information sets of weak form, semistrong form, and strong form efficiency are represented by the blue, green, and yellow circles, respectively.

Not all market participants believe that the stock market is semistrong form efficient. Technical analysts, who look for patterns in stock prices, do not believe the market is even weak form efficient. Mutual fund managers and fundamental analysts, such as those who work for brokerages and make stock recommendations, believe that mispricing can be uncovered by careful analysis of company fundamentals. There is evidence that traders with inside information about upcoming merger or earnings announcements can make abnormal returns by trading (illegally) on that information, so the market is clearly not strong form efficient.

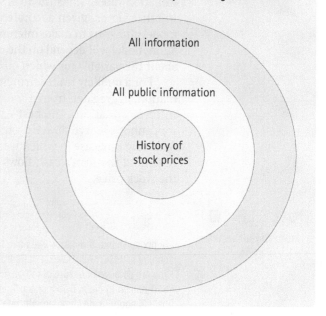

What happens when new information about a stock arrives? The answer depends on the degree of competition, that is, on the number of investors who have access to this new information. Consider two important cases.

Public, Easily Interpretable Information. Information that is available to all investors includes information in news reports, financial statements, corporate press releases, or other public data sources. If investors can readily ascertain the effects of this information on the firm's future cash flows, then all investors can determine how this information will change the firm's value.

In this situation, we expect competition among investors to be fierce and the stock price to react nearly instantaneously to such news. A few lucky investors might be able to trade a small quantity of shares before the price has fully adjusted. Most investors, however, would find that the stock price already reflected the new information before they were able to trade on it. In other words, the efficient markets hypothesis holds very well with respect to this type of information.

EXAMPLE 10.7

Stock Price Reactions
to Public Information

MyFinanceLab

PROBLEM

Myox Labs announces that it is pulling one of its leading drugs from the market, owing to the potential side effects associated with the drug. As a result, its future expected free cash flow will decline by $85 million per year for the next 10 years. Myox has 50 million shares outstanding, no debt, and an equity cost of capital of 8%. If this news came as a complete surprise to investors, what should happen to Myox's stock price upon the announcement?

SOLUTION

PLAN

In this case, we can use the discounted free cash flow method. With no debt, $r_{wacc} = r_E = 8\%$. The effect on the Myox's enterprise value will be the loss of a 10-year annuity of $85 million. We can compute the effect today as the present value of that annuity.

EXECUTE

Using the annuity formula, the decline in expected free cash flow will reduce Myox's enterprise value by

$$\$85 \text{ million} \times \frac{1}{0.08}\left(1 - \frac{1}{1.08^{10}}\right) = \$570.36 \text{ million}$$

Thus, the stock price should fall by 570.36 = $11.41 per share.

EVALUATE

Because this news is public and its effect on the firm's expected free cash flow is clear, we would expect the stock price to drop by $11.41 per share nearly instantaneously.

Private or Difficult-to-Interpret Information. Of course, some information is not publicly available. For example, an analyst might spend considerable time and effort gathering information from a firm's employees, competitors, suppliers, or customers that is relevant to the firm's future cash flows. This information is not available to other investors who have not devoted a similar effort to gathering it.

Even when information is publicly available, it may be difficult to interpret. Non-experts in the field may find it challenging to evaluate research reports on new technologies, for example. It may take a great deal of legal and accounting expertise and effort to understand the full consequences of a highly complicated business transaction. Certain consulting experts may have greater insight into consumer tastes and the likelihood of a product's acceptance. In these cases, while the fundamental information may be public, the *interpretation* of how that information will affect the firm's future cash flows is itself private information.

As an example, imagine that Phenyx Pharmaceuticals has announced the development of a new drug for which the company is seeking approval from the U.S. Food and Drug Administration (FDA). If the drug is approved and subsequently launched in the U.S. market, the future profits from the new drug will increase Phenyx's market value by $750 million, or $15 per share given its 50 million shares outstanding. Assume that the development of this drug comes as a surprise to investors, and that the average likelihood of FDA approval is 10%. In that case, because many investors probably know the chance of FDA approval is 10%, competition should lead to an immediate jump in Phenyx's stock price of 10% × $15 = $1.50 per share. Over time, however, analysts and experts in the field will likely make their own assessments of the probable efficacy of the drug. If they conclude that the drug looks more promising than average, they will begin to trade on their private information and buy the stock, and the firm's price will tend to drift higher over time. However, if the experts conclude that the drug looks less promising than average, they will tend to sell the stock, and the firm's price will drift lower over time. Of course, at the time of the announcement, uninformed investors do not know which way it will go. Examples of possible price paths are shown in Figure 10.6.

FIGURE 10.6

Possible Stock Price
Paths for Phenyx
Pharmaceuticals

Phenyx's stock price jumps on the announcement based on the average likelihood of FDA approval. The stock price then drifts up (green path) or down (orange path) as informed traders trade on their more accurate assessment of the drug's likelihood of approval and hence entry into the U.S. market. At the time of the announcement, uninformed investors do not know which way the stock will go.

When private information is in the hands of a relatively small number of investors, these investors may be able to profit by trading on their information.[3] In this case, the efficient markets hypothesis will not hold in the strict sense. However, as these informed traders begin to trade, their actions will tend to move prices, so over time prices will begin to reflect their information as well.

If the profit opportunities from having this type of information are large, other individuals will attempt to gain the expertise and devote the resources needed to acquire it. As more individuals become better informed, competition to exploit this information will increase. Thus, in the long run, we should expect that the degree of "inefficiency" in the market will be limited by the costs of obtaining the information.

Lessons for Investors and Corporate Managers

The effect of competition based on information about stock prices has important consequences for both investors and corporate managers.

Consequences for Investors. As in other markets, investors should be able to identify positive-NPV trading opportunities in securities markets only if some barrier or restriction to free competition exists. An investor's competitive advantage may take several forms. For

---

[3]Even with private information, informed investors may find it difficult to profit from that information, because they must find others who are willing to trade with them; that is, the market for the stock must be sufficiently *liquid*. A liquid market requires that other investors in the market have alternative motives to trade (for example, selling shares of a stock to purchase a house) and so are willing to trade even when facing the risk that other traders may be better informed.

instance, the investor may have expertise or access to information known only to a few people. Alternatively, the investor may have lower trading costs than other market participants and so can exploit opportunities that others would find unprofitable. In all cases, the source of the positive-NPV trading opportunity must be something that is difficult to replicate; otherwise, any gains would be competed away in short order.

While the fact that positive-NPV trading opportunities are hard to come by may be disappointing, there is some good news as well. If stocks are fairly priced according to our valuation models, then investors who buy stocks can expect to receive future cash flows that fairly compensate them for the risk of their investment. In such cases, the average investor can invest with confidence, even if he or she is not fully informed.

Implications for Corporate Managers. If stocks are fairly valued according to the models we have described in this chapter and in Chapter 7, then the value of the firm is determined by the cash flows that it can pay to its investors. This result has several key implications for corporate managers:

- *Focus on NPV and free cash flow.* A manager seeking to boost the price of her firm's stock should make investments that increase the present value of the firm's free cash flow. Thus, the capital budgeting methods outlined in Chapter 9 are fully consistent with the objective of maximizing the firm's share price.

- *Avoid accounting illusions.* Many managers make the mistake of focusing on accounting earnings as opposed to free cash flows. According to the efficient markets hypothesis, the accounting consequences of a decision do not directly affect the value of the firm and should not drive decision making.

- *Use financial transactions to support investment.* With efficient markets, the firm can sell its shares at a fair price to new investors. As a consequence, the firm should not be constrained from raising capital to fund positive-NPV investment opportunities.

The Efficient Markets Hypothesis Versus No Arbitrage

There is an important distinction between the efficient markets hypothesis and the notion of no arbitrage that we introduced in Chapter 3. An arbitrage opportunity is a situation in which two securities (or portfolios) with *identical* cash flows have different prices. Because anyone can earn a sure profit in this situation by buying the low-priced security and selling the high-priced one, we expect investors to exploit and eliminate these opportunities immediately. Thus, arbitrage opportunities will not be found.

The efficient markets hypothesis states that the best estimate of the value of a share of stock is its market price. That is, investors' own estimates of value are not as accurate as the market price. But that does not mean that the market price always correctly estimates the value of a share of stock. There is a difference between the best estimate and being correct. Thus, there is no reason to expect the market price to always assess value accurately; rather, the price is best viewed as an approximation. However, because the price is the best estimate, the efficient market hypothesis implies that you cannot tell which prices overestimate and which underestimate the true value of the stock.

Concept
Check

5. State the efficient markets hypothesis.

6. What are the implications of the efficient markets hypothesis for corporate managers?

10.5   ## Individual Biases and Trading

Not all investors accept the notion that second guessing the stock prices requires specialized knowledge and unusual skills. Instead, they attempt to make money by trading and in most cases end up losing money. In this next section, we will briefly discuss some common psychological biases and consider how they affect individuals' trading behavior. In an efficient market, these biases can be costly, resulting in lower realized returns and reduced wealth.

Excessive Trading and Overconfidence

Trading is expensive; you must pay commissions on top of the difference between the bid and ask price, called the *spread*. Given how hard it should be to identify over- and under-valued stocks, you might then expect individual investors to take a conservative approach to trading. However, in an influential study of the trading behavior of individual investors that held accounts at a discount brokerage, researchers Brad Barber and Terrance Odean found that individual investors tend to trade very actively, with average turnover almost 50% above the average of all investors including institutions during the time period of their study.[4]

What might explain this trading behavior? Psychologists have known since the 1960s that uninformed individuals tend to overestimate the precision of their knowledge. For example, many sports fans sitting in the stands confidently second-guess the coaching decisions on the field, truly believing that they can do a better job. In finance we call investors' presumptuousness of their ability to beat the market by overtrading the **overconfidence hypothesis**. Barber and Odean hypothesized that this kind of behavior also characterizes individual investment decision making: Like sports fans, individual investors believe they can pick winners and losers when, in fact, they cannot; this overconfidence leads them to trade too much.

An implication of this overconfidence hypothesis is that, assuming they have no true ability, investors who trade more will not earn higher returns. Instead, their performance will be worse once we take into account the costs of trading (due to both commissions and bid-ask spreads). Figure 10.7 documents precisely this result, showing that much investor trading appears not to be based on rational assessments of performance.

overconfidence hypothesis The tendency of individual investors to trade too much based on the mistaken belief that they can pick winners and losers better than investment professionals.

Hanging On to Losers and the Disposition Effect

Investors tend to hold on to stocks that have lost value and sell stocks that have risen in value since the time of purchase. We call this tendency to keep losers and sell winners the **disposition effect**. Researchers Hersh Shefrin and Meir Statman, building on the work of psychologists Daniel Kahneman and Amos Tversky, suggest that this effect arises due to investors' increased willingness to take on risk in the face of possible losses.[5] It may also reflect a reluctance to admit a mistake by taking the loss.

Researchers have verified the disposition effect in many studies. For example, in a study of all trades in the Taiwanese stock market from 1995–1999, investors in aggregate were twice as likely to realize gains as they were to realize losses. Also, nearly 85% of

disposition effect The tendency to hold on to stocks that have lost value and sell stocks that have risen in value since the time of purchase.

---

[4]B. Barber and T. Odean, "Trading Is Hazardous to Your Wealth: The Common Stock Investment Performance of Individual Investors," *Journal of Finance* 55 (2000) 773–806.

[5]H. Shefrin and M. Statman, "The Disposition to Sell Winners Too Early and Ride Losers Too Long: Theory and Evidence," *Journal of Finance* 40 (1985): 777–790, and D. Kahneman and A. Tversky, "Prospect Theory: An Analysis of Decision under Risk," *Econometrica* 47 (1979): 263–291.

FIGURE 10.7

Individual Investor
Returns Versus
Portfolio Turnover

The plot shows the average annual return (net of commissions and trading costs) for individual investors at a large discount brokerage from 1991–1997. Investors are grouped into quintiles based on their average annual turnover. While the least-active investors had slightly (but not significantly) better performance than the S&P 500, performance declined with the rate of turnover.

Source: B. Barber and T. Odean, "Trading Is Hazardous to Your Wealth: The Common Stock Investment Performance of Individual Investors," *Journal of Finance* 55 (2000) 773–806.

individual investors were subject to this bias.[6] On the other hand, mutual funds and foreign investors did not exhibit the same tendency, and other studies have shown that more sophisticated investors appear to be less susceptible to the disposition effect.[7]

This behavioral tendency to sell winners and hang on to losers is costly from a tax perspective. Because capital gains are taxed only when the asset is sold, it is optimal for tax purposes to postpone taxable gains by continuing to hold profitable investments; delaying the tax payment reduces its present value. On the other hand, investors should capture tax losses by selling their losing investments, especially near the year's end, in order to accelerate the tax write-off.

Of course, keeping losers and selling winners might make sense if investors forecast that the losing stocks would ultimately "bounce back" and outperform the winners going forward. While investors may in fact have this belief, it does not appear to be justified—if anything, the losing stocks that investors continue to hold tend to *underperform* the winners they sell. According to one study, losers underperformed winners by 3.4% over the year after the winners were sold.[8]

Investor Attention, Mood, and Experience

Individual investors generally are not full-time traders. As a result, they have limited time and attention to spend on their investment decisions and may be influenced by attention-grabbing news stories or other events. Studies show that individuals are

---

[6]B. Barber, Y. T. Lee, Y. J. Liu, and T. Odean, "Is the Aggregate Investor Reluctant to Realize Losses? Evidence from Taiwan," *European Financial Management*, 13 (2007): 423–447.

[7]R. Dhar and N. Zhu, "Up Close and Personal: Investor Sophistication and the Disposition Effect," *Management Science*, 52 (2006): 726–740.

[8]T. Odean, "Are Investors Reluctant to Realize Their Losses?" *Journal of Finance* 53 (1998): 1775–1798.

more likely to buy stocks that have recently been in the news, engaged in advertising, experienced exceptionally high trading volume, or have had extreme (either positive or negative) returns.[9]

Investment behavior also seems to be affected by investors' moods. For example, sunshine generally has a positive effect on mood, and studies have found that stock returns tend to be higher when it is a sunny day at the location of the stock exchange. In New York City, the annualized market return on perfectly sunny days is approximately 24.8% per year versus 8.7% per year on perfectly cloudy days.[10] Further evidence of the link between investor mood and stock returns comes from the effect of major sports events on returns. One recent study estimates that a loss in the World Cup elimination stage lowers the next day's stock returns in the losing country by about 0.50%, presumably due to investors' poor moods.[11]

Finally, investors appear to put too much weight on their own experience rather than considering all the historical evidence. As a result, people who grow up and live during a time of high stock returns are more likely to invest in stocks than people who grow up and live during a time of low stock returns.[12]

Why would investors continue to make such mistakes? Even if they started with such misconceptions, wouldn't they be able to learn over time the cost of these errors? The challenge is that stock returns are extremely volatile, and this volatility masks the small differences in returns from different trading strategies. We will start Chapter 11 with a review of the historical evidence on average stock returns and their volatility. You will see how variable returns are and how there have been long stretches of good returns, as in the 1990s, and stretches in which the total return was negative, as in the 2000s.

Concept Check

7. What are several systematic behavioral biases that individual investors fall prey to?

8. Why would excessive trading lead to lower realized returns?

---

[9]See G. Grullon, G. Kanatas, and J. Weston, "Advertising, Breadth of Ownership, and Liquidity," *Review of Financial Studies*, 17 (2004): 439–461; M. Seasholes and G. Wu, "Predictable Behavior, Profits, and Attention," *Journal of Empirical Finance*, 14 (2007): 590–610; B. Barber and T. Odean, "All That Glitters: The Effect of Attention and News on the Buying Behavior of Individual and Institutional Investors," *Review of Financial Studies*, 21 (2008): 785–818.

[10]Based on data from 1982–1997; see D. Hirshleifer and T. Shumway, "Good Day Sunshine: Stock Returns and the Weather," *Journal of Finance*, 58 (2003): 1009–1032.

[11]A. Edmans, D. Garcia, and O. Norli, "Sports Sentiment and Stock Returns," *Journal of Finance*, 62 (2007): 1967–1998.

[12]U. Malmendier and S. Nagel, "Depression Babies: Do Macroeconomic Experiences Affect Risk-Taking?" NBER working paper no. 14813.

MyFinanceLab

Here is what you should know after reading this chapter. MyFinanceLab will help you identify what you know, and where to go when you need to practice.

Key Points and Equations	Key Terms	Online Practice
10.1 The Discounted Free Cash Flow Model • When a firm has leverage, it is more reliable to use the discounted free cash flow model. In this model, the enterprise value of the firm equals the present value of the firm's future free cash flow: $$V_0 = PV(\text{Future Free Cash Flow of Firm}) \quad (10.3)$$ • We discount cash flows using the weighted average cost of capital, which is the expected return the firm must pay to investors to compensate them for the risk of holding the firm's debt and equity together. • We can estimate a terminal enterprise value by assuming free cash flow grows at a constant rate (typically equal to the rate of long-run revenue growth). • We determine the stock price by subtracting debt and adding cash to the enterprise value, and then dividing by the initial number of shares outstanding of the firm: $$P_0 = \frac{V_0 + \text{Cash}_0 - \text{Debt}_0}{\text{Shares Outstanding}_0} \quad (10.4)$$	discounted free cash flow model, p. 300 weighted average cost of capital (WACC), p. 301	MyFinanceLab Study Plan 10.1 Interactive Discounted Cash Flow Valuation
10.2 Valuation Based on Comparable Firms • We can also value stocks by using valuation multiples based on comparable firms. Multiples commonly used for this purpose include the P/E ratio and the ratio of enterprise value (EV) to EBITDA. When we use multiples, we assume that comparable firms have the same risk and future growth as the firm being valued. • No valuation model provides a definitive value for the stock. It is best to use several methods to identify a reasonable range for the value.	forward earnings, p. 306 forward P/E, p. 306 method of comparables, p. 304 trailing earnings, p. 306 trailing P/E, p. 306 valuation multiple, p. 304	MyFinanceLab Study Plan 10.2
10.3 Stock Valuation Techniques: The Final Word • All valuation approaches require assumptions or forecasts that are too uncertain to provide a definitive assessment of the firm's value. • You can be more confident if the valuation is consistent across a variety of methods.		
10.4 Information, Competition, and Stock Prices • Stock prices aggregate the information of many investors. Therefore, if our valuation disagrees with the stock's market price, it is most likely an indication that our assumptions about the firm's cash flows are wrong.	efficient markets hypothesis, p. 314	MyFinanceLab Study Plan 10.3

- Competition between investors tends to eliminate positive-NPV trading opportunities. Competition will be strongest when information is public and easy to interpret. Privately informed traders may be able to profit from their information, which is reflected in prices only gradually.
- The efficient markets hypothesis states that competition eliminates all positive-NPV trades, which is equivalent to stating that securities with equivalent risk have the same expected returns.
- In an efficient market, investors will not find positive-NPV trading opportunities without some source of competitive advantage. By contrast, the average investor will earn a fair return on his or her investment.
- In an efficient market, to raise the stock price, corporate managers should focus on maximizing the present value of the free cash flow from the firm's investments, rather than accounting consequences or financial policy.

10.5 Individual Biases and Trading	disposition effect, p. 318	MyFinanceLab Study Plan 10.4
• Individual investors display many biases, including overconfidence, disposition effect, limited attention, and mood affects.	overconfidence hypothesis, p. 318	
• In an efficient market, these biases can lead to trading losses through excessive trading or biases in valuations.		

CRITICAL THINKING

1. What are the advantages of valuing a stock based on discounted free cash flows?

2. Explain the connection between the FCF valuation model and capital budgeting.

3. What is the intuition behind valuation by multiples and what are the major assumptions?

4. What are the limitations of valuation by multiples?

5. What is an efficient market?

6. How do interactions in a market lead to information being incorporated into stock prices?

7. Why does market efficiency lead a manager to focus on NPV and free cash flow?

8. Why don't investors always trade rationally?

9. What are some of the major behavioral trading biases?

PROBLEMS

All problems in this chapter are available in MyFinanceLab. An asterisk * indicates problems with a higher level of difficulty.

The Discounted Free Cash Flow Model

1. This year, FCF, Inc., has earnings before interest and taxes of $10 million, depreciation expenses of $1 million, capital expenditures of $1.5 million, and has increased its net working capital by $500,000. If its tax rate is 35%, what is its free cash flow?

2. Victoria Enterprises expects earnings before interest and taxes (EBIT) next year of $1 million. Its depreciation and capital expenditures will both be $300,000, and it

expects its capital expenditures to always equal its depreciation. Its working capital will increase by $50,000 over the next year. Its tax rate is 40%. If its WACC is 10% and its FCFs are expected to increase at 4% per year in perpetuity, what is its enterprise value?

3. The present value of JECK Co.'s expected free cash flows is $100 million. If JECK has $30 million in debt, $6 million in cash, and 2 million shares outstanding, what is its share price?

4. Portage Bay Enterprises has $1 million in excess cash, no debt, and is expected to have free cash flow of $10 million next year. Its FCF is then expected to grow at a rate of 3% per year forever. If Portage Bay's equity cost of capital is 11% and it has 5 million shares outstanding, what should be the price of Portage Bay stock?

5. Heavy Metal Corporation is expected to generate the following free cash flows over the next five years:

Year	1	2	3	4	5
FCF ($ million)	53	68	78	75	82

After 5 years, the free cash flows are expected to grow at the industry average of 4% per year. Using the discounted free cash flow model and a weighted average cost of capital of 14%:
a. Estimate the enterprise value of Heavy Metal.
b. If Heavy Metal has no excess cash, debt of $300 million, and 40 million shares outstanding, estimate its share price.

*6. Covan, Inc., is expected to have the following free cash flows:

Year	1	2	3	4	...
FCF	10	12	13	14	Grow by 4% per year

a. Covan has 8 million shares outstanding, $3 million in excess cash, and it has no debt. If its cost of capital is 12%, what should its stock price be?
b. Covan reinvests all its FCF and has no plans to add debt or change its cash holdings. If you plan to sell Covan at the beginning of year 2, what should you expect its price to be?
c. Assume you bought Covan stock at the beginning of year 1. What is your expected return from holding Covan stock until year 2?

7. Sora Industries has 60 million outstanding shares, $120 million in debt, $40 million in cash, and the following projected free cash flow for the next four years (*see MyFinanceLab for the data in Excel format*):

	Year	0	1	2	3	4
1						
2	**Earnings and FCF Forecast ($ million)**					
3	Sales	433.0	468.0	516.0	547.0	574.3
4	*Growth Versus Prior Year*		*8.1%*	*10.3%*	*6.0%*	*5.0%*
5	Cost of Goods Sold		−313.6	−345.7	−366.5	−384.8
6	**Gross Profit**		154.4	170.3	180.5	189.5
7	Selling, General, and Administrative		−93.6	−103.2	−109.4	−114.9
8	Depreciation		−7.0	−7.5	−9.0	−9.5
9	**EBIT**		53.8	59.6	62.1	65.2
10	Less: Income Tax at 40%		−21.5	−23.8	−24.8	−26.1
11	Plus: Depreciation		7.0	7.5	9.0	9.5
12	Less: Capital Expenditures		−7.7	−10.0	−9.9	−10.4
13	Less: Increase in NWC		−6.3	−8.6	−5.6	−4.9
14	**Free Cash Flow**		25.3	24.6	30.8	33.3

a. Suppose Sora's revenues and free cash flow are expected to grow at a 5% rate beyond year 4. If Sora's weighted average cost of capital is 10%, what is the value of Sora stock based on this information?

b. Sora's cost of goods sold was assumed to be 67% of sales. If its cost of goods sold is actually 70% of sales, how would the estimate of the stock's value change?

c. Return to the assumptions of part (a) and suppose Sora can maintain its cost of goods sold at 67% of sales. However, the firm reduces its selling, general, and administrative expenses from 20% of sales to 16% of sales. What stock price would you estimate now? (Assume no other expenses, except taxes, are affected.)

*d. Sora's net working capital needs were estimated to be 18% of sales (their current level in year 0). If Sora can reduce this requirement to 12% of sales starting in year 1, but all other assumptions remain as in part (a), what stock price do you estimate for Sora? (*Hint*: This change will have the largest effect on Sora's free cash flow in year 1.)

8. Consider the valuation of Nike given in Example 10.1.
   a. Suppose you believe Nike's initial revenue growth rate will be between 7% and 11% (with growth always slowing linearly to 5% by year 2018). What range of prices for Nike stock is consistent with these forecasts?
   b. Suppose you believe Nike's initial revenue EBIT margin will be between 9% and 11% of sales. What range of prices for Nike stock is consistent with these forecasts?
   c. Suppose you believe Nike's weighted average cost of capital is between 9.5% and 12%. What range of prices for Nike stock is consistent with these forecasts?
   d. What range of stock prices is consistent if you vary the estimates as in parts (a), (b), and (c) simultaneously?

Valuation Based on Comparable Firms

9. You are evaluating the stock price of Kroger, a grocery store chain. It has forward earnings per share of $3. You notice that its competitor Safeway has a P/E ratio of 13. What is a good estimate of Kroger's stock price?

10. You notice that Coca-Cola has a stock price of $41.09 and EPS of $1.89. Its competitor PepsiCo has EPS of $3.90. But, Jones Soda, a small batch Seattle-based soda producer has a P/E ratio of 35. Based on this information, what is one estimate of the value of a share of PepsiCo stock?

11. CSH has EBITDA of $5 million. You feel that an appropriate EV/EBITDA ratio for CSH is 9. CSH has $10 million in debt, $2 million in cash, and 800,000 shares outstanding. What is your estimate of CSH's stock price?

12. Next year, BHH Co. is expected to pay a dividend of $3 per share from earnings of $5 per share. The equity cost of capital for BHH is 12%. What should BHH's forward P/E ratio be if its dividend growth rate is expected to be 4% for the foreseeable future?

13. GHL, Inc., has a dividend payout ratio of 50%. Its cost of equity is 11% and its dividend growth rate is 5%. If its forward EPS is $6, what is your estimate of its stock price?

14. SLYMN Enterprises has a P/E ratio of 12 and a dividend payout ratio of 40%. If its equity cost of capital is 13%, what growth rate is its P/E ratio consistent with?

15. After researching the competitors of EJH Enterprises, you determine that most comparable firms have the following valuation ratios (*see MyFinanceLab for the data in Excel format*):

	Comp 1	Comp 2	Comp 3	Comp 4
EV/EBITDA	12	11	12.5	10
P/E	19	18	20	17

EJH Enterprises has EPS of $2, EBITDA of $300 million, $30 million in cash, $40 million in debt, and 100 million shares outstanding. What range of prices is consistent with both sets of multiples?

16. Suppose that in July 2013, Nike had EPS of $2.52 and a book value of equity of $12.48 per share.

    a. Using the average P/E multiple in Table 10.1, estimate Nike's share price.

    b. What range of share prices do you estimate based on the highest and lowest P/E multiples in Table 10.1?

    c. Using the average price-to-book value multiple in Table 10.1, estimate Nike's share price.

    d. What range of share prices do you estimate based on the highest and lowest price-to-book value multiples in Table 10.1?

17. Suppose that in July 2013, Nike had sales of $25,313 million, EBITDA of $3,254 million, excess cash of $3,337 million, $1,390 million of debt, and 893.6 million shares outstanding.

    a. Using the average enterprise value to sales multiple in Table 10.1, estimate Nike's share price.

    b. What range of share prices do you estimate based on the highest and lowest enterprise value to sales multiples in Table 10.1?

    c. Using the average enterprise value to EBITDA multiple in Table 10.1, estimate Nike's share price.

    d. What range of share prices do you estimate based on the highest and lowest enterprise value to EBITDA multiples in Table 10.1?

*18. Suppose Rocky Brands has earnings per share of $2.30 and EBITDA of $30.7 million. The firm also has 5.4 million shares outstanding and debt of $125 million (net of cash). You believe Deckers Outdoor Corporation is comparable to Rocky Brands in terms of its underlying business, but Deckers has no debt. If Deckers has a P/E of 13.3 and an enterprise value to EBITDA multiple of 7.4, estimate the value of Rocky Brands stock using both multiples. Which estimate is likely to be more accurate?

Information, Competition, and Stock Prices

19. Summit Systems has an equity cost of capital of 11%, will pay a dividend of $1.50 in one year and its dividends had been expected to grow by 6% per year. You read in the paper that Summit has revised its growth prospects and now expects its dividends to grow at a rate of 3% per year forever.

    a. What is the drop in the value of a share of Summit Systems stock based on this information?

    b. If you tried to sell your Summit Systems stock after reading this news, what price would you be likely to get? Why?

20. Assume that Cola Co. has a share price of $43. The firm will pay a dividend of $1.24 in one year, and you expect Cola Co. to raise this dividend by approximately 7% per year in perpetuity.

    a. If Cola Co.'s equity cost of capital is 8%, what share price would you expect based on your estimate of the dividend growth rate?

    b. Given Cola Co.'s share price, what would you conclude about your assessment of Cola Co.'s future dividend growth?

21. Roybus, Inc., a manufacturer of flash memory, just reported that its main production facility in Taiwan was destroyed in a fire. Although the plant was fully insured, the loss of production will decrease Roybus's free cash flow by $180 million at the end of this year and by $60 million at the end of next year.

a. If Roybus has 35 million shares outstanding and a weighted average cost of capital of 13%, what change in Roybus's stock price would you expect upon this announcement? (Assume the value of Roybus's debt is not affected by the event.)

b. Would you expect to be able to sell Roybus stock on hearing this announcement and make a profit? Explain.

*22. Apnex, Inc., is a biotechnology firm that is about to announce the results of its clinical trials of a potential new cancer drug. If the trials were successful, Apnex stock will be worth $70 per share. If the trials were unsuccessful, Apnex stock will be worth $18 per share. Suppose that the morning before the announcement is scheduled, Apnex shares are trading for $55 per share.

a. Based on the current share price, what sort of expectations do investors seem to have about the success of the trials?

b. Suppose hedge fund manager Paul Kliner has hired several prominent research scientists to examine the public data on the drug and make their own assessment of the drug's promise. Would Kliner's fund be likely to profit by trading the stock in the hours prior to the announcement?

c. Which factors would limit the ability of Kliner's fund to profit on its information?

Individual Biases and Trading

23. You have a $100,000 portfolio made up of 15 stocks. You trade each stock five times this year and each time you trade, you pay about $30 in commissions and spread. You have no special knowledge, so you earn only the average market return of 12% on your investments. How much lower will your total return be because of your trades?

24. Assume the annual return for the lowest turnover portfolio is 18% and the annual return for the highest turnover portfolio is 12%. If you invest $100,000 and have the highest turnover, how much lower will the value of your portfolio be at the end of 10 years than if you had had the lowest turnover?

DATA CASE

As a new junior analyst for a large brokerage firm, you are excited to demonstrate the skills you learned in college and prove that you are worth your attractive salary. Your first assignment is to analyze General Electric stock. Your boss recommends determining prices based on both the discounted free cash flow valuation method and the comparable P/E ratio method. You are a little concerned about your boss's recommendation because your finance professor explained that these two valuation methods can result in widely differing estimates when applied to real data. You are really hoping the two methods will reach similar prices. Good luck with that!

1. Go to Reuters (http://www.reuters.com) and enter the symbol for General Electric (GE) in the "Search News & Quotes" box. From the main page for GE, click "View Full Quote," gather the following information, and enter it into a spreadsheet:
   a. The current stock price (on the left side of the page)
   b. The EPS (TTM)
   c. The number of shares of stock outstanding
   d. The industry P/E (TTM) ratio

2. Click the "Analysts" tab. On the Analyst page, scroll down to find the LT (Long-Term) Growth Rate and enter it into your spreadsheet.

3. Go to MSN Money (http://money.msn.com/) and type "GE" into the "Get Quote" box.

4. Under "Financials," Click Income Statement. Copy and paste the most recent three years' worth of income statements into a new worksheet in your existing Excel file.

Repeat this process for both the balance sheet and the cash flow statement for General Electric. Keep all of the different statements in the same Excel worksheet. *Note*: Make sure you are collecting annual data, rather than interim data.

5. To determine the stock value based on the discounted free cash flow method:
   a. Forecast the free cash flows using the historical data from the financial statements downloaded from Yahoo! Finance to compute the three-year average of the following ratios:
      i. EBIT/sales
      ii. Tax rate (income tax expense/income before tax)
      iii. Property plant and equipment/sales
      iv. Depreciation/property plant and equipment
      v. Net working capital/sales
   b. Create an empty timeline for the next five years.
   c. Forecast future sales based on the most recent year's total revenue growing at the LT growth rate from Reuters for the first five years.
   d. Use the average ratios computed in part (a) to forecast EBIT, property, plant and equipment, depreciation, and net working capital for the next five years.
   e. Forecast the free cash flow for the next five years using Eq. 10.2.
   f. Determine the horizon enterprise value for year 5 using Eq. 10.6 and a long-run growth rate of 4% and a cost of capital for GE of 11%.
   g. Determine the enterprise value of the firm as the present value of the free cash flows.
   h. Determine the stock price using Eq. 10.4. Note that your enterprise value is in $ thousands and the number of shares outstanding is in billions.

6. To calculate an estimate of GE's price based on a comparable P/E ratio, multiply the industry average P/E ratio by GE's EPS.

7. Compare the stock prices produced by the two methods to the actual stock price. What recommendations can you make as to whether clients should buy or sell GE stock based on your price estimates?

8. Explain to your boss why the estimates from the two valuation methods differ. Specifically address the assumptions implicit in the models themselves as well as the assumptions you made in preparing your analysis. Why do these estimates differ from the actual stock price of GE?

3 Integrative Case

This case draws on material from this and earlier chapters.

Nanovo, Inc., is a manufacturer of low-cost micro batteries for use in a wide variety of compact electronic devices such as children's toys, wireless transmitters, and sensors. The growth in the use of these devices has steadily increased, leading to an ever greater demand for Nanovo's products. Nanovo has responded to this increase in demand by expanding its production capacity, more than doubling the firm's size over the last decade. Despite this growth, however, Nanovo does not have sufficient capacity to meet the current demand for its ultra-long-life, low-voltage batteries. You have been asked to evaluate two proposals to expand one of Nanovo's existing plants, and make a recommendation.

Proposal 1

The current plant has a capacity of 25,000 cases per month. The first proposal is for a major expansion that would double the plant's current capacity to 50,000 cases per month. After talking with the firm's design engineers, sales managers, and plant operators, you have prepared the following estimates:

- Expanding the plant will require the purchase of $3.6 million in new equipment, and entail up-front design and engineering expenses of $3.9 million. These costs will be paid immediately when the expansion begins.

- Installing the new equipment and redesigning the plant to accommodate the higher capacity will require shutting down the plant for nine months. During that time, the plant's production will cease. After the expansion is finished, the plant will operate at double its original capacity.

- Marketing and selling the additional volume will lead to $1 million per year in additional sales, marketing, and administrative costs. These costs will begin in the first year (even while the plant is under construction and shut down).

Proposal 2

The engineers have put forth a second proposal for a minor expansion that will increase the firm's capacity by only 50%, to 37,500 cases per month. While the capacity is smaller, such an expansion would be cheaper and less disruptive:

- The smaller expansion will require only $2.4 million in new equipment, and $1.5 million in design and engineering expenses.

- The existing plant will need to be shut down for only four months.

- Sales, marketing, and administrative costs will only increase by $500,000.

Nanovo believes that with or without any expansion, the technology used at the plant will be obsolete after six years and will have no salvage value, and the plant itself will need to be completely overhauled at that time. You also have the following additional general information:

- With or without either proposed expansion, Nanovo will be able to sell all it can produce at an average wholesale price of $80 per case. This price is not expected to change during the next six years.
- Nanovo has a gross profit margin of 55% on these batteries.
- Nanovo's average net working capital at the end of each year will equal 15% of its annual revenue.
- Nanovo pays a 40% corporate tax rate.
- While all design and engineering costs are immediately deductible as operating expenses, all capital expenditures will be straight-line depreciated for tax purposes over the subsequent six years.

Management believes the risk of the expansion is similar to the risk of Nanovo's existing projects, and because Nanovo is all equity financed, the risk of the expansion is also similar to the risk of Nanovo stock. You have the following additional information about the stock:

- Nanovo has no debt and has 2 million shares outstanding. The firm's current share price is $75 per share.
- Analysts are expecting Nanovo to pay a $3 dividend at the end of this year, and to raise its dividend at an average rate of 8% per year in the future.

Based on this information, you have been tasked with preparing expansion recommendations for Nanovo (using Excel is optional but recommended).

Case Questions

1. Determine the annual incremental free cash flow associated with each expansion proposal relative to the status quo (no expansion).
2. Compute the IRR and payback period of each expansion proposal. Which plan has a higher IRR? Which has a shorter payback period?
3. Estimate Nanovo's equity cost of capital. Use it to determine the NPV associated with each expansion proposal. Which plan has a higher NPV?
4. Should Nanovo expand the plant? If so, which proposal should Nanovo adopt? Explain.
5. Suppose Nanovo decides to do the major expansion. If investors are not expecting this expansion, and if they agree with the forecasts above, how will the stock price change when the expansion is announced?
6. Suppose Nanovo announces the major expansion and the stock price reacts as in Question 5. Nanovo then issues new shares at this price to cover the up-front free cash flow required to launch the expansion, and thereafter pays out as dividends the total amount it expected to pay prior to the expansion, plus the additional free cash flow associated with the expansion. What dividend per share will Nanovo pay over the next eight years? What is the fair price today for Nanovo stock given these dividends?

PART 4

Risk and Return

Valuation Principle Connection. To apply the Valuation Principle, we must be able to discount the future costs and benefits of a decision. To do so, we need a discount rate that should reflect the risk, or uncertainty, surrounding those future costs and benefits. Our objective in this part of the book is to explain how to measure and compare risks across investment opportunities and use that knowledge to determine a discount rate, or cost of capital, for each investment opportunity. Chapter 11 introduces the key insight that investors only demand a risk premium for risk they cannot costlessly remove themselves by diversifying their portfolios. Hence, only non-diversifiable risk will matter when comparing investment opportunities. In Chapter 12, we quantify this idea, leading to the Capital Asset Pricing Model (CAPM), the central model of financial economics that quantifies what an equivalent risk is and in doing so provides the relation between risk and return. In Chapter 13, we apply what we've learned to estimate a company's overall cost of capital.

11

Risk and Return in Capital Markets

LEARNING OBJECTIVES

- Identify which types of securities have historically had the highest returns and which have been the most volatile

- Compute the average return and volatility of returns from a set of historical asset prices

- Understand the tradeoff between risk and return for large portfolios versus individual stocks

- Describe the difference between common and independent risk

- Explain how diversified portfolios remove independent risk, leaving common risk as the only risk requiring a risk premium

notation

Div_t	dividend paid on date t	$\bar{R}$	average return
P_t	price on date t	$SD(R)$	standard deviation of return R
R_t	realized or total return of a security from date $t-1$ to t	$Var(R)$	variance of return R

Over the 10-year period of 2003 through 2012, Investors in Consolidated Edison, Inc. (an electric utility) earned an average return of over 10% per year. Within this period there was considerable variation, with the annual return ranging from −16% in 2008 to nearly 31% in 2011. Over the same period, investors in Yahoo! Inc. earned an average return of 21%. However, the road was rocky—these investors gained 175% in 2003, but lost 48% in 2008. At the same time, investors in three-month U.S. Treasury bills earned an average return of 2% during the period, with a high of 5% in 2006 and a low of 0.04% in 2011. Thus, these three investments offered investors returns that were very different in terms of their average level and their variability. While Yahoo! stock paid the highest return on average, its returns were also the most volatile.

In this chapter, our goal is to develop an understanding of how risk relates to return. In the last three chapters, we established that value in projects, and hence in the firm, is determined by the present value of free cash flows. Up until now, we have focused on how to forecast and discount those cash flows. In this chapter and the two that follow, we turn our attention to the discount rate. As we have emphasized, the discount rate should be our cost of capital, and our cost of capital is determined by the risk of the project. But how exactly do we measure risk and how does a particular level of risk imply a specific cost of capital?

We will see how holding many assets together affects our risk exposure. In Chapter 12, we will build on this foundation to develop a theory that explains how to determine the cost of capital for any investment opportunity. Then, in Chapter 13, we will apply what we've learned about the relation between risk and return to the cost of capital for a company as a whole.

We begin our investigation of the relationship between risk and return by looking at historical data for publicly traded securities. We will see, for example, that while stocks are riskier investments than bonds, they have also earned higher average annual returns. We interpret the higher average return on stocks versus bonds as compensation to investors for the greater risk they are taking. But we will also find that not all risk needs to be compensated. By holding a portfolio of many different investments, investors can eliminate risks that are specific to individual securities. Only risks that cannot be eliminated by holding a large portfolio determine the risk premium investors will require.

11.1 A First Look at Risk and Return

If your great-grandparents had invested only $100 in a portfolio of small companies in 1925, your family could be worth over $3 million today! As we will see, however, such a decision would have carried considerable risk and it is only with 20/20 hindsight that we know it would have been a profitable one.

We begin our look at risk and return by illustrating how the risk premium affects investor decisions and returns. Suppose your great-grandparents had indeed invested $100 on your behalf at the end of 1925. They instructed their broker to reinvest any dividends or interest earned in the account until the end of 2012. How would that $100 have grown if it were invested in one of the following?

1. Standard & Poor's 500 (S&P 500): A portfolio, constructed by Standard & Poor's, comprising 90 U.S. stocks up to 1957 and 500 U.S. stocks after that. The firms represented are leaders in their respective industries and are among the largest firms, in terms of market capitalization (share price times the number of shares in the hands of the shareholders), traded on U.S. markets.

2. Small stocks: A portfolio, updated quarterly, of U.S. stocks traded on the NYSE with market capitalizations in the bottom 20%.

3. World portfolio: A portfolio of international stocks from all of the world's major stock markets in North America, Europe, and Asia.

4. Corporate bonds: A portfolio of long-term, AAA-rated U.S. corporate bonds with maturities of approximately 20 years.[1]

5. Treasury bills: An investment in one-month U.S. Treasury bills (reinvested as the bills mature).

Figure 11.1 shows the result, through the end of 2012, of investing $100 at the end of 1925 for each of these five different investment portfolios. The results are striking—had your grandparents invested $100 in the small-stock portfolio, the investment would have been worth over $3 million at the end of 2012! On the other hand, if they had invested in Treasury bills, the investment would have been worth only $2042.

---

[1] Based on Moody's AAA Corporate Bond Index.

FIGURE 11.1

Value of $100 Invested at the End of 1925 in Small Stocks, U.S. Large Stocks (S&P 500), World Portfolio, Corporate Bonds, and Treasury Bills

Note that the investments that performed the best in the long run also had the greatest fluctuations from year to year. The change in the Consumer Price Index (CPI) is shown as a reference point.

Source: Global Financial Data.

For comparison, consider how prices have changed during the same period based on the Consumer Price Index (CPI), the bottom line in Figure 11.1. From 1925–2012, small stocks in the United States experienced the highest long-term return, followed by the large stocks in the S&P 500, the international stocks in the world portfolio, corporate bonds, and finally Treasury bills. All of the investments grew faster than inflation (as measured by the CPI).

There is a second pattern evident in Figure 11.1. While the small-stock portfolio performed the best in the long run, its value also experienced the largest fluctuations. For example, investors in small stocks had the largest loss during the Depression era of the 1930s. To illustrate, suppose that in 1925 your great-grandparents put the $100 in a small-stock portfolio intended for their own retirement 15 years later in 1940. They would have had only $144 with which to retire, compared with $217 from an investment in corporate bonds. Moreover, during the 15-year period, they would have seen the value of their investment drop as low as $15. Yet if they had invested in Treasury bills, they would not have experienced any losses during the Depression period, but would have enjoyed steady—though modest—gains each year. Indeed, when ranking the investments by the size of their increases and decreases in value, we have the same ranking as before: small stocks had the most variable returns, followed by the S&P 500, the world portfolio, corporate bonds, and finally Treasury bills.

Investors are averse to fluctuations in the value of their investments, so they demand that riskier investments have higher expected returns. But even more importantly, when times are bad, investors do not like to have their problems exacerbated by experiencing losses on their investments. In fact, even if your great-grandparents had actually put the $100 into a small-stock portfolio in 1925, it is unlikely you would have received the proceeds. More likely, in the depths of the Great Depression your great-grandparents would have turned to their investments to supplement their income. Table 11.1 presents the first 10 years of returns that correspond to several of the investments in Figure 11.1. Negative returns (losses) are in red. Notice the string of large, negative returns from 1929–1931 for small stocks. Unfortunately, your great-grandparents' small-stock portfolio would have been of little help to them in the Great Depression—in June 1932 their original $100 investment would have been worth only $15. With the benefit of 85 years of hindsight, the small-stock portfolio looks like a great investment, but in 1932 it would have seemed like a huge mistake. Perhaps this is the reason your great-grandparents did not actually invest money for you in small stocks. The pleasure of knowing that their great-grandchild might one day be a millionaire does not really make up for the pain of the investment going bust at precisely the time that the money is needed for other things.

TABLE 11.1

Realized Returns, in Percent (%) for Small Stocks, the S&P 500, Corporate Bonds, and Treasury Bills, 1926–1935

Year	Small Stocks	S&P 500	Corp Bonds	Treasury Bills
1926	7.20	11.14	6.29	3.19
1927	25.75	37.13	6.55	3.12
1928	46.87	43.31	3.38	3.82
1929	50.47	8.91	4.32	4.74
1930	45.58	25.26	6.34	2.35
1931	50.22	43.86	2.38	1.02
1932	8.70	8.86	12.20	0.81
1933	187.20	52.89	5.26	0.29
1934	25.21	2.34	9.73	0.15
1935	64.74	47.21	6.86	0.17

Source: Global Financial Data.

We have established the general principle that investors do not like risk and therefore demand a risk premium to bear it. Our goal in this chapter is to further understand that because investors can eliminate some risk by holding large portfolios of stocks, not all risk is entitled to a risk premium. To show this, we must first develop tools that will allow us to measure risk and return.

Concept Check

1. Historically, which types of investments have had the highest average returns and which have been the most volatile from year to year? Is there a relation?

2. Why do investors demand a higher return when investing in riskier securities?

11.2 Historical Risks and Returns of Stocks

In this section, we explain how to compute average returns and a measure of risk, or volatility, using historical stock market data. The distribution of past returns can be useful in estimating the possible future returns for investors. We start by explaining how to compute historical returns.

Computing Historical Returns

realized return The total
return that occurs over a
particular time period.

We begin with *realized returns* for an individual investment and a portfolio. The **realized return** is the total return that occurs over a particular time period.

Individual Investment Realized Return. Suppose you invested $10 in a stock a month ago. Today, it paid a dividend of $0.50 and you then sold it for $11. What was your return? Your return came from two sources: the dividend and the change in price. You earned $0.50 on your $10 investment through the dividend, for a return of $0.50/$10 = 5%, and you earned $1 from the increase in price, for a return of $1/$10 or 10%. Your total return was 15%:

$$\text{Return} = \frac{\$0.50}{\$10} + \frac{(\$11 - \$10)}{\$10} = 5\% + 10\% = 15\%$$

In general, assume you buy a stock on date t for price P_t. If the stock pays a dividend, Div_{t+1}, on date $t + 1$, and you sell the stock at that time for price P_{t+1}, then the timeline of your cash flows for the stock looks like this:

The realized return from your investment in the stock from t to $t + 1$ is:

$$R_{t+1} = \frac{Div_{t+1} + P_{t+1} - P_t}{P_t} = \frac{Div_{t+1}}{P_t} + \frac{P_{t+1} - P_t}{P_t}$$

$$= \text{Dividend Yield} + \text{Capital Gain Yield} \qquad (11.1)$$

Your realized return for the period from t to $t + 1$ is the total of the dividend yield and the capital gain (as a percentage of the initial price); as discussed in Chapter 7, it is also called the *total return*. For each dollar invested at date t, you will have $1 + R_{t+1}$ at date $t + 1$. We can compute the total return for any security in the same way, by replacing the dividend payments with any cash flows paid by the security (for example, with a bond, coupon payments would replace dividends).

EXAMPLE 11.1

Realized Return

MyFinanceLab

PROBLEM

Microsoft paid a one-time special dividend of $3.08 on November 15, 2004. Suppose you bought Microsoft stock for $28.08 on November 1, 2004, and sold it immediately after the dividend was paid for $27.39. What was your realized return from holding the stock?

SOLUTION

PLAN

We can use Eq. 11.1 to calculate the realized return. We need the purchase price ($28.08), the selling price ($27.39), and the dividend ($3.08) and we are ready to proceed.

EXECUTE

Using Eq. 11.1, the return from Nov 1, 2004, until Nov 15, 2004, is equal to:

$$R_{t+1} = \frac{Div_{t+1} + P_{t+1} - P_t}{P_t} = \frac{3.08 + (27.39 - 28.08)}{28.08} = 0.0851, \text{ or } 8.51\%$$

(Continued)

This 8.51% can be broken down into the dividend yield and the capital gain yield:

$$\text{Dividend Yield} = \frac{Div_{t+1}}{P_t} = \frac{3.08}{28.08} = .1097, \text{ or } 10.97\%$$

$$\text{Capital Gain Yield} = \frac{P_{t+1} - P_t}{P_t} = \frac{27.39 - 28.08}{28.08} = -0.0246, \text{ or } -2.46\%$$

EVALUATE

These returns include both the capital gain (or in this case a capital loss) and the return generated from receiving dividends. Both dividends and capital gains contribute to the total realized return—ignoring either one would give a very misleading impression of Microsoft's performance.

If you hold the stock beyond the date of the first dividend, then to compute your return we must specify how you invest any dividends you receive in the interim. To focus on the returns of a single security, we assume that *all dividends are immediately reinvested and used to purchase additional shares of the same stock or security*. In this case, we can use Eq. 11.1 to compute a stock's return between dividend payments and then compound the returns from each dividend interval to compute the return over a longer horizon. If a stock pays dividends at the end of each quarter, with realized returns $R_1, \ldots, R_4$ each quarter, then we show the four quarterly returns for this stock as:

Its annual realized return, R_{annual}, is:

$$1 + R_{\text{annual}} = (1 + R_1)(1 + R_2)(1 + R_3)(1 + R_4) \tag{11.2}$$

EXAMPLE 11.2
Compounding
Realized Returns

MyFinanceLab

PROBLEM

Suppose you purchased Microsoft stock (MSFT) on Nov 1, 2004, and held it for one year, selling on Oct 31, 2005. What was your annual realized return?

SOLUTION

PLAN

We need to analyze the cash flows from holding MSFT stock for each quarter. In order to obtain the cash flows, we must look up MSFT's stock price data at the purchase date and selling date, as well as at any dividend dates (see Chapter 7 and the book's Web site for online sources of stock price and dividend data). From the data, we can construct the following table to fill out our cash flow timeline:

Date	Price	Dividend
Nov 01 04	28.08	
Nov 15 04	27.39	3.08
Feb 15 05	25.93	0.08
May 16 05	25.49	0.08
Aug 15 05	27.13	0.08
Oct 31 05	25.70	

Next, compute the realized return between each set of dates using Eq. 11.1. Then determine the annual realized return similarly to Eq. 11.2 by compounding the returns for all of the periods in the year.

EXECUTE

In Example 11.1, we already computed the realized return for November 1, 2004, to November 15, 2004, as 8.51%. We continue as in that example, using Eq. 11.1 for each period until we have a series of realized returns. For example, from November 15, 2004, to February 15, 2005, the realized return is:

$$R_{t+1} = \frac{Div_{t+1} + P_{t+1} - P_t}{P_t} = \frac{0.08 + (25.93 - 27.39)}{27.39} = -0.0504, \text{ or } -5.04\%$$

The following table includes the realized return in each period

Date	Price	Dividend	Return
Nov 01 04	28.08		
Nov 15 04	27.39	3.08	8.51%
Feb 15 05	25.93	0.08	−5.04%
May 16 05	25.49	0.08	−1.39%
Aug 15 05	27.13	0.08	6.75%
Oct 31 05	25.70		−5.27%

We then determine the one-year return by compounding.

Note that to use the method in Eq. 11.2, we must have an investment to compound, so just as in Chapter 3, when we compounded interest, we add 1 as if we are computing the outcome of investing $1. The first return is 8.51%, giving us 1 + .0851 or 1.0851. The same is true when the return is negative: The second return is −5.04%, giving us 1 + (−.0504) or 0.9496. To compute the annual realized return, we simply subtract the initial $1, leaving only the return:

$$1 + R_{annual} = (1 + R_1)(1 + R_2)(1 + R_3)(1 + R_4)(1 + R_5)$$
$$1 + R_{annual} = (1.0851)(0.9496)(0.9861)(1.0675)(0.9473) - 1.0275$$
$$R_{annual} = 1.0275 - 1 = 0.0275 \text{ or } 2.75\%$$

EVALUATE

By repeating these steps, we have successfully computed the realized returns for an investor holding MSFT stock over this one-year period. From this exercise we can see that returns are risky. MSFT fluctuated up and down over the year and ended only slightly up (2.75%) at the end.

It is unlikely that anyone investing in Microsoft on November 1, 2004, expected to receive exactly the realized return we calculated in Example 11.2. In any given year we only observe one actual realized return from all of the possible returns that could have been realized. However, we can observe realized returns over many years. By counting the number of times the realized return falls in a particular range, we can start to graph the distribution of possible returns. Let's illustrate this process with the data in Table 11.1.

In Figure 11.2, we plot the annual returns for each U.S. investment in Table 11.1 in a histogram. In this histogram, the height of each bar represents the number of years that the annual returns were in each range indicated on the x-axis. Notice how much more variable stock returns are compared to Treasury bills.

Average Annual Returns

average annual return
The arithmetic average of an investment's realized returns for each year.

Out of the distribution of possible returns for each security depicted in Figure 11.2, we want to know the most likely return, represented by the average. The **average annual return** of an investment during some historical period is simply the average of the realized returns

FIGURE 11.2

The Distribution of
Annual Returns for U.S.
Large Company Stocks
(S&P 500), Small
Stocks, Corporate
Bonds, and Treasury
Bills, 1926–2012

The height of each bar represents the number of years that the annual returns were in each range.
For example, the bar in the T-bills chart indicates that in more than 50% of the years, the annual
return on one-month Treasury bills was between 0 and 5%. Note the greater variability of stock returns
(especially small stocks) compared to the returns of corporate bonds or Treasury bills.

for each year. That is, if R_t is the realized return of a security in each year t, then the average annual return for years 1 through T is:

Average Annual Return of a Security

$$\overline{R} = \frac{1}{T}(R_1 + R_2 + \cdots + R_T) \tag{11.3}$$

If we assume that the distribution of possible returns is the same over time, the average return provides an estimate of the return we should expect in any given year—the expected return. This idea is not unique to returns. For example, a Starbucks manager cannot know exactly how many customers she will have today, but by looking at the average number of customers who have come in historically, she can form an expectation to use in staffing and stocking.

We can use Eq. 11.3 to calculate the average return for the S&P 500 for the years 2005–2009. The returns are:

2005	2006	2007	2008	2009
4.9%	15.8%	5.5%	−37.0%	26.5%

and the average return is:

$$\frac{1}{5}\left(4.9\% + 15.8\% + 5.5\% - 37.0\% + 26.5\%\right) = 3.1\%$$

The average Treasury bill return during the same period was 2.0%. Therefore, investors earned 1.1% $(3.1\% - 2.0\%)$ more on average holding the S&P 500 than investing in Treasury bills during this period. This average is computed over just five years of data. Naturally, our estimate of the true average of the distribution is more precise the more data we use. We display the average returns for different U.S. investments from 1926–2012 in Figure 11.3.

Arithmetic Average Returns Versus Compound Annual Returns

In Figure 11.1, we saw that $100 invested in the S&P 500 at the end of 1925 would have grown to $319,287 by the end of 2012. What if we wanted to know the average compound annual return for that investment? That's the same as asking what return, earned each year for 87 years, would have caused our $100 to grow into $319,287. We know that the formula for future value tells us that:

$$FV = PV(1 + R)^n$$

Thus:

$$\$319,287 = \$100(1 + R)^{87}$$

Solving for R, we get 9.718% (rounded).

But Figure 11.3 shows that the average annual return for the S&P 500 for this period was 11.70%. How can the two answers be different?

The difference is due to the fact that returns are volatile. To see the effect of volatility, suppose an investment has annual returns of +20% one year and −20% the next. The average annual return is:

$$\frac{20\% + (-20\%)}{2} = 0\%$$

But the value of $1 invested after two years is:

$$\$1 \times (1 + 0.20) \times (1 - 0.20) = \$0.96$$

This tells us that an investor would have lost money. Why? Because the 20% gain happens on a $1 investment for a total of 20 cents, whereas the 20% loss happens on a larger investment of $1.20. The loss is 20% of $1.20, or 24 cents.

$1.20
+20%($1) = +$0.20   −20%($1.20) = −$0.24
$1.00
$0.96

In this case, the compound annual return is

$$\$0.96 = \$1(1 + R)^2$$

so solving for R:

$$R = (0.96)^{1/2} - 1 = -2\%$$

We calculated the 11.70% average for the S&P 500 as a simple arithmetic average of the realized returns, while we calculated 9.7% as the average annual compound return that corresponds to the total gain on our $100 investment (called the *geometric average*).

Which is a better description of an investment's return? The compound annual return is a better description of the long-term *historical performance* of an investment. It describes the average annual compound return for that particular history of returns. The ranking of the long-term performance of different investments coincides with the ranking of their compound annual returns. Thus, the compound annual return is the return that is most often used for comparison purposes. For example, mutual funds generally report their compound annual returns over the last five or ten years.

On the other hand, the arithmetic average return should be used when trying to estimate an investment's *expected* return over a *future* horizon based on its past performance. If we view past annual returns as independent realizations of actual returns from the same set of possible returns, then we know from statistics that the arithmetic average provides the best estimate of the true mean. If the investment above is equally likely to have annual returns of +20% and −20% in the future, then the payoff from a $1 investment after two years will be:

25% of the time: $1 × (1.20) × (1.20) = $1.44
50% of the time: $1 × (1.20) × (0.80)
$$= (0.80) \times (1.20) = \$0.96$$
25% of the time: $1 × (0.80) × (0.80) = $0.64

The expected payoff is

$$25\%\,(1.44) + 50\%\,(0.96) + 25\%\,(0.64) = \$1$$

which is consistent with the arithmetic average return of 0%.

FIGURE 11.3

Average Annual
Returns of U.S. Small
Stocks, Large Stocks
(S&P 500), Corporate
Bonds, and Treasury
Bills, 1926–2012

Each bar represents an investment's average return.

The Variance and Volatility of Returns

Looking at Figure 11.2, we can see that the variability of the returns is very different for each investment. The distribution of small stocks' returns is the most widely dispersed—if you had invested in these stocks, you would have lost more than 50% in some years and gained more than 100% in some years! The large company stocks in the S&P 500 have returns that vary less than small company stocks, but much more than corporate bonds or Treasury bills. While we can see these differences in variability in the chart, we need a way to formally quantify them. To determine the variability of returns, we calculate the *standard deviation* of the distribution of realized returns. The **standard deviation** is the square root of the *variance* of the distribution of realized returns. **Variance** measures the variability in returns by taking the differences of the returns from the average return and squaring those differences. We have to square the difference of each return from the average because, by definition, the unsquared differences from an average must sum to zero. Because we square the returns, the variance is in units of "%^{2}" or percent-squared. That is not very useful to us, so we take the square root, to get the standard deviation, in units of %.

While that sounds a bit abstract, standard deviation simply indicates the tendency of the historical returns to be different from their average and how far from the average they tend to be. Standard deviation therefore captures our intuition of risk: How often will we miss the mark and how far off will we be? Formally, we calculate the variance with the following equation:[2]

standard deviation A common method used to measure the risk of a probability distribution; it is the square root of the variance.

variance A method to measure the variability of returns; it is the expected squared deviation of returns from the mean.

Variance Estimate Using Realized Returns

$$Var(R) = \frac{1}{T-1}\left[(R_1 - \bar{R})^2 + (R_2 - \bar{R})^2 + \cdots + (R_T - \bar{R})^2 \right] \qquad (11.4)$$

[2]You may wonder why we divide by $T - 1$ rather than T here. The reason is that we are not computing deviations from the true expected return; instead, we are computing deviations from the estimated average return $\bar{R}$. Because the average return is derived from the same data, we lose a degree of freedom (in essence, we have used up one of the data points), so that when computing the variance there are really only $T - 1$ additional data points on which to base it.

The standard deviation, which we will call the *volatility*, is the square root of the variance:[3]

$$SD(R) = \sqrt{Var(R)} \tag{11.5}$$

EXAMPLE 11.3

Computing Historical Volatility

MyFinanceLab

PROBLEM

Using the following data, what is the standard deviation of the S&P 500's returns for the years 2005–2009?

2005	2006	2007	2008	2009
4.9%	15.8%	5.5%	−37.0%	26.5%

SOLUTION

PLAN

With the five returns, compute the average return using Eq. 11.3 because it is an input to the variance equation. Next, compute the variance using Eq. 11.4 and then take its square root to determine the standard deviation, as shown in Eq. 11.5.

EXECUTE

In the previous section we computed the average annual return of the S&P 500 during this period as 3.1%, so we have all of the necessary inputs for the variance calculation:

Applying Eq.11.4, we have:

$$Var(R) = \frac{1}{T-1}[(R_1 - \bar{R})^2 + (R_2 - \bar{R})^2 + \ldots + (R_T - \bar{R})^2]$$

$$= \frac{1}{5-1}[(.049 - .031)^2 + (.158 - .031)^2 + (.055 - .031)^2$$

$$+ (-.370 - .031)^2 + (.265 - .031)^2]$$

$$= .058$$

Alternatively, we can break out the calculation of this equation as follows:

	2005	2006	2007	2008	2009
Return	0.049	0.158	0.055	−0.370	0.265
Average	0.031	0.031	0.031	0.031	0.031
Difference	0.018	0.127	0.024	−0.401	0.234
Squared	0.000	0.016	0.001	0.161	0.055

Summing the squared differences in the last row, we get 0.233.

Finally, dividing by $(5 - 1 = 4)$ gives us 0.233/4 = 0.058. The standard deviation is therefore:

$$SD(R) = \sqrt{Var(R)} = \sqrt{.058} = 0.241, \text{ or } 24.1\%$$

EVALUATE

Our best estimate of the expected return for the S&P 500 is its average return, 3.1%, but it is risky, with a standard deviation of 24.1%.

---

[3]If the returns used in Eq. 11.4 are not annual returns, it is conventional to convert the variance to annual terms by multiplying the number of returns per year. Thus, when using monthly returns, we multiply the variance by 12, and equivalently, the standard deviation by $\sqrt{12}$.

COMMON MISTAKE | **Mistakes When Computing Standard Deviation**

Example 11.3 highlights two missteps often made in computing standard deviations.

1. Remember to divide by ONE LESS than the number of returns you have ($T - 1$, NOT T).

2. Don't forget to take the square root of the variance to obtain the standard deviation. You are not done when you calculate the variance—you have one more step to go.

We began our review of statistics with the goal of being able to quantify the difference in the variability of the distributions that we observed in Figure 11.2. We can now do so with the standard deviation of the returns on the U.S. investments as shown in Figure 11.4.

Comparing the standard deviations in Figure 11.4 we see that, as expected, small companies have had the most variable historical returns, followed by large companies. The returns of corporate bonds and Treasury bills are much less variable than stocks, with Treasury bills being the least volatile investment category.

USING EXCEL

Computing the Standard Deviation of Historical Returns

1. Enter or import the historical returns into Excel.

2. Next, highlight the cell where you want to produce the standard deviation and select **Function** from the **Insert** tab.

3. Select the "**STDEV**" function, highlight the returns for which you want to compute the average, and click **OK**.

4. *Make sure that you use the STDEV function and NOT the STDEVP function.* STDEV calculates the sample standard deviation as in Eqs. 11.4 and 11.5, by dividing by $T - 1$. STDEVP assumes that you know with certainty the true mean and calculates the standard deviation by dividing by T. See footnote 1 for more discussion of this important distinction.

FIGURE 11.4

Volatility (Standard Deviation) of U.S. Small Stocks, Large Stocks (S&P 500), Corporate Bonds, and Treasury Bills, 1926–2012

Each bar represents the standard deviation of the investment's returns.

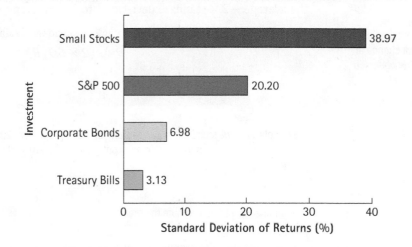

The Normal Distribution

normal distribution A symmetric probability distribution that is completely characterized by its average and standard deviation. About 95% of all possible outcomes fall within two standard deviations above and below the average.

The standard deviations that we have computed in Figure 11.4 are useful for more than just ranking the investments from most to least risky. The standard deviation also plays an important role in describing a **normal distribution**, shown in Figure 11.5, which is a symmetric probability distribution that is completely characterized by its average and standard deviation. Importantly, about two-thirds of all possible outcomes fall within one standard deviation above or below the average, and about 95% of all possible outcomes fall within two standard deviations above and below the average. Figure 11.5 shows these outcomes for small company stocks.

FIGURE 11.5

Normal Distribution

The height of the line reflects the likelihood of each return occurring. Using the data from Figures 11.3 and 11.4, if the returns of small companies are normally distributed, then about two-thirds of all possible outcomes should lie within one standard deviation of the average return of 18.74% (given in Figure 11.3) and about 95% should lie within two standard deviations. Figure 11.4 shows the standard deviation to be 38.97%, so that puts 95% of possible outcomes between −59.21% and +96.68% (the shaded area of the distribution).

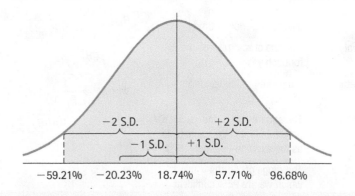

prediction interval A range of values that is likely to include a future observation. A 95% prediction interval should have a 95% chance of including the observed future observation.

Because about 95% of the time, next year's return will be within two standard deviations of the average, we say that the 95% **prediction interval** runs from [the average − 2 × standard deviation] to [the average + 2 × standard deviation]:

$$\text{Average} \pm (2 \times \text{standard deviation})$$
$$\overline{R} \pm (2 \times SD(R)) \tag{11.6}$$

EXAMPLE 11.4
Prediction Intervals

MyFinanceLab

PROBLEM

In Example 11.3, we found the average return for the S&P 500 from 2005 to 2009 to be 3.1% with a standard deviation of 24.1%. What is a 95% prediction interval for 2010's return?

SOLUTION

PLAN

We can use Eq. 11.6 to compute the prediction interval.

EXECUTE

Using Eq. 11.6, we have:

$$\text{Average} \pm (2 \times \text{standard deviation}) = 3.1\% - (2 \times 24.1\%) \text{ to } 3.1\% + (2 \times 24.1\%)$$
$$= -45.1\% \text{ to } 51.3\%.$$

EVALUATE

Even though the average return from 2005 to 2009 was 3.1%, the S&P 500 was volatile, so if we want to be 95% confident of 2010's return, the best we can say is that it will lie between −45.1% and +51.3%.

Table 11.2 summarizes the central concepts and equations that we developed in this section. Calculating historical averages and volatilities indicates how investments performed in the past and might perform in the future. Of course, using the past to predict the future is fraught with uncertainty. In the next section, we will discuss that uncertainty.

TABLE 11.2

Summary of Tools for Working with Historical Returns

Concept	Definition	Formula
Realized Returns	Total return earned over a particular period of time	$R_{t+1} = \dfrac{Div_{t+1} + P_{t+1} - P_t}{P_t}$
Average Annual Return	Average of realized returns for each year	$\overline{R} = \dfrac{1}{T}(R_1 + R_2 + \ldots + R_T)$
Variance of Returns	A measure of the variability of returns	$Var(R) = \dfrac{1}{T-1}[(R_1 - \overline{R})^2 + (R_2 - \overline{R})^2 + \ldots + (R_T - \overline{R})^2]$
Standard Deviation or Volatility of Returns	The square root of the variance (which puts it in the same units as the average—namely "%")	$SD(R) = \sqrt{Var(R)}$
95% Prediction Interval	The range of returns within which we are 95% confident that next period's return will lie	$\overline{R} \pm 2 \times SD(R)$

Concept
Check

3. For what purpose do we use the average and standard deviation of historical stock returns?

4. How does the standard deviation of historical returns affect our confidence in predicting the next period's return?

11.3 The Historical Tradeoff Between Risk and Return

Would you intentionally choose to accept additional risk without additional reward? In other words, are you willing to pursue riskier investments if they do not have the potential to generate higher returns? The answer to both of these questions is most likely "no." In this section, we will examine the historical tradeoff between risk (as measured by price volatility) and reward (as measured by returns) to see if historically investors behaved as you would.

The Returns of Large Portfolios

In Figures 11.3 and 11.4, we showed the historical average returns and volatilities for a number of different types of investments. In Figure 11.6, we plot the average return versus the volatility of each type of investment from those tables. We also include the world portfolio from Figure 11.1. Note that the investments with higher volatility, measured here with standard deviation, have rewarded investors with higher average returns. Figure 11.6 is consistent with our view that investors are risk averse. Riskier investments must offer investors higher average returns to compensate for the risk they are taking.

FIGURE 11.6

The Historical
Tradeoff Between
Risk and Return in
Large Portfolios,
1926–2011

Using quarterly data from 1926–2011, this figure graphs the relation between risk and return for 500 individual stocks, Treasury bills, corporate bonds, the S&P 500, and the small stock portfolio, as well as a world portfolio of large company stocks from North America, Europe, and Asia. Note the general increasing relationship between historical volatility (standard deviation) and average return for these large portfolios. However, note that there is no clear relation between the risk and return of individual stocks.

Source: Global Financial Data and authors' calculations.

The Returns of Individual Stocks

Figure 11.6 suggests the following simple model of the risk premium: Investments with higher volatility should have a higher risk premium and therefore higher returns. Indeed, looking at Figure 11.6 it is tempting to draw a line through the portfolios and conclude that all investments should lie on or near this line—that is, expected return should rise proportionately with volatility. This conclusion appears to be approximately true for the large portfolios we have looked at so far. Is it correct? Does it apply to individual stocks?

Actually, the answer to both questions is no. There is no clear relationship between volatility and returns for individual stocks. Although it will take more work to establish the relation between risk and return for individual stocks, the following is true:

1. There is a relationship between size and risk—on average larger stocks have lower volatility than smaller stocks.

2. Even the largest stocks are typically more volatile than a portfolio of large stocks, such as the S&P 500.

3. All individual stocks have lower returns and/or higher risk than the portfolios in Figure 11.6.

Thus, while volatility (standard deviation) seems to be a reasonable measure of risk when evaluating a large portfolio, the volatility of an individual security doesn't explain the size of its average return. What are we to make of this? Why wouldn't investors demand a higher return from stocks with a higher volatility? And how is it that the S&P 500, a portfolio of 500 large stocks, is so much less risky than almost all of the 500 stocks individually? To answer these questions, we need to think more carefully about how to measure risk for an investor.

Concept Check

5. What is the relation between risk and return for large portfolios? How are individual stocks different?

6. Do portfolios or the stocks in the portfolios tend to have the lower volatility?

11.4 Common Versus Independent Risk

In this section, we explain why the risk of an individual security differs from the risk of a portfolio composed of similar securities. We begin with an example from the insurance industry to understand how the portfolio of insurance products performs for the insurance company offering them.

Theft Versus Earthquake Insurance: An Example

Consider two types of home insurance an insurance company might offer: theft insurance and earthquake insurance. Let's assume, for the purpose of illustration, that the risk of each of these two hazards is similar for a given home in the San Francisco area—each year there is about a 1% chance the home will be robbed and also a 1% chance that the home will be damaged by an earthquake. In this case, the chance the insurance company will pay a claim for a single home is the same for the two types of insurance policies. Suppose an insurance company writes 100,000 policies of each type for homeowners in San Francisco. We know the risks of the individual policies are similar, but are the risks of the portfolios of 100,000 policies similar?

First consider theft insurance. Because the chance of a theft for any given home is 1%, we would expect about 1% of the 100,000 homes to experience a robbery. Thus, the number of theft claims will be about 1000 per year. The actual number of claims may be a bit higher or lower each year, but not by much. In this case, if the insurance company holds reserves sufficient to cover 1200 claims, it will almost certainly have enough to cover its obligations on its theft insurance policies.

Now consider earthquake insurance. There is a 99% chance that an earthquake will not occur. All the homes are in the same city, so if an earthquake does occur, all homes are likely to be affected and the insurance company can expect 100,000 claims. As a result, the insurance company can expect either 0 claims or 100,000 claims. Because it may have 100,000 claims, it will have to hold reserves of cash (or other investments) sufficient to cover claims on all 100,000 policies it wrote in order to meet its obligations if an earthquake occurs.

Thus, earthquake and theft insurance lead to portfolios with very different risk characteristics. For earthquake insurance, the percentage of claims is very risky—it will most likely be 0, but there is a 1% chance that the insurance company will have to pay claims on *all* the policies it wrote. So the risk of the portfolio of earthquake insurance policies is no different from the risk of any single policy. On the other hand, we've seen that for theft insurance the number of claims in a given year is quite predictable. Year in and year out, it will be very close to 1% of the total number of policies, or 1000 claims. The portfolio of theft insurance policies has almost no risk! That is, the insurance company's payouts are quite stable and predictable over time.

Types of Risk

common risk Risk that is linked across outcomes.

independent risk Risks that bear no relation to each other. If risks are independent, then knowing the outcome of one provides no information about the other.

diversification The averaging of independent risks in a large portfolio.

Why are the portfolios of insurance policies so different when the individual policies themselves are quite similar? Intuitively, the key difference between them is that an earthquake affects all houses simultaneously, and so the risk is linked across homes, meaning either all homes are damaged or all homes are not damaged. We call risk that is linked in this way **common risk**. In contrast, we have assumed that thefts in different houses are not related to each other—whether one house is burglarized has no effect on another house's chance of being burglarized. **Independent risk**, such as the risk of theft, is not linked across homes. When risks are independent, some individual homeowners are unlucky, others are lucky, but overall the number of claims is similar. The averaging out of risks in a large portfolio is called **diversification**.[4] Table 11.3 summarizes our discussion of common and independent risk.

The principle of diversification is used routinely in the insurance industry. In addition to theft insurance, many other forms of insurance (life, health, auto) rely on the fact that the number of claims is relatively predictable in a large portfolio. Even in the case of earthquake insurance, insurers can achieve some diversification by selling policies in different geographical regions, or by combining different types of policies. Diversification is used to reduce risk in many other settings. For example, many systems are designed with redundancy to decrease the risk of a disruption. For example, firms often add redundancy to critical parts of the manufacturing process: NASA puts more than one antenna on its space probes, and automobiles contain spare tires.

TABLE 11.3

Summary of Types of Risk

Type of Risk	Definition	Example	Risk Diversified in Large Portfolio?
Common Risk	Linked across outcomes	Risk of earthquake	No
Independent Risk	Risks that bear no relation to each other	Risk of theft	Yes

[4]Harry Markowitz was the first to formalize the benefits from diversification. See Markowitz, H. M., "Portfolio Selection," *Journal of Finance* 7(1) (1952): 77–91.

In many settings, the risks lie somewhere between the common risks and independent risks. For example, you probably applied to more than one college. Your chances of being accepted (or rejected) at any one school are not perfectly linked across schools because schools have different admissions criteria and are looking for different types of students. However, your risk of rejection is not completely independent, either; all schools look at your high school grades and SAT/ACT scores, so their decisions will be related.

EXAMPLE 11.5

Diversification

MyFinanceLab

PROBLEM

You are playing a very simple gambling game with your friend: a $1 bet based on a coin flip. That is, you each bet $1 and flip a coin: heads you win your friend's $1, tails you lose and your friend takes your dollar. How is your risk different if you play this game 100 times versus just betting $100 (instead of $1) on a single coin flip?

SOLUTION

PLAN

The risk of losing one coin flip is independent of the risk of losing the next one: Each time you have a 50% chance of losing, and one coin flip does not affect any other coin flip. We can compute the expected outcome of any flip as a weighted average by weighting your possible winnings ($+\$1$) by 50% and your possible losses ($-\$1$) by 50%. We can then compute the probability of losing all $100 under either scenario.

EXECUTE

If you play the game 100 times, you should lose 50 times and win 50 times, so your expected outcome is $50 \times (+\$1) + 50 \times (-\$1) = \$0$. You should break even. But even if you don't win exactly half of the time, the probability that you would lose all 100 coin flips (and thus lose $100) is exceedingly small (in fact, it is 0.50^{100}, which is far less than even 0.0001%). If it happens, you should take a very careful look at the coin!

If instead you make a single $100 bet on the outcome of one coin flip, you have a 50% chance of winning $100 and a 50% chance of losing $100, so your expected outcome will be the same: break-even. However, there is a 50% chance you will lose $100, so your risk is far greater than it would be for 100 one-dollar bets.

EVALUATE

In each case, you put $100 at risk, but by spreading out that risk across 100 different bets, you have diversified much of your risk away, compared to placing a single $100 bet.

Concept Check

7. What is the difference between common and independent risk?

8. How does diversification help with independent risk?

11.5 Diversification in Stock Portfolios

As the insurance example indicates, the risk of a portfolio depends upon whether the individual risks within it are common or independent. Independent risks are diversified in a large portfolio, whereas common risks are not. Our goal is to understand the relation between risk and return in the capital markets, so let's consider the implication of this distinction for the risk of stock portfolios.

Unsystematic Versus Systematic Risk

Over any given time period, the risk of holding a stock is that the dividends plus the final stock price will be higher or lower than expected, which makes the realized return risky.

What causes dividends or stock prices, and therefore returns, to be higher or lower than we expect? Usually, stock prices and dividends fluctuate due to two types of news:

1. *Company or industry-specific news*: This is good or bad news about a company (or industry) itself. For example, a firm might announce that it has been successful in gaining market share within its industry. Or, the home-building industry may be damaged by a real estate slowdown.

2. *Market-wide news*: This is news that affects the economy as a whole and therefore affects all stocks. For instance, the Federal Reserve might announce that it will lower interest rates in an attempt to boost the economy.

Fluctuations of a stock's return that are due to company- or industry-specific news are independent risks. Similar to theft across homes, these are unrelated across stocks. This type of risk is also referred to as **unsystematic risk**.

unsystematic risk
Fluctuations of a stock's return that are due to company- or industry-specific news and are independent risks unrelated across stocks.

On the other hand, fluctuations of a stock's return that are due to market-wide news represent common risk. As with earthquakes, all stocks are affected simultaneously. This type of risk is also called **systematic risk**.

systematic risk
Fluctuations of a stock's return that are due to market-wide news representing common risk.

When we combine many stocks in a large portfolio, the unsystematic risks for each stock will average out and be eliminated by diversification. Good news will affect some stocks and bad news will affect others, but the amount of good or bad news overall will be relatively constant. The systematic risk, however, will affect all firms—and therefore the entire portfolio—and will not be eliminated by diversification.

Let's consider a hypothetical example. Suppose type S firms are *only* affected by the systematic risk of the strength of the economy, which has a 50-50 chance of being either strong or weak. If the economy is strong, type S stocks will earn a return of 40%, and if the economy is weak, their return will be −20%. Because the risk these firms face (the strength of the economy) is systematic risk, holding a large portfolio of type S stocks will not diversify the risk. When the economy is strong, the portfolio will have the same return of 40% as each type S firm. When the economy is weak, the portfolio will also have a return of −20%.

Now consider type U firms, which are only affected by unsystematic risks. Their returns are equally likely to be 35% or −25%, based on factors specific to each firm's local market. Because these risks are firm-specific, if we hold a portfolio of many type U stocks, the risk is diversified. About half of the firms will have returns of 35%, and half will have returns of −25%. The return of the portfolio will be the average return of $50\% (0.35) + 50\% (-0.25) = .05$ or 5%, no matter whether the economy is strong or weak.

Figure 11.7 illustrates how volatility, measured by standard deviation, declines with the size of the portfolio for type S and type U firms. Type S firms have only systematic risk. Similar to earthquake insurance, the volatility of the portfolio does not change as we increase the number of firms. Type U firms have only unsystematic risk. As with theft insurance, the risk is diversified as the number of firms increases, and volatility declines. As is evident from Figure 11.7, with a large number of firms, Type U firms' risk is, essentially, completely eliminated.

Of course, actual firms are not similar to type S or type U firms. Firms are affected by both systematic, market-wide risks, as well as unsystematic risks. Figure 11.7 also shows how the volatility changes with the number of stocks in a portfolio of typical firms. *When firms carry both types of risk, only the unsystematic risk will be eliminated by diversification when we combine many firms into a portfolio. The volatility will therefore decline until only the systematic risk, which affects all firms, remains.*

This example explains one of the puzzles from Section 11.3. There we saw that the S&P 500 had much lower volatility than any of the individual stocks. Now we can see why—the individual stocks each contain unsystematic risk, which is eliminated when we combine

FIGURE 11.7

Volatility of
Portfolios of Type S
and Type U Stocks

Because type S firms have only systematic risk, the volatility of the portfolio does not change. Type U firms have only unsystematic risk, which is diversified and eliminated as the number of firms in the portfolio grows. Typical stocks carry a mix of both types of risk, so that the risk of the portfolio declines as unsystematic risk is diversified, but systematic risk remains.

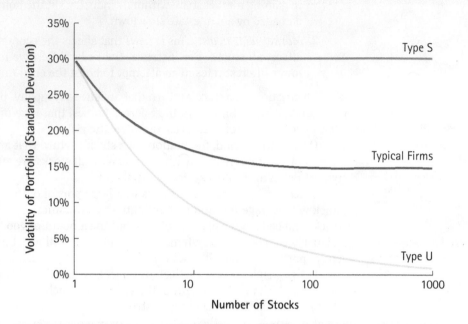

them into a large portfolio. Thus, the portfolio can have lower volatility than each of the stocks within it. Figure 11.8 illustrates this fact. The dotted lines show the extremes of the range of returns of a portfolio of Yahoo! and Consolidated Edison. The returns of each of the two stocks in the portfolio cross at least one of these extremes. Thus, the volatility of the portfolio is lower than the volatility of both of the stocks in the portfolio.

Diversifiable Risk and the Risk Premium

What if you hold only one or two stocks—wouldn't you be exposed to unsystematic risk and demand a premium for it? If the market compensated you with an additional risk premium for choosing to bear diversifiable risk, then other investors could buy the same stocks, earn the additional premium, while putting them in a portfolio so that they could diversify and eliminate the unsystematic risk. By doing so, investors could earn an additional premium without taking additional risk!

This opportunity to earn something for nothing is an arbitrage opportunity as we discussed in Chapter 3, and so it is something investors would find very attractive. As more and more investors take advantage of this situation and purchase shares that pay a risk premium for diversifiable, unsystematic risk, the current share price of those firms would rise, lowering their expected return—recall that the current share price P_t is the denominator when computing the stock's return as in Eq. 11.1. This trading would stop only when the risk premium for diversifiable risk dropped to zero. Competition among investors ensures that no additional return can be earned for diversifiable risk. The result is that

The risk premium of a stock is not affected by its diversifiable, unsystematic risk.

This argument is essentially an application of the Valuation Principle's Law of One Price. Imagine a large portfolio of type U firms, which have no systematic risk. As depicted in Figure 11.7, a large portfolio of type U firms eliminates all unsystematic risk, leaving no

FIGURE 11.8

The Effect of
Diversification on
Portfolio Volatility

While Hasbro and Nike are each very volatile, some of their movements offset each other. If they are in a portfolio together, as represented by the green bars, the total movement of the portfolio is muted relative to the movement of either of the individual stocks. The dotted line shows the lowest return of the portfolio—note that the portfolio's worst return is better than the worst return of either stock on its own.

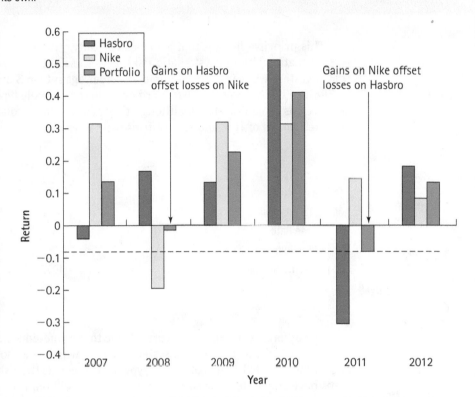

additional risk. Since that portfolio has no risk, it cannot earn a risk premium and instead must earn the risk-free interest rate. This line of reasoning suggests the following more general principle:

> *The risk premium for diversifiable risk is zero. Thus, investors are not compensated for holding unsystematic risk.*

The Importance of Systematic Risk

Because investors can eliminate unsystematic risk "for free" by diversifying their portfolios, they will not require (nor deserve) a reward or risk premium for bearing it. On the other hand, diversification does not reduce systematic risk: Even when holding a large portfolio, an investor will be exposed to risks that affect the entire economy and therefore affect all securities. We can reduce the systematic risk of a portfolio by selling stocks and investing in risk-free bonds, but at the cost of giving up the higher expected return of stocks. Because unsystematic risk can be eliminated for free by diversifying, whereas systematic risk can only be eliminated by sacrificing expected returns, it is a security's systematic risk that determines the risk premium investors require to hold it. This fact, summarized in Table 11.4, leads to the second key principle:

> *The risk premium of a security is determined by its systematic risk and does not depend on its diversifiable risk.*

TABLE 11.4

Systematic Risk Versus
Unsystematic Risk

	Diversifiable?	Requires a Risk Premium?
Systematic Risk	No	Yes
Unsystematic Risk	Yes	No

This principle implies that a stock's volatility, which is a measure of total risk (that is, systematic risk + unsystematic risk), is not useful in determining the risk premium that investors will earn. For example, consider again type S and type U firms. As shown in Figure 11.7, the volatility (standard deviation) of a single type S or type U firm is 30%. However, as Table 11.5 shows, although they have the same volatility, type S firms have an expected return of 10% and type U firms have an expected return of 5%.

TABLE 11.5

The Expected Return
of Type S and Type U
Firms, Assuming the
Risk-Free Rate Is 5%

	S Firm	U Firm
Volatility (standard deviation)	30%	30%
Risk-Free Rate	5%	5%
Risk Premium	5%	0%
Expected Return	10%	5%

The difference in expected returns is due to the difference in the kind of risk each firm bears. Type U firms have only unsystematic risk, which does not require a risk premium, and so the expected return of 5% for type U firms equals the risk-free interest rate. Type S firms have only systematic risk. Because investors will require compensation for this risk, the expected return of 10% for type S firms provides investors with a 5% risk premium above the risk-free interest rate.

We now have an explanation for the second puzzle from Section 11.3. While volatility or standard deviation might be a reasonable measure of risk for a large portfolio, it is not appropriate for an individual security.

Thus, there is no relationship between volatility and average returns for individual securities.

Consequently, to estimate a security's expected return we need to find a measure of a security's systematic risk.

We began this chapter by showing in Figure 11.1 that your great-grandparents' investment in small stocks would have lost a lot of money in the Depression, potentially leaving them in dire straits. Thus, risk-averse investors will demand a premium to invest in securities that will do poorly in bad times. This idea coincides with the notion of systematic risk we have defined in this chapter. Economy-wide risk, the risk of recessions and booms, is systematic risk that cannot be diversified. Therefore, an asset that moves with the economy contains systematic risk and so requires a risk premium. In Chapter 12, we will discuss how to measure an investment's systematic risk and then use that measure to compute its expected return. We can then apply that return expected by investors as our cost of capital.

COMMON MISTAKE — A Fallacy of Long-Run Diversification

We have seen that investors can greatly reduce risk by dividing their investment dollars over many different investments, eliminating the diversifiable risk in their portfolios. It is sometimes argued that the same logic applies over time: By investing for many years, we can also diversify the risk we face during any particular year. Thus, young investors should choose risky portfolios because they have more time to make up their losses. Is this correct? In the long run, does risk still matter?

It is true that if returns each year are independent, the volatility of the average annual return does decline with the number of years that we invest. But, as long-term investors, we don't care about the volatility of our *average* return; instead we care about the volatility of our *cumulative* return over the period. This volatility grows with the investment horizon, as illustrated in the following example.

In 1925, large U.S. stocks increased in value by about 30%. So, a $77 investment at the start of 1925 would have grown to $77 × 1.30 = $100 by the end of the year. We see from Figure 11.1 that if that $100 were invested in the S&P 500 from 1926 onward, it would have grown to about $319,287 by the start of 2013. But suppose instead that mining and transportation strikes had caused stocks to drop by 35% in 1925. Then the initial $77

invested would only be worth $77 × (1 − 0.35) = $50 at the start of 1926. If returns from then on were unchanged, the investment would be worth half as much in 2013, or $159,643.50.

Thus, if future returns are not affected by today's return, then an increase or decline in the value of our portfolio today will translate into the same percentage increase or decrease in the value of our portfolio in the future, and so there is no diversification over time. The only way the length of the time horizon can reduce risk is if a below-average return this year implies that returns are more likely to be above average in the future (and vice versa). If this were true, past low returns can be used to predict future high returns in the stock market.

For short horizons of a few years, there is no evidence of this predictability in the stock market. For longer horizons, there is some evidence of this historically, but it is not clear how reliable this evidence is (there are not enough decades of accurate stock market data available) or whether the pattern will continue. But even if there is long-run reversal in stock returns, a buy-and-hold diversification strategy is still not optimal: If past returns can be used to predict future returns, it is optimal to invest more in stocks when returns are predicted to be high, and less when they are predicted to be low. Note that this strategy is very different from the diversification we achieve by holding many stocks, where we cannot predict which stocks will have good or bad unsystematic shocks.

Concept Check

9. Why is the risk of a portfolio usually less than the average risk of the stocks in the portfolio?

10. Does systematic or unsystematic risk require a risk premium? Why?

MyFinanceLab

Here is what you should know after reading this chapter. MyFinanceLab will help you identify what you know, and where to go when you need to practice.

Key Points and Equations	Key Terms	Online Practice
11.1 A First Look at Risk and Return • While in hindsight some investments have had very high returns, they have also had the most volatility over time.		MyFinanceLab Study Plan 11.1
11.2 Historical Risks and Returns of Stocks • The realized return from investing in a stock from time t to $t+1$ is: $$R_{t+1} = \frac{Div_{t+1} + P_{t+1} - P_t}{P_t} = \frac{Div_{t+1}}{P_t} + \frac{P_{t+1} - P_t}{P_t}$$ $$= \text{Dividend Yield} + \text{Capital Gain Yield} \quad (11.1)$$	average annual return, p. 339 normal distribution, p. 345 prediction interval, p. 346 realized return, p. 337 standard deviation, p. 342 variance, p. 342	MyFinanceLab Study Plan 11.2 Using Excel: Standard Deviation of Historical Returns

- We can calculate the average annual return and variance of realized returns:

$$\bar{R} = \frac{1}{T}(R_1 + R_2 + \ldots + R_T) \qquad (11.3)$$

$$Var(R) = \frac{1}{T-1}\big[(R_1 - \bar{R})^2 + (R_2 - \bar{R})^2$$
$$+ \ldots + (R_T - \bar{R})^2\big] \qquad (11.4)$$

- The square root of the estimated variance is the standard deviation, an estimate of the volatility of returns.
- Based on historical data, small stocks have had higher volatility and higher average returns than large stocks, which have higher volatility and higher average returns than bonds.
- About 95% of possible outcomes lie within two standard deviations above or below the average outcome.

11.3 The Historical Tradeoff Between Risk and Return

- There is no clear relationship between the volatility (standard deviation) and return of individual stocks.
- Larger stocks tend to have lower overall volatility, but even the largest stocks are typically more risky than a portfolio of large stocks.
- All stocks seem to have higher risk and lower returns than would be predicted based on extrapolation of data for large portfolios.

MyFinanceLab
Study Plan 11.3

11.4 Common Versus Independent Risk

- Common risk is risk that is perfectly linked across investments.
- Independent risks are unrelated across investments.
- Diversification is the averaging of risks in a large portfolio.

common risk, p. 349
diversification, p. 349
independent risk,
    p. 349

MyFinanceLab
Study Plan 11.4

11.5 Diversification in Stock Portfolios

- The total risk of a security represents both unsystematic risk and systematic risk.
- Variation in a stock's return due to industry-specific or a firm's news is called unsystematic risk.
- Systematic risk is risk due to market-wide news that affects all stocks simultaneously.
- Diversification eliminates unsystematic risk but does not eliminate systematic risk.
- Because investors can eliminate unsystematic risk, they do not require a risk premium for it.
- Because investors cannot eliminate systematic risk, they must be compensated for it. So, the risk premium for a stock depends upon the amount of its systematic risk rather than its total risk.

systematic risk, p. 351
unsystematic risk,
    p. 351

MyFinanceLab
Study Plan 11.5

Interactive Risk
and Portfolio
Diversification
Analysis

CRITICAL THINKING

1. What does the historical relation between volatility and return tell us about investors' attitude toward risk?

2. What are the components of a stock's realized return?

3. What is the intuition behind using the average annual return as a measure of expected return?

4. How does standard deviation relate to the general concept of risk?

5. How does the relationship between the average return and the historical volatility of individual stocks differ from the relationship between the average return and the historical volatility of large, well-diversified, portfolios?

6. Consider two local banks. Bank A has 100 loans outstanding, each for $1 million, that it expects will be repaid today. Each loan has a 5% probability of default, in which case the bank is not repaid anything. The chance of default is independent across all the loans. Bank B has only one loan of $100 million outstanding that it also expects will be repaid today. It also has a 5% probability of not being repaid. Explain the difference between the type of risk each bank faces. Assuming you are averse to risk, which bank would you prefer to own?

7. What is meant by diversification and how does it relate to common versus independent risk?

8. Which of the following risks of a stock are likely to be unsystematic, diversifiable risks and which are likely to be systematic risks? Which risks will affect the risk premium that investors will demand?
   a. The risk that the founder and CEO retires
   b. The risk that oil prices rise, increasing production costs
   c. The risk that a product design is faulty and the product must be recalled
   d. The risk that the economy slows, reducing demand for the firm's products
   e. The risk that your best employees will be hired away
   f. The risk that the new product you expect your R&D division to produce will not materialize

9. What is the difference between systematic and unsystematic risk?

10. There are three companies working on a new approach to customer-tracking software. You work for a software company that thinks this could be a good addition to its software line. If you invest in one of them versus all three of them:
   a. Is your systematic risk likely to be very different?
   b. Is your unsystematic risk likely to be very different?

11. If you randomly select 10 stocks for a portfolio and 20 other stocks for a different portfolio, which portfolio is likely to have the lower standard deviation? Why?

12. Why doesn't the risk premium of a stock depend on its diversifiable risk?

13. Your spouse works for Southwest Airlines and you work for a grocery store. Is your company or your spouse's company likely to be more exposed to systematic risk?

PROBLEMS

*All problems in this chapter are available in MyFinanceLab. An asterisk * indicates problems with a higher level of difficulty.*

Historical Risks and Returns of Stocks

1. You bought a stock one year ago for $50 per share and sold it today for $55 per share. It paid a $1 per share dividend today. What was your realized return?

2. How much of the return in Problem 1 came from dividend yield and how much came from capital gain?

3. Repeat Problems 1 and 2 assuming instead that the stock fell $5 to $45.
   a. Is your capital gain different? Why or why not?
   b. Is your dividend yield different? Why or why not?

4. Your portfolio consists of 100 shares of CSH and 50 shares of EJH, which you just bought at $20 and $30 per share, respectively.
   a. What fraction of your portfolio is invested in CSH? In EJH?
   b. If CSH increases to $23 and EJH decreases to $29, what is the return on your portfolio?

5. You have just purchased a share of stock for $20. The company is expected to pay a dividend of $0.50 per share in exactly one year. If you want to earn a 10% return on your investment, what price do you need if you expect to sell the share immediately after it pays the dividend?

6. The following table contains prices and dividends for a stock. All prices are after the dividend has been paid. If you bought the stock on January 1 and sold it on December 31, what is your realized return?

	Price	Dividend
Jan 1	10.00	
Mar 31	11.00	0.20
Jun 30	10.50	0.20
Sep 30	11.10	0.20
Dec 31	11.00	0.20

7. Using the data in the following table, calculate the return for investing in Boeing stock (BA) from January 2, 2008, to January 2, 2009, and also from January 3, 2011, to January 3, 2012, assuming all dividends are reinvested in the stock immediately.

Historical Stock and Dividend Data for Boeing

Date	Price	Dividend	Date	Price	Dividend
1/2/2008	86.62		1/3/2011	66.40	
2/6/2008	79.91	0.40	2/9/2011	72.63	0.42
5/7/2008	84.55	0.40	5/11/2011	79.08	0.42
8/6/2008	65.40	0.40	8/10/2011	57.41	0.42
11/5/2008	49.55	0.40	11/8/2011	66.65	0.42
1/2/2009	45.25		1/3/2012	74.22	

8. The last four years of returns for a stock are as follows:

1	2	3	4
−4%	+28%	+12%	+4%

   a. What is the average annual return?
   b. What is the variance of the stock's returns?
   c. What is the standard deviation of the stock's returns?

9. Use the data in SBUX_GOOG.xlsx on MFL to answer the following questions:
   a. What is the return for SBUX over the period without including its dividends? With the dividends?
   b. What is the return for GOOG over the period?
   c. If you have 30% of your portfolio in SBUX and 70% in GOOG, what was the return on your portfolio?

10. Download the spreadsheet from the book's Web site containing the data for Figure 11.1.
    a. Compute the average return for each of the assets from 1929 to 1940 (the Great Depression).
    b. Compute the variance and standard deviation for each of the assets from 1929 to 1940.
    c. Which asset was riskiest during the Great Depression? How does that fit with your intuition?

11. Ten annual returns are listed in the following table.

−19.9%	16.6%	18.0%	−50.0%	43.3%	1.2%	−16.5%	45.6%	45.2%	−3.0%

   a. What is the arithmetic average return over the 10-year period?
   *b. What is the geometric average return over the 10-year period?
   c. If you invested $100 at the beginning, how much would you have at the end?

12. Using the data in the following table, calculate the return for investing in this stock from January 1 to December 31. Prices are after the dividend has been paid (*see MyFinanceLab for the data in Excel format*).

Stock and Dividend Data

Date	Price	Dividend
Jan 1	33.88	
Feb 5	30.67	0.17
May 14	29.49	0.17
Aug 13	32.38	0.17
Nov 12	39.07	0.17
Dec 31	41.99	

13. What was your dividend yield from investing in the stock in Problem 11? What was your capital gain?

14. Consider the following five monthly returns:

0.05	−0.02	0.04	0.08	−0.01

   a. Calculate the arithmetic average monthly return over this period.
   *b. Calculate the geometric average monthly return over this period.
   c. Calculate the monthly variance over this period.
   d. Calculate the monthly standard deviation over this period.

15. Explain the difference between the arithmetic average return you calculated in Problem 13a and the geometric average return you calculated in Problem 13b. Are both numbers useful? If so, explain why.

16. The last four years of returns for a stock are as follows:

1	2	3	4
−4%	+28%	+12%	+4%

    a. What is the average annual return?
    b. What is the variance of the stock's returns?
    c. What is the standard deviation of the stock's returns?

17. Calculate the 95% prediction intervals for the four different investments included in Figures 11.3 and 11.4.

18. You are choosing between the four investments from Problem 16 and you want to be 95% certain that you do not lose more than 8% on your investment. Which investments should you choose?

19. If returns of S&P 500 stocks are normally distributed, what range of returns would you expect to see 95% of the time? Base your answer on Figures 11.3 and 11.4.

20. You observe a portfolio for five years and determine that its average return is 12% and the standard deviation of its returns is 20%. Can you be 95% confident that this portfolio will not lose more than 30% of its value next year?

Common Versus Independent Risk

*21. Using the data in Critical Thinking Question 6, calculate the following:
    a. The expected overall payoff of each bank
    b. The standard deviation of the overall payoff of each bank

Diversification in Stock Portfolios

22. You are a risk-averse investor who is considering investing in one of two economies. The expected return and volatility of all stocks in both economies are the same. In the first economy, all stocks move together—in good times all prices rise together and in bad times they all fall together. In the second economy, stock returns are independent—one stock increasing in price has no effect on the prices of other stocks. Which economy would you choose to invest in? Explain.

DATA CASE

Today is July 31, 2013, and you have just started your new job with a financial planning firm. In addition to studying for all your license exams, you have been asked to review a portion of a client's stock portfolio to determine the risk/return profiles of 12 stocks in the portfolio. Unfortunately, your small firm cannot afford the expensive databases that would provide all this information with a few simple keystrokes, but that's why they hired you. Specifically, you have been asked to determine the monthly average returns and standard deviations for the 12 stocks for the past five years.

The stocks (with their symbols in parentheses) are:

Archer Daniels Midland (ADM)
Boeing (BA)
Caterpillar (CAT)
Deere & Co. (DE)
General Mills, Inc. (GIS)
Google Inc. (GOOG)

Hershey (HSY)
International Business Machines Corporation (IBM)
JPMorgan Chase & Co. (JPM)
Microsoft (MSFT)
Procter and Gamble (PG)
Walmart (WMT)

1. Collect price information for each stock from Yahoo! Finance (finance.yahoo.com) as follows:
   a. Enter the stock symbol. On the page for that stock, click "Historical Prices" on the left side of the page.
   b. Enter the "start date" as July 31, 2008, and the "end date" as July 31, 2013, to cover the five-year period. Make sure you click "monthly" next to the date.
   c. After hitting "Get Prices," scroll to the bottom of the first page and click "Download to Spreadsheet." If you are asked if you want to open or save the file, click open.
   d. Copy the entire spreadsheet, open Excel, and paste the Web data into a spreadsheet. Delete all the columns except the date and the adjusted close (the first and last columns).
   e. Keep the Excel file open and go back to the Yahoo! Finance Web page and hit the back button. If you are asked if you want to save the data, click no.
   f. When you return to the prices page, enter the next stock symbol and hit "Get Prices" again. Do not change the dates or frequency, but make sure you have the same dates for all the stocks you will download. Again, click "Download to Spread-sheet" and then open the file. Copy the last column, "Adj. Close," paste it into the Excel file and change "Adj. Close" to the stock symbol. Make sure that the first and last prices are in the same rows as the first stock.
   g. Repeat these steps for the remaining 10 stocks, pasting each closing price right next to the other stocks, again making sure that the correct prices on the correct dates all appear on the same rows.

2. Convert these prices to monthly returns as the percentage change in the monthly prices. (*Hint*: Create a separate worksheet within the Excel file.) Note that to compute a return for each month, you need a beginning and ending price, so you will not be able to compute the return for the first month.

3. Compute the mean monthly returns and standard deviations for the monthly returns of each of the stocks.[5] Convert the monthly statistics to annual statistics for easier interpretation (muliply the mean monthly return by 12, and multiply the monthly standard deviation by $\sqrt{12}$).

4. Add a column in your Excel worksheet with the average return across stocks for each month. This is the monthly return to an equally weighted portfolio of these 12 stocks. Compute the mean and standard deviation of monthly returns for the equally weighted portfolio. Double-check that the average return on this equally weighted portfolio is equal to the average return of all of the individual stocks. Convert these monthly statistics to annual statistics (as described in step 3) for interpretation.

---

[5]In Eq. 11.1, we showed how to compute returns with stock price and dividend data. The "adjusted close" series from Yahoo! Finance is already adjusted for dividends and splits, so we may compute returns based on the percentage change in monthly adjusted prices.

5. Using the annual statistics, create an Excel plot with standard deviation (volatility) on the *x*-axis and average return on the *y*-axis as follows:
   a. Create three columns on your spreadsheet with the statistics you created in Questions 3 and 4 for each of the individual stocks and the equally weighted portfolio. The first column will have the ticker, the second will have annual standard deviation, and the third will have the annual mean return.
   b. Highlight the data in the last two columns (standard deviation and mean), choose > Insert > Chart > XY Scatter Plot. Complete the chart wizard to finish the plot.

6. What do you notice about the average of the volatilities of the individual stocks, compared to the volatility of the equally weighted portfolio?

12

Systematic Risk and the Equity Risk Premium

LEARNING OBJECTIVES

- Calculate the expected return and volatility (standard deviation) of a portfolio

- Understand the relation between systematic risk and the market portfolio

- Measure systematic risk

- Use the Capital Asset Pricing Model (CAPM) to compute the cost of equity capital for a stock

In Chapter 11, we started our exploration of the tradeoff between risk and return. We found that for large portfolios, while investors should expect to experience higher returns for higher risk, the same does not hold true for individual stocks. Stocks have both unsystematic, diversifiable risk and systematic, undiversifiable risk; only the systematic risk is rewarded with higher expected returns. With no reward for bearing unsystematic risk, rational investors should choose to diversify.

Put yourself in the role of a financial manager at a company such as Apple. One part of your job would be to calculate Apple's cost of equity capital so that its managers know what return its equity investors require. Recall that in Chapter 5 we defined the cost of capital as the best available expected return offered in the market on an investment of comparable risk and term. Since only systematic risk contributes to expected returns, we need to measure the systematic risk of Apple and map it into an expected return for Apple. To do so, we need to think about Apple's stock the way our investors would—as part of a portfolio. As a result, we begin where we left off in Chapter 11: with portfolios. After learning how to calculate the risk and expected return of a portfolio, we will focus on the biggest portfolio of them all: the portfolio of *all* risky securities. This portfolio has no diversifiable risk left and can be used as a baseline for measuring systematic risk. From there, we will develop a simple, powerful model that relates the systematic risk of an investment to its expected return. In other words, the model says that the return we should expect on any investment is equal to the risk-free rate of return plus a risk premium proportional to the amount of systematic risk in the investment.

12.1 The Expected Return of a Portfolio

In Chapter 11, we learned the important role that portfolios play in reducing unsystematic risk. As financial managers, we have to be mindful that investors hold our company's stock as part of a larger portfolio. Thus, it is important to understand how portfolios work and the implications for the return our investors expect on the stock of our company and the projects we undertake in that company.

Portfolio Weights

We begin by calculating the return and expected return of a portfolio. For example, consider a portfolio with 200 shares of Apple worth $200 per share ($40,000 total), and 1000 shares of Coca-Cola worth $60 per share ($60,000 total). The total value of the portfolio is $100,000, so Apple is 40% of the portfolio and Coca-Cola is 60% of the portfolio. More generally, we can describe a portfolio by its **portfolio weights**, which are the fractions of the total investment in a portfolio held in each individual investment in the portfolio:

portfolio weights The fraction of the total investment in a portfolio held in each individual investment in the portfolio.

$$w_i = \frac{\text{Value of Investment } i}{\text{Total Value of Portfolio}} \tag{12.1}$$

These portfolio weights add up to 100% (that is, $w_1 + w_2 + \ldots + w_N = 100\%$), so that they represent the way we have divided our money between the different individual investments in the portfolio. We can confirm the portfolio weights for our portfolio of Apple and Coca-Cola:

$$w_{Apple} = \frac{200 \times \$200}{\$100,000} = 40\% \text{ and } w_{Coca\text{-}Cola} = \frac{1000 \times \$60}{\$100,000} = 60\%$$

Portfolio Returns

Once you know the portfolio weights, you can calculate the return on the portfolio. For example, take the portfolio of Apple and Coca-Cola. If Apple earns a 10% return and Coca-Cola earns a 15% return, then 40% of the portfolio earns 10% and 60% of the portfolio earns 15%, so the portfolio as a whole earns: $(0.40)(10\%) + (0.60)(15\%) = 13\%$.

return of a portfolio The weighted average of the returns on the investments in a portfolio, where the weights correspond to the portfolio weights.

The **return of a portfolio** *is the weighted average of the returns on the investments in the portfolio, where the weights correspond to the portfolio weights.*

Formally, suppose $w_1, \ldots, w_n$ are the portfolio weights of the n investments in a portfolio and these investments have returns $R_1, \ldots, R_n$, then the formula for the return on the portfolio is:

$$R_p = w_1 R_1 + w_2 R_2 + \ldots + w_n R_n \tag{12.2}$$

EXAMPLE 12.1

Calculating Portfolio
Returns

MyFinanceLab

PROBLEM

Suppose you invest $100,000 and buy 200 shares of Apple at $200 per share ($40,000) and 1000 shares of Coca-Cola at $60 per share ($60,000). If Apple's stock rises to $240 per share and Coca-Cola stock falls to $57 per share and neither paid dividends, what is the new value of the portfolio? What return did the portfolio earn? Show that Eq. 12.2 is true by calculating the individual returns of the stocks and multiplying them by their weights in the portfolio. If you don't buy or sell any shares after the price change, what are the new portfolio weights?

SOLUTION

PLAN

Your portfolio: 200 shares of Apple: $200 → $240 ($40 capital gain per share)
                      1000 shares of Coca-Cola: $60 → $57 ($3 capital loss per share)

A. To calculate the return on your portfolio, compute its value using the new prices and compare it to the original $100,000 investment.
B. To confirm that Eq. 12.2 is true, compute the return on each stock individually using Eq. 11.1 from Chapter 11, multiply those returns by their original weights in the portfolio, and compare your answer to the return you just calculated for the portfolio as a whole.

EXECUTE

The new value of your Apple stock is $200 \times \$240 = \$48,000$ and the new value of your Coca-Cola stock is $1000 \times \$57 = \$57,000$. So, the new value of your portfolio is $\$48,000 + 57,000 = \$105,000$, for a gain of $5000 or a 5% return on your initial $100,000 investment.

Since neither stock paid any dividends, we calculate their returns simply as the capital gain or loss divided by the purchase price. The return on Apple stock was $40/$200 = 20%, and the return on Coca-Cola stock was −$3/$60 = −5%.

The initial portfolio weights were $40,000/$100,000 = 40% for Apple and $60,000/$100,000 = 60% for Coca-Cola, so we can also compute the return of the portfolio from Eq. 12.2 as:

$$R_p = w_{Apple} R_{Apple} + w_{Coke} R_{Coke} = 0.40 \, (20\%) + 0.60 \, (-5\%) = 5\%$$

After the price change, the new portfolio weights are equal to the value of your investment in each stock divided by the new portfolio value:

$$w_{Apple} = \frac{200 \times \$240}{105,000} = 45.71\% \text{ and } w_{Coca\text{-}Cola} = \frac{1000 \times \$57}{105,000} = 54.29\%$$

As a check on your work, always make sure that your portfolio weights sum to 100%!

EVALUATE

The $3000 loss on your investment in Coca-Cola was offset by the $8000 gain in your investment in Apple, for a total gain of $5,000 or 5%. The same result comes from giving a 40% weight to the 20% return on Apple and a 60% weight to the −5% loss on Coca-Cola—you have a total net return of 5%.

After a year, the portfolio weight on Apple has increased and the weight on Coca-Cola has decreased. Note that without trading, the portfolio weights will increase for the stock(s) in the portfolio whose returns are above the overall portfolio return. The charts below show the initial and ending weights on Apple (shown in yellow) and Coca-Cola (shown in red).

Expected Portfolio Return

expected return of a portfolio The weighted average of the expected returns of the investments in a portfolio, where the weights correspond to the portfolio weights.

As we showed in Chapter 11, you can use the historical average return of a security as its expected return. With these expected returns, you can compute the **expected return of a portfolio**, which is simply the weighted average of the expected returns of the investments within it, using the portfolio weights:

$$E[R_P] = w_1 E[R_1] + w_2 E[R_2] + \ldots + w_n E[R_n] \tag{12.3}$$

We started by stating that you can describe a portfolio by its weights. These weights are used in computing both a portfolio's return and its expected return. Table 12.1 summarizes these concepts.

TABLE 12.1

Summary of Portfolio Concepts

Term	Concept	Equation
Portfolio weight	The relative investment in your portfolio	$w_i = \dfrac{\text{Value of Investment } i}{\text{Total Value of Portfolio}}$
Portfolio return	The total return earned on your portfolio, accounting for the returns of all of the securities in the portfolio and their weights	$R_P = w_1 R_1 + w_2 R_2 + \cdots + w_n R_n$
Portfolio expected return	The return you can expect to earn on your portfolio, given the expected returns of the securities in that portfolio and the relative amount you have invested in each	$E[R_P] = w_1 E[R_1] + w_2 E[R_2] + \cdots + w_n E[R_n]$

EXAMPLE 12.2

Portfolio Expected Return

MyFinanceLab

PROBLEM

Suppose you invest $10,000 in Boeing (BA) stock, and $30,000 in Merck (MRK) stock. You expect a return of 10% for Boeing and 16% for Merck. What is the expected return for your portfolio?

SOLUTION

PLAN

You have a total of $40,000 invested:

$10,000/$40,000 = 25% in Boeing and: $E[R_{BA}] = 10\%$

$30,000/$40,000 = 75% in Merck and: $E[R_{MRK}] = 16\%$

Using Eq. 12.3, compute the expected return on your whole portfolio by multiplying the expected returns of the stocks in your portfolio by their respective portfolio weights.

EXECUTE

The expected return on your portfolio is:

$$E[R_P] = w_{BA} E[R_{BA}] + w_{MRK} E[R_{MRK}]$$
$$E[R_P] = 0.25 \times 10\% + 0.75 \times 16\% = 14.5\%$$

EVALUATE

The importance of each stock for the expected return of the overall portfolio is determined by the relative amount of money you have invested in it. Most (75%) of your money is invested in Merck, so the overall expected return of the portfolio is much closer to Merck's expected return than it is to Boeing's.

Concept
Check

1. What do the weights in a portfolio tell us?

2. How is the expected return of a portfolio related to the expected returns of the stocks in the portfolio?

12.2 The Volatility of a Portfolio

Investors in a company such as Apple care not only about the return, but also about the risk of their portfolios. Understanding how Apple's investors think about risk requires us to understand how to calculate the risk of a portfolio. As we explained in Chapter 11, when we combine stocks in a portfolio, some of their risk is eliminated through diversification. The amount of risk that will remain depends upon the degree to which the stocks share common risk. The **volatility of a portfolio** is the total risk, measured as standard deviation, of the portfolio. In this section, we describe the tools to quantify the degree to which two stocks share risk and to determine the volatility of a portfolio.

volatility of a portfolio
The total risk, measured as standard deviation, of a portfolio.

Diversifying Risks

Let's begin with a simple example of how risk changes when stocks are combined in a portfolio. Table 12.2 shows returns for three hypothetical stocks, along with their average returns and volatilities. Note that while the three stocks have the same volatility and average return, the pattern of returns differs. In years when the airline stocks performed well, the oil stock tended to do poorly (see 2008–2009), and when the airlines did poorly, the oil stock tended to do well (2011–2012).

Table 12.2 also shows the returns for two portfolios of the stocks. The first portfolio is an equal investment in the two airlines, North Air and West Air. The second portfolio is an equal investment in West Air and Tex Oil. The bottom two rows display the average return and volatility for each stock and portfolio of stocks. Note that the 10% average return of both portfolios is equal to the 10% average return of the stocks, consistent with Eq. 12.3. However, as Figure 12.1 illustrates, their volatilities (standard deviations)—12.1% for portfolio 1 and 5.1% for portfolio 2—are very different from the 13.4% volatility for the individual stocks *and* from each other.

This example demonstrates two important things that we learned in Chapter 11. *First, by combining stocks into a portfolio, we reduce risk through diversification.* Because the stocks do not move identically, some of the risk is averaged out in a portfolio. As a result, both portfolios have lower risk than the individual stocks.

Second, the amount of risk that is eliminated in a portfolio depends upon the degree to which the stocks face common risks and move together. Because the two airline stocks tend to perform well or poorly at the same time, the portfolio of airline stocks has a volatility that is only slightly lower than the volatility of the individual stocks. The airline and

TABLE 12.2

Returns for Three Stocks, and Portfolios of Pairs of Stocks

	Stock Returns			Portfolio Returns	
				(1) Half N.A. and Half W.A.	(2) Half W.A. and Half T.O.
Year	North Air	West Air	Tex Oil		
2008	21%	9%	−2%	15.0%	3.5%
2009	30%	21%	−5%	25.5%	8.0%
2010	7%	7%	9%	7.0%	8.0%
2011	−5%	−2%	21%	−3.5%	9.5%
2012	−2%	−5%	30%	−3.5%	12.5%
2013	9%	30%	7%	19.5%	18.5%
Avg. Return	10.0%	10.0%	10.0%	10.0%	10.0%
Volatility	13.4%	13.4%	13.4%	12.1%	5.1%

FIGURE 12.1

Volatility of Airline
and Oil Portfolios

The figures graph the portfolio returns from Table 12.2. In Panel (a), we see that the airline stocks move in synch, so that a portfolio made up of the two airline stocks does not achieve much diversification. In Panel (b), because the airline and oil stocks often move opposite each other, a portfolio of West Air and Texas Oil achieves greater diversification and lower portfolio volatility. Because both stocks have an average return of 10%, so does the portfolio, but it achieves that return with much less volatility than either of the individual stocks.

Panel (a): Portfolio split equally between West Air and North Air

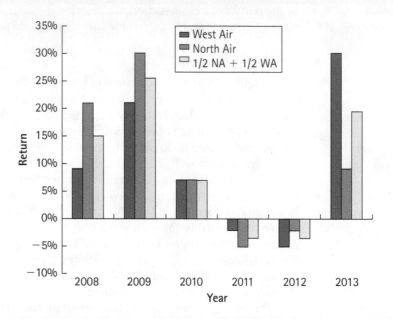

Panel (b): Portfolio split equally between West Air and Texas Oil

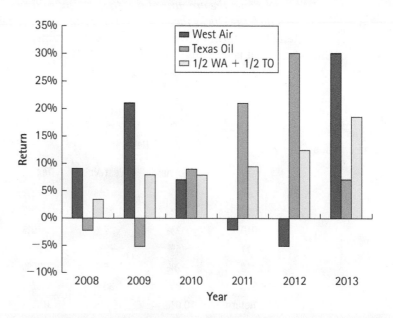

oil stocks, on the other hand, do not move together. Indeed, they tend to move in opposite directions. As a result, more risk is canceled out, making that portfolio much less risky.

Measuring Stocks' Co-Movement: Correlation

Figure 12.1 emphasizes the fact that to find the risk of a portfolio, we need to know more than just the risk of the component stocks: We need to know the degree to which the stocks' returns move together. The stocks' *correlation* is such a measure, ranging from -1 to $+1$.[1]

correlation A measure of the degree to which returns share common risk. It is calculated as the covariance of the returns divided by the product of the standard deviations of each return.

As Figure 12.2 shows, **correlation** is a barometer of the degree to which the returns share common risk. The closer the correlation is to $+1$, the more the returns tend to move together as a result of common risk. When the correlation equals 0, the returns are *uncorrelated*; that is, they have no tendency to move together or opposite of one another. Independent risks are uncorrelated. Finally, the closer the correlation is to -1, the more the returns tend to move in opposite directions.

When will stock returns be highly correlated with each other? Stock returns will tend to move together if they are affected similarly by economic events. Thus, stocks in the same industry tend to have more highly correlated returns than stocks in different industries. This tendency is illustrated in Table 12.3, which shows the volatility (standard deviation) of individual stock returns and the correlation between them for several common stocks. The blue-shaded boxes along the diagonal show the correlation of a stock with itself—which has to be 1 (a stock is perfectly correlated with itself). The table can be read across the rows or down the columns. Each correlation appears twice. For example, reading across the Ford row, the correlation between Ford and Goodyear Tire (red box) is 0.58, which you could also find by reading across the Goodyear row for the correlation between Goodyear and Ford. Goodyear and Ford have the highest correlation in the table, 0.58, because new

FIGURE 12.2

Correlation

The correlation measures how returns move in relation to each other. The correlation is between $+1$ (returns always move together) and -1 (returns always move oppositely). Independent risks have no tendency to move together and have zero correlation. The correlations of Ford with Apple and Goodyear Tire are indicated on the continuum. Note that car manufacturer Ford is more correlated with a tire company than with an electronics company. See Table 12.3 for more examples of correlations.

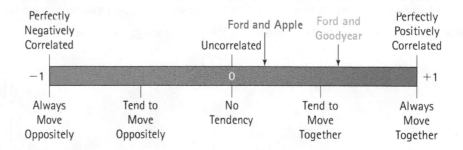

Source: Authors' calculations based on data from moneycentral.msn.com.

---

[1]Correlation is scaled covariance and is defined as:

$$Corr(R_i, R_j) = \frac{Covariance(R_i, R_j)}{SD(R_i)\,SD(R_j)}$$

TABLE 12.3

Estimated Annual Volatilities and Correlations for Selected Stocks
(Based on Monthly Returns, January 2001–December 2012)

	Apple	Microsoft	Target	Starbucks	Goodyear	Ford	Berkshire Hathaway
Standard Deviation	41%	28%	26%	32%	56%	59%	17%
Apple	1	0.48	0.38	0.38	0.31	0.23	0.06
Microsoft	0.48	1	0.39	0.36	0.33	0.36	0.16
Target	0.38	0.39	1	0.39	0.50	0.46	0.27
Starbucks	0.38	0.36	0.39	1	0.41	0.27	0.20
Goodyear	0.31	0.33	0.50	0.41	1	0.58	0.38
Ford	0.23	0.36	0.46	0.27	0.58	1	0.27
Berkshire Hathaway	0.06	0.16	0.27	0.20	0.38	0.27	1

Source: Authors' calculations based on data from moneycentral.msn.com.

cars come with tires, so both companies benefit from increased spending on new cars. All of the correlations are positive, however, showing the general tendency of stocks to move together. The lowest correlation is shown in the green boxes for Apple and Berkshire Hathaway, which is 0.06, showing that there is little relation between a consumer electronics company and Warren Buffet's insurance-based conglomerate. Figure 12.3 shows scatter plots of monthly returns for Apple and Berkshire Hathaway and for Goodyear and Ford. While there is a clear positive relation between the returns of Ford and Goodyear, the plot for Apple and Berkshire Hathaway looks like an unrelated cloud of returns.

FIGURE 12.3

Scatterplots of Returns

Plots of pairs of monthly returns for Apple and Berkshire Hathaway and for Ford and Goodyear. Notice the clear positive relation between Ford and Goodyear, which tend to move up and down together, versus the lack of a relation between Apple and Berkshire Hathaway.

Panel (a): Monthly Returns for Apple and Berkshire Hathaway   Panel (b): Monthly Returns for Ford and Goodyear

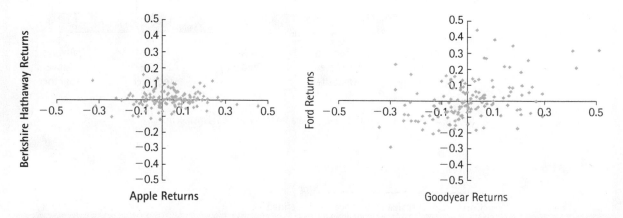

Source: Authors' calculations based on data from moneycentral.msn.com.

USING EXCEL

Calculating the
Correlation Between
Two Sets of Returns

The correlations presented in Table 12.3 were calculated by comparing the returns of two stocks. Here we describe how you can use Excel to calculate these correlations.

1. Enter or import the historical returns for the two stocks into Excel.
2. Next, from the Data Group, select **Data Analysis**, and then select **Correlation**.
3. For the "Input Range" field, highlight the two columns of returns, as shown in the screenshot.
4. Click **OK**.
5. The answer will appear in a new worksheet as the correlation between "column 1" and "column 2."

Note that if you don't have the Analysis Toolpak installed, you can use the CORREL function. In this case, you would type: =CORREL(B2:B145,C2:C145) into any empty cell. The function would return the correlation. The cell ranges B2:B145 and C2:C145 are the returns of Apple and Microsoft, respectively.

Computing a Portfolio's Variance and Standard Deviation

We now have the tools to formally compute portfolio variance. The formula for the variance of a two-stock portfolio is:

$$
Var(R_p) = \underbrace{w_1^2 SD(R_1)^2}_{\substack{\text{Accounting} \\ \text{for the risk} \\ \text{of stock 1}}} + \underbrace{w_2^2 SD(R_2)^2}_{\substack{\text{Accounting} \\ \text{for the risk} \\ \text{of stock 2}}} + \underbrace{2w_1 w_2 Corr(R_1, R_2) SD(R_1) SD(R_2)}_{\substack{\text{Adjustment for} \\ \text{how much the two stocks move together}}} \quad (12.4)
$$

Each part of Eq. 12.4 accounts for an important determinant of the overall variance of the portfolio: the risk of stock 1, the risk of stock 2, and an adjustment for how much the two stocks move together (their correlation, given as $Corr(R_1, R_2)$.[2] The equation demonstrates

---

[2]For three stocks, the formula is

$$
Var(R_p) = w_1^2 SD(R_1)^2 + w_2^2 SD(R_2)^2 + w_3^2 SD(R_3)^2 + 2w_1 w_2 Corr(R_1, R_2) SD(R_1) SD(R_2)
$$
$$
+ 2w_2 w_3 Corr(R_2, R_3) SD(R_2) SD(R_3) + 2w_1 w_3 Corr(R_1, R_3) SD(R_1) SD(R_3)
$$

and for n stocks, it is:

$$
\sum_{i=1}^{n} \sum_{j=1}^{n} w_i w_j Corr(R_i, R_j) SD(R_i) SD(R_j)
$$

that with a positive amount invested in each stock, the more the stocks move together and the higher their correlation, the more volatile the portfolio will be. The portfolio will have the greatest variance if the stocks have a perfect positive correlation of +1. In fact, when combining stocks into a portfolio, unless the stocks all have a perfect positive correlation of +1 with each other, the risk of the portfolio will be lower than the weighted average volatility of the individual stocks (as shown in Figure 12.1). Contrast this fact with a portfolio's expected return. *The expected return of a portfolio is equal to the weighted average expected return of its stocks, but the volatility of a portfolio is less than the weighted average volatility. As a result, it is clear that we can eliminate some volatility by diversifying.* Equation 12.4 formalized the concept of diversification introduced in Chapter 11. In the following example, we use it to compute the volatility of a portfolio.

EXAMPLE 12.3

Computing the Volatility of a Two-Stock Portfolio

MyFinanceLab

PROBLEM

Using the data from Table 12.3, what is the volatility (standard deviation) of a portfolio with equal amounts invested in Apple and Microsoft stock? What is the standard deviation of a portfolio with equal amounts invested in Apple and Starbucks stock?

SOLUTION

PLAN

	Weight	Volatility	Correlation with Apple
Apple	0.50	0.41	1
Microsoft	0.50	0.28	0.48
Apple	0.50	0.41	1
Starbucks	0.50	0.32	0.38

A. With the portfolio weights, volatility, and correlations of the stocks in the two portfolios, we have all the information we need to use Eq. 12.4 to compute the variance of each portfolio.
B. After computing the portfolio's variance, we can take the square root to get the portfolio's standard deviation.

EXECUTE

For Apple and Microsoft, from Eq. 12.4 the portfolio's variance is:

$$Var(R_P) = w_{AAPL}^2 SD(R_{AAPL})^2 + w_{MSFT}^2 SD(R_{MSFT})^2$$
$$+ 2w_{AAPL}w_{MSFT}Corr(R_{AAPL}, R_{MSFT})SD(R_{AAPL})SD(R_{MSFT})$$
$$= (.50)^2(.41)^2 + (.50)^2(.28)^2 + 2(.50)(.50)(.48)(.41)(.28)$$
$$= 0.08918$$

The standard deviation is therefore:

$$SD(R_P) = \sqrt{Var(R_P)} = \sqrt{0.08918} = 0.299, \text{ or } 29.9\%$$

For the portfolio of Apple and Starbucks:

$$Var(R_P) = w_{AAPL}^2 SD(R_{AAPL})^2 + w_{SBUX}^2 SD(R_{SBUX})^2$$
$$+ 2w_{AAPL}w_{SBUX}Corr(R_{AAPL}, R_{SBUX})SD(R_{AAPL})SD(R_{SBUX})$$
$$= (.50)^2(.41)^2 + (.50)^2(.32)^2 + 2(.50)(.50)(.38)(.41)(.32)$$
$$= 0.09255$$

The standard deviation in this case is:

$$SD(R_P) = \sqrt{Var(R_P)} = \sqrt{0.09255} = 0.304, \text{ or } 30.4\%.$$

EVALUATE

The weights, standard deviations, and correlation of the two stocks are needed to compute the variance and then the standard deviation of the portfolio. Here, we computed the standard deviation of the portfolio of Apple and Microsoft to be 29.9% and of Apple and Starbucks to be 30.4%. Note that the portfolio of Apple and Starbucks is less volatile than either of the individual stocks. It is also about equally volatile as the portfolio of Apple and Microsoft. Even though Starbucks is more volatile than Microsoft, its lower correlation with Apple leads to greater diversification benefits in the portfolio, which offsets Starbuck's higher volatility.

In the next example, we show how portfolios can be used to reduce risk without giving up too much expected return.

EXAMPLE 12.4

Reducing Risk Without Sacrificing Return

MyFinanceLab

PROBLEM

Based on historical data, your expected annual return for Target is 6% and for Berkshire Hathaway is 5%. What is the expected return and risk (standard deviation) of your portfolio if you hold only Target? If you split your money evenly between Target and Berkshire, what is the expected return and risk of your portfolio?

SOLUTION

PLAN

A. From Table 12.3 we can get the standard deviations of Target and Berkshire stock along with their correlation:

$$SD(R_{TGT}) = 0.26, \quad SD(R_{BRK}) = 0.17 \quad Corr(R_{TGT}, R_{BRK}) = 0.28$$

B. With this information and the information from the problem, we can compute the expected return of the portfolio using Eq. 12.3 and its variance using Eq. 12.4.

EXECUTE

For the all-Target portfolio, we have 100% of our money in Target stock, so the expected return and standard deviation of our portfolio is simply the expected return and standard deviation of that stock:

$$E[R_{TGT}] = .06, \quad SD(R_{TGT}) = 0.26$$

However, when we invest our money 50% in Berkshire and 50% in Target, the expected return is:

$$E[R_P] = w_{BRK}E[R_{BRK}] + w_{TGT}E[R_{TGT}] = 0.5(.05) + 0.5(.06) = 0.055$$

and the variance is:

$$Var(R_P) = w_{BRK}^2 SD(R_{BRK})^2 + w_{TGT}^2 SD(R_{TGT})^2$$

$$+ 2w_{BRK}w_{TGT} Corr(R_{BRK}, R_{TGT}) SD(R_{BRK}) SD(R_{TGT})$$

$$= (.50)^2(.17)^2 + (.50)^2(.26)^2 + 2(.50)(.50)(.26)(.17)(.28)$$

$$= 0.0303$$

The standard deviation is therefore:

$$SD(R_P) = \sqrt{Var(R_P)} = \sqrt{0.0303} = 0.1741$$

EVALUATE

For a very small reduction in expected return, we gain a large reduction in risk. This is the advantage of portfolios: By selecting stocks with low correlation but similar expected returns, we achieve our desired expected return at the lowest possible risk.

The Volatility of a Large Portfolio

We can gain additional benefits of diversification by holding more than two stocks in our portfolio. As we add more stocks to our portfolio, the diversifiable firm-specific risk for each stock matters less and less. Only risk that is common to all of the stocks in the portfolio continues to matter.

In Figure 12.4, we graph the volatility for an *equally weighted portfolio* with different numbers of stocks. In an **equally weighted portfolio**, the same amount of money is invested in each stock. Note that the volatility declines as the number of stocks in the portfolio grows. In fact, nearly half the volatility of the individual stocks is eliminated in a large portfolio by diversification. The benefit of diversification is most dramatic initially—the decrease in volatility going from one to two stocks is much larger than the decrease going from 100 to 101 stocks. Even for a very large portfolio, however, we cannot eliminate all of the risk—the systematic risk remains.

equally weighted portfolio A portfolio in which the same amount of money is invested in each stock.

FIGURE 12.4

Volatility of an Equally Weighted Portfolio Versus the Number of Stocks

The graph in Panel (b) is based on the data in Panel (a). Note that the volatility declines as we increase the number of stocks in the portfolio. Yet even in a very large portfolio, systematic (market) risk remains. Also note that the volatility declines at a decreasing rate (the effect of going from one to two stocks—an 8-percentage point decrease in volatility—is bigger than the effect of going from four to five stocks, which is a 1.1-percentage point decrease). The graph is formed based on the assumption that each stock has a volatility of 40% and a correlation with other stocks of 0.28. Both are average for large stocks in the United States.

Panel (a)

No. Stocks	Portfolio Volatility
1	40.0%
2	32.0%
3	28.8%
4	27.1%
5	26.0%
10	23.7%
15	22.9%
20	22.5%
25	22.2%
30	22.1%
50	21.7%
100	21.5%
1000	21.2%

Panel (b)

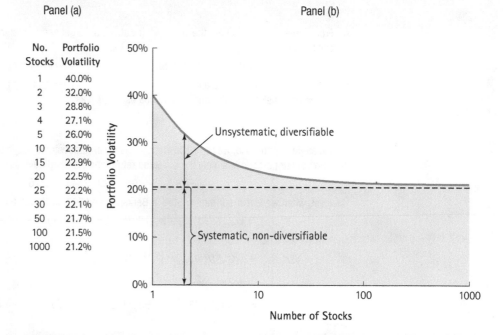

Concept Check

3. What determines how much risk will be eliminated by combining stocks in a portfolio?

4. When do stocks have more or less correlation?

12.3   Measuring Systematic Risk

Our goal is to understand the impact of risk on the firm's investors. By understanding how they view risk, we can quantify the relation between risk and required return to produce a discount rate for our present value calculations. In Chapter 11, we established that the only risk that is related to return is systematic risk, but standard deviation measures *total* risk, including the unsystematic part. We need a way to measure just the systematic risk of an investment opportunity. The previous section contains two important insights that we will now build on to determine the sensitivity of individual stocks to risk. To recap:

1. *The amount of a stock's risk that is removed by diversification depends on its correlation with other stocks in the portfolio.* For example, in Example 12.3 we showed that much less of Apple's risk is diversified away in a portfolio with Microsoft than in a portfolio with Starbucks.

2. *If you build a large enough portfolio, you can remove all unsystematic risk by diversification, but you will still be left with systematic risk.* Figure 12.4 shows that as the number of stocks in your portfolio grows, the unsystematic positive and negative events affecting only a few stocks will cancel out, leaving systematic events as the only source of risk for the portfolio.

Role of the Market Portfolio

As we explained in Chapter 11, investors should diversify their portfolios in order to reduce their risk. If investors choose their portfolios optimally, they will do so until no further diversifiable risk is present, and only systematic risk remains. Let's assume that all investors behave in this way; that is

Suppose all investors hold portfolios that contain only systematic risk.

If that is the case, then consider the portfolio we obtain by combining the portfolios of every investor. Because each investor's portfolio contains only systematic risk, the same is true for this "aggregate" portfolio. So, the aggregate portfolio held by all investors is a fully diversified, optimal portfolio. Moreover, we can identify this portfolio: Because all securities are held by someone, the aggregate portfolio contains all shares outstanding of

market portfolio The portfolio of all risky investments, held in proportion to their value.

every risky security. We call this portfolio the **market portfolio**.

To illustrate, imagine that there are only two companies in the world, each with 1000 shares outstanding:

	Number of Shares Outstanding	Price per Share	Market Capitalization
Company A	1000	$40	$40,000
Company B	1000	$10	$10,000

In this simple setting, the market portfolio consists of 1000 shares of each stock and has a total value of $50,000. Stock A's portfolio weight is therefore 80% ($40,000/$50,000) and B's is 20% ($10,000/$50,000). Because all of the shares of A and all of the shares of B must be held by someone, the sum of all investors' portfolios must equal this market portfolio. Note from this example that the portfolio weight of each stock is proportional to the total market value of its outstanding shares, which is called its **market capitalization**:

market capitalization The total market value of a firm's equity; equals the market price per share times the number of shares.

$$\text{Market Capitalization} = (\text{Number of Shares Outstanding})$$
$$\times (\text{Price per Share}) \qquad (12.5)$$

Generally, the market portfolio will consist of all risky securities in the market, with portfolio weights proportional to their market capitalization. Thus, for example, if Microsoft's market capitalization were equal to 3% of the total market value of all securities, then it would have a 3% weight in the market portfolio. Because stocks are held in proportion to their market capitalization (value), we say that the market portfolio is **value weighted**.

value-weighted portfolio A portfolio in which each security is held in proportion to its market capitalization.

Because the market portfolio only contains systematic risk, we can use it to measure the amount of systematic risk of other securities in the market. In particular, any risk that is correlated with the market portfolio must be systematic risk. Therefore, by looking at the sensitivity of a stock's return to the overall market, we can calculate the amount of systematic risk the stock has.

Stock Market Indexes as the Market Portfolio

While the market portfolio is easy to identify, actually constructing it is a different matter. Because it should contain all risky securities, we need to include all stocks, bonds, real estate, commodities, etc., both in the United States and around the world. Clearly, it would be impractical, if not impossible, to collect and update returns on all risky assets everywhere. In practice, we use a **market proxy**—a portfolio whose return should track the underlying, unobservable market portfolio. The most common proxy portfolios are *market indexes*, which are broadly used to represent the performance of the stock market. A **market index** reports the value of a particular portfolio of securities. We list the most popular indexes below, but you can also read the box on page 19 in Section 1.5 of Chapter 1 that compares the different market indexes.

market proxy A portfolio whose return should closely track the true market portfolio.

market index The market value of a broad-based portfolio of securities.

Dow Jones Industrial Average. The most familiar stock index in the United States is the Dow Jones Industrial Average, or DJIA. This index consists of a portfolio of 30 large stocks. While these stocks are chosen to be representative of different sectors of the economy, they clearly do not represent the entire market. Despite being non-representative of the entire market, the DJIA remains widely cited because it is one of the oldest stock market indexes (it was first published in 1884).

S&P 500. A better representation of the entire U.S. stock market is the S&P 500, a value-weighted portfolio of 500 of the largest U.S. stocks.[3] The S&P 500 was the first widely publicized value-weighted index (S&P began publishing its index in 1923), and it is a standard benchmark for professional investors. This index is the most commonly cited index when evaluating the overall performance of the U.S. stock market. It is also the standard portfolio used to represent "the market" in practice. As we show in Figure 12.5, even though the S&P 500 includes only 500 of more than 7000 individual U.S. stocks, because the S&P 500 includes the largest stocks, it represents more than 70% of the U.S. stock market in terms of market capitalization.

Market Risk and Beta

Now that we have established that the market portfolio is a good basis for measuring systematic risk, we can use the relation between an individual stock's returns and the market portfolio's returns to measure the amount of systematic risk present in that stock. The intuition is that if a stock's returns are highly sensitive to the market portfolio's returns,

---

[3]There is no precise formula for determining which stocks will be included in the S&P 500. Standard & Poor's periodically replaces stocks in the index (on average about seven or eight stocks per year). While size is one criterion, Standard & Poor's also tries to maintain appropriate representation of different segments of the economy and chooses firms that are leaders in their industries.

FIGURE 12.5

The S&P 500

The Panel (a) pie chart shows the 500 firms in the S&P 500 as a fraction of the approximately 7000 U.S. public firms. Panel (b) shows the S&P 500 firms' importance in terms of market capitalization—these 500 firms represent approximately 70% of the total capitalization of the 7000 public firms.

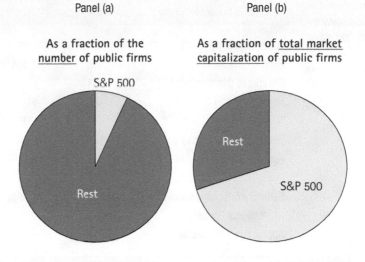

Panel (a)

Panel (b)

As a fraction of the number of public firms

As a fraction of total market capitalization of public firms

S&P 500

Rest

Rest

S&P 500

Index Funds

One easy way investors can buy (an approximation of) the market portfolio is to invest in an *index fund*, which invests in stocks and other securities with the goal of matching the performance of a particular market index. The Vanguard Group was the largest mutual fund company in 2013 and it specializes in index funds. Vanguard was founded in 1974 by John Bogle, who advocates the benefits of index funds for individual investors. Comparing index funds to the strategy of trying to pick hot stocks, Bogle reportedly said, "What's the point of looking for the needle in the haystack? Why not own the haystack?"

In August of 1976, Vanguard created its well-known S&P 500 Index Fund, which tries to match the performance of the S&P 500 index as closely as possible. As of July 2013, this fund had nearly $275 billion in assets. Vanguard's Total Stock Market Index Fund is designed to track the performance of the MSCI US Broad Market index, an index that measures the performance of all U.S. stocks with available price data.

then that stock is highly sensitive to systematic risk. That is, events that are systematic and affect the whole market are also strongly reflected in that stock's returns. If a stock's returns do not depend on the market's returns, then it has little systematic risk—when systematic events happen, they are not strongly reflected in its returns. So stocks whose returns are volatile *and* are highly correlated with the market's returns are the riskiest in the sense that they have the most systematic risk.

Specifically, we can measure a stock's systematic risk by estimating the stock's sensitivity to the market portfolio, which we refer to as its **beta** (β):

beta (β) The expected percentage change in the excess return of a security for a 1% change in the excess return of the market (or other benchmark) portfolio.

> *A stock's beta (β) is the percentage change in its return that we expect for each 1% change in the market's return.*

There are many data sources that provide estimates of beta based on historical data. Typically, these data sources estimate betas using two-to-five years of weekly or monthly returns and use the S&P 500 as the market portfolio. Table 12.4 shows estimates of betas for a number of large stocks and their industries. You can find the betas of other companies

TABLE 12.4

Average Betas for Stocks by Industry and the Betas of a Selected Company in Each Industry

Industry	Average Beta	Ticker	Company	Beta
Electric Utilities	0.7	EIX	Edison International	0.6
Personal & Household Prods.	0.4	PG	The Procter & Gamble Company	0.5
Food Processing	0.6	CPB	Campbell Soup Co.	0.3
Restaurants	0.4	SBUX	Starbucks Corporation	1.2
Beverages (Nonalcoholic)	0.4	KO	The Coca-Cola Company	0.5
Retail (Grocery)	0.7	SWY	Safeway Inc.	0.8
Major Drugs	0.9	PFE	Pfizer Inc.	0.7
Beverages (Alcoholic)	0.8	SAM	Boston Beer Company Inc.	0.9
Apparel/Accessories	0.8	ANF	Abercrombie & Fitch	1.7
Retail (Home Improvement)	0.7	HD	Home Depot Inc.	0.8
Software & Programming	1.0	MSFT	Microsoft Corporation	1.0
Recreational Products	1.3	HOG	Harley-Davidson Inc.	2.2
Auto & Truck Manufacturers	1.3	F	Ford Motor Company	2.1
Communications Equipment	1.0	CSCO	Cisco Systems Inc.	1.2
Forestry & Wood Products	1.1	WY	Weyerhaeuser Company	1.5
Computer Services	0.8	GOOG	Google	0.9
Computer Hardware	1.2	HPQ	Hewlett Packard	1.2
Semiconductors	1.3	INTC	Intel Corporation	1.0

Source: Reuters, July 2013.

by going to http://finance.google.com or http://finance.yahoo.com. Note that because different Web sites use different time frames for estimating betas, they can display different betas from each other and from your own calculation for a stock's beta.

As we explain below, the beta of the overall market portfolio is 1, so you can think of a beta of 1 as representing average exposure to systematic risk. However, as the table demonstrates, many industries and companies have betas much higher or lower than 1. The differences in betas by industry are related to the sensitivity of each industry's profits to the general health of the economy. For example, Hewlett Packard, Starbucks, and Harley-Davidson all have high betas (near or above 1.2) because demand for their products usually varies with the business cycle (cyclical stocks): People tend to indulge in new computers, expensive coffee, and high-end motorcycles when times are good, but cut back on these purchases when the economy slows. Thus, systematic events have a greater-than-average impact on these firms and their exposure to systematic risk is greater than average. On the other hand, the demand for personal and household products such as shampoo has very little relation to the state of the economy (stocks of companies providing these types of products are often called *defensive stocks*). Firms producing these types of goods, such as Procter & Gamble, tend to have low betas (near 0.5). Note also that even within an industry, each company's specific strategy and focus can lead to different exposures to systematic events, so that there is variation in beta even within industries (see, for example, how different Abercrombe & Fitch's beta is than the average beta in the apparel industry).

Mixing Standard Deviation and Beta

Volatility (standard deviation) and beta are measured in different units (standard deviation is measured in % and beta is unitless). So even though total risk (volatility) is equal to the sum of systematic risk (measured by beta) and firm-specific risk, our measure of volatility does not have to be a bigger number than our measure for beta. To illustrate, consider Microsoft. It has total risk (volatility), measured as standard deviation, of 28% or 0.28 (see Table 12.3), but Table 12.4 shows that it has systematic risk, measured as a beta, of 1.0, which is greater than 0.28. Volatility (standard deviation) is measured in percentage terms, but beta is not, so 0.28 does not have to be greater than 1.0. For the same reason, it is possible for Boston Beer Company to have a higher standard deviation than Microsoft (35%), but a lower beta (0.9). Figure 12.6 illustrates one possible breakdown of total risk for Microsoft and Boston Beer Company that would be consistent with these data.

FIGURE 12.6

Systematic Versus Firm-Specific Risk in Boston Beer and Microsoft

Beta, measuring systematic risk, and standard deviation, measuring total risk, are in different units. Even though Microsoft's total risk (standard deviation) is 0.28 (28%), its beta, measuring only systematic risk, is 1.0. In this case, the beta of 1.0 corresponds to a breakdown in total risk as depicted in the figure. Formally, the portion of Microsoft's total risk that is in common with the market is calculated by multiplying the correlation between Microsoft and the market by the standard deviation (total risk) of Microsoft. We can do a similar breakdown of Boston Beer's risk. Note that Boston Beer has more total, but less systematic, risk than Microsoft.

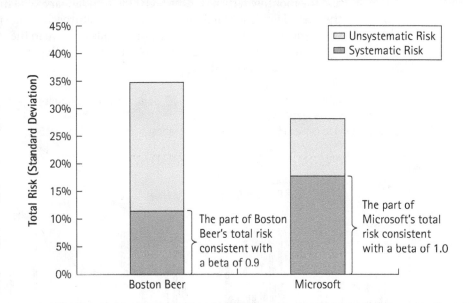

EXAMPLE 12.5

Total Risk Versus Systematic Risk

MyFinanceLab

PROBLEM

Suppose that in the coming year, you expect SysCo's stock to have a standard deviation of 30% and a beta of 1.2, and UniCo's stock to have a standard deviation of 41% and a beta of 0.6. Which stock carries more total risk? Which has more systematic risk?

SOLUTION

PLAN

	Standard Deviation (Total Risk)	Beta (β) (Systematic Risk)
SysCo	30%	1.2
UniCo	41%	0.6

(Continued)

Total risk is measured by standard deviation; therefore, UniCo's stock has more total risk. Systematic risk is measured by beta. SysCo has a higher beta, and so has more systematic risk.

EVALUATE

As we discuss in the Common Mistake box on p. 379, a stock can have high total risk, but if a lot of it is diversifiable, it can still have low or average systematic risk.

Estimating Beta from Historical Returns

A security's beta is the expected percentage change in the return of the security for a 1% change in the return of the market portfolio. That is, beta represents the amount by which risks that affect the overall market are amplified or dampened in a given stock or investment. As demonstrated in Table 12.4, securities whose returns tend to move one for one with the market on average have a beta of one. Securities that tend to move more than the market have higher betas, while those that move less than the market have lower betas.

For example, let's look at Apple's stock. Figure 12.7 shows the monthly returns for Apple and the monthly returns for the S&P 500 from January 2008 through December 2012. Note the overall tendency for Apple to have a high return when the market is up and a low return when the market is down. Indeed, Apple tends to move in the same direction as the market, but its movements are larger. The pattern suggests that Apple's beta is greater than one.

FIGURE 12.7

Monthly Excess Returns for Apple Stock and for the S&P 500, January 2008 through December 2012

Note that Apple's returns tend to move in the same direction but farther than those of the S&P 500.

We can see Apple's sensitivity to the market even more clearly by plotting Apple's return as a function of the S&P 500 return, as shown in Figure 12.8. Each point in this figure represents the returns of Apple and the S&P 500 for one of the months in Figure 12.7. For example, in May 2009, Apple's return was 7.9% and the S&P 500's was 5.3%.

As the scatterplot makes clear, Apple's returns have a positive correlation with the market: Apple tends to be up when the market is up, and vice versa. In practice, we use linear regression to estimate the relation between Apple's returns and the market's return. The output of the linear regression analysis is the best-fitting line that represents the historical relation between the stock and the market. The slope of this line is our estimate of its beta. That slope tells us how much, on average, the stock's return changes for a 1% change in the market's return.[4]

For example, in Figure 12.8, the best-fitting line shows that a 1% change in the market's return corresponds to about a 1.2% change in Apple's return. That is, Apple's return moves about 1.2 times the overall market's movement, and so Apple's beta is about 1.2.

To fully understand this result, recall that beta measures the systematic, market risk of a security. The best-fitting line in Figure 12.8 captures the components of a security's returns that can be explained by market-risk factors. In any individual month, the security's returns will be higher or lower than the best-fitting line. Such deviations from the best-fitting line result from risk that is not related to the market as a whole. This risk is diversifiable risk that averages out in a large portfolio.

But what is the beta of the market portfolio? Imagine plotting the returns of the S&P 500 against themselves. You would have a line with a slope of one and no deviations from that line. Thus, the beta of the market portfolio is 1. What about a risk-free investment?

FIGURE 12.8

Scatterplot of Monthly Returns for Apple Versus the S&P 500, January 2008 through December 2012

Beta corresponds to the slope of the best-fitting line. Beta measures the expected change in Apple's return per 1% change in the market's return. Deviations from the best-fitting line, such as in November 2008, correspond to diversifiable, unsystematic risk.

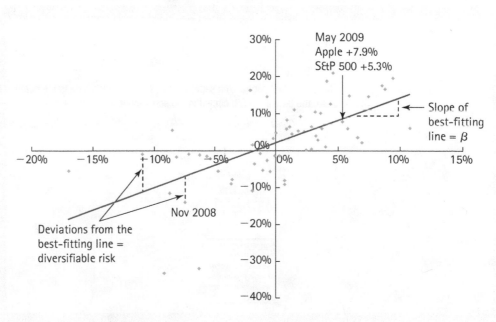

[4]Formally, the beta of an investment is defined as:

$$\beta_i = \frac{\overbrace{SD\,(R_i) \times Corr\,(R_i, R_{Mkt})}^{\text{Volatility of } i \text{ that is common with the market}}}{SD\,(R_{Mkt})} = \frac{Covariance\,(R_i, R_{Mkt})}{Var\,(R_{Mkt})}$$

Because the risk-free return is the return earned on a Treasury bond and is therefore known in advance, it has no volatility and hence no correlation with the market. Therefore, the beta of the risk-free investment is 0.

Calculating a Stock's Beta

1. Enter or import the historical returns for the stock and the S&P 500 into Excel.
2. Next, from the Data Tab, select **Data Analysis**, and then select **Regression**.
3. For the "Input Y Range" box, highlight the stock's returns.
4. For the "Input X Range" box, highlight the S&P 500's returns, as shown in the screenshot.
5. Click **OK**.

6. The output will appear in a separate sheet. The stock's beta is the coefficient on "X Variable 1." In this case, the beta is 1.209, circled in the screenshot.

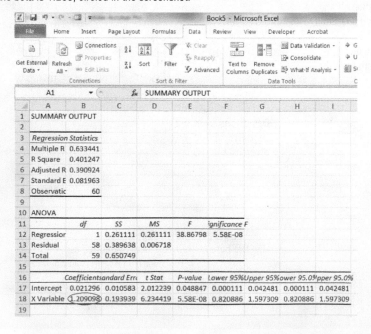

Concept
Check

5. What is the market portfolio?
6. What does beta (β) tell us?

12.4 Putting It All Together: The Capital Asset Pricing Model

One of our goals in this chapter is to compute the cost of equity capital for Apple, which is the best available expected return offered in the market on an investment of comparable risk and term. Thus, in order to compute the cost of capital, we need to know the relation between Apple's risk and its expected return. In the last three sections, we have laid the foundation for a practical way of measuring this relation. In this section, we put all the pieces together to build a model for determining the expected return of any investment.

The CAPM Equation Relating Risk to Expected Return

As we have learned, only common, systematic risk determines expected returns—firm-specific risk is diversifiable and does not warrant extra return. In the introduction to this chapter, we stated that, intuitively, the expected return on any investment should come from two components:

1. A baseline risk-free rate of return that we would demand to compensate for inflation and the time value of money, even if there were no risk of losing our money.
2. A risk premium that varies with the amount of systematic risk in the investment.

Expected Return = Risk-Free Rate + Risk Premium for Systematic Risk

We devoted the last section to measuring systematic risk. Beta is our measure of the amount of systematic risk in an investment:

Expected Return for Investment i =
Risk-Free Rate + $\beta_i \times$ Risk Premium per Unit of Systematic Risk $(per\ unit\ of\ \beta)$.

But what is the risk premium per unit of systematic risk? Well, we know that the market portfolio, by definition, has exactly one unit of systematic risk (it has a beta of 1). So, a natural estimate of the risk premium per unit of systematic risk is the historical average excess return on the market portfolio, also known as the **market** or **equity risk premium**. Historically, the average excess return of the S&P 500 over the return on U.S. Treasury bonds (the risk-free rate) has been 5% to 7%, depending on the period of measurement (we'll discuss issues in determining the risk premium and risk-free rate in Chapter 13). With this last piece of the puzzle, we can write the equation for the expected return of an investment:

market risk premium (equity risk premium) The historical average excess returns on the market portfolio.

Capital Asset Pricing Model

$$E[R_i] = r_f + \underbrace{\beta_i(E[R_{Mkt}] - r_f)}_{\text{Risk premium for security } i}$$

(12.6)

Capital Asset Pricing Model (CAPM) An equilibrium model of the relationship between risk and return that characterizes a security's expected return based on its beta with the market portfolio.

This equation for the expected return of any investment is the **Capital Asset Pricing Model (CAPM)**. In words, the CAPM simply says that the return we should expect on any investment is equal to the risk-free rate of return plus a risk premium proportional to the amount of systematic risk in the investment. Specifically, the risk premium of an investment is equal to the market risk premium $(E[R_{Mkt}] - r_f)$ multiplied by the amount of systematic (market) risk present in the investment, measured by its beta with the market (β_i).

required return The expected return of an investment that is necessary to compensate for the risk of undertaking the investment.

Because investors will not invest in this security unless they can expect at least the return given in Eq. 12.6, we also call this return the investment's **required return**.

The CAPM is the main method used by most major corporations to determine the equity cost of capital. In a survey of CFOs, Graham and Harvey found that more than 70% rely on the CAPM, and Bruner, Eades, Harris, and Higgins reported that 85% of a sample of large firms rely on it.[5] It has become the most important model of the relationship between risk and return, and for his contributions to the theory, William Sharpe was awarded the Nobel Prize in Economics in 1990.

EXAMPLE 12.6
Computing the Expected Return of a Stock

MyFinanceLab

PROBLEM

Suppose the risk-free return is 3% and you measure the market risk premium to be 6%. Apple has a beta of 1.2. According to the CAPM, what is its expected return?

SOLUTION

PLAN

We can use Eq. 12.6 to compute the expected return according to the CAPM. For that equation, we will need the market risk premium, the risk-free return, and the stock's beta. We have all of these inputs, so we are ready to go.

EXECUTE

Using Eq. 12.6:

$$E[R_{AAPL}] = r_f + \beta_{AAPL}(E[R_{Mkt}] - r_f) = 3\% + 1.2(6\%)$$
$$= 10.2\%$$

EVALUATE

Because of Apple's beta of 1.2, investors will require a risk premium of 7.2% over the risk-free rate for investments in its stock to compensate for the systematic risk of Apple stock. This leads to a total expected return of 10.2%.

---

[5]J. Graham and C. Harvey, "The Theory and Practice of Corporate Finance: Evidence from the Field," *Journal of Financial Economics* 60 (2001): 187–243; and R. Bruner, K. Eades, R. Harris, and R. Higgins, "Best Practices in Estimating the Cost of Capital: Survey and Synthesis," *Financial Practice and Education* 8 (1998): 13–28.

William Sharpe

The CAPM was proposed as a model of risk and return by William Sharpe in a 1964 paper, and in related papers by Jack Treynor (1961), John Lintner (1965), and Jan Mossin (1966).*

Below is an excerpt from a 1998 interview with William Sharpe:

Portfolio Theory focused on the actions of a single investor with an optimal portfolio. I said what if everyone was optimizing? They've all got their copies of Markowitz and they're doing what he says. Then some people decide they want to hold more IBM, but there aren't enough shares to satisfy demand. So they put price pressure on IBM and up it goes, at which point they have to change their estimates of risk and return, because now they're paying more for the stock. That process of upward and downward pressure on prices continues until prices reach an equilibrium and everyone collectively wants to hold what's available. At that point, what can you say about the relationship between risk and return? The answer is that expected return is proportionate to beta relative to the market portfolio.

The CAPM was and is a theory of equilibrium. Why should anyone expect to earn more by investing in one security as opposed to another? You need to be compensated for doing badly when times are bad. The security that is going to do badly just when you need money when

times are bad is a security you have to hate, and there had better be some redeeming virtue or else who will hold it? That redeeming virtue has to be that in normal times you expect to do better. The key insight of the Capital Asset Pricing Model is that higher expected returns go with the greater risk of doing badly in bad times. Beta is a measure of that. Securities or asset classes with high betas tend to do worse in bad times than those with low betas.

Source: Jonathan Burton, "Revisiting the Capital Asset Pricing Model." *Dow Jones Asset Manager* (May/June 1998): 20–28.

---

*W. F. Sharpe: "Capital Asset Prices: A Theory of Market Equilibrium Under Conditions of Risk." *Journal of Finance* 19 (September 1964): 425–442.

Jack Treynor, "Toward a Theory of the Market Value of Risky Assets." Unpublished manuscript (1961).

J. Lintner: "The Valuation of Risk Assets and the Selection of Risky Investments in Stock Portfolios and Capital Budgets." *Review of Economics and Statistics* 47 (February 1965): 13–37.

J. Mossin "Equilibrium in a Capital Asset Market." *Econometrica* 34 (4) (1966): 768–783.

The Security Market Line

Figure 12.9 graphs the relations between expected return and both total risk and systematic risk (beta) for the stocks in Table 12.4. Recall from Chapter 11 that there is no clear relation between a stock's standard deviation (total risk) and its expected return, as shown in Panel (a). However, the CAPM equation (Eq. 12.6) implies that there is a linear relation between a stock's beta and its expected return. This line is graphed in Panel (b) as the line through the risk-free investment (with a beta of zero) and the market (with a beta of one); it is called the **security market line (SML)**. We see that the relation between risk and return for individual securities is only evident when we measure market risk as in Panel (b), rather than total risk as in Panel (a).

The security market line in Figure 12.9 raises the subject of negative beta stocks. While the vast majority of stocks have a positive beta, it is possible to have returns that co-vary negatively with the market. Firms that provide goods or services that are in greater demand in economic contractions than in booms fit this description.

security market line (SML) The pricing implication of the CAPM; it specifies a linear relation between the risk premium of a security and its beta with the market portfolio.

FIGURE 12.9

Expected Return,
Volatility, and Beta

Panel (a) Expected Return and Total Risk (Standard Deviation)
The graph compares the standard deviation and expected returns of the stocks in Table 12.4, as well as Apple. There is no relation between total risk and expected return. Some of the stocks are identified. It is clear that we could not predict Boston Beer's expected return using its total risk (volatility).

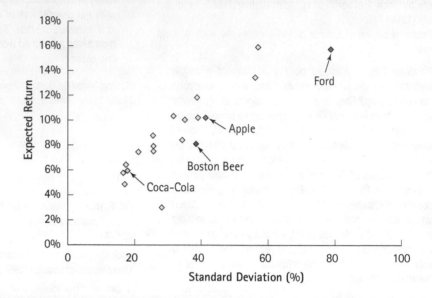

Panel (b) Expected Return and Beta
The security market line shows the expected return for Apple and each security in Table 12.4 as a function of its beta with the market. According to the CAPM, all stocks and portfolios (including the market portfolio) should lie on the security market line. Thus, Apple's expected return can be determined by its beta, which measures its systematic risk.

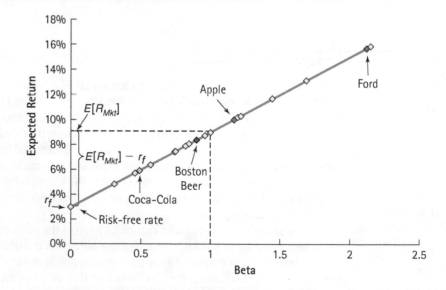

EXAMPLE 12.7
A Negative Beta Stock

MyFinanceLab

PROBLEM

Suppose the stock of Bankruptcy Auction Services Inc. (BAS) has a negative beta of -0.30. How does its expected return compare to the risk-free rate, according to the CAPM? Does your result make sense?

SOLUTION

PLAN

We can use the CAPM equation, Eq. 12.6, to compute the expected return of this negative beta stock just as we would with a positive beta stock. We don't have the risk-free rate or the market risk premium, but the problem doesn't ask us for the exact expected return, just whether or not it will be more or less than the risk-free rate. Using Eq. 12.6, we can answer that question.

EXECUTE

Because the expected return of the market is higher than the risk-free rate, Eq. 12.6 implies that the expected return of Bankruptcy Auction Services (BAS) will be *below* the risk-free rate. As long as the market risk premium is positive (as long as people demand a higher return for investing in the market than for a risk-free investment), then the second term in Eq. 12.6 will have to be negative if the beta is negative. For example, if the risk-free rate is 4% and the market risk premium is 6%:

$$E[R_{BAS}] = 4\% - 0.30\,(6\%) = 2.2\%.$$

(See Figure 12.9—the security market line drops below r_f for $\beta < 0$.)

EVALUATE

This result seems odd—why would investors be willing to accept a 2.2% expected return on this stock when they can invest in a safe investment and earn 4%? The answer is that a savvy investor will not hold BAS alone; instead, the investor will hold it in combination with other securities as part of a well-diversified portfolio. These other securities will tend to rise and fall with the market. But because BAS has a negative beta, its correlation with the market is negative, which means that BAS tends to perform well when the rest of the market is doing poorly. Therefore, by holding BAS, an investor can reduce the overall market risk of the portfolio. In a sense, BAS is "recession insurance" for a portfolio, and investors will pay for this insurance by accepting a lower expected return.

The CAPM and Portfolios

Because the security market line applies to all securities, we can apply it to portfolios as well. For example, the market portfolio is on the SML, and according to the CAPM, other portfolios (such as mutual funds) are also on the SML. Therefore, the expected return of a portfolio should correspond to the portfolio's beta. We calculate the beta of a portfolio made up of securities each with weight w_i as follows:

$$\beta_P = w_1\beta_1 + w_2\beta_2 + \cdots + w_n\beta_n \tag{12.7}$$

That is, the *beta of a portfolio is the market value weighted average beta of the securities in the portfolio.*

EXAMPLE 12.8
The Expected Return of a Portfolio

MyFinanceLab

PROBLEM

Suppose drug-maker Pfizer (PFE) has a beta of 0.7, whereas the beta of Google (GOOG) is 0.9. If the risk-free interest rate is 3% and the market risk premium is 6%, what is the expected return of an equally weighted portfolio of Pfizer and Google, according to the CAPM?

SOLUTION

PLAN

We have the following information:

$$r_f = 3\%, \qquad E[R_{Mkt}] - r_f = 6\%$$

PFE: $\quad \beta_{PFE} = 0.7, \quad w_{PFE} = 0.50$

GOOG: $\quad \beta_{GOOG} = 0.9, \quad w_{GOOG} = 0.50$

(Continued)

We can compute the expected return of the portfolio two ways. First, we can use the CAPM (Eq. 12.6) to compute the expected return of each stock and then compute the expected return of the portfolio using Eq. 12.3.

Or, we can compute the beta of the portfolio using Eq. 12.7 and then use the CAPM (Eq. 12.6) to find the portfolio's expected return.

EXECUTE

Using the first approach, we compute the expected return for PFE and GOOG:

$$E[R_{PFE}] = r_f + \beta_{PFE}(E[R_{Mkt}] - r_f) \qquad E[R_{GOOG}] = r_f + \beta_{GOOG}(E[R_{Mkt}] - r_f)$$

$$E[R_{PFE}] = 3\% + 0.7(6\%) = 7.2\% \qquad E[R_{GOOG}] = 3\% + 0.9(6\%) = 8.4\%$$

Then the expected return of the equally weighted portfolio P is:

$$E[R_P] = 0.5(7.2\%) + 0.5(8.4\%) = 7.8\%$$

Alternatively, we can compute the beta of the portfolio using Eq.12.7:

$$\beta_P = w_{PFE}\beta_{PFE} + w_{GOOG}\beta_{GOOG}$$
$$\beta_P = (0.5)(0.7) + (0.5)(0.9) = 0.8$$

We can then find the portfolio's expected return from the CAPM:

$$E[R_P] = r_f + \beta_P(E[R_{Mkt}] - r_f)$$
$$E[R_P] = 3\% + 0.8(6\%) = 7.8\%$$

EVALUATE

The CAPM is an effective tool for analyzing securities and portfolios of those securities. You can compute the expected return of each security using its beta and then compute the weighted average of those expected returns to determine the portfolio's expected return. Or, you can compute the weighted average of the securities' betas to get the portfolio's beta and then compute the expected return of the portfolio using the CAPM. Either way, you will get the same answer.

Summary of the Capital Asset Pricing Model

The CAPM is a powerful tool that is widely used to estimate the expected return on stocks and investments within companies. To summarize the model and its use:

- Investors require a risk premium proportional to the amount of *systematic* risk they are bearing.
- We can measure the systematic risk of an investment by its β, which is the sensitivity of the investment's return to the market's return. For each 1% change in the market portfolio's return, the investment's return is expected to change by β percent due to risks that it has in common with the market.
- The most common way to estimate a stock's beta is to regress its historical returns on the market's historical returns. The stock's beta is the slope of the line that best explains the relation between the market's return and the stock's return.
- The CAPM says that we can compute the expected, or required, return for any investment using the following equation:

$$E[R_i] = r_f + \beta_i(E[R_{Mkt}] - r_f)$$

which when graphed is called the *security market line*.

The Big Picture

The CAPM marks the culmination of our examination of how investors in capital markets trade off risk and return. It provides a powerful and widely used tool to quantify the return that should accompany a particular amount of systematic risk. We have already reached our goal (in Example 12.6) of estimating the cost of equity capital for Apple. While our finding that equity investors in Apple should reasonably expect (and therefore require) a return of 10.2% on their investments is an important piece of information to Apple's managers, it is not the whole picture. While some firms have only equity investors, most have debt investors as well. In Chapters 13, we will apply what we have learned here and in Chapters 6, 7, and 10 on bonds and stocks to develop the overall cost of capital for a company. The Valuation Principle tells us to use this cost of capital to discount the future expected cash flows of a firm to arrive at the value of the firm. Thus, the cost of capital is an essential input to the financial manager's job of analyzing investment opportunities, and so knowing this overall cost of capital is critical to the company's success at creating value for its investors.

Concept Check

7. What does the CAPM say about the required return of a security?
8. What is the security market line?

MyFinanceLab

Here is what you should know after reading this chapter. MyFinanceLab will help you identify what you know, and where to go when you need to practice.

Key Points and Equations	Key Terms	Online Practice
12.1 The Expected Return of a Portfolio • The portfolio weight is the initial fraction w_i of an investor's money invested in each asset. Portfolio weights add up to one: $$w_i = \frac{\text{Value of Investment } i}{\text{Total Value of Portfolio}} \quad (12.1)$$ • The expected return of a portfolio is the weighted average of the expected returns of the investments within it, using the portfolio weights: $$E[R_P] = w_1 E[R_1] + w_2 E[R_2] + \cdots + w_n E[R_n] \quad (12.3)$$	expected return of a portfolio, p. 366 portfolio weights, p. 364 return of a portfolio, p. 364	MyFinanceLab Study Plan 12.1
12.2 The Volatility of a Portfolio • To find the risk of a portfolio, we need to know the degree to which stock returns move together. Correlation measures the co-movement of returns. The correlation is always between -1 and $+1$. It represents the fraction of the volatility due to risk that is common to the securities. • The variance of a portfolio depends on the correlation of the stocks. For a portfolio with two stocks, the portfolio variance is: $Var(R_p)$ $= w_1^2 SD(R_1)^2 + w_2^2 SD(R_2)^2$ $\quad + 2w_1 w_2 Corr(R_1, R_2) SD(R_1) SD(R_2) \quad (12.4)$ • As we lower the correlation between the two stocks in a portfolio, we lower the portfolio variance. • Diversification eliminates independent, firm-specific risks, and the volatility of a large portfolio results from the common systematic risk between the stocks in the portfolio.	correlation, p. 369 equally weighted portfolio, p. 374 volatility of a portfolio, p. 367	MyFinanceLab Study Plan 12.2 Using Excel: Correlation Between Two Sets of Returns

12.3 Measuring Systematic Risk

- The market portfolio in theory is a value-weighted index of all risky investments. In practice, we often use a stock market index such as the S&P 500 to represent the market.
- A stock's beta is the percentage change in its return that we expect for each 1% change in the market's return.
- To estimate beta, we often use historical returns. Most data sources use five years of monthly returns to estimate beta.
- Beta also corresponds to the slope of the best-fitting line in the plot of a security's excess returns versus the market's excess returns. We use linear regression to find the best-fitting line.
- The beta of a portfolio is the weighted-average beta of the securities in the portfolio.

beta (β), p. 377
market capitalization, p. 375
market index, p. 376
market portfolio, p. 375
market proxy, p. 376
value-weighted portfolio, p. 376

MyFinanceLab
Study Plan 12.3

Interactive Beta Calculation,
Using Excel: Calculating a Stock's Beta

12.4 Putting It All Together: The Capital Asset Pricing Model

- According to the CAPM, the risk premium of any security is equal to the market risk premium multiplied by the beta of the security. This relationship is called the security market line (SML), and it determines the expected or required return for an investment:

$$E[R_i] = r_f + \underbrace{\beta_i(E[R_{Mkt}] - r_f)}_{\text{Risk premium for security } i} \quad (12.6)$$

Capital Asset Pricing Model (CAPM), p. 383
market or equity risk premium, p. 383
required return, p. 384
security market line (SML), p. 385

MyFinanceLab
Study Plan 12.4

CRITICAL
THINKING

1. What information do you need to compute the expected return of a portfolio?

2. What does correlation tell us?

3. Why isn't the total risk of a portfolio simply equal to the weighted average of the risks of the securities in the portfolio?

4. What does beta measure? How do we use beta?

5. What, intuitively, does the CAPM say drives expected return?

6. What relation is described by the security market line?

PROBLEMS

*All problems in this chapter are available in MyFinanceLab. An asterisk * indicates problems with a higher level of difficulty.*

The Expected Return of a Portfolio

1. You buy 100 shares of Tidepool Co. for $40 each and 200 shares of Madfish, Inc., for $15 each. What are the weights in your portfolio?

2. Fremont Enterprises has an expected return of 15% and Laurelhurst News has an expected return of 20%. If you put 70% of your portfolio in Laurelhurst and 30% in Fremont, what is the expected return of your portfolio?

3. You are considering how to invest part of your retirement savings. You have decided to put $200,000 into three stocks: 50% of the money in GoldFinger (currently

$25/share), 25% of the money in Moosehead (currently $80/share), and the remainder in Venture Associates (currently $2/share). If GoldFinger stock goes up to $30/share, Moosehead stock drops to $60/share, and Venture Associates stock rises to $3 per share,

a. What is the new value of the portfolio?
b. What return did the portfolio earn?
c. If you don't buy or sell shares after the price change, what are your new portfolio weights?

4. You have $70,000. You put 20% of your money in a stock with an expected return of 12%, $30,000 in a stock with an expected return of 15%, and the rest in a stock with an expected return of 20%. What is the expected return of your portfolio?

5. There are two ways to calculate the expected return of a portfolio: Either calculate the expected return using the value and dividend stream of the portfolio as a whole, or calculate the weighted average of the expected returns of the individual stocks that make up the portfolio. Which return is higher?

The Volatility of a Portfolio

6. If the returns of two stocks have a correlation of 1, what does this imply about the relative movements in the stock prices?

 7. Stocks A and B have the following returns (*see MyFinanceLab for the data in Excel format*):

	Stock A	Stock B
1	0.10	0.06
2	0.07	0.02
3	0.15	0.05
4	−0.05	0.01
5	0.08	−0.02

a. What are the expected returns of the two stocks?
b. What are the standard deviations of the returns of the two stocks?
c. If their correlation is 0.46, what is the expected return and standard deviation of a portfolio of 70% stock A and 30% stock B?

 8. Using the data in the following table, estimate the average return and volatility for each stock (*see MyFinanceLab for the data in Excel format*).

	Realized Returns	
Year	Stock A	Stock B
2008	−10%	21%
2009	20%	30%
2010	5%	7%
2011	−5%	−3%
2012	2%	−8%
2013	9%	25%

9. Using your estimates from Problem 8 and the fact that the correlation of A and B is 0.48, calculate the volatility (standard deviation) of a portfolio that is 70% invested in stock A and 30% invested in stock B.

10. The following spreadsheet contains monthly returns for Cola Co. and Gas Co. for 2013. Using these data, estimate the average monthly return and volatility for each stock (*see MyFinanceLab for the data in Excel format*).

Date	Cola Co.	Gas Co.
Jan	−10.84%	−6.00%
Feb	2.36%	1.28%
Mar	6.60%	−1.86%
Apr	2.01%	−1.90%
May	18.36%	7.40%
June	−1.22%	−0.26%
July	2.25%	8.36%
Aug	−6.89%	−2.46%
Sep	−6.04%	−2.00%
Oct	13.61%	0.00%
Nov	3.51%	4.68%
Dec	0.54%	2.22%

 11. Using the spreadsheet from Problem 10 and the fact that Cola Co. and Gas Co. have a correlation of 0.6083, calculate the volatility (standard deviation) of a portfolio that is 55% invested in Cola Co. stock and 45% invested in Gas Co. stock. Calculate the volatility by
a. Using Eq. 12.4.
b. Calculating the monthly returns of the portfolio and computing its volatility directly.
c. How do your results compare?

12. Using the data in Table 12.2,
a. Compute the annual returns for a portfolio with 25% invested in North Air, 25% invested in West Air, and 50% invested in Texas Oil.
b. What is the lowest annual return for your portfolio in part a? How does it compare with the lowest annual return of the individual stocks or portfolios in Table 12.2?

13. Using the data from Table 12.3, what is the volatility of an equally weighted portfolio of Microsoft and Ford stock?

14. Suppose Johnson & Johnson and the Walgreen Company have the expected returns and volatilities shown below, with a correlation of 22%.

	E[R]	SD[R]
Johnson & Johnson	7%	16%
Walgreen Company	10%	20%

For a portfolio that is equally invested in Johnson & Johnson's and Walgreen's stock, calculate
a. The expected return.
b. The volatility (standard deviation).

15. Arbor Systems and Gencore stocks both have a volatility of 40%. Compute the volatility of a portfolio with 50% invested in each stock if the correlation between the stocks is (a) +1, (b) 0.50, (c) 0, (d) −0.50, and (e) −1.0. In which cases is the volatility lower than that of the original stocks?

16. Suppose Wesley Publishing stock has a volatility of 60%, while Addison Printing stock has a volatility of 30%. If the correlation between these stocks is 25%, what is the volatility of the following portfolios of Addison and Wesley: (a) 100% Addison, (b) 75% Addison and 25% Wesley, and (c) 50% Addison and 50% Wesley?

17. You have a portfolio with a standard deviation of 30% and an expected return of 18%. You are considering adding one of the two stocks in the following table. If after adding the stock you will have 20% of your money in the new stock and 80% of your money in your existing portfolio, which one should you add?

	Expected Return	Standard Deviation	Correlation with Your Portfolio's Returns
Stock A	15%	25%	0.2
Stock B	15%	20%	0.6

18. Your client has $100,000 invested in stock A. She would like to build a two-stock portfolio by investing another $100,000 in either stock B or C. She wants a portfolio with an expected return of at least 14% and as low a risk as possible, but the standard deviation must be no more than 40%. What do you advise her to do, and what will be the portfolio's expected return and standard deviation?

	Expected Return	Standard Deviation	Correlation with A
A	15%	50%	1
B	13%	40%	0.2
C	13%	40%	0.3

Measuring Systematic Risk

19. Suppose all possible investment opportunities in the world are limited to the five stocks listed in the following table. What are the market portfolio weights (*see MyFinanceLab for the data in Excel format*)?

Stock	Price/Share ($)	Number of Shares Outstanding (millions)
A	10	10
B	20	12
C	8	3
D	50	1
E	45	20

20. Given $100,000 to invest, construct a value-weighted portfolio of the four stocks listed below (*see MyFinanceLab for the data in Excel format*).

Stock	Price/Share ($)	Number of Shares Outstanding (millions)
Golden Seas	13	1.00
Jacobs and Jacobs	22	1.25
MAG	43	30
PDJB	5	10

21. If one stock in a value-weighted portfolio goes up in price and all other stock prices remain the same, what trades are necessary to keep the portfolio value weighted?

22. You hear on the news that the S&P 500 was down 2% today relative to the risk-free rate (the market's excess return was −2%). You are thinking about your portfolio and your investments in Zynga and Procter & Gamble.
    a. If Zynga's beta is 1.4, what is your best guess as to Zynga's excess return today?
    b. If Procter & Gamble's beta is 0.5, what is your best guess as to P&G's excess return today?

23. Go to Chapter Resources on MyFinanceLab and use the data in the spreadsheet provided to estimate the beta of Nike stock using linear regression.

24. The Chapter Resources section of MyFinanceLab has data on Microsoft and the S&P 500 from 1986 to 2006.
    a. Estimate Microsoft's beta using linear regression over the periods 1987–1991, 1992–1996, 1997–2001, and 2002–2006.
    b. Compare the four estimated betas. What do you conclude about how Microsoft's exposure to systematic risk changed over that 20-year period? What do you think explains the change?

Putting It All Together: The Capital Asset Pricing Model

25. Suppose the risk-free return is 4% and the market portfolio has an expected return of 10% and a standard deviation of 16%. Johnson & Johnson Corporation stock has a beta of 0.32. What is its expected return?

26. What is the sign of the risk premium of a negative-beta stock? Explain. (Assume the risk premium of the market portfolio is positive.)

27. EJH has a beta of 1.2, CSH has a beta of 0.6, and KMS has a beta of 1.0. If you put 25% of your money in EJH, 25% in CSH, and 50% in KMS, what is the beta of your portfolio?

28. Suppose Autodesk stock has a beta of 2.16, whereas Costco stock has a beta of 0.69. If the risk-free interest rate is 4% and the expected return of the market portfolio is 10%, what is the expected return of a portfolio that consists of 60% Autodesk stock and 40% Costco stock, according to the CAPM?

29. Suppose Intel stock has a beta of 1.6, whereas Boeing stock has a beta of 1. If the risk-free interest rate is 4% and the expected return of the market portfolio is 10%, according to the CAPM,
    a. What is the expected return of Intel stock?
    b. What is the expected return of Boeing stock?
    c. What is the beta of a portfolio that consists of 60% Intel stock and 40% Boeing stock?
    d. What is the expected return of a portfolio that consists of 60% Intel stock and 40% Boeing stock? (Show both ways to solve this.)

*30. You are thinking of buying a stock priced at $100 per share. Assume that the risk-free rate is about 4.5% and the market risk premium is 6%. If you think the stock will rise to $117 per share by the end of the year, at which time it will pay a $1 dividend, what beta would it need to have for this expectation to be consistent with the CAPM?

*31. You are analyzing a stock that has a beta of 1.2. The risk-free rate is 5% and you estimate the market risk premium to be 6%. If you expect the stock to have a return of 11% over the next year, should you buy it? Why or why not?

32. You have risen through the ranks of a coffee company, from the lowly green-apron barista to the coveted black apron, and all the way to CFO. A quick Internet check

shows that your company's beta is 0.6. The risk-free rate is 5% and you believe the market risk premium to be 5.5%. What is your best estimate of investors' expected return on your company's stock (its cost of equity capital)?

33. At the beginning of 2007, Apple's beta was 1.4 and the risk-free rate was about 4.5%. Apple's price was $84.84. Apple's price at the end of 2007 was 198.08. If you estimate the market risk premium to have been 6%, did Apple's managers exceed their investors' required return as given by the CAPM?

*34. You want to invest $50,000 in a portfolio with a beta of no more than 1.4 and an expected return of 12.4%. Bay Corp. has a beta of 1.2 and an expected return of 11.2%, and City Inc. has a beta of 1.8 and an expected return of 14.8%. The risk-free rate is 4%. You can invest in Bay Corp. and City Inc. How much will you invest in each?

Chapter 12
APPENDIX

Alternative Models of Systematic Risk

While the CAPM is the most widely used model for estimating the cost of capital in practice, recently some practitioners have tried to improve on the CAPM.

Problems with the CAPM in Practice

Researchers have found that using only the S&P 500, or some other simple proxy for the true market portfolio, has led to consistent pricing errors from the CAPM. That is, some stocks and portfolios of stocks earn consistently higher or lower returns than the CAPM would predict. For example, researchers have found that small stocks, stocks with high ratios of book-to-market value of equity, and stocks that have recently performed very well have consistently earned higher returns than the CAPM would predict using a simple stock market proxy for the market portfolio.

Multi-Factor Models

risk factors Different components of systematic risk (used in a multi-factor model).

multi-factor model A model that uses more than one portfolio to capture systematic risk. Each portfolio can be thought of as either the risk factor itself or a portfolio of stocks correlated with an unobservable risk factor.

These findings have led researchers to add new portfolios to the CAPM pricing equation in an attempt to construct a better proxy for the true market portfolio. The goal is a proxy that captures the components of systematic risk that just using the S&P 500 alone misses. Although we might not be able to identify a perfect proxy for the true market portfolio, the market portfolio can be constructed from other portfolios. This observation implies that as long as the market portfolio can be constructed from a collection of portfolios, the collection itself can be used to measure risk. *Thus, it is not actually necessary to identify the market portfolio itself.* All that is required is to identify a collection of portfolios from which it can be constructed.

Thus, we can use a collection of portfolios to capture the components of systematic risk, referred to as **risk factors**. A model with more than one portfolio to capture risk is known as a **multi-factor model**. Each portfolio can be thought of as either the risk factor itself or a portfolio of stocks correlated with an unobservable risk factor. This particular form of the multi-factor model was originally developed by Professor Stephen Ross, but

Professor Robert Merton developed an alternative multi-factor model earlier.[6] The model is also referred to as the **Arbitrage Pricing Theory (APT)**.

Fama-French-Carhart Factor Specification

Practitioners have added portfolios specifically to address the CAPM pricing errors. One such portfolio is constructed by buying small firms and selling large firms. This portfolio is widely known as the *small-minus-big (SMB) portfolio*. A second portfolio buys high book-to-market firms and sells low book-to-market firms, and we call it the *high-minus-low (HML) portfolio*. A third portfolio buys stocks that have recently done extremely well and sells those that have done extremely poorly. Since this portfolio addresses the problem that this extremely good and bad performance continues in the short run, it is called the *prior 1-year (PR1YR) momentum portfolio*.

The collection of these four portfolios—the stock market (Mkt), SMB, HML, and PR1YR—is the most popular collection of portfolios used as an alternative model to the CAPM and is one example of a multi-factor model. Using this collection, the expected return of security i is given by:

$$E[R_i] = r_f + \beta_i^{Mkt}(E[R_{Mkt}] - r_f) + \beta_i^{SMB}E[R_{SMB}] + \beta_i^{HML}E[R_{HML}]$$
$$+ \beta_i^{PR1YR}E[R_{PR1YR}] \tag{12.8}$$

where β_i^{Mkt}, β_i^{SMB}, β_i^{HML}, and β_i^{PR1YR} are the factor betas of stock i and measure the sensitivity of the stock to each portfolio. Because the collection of portfolios in Eq. 12.8 (Mkt, SMB, HML, and PR1YR) were identified by Professors Eugene Fama, Kenneth French, and Mark Carhart, we refer to this collection of portfolios as the **Fama-French-Carhart (FFC) factor specification**.

The average monthly returns for each of the four portfolios in the FFC factor specification are given in Table 12.5.

TABLE 12.5

FFC Portfolio Average Monthly Returns (1926–2008)

	Average Monthly Return (%)
Mkt−r_f	0.61
SMB	0.25
HML	0.38
PR1YR	0.70

Source: Kenneth French: http://mba.tuck.dartmouth.edu/pages/faculty/ken.french/data_library.html.

EXAMPLE 12.9

Using the FFC Factor Specification to Calculate the Cost of Capital

MyFinanceLab

PROBLEM

You are currently considering making an investment in the fast food industry. You determine the project has the same level of non-diversifiable risk as investing in McDonald's stock. You use data over the past nine years to estimate the factor betas of McDonald's stock (ticker symbol: MCD). Specifically, you regress the

---

[6]See Stephen A. Ross, "The Arbitrage Theory of Capital Asset Pricing," *Journal of Economic Theory* 3 (December 1976): 343–362, and Robert C. Merton "An Intertemporal Capital Asset Pricing Model," *Econometrica* 41 (1973): 867–887.

monthly excess return (the realized return in each month minus the risk-free rate) of McDonald's stock on the return of each of the four-factor portfolios. You determine that the factor betas for MCD are:

$$\beta_{MCD}^{Mkt} = 0.687$$

$$\beta_{MCD}^{SMB} = -0.299$$

$$\beta_{MCD}^{HML} = -0.156$$

$$\beta_{MCD}^{PR1YR} = 0.123$$

The current risk-free monthly rate is 1.5%/12 = 0.125%. Determine the cost of capital by using the FFC factor specification.

SOLUTION

PLAN

First, gather the information you have. Combining the information in the problem with the data in Table 12.5, you have:

	Average Monthly Return (%)	MCD's β with Factor
Mkt−r_f	0.61	0.687
SMB	0.25	−0.299
HML	0.38	−0.156
PR1YR	0.70	0.123

Using the information you have collected along with the monthly risk-free rate of 0.125%, you can use Eq. 12.8 to calculate the monthly expected return for investing in McDonald's. From there, you can multiply by 12 to get the annual expected return, represented as an APR.

EXECUTE

Using Eq. 12.8, the monthly expected return of investing in McDonald's is:

$$E[R_{MCD}] = r_f + \beta_{MCD}^{Mkt}(E[R_{Mkt}] - r_f) + \beta_{MCD}^{SMB}E[R_{SMB}] + \beta_{MCD}^{HML}E[R_{HML}] + \beta_{MCD}^{PR1YR}E[R_{PR1YR}]$$

$$= 0.125\% + 0.687 \times 0.61\% - 0.299 \times 0.25\% - 0.156 \times 0.38\% + 0.123 \times 0.70\%$$

$$= 0.496\%$$

Expressed as an APR, the expected return is 0.496% × 12 = 5.95%

EVALUATE

By gathering all of the inputs and applying the FFC factor specification in the same way we would apply the CAPM, we can calculate this alternative estimate of the cost of capital for McDonald's stock. According to this approach, we would conclude that the annual cost of capital of the investment opportunity is about 5.95%.

As a comparison, a standard CAPM regression over the same time period leads to an estimated market beta of 0.54 for McDonald's—the market beta differs from the estimate of 0.687 above because we are using only a single factor in the CAPM regression. Using the historical excess return on the market implies an expected return of 0.125% + 0.54 × 0.61% = 0.454% per month, or about 5.5% per year.

The Cost of Capital

LEARNING OBJECTIVES

- Understand the drivers of the firm's overall cost of capital

- Measure the costs of debt, preferred stock, and common stock

- Compute a firm's overall, or weighted average, cost of capital

- Apply the weighted average cost of capital to value projects

- Adjust the cost of capital for the risk associated with the project

- Account for the direct costs of raising external capital

notation

$D\%$	fraction of the firm financed with debt	P_{pfd}	price of preferred stock
Div_1	dividend due in one year	r_D	required return (cost of capital) for debt
Div_{pfd}	dividend on preferred stock	r_E	required return (cost of capital) of levered equity
$E\%$	fraction of the firm financed with equity	r_{pfd}	required return (cost of capital) for preferred stock
FCF_t	incremental free cash flow in year t		
g	expected growth rate for dividends	r_{wacc}	weighted average cost of capital
$P\%$	fraction of the firm financed with preferred stock	T_C	marginal corporate tax rate
P_E	price of common stock equity	V_0^L	initial levered value

In Chapter 12, we learned how to determine a firm's equity cost of capital. In reality, most firms are financed with a combination of equity, debt, and other securities such as preferred stock. As a result, financial managers must determine their firm's overall cost of capital based on all sources of financing. This overall cost of capital is a critical input into the capital budgeting process. The Valuation Principle tells us that the value of a project is the present value of its benefits net of the present value of its costs. In capital budgeting, we implement this important concept with net present value (NPV). To calculate a project's NPV, we need a cost of capital to use as a discount rate.

In this chapter, we will learn how to calculate and use the firm's overall cost of capital, which is typically referred to as its *weighted average cost of capital (WACC)*. We will see that the WACC is a weighted average of the costs of capital from each of the firm's different financing sources. After we have learned how to estimate the WACC, we will apply it in capital budgeting. As part of that discussion, we will learn the conditions under which we can use the firm's overall cost of capital as a discount rate and identify those situations in which we will instead need to determine a cost of capital specific to a project or division of the firm.

13.1 A First Look at the Weighted Average Cost of Capital

Most firms draw on some combination of equity, debt, and other securities to raise the funds they need for investment. In this section, we examine the role of financing sources in determining the firm's overall cost of capital. We begin by stepping back to assess these financing sources in the context of the firm's balance sheet.

The Firm's Capital Structure

capital A firm's sources of financing—debt, equity, and other securities that it has outstanding.

A firm's sources of financing, which usually consist of debt and equity, represent its **capital**. The typical firm raises funds to invest by selling shares to stockholders (its equity) and borrowing from lenders (its debt). Recall the most basic form of the balance sheet, as represented in Figure 13.1. The left side of the balance sheet lists the firm's assets, and the right side describes the firm's capital.

capital structure The relative proportions of debt, equity, and other securities that a firm has outstanding.

The relative proportions of debt, equity, and other securities that a firm has outstanding constitute its **capital structure**. When corporations raise funds from outside investors, they must choose which type of security to issue. The most common choices are financing through equity alone and financing through a combination of debt and equity. Figure 13.2 shows the capital structures of Apple and Southwest Airlines. Capital structures vary widely across firms. In Chapter 16, we will discuss how a firm sets its capital structure.

Opportunity Cost and the Overall Cost of Capital

Financial managers take into account each component of the firm's capital structure when determining the firm's overall cost of capital. Throughout the discussion that follows, keep in mind the intuition behind the term "cost of capital." When investors buy the stock

FIGURE 13.1

A Basic Balance Sheet

This figure provides a very basic balance sheet for reference. As discussed in Chapter 2, the two sides of the balance sheet must equal each other: Assets = Liabilities + Equity. The right side represents the way the assets are financed. In this chapter, we will focus on the required returns for the different forms of financing found on the right side of the balance sheet.

Assets	Liabilities and Equity
Current Assets	Debt
Long-Term Assets	Preferred Stock
	Equity

FIGURE 13.2

Two Capital Structures

This figure shows the capital structures of two real firms. Apple is financed 96% with common equity, shown in blue, while Southwest Airlines is financed 74% with common equity and 26% with debt, shaded in beige.

Source: Authors' calculations based on publicly available data in 2013.

or bonds of a company, they forgo the opportunity to invest that money elsewhere. The expected return from those alternative investments constitutes an opportunity cost to them. Thus, to attract their investments as capital to the firm, the firm must offer potential investors an expected return equal to what they could expect to earn elsewhere for assuming the same level of risk. Providing this return is the cost a company bears in exchange for obtaining capital from investors.

Weighted Averages and the Overall Cost of Capital

Intuitively, the firm's overall cost of capital should be a blend of the costs of the different sources of capital. In fact, we calculate the firm's overall cost of capital as a weighted average of its equity and debt costs of capital, known as the firm's **weighted average cost of capital (WACC)**.

weighted average cost of capital (WACC) The average of a firm's equity and debt costs of capital, weighted by the fractions of the firm's value that correspond to equity and debt, respectively.

But what should the weights be? Imagine you owned all of the stock and all of the debt of the firm. If that was all you had in your portfolio, the return on your portfolio would be the total return of the firm. As we showed in Chapter 12, a portfolio return is the weighted average of the returns of the securities in the portfolio. In this case, the return on your portfolio—the total return of the firm—is a weighted average of the return you earn holding all the stock of the firm and the return you earn holding all of the debt. Since you hold all of each, your portfolio weights are just the relative amount of debt and equity issued by the firm. Thus, the weights we use in the WACC are the proportions of debt and equity used in the firm's capital structure. For example, if the firm is financed 30% by debt and 70% by equity, then the weights used in its WACC would be 30% on the debt cost of capital and 70% on the equity cost of capital.

This example suggests that you can determine the weights by looking at the right side of the firm's balance sheet. That assumption is correct, with one important modification: You must use the *market values* of the debt and equity to determine the proportions, not the accounting-based *book values* listed on the balance sheet. Recall from Chapter 2 that book values reflect historical costs, but market values are forward-looking, based on what the assets are expected to produce in the future. Holders of the firm's financial claims—equity and, if the firm has it, debt—assess the firm based on the market value of its assets, not the book value.

market-value balance sheet Similar to an accounting balance sheet, but all values are current market values rather than historical costs.

In fact, it is useful to think about the **market-value balance sheet**, where the assets, debt, and equity are all listed in terms of their market values, instead of their book values. Of course, the market-value balance sheet must still balance:

$$\text{Market Value of Equity} + \text{Market Value of Debt} = \text{Market Value of Assets} \quad (13.1)$$

Equation 13.1 states that the total market value of all the claims (equity and debt) issued by the firm must be equal to the total market value of all its assets. This equality drives home the point that the equity and debt issued by the firm derive their value from the underlying assets they claim. The risk, and hence the required return, of the debt and equity of the firm are determined by the risk of the firm's assets. This point will be useful as we derive the firm's WACC.

Weighted Average Cost of Capital Calculations

In this section, we will develop the intuition behind the use of market-value weights as well as the link between the risk of the assets and the risk of the debt and equity claims on those assets.

unlevered A firm that does not have debt outstanding.

levered A firm that has debt outstanding.

leverage The relative amount of debt on a firm's balance sheet.

We begin with the straightforward case of the firm that does not issue debt—the **unlevered** firm that pays out all of the free cash flows generated by its assets to its equity holders. When some of a firm's financing comes from debt, we say the firm is **levered**. Just as a lever allows you to lift a heavy object by exerting relatively little force, so borrowing money through debt allows equity holders to control highly valued assets with relatively little investment of their own money. We refer to the relative amount of debt on the balance sheet as the firm's **leverage**.

The Weighted Average Cost of Capital: Unlevered Firm. If a firm is unlevered, so that it has no debt, all of the free cash flows generated by its assets are ultimately paid out to its equity holders. Because the free cash flows to the equity holders are the same as the free cash flows from the assets, the Valuation Principle tells us that the market value, risk, and cost of capital for the firm's equity are equal to the corresponding amounts for its assets. Given this relationship, we can estimate the firm's equity cost of capital using the Capital Asset Pricing Model (CAPM). The resulting estimate is the cost of capital for the firm as a whole. For example, Zynga does do not issue debt, so the cost of capital for Zynga's assets is the same as Zynga's cost of equity.

The Weighted Average Cost of Capital: Levered Firm. But what if the firm has debt? How should we incorporate the cost of this debt to determine the cost of capital for the firm's assets as a whole? The market-value balance sheet provides the answer. We can interpret the equality in Eq. 13.1 in terms of a portfolio: By holding a portfolio of the firm's equity and debt, we can get the same cash flows as if we held the assets directly. Because the return of a portfolio is equal to the weighted average of the returns of the securities in it, this equality implies the following relationship between the required returns (costs) of equity, debt, and assets:

Weighted Average Cost of Capital (Pretax)

$$r_{wacc} = \left(\begin{array}{c} \text{Fraction of Firm Value} \\ \text{Financed by Equity} \end{array} \right) \left(\begin{array}{c} \text{Equity} \\ \text{Cost of Capital} \end{array} \right)$$

$$+ \left(\begin{array}{c} \text{Fraction of Firm Value} \\ \text{Financed by Debt} \end{array} \right) \left(\begin{array}{c} \text{Debt} \\ \text{Cost of Capital} \end{array} \right)$$

$$= \left(\begin{array}{c} \text{Asset} \\ \text{Cost of Capital} \end{array} \right) \quad (13.2)$$

We now have the justification for our intuition that the overall cost of capital for a firm should be a weighted average of its equity and debt costs of capital. Eq. 13.2 shows that we can calculate the cost of capital of the firm's assets by computing the weighted average of the firm's equity and debt cost of capital. In the next section, we explore how to estimate the firm's costs of equity and debt capital.

EXAMPLE 13.1

Calculating the Weights in the WACC

MyFinanceLab

PROBLEM

Suppose Kenai Corp. has debt with a book (face) value of $10 million, trading at 95% of face value. It also has book equity of $10 million, and 1 million shares of common stock trading at $30 per share. What weights should Kenai use in calculating its WACC?

SOLUTION

PLAN

Equation 13.2 tells us that the weights are the fractions of Kenai financed with debt and financed with equity. Furthermore, these weights should be based on market values because the cost of capital is based on investors' current assessment of the value of the firm, not on accounting-based book values. As a consequence, we can ignore the book values of debt and equity.

EXECUTE

$10 million in debt trading at 95% of face value is $9.5 million in market value. One million shares of stock at $30 per share is $30 million in market value. So, the total market value of the firm is $39.5 million.

The weights are

$$9.5 \div 39.5 = 24.1\% \text{ for debt and } 30 \div 39.5 = 75.9\% \text{ for equity.}$$

EVALUATE

When calculating its overall cost of capital, Kenai will use a weighted average of the cost of its debt capital and the cost of its equity capital, giving a weight of 24.1% to its cost of debt and a weight of 75.9% to its cost of equity.

Concept Check

1. Why does a firm's capital have a cost?

2. Why do we use market-value weights in the weighted average cost of capital?

13.2 The Firm's Costs of Debt and Equity Capital

Section 13.1 made it clear that to measure the firm's overall cost of capital, we need to start by determining the cost of each type of capital a firm might use. We now turn to how a company measures the costs of its debt, preferred stock, and common stock. We will use DuPont, a global chemical company, as an example.

Cost of Debt Capital

We will start at the top of the right side of the balance sheet with the cost of the firm's debt. A firm's cost of debt is the interest rate it would have to pay to refinance its existing debt, such as through new bond issues. This rate differs from the coupon rate on the firm's existing debt, which reflects the interest rate the firm had to offer at the time the debt was issued.

Yield to Maturity and the Cost of Debt. Existing debt trades in the marketplace, so its price fluctuates to reflect both changes in the overall credit environment and changes in the risk specifically associated with the firm. As we learned in Chapter 6, the market price of the firm's existing debt implies a yield to maturity, which is the return that current purchasers of the debt would earn if they held the debt to maturity and received all of the payments as promised. So, we can use the yield to maturity to estimate the firm's current cost of debt: It is the yield that investors demand to hold the firm's debt (new or existing).[1]

Suppose DuPont has debt due in 2020 with a coupon rate of 4.63% priced at $1167.80 per $1000 face value. Because the market price of the debt is above its face value, investors in debt earn a yield that is lower than the 4.63% coupon rate. In fact, based on the timing of the remaining payments, this price implies a yield to maturity of 2.81%, which is an estimate of DuPont's current cost of debt. You would not need to actually compute the yield to maturity yourself because prices and their implied yields to maturity are always quoted together in the bond market.[2]

COMMON MISTAKE — Using the Coupon Rate as the Cost of Debt

A common mistake in estimating a company's overall cost of capital is to use the coupon rate on its existing debt as its debt cost of capital. The company's cost of capital is forward-looking and based on current conditions. By contrast, the coupon rate on existing debt is historical and set under potentially very different conditions. A better estimate of the firm's debt cost of capital is the yield to maturity of its existing debt, which is the promised return its lenders currently demand. As we mention in the text, it would be even better to adjust the promised yield to maturity for expected losses to get an estimate of investors' actual expected return.

Consider KB Homes as an example. KB has bonds due in 2014 that were originally issued in 2004; these bonds have a coupon rate of 5.75%. With the collapse of the U.S. real estate market in 2008, KB Homes' performance suffered and the risk that it

might not be able to meet all of its debt obligations increased. By mid-2010, those 5.75% coupon bonds were rated BB (below investment grade) and trading at a yield to maturity of about 8.6%. Thus, to be willing to take a creditor position in KB, investors demanded a yield to maturity of 8.6%. Taking into account the probability of default and the expected loss in default, BB-rated bonds had an average expected loss of 1.3%. Thus, the true expected return was closer to 7.3% (8.6% promised minus 1.3% expected loss).

So, which is a better estimate of the cost of debt capital for KB in 2010: the 5.75% coupon or something based on the 8.6% yield to maturity? It would be a mistake for KB to use 5.75% as its cost of debt capital. The 5.75% rate, which was set under different circumstances, is not a relevant measure of KB's debt holders' required return in 2010, so it should not enter into the WACC calculation. Because of the default risk, the 7.3% we calculated would be a much better estimate of KB's cost of debt capital.

Taxes and the Cost of Debt. In the case of debt, the return paid to the debt holders is not the same as the cost to the firm. How could this be? The difference arises because interest paid on debt is a tax-deductible expense. When a firm uses debt financing, the cost of the interest it must pay is offset to some extent by the tax savings from the tax deduction.

For example, suppose a firm with a 35% tax rate borrows $100,000 at 10% interest per year. Then its net cost at the end of the year is calculated as follows:

		Year-End
Interest expense	$r_D \times \$100,000 =$	$10,000
Tax savings	$-\text{ Tax Rate} \times r_D \times \$100,000 =$	−$3500
Effective after-tax interest expense	$r_D \times (1 - \text{Tax Rate}) \times \$100,000 =$	$6500

effective cost of the debt A firm's net cost of interest on its debt after accounting for the interest tax deduction.

The **effective cost of the debt**—the firm's net cost of interest on its debt after taxes—is only $6500/$100,000 = 6.50% of the loan amount, rather than the full 10% interest. Thus, the tax deductibility of interest lowers the effective cost of debt financing for the firm.

---

[1]In fact, the yield to maturity is the *most* the firm will pay because there is some risk the firm may not repay its debt. The expected return on the bond can be significantly less than the *promised* yield to maturity during times when the firm might be close to financial distress. However, outside of these times, the yield on an A-rated bond such as DuPont's provides a reasonable estimate of its expected return.

[2]Chapter 6 demonstrated how to find current prices and yields to maturity for corporate bonds online using the Web site http://www.finra.org/marketdata.

More generally, with tax-deductible interest and denoting the corporate tax rate as T_C, the effective after-tax borrowing rate is

$$r_D(1 - T_C) \qquad (13.3)$$

EXAMPLE 13.2

Effective Cost of Debt

MyFinanceLab

PROBLEM

By using the yield to maturity on DuPont's debt, we found that its pretax cost of debt is 2.81%. If DuPont's tax rate is 35%, what is its effective cost of debt?

SOLUTION

PLAN

We can use Eq. 13.3 to calculate DuPont's effective cost of debt:

$$r_D = 0.0281 \,(\text{pretax cost of debt})$$
$$T_C = 0.35 \,(\text{corporate tax rate})$$

EXECUTE

DuPont's effective cost of debt is $0.0281\,(1 - 0.35) = 0.01827 = 1.827\%$.

EVALUATE

For every new $1000 it borrows, DuPont would pay its bondholders $0.0281\,(\$1000) = \$28.10$ in interest every year. Because it can deduct that $28.10 in interest from its income, every dollar in interest saves DuPont 35 cents in taxes, so the interest tax deduction reduces the firm's tax payment to the government by $0.35\,(\$28.10) = \$9.83$. Thus, DuPont's net cost of debt is the $28.10 it pays minus the $9.83 in reduced tax payments, which is $18.27 per $1000 or 1.827%.

We have used corporate bonds as an example for estimating the cost of debt. Many smaller companies do not have access to the bond market and use bank debt instead. In their case, they typically have a good sense of their cost of debt from discussions with their banker about interest rates on new loans.

Cost of Preferred Stock Capital

Firms may also raise capital by issuing preferred stock. Typically, holders of the preferred stock are promised a fixed dividend, which must be paid "in preference to" (i.e., before) any dividends can be paid to common stockholders.

If the preferred dividend is known and fixed, we can estimate the preferred stock's cost of capital using Eq. 7.7 of Chapter 7,

$$r_E = \frac{Div_1}{P_0} + g$$

where the growth rate $g = 0$. Thus,

$$\text{Cost of Preferred Stock Capital} = \frac{\text{Preferred Dividend}}{\text{Preferred Stock Price}} = \frac{Div_{pfd}}{P_{pfd}} \qquad (13.4)$$

For example, assume DuPont's class A preferred stock has a price of $85.83 and an annual dividend of $3.50. Its cost of preferred stock, therefore, is $3.50 \div 85.83 = 4.08\%$.[3]

---

[3]DuPont has a second class of preferred stock (B) with a $4.50 annual dividend, also priced to imply a cost near 4.08%.

Cost of Common Stock Capital

As we learned in Chapter 12, a company cannot directly observe its cost of common stock (equity), but must instead estimate it. We now present and compare the two major methods for doing so.

Capital Asset Pricing Model. The most common approach is to use the CAPM as presented in Chapter 12. To summarize that approach:

1. Estimate the firm's beta of equity, typically by regressing 60 months of the company's returns against 60 months of returns for a market proxy such as the S&P 500.
2. Determine the risk-free rate, typically by using the yield on Treasury bills or bonds.
3. Estimate the market risk premium, typically by comparing historical returns on a market proxy to historical risk-free rates.
4. Apply the CAPM:

$$\text{Cost of Equity} = \text{Risk-Free Rate} + \text{Equity Beta} \times \text{Market Risk Premium}$$

For example, suppose the equity beta of DuPont is 1.60, the yield on 10-year Treasury notes is 3%, and you estimate the market risk premium to be 6%. DuPont's cost of equity is $3\% + 1.60 \times 6\% = 12.60\%$.

Constant Dividend Growth Model. Another way to estimate a company's cost of equity comes from the constant dividend growth model (CDGM) introduced in Chapter 7. Equation 7.7 from Chapter 7 shows that

$$\text{Cost of Equity} = \frac{\text{Dividend (in one year)}}{\text{Current Price}} + \text{Dividend Growth Rate} = \frac{Div_1}{P_E} + g \quad (13.5)$$

Thus, to estimate the cost of equity, we need the current price of the stock, the expected dividend in one year, and an estimate of the dividend growth rate. The current price of the stock is easy to obtain online. We may even have a reasonable estimate of next year's dividend. However, as we discussed in Chapter 7, estimating the future dividend growth rate can be very difficult. For example, DuPont's recent annual dividend history is $1.40 (1998–2004), $1.48 (2005–2007), $1.64 (2008–2011), $1.72 (2012) and $1.80 (2013). Perhaps it is reasonable to assume that 2014's dividend will also be $1.80 per year, but what about the dividend's long-term growth rate? The historical growth has been uneven.

Rather than looking backward at historical growth, one common approach is to use estimates produced by stock analysts, as these estimates are forward-looking. As discussed in Chapter 7, if DuPont keeps its dividend payout rate constant, then the long-run growth in dividends will equal the long-run growth in earnings. In mid-2013, the average forecast for DuPont's long-run earnings growth rate was 7.9%. Thus, with an expected dividend in one year of $1.80, a price of $57.66, and long-run dividend growth of 7.9%, the CDGM estimates DuPont's cost of equity as follows (using Eq. 13.5):

$$\text{Cost of Equity} = \frac{Div_1}{P_E} + g = \frac{\$1.80}{\$57.66} + 0.079 = 0.110, \text{ or } 11.0\%$$

We should not be surprised that the two estimates of DuPont's cost of equity (12.6% and 11.0%) do not match, because each was based on different assumptions. Furthermore, even given an estimate of future growth of dividends, Eq. 13.5 makes an assumption that future dividend growth will continue at a constant rate. This assumption is unlikely to be valid for most firms. Looking again at DuPont, its dividend was constant for seven years and then increased four times in eight years. Also note that many young, growing firms do not pay a dividend and have no plans to do so in the near future.

TABLE 13.1

Estimating the Cost of Equity

	Capital Asset Pricing Model	Constant Dividend Growth Model
Inputs	Equity beta	Current stock price
	Risk-free rate	Expected dividend next year
	Market risk premium	Future dividend growth rate
Major Assumptions	Estimated beta is correct	Dividend estimate is correct
	Market risk premium is accurate	Growth rate matches market expectations
	CAPM is the correct model	Future dividend growth is constant

We could use any model relating a firm's stock price to its future cash flows to estimate its cost of equity—the CDGM is just one of the possible models. For example, we could use the discounted free cash flow model from Chapter 10 to solve for the firm's cost of equity.

CAPM and CDGM Comparison. Because of the difficulties with the CDGM, the CAPM is the most popular approach for estimating the cost of equity. Table 13.1 compares the two approaches.

EXAMPLE 13.3

Estimating the Cost of Equity

MyFinanceLab

PROBLEM

Assume the equity beta for Johnson & Johnson (ticker: JNJ) is 0.55. The yield on 10-year treasuries is 3%, and you estimate the market risk premium to be 6%. Furthermore, Johnson & Johnson issues dividends at an annual rate of $2.81. Its current stock price is $92.00, and you expect dividends to increase at a constant rate of 4% per year. Estimate J&J's cost of equity in two ways.

SOLUTION

PLAN

The two ways to estimate J&J's cost of equity are to use the CAPM and the CDGM.

1. The CAPM requires the risk-free rate, an estimate of the equity's beta, and an estimate of the market risk premium. We can use the yield on 10-year Treasury notes as the risk-free rate.
2. The CDGM requires the current stock price, the expected dividend next year, and an estimate of the constant future growth rate for the dividend.

Risk-free rate: 3%	Current price: $92.00
Equity beta: 0.55	Expected dividend: $2.81
Market risk premium: 6%	Estimated future dividend growth rate: 4%

We can use the CAPM from Chapter 12 to estimate the cost of equity using the CAPM approach and Eq. 13.5 to estimate it using the CDGM approach.

EXECUTE

1. The CAPM says that

$$\text{Cost of Equity} = \text{Risk-Free Rate} + \text{Equity Beta} \times \text{Market Risk Premium}$$

For J&J, this implies that its cost of equity is $3\% + 0.55 \times 6\% = 6.3\%$.

2. The CDGM says

$$\text{Cost of Equity} = \frac{\text{Dividend (in one year)}}{\text{Current Price}} + \text{Dividend Growth Rate} = \frac{\$2.81}{\$92.00} + 4\% = 7.1\%$$

EVALUATE

According to the CAPM, the cost of equity capital is 6.3%; the CDGM produces a result of 7.1%. Because of the different assumptions we make when using each method, the two methods do not have to produce the same answer—in fact, it would be highly unlikely that they would. When the two approaches produce

(Continued)

different answers, we must examine the assumptions we made for each approach and decide which set of assumptions is more realistic. We can also see what assumption about future dividend growth would be necessary to make the answers converge. By rearranging the CDGM and using the cost of equity we estimated from the CAPM, we have

$$\text{Dividend Growth Rate} = \text{Cost of Equity} - \frac{\text{Dividend (in one year)}}{\text{Current Price}} = 6.3\% - 3.1\% = 3.2\%$$

Thus, if we believe that J&J's dividends will grow at a rate of 3.2% per year, the two approaches would produce the same cost of equity estimate.

Concept Check

3. How can you measure a firm's cost of debt?

4. What are the major tradeoffs in using the CAPM versus the CDGM to estimate the cost of equity?

13.3 A Second Look at the Weighted Average Cost of Capital

Now that we have estimated the costs of DuPont's different sources of capital, we are ready to calculate the firm's overall WACC. The weights are the percentage of the firm's value financed by equity, preferred stock, and debt. We can represent these as $E\%$, $P\%$, and $D\%$, respectively, and note that they must sum to 100% (i.e., we must account for all the sources of financing).

WACC Equation

Formally, denoting the cost of equity, preferred and debt capital as r_E, r_{pfd}, and r_D, and the corporate tax rate as T_C, the WACC is

Weighted Average Cost of Capital

$$r_{wacc} = r_E E\% + r_{pfd} P\% + r_D (1 - T_C) D\% \tag{13.6}$$

For a company that does not have preferred stock, the WACC condenses to

$$r_{wacc} = r_E E\% + r_D (1 - T_C) D\% \tag{13.7}$$

For example, in mid-2013, the market values of DuPont's common stock, preferred stock, and debt were $53,240 million, $221 million, and $14,080 million, respectively. Its total value was, therefore, $53,240 million + $221 million + $14,080 million = $67,541 million. Given the costs of common stock (CAPM estimate), preferred stock, and debt we have already computed, DuPont's WACC in mid-2013 was

$$r_{wacc} = r_E E\% + r_{pfd} P\% + r_D (1 - T_C) D\%$$

$$r_{wacc} = 12.6\% \left(\frac{53,240}{67,541} \right) + 4.08\% \left(\frac{221}{67,541} \right) + 2.81\% (1 - 0.35) \left(\frac{14,080}{67,541} \right)$$

$$r_{wacc} = 10.33\%$$

EXAMPLE 13.4

Computing the WACC

MyFinanceLab

PROBLEM

Assume the expected return on Target's equity is 11.5%, and the firm has a yield to maturity on its debt of 6%. Debt accounts for 18% and equity for 82% of Target's total market value. If its tax rate is 35%, what is an estimate of this firm's WACC?

SOLUTION

PLAN

We can compute the WACC using Eq. 13.7. To do so, we need to know the costs of equity and debt, their proportions in Target's capital structure, and the firm's tax rate. We have all that information, so we are ready to proceed.

EXECUTE

$$r_{wacc} = r_E E\% + r_D(1 - T_C)D\% = (0.115)(0.82) + (0.06)(1 - 0.35)(0.18)$$
$$= 0.101, \text{ or } 10.1\%$$

EVALUATE

Even though we cannot observe the expected return of Target's investments directly, we can use the expected return on its equity and debt and the WACC formula to estimate it, adjusting for the tax advantage of debt. Target needs to earn at least a 10.1% return on its investment in current and new stores to satisfy both its debt and equity holders.

Weighted Average Cost of Capital in Practice

The WACC is driven by the risk of a company's line of business and, because of the tax effect of interest, its leverage. As a result, WACCs vary widely across industries and companies. Figure 13.3 presents the WACC for several real companies to provide a sense of the degree to which the cost of capital can vary. Some lines of business are clearly riskier than others.

FIGURE 13.3

WACCs for Real Companies

The cost of equity is computed using the company's equity beta, a risk-free rate of 3%, and a market risk premium of 6%. The cost of debt is based on market yield to maturities of the debt. The percent equity and percent debt are determined from the company's market capitalization and balance sheet. The WACC is computed using Eq. 13.7 with a 35% tax rate and is shown in the accompanying bar graph. "N/A" means that the cost of debt is not applicable and refers to companies that have no debt.

	Beta	Cost of Equity	Cost of Debt	% Equity	% Debt	WACC
Hershey Company	0.17	4.0%	3.3%	91.8%	8.2%	3.9%
Exxon Mobil	0.50	6.0%	2.9%	96.9%	3.1%	5.9%
Johnson & Johnson	0.55	6.3%	3.3%	94.3%	5.7%	6.1%
Target	0.89	8.3%	3.2%	75.8%	24.2%	6.8%
Amazon.com	0.80	7.8%	3.5%	97.3%	2.7%	7.6%
Nike	0.83	8.0%	3.2%	98.0%	2.0%	7.9%
Microsoft	0.99	8.9%	3.3%	94.4%	5.6%	8.6%
Apple	0.98	8.9%	2.8%	95.9%	4.1%	8.6%
Boeing	1.13	9.8%	4.0%	90.1%	9.9%	9.1%
Starbucks	1.17	10.0%	1.8%	99.0%	1.0%	9.9%
Weyerhaeuser	1.47	11.8%	5.4%	80.2%	19.8%	10.2%
Nordstrom	1.63	12.8%	3.3%	79.3%	20.7%	10.6%
AMD	2.32	16.9%	7.9%	57.1%	42.9%	11.9%
BlackBerry Ltd	1.71	13.3%	N/A	100.0%	0.0%	13.3%

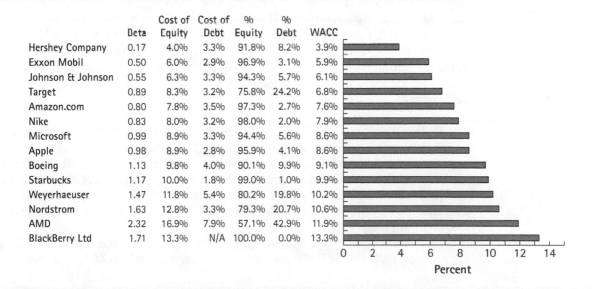

Source: Authors' calculations based on publicly available information in 2013.

For example, selling chocolate, as Hershey does, is a fairly low-risk proposition, but selling high-end cellular phones (as Apple and BlackBerry Ltd. do) is much riskier.

Methods in Practice

We now turn to some issues that arise for financial managers when they are estimating the WACC in practice.

net debt Total debt outstanding minus any cash balances.

Net Debt. When calculating the weights for the WACC, it is increasingly common practice to make an adjustment to the debt. Many practitioners now use **net debt**, the total debt outstanding minus any cash balances:

$$\text{Net Debt} = \text{Debt} - \text{Cash and Risk-Free Securities} \tag{13.8}$$

Why subtract a company's cash from its debt? The assets on a firm's balance sheet include any holdings of cash or risk-free securities. If a firm holds $1 in cash and has $1 of risk-free debt, then the interest earned on the cash will equal the interest paid on the debt. The cash flows from each source cancel each other, just as if the firm held no cash and no debt. In fact, we can view cash as being equivalent to negative debt. Significant excess cash on a firm's balance sheet can complicate the assessment of the risk (and hence the cost of capital) of the assets the firm actually uses in the course of business. Thus, when trying to evaluate a firm's business assets separate from any cash holdings, practitioners often measure the leverage of the firm in terms of its net debt and measure the market value of a firm's business assets using its enterprise value. Recall Chapter 2's definition of the enterprise value as the market value of its equity plus its net debt.

Using this approach, the weights in the WACC would then be

$$\left(\frac{\text{Market Value of Equity}}{\text{Enterprise Value}} \right) \text{ and } \left(\frac{\text{Net Debt}}{\text{Enterprise Value}} \right)$$

For firms with substantial excess cash reserves, this adjustment could be important. For firms with relatively low levels of cash, it will not have a large effect on the overall WACC estimate.

The Risk-Free Interest Rate. Estimating the equity cost of capital using the CAPM requires the risk-free interest rate. The risk-free interest rate is generally determined using the yields of U.S. Treasury securities, which are free from default risk. But which horizon should we choose? The CAPM states that we should use the risk-free interest corresponding to the investment horizon of the firm's investors. When surveyed, the vast majority of large firms and financial analysts report using the yields of long-term (10- to 30-year) bonds to determine the risk-free rate.[4]

The Market Risk Premium. Using the CAPM also requires an estimate of the market risk premium. As mentioned in Chapter 11, one way to estimate the market risk premium is to look at historical data. Because we are interested in the *future* market risk premium, we face a tradeoff in terms of the amount of data we use. As noted in Chapter 11, it takes many years of data to produce even moderately accurate estimates of expected returns—yet data that are very old may have little relevance for investors' expectations of the market risk premium today.

Table 13.2 reports excess returns of the S&P 500 versus one-year and 10-year Treasury rates. Since 1926, the S&P 500 has produced an average return of 7.7% above the rate

---

[4]See Robert Bruner, et al., "Best Practices in Estimating the Cost of Capital: Survey and Synthesis," *Financial Practice and Education* 8 (1998): 13–28.

TABLE 13.2

Historical Excess
Returns of the S&P 500
Compared to One-Year
Treasury Bills
and 10-Year U.S.
Treasury Securities

S&P 500 Excess Return Versus	Period	
	1926–2012	1962–2012
One-year Treasury	7.7%	5.5%
10-year Treasury*	5.9%	3.8%

*Based on a comparison of compounded returns over a 10-year holding period.

for one-year Treasury securities. However, some evidence indicates that the market risk premium has declined over time. Since 1962, the S&P 500 has shown an excess return of only 5.5% over the rate for one-year Treasury securities. Compared with 10-year Treasury securities, the S&P 500 had an average excess return of only 3.8% (due primarily to the fact that 10-year Treasury bond rates tend to be higher than one-year rates).

How can we explain this decline? One explanation may be that as more investors have begun to participate in the stock market and the costs of constructing a diversified portfolio have declined, investors have tended to hold less risky portfolios. As a result, the return they require as compensation for taking on that risk has diminished. In addition, the overall volatility of the market has declined over time. Some researchers believe that the future expected returns for the market are likely to be even lower than these historical numbers, in a range of 3% to 5% over Treasury bills.[5] Consequently, many financial managers currently use market risk premiums closer to 5%, rather than 7%.

Concept Check

5. Why do different companies have different WACCs?

6. What are the tradeoffs in estimating the market risk premium?

13.4 Using the WACC to Value a Project

A project's cost of capital depends on its risk. When the market risk of the project is similar to the average market risk of the firm's investments, then its cost of capital is equivalent to the cost of capital for a portfolio of all the firm's securities. In other words, the project's cost of capital is equal to the firm's WACC. As shown in Eq. 13.6, the WACC incorporates the benefit of the interest tax deduction by using the firm's *after-tax* cost of capital for debt.

Because the WACC incorporates the tax savings from debt, we can compute the value of an investment including the benefit of the interest tax deduction given the firm's leverage policy, sometimes called the investment's **levered value**. To do so, we discount the firm's future incremental free cash flow using the WACC, a process we refer to as the **WACC method**. Specifically, if FCF_t is the expected incremental free cash flow of an investment at the end of year t, then the Valuation Principle tells us that the investment's levered value, V_0^L, is

levered value The value of an investment, including the benefit of the interest tax deduction, given the firm's leverage policy.

WACC method Discounting future incremental free cash flows using the firm's WACC. This method produces the levered value of a project.

$$V_0^L = FCF_0 + \frac{FCF_1}{1 + r_{wacc}} + \frac{FCF_2}{(1 + r_{wacc})^2} + \frac{FCF_3}{(1 + r_{wacc})^3} + \cdots \qquad (13.9)$$

The intuition for the WACC method is that the firm's WACC represents the average return the firm must pay to its investors (both debt and equity holders) on an after-tax basis. Thus, to have a positive NPV, a project with the same risk as the average risk for the firm's projects should generate an expected return of at least the firm's WACC.

---

[5]See I. Welch, "Views of Financial Economists on the Equity Premium and Other Issues," *Journal of Business* 73 (2000): 501–537 (with 2009 update), and J. Graham and C. Harvey, "The Equity Risk Premium in 2008: Evidence from the Global CFO Outlook Survey," SSRN 2008.

EXAMPLE 13.5

The WACC Method

MyFinanceLab

PROBLEM

Suppose Anheuser-Busch InBev is considering introducing a new ultra-light beer with zero calories to be called BudZero. The firm believes that the beer's flavor and appeal to calorie-conscious drinkers will make it a success. The cost of bringing the beer to market is $200 million, but Anheuser-Busch InBev expects first-year incremental free cash flows from BudZero to be $100 million and to grow at 3% per year thereafter. If Anheuser-Busch InBev's WACC is 5.7%, should it go ahead with the project?

SOLUTION

PLAN

We can use the WACC method shown in Eq. 13.9 to value BudZero and then subtract the up-front cost of $200 million. We will need Anheuser-Busch InBev's WACC, which is 5.7%.

EXECUTE

The cash flows for BudZero are a growing perpetuity. Applying the growing perpetuity formula with the WACC method, we have

$$V_0^L = FCF_0 + \frac{FCF_1}{r_{wacc} - g} = -\$200 \text{ million } + \frac{\$100 \text{ million}}{0.057 - 0.03} = \$3,503.7 \text{ million } (\$3.5 \text{ billion})$$

EVALUATE

The BudZero project has a positive NPV because it is expected to generate a return on the $200 million far in excess of Anheuser-Busch InBev's WACC of 5.7%. As discussed in Chapter 8, taking positive-NPV projects adds value to the firm. Here, we can see that the value is created by exceeding the required return of the firm's investors.

Key Assumptions

While it is common practice to use the WACC as the discount rate in capital budgeting, it is important to be aware of the underlying assumptions. We examine the critical assumptions here and then explore these assumptions further in the context of an application.

Assumption 1: Average Risk. We assume initially that the market risk of the project is equivalent to the average market risk of the firm's investments. In that case, we assess the project's cost of capital based on the risk of the firm.

Assumption 2: Constant Debt-Equity Ratio. We assume that the firm adjusts its leverage continuously to maintain a constant ratio of the market value of debt to the market value of equity—a relationship referred to as the **debt-equity ratio**. This policy determines the amount of debt the firm will take on when it accepts a new project. It also implies that the risk of the firm's equity and debt, and therefore its WACC, will not fluctuate owing to leverage changes.

debt-equity ratio A ratio of the market value of debt to the market value of equity.

Assumption 3: Limited Leverage Effects. We assume initially that the main effect of leverage on valuation follows from the interest tax deduction. We assume that any other factors (such as possible financial distress) are not significant at the level of debt chosen. We discuss these other factors in detail in Chapter 16.

Assumptions in Practice. These assumptions are reasonable for many projects and firms. The first assumption is likely to fit typical projects of firms with investments concentrated in a single industry. In that case, the market risk of both the project and the firm will primarily depend on the sensitivity of the industry to the overall economy. The second assumption, while unlikely to hold exactly, reflects the fact that firms tend to increase their levels of debt as they grow larger; some may even have an explicit target for their debt-equity ratio.[6] Finally, for firms without very high levels of debt, the interest tax deduction is likely to be the most important factor affecting the capital budgeting decision. Hence, the third assumption is a reasonable starting point to begin our analysis.

Of course, while these three assumptions may be a reasonable approximation in many situations, there are certainly projects and firms for which they do not apply. In the following section, we apply the WACC method under all three assumptions. Next, we relax the first assumption, which states that the project has average risk. (We will relax the other two assumptions in later chapters.)

WACC Method Application: Extending the Life of a DuPont Facility

Let's apply the WACC method to value a project. Suppose DuPont is considering an investment that would extend the life of one of its facilities for four years. The project would require up-front costs of $6.67 million plus a $24 million investment in equipment. The equipment will be obsolete in four years and will be depreciated via the straight-line method over that period. During the next four years, however, DuPont expects annual sales of $60 million per year from this facility. Material costs and operating expenses are expected to total $25 million and $9 million, respectively, per year. Finally, DuPont expects no net working capital requirements for the project, and it pays a corporate tax rate of 35%.

Using this information, the spreadsheet in Table 13.3 forecasts the project's expected free cash flow. Assume that the market risk of the project of extending the life of the facility is the same as that for DuPont's overall business. As a consequence, we can use DuPont's WACC to compute the NPV of the project.

We can determine the value of the project, including the present value of the interest tax deduction from the debt, by calculating the present value of its future free cash flows, V_0^L, using the WACC method and DuPont's WACC of 10.33%, which we computed in Section 13.3:

$$V_0^L = \frac{19}{1.1033} + \frac{19}{1.1033^2} + \frac{19}{1.1033^3} + \frac{19}{1.1033^4} = \$59.80 \text{ million}$$

TABLE 13.3

Expected Free Cash Flow from DuPont's Facility Project

1	Year	0	1	2	3	4
2	**Incremental Earnings Forecast ($million)**					
3	Sales	—	60.00	60.00	60.00	60.00
4	Cost of Goods Sold	—	−25.00	−25.00	−25.00	−25.00
5	**Gross Profit**	—	35.00	35.00	35.00	35.00
6	Operating Expenses	−6.67	−9.00	−9.00	−9.00	−9.00
7	Depreciation	—	−6.00	−6.00	−6.00	−6.00
8	**EBIT**	−6.67	20.00	20.00	20.00	20.00
9	Income Tax at 35%	2.33	−7.00	−7.00	−7.00	−7.00
10	**Unlevered Net Income**	−4.34	13.00	13.00	13.00	13.00
11	**Incremental Free Cash Flow ($ million)**					
12	Plus: Depreciation	—	6.00	6.00	6.00	6.00
13	Less: Capital Expenditures	−24.00	—	—	—	—
14	Less: Increases in NWC	—	—	—	—	—
15	**Incremental Free Cash Flow**	−28.34	19.00	19.00	19.00	19.00

---

[6]We discuss the tradeoff between debt and equity and the concept of a target debt-equity ratio in Chapter 16.

Because the up-front after-tax cost of extending the facility's life is only $28.34 million, this project is a good idea. Taking the project results in an NPV of $59.80 million − $28.34 million = $31.46 million for the firm.

Summary of the WACC Method

To summarize, the key steps in the WACC valuation method are as follows:

1. Determine the incremental free cash flow of the investment.
2. Compute the weighted average cost of capital using Eq. 13.6.
3. Compute the value of the investment, including the tax benefit of leverage, by discounting the incremental free cash flow of the investment using the WACC.

In many firms, the corporate treasurer performs the second step, calculating the firm's WACC. This rate can then be used throughout the firm as the companywide cost of capital for new investments *that are of comparable risk to the rest of the firm and that will not alter the firm's debt-equity ratio.* Employing the WACC method in this way is very simple and straightforward. As a result, this method is the most commonly used in practice for capital budgeting purposes.

Concept Check

7. What are the main assumptions you make when you use the WACC method?
8. What inputs do you need to be ready to apply the WACC method?

13.5 Project-Based Costs of Capital

Up to this point we have assumed that both the risk and the leverage of the project under consideration matched those characteristics for the firm as a whole. This assumption allowed us, in turn, to assume that the cost of capital for a project matched the firm's cost of capital.

In reality, specific projects often differ from the average investment made by the firm. Consider General Electric Company (GE), a large firm with many divisions that operate in completely different lines of business. Projects in GE's health-care division are likely to have different market risk than projects in its air transportation equipment division or in its appliance division. Projects may also vary in terms of the amount of leverage they will support—for example, acquisitions of real estate or capital equipment are often highly levered, while investments in intellectual property are not. We will study the effect of leverage on the cost of capital when we cover the leverage decision in Chapter 16. In this section, we show how to calculate the cost of capital for the project's cash flows when a project's risk differs from the firm's overall risk.

Cost of Capital for a New Acquisition

We begin by explaining how to calculate the cost of capital of a project with market risk that is different from the risk for the rest of the firm. Suppose DuPont wants to use its materials expertise to enter the athletic shoe business. To do so, it is considering acquiring Nike, a company that is focused on that business. Nike faces different market risks than DuPont does in its chemicals and materials business. What cost of capital should DuPont use to value a possible acquisition of Nike?

Because the risks are different, DuPont's WACC would be inappropriate for valuing Nike. Instead, DuPont should calculate and use Nike's WACC when assessing the acquisition. In Figure 13.3, we find the following information for Nike, where the WACC is based on a tax rate of 35%:

	Beta	Cost of Equity	Cost of Debt	% Equity	% Debt	WACC
Nike	0.83	8.0%	3.2%	98%	2%	7.9%

Assuming that DuPont will find it appropriate to continue to finance Nike with the same mix of debt and equity after it buys Nike,[7] we can use Nike's WACC as the cost of capital for acquiring it. Thus, DuPont would use a cost of capital of 7.9% to value Nike for purchase.

Divisional Costs of Capital

Now assume DuPont makes a different decision: It decides to create an athletic shoes division internally, rather than buying Nike. What should the cost of capital for the new division be? If DuPont plans to finance the division with the same proportion of debt as is used by Nike, then DuPont would use Nike's WACC as the WACC for its new division. Because Nike's WACC is the right cost of capital given the risks of athletic shoes and 2% debt financing, it has to be the right cost of capital for an internally created athletic shoes division that is financed 2% with debt.

In most cases, firms with more than one division should not use a single company-wide WACC to evaluate projects. More typically, they perform analyses similar to DuPont's analysis of Nike. Multidivisional firms benchmark their own divisions off of companies that compete with their division and are focused in that single line of business. By performing the same analysis as we did in Figure 13.3, the multidivisional firm can estimate the WACCs of its divisions' competitors—adjusting for different financing if necessary—to estimate the cost of capital for each division.

EXAMPLE 13.6 A Project in a New Line of Business MyFinanceLab	### PROBLEM You are working for Microsoft evaluating the possibility of selling digital video recorders (DVRs). Microsoft's WACC is 8.6%. DVRs would be a new line of business for Microsoft, however, so the systematic risk of this business would likely differ from the systematic risk of Microsoft's current business. As a result, the assets of this new business should have a different cost of capital. You need to find the cost of capital for the DVR business. Assuming that the risk-free rate is 3% and the market risk premium is 6%, how would you estimate the cost of capital for this type of investment? ### SOLUTION #### PLAN The first step is to identify a company operating in Microsoft's targeted line of business. TiVo, Inc., is a well-known marketer of DVRs. In fact, that is its sole business. Thus, the cost of capital for TiVo would be a good estimate of the cost of capital for Microsoft's proposed DVR business. Many Web sites are available that provide betas for traded stocks, including http://finance.yahoo.com. Suppose you visit that site and find that the beta of TiVo stock is 1.45. With this beta, the risk-free rate, and the market risk premium, you can use the CAPM to estimate the cost of equity for TiVo. Fortunately for us, TiVo has no debt, so its cost of equity is the same as its cost of capital for its assets. #### EXECUTE Using the CAPM, we have TiVo's Cost of Equity = Risk-Free Rate + TiVo's Equity Beta × Market Risk Premium = 3% + 1.45 × 6% = 11.7% Because TiVo has no debt, its WACC is equivalent to its cost of equity. #### EVALUATE The correct cost of capital for evaluating a DVR investment opportunity is 11.7%. If we had used the 8.6% cost of capital that is associated with Microsoft's *existing* business, we would have mistakenly used too low of a cost of capital. That could lead us to go ahead with the investment, even if it truly had a negative NPV.

---

[7]We consider what to do if DuPont wants to change Nike's financing mix in Chapter 16.

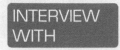

INTERVIEW WITH SHELAGH GLASER

Shelagh Glaser is the Finance Director for Intel's Mobility Group, which provides solutions for the mobile computing market. Prior to that she was Group Controller for Sales & Marketing and Co-Group Controller for Digital Enterprise Group.

QUESTION: *Does Intel set the discount rate at the corporate or project level?*

ANSWER: We typically set the discount rate at the corporate level. As a company, Intel makes a broad set of products that sell into similar markets, so one hurdle rate makes sense for our core business. To justify an investment, every project has to earn or exceed that level of return for our shareholders.

We may use a different discount rate for mergers and acquisitions. For example, recently we've done more software acquisitions. That industry is very different from semiconductors and has different risk factors, so we take those considerations into account to set the hurdle rate.

QUESTION: *How does Intel compute the cost of capital for new investment opportunities?*

ANSWER: We reexamine our weighted average cost of capital (WACC) each year to see that we have the right inputs and if any have changed: What is the current market risk premium? Are we using the right risk-free rate? How should we weight historical data? We use the CAPM to determine beta but consider whether to continue using the five-year weekly beta or to change to a daily or monthly beta in the calculation. We also look at the latest studies from academia on what the inputs should be.

Once we have estimated the WACC, we think about the appropriate hurdle rate for our circumstances. We have not changed the hurdle rate in recent years—even though the WACC may have changed—and continue to use a hurdle rate that is above the WACC. This higher hurdle rate reflects our ability to time our investments and helps us choose projects that maximize our expected returns. Intel has more projects with returns above our hurdle than we can invest in, so assessing opportunity cost is a significant aspect of decision making. We may invest in some projects with NPVs below the hurdle rate if they are of strategic importance.

QUESTION: *How do project-specific considerations affect Intel's cost of capital calculation?*

ANSWER: When deciding whether to invest billions in wafer fabrication plants, Intel considers both the physical plant and the product line. We calculate the margin we would need from the product and develop a comprehensive set of metrics to justify the large capital investment. Typically we use our standard hurdle rate and also look at risk factors and the timing of the product launch. Intel's business is driven by the economics of Moore's Law, allowing us to double transistors every two years. Each generation of new technology creates cost reductions that enable new fabrication plants to clear the hurdle rate. These plants produce our leading-edge product, which earn our highest margins. To get a premium price, our customers require a product that takes advantage of the performance and power efficiency of the latest technology.

QUESTION: *Did the 2008 financial crisis affect how you evaluate investment opportunities?*

ANSWER: In 2008, the market was very depressed. We continued making R&D investments and reduced spending in other areas, such as marketing and short-term promotion. Cutting R&D would have left us with a gap in our product line in several years, because product development cycles typically run four years. In this industry, not keeping the R&D machine flowing, to boost short-term earnings, will harm the company's long-term viability. R&D is critical to our fundamental business model, which may require long-term decisions that negatively impact short-term results.

Intel has a long history of investing to maintain performance leadership during downturns. Intel carries almost no debt. Our capital policy is to maintain sufficient cash for fabrication plants and multiple years of R&D expenses, to avoid depending on capital markets to finance ongoing operations. A painful experience in the 1980s, when Intel's access to capital markets was curtailed, highlighted how this conservative capital policy pays off. Going into this crisis with no debt and an extremely strong cash position has served us well.

Concept Check

9. When evaluating a project in a new line of business, which assumptions for the WACC method are most likely to be violated?

10. How can you estimate the WACC to be used in a new line of business?

13.6 When Raising External Capital Is Costly

So far, we have assumed that there are no important factors to consider in seeking capital other than taxes. Among other things, this implies that we can raise external capital without any extra costs associated with the capital-raising transaction. As a consequence, we have no reason to treat a project financed with new external funds any differently than a project financed with internal funds (retained earnings).

In reality, issuing new equity or bonds carries a number of costs. These costs include the costs of filing and registering with the Securities and Exchange Commission and the fees charged by investment bankers to place the securities. We will discuss the process for issuing equity and bonds in detail in Chapters 14 and 15. Here, we mention it briefly in the context of the cost of capital.

Because of these issuing costs, a project that can be financed from internal funds will be less costly overall than the same project if it were financed with external funds. One approach would be to adjust the costs of equity and debt capital in the WACC to incorporate the issuing costs. A better and far more direct route is to simply treat the issuing costs as what they are—cash outflows that are necessary to the project. We can then incorporate this additional cost as a negative cash flow in the NPV analysis.

EXAMPLE 13.7

Evaluating an Acquisition with Costly External Financing

MyFinanceLab

PROBLEM

You are analyzing DuPont's potential acquisition of Nike. DuPont plans to offer $65 billion as the purchase price for Nike, and it will need to issue additional debt and equity to finance such a large acquisition. You estimate that the issuance costs will be $800 million and will be paid as soon as the transaction closes. You estimate the incremental free cash flows from the acquisition will be $3.3 billion in the first year and will grow at 3% per year thereafter. What is the NPV of the proposed acquisition?

SOLUTION

PLAN

We know from Section 13.5 that the correct cost of capital for this acquisition is Nike's WACC. We can value the incremental free cash flows as a growing perpetuity:

$$PV = \frac{FCF_1}{r - g}$$

where

$$FCF_1 = \$3.3 \text{ billion}$$
$$r = \text{Nike's WACC} = 0.079 \text{ (from Figure 13.3)}$$
$$g = 0.03$$

The NPV of the transaction, including the costly external financing, is the present value of this growing perpetuity net of both the purchase cost and the transaction costs of using external financing.

EXECUTE

Noting that $800 million is $0.8 billion,

$$NPV = -\$65 - \$0.8 + \frac{\$3.3}{0.079 - 0.03} = \$1.547 \text{ billion}$$

EVALUATE

It is not necessary to try to adjust Nike's WACC for the issuance costs of debt and equity. Instead, we can subtract the issuance costs from the NPV of the acquisition to confirm that the acquisition remains a positive-NPV project even if it must be financed externally.

In this chapter, we learned what a firm's cost of capital is, where it comes from, and how it is used in capital budgeting. The role of capital budgeting is to identify positive-NPV projects that allow a firm to cover the costs of its various types of capital. Now, we turn to another aspect of capital financing—where the firm gets that capital. In Chapters 14 through 16, we explore how a firm raises equity and debt capital and how it decides the proportion of each to have in its capital structure.

Concept Check

11. What types of additional costs does a firm incur when accessing external capital?

12. What is the best way to incorporate these additional costs into capital budgeting?

Key Points and Equations	Key Terms	Online Practice
13.1 A First Look at the Weighted Average Cost of Capital • A firm's debt and equity represent its capital. The relative proportions of debt, equity, and other securities that a firm has outstanding constitute its capital structure. • Investors of each type of capital have a required return. Providing this return is the cost a company bears to obtain capital from investors. • We calculate the firm's overall cost of capital as a weighted average of its equity and debt costs of capital, referred to as the firm's weighted average cost of capital. • The weights in the WACC must be based on the market values of both the firm's debt and equity, not the book values.	capital, p. 400 capital structure, p. 400 leverage, p. 402 levered, p. 402 market-value balance sheet, p. 402 unlevered, p. 402 weighted average cost of capital (WACC), p. 401	MyFinanceLab Study Plan 13.1
13.2 The Firm's Costs of Debt and Equity Capital • To estimate the cost of capital for a company as a whole, we usually start by estimating the cost of each of the company's sources of capital. • The cost of debt is the interest a firm would need to pay on *new* debt. Generally, it will differ from the coupon rate on existing debt, but can be estimated from the yield to maturity on existing debt. • The cost of preferred stock is straightforward to estimate because of its constant and known dividend: $$\text{Cost of Preferred Stock Capital} = \frac{Div_{pfd}}{P_{pfd}} \quad (13.4)$$ • The Capital Asset Pricing Model (CAPM) is the most common approach for estimating the cost of equity capital. To apply the CAPM, we need an estimate of the firm's equity beta, the market risk premium, and the risk-free rate: $$\text{Cost of Equity} = \text{Risk-Free Rate} + \text{Equity Beta} \\ \times \text{Market Risk Premium}$$ • Another approach to estimating the cost of equity is to use the constant dividend growth model (CDGM). To apply this model, we need the current stock price, the expected future dividend, and an estimate of the dividend's constant growth rate: $$\text{Cost of Equity} = \frac{Div_1}{P_E} + g \quad (13.5)$$	effective cost of the debt, p. 404	MyFinanceLab Study Plan 13.2

13.3 A Second Look at the Weighted Average Cost of Capital • The WACC equation is $$r_{wacc} = r_E E\% + r_{pfd} P\% + r_D(1 - T_C)D\% \quad (13.6)$$ • For a company that does not have preferred stock, the WACC equation condenses to $$r_{wacc} = r_E E\% + r_D(1 - T_C)D\% \quad (13.7)$$ • The WACC is driven by the risk of a company's line of business and, because of the tax effect of interest, its leverage. As a result, WACCs vary widely across industries and companies.	net debt, p. 410	MyFinanceLab Study Plan 13.3
13.4 Using the WACC to Value a Project • Assuming a project has average risk for the firm, that the firm will maintain its current leverage ratio, and that a firm's leverage affects its value only through taxes, the WACC can be used to value the cash flows from a new project.	debt-equity ratio, p. 412 levered value, p. 411 WACC method, p. 411	MyFinanceLab Study Plan 13.4 Spreadsheet Table 13.3
13.5 Project-Based Costs of Capital • If the project's risk differs from the average risk for the firm, the WACC will not be the appropriate discount rate for the project. Instead, you must estimate the WACC from the WACC of other firms operating in the same line of business as the new project.		MyFinanceLab Study Plan 13.5
13.6 When Raising External Capital Is Costly • The WACC is calculated without accounting for the direct costs of raising external financing. Rather than adjusting the WACC, the correct way to account for these costs is to subtract their present value from the NPV of the project.		MyFinanceLab Study Plan 13.6

CRITICAL
THINKING

1. What does the WACC measure?

2. Why are market-based weights important?

3. Why is the coupon rate of existing debt irrelevant for finding the cost of debt capital?

4. Why is it easier to determine the costs of preferred stock and of debt than it is to determine the cost of common equity?

5. Describe the steps involved in the CAPM approach to estimating the cost of equity.

6. Why would the CDGM and CAPM produce different estimates of the cost of equity capital?

7. Under what assumptions can the WACC be used to value a project?

8. What possible problems might be associated with the assumptions used in applying the WACC method?

9. How should you value a project in a line of business with risk that is different than the average risk of your firm's projects?

10. What is the right way to adjust for the costs of raising external financing?

PROBLEMS

All problems in this chapter are available in MyFinanceLab.

A First Look at the Weighted Average Cost of Capital

1. MV Corporation has debt with market value of $100 million, common equity with a book value of $100 million, and preferred stock worth $20 million outstanding. Its common equity trades at $50 per share, and the firm has 6 million shares outstanding. What weights should MV Corporation use in its WACC?

2. Andyco, Inc., has the following balance sheet and an equity market-to-book ratio of 1.5. Assuming the market value of debt equals its book value, what weights should it use for its WACC calculation?

Assets	Liabilities and Equity	
1000	Debt	400
	Equity	600

3. Book Co. has 1 million shares of common equity with a par (book) value of $1, retained earnings of $30 million, and its shares have a market value of $50 per share. It also has debt with a par value of $20 million that is trading at 101% of par.
   a. What is the market value of its equity?
   b. What is the market value of its debt?
   c. What weights should it use in computing its WACC?

4. Consider a simple firm that has the following market-value balance sheet:

Assets	Liabilities and Equity	
1000	Debt	400
	Equity	600

Next year, there are two possible values for its assets, each equally likely: $1200 and $960. Its debt will be due with 5% interest. Because all of the cash flows from the assets must go either to the debt or the equity, if you hold a portfolio of the debt and equity in the same proportions as the firm's capital structure, your portfolio should earn exactly the expected return on the firm's assets. Show that a portfolio invested 40% in the firm's debt and 60% in its equity will have the same expected return as the assets of the firm. That is, show that the firm's pretax WACC is the same as the expected return on its assets.

The Firm's Costs of Debt and Equity Capital

5. Avicorp has a $10 million debt issue outstanding, with a 6% coupon rate. The debt has semiannual coupons, the next coupon is due in six months, and the debt matures in five years. It is currently priced at 95% of par value.
   a. What is Avicorp's pretax cost of debt?
   b. If Avicorp faces a 40% tax rate, what is its after-tax cost of debt?

6. Laurel, Inc., has debt outstanding with a coupon rate of 6% and a yield to maturity of 7%. Its tax rate is 35%. What is Laurel's effective (after-tax) cost of debt?

7. Dewyco has preferred stock trading at $50 per share. The next preferred dividend of $4 is due in one year. What is Dewyco's cost of capital for preferred stock?

8. Steady Company's stock has a beta of 0.20. If the risk-free rate is 6% and the market risk premium is 7%, what is an estimate of Steady Company's cost of equity?

9. Wild Swings Inc.'s stock has a beta of 2.5. Given the information in Problem 8, what is an estimate of Wild Swings' cost of equity?

10. HighGrowth Company has a stock price of $20. The firm will pay a dividend next year of $1, and its dividend is expected to grow at a rate of 4% per year thereafter. What is your estimate of HighGrowth's cost of equity capital?

11. Slow 'n Steady, Inc., has a stock price of $30, will pay a dividend next year of $3, and has expected dividend growth of 1% per year. What is your estimate of Slow 'n Steady's cost of equity capital?

12. Mackenzie Company has a price of $36 and will issue a dividend of $2 next year. It has a beta of 1.2, the risk-free rate is 5.5%, and it estimates the market risk premium to be 5%.
    a. Estimate the equity cost of capital for Mackenzie.
    b. Under the CGDM, at what rate do you need to expect Mackenzie's dividends to grow to get the same equity cost of capital as in part (a)?

A Second Look at the Weighted Average Cost of Capital

13. CoffeeCarts has a cost of equity of 15%, has an effective cost of debt of 4%, and is financed 70% with equity and 30% with debt. What is this firm's WACC?

14. AllCity, Inc., is financed 40% with debt, 10% with preferred stock, and 50% with common stock. Its pretax cost of debt is 6%, its preferred stock pays an annual dividend of $2.50 and is priced at $30. It has an equity beta of 1.1. Assume the risk-free rate is 2%, the market risk premium is 7% and AllCity's tax rate is 35%. What is its after-tax WACC?

15. Pfd Company has debt with a yield to maturity of 7%, a cost of equity of 13%, and a cost of preferred stock of 9%. The market values of its debt, preferred stock, and equity are $10 million, $3 million, and $15 million, respectively, and its tax rate is 40%. What is this firm's WACC?

16. Growth Company's current share price is $20 and it is expected to pay a $1 dividend per share next year. After that, the firm's dividends are expected to grow at a rate of 4% per year.
    a. What is an estimate of Growth Company's cost of equity?
    b. Growth Company also has preferred stock outstanding that pays a $2 per share fixed dividend. If this stock is currently priced at $28, what is Growth Company's cost of preferred stock?
    c. Growth Company has existing debt issued three years ago with a coupon rate of 6%. The firm just issued new debt at par with a coupon rate of 6.5%. What is Growth Company's pretax cost of debt?
    d. Growth Company has 5 million common shares outstanding and 1 million preferred shares outstanding, and its equity has a total book value of $50 million. Its liabilities have a market value of $20 million. If Growth Company's common and preferred shares are priced as in parts (a) and (b), what is the market value of Growth Company's assets?
    e. Growth Company faces a 35% tax rate. Given the information in parts (a) through (d), and your answers to those problems, what is Growth Company's WACC?

Using the WACC to Value a Project

17. A retail coffee company is planning to open 100 new coffee outlets that are expected to generate $15 million in free cash flows per year, with a growth rate of 3% in perpetuity. If the coffee company's WACC is 10%, what is the NPV of this expansion?

18. RiverRocks, Inc., is considering a project with the following projected free cash flows:

0	1	2	3	4
−50	10	20	20	15

The firm believes that, given the risk of this project, the WACC method is the appropriate approach to valuing the project. RiverRocks' WACC is 12%. Should it take on this project? Why or why not?

Project-Based Costs of Capital

19. RiverRocks (whose WACC is 12%) is considering an acquisition of Raft Adventures (whose WACC is 15%). What is the appropriate discount rate for RiverRocks to use to evaluate the acquisition? Why?

20. RiverRocks' purchase of Raft Adventures (from Problem 19) will cost $100 million, and will generate cash flows that start at $15 million in one year and then grow at 4% per year forever. What is the NPV of the acquisition?

21. Your firm is planning to invest in an automated packaging plant. Harburtin Industries is an all-equity firm that specializes in this business. Suppose Harburtin's equity beta is 0.85, the risk-free rate is 4%, and the market risk premium is 5%. If your firm's project is all equity financed, estimate its cost of capital.

22. CoffeeStop primarily sells coffee. It recently introduced a premium coffee-flavored liquor. Suppose the firm faces a tax rate of 35% and collects the following information. If it plans to finance 11% of the new liquor-focused division with debt and the rest with equity, what WACC should it use for its liquor division? Assume a cost of debt of 4.8%, a risk-free rate of 3%, and a risk premium of 6%.

	Beta	% Equity	% Debt
CoffeeStop	0.61	96%	4%
BF Liquors	0.26	89%	11%

23. Your company has two divisions: One division sells software and the other division sells computers through a direct sales channel, primarily taking orders over the Internet. You have decided that Dell Computer is very similar to your computer division, in terms of both risk and financing. You go online and find the following information: Hewlett Packard's beta is 1.21, the risk-free rate is 4.5%, its market value of equity is $67 billion, and it has $700 million worth of debt with a yield to maturity of 6%. Your tax rate is 35% and you use a market risk premium of 5% in your WACC estimates.
    a. What is an estimate of the WACC for your computer sales division?
    b. If your overall company WACC is 12% and the computer sales division represents 40% of the value of your firm, what is an estimate of the WACC for your software division?

When Raising External Capital Is Costly

24. RiverRocks realizes that it will have to raise the financing for the acquisition of Raft Adventures (described in Problem 20) by issuing new debt and equity. The firm

estimates that the direct issuing costs will come to $7 million. How should it account for these costs in evaluating the project? Should RiverRocks go ahead with the project?

25. You are planning to issue debt to finance a new project. The project will require $20 million in financing and you estimate its NPV to be $15 million. The issue costs for the debt will be 3% of face value. Taking into account the costs of external financing, what is the NPV of the project?

DATA CASE

You work in Walt Disney Company's corporate finance and treasury department and have been assigned to the team estimating Disney's WACC. You must estimate this WACC in preparation for a team meeting later today. You quickly realize that the information you need is readily available online.

1. Go to http://finance.yahoo.com. Under "Market Summary," you will find the yield to maturity for 10-year Treasury bonds listed as "10 Yr Bond(%)." Collect this number as your risk-free rate.

2. In the box next to the "Get Quotes" button, type Walt Disney's ticker symbol (DIS), and click "Search". Once you see the basic information for Disney, find and click "Key Statistics" on the left side of the screen. From the key statistics, collect Disney's market capitalization (its market value of equity), enterprise value (market value equity + net debt), cash, and beta.

3. To get Disney's cost of debt and the market value of its long-term debt, you will need the price and yield to maturity on the firm's existing long-term bonds. Go to http://www.finra.org, click 'Investors' and then under "Market Data," click 'Bonds'. Under "Quick Bond Search," click "Corporate," type Disney's ticker symbol (DIS), and click "Search". A list of Disney's outstanding bond issues will appear. Assume that Disney's policy is to use the yield to maturity on non-callable 10-year obligations as its cost of debt. Find the non-callable bond issue that is as close to 10 years from maturity as possible. (*Hint*: You will see a column titled "Callable"; make sure the issue you choose has "No" in this column.) You may have to choose a bond issued by one of its subsidiaries, like ABC. Find the yield to maturity for your chosen bond issue (it is in the column titled "Yield") and enter that yield as your pretax cost of debt into your spreadsheet. Next, copy and paste the data in the entire table into Excel.

4. You now have the price for each bond issue, but you need to know the size of the issue. Returning to the Web page, go to the row of the bond you chose and click the Issuer Name in the first column (this will either be Walt Disney Company or ABC or another subsidiary). This brings up a Web page with all of the information about the bond issue. Scroll down until you find "Amount Outstanding" on the right side. Noting that this amount is quoted in thousands of dollars (e.g., $60,000 means $60 million = $60,000,000), record the issue amount in the appropriate row of your spreadsheet. Repeat this step for all of the bond issues.

5. The price for each bond issue in your spreadsheet is reported as a percentage of the bond's par value. For example, 104.50 means that the bond issue is trading at 104.5% of its par value. You can calculate the market value of each bond issue by multiplying the amount outstanding by (Price ÷ 100). Do so for each issue and then calculate the total of all the bond issues. This is the market value of Disney's debt.

6. Compute the weights for Disney's equity and debt based on the market value of equity and Disney's market value of debt, computed in step 5.

7. Calculate Disney's cost of equity capital using the CAPM, the risk-free rate you collected in step 1, and a market risk premium of 5%.

8. Assuming that Disney has a tax rate of 35%, calculate its effective cost of debt capital.

9. Calculate Disney's WACC.

10. Calculate Disney's net debt by subtracting its cash (collected in step 2) from its debt. Recalculate the weights for the WACC using the market value of equity, net debt, and enterprise value. Recalculate Disney's WACC using the weights based on the net debt. How much does it change?

11. How confident are you of your estimate? Which implicit assumptions did you make during your data collection efforts?

4

Integrative Case

This case draws on material from Chapters 11–13.

You work for HydroTech, a large manufacturer of high-pressure industrial water pumps. The firm specializes in natural disaster services, ranging from pumps that draw water from lakes, ponds, and streams in drought-stricken areas to pumps that remove high water volumes in flooded areas. You report directly to the CFO. Your boss has asked you to calculate HydroTech's WACC in preparation for an executive retreat. Too bad you're not invited, as water pumps and skiing are on the agenda in Sun Valley, Idaho. At least you have an analyst on hand to gather the following required information:

1. The risk-free rate of interest, in this case, the yield of the 10-year government bond, which is 3%

2. HydroTech's:
   a. Market capitalization (its market value of equity), $100 million
   b. CAPM beta, 1.2
   c. Total book value of debt outstanding, $50 million
   d. Cash, $10 million

3. The cost of debt (using the quoted yields on HydroTech's outstanding bond issues), which is 5%

With this information in hand, you are now prepared to undertake the analysis.

Case Questions

1. Calculate HydroTech's net debt.
2. Compute HydroTech's equity and (net) debt weights based on the market value of equity and the book value of net debt.
3. Calculate the cost of equity capital using the CAPM, assuming a market risk premium of 5%.
4. Using a tax rate of 35%, calculate HydroTech's effective cost of debt capital.
5. Calculate HydroTech's WACC.
6. When is it appropriate to use this WACC to evaluate a new project?

GUIDE TO FINANCE 320
Financial Management I

Part 1: Introduction

Part 2: Required Competencies for Finance 320

Part 3: The Departmental Valuation Exam

Part 4: The Comprehensive Departmental Final Exam

Department of Finance

Mihaylo College of Business and Economics

California State University Fullerton

PART 1

INTRODUCTION

FIN 320 Financial Management I

DEPARTMENT WEB PAGE FOR FIN 320
http://business.fullerton.edu/finance/finance320.htm

FIN 320 Financial Management I (3 units)

Prerequisite: Accounting 201A. Corequisites: ISDS 361A and BUAD 301.
COURSE DESCRIPTION: Financial statement analysis. Interest rates and valuing cash flows (w/valuing stocks & bonds). Investment decision rules and capital budgeting. Risk and return (CAPM) and WACC. International corporate finance.

Financial Management I addresses international corporate finance as an integrated topic throughout many of the topics in the course. It does not address this topic with a single chapter from the text.

BUSINESS CORE COURSE

FIN 320 is one of the Upper Division Core course requirements for the B.A. in Business Administration and for the B.A. in International Business within the Mihaylo College of Business and Economics.

ASSESSMENT

The main purpose of the degree program at the Mihaylo College of Business and Economics (College) at California State University Fullerton (CSUF) is to provide you with the knowledge and skills that prepare you for a successful career in business. In order to assist us in achieving this goal, we will use a number of assessment tools to track your progress throughout the College curriculum. Please expect to participate in College assessment activities in several of your courses while at CSUF. As you do so, you will assist us in identifying our program's strengths and weaknesses as well as areas for potential improvement. In other words, you are making an important investment in the value of your degree.

COMMON FEATURES FOR ALL FIN 320 SECTIONS

This course is required of all students with a major in business. As a result, the Department of Finance has decided to ensure that there are several **common elements/requirements in all sections of FIN 320 taught each semester**, including:

1. A common (custom) textbook for the course as based upon the 3rd Edition of **Fundamentals of Corporate Finance**, by Jonathan Berk, Peter DeMarzo and Jarrad Harford, and published by Prentice Hall (a division of Pearson).
2. All students use **MyFinanceLab** (required homework and quiz assignments).
3. All sections have **two common Departmental exams**, including a:
   a. **Valuation Exam** (covering Chapters 3, 4, 6 and 7 of the text), and
   b. **Comprehensive Final Exam** (covering all assigned chapters).
4. There are suggested weights on exams and quizzes/homework for all sections – though individual faculty may vary these weights.

5. All students are strongly encouraged to use **financial calculators** (either the HP 10BII or the Texas Instruments BAII PLUS).

6. Students are permitted to use a **Formula Sheet** and **only this sheet**, provided by the Department of Finance during the two common exams. The formula sheet may be used during other midterm exams, at the discretion of the individual instructor. **No other notes are permitted to be brought into or used during exams by any student in any section of FIN 320**.

7. All students should use Scantrons on exams – ask your instructor which form to bring.

8. <u>Note</u>: that most or all sections of FIN 320 will have **two additional midterms**, but these exams are **not common exams**. These exams will be written and administered by your instructor.

COMMITMENT TO MAINTAINING REASONABLE COSTS FOR STUDENT TEXTBOOKS

The **custom edition** of this text for MCBE students only includes Parts 1–4 (Chapters 1–13) of the hardcover version and is packaged along with MyFinanceLab, which together cost about $100. Total list price for the hard version of the text and MyFinanceLab would be about $290. The Department of Finance has made the decision to use a common customized text in order to keep your text costs reasonable.

You have the option of purchasing an "e–text" along with MyFinanceLab for $100, or MyFinanceLab code (without e-text) for $55.

THE FIN 320/321 SEQUENCE FOR FINANCE MAJORS

Chapters 14 – 18 of the text, **Fundamentals of Corporate Finance**, serve as the foundation for the second course in finance, FIN 321, Financial Management II. FIN 321 is required of all finance majors (either in the Finance Concentration or in the Joint Emphasis in Accounting and Finance). Additional material will be required in FIN 321 along with brief reviews of some chapters covered in FIN 320 (e.g., Chapters 8 – 13), but any additional required material (topics) will be available both in the Custom Edition and in MyFinanceLab.

VALUATION EXAM

This exam will be administered after your instructor has completed Part 2 of the text (e.g., after finishing Chapter 7, Stock Valuation). This exam will be administered through MyFinanceLab. See your instructor's syllabus for your class test dates. Primary topics for this exam include those covered in **Chapters 3, 4, 6 and 7**. This exam is important because it focuses on the principles which illustrate the time value of money as the foundation for valuing (pricing) stocks and bonds, the two most important means for financing any company. The word 'finance' directly relates to the balance sheet, because the right hand–side, liabilities (debt) and equity **finances** the left hand–side, assets. This exam typically includes 25 questions to be completed in 75 minutes and are all calculation problems (requiring the use of a financial calculator).

COMPREHENSIVE DEPARTMENT FINAL EXAM

The department final exam will take place during the week scheduled for final exams by CSUF. It is a comprehensive exam, covering concepts and calculation principles from Chapters 1 – 9 and 11 – 13. While **Chapter 10 is not covered on the Final Exam**, your instructor may review important topics from this chapter in class, and those topics are likely to be covered in the second mid–term exam written and administered by your instructor. You will have the normal amount of time to complete this final exam (1 hour and 50 minutes). See the CSUF Exam Schedule and/or your FIN 320 syllabus for the date and time that your section will take the final exam. Required competencies and study tips for this comprehensive final exam are provided in Part 4 of this Guide. There are typically 50 questions on the exam, which tend to be more heavily weighted toward conceptual questions (about 70% conceptual and 30% calculations). Usually the instructor's midterm exams, along with the Valuation Exam, are more heavily weighted toward calculation problems. The final exam includes questions similar to those that you see all semester long, but since it is comprehensive, most students find that it is more difficult. **Regular studying – every week – during the semester** is the best way to prepare for the final exam.

Resources for Finance 320 Students
CALCULATORS
- **Tutorial for the Texas Instruments BAII Plus Financial Calculator: <u>Appendix A</u>** in the textbook supplement provides a brief guide for using this calculator.
- **The Appendix for Chapter 4 of the Text (pg. 114)** provides basic instructions for using the HP 10BII and the TI BAII Plus (or Professional).
- **The textbook webpage includes Tutorials for both recommended calculators.** Just click on the <u>Textbook Resources</u> link in **MyFinanceLab** to find these tutorials.
- **There are many free on–line guides for calculators, just do a simple search!**
- **Your calculator comes with a guide – these are also useful.**

A **Formula Sheet** provided by the Department of Finance will be made available for all students for use during the two common exams, the Valuation Exam and the Comprehensive Final Exam. The FIN 320 Syllabus, to be provided within MyFinanceLab (and on Titanium at the discretion of the individual instructors), will include the Departmental Formula Sheet and it will also be available on the FIN 320 website.

<u>MyFinanceLab</u>
The Pearson web site includes direct access to MyFinanceLab:

> http://www.myfinancelab.com

Click on Register to set up your student account. To register, you will need your <u>Course ID</u> provided by your instructor (in class and on the syllabus). Once you are registered, you will sign in from this same page from the Sign In link using your username and password. There are MANY resources available for you at the textbook webpage in <u>MyFinanceLab</u>, all of which are on–line. Once you have started My Finance Lab, the navigation links appear on the left–hand side of the screen, as pictured here:

To find resources, click on the **Chapter Resources** link and select a chapter to find options for you to organize your studying:

You may also click on <u>Multimedia Resources</u> and select a chapter to access additional resources such as the financial calculator, etc.

Finance 320 Webpage

Where to Find the Finance 320 Webpage
http://business.fullerton.edu/finance/finance320.htm

What You Will Find on the Webpage:
1. The Departmental **Formula Sheet** that may be used during common exams. It may be used during the other mid–term exams at the discretion of your instructor. **No other**

2. **A sample Valuation Exam**. This exam is an actual exam given in a prior semester. ***This exam is a sample only.*** The exam that you will take will cover the same topics but the questions will be different. The best way to study for the exam is to use the _Guide to Finance 320_ in conjunction with working with the materials available to you at *MyFinanceLab*.

3. **A sample Comprehensive Department Final Exam**. This is an actual exam that was given in a prior semester. ***Any exams provided are samples only.*** The exam that you will take will cover the same topics but the questions will be different. The best way to study for the exam is to use the _Guide to Finance 320_ in conjunction with your textbook and any notes that you take from your professor's lectures. The main reason a sample of the exam is provided is to illustrate the format of the exam.

4. **GUIDE TO FINANCE 320. This is an electronic version of the guide you are reading in your Custom text for the course.**

PART 2

REQUIRED

COMPETENCIES

FOR FIN 320

PART 2
Required Competencies

Finance 320 Financial Management I is an important and practical course. It includes concepts and techniques needed for success in managing any type of company, whether large or small, public or private, including all areas of business such as Accounting, Finance, Management and Marketing. The competencies listed below reflect the minimum knowledge that you will be expected to acquire and represent the core competencies that you are expected to master. Professors enrich their courses with additional materials and learning objectives.

The Comprehensive Departmental Final Exam will be based upon these competencies. No notes are allowed during common exams, other than the Departmental **Formula Sheet**. NEITHER textbook nor calculator manuals are allowed. Naturally, you may use text book and PPT files provided by your instructor for any assignments completed on–line through MyFinanceLab. This document will help you prepare for the Comprehensive Department Exam that is given to all Finance 320 students during the final exam week at the end of the semester.

COURSE COMPETENCIES
The competencies that you are to master are presented here and are organized by the chapters in the textbook for this class, ***Fundamentals of Corporate Finance*** by Berk, DeMarzo and Harford, Custom Edition for Finance 320, California State University, Fullerton.

The textbook is the single most important aid you have to master the competencies of this course. In most cases, the materials available in the text provide adequate coverage and it is not necessary for the professor to spend valuable class time on each and every competency. In a few cases you may have to review sections of the textbook that are not included in the assignment. *It is your responsibility to read the book carefully and learn the material. Your professor's lectures are not a substitute for the reading assignment. It is not possible to cover every single topic in class and you should expect to see questions on exam that have not been discussed thoroughly in class.*

MyFinanceLab is also an essential tool that you should use in studying. Please see above for registration details and the initial windows and navigation panes you will see after logging on to MyFinanceLab. The **Study Plan** feature in MyFinanceLab is very useful.

FOCUS OF FIN 320 FINANCIAL MANAGEMENT I
The central focus of the course is the same as the text, Fundamentals of Corporate Finance, namely:

> **The Valuation Principle** (pg. 74):
> The value of a commodity or an asset to the firm or its investors is determined by its competitive market price. The benefits and costs of a decision should be evaluated using those market prices. When the value of

the benefits exceeds the value of the costs, the decision will increase the market value of the firm.

Market prices remain competitive through supply and demand, and there can only be one price for goods or securities which are the same. The pressure for only one price to exist for the same good is the **Law of One Price**, and it is this "law" which makes the valuation principle effective. If prices for goods which are the same deviate from one another, an **arbitrage opportunity** may easily occur. For example, if you knew that Apple stock was being sold in Hong Kong for $520 a share and for only $500 a share in New York, and you could make a contract to buy in NY and sell in HK simultaneously (at the given prices), so that you wouldn't need to make any investment, you would make a $20/share profit. You could make $2,000 in a couple seconds without any risk or investment, should an opportunity like this arise. Any time it is possible to make a profit without taking any risk or making any investment, you have an arbitrage opportunity. Naturally, such opportunities are rare for ordinary investors, but the underlying forces drive prices for the same goods to one price.

A. CORPORATE FINANCE AND THE FINANCIAL MANAGER (Chapter 1)

1. **Explain and evaluate the importance of financial information for businesses and individuals.**
2. **Distinguish among the four different types of firms (Table 1.1).**
3. **Understand and explain the Financial Manager's position and responsibilities.**
4. **Explain and evaluate the concept of shareholder wealth maximization and how it relates to other possible objectives of the firm's management.**
5. **Explain the main features of the stock market.**
6. **Explain how financial institutions fit into the free–market economy (Table 1.2).**

- **Sample Focus Questions**: What is wrong with profit maximization as an objective? Why is stockholder wealth maximization a better objective? What does it mean to maximize stockholder wealth? What is the agency problem and how does it relate to stockholder wealth maximization? How do ethical considerations enter into the desire to maximize stockholder wealth? Why do financial markets exist and how important are they to American firms? What are the key components of the U.S. financial market system? How is financial capital moved from savers to ultimate users of the funds? Which securities have been used most frequently by American firms? How do primary and secondary financial markets differ? What are the examples of each type of market? What is the difference between the money market and the capital market? Which instruments are traded in each type of market? How do over-the-counter markets differ from organized securities exchanges?

- **Chapter Summary**: See pages 22–23 of text.

B. INTRODUCTION TO FINANCIAL STATEMENT ANALYSIS (Chapter 2)

1. Understand why firms file financial statements (10–Ks and Annual Reports).
2. Understand and be able to analyze (using relevant financial ratios) balance sheet accounts (Table 2.4) to diagnose the firm's financial health.
3. Understand and be able to analyze (using relevant financial ratios) income statement accounts (Table 2.4) to diagnose the firm's financial health.
4. Understand Other Related Elements of a Firm's Financial Position (Statement of Cash Flows, Management Discussion, Notes to the Financial Statement, the role of Sarbanes–Oxley Act).

- **Sample Focus Questions**: What is an income statement and what information does it contain? What is the difference in the information contained in operating income (EBIT) and net income available to common stockholders? How do interest payments affect taxes? How do preferred and common dividends affect taxes? What are the major categories on the right and left sides of the balance sheet? What does the balance sheet tell us about the firm? What does the cash flow statement tell us about the firm? What are cash flows from operations? What are cash flows from investing activities? What are cash flows from financing activities? How are cash flows and net income (profits) different? How can you interpret the cash flow statement? Which ratios help answer which questions? How is each ratio computed? What comparisons can be made in financial ratio analysis? What are the limitations of financial ratio analysis?

- **Chapter Summary**: See pages 55–57 of text.

C. TIME VALUE OF MONEY: AN INTRODUCTION (Chapter 3)

1. Understand the decision making process in competitive markets (using cost-benefit analysis).
2. Understand the concept of time value of money and interest rates.
3. Explain the concepts of compounding and discounting and show how they can be used to calculate the future value and present value. Learn how to value cash flows at different points in time.
4. Learn the three basic rules of the Time Value of Money: (1) Comparing and Combining Values, (2) Compounding, and (3) Discounting.

- **Sample Focus Questions**: What are the roles of financial manager? By analyzing incremental costs and benefits, how to define a good decision? What is the Valuation Principle? What is time value of money? What is meant by compounding and discounting? Why is $100 invested for three years at 10% worth $133.10 rather than $130? How can the equation for computing present value be derived from the equation for computing future value?

- **Chapter Summary**: See pages 86–87 of text.

D. TIME VALUE OF MONEY: VALUING CASH FLOW STREAMS (Chapter 4)

1. Explain how to value a stream of cash flows.
2. Understand and be able to value annuity, perpetuity and growing cash flows.
3. Compute time value of money variables other than present and future values.

- **Sample Focus Questions:** How to compute the present value of an uneven stream? How to compute the present value of an annuity? How to compute the present value of perpetuity? How to compute the present value of growing cash flows? How to compute annual interest rate, annuity payment, and time periods?

- **Chapter Summary:** See pages 116–117 of text.

E. INTEREST RATES (Chapter 5)

1. Understand the Basic Features of Interest Rates, including the Effective Annual Rate (EAR) and the Annual Percentage Rate (APR).
2. Compute equal loan payments and the remaining balance on an amortizing loan.
3. Describe how interest rates are determined, and the relation of interest rates to the opportunity cost of capital.

- **Sample Focus Questions:** What is Effective Annual Rate (EAR)? What is Annual Percentage Rate (APR)? How to compute EAR given APR? What is an amortizing loan? For an amortizing loan, how to calculate equal loan payments and the outstanding loan balance? How does the nominal rate of interest differ from the real rate of interest? Which factors determine the nominal rate of interest? What is the relationship between a debt security's rate of return and the length of time until the debt matures? What is the opportunity cost of capital?

- **Chapter Summary:** See pages 148–149 of text.

F. BONDS (Chapter 6)

1. Describe the characteristics (terminology) of bonds.
2. Explain how zero-coupon bonds and coupon bonds are valued and compute the value of these bonds.
3. Compute bond yields.
4. Explain the important relationships of bond valuation.
5. Understand bond ratings and the yield curve.

- **Sample Focus Questions**: What are the definitions of book value, liquidation value, market value and intrinsic (economic) value? What is the relationship between the concept of market value and Efficient Capital Markets? What would be the relationship between market value and intrinsic value in an efficient capital market? What determines the value of an asset? What is a bond? What is the nature of the bondholders' claim on the assets and income of the firm? What is the meaning of par value, coupon interest rate, maturity and current yield? What is an indenture? What risk is measured by bond ratings? What are the ranking categories used by Standard and Poor? What are zero-coupon and coupon- bonds? What are the cash flows associated with the zero-coupon and coupon bonds? How to value these two types of bonds? What adjustment is made for semiannual interest payments? What is expected rate of return and how does it relate to the concept of a bond's yield to maturity? How is yield to maturity computed? During a period of inflation, what would you expect to happen to interest rates and bond prices? What is the relation between coupon rate, yield to maturity, and the bond value? What happens to the value of a bond as it approaches its maturity date? Why?

- **Chapter Summary**: See pages 181-182 of text.

G. STOCK VALUATION (Chapter 7)

1. Explain the characteristics of common stock and preferred stock.
2. Describe the factors in the dividend discount model that determine the value of stock, and show how these factors can be combined to calculate the value of preferred stock and common stock.
3. Calculate the expected rate of return on preferred stock and common stock.
4. Understand the primary drawback of dividend discount model.
5. Understand the basics of share repurchases.

- **Sample Focus Questions:** What are the major features of preferred stock? What are the major features of common stock? How does preferred stock differ from common stock? How do trades on the NYSE and NASDAQ work? How is the value of preferred stock computed? How to value common stock by using the dividend discount model? What would make common stock go up in value? Why might common stock go down in value? What is the primary drawback of the dividend discount model? How do share repurchases and total payout model work?

- **Chapter Summary**: See pages 212–213 of text.

H. INVESTMENT DECISION RULES (Chapter 8)

1. Describe NPV, IRR, payback period and evaluate the advantages and disadvantages of each of these techniques.

2. Compute NPV, IRR and payback period.
3. Discuss the cases where NPV and IRR give different decisions.
4. Describe how to choose between mutually exclusive projects.
5. Compute equivalent annual annuity (EAA) and profitability index (PI) and describe how they can be used to choose between projects with different resource requirements and lives.

- **Sample Focus Questions:** What is NPV? What does a positive NPV signify and why? What does a negative NPV mean? What is IRR? How is IRR used to make capital budgeting decisions? Why is it true that NPV and IRR will give the same decisions (except under unusual circumstances)? What is payback period? What are the advantages and disadvantages of each technique? Should capital budgeting decisions be based on NPV or IRR when choosing among projects with different scales and timing of cash flows? Why? What is equivalent annual annuity (EAA)? How is EAA used to choose between projects with different lives? What is profitability index (PI)? How is PI used to choose between projects with different resource requirements?

- **Chapter Summary:** See pages 251–252 of text (and Table 8–5, pg. 250).

I. FUNDAMENTALS OF CAPITAL BUDGETING (Chapter 9)

1. Describe the goal of the capital budgeting process.
2. Evaluate the guidelines for estimating/forecasting incremental earnings associated with capital budgeting alternatives.
3. Calculating Incremental Free Cash Flows (FCFs), and evaluating the project with the decision rules (NPV, IRR, etc.).
4. Discuss the effects of opportunity costs, project externalities and sunk costs on incremental free cash flows.
5. Describe sensitivity analysis, break-even analysis and scenario analysis and discuss how they help with making capital budgeting decisions.

- **Sample Focus Questions:** What is capital budgeting? How do you estimate incremental earnings? How do you use incremental earnings estimates to calculate incremental free cash flows? What is meant by incremental cash flows? Why are incremental rather than total cash flows used? Why are incremental free cash flows rather than incremental earnings used? How do capital expenditures, depreciation and changes in net working capital affect free cash flows? What are opportunity costs and how should they be incorporated into the analysis? What are project externalities and how do they affect free cash flows? What are sunk costs and how are they handled? What is salvage value and how does it affect the free cash flows? What are sensitivity, break-even and scenario analyses? How are they used?

- **Chapter Summary:** See pages 287–288 of text.

J. STOCK VALUATION: A SECOND LOOK (Chapter 10)

NOTE: <u>Chapter 10 will not be covered on the common Comprehensive Departmental Final Exam.</u> Your instructor may review some sections in this Chapter, as a result questions on a second mid–term exam may cover these sections.

1. Describe and implement the discounted free cash flow model (DCF) to find the firm's enterprise and equity value.
2. Explain how DCF is related to the NPV decision rule used in capital budgeting.
3. Discuss how valuation multiples of comparable firms can be used to estimate enterprise and equity value.
4. Compare DCF and valuation multiple methods, and discuss strengths and weaknesses of each method.
5. Explain the efficient markets hypotheses (EMH) and discuss what it implies for stock prices.
6. Describe the implications of the EMH for investors and corporate managers.
7. Describe individual biases when trading and their effects on stock prices.

- **Sample Focus Questions:**
  Why is the Dividend Discount Model not very useful for stock valuation in the real world? What is the discounted free cash flow model (DCF)? What is the definition of Enterprise Value (EV)? How is it EV related to free cash flows (FCF)? How are FCFs of a firm calculated? What is terminal value (TV) of the enterprise and how is it calculated? What rate is used to discount the FCFs and TV and why? What is the method of valuation multiples of comparable firms? What are valuation multiples? Define the price-earnings-ratio and enterprise value multiples. What is the advantage of using enterprise value multiples? What are the limitations of multiples? What are its strengths and weaknesses compared to the DCF method? What is the efficient markets hypothesis (EMH)? List the different versions of EMH and explain how they are different from each other? What is the implication of EMH for investors and corporate managers? List the common psychological biases exhibited by the investors. What is overconfidence and how does it affect trading? What is the disposition effect and how does it influence the stock prices? How does investor attention, mood and experience affect trading?

- **Chapter Summary:** See pages 321–322 of text.

K. RISK AND RETURN IN CAPITAL MARKETS (Chapter 11)

1. Define and measure the expected rate of return of an individual investment and a portfolio of assets.
2. Define and measure the riskiness of an individual investment.

3. **Define and measure the investment risk of a portfolio of assets and evaluate the merits of diversification.**

*   **Sample Focus Questions:** Why is the Risk-Return Tradeoff important? What is expected return and how does it relate to the statistical concept of expected value? How is expected return measured? Why isn't each possible return given the same weight in the computational procedure? What is investment risk? Using Figures 11-1 to 11-3 as a frame of reference, why are some investments are more risky? Why is standard deviation a good measure of risk of an individual investment and how is it computed? Why would a firm choose an investment with relatively high risk? What are the two types of risk associated with holding a portfolio of investments? How is each measure of risk defined? Which risks can be diversified away and which can't? How large does a portfolio have to be in order to diversify away company-unique risk? Why does some risk remain even after diversification? What does beta measure? What does it mean if a stock has a beta of less than one; equal to one; or greater than one?   How is a portfolio beta computed?

*   **Chapter Summary**: See pages 355–356 of text.

L. SYSTEMATIC RISK AND THE EQUITY RISK PREMIUM (Chapter 12)

1. **What is the expected return and risk (volatility) of a portfolio? How do investors diversity their risks? How do investors measure the co–movement of stock returns?**
2. **How is systematic risk measured?**
3. **How do investors and financial managers estimate a company's beta?**
4. **Explain the concept of Capital Asset Pricing Model (CAPM) and show the relationship between risk and return on the Security Market Line (SML).**

*   **Sample Focus Questions:**   Why would we want to know the required rate of return? What is the meaning of Equation 12-6? What is the meaning of each term in equation 12-6? How does Equation 12-6 relate to the Risk-Return Tradeoff? How can one use Figure 12-6 to find the market risk premium and the risk free rate of return? What is a company's beta? What is the primary use of the security market line for financial managers?

*   **Chapter Summary**: See pages 389–390 of text.

M. THE COST OF CAPITAL (Chapter 13)

1. **What is a firm's weighted cost of capital? How do financial managers calculate their company's WACC?**

2. **What are the components of a firm's WACC? How do financial managers estimate (calculate) their firm's cost of equity, cost of debt and cost of preferred stock?**
3. **How should financial managers use the WACC to value the firm's projects?**

- **Sample Focus Questions:** What is the cost of capital? How is it similar and how is it different from the investors' required rate of return? What are the components of the capital structure in the cost of capital? Why is the cost of capital a weighted average rather than a simple average? How is the cost of capital used in conjunction with investment schedules to make asset acquisition choices? Why should the firm not use a single cost of financing as the hurdle rate (discount rate) for making capital-budgeting decisions?

- **Chapter Summary:** See pages 418–419 of text.

PART 3

THE DEPARTMENTAL

VALUATION EXAM

The Departmental Valuation Exam

One of the departmental requirements for all students taking *Finance 320 Financial Management I* is the Valuation Exam. The exam is typically administered through MyFinanceLab. You will have up to two attempts to take the 25 question exam. Your highest score on these two attempts will be your score for this exam. In each case you have up to 75 minutes to complete the exam, using any text or PPT materials available to you. Relying on others for assistance on this exam is cheating and any cheating detected will be addressed following both Departmental and University Policy.

Solving problems using the basic time value of money formulas provides the foundation for understanding the key principles of modern finance, especially as they focus around the valuation of common stock (Chapter 7, along with a more detailed analysis in Chapter 10, later in the semester). The fundamental valuation principle requires all investors to estimate the present value (today) of cash flows that you expect to receive in the future. In the case of common stock, the future cash flows can always be considered to be dividends. In the case of bonds, the primary future cash flows include interest payments along with the repayment of the principal. The question is whether a purchase or sale today provides you with an expected gain in wealth. It is only through the careful use of the time value of money formulas/principles that questions like this can be answered. This is why the **Valuation Exam** is a central feature of FIN 320.

Which Topics Are Included on the Exam? All topics included in Part 2 of the Berk/DeMarzo/Harford text (Chapters 3, 4, 6, 7) are eligible as questions on the exam. The following list includes main principles from these chapters.

IMPORTANT STUDY TIPS
- All Problems listed in the Text are also available in My Finance Lab!
- **Brief Reviews (Key Points and Equations)** are printed in the text the end of each chapter. The reviews are tied directly to My Finance Lab (your **Study Plan**). For the Valuation Exam, these reviews are on the following pages:
    1. **Chapter 3** – Time Value of Money: pgs. 86–87.
    2. **Chapter 4** – TVM – Valuing Cash Flow Streams: pgs. 116–117.
    3. **Chapter 6** – Bonds: pgs. 181–182.
    4. **Chapter 7** – Stocks: pgs. 212–213.

CHAPTER 3 – INTRODUCTION TO THE TIME VALUE OF MONEY
1) Cost – Benefit Analysis
2) Market Prices and the Valuation Principle
3) Time Value of Money and Interest Rates
4) Valuing Cash Flows at Different Points in Time

5) Solving for Variables other than PV or FV
   a) Cash Flows
   b) Rate of Return (discount rate)
   c) Number of Periods

CHAPTER 6 – BONDS
1) Zero – Coupon Bonds
2) Coupon Bonds

a) Comparing/Combining Values
b) Future Value – Compounding
c) Present Value – Discounting

CHAPTER 4 – TIME VALUE OF MONEY – VALUING CASH FLOW STREAMS
1) Valuing a Stream of Cash Flows
2) Perpetuities
3) Annuities
   a) Present Value
   b) Future Value
4) Growing Cash Flows
   a) Growing Perpetuity
   b) Growing Annuity

3) Why Bond Prices Change
   • Estimating Bond Value
   • Estimating Coupon Payment
   • Estimating Coupon Rate
   • Current Yield of a Bond

CHAPTER 7 – STOCKS
1) The Dividend Discount Model (DDM) and Equation
2) Estimating Dividends in the DDM
   a) Cost of Equity
   b) Valuing Stock with Constant Growth
   c) Estimating Stock Yield
   d) Estimating Stock Growth

How Have Students Done on Past Valuation Exams (the old name for this exam was the FinCoach Exam)? Students have been quite successful, though as we move to a different text, topics and procedure for this exam, average scores may change. The Department of Finance will carefully monitor students' results on the Valuation Exam.

What Will the Valuation Exam Look Like? There is a sample exam on the Finance 320 Web Page. The exam that you take will have the same format and cover the same topics but the questions will be different. **The best way to prepare for the exam is to master all specified topics in Part 2 of the Text.** To accomplish this, study and use **MyFinanceLab** to assist you in your preparation. The **Study Plan** link (tool) in MyFinanceLab is particularly useful.

Should Students Use a Financial Calculator? Absolutely! And since you will most likely take this exam at home (on–line) you may also use **Excel**. It is important to learn the financial calculator for exams, and knowledge of how to use a financial calculator will improve job performance in many business-related occupations. Using a financial calculator will also improve your performance in most other business courses.

EXCEL The Department of Finance is attempting to introduce the use of Excel for solving finance problems (time value of money, stock and bond valuation, etc.) into all relevant courses when feasible. As a result, FIN 320 will focus on the use of Excel as much as possible – with the assistance of the Text and **MyFinanceLab**. Excel is the most important software tool generally available to finance professionals. Becoming an expert in Excel will enable your initial success on the job.

TYPES OF PROBLEMS THAT WILL APPEAR ON THE VALUATION EXAM

THIS SECTION GIVES SPECIFIC INFORMATION FOR EACH OF THE BASIC TIME VALUE OF MONEY TOPICS COVERED ON THE EXAM *(Does not include Chapter 5, Interest Rates)*

1. **Single Cash Flows**
- **Future Value of a Single Cash Flow**

    Types of Problems: You will be asked to compute the future value (*FV*) of a single cash flow, given annual compounding or nonannual compounding.

- **Present Value of a Single Cash Flow**

    Types of Problems: You will be asked to solve for the present value (*PV*) of a single cash flow, given annual compounding or nonannual compounding. Look at a fairly large number of this type of problems because there are many different ways of phrasing the present value problem.

- **Single Cash Flow: Solving for Discount Rate**

    Types of Problems: You will sometimes be asked to compute either: (1) the underlying interest rate, (2) the underlying discount rate, (3) the underlying rate of return, or (4) several other variations. They all basically refer to the same thing – the growth rate of money between the present point in time and some specified future point in time. Note that the techniques discussed in this section could also be generalized to apply to problems such as the rate of growth in sales, income, employment or whatever.

2. **Finite Cash Flows**

- **Future Value of an Annuity**

    Types of Problems: You will be asked to compute the future value of an annuity, i.e. a series of cash flows of equal amount, at fixed intervals, and for a specified number of periods. The cash flows may occur on annual basis, or on nonannual basis, such as weekly, monthly or quarterly.

- **Present Value of an Annuity**

    Types of Problems: You will be asked to find the present value of an annuity, given annual compounding or nonannual compounding. A very important application of this topic is to deal with amortized loans. An amortized loan is repaid with equal periodic payments; therefore, the payments of the loan represent an annuity. In an amortized loan problem, the loan amount is *PV* while the periodic payment is *PMT*. If the loan calls for nonannual payments, make sure that *n* and *i* are consistent with the payment pattern.

- **Annuities: Solving for Discount Rate**

  Types of Problems: There are two types of problems that will ask you to solve for *i*. For example, you may be given the amount that is borrowed in an amortized loan (i.e. *PV*) and the periodic payments (i.e. *PMT*). Your job is to find the interest rate on the loan. Note that if you are asked to compute the **APR** (annual percentage rate) and the payments are on nonannual basis, you must annualize the periodic interest rate. The problem may also be approached from the perspective of achieving a financial goal. Suppose you expect to accumulate certain amount of money at a future point in time by making a series of equal periodic deposits. In this case you will be asked to compute the annual rate of return on the savings.

- **Annuities: Solving for Time or Payment**

  Types of Problems: The types of problems are similar to those described in the previous sections. However, you will be asked to solve for *n* or *PMT*. For example, you may be asked to find out how many years it takes to reach a specified financial goal (*FV*), or how long it takes to pay off an amortized loan (*PV*). The problems may also ask you how much each periodic payment is to pay off a loan (*PV*), or how much each deposit is required to accumulate certain amount of money in the future (*FV*).

3. **Infinite Cash Flows**

- **Present Value of a Perpetuity**

  Types of Problems: You will be asked to find the present value of a perpetuity (i.e. an annuity that continues forever). The problem may or may not mention the term "perpetuity," so it is important that you recognize the pattern of cash flows described in the problem.

- **Present Value of a Growth Perpetuity**

  Types of Problems: In these problems you will be asked to compute the present value of a perpetuity whose cash flows grow at a constant rate forever, i.e. the growth perpetuity. Some problems may require you to combine the present value computation and the basic valuation concept. For example, if someone offers you an investment opportunity that will provide you with payments that grow at a constant rate and last forever, how much should you pay for this investment now? Since the value of the investment is equal to the present value of its expected future cash flows, the maximum amount you should pay for the investment is the *PV* of a growth perpetuity.

4. **Bond Valuation**

- **Estimating Bond Value**

  Types of Problems: You will be asked to compute the intrinsic value of a bond. The interest payments (most bonds pay interest semiannually) and the par value of the bond are given. A discount rate that is usually called the required rate of return or the market interest rate on the bond is also given. You are to compute the present value of the cash flows generated by the bond. Conceptually, this type of problem is a combination of the present value of an annuity (periodic interest payments) and the present value of a single lump sum received in the future (the par value). If you use a financial calculator, this is all computed at the same time. Note that in some cases, the dollar interest payment is given; in other cases, the dollar interest amount must be computed (the coupon rate times the par value equals the dollar interest payment).

- **Estimating the Coupon Payment or Coupon Rate**

   Types of Problems: Some problems may ask you to compute the coupon payment of a bond. In these cases, you will be given the bond price (*PV*), the par value (*FV*), the term to maturity (*n*), and the yield to maturity or required rate of return (*i*); the unknown is *PMT*. If the bond pays semiannual interest, don't forget to adjust your inputs for *n* and *i*. Additionally, pay attention to the proper signs of *PV* and *FV*. Some problems may ask you to compute the annual coupon rate of the bond. You first need to find the bond's periodic coupon payment. If the payment is on semiannual basis, multiply it by 2 to get the annual coupon payment. Divide the annual coupon payment by the par value to derive the annual coupon rate.

- **Yield to Maturity of a Bond**

   Types of Problems: Yield to maturity (YTM) is also called the expected or required rate of return on the bond. If the problem asks you to find the yield to maturity, use the financial calculator to solve for *i* by entering the values for *n*, *PV*, *PMT* and *FV*. Make sure you use proper signs for *PV*, *PMT* and *FV*. Since YTMs are stated on annual basis, you must multiply the calculated *i* by 2 for semiannual bonds.

- **Current Yield of a Bond**

   Types of Problems: If the problem asks you to find the current yield of a bond, simply take the annual interest payment and divide it by the bond price.

5. **Stock Valuation**

- **Valuing Stock with Constant Growth**

   Types of Problems: The problem will ask you to calculate the value of a constant growth common stock. For these problems you are given a dividend, a required rate of return, and a dividend growth rate. This is an important problem in finance because it highlights the combined impacts of cash flows to the stockholder (dividends and growth in dividends) and the risk borne by stockholders (required rate of return).

- **Estimating Stock Yield**

   Types of Problems: You will be asked to compute the required rate of return on a common stock. The problem will provide you with information about dividends and the price of the stock.

- **Estimating Stock Growth**

  Types of Problems: You will be asked to calculate the implied growth rate in dividends when the price of the stock is known and the dividend is known.

PART 4

COMMON DEPARTMENTAL

COMPREHENSIVE FINAL EXAM

DEPARTMENTAL COMPREHENSIVE FINAL EXAM

A department requirement of FIN 320 is the common Comprehensive Final Exam, to be administered at the standard time during final exam week (see CSUF Exam Schedule): http://www.fullerton.edu/admissions/CurrentStudent/FinalExaminations.asp

KEY FEATURES OF FINAL EXAM
- The Departmental Final Exam for FIN 320 is a common exam, with many different versions, typically consisting of 50 questions. It will be in your usual classroom.
- Bring a Scantron to the Final Exam – ask your instructor for the type of Scantron sheet.
- You have the "normal" amount of time for a final exam: 1 hour and 50 minutes.
- Please do not wait until the end of the exam to start filling in your Scantron – all exams are collected at the same time. Penalties are assessed for not following directions.
- <u>No notes are allowed on the final exam</u>. As a result you should ensure that you practice and remember crucial formulas. You will be permitted to use the **Formula Sheet**.
- The exam is comprehensive and any material covered during the semester or in the assigned chapters/sections from the textbook may be on the exam.

PREPARING FOR THE FINAL EXAM
- The exam covers Chapters 1 – 9, and 11 – 13.
- It is best to prepare for the final exam by **studying every week** during the semester. Those who wait until finals week to review have a **high probability of performing much lower** than their average during the semester and of having to retake FIN 320. Approximately 10–15 % of students from any given semester end up having to retake FIN 320 again. Our goal is to assist you in a reasonable manner to ensure that you learn the material the first time around!
- Some instructors provide a variety of ways to earn extra credit. It is a good idea to take advantage of these opportunities – given the facts and examples provided next.
- Historically, the average score for all students over many years of administering final exams in FIN 320 to thousands of students is less than 70%. **Is the exam difficult? Yes, but that is primarily because it is comprehensive**. The questions are almost always similar (and some will be identical) to those that you have already had on mid–term exams, on quizzes and homework assignments in My Finance Lab and on the Valuation Exam.
- **You need at least a C grade to "pass" FIN 320** (74% or higher course average – this average may vary slightly by instructor). Since the average score on the final exam is usually lower than this, the best strategy is to have a higher average going into the final exam. **Consider a few examples**:
  1. You have an average course grade going into the final exam of 78%. If the final exam counts for 25% of the course grade, you will need at least a 62% score on your final exam to achieve a 74% course average.

2. You have a 75% (passing) average going into the final exam. Suppose that your final exam score is 67%. Will you pass the course (so that you don't have to re–take FIN 320)? No you will not pass FIN 320, because your average is only 73%.

3. You have an 80% average going into the final and are confident! But you don't really study enough. You earn a 50% on the final exam – and your course average is 72.5%, which means that you will have to re–take FIN 320.

	Number of Owners	Liability for Firm's Debts	Owners Manage the Firm	Ownership Change Dissolves Firm	Taxation
Sole Proprietorship	One	Yes	Yes	Yes	Personal
Partnership	Unlimited	Yes; each partner is liable for the entire amount	Yes	Yes	Personal
Limited Partnership	At least one general partner (GP), no limit on limited partners (LP)	GP-Yes LP-No	GP-Yes LP-No	GP-Yes LP-No	Personal
Limited Liability Company	Unlimited	No	Yes	No*	Personal
S Corporation	At most 100	No	No (but they legally may)	No	Personal
C Corporation	Unlimited	No	No (but they legally may)	No	Double

*However, most LLCs require the approval of the other members to transfer your ownership.

TVM Formulas

$$FV_n = C*(1+r)^n \qquad \text{Eq.3.1}$$

$$PV_0 = \frac{C}{(1+r)^n} \qquad \text{Eq.3.2}$$

$$PV = C_0 + \frac{C_1}{(1+r)1} + \frac{C_2}{(1+r)2} + \cdots + \frac{C_N}{(1+r)N} \qquad \text{Eq.4.3} \approx \text{Eq.5.7}$$

$$PV(C \ in \ Perpetuity) = \frac{C}{r} \qquad \text{Eq.4.4}$$

$$PV(Annuity) = C*\frac{1}{r}*(1 - \frac{1}{(1+r)N}) \qquad \text{Eq.4.5}$$

$$FV(Annuity) = C*\frac{1}{r}*((1+r)N - 1) \qquad \text{Eq.4.6}$$

$$PV(Growing \ Perpetuity) = \frac{C}{r-g} \qquad \text{Eq.4.7}$$

$$PV(Growing \ Annuity) = C\frac{1}{r-g}(1 - (\frac{1+g}{1+r})^N) \quad \text{Eq.4.8}$$

Equivalent n-period discount rate $= (1+r)^n - 1$ Eq. 5.1

EAR to periodic rate: $\frac{i}{m} = (1+EAR)^{\frac{1}{m}} - 1$

$$EAR = \left(1 + \frac{APR}{m}\right)^m - 1 \qquad \text{Eq. 5.3}$$

$$Real \ Interest \ Rate = \frac{Nominal \ Rate - Inflation \ Rate}{1 + Inflation \ Rate} \quad \text{Eq. 5.5}$$

Stocks, Bonds, & Capital Budgeting Formulas

$$Bond \ P_0 = \frac{CPN_1}{(1+y)1} + \frac{CPN_2}{(1+y)2} + \cdots + \frac{CPN_N + FV}{(1+y)N}$$

$$Bond \ P_0 = CPN*\frac{1}{y}*(1 - \frac{1}{(1+y)N}) + \frac{FV}{(1+y)N} \quad \text{Eq. 6.3}$$

$$Stock \ P_0 = \frac{Div_1}{(1+r_E)1} + \cdots + \frac{Div_N}{(1+r_E)N} + \frac{P_N}{(1+r_E)N} \quad \text{Eq. 7.4}$$

$$Stock \ P_0 \ (Constant \ Growth) = \frac{Div_1}{r_E - g} \qquad \text{Eq. 7.6}$$

$$R_{t+1} = \frac{Div_{t+1} + P_{t+1} - P_t}{P_t} \qquad \text{Eq.11.1}$$

$$Cost \ of \ Equity \ Capital = r_E = \frac{Div_1}{P_0} + g \quad \text{Eq. 7.7}$$

$$g = Retention \ Rate * Return \ on \ New \ Investment \qquad \text{Eq. 7.12}$$

$$NPV = -I_0 + \frac{CF_1}{(1+r)1} + \frac{CF_2}{(1+r)2} + \cdots + \frac{CF_N}{(1+r)N} \qquad \text{Eq. 8.2}$$

Annual Realized Return:
$$R_{Annual} = (1+R_1)(1+R_2)(1+R_3)(1+R_4) - 1 \qquad \text{Eq.11.2}$$

Average Annual Return: $\overline{R} = \frac{1}{T}(R_1 + R_2 + \ldots + R_T)$ Eq.11.3

$$VAR(R) = \frac{1}{T-1}((R_1 - \overline{R})^2 + (R_2 - \overline{R})^2 + \ldots + (R_T - \overline{R})^2) \ \text{Eq.11.4}$$

$$Std(R) = \sqrt{VAR(R)} \qquad \text{Eq.11.5}$$

CAPM or SML: $E[R_i] = r_f + \beta_i*(E[R_{Mkt}] - r_f)$ Eq.12.6

$$WACC = r_D*(1-T)*D\% + r_{pfd}*P\% + r_E*E\% \qquad \text{Eq.13.6}$$

$$CFs \ Operations = EBIT(1-T) + depreciation \ expense \quad \text{Eq. 9.6}$$

$$FCF = CFs \ Operations - CapEx - Change \ in \ NWC \quad \text{Eq. 9.6}$$

Financial Ratios

$$Market-to-Book \ Ratio = \frac{Market \ Value \ of \ Equity}{Book \ Value \ of \ Equity}$$

$$Book \ Debt-to-Equity \ Ratio = \frac{LT \ \& \ ST \ Debt}{Book \ Value \ of \ Equity}$$

$$Market \ Debt-to-Equity \ Ratio = \frac{LT \ \& \ ST \ Debt}{Market \ Value \ of \ Equity}$$

$$Enterprise \ Value = Mkt \ Value \ of \ Equity + LT \ \& \ ST \ Debt - Cash$$

$$Current \ Ratio = \frac{Current \ Assets}{Current \ Liabilities}$$

$$Quick \ Ratio = \frac{Current \ Assets - Inventory}{Current \ Liabilities}$$

$$Gross \ Margin = \frac{Gross \ Profit}{Sales}$$

$$Operating \ Margin = \frac{Operating \ Income}{Sales}$$

$$Net \ Profit \ Margin = \frac{Net \ Income}{Sales}$$

$$Interest \ Coverage \ Ratio = \frac{Operating \ Income}{Interest \ Expense}$$

$$Return \ on \ Equity = \frac{Net \ Income}{Book \ Value \ of \ Equity}$$

$$Return \ on \ Assets = \frac{Net \ Income}{Total \ Assets}$$

$$Price-to-Earnings \ Ratio = \frac{Share \ Price}{Earnings \ per \ Share}$$

$$Accounts \ Receivable \ Days = \frac{Accounts \ Receivable}{Average \ Daily \ Sales}$$

$$Inventory \ Turnover = \frac{Cost \ of \ Goods \ Sold}{Inventory}$$

$$Fixed \ Asset \ Turnover = \frac{Sales}{Fixed \ Assets}$$

$$Total \ Asset \ Turnover = \frac{Sales}{Total \ Assets}$$

1. What is the yield to maturity of a ten − year, $1000 bond with a 5.2% coupon rate and semiannual coupons if this bond is currently trading for a price of $884?

   ○A. 6.82%

   ○B. 6.23%

   ○C. 12.46%

   ○D. 5.02%

2. Sara wants to have $500,000 in her savings account when she retires. How much must she put in the account now, if the account pays a fixed interest rate of 8%, to ensure that she has $500,000 in 20 years time?

   ○A. $231,480

   ○B. $144,616

   ○C. $107,274

   ○D. $180,884

3. A risk − free, zero − coupon bond with a $5000 face value has ten years to maturity. The bond currently trades at $3650. What is the yield to maturity of this bond?

   ○A. 3.465%

   ○B. 3.699%

   ○C. 3.284%

   ○D. 3.197%

4. What is the present value (PV) of $100,000 received five years from now, assuming the interest rate is 8% per year?

   ○A. $60,000.00

   ○B. $82,609.42

   ○C. $73,502.99

   ○D. $68,058.32

5.   What is the future value (FV) of $60,000 in five years, assuming the interest rate is 5% per year?

    ○A. $62,500.00

    ○B. $76,576.89

    ○C. $75,000.00

    ○D. $72,674.86

6.   If $15,000 is invested at 10% per year, in approximately how many years will the investment double?

    ○A. 8.4 years

    ○B. 10.6 years

    ○C. 7.3 years

    ○D. 14.8 years

7.   An annuity is set up that will pay $1500 per year for ten years. What is the present value (PV) of this annuity given that the discount rate is 6%?

    ○A. $11,040

    ○B. $19,771

    ○C. $14,721

    ○D. $8441

8.   Von Bora Corporation (VBC) is expected to pay a $2.00 dividend at the end of this year. If you expect VBC's dividend to grow by 5% per year forever and VBC's equity cost of capital is 13%, then the value of a share of VBS stock is closest to:

    ○A. $11.10

    ○B. $15.40

    ○C. $25.00

    ○D. $40.00

9.   You are interested in purchasing a new automobile that costs $35,000. The dealership offers you a special financing rate of 6% APR (0.5%) per month for 48 months. Assuming that you do not make a down payment on the auto and you take the dealer's financing deal, then your monthly car payments would be closest to:

  ○A. $729

  ○B. $822

  ○C. $647

  ○D. $842

10.   What must be the price of a $10,000 bond with a 6.5% coupon rate, semiannual coupons, and two years to maturity if it has a yield to maturity of 8% APR?

  ○A. $9727.76

  ○B. $10,754.44

  ○C. $10,619.63

  ○D. $9819.74

11.   If $10,000 is invested in a certain business at the start of the year, the investor will receive $3000 at the end of each of the next four years. What is the present value of this business opportunity if the interest rate is 7% per year?

  ○A. $178.88

  ○B. $172.45

  ○C. $148.53

  ○D. $161.63

12. Consider the following timeline detailing a stream of cash flows:

Date

| 0 | 1 | 2 | 3 | 4 |

? $5000 $6000 $7000 $8000

Cash flow

If the current market rate of interest is 8%, then the present value (PV) of this stream of cash flows is closest to:

○A. $21,211

○B. $22,871

○C. $26,000

○D. $24,074

13. NoGrowth Industries presently pays an annual dividend of $1.50 per share and it is expected that these dividend payments will continue indefinitely. If NoGrowth's equity cost of capital is 12%, then the value of a share of NoGrowth's stock is closest to:

○A. $12.50

○B. $14.00

○C. $15.00

○D. $10.00

14.

| 0 | 1 | 2 | 3 | 59 | 60 |

$62.50 $62.50 $62.50 $62.50 $62.50 + $5,000

A corporation issues a bond that generates the above cash flows. If the periods shown are 3 months, which of the following best describes that bond?

○A. a 60 − year bond with a notional value of $5000 and a coupon rate of 5% paid quarterly

○B. a 15 − year bond with a notional value of $5000 and a coupon rate of 5% paid quarterly

○C. a 15 − year bond with a notional value of $5000 and a coupon rate of 1.25% paid annually

○D. a 30 − year bond with a notional value of $5000 and a coupon rate of 3.75% paid semiannually

15. How much will the coupon payments be of a 30 − year $10,000 bond with a 4.5% coupon rate and semiannual payments?

- A. $450
- B. $30
- C. $350
- D. $225

16. A stock is expected to pay $3.20 per share every year indefinitely and the equity cost of capital for the company is 10%. What price would an investor be expected to pay per share next year?

- A. $8.00
- B. $16.00
- C. $32.00
- D. $24.00

17. Jumbuck Exploration has a current stock price of $2.00 and is expected to sell for $2.10 in one year's time, immediately after it pays a dividend of $0.26. Which of the following is closest to Jumbuck Exploration's equity cost of capital?

- A. 9%
- B. 12%
- C. 18%
- D. 22%

18. Gremlin Industries will pay a dividend of $1.80 per share this year. It is expected that this dividend will grow by 4% per year each year in the future. The current price of Gremlin's stock is $22.40 per share. What is Gremlin's equity cost of capital?

- A. 14%
- B. 16%
- C. 12%
- D. 11%

19. A lender lends $10,000, which is to be repaid in annual payments of $2,000 for 6 years. Which of the following shows the timeline of the loan from the lender's perspective?

A.

Year 0	Year 1	Year 2	Year 3	Year 4	Year 5	Year 6
-$10,000	$2000	$4000	$6000	$8000	$10,000	$12,000

B.

Year 0	Year 1	Year 2	Year 3	Year 4	Year 5	Year 6
-$10,000	$2000	$2000	$2000	$2000	$2000	$2000

C.

Year 1	Year 2	Year 3	Year 4	Year 5	Year 6
0	$2000	$2000	$2000	$2000	$2000

D.

Year 1	Year 2	Year 3	Year 4	Year 5	Year 6
-$10,000	$2000	$2000	$2000	$2000	$2000

20. Dan buys a property for $250,000. He is offered a 20 − year loan by the bank, at an interest rate of 6% per year. What is the annual loan payment Dan must make?

A. $24,864.98

B. $32,684.66

C. $21,796.14

D. $64,486.34

21. A risk − free, zero − coupon bond with a face value of $1,000 has 15 years to maturity. If the YTM is 5.8%, which of the following would be closest to the price this bond will trade at?

A. $525

B. $721

C. $429

D. $686

22. Clarissa wants to fund a growing perpetuity that will pay $5000 per year to a local museum, starting next year. She wants the annual amount paid to the museum to grow by 5% per year. Given that the interest rate is 8%, how much does she need to fund this perpetuity?

   ○A. $166,666.67

   ○B. $143,445.65

   ○C. $62,500.00

   ○D. $102,112.33

23. A company has stock which costs $42.00 per share and pays a dividend of $2.50 per share this year. The company's cost of equity is 8%. What is the expected annual growth rate of the company's dividends?

   ○A. 11%

   ○B. 2%

   ○C. 4%

   ○D. 8%

24. You are saving money to buy a car. If you save $300 per month starting one month from now at an interest rate of 4%, how much will you be able to spend on the car after saving for 4 years?

   ○A. $13,286.65

   ○B. $15,587.88

   ○C. $15,287.27

   ○D. $41,778.96

25. What is the coupon rate of a two − year, $10,000 bond with semiannual coupons and a price of $9543.45, if it has a yield to maturity of 6.8%?

   ○A. 4.32%

   ○B. 8.44%

   ○C. 5.60%

   ○D. 6.25%

1.   A

2.   C

3.   D

4.   D

5.   B

6.   C

7.   A

8.   C

9.   B

10.   A

11.   D

12.   A

13.   A

14.   B

15.   D

16.   C

17.   C

18.   C

19.   B

20.   C

21.   C

22.   A

23.   B

24.   B

25.   A

Chapters: 1, 2, 3, 4, 5, 6, 7, 8, 9, 11, 12, and 13

1) A C corporation earns $4.50 per share before taxes. The corporate tax rate is 35%, the personal tax rate on dividends is 20%, and the personal tax rate on non–dividend income is 39%. What is the total amount of taxes paid if the company pays a $2.00 dividend?
    A) $2.48   B) $1.98   C) $0.90   D) $1.58

2) Why in general do financial managers make financial decisions in a corporation, rather than the owners making these decisions themselves?
    A) The interests of the various owners may conflict with each other.
    B) It is best for the control of the finances of a corporation to be in the hands of a disinterested third party.
    C) The owners may not be U.S. citizens or residents.
    D) There are often many owners, and they can often change as they buy and sell stock.

3) Which of the following is NOT a function of the board of directors?
    A) answering to shareholders of the company
    B) monitoring the performance of the company
    C) determining how top executives should be compensated
    D) day–to–day running of the company

4) Which of the following is a measure of the aggregate price level of collections of pre–selected stocks?
    A) Euronext   B) NYSE   C) S&P 500   D) NASDAQ

5) Which of the following is not a role of financial institutions?
    A) Printing money for borrowers.   B) Moving funds from savers to borrowers.
    C) Spreading out risk–bearing.   D) Moving funds though time.

6) In the United States, publicly traded companies can choose whether or not they wish to release periodic financial statements.
    A) True   B) False

7) A company that produces drugs is preparing a balance sheet. Which of the following would be most likely to be considered a long–term asset on this balance sheet?
    A) a patent for a drug held by the company
    B) the cash reserves of the company
    C) commercial paper held by the company
    D) the inventory of chemicals used to produce the drugs made by the company

Luther Corporation
Consolidated Balance Sheet
December 31, 2006 and 2005 (in $ millions)

Assets	2006	2005	Liabilities and Stockholders' Equity	2006 2005
Current Assets			*Current Liabilities*	
Cash	63.6	58.5	Accounts payable	87.6 73.5
Accounts receivable	55.5	39.6	Notes payable / short-term debt	10.5 9.6
Inventories	45.9	42.9	Current maturities of long-term debt	39.9 36.9
Other current assets	6.0	3.0	Other current liabilities	6.0 12.0
Total current assets	171.0	144.0	Total current liabilities	144.0 132.0
Long–Term Assets			*Long–Term Liabilities*	
Land	66.6	62.1	Long-term debt	239.7 168.9
Buildings	109.5	91.5	Capital lease obligations	--- ---
Equipment	119.1	99.6	Total Debt	239.7 168.9
Less accumulated depreciation	(56.1)	(52.5)	Deferred taxes	22.8 22.2
Net property, plant, and equipment	239.1	200.7	Other long-term liabilities	--- ---
Goodwill	60.0	--	Total long-term liabilities	262.5 191.1
Other long-term assets	63.0	42.0	Total liabilities	406.5 323.1
Total long-term assets	362.1	242.7	Stockholders' Equity	126.6 63.6
Total Assets	**533.1**	**386.7**	**Total liabilities and Stockholders' Equity**	**533.1 386.7**

8) Refer to the balance sheet above. If in 2006 Luther has 10.2 million shares outstanding and these shares are trading at $16 per share, then Luther's market-to-book ratio would be closest to:
   A) 0.39   B) 0.76   C) 1.29   D) 2.57

9) Which of the following statements regarding the income statement is INCORRECT?
   A) The first line of an income statement lists the revenues from the sales of products or services.
   B) The income statement shows the earnings and expenses at a given point in time.
   C) The income statement shows the flow of earnings and expenses generated by the firm between two dates.
   D) The last or "bottom" line of the income statement shows the firm's net income.

Luther Corporation
Consolidated Income Statement
Year ended December 31 (in $ millions)

	2006	2005
Total sales	610.1	578.3
Cost of sales	(500.2)	(481.9)
Gross profit	109.9	96.4
Selling, general, and administrative expenses	(40.5)	(39.0)
Research and development	(24.6)	(22.8)
Depreciation and amortization	(3.6)	(3.3)
Operating income	41.2	31.3
Other income	---	---
Earnings before interest and taxes (EBIT)	41.2	31.3
Interest income (expense)	(25.1)	(15.8)
Pretax income	16.1	15.5
Taxes	(5.5)	(5.3)
Net income	10.6	10.2
Price per share	$16	$15
Shares outstanding (millions)	10.2	8.0
Stock options outstanding (millions)	0.3	0.2
Stockholders' Equity	126.6	63.6
Total Liabilities and Stockholders' Equity	533.1	386.7

10) Refer to the income statement above. Luther's operating margin for the year ending December 31, 2005 is closest to:

A) 1.8%   B) 2.7%   C) 5.4%   D) 16.7%

11) Allen Company bought a new copy machine to be depreciated straight line for three years for use by sales personnel. Where would this purchase be reflected on the Statement of Cash Flows?

A) It would be an addition to property, plant and equipment, so it would be an investing activity.
B) It would be an addition to cash, so would be reflected in the change in cash.
C) It would be an expense on the income statement, so it would be reflected in operating cash flows.
D) None of the above answers is correct.

12) If the risk–free rate of interest (r_f) is 6%, then you should be indifferent between receiving $250 today or

A) $250.00 in one year.   B) $265.00 in one year.
C) $235.85 in one year.   D) none of the above

13) A dollar today and a dollar in one year may be considered to be equivalent.

A) True   B) False

14) An investment will pay you $100 in one year and $200 in two years. If the interest rate is 5%, what is the present value of these cash flows?

A) $285.71   B) 258.32   C) $276.65   D) $305.00

15) A homeowner in a sunny climate has the opportunity to install a solar water heater in his home for a cost of $2400. After installation the solar water heater will produce a small amount of hot water every day, forever, and will require no maintenance. How much must the homeowner save on water heating costs every year if this is to be a sound investment? (The interest rate is 9% per year.)

    A) $262   B) $216   C) $248   D) $240

16) Which of the following would be LEAST likely to lower the interest rate that a bank offers a borrower?
    A) The expected inflation rate is expected to be low.
    B) The investment will be for a long period of time.
    C) The borrower is judged to have a low degree of risk.
    D) The number of borrowers seeking funds is low.

17) The effective annual rate (EAR) for a loan with a stated APR of 8% compounded monthly is closest to:
    A) 8.33%   B) 8.00%   C) 8.30%   D) 8.24%

18) You are considering purchasing a new truck that will cost you $34,000. The dealer offers you 1.9% APR financing for 48 months (with payments made at the end of the month). Assuming you finance the entire $34,000 and finance through the dealer, your monthly payments will be closest to:
    A) $736   B) $708   C) $1086   D) $594

19)
Term:	1 year	2 years	3 years	5 years	10 years	20 years
Rate:	5.00%	5.20%	5.40%	5.50%	5.76%	5.9%

Given the above term structure of interest rates, which of the following is most likely in the future?
Option I.   Interest rates will rise.
Option II.   Economic growth will slow.
Option III.   Long-term rates will fall relative to short term rates.
    A) Options I and II   B) Option II only   C) Option III only   D) Option I only

20) Which of the following is true about the face value of a bond?
    A) It is the amount that is repaid at maturity.
    B) It is the notional amount we use to compute coupon payments.
    C) It is usually denominated in standard increments, such as $1,000.
    D) All of the above are true.

21) Which of the following statements is FALSE?
    A) Treasury bills are U.S. government bonds with a maturity of up to one year.
    B) The amount of each coupon payment is determined by the coupon rate of the bond.
    C) The simplest type of bond is a zero-coupon bond.
    D) Prior to its maturity date, the price of a zero-coupon bond is always greater than its face value.

22) What is the yield to maturity of a ten-year, $1000 bond with a 5.2% coupon rate and semiannual coupons if this bond is currently trading for a price of $884?
    A) 6.23%   B) 5.02%   C) 6.82%   D) 12.46%

23) Which of the following statements are true?
    A) A fall in bond prices causes interest rates to fall.
    B) A rise in interest rates causes bond prices to fall.
    C) Bond prices and interest rates are not connected.
    D) A fall in interest rates causes a fall in bond prices.

24) A corporate bond which receives a BBB rating from Standard and Poor's is considered
    A) an investment grade bond.   B) a defaulted bond.
    C) a high–yield bond.   D) a junk bond.

25) Which of the following formulas is INCORRECT?

    A) g = retention rate × return on new investment   B) $r_E = \dfrac{Div_1}{P_0} - g$

    C) $Div_t = EPS_t$ × Dividend Payout Rate   D) $P_0 = \dfrac{Div_1}{r_E - g}$

26) Von Bora Corporation (VBC) is expected to pay a $2.00 dividend at the end of this year. If you expect VBC's dividend to grow by 5% per year forever and VBC's equity cost of capital is 13%, then the value of a share of VBS stock is closest to:
    A) $40.00   B) $25.00   C) $11.10   D) $15.40

27) Stocks that do not pay a dividend must have a value of $0.
    A) True   B) False

28) An auto–parts company is deciding whether to sponsor a racing team for a cost of $1 million. The sponsorship would last for three years and is expected to increase cash flows by $580,000 per year. If the discount rate is 7.5%, what will be the change in the value of the company if it chooses to go ahead with the sponsorship?
    A) $508,305   B) $740,000   C) $863,000   D) $808,786

29) Which of the following statements is FALSE?
    A) If the cost of capital estimate is more than the internal rate of return (IRR), the net present value (NPV) will be positive.
    B) The internal rate of return (IRR) can provide information on how sensitive your analysis is to errors in the estimate of your cost of capital.
    C) In general, the difference between the cost of capital and the internal rate of return (IRR) is the maximum amount of estimation error in the cost of capital estimate that can exist without altering the original decision.
    D) If you are unsure of your cost of capital estimate, it is important to determine how sensitive your analysis is to errors in this estimate.

30) According to Graham and Harvey's 2001 survey (Figure 8.2 in the text), the most popular decision rules for capital budgeting used by CFOs are:
    A) IRR, NPV, Payback period   B) MIRR, IRR, Payback period
    C) NPV, IRR, MIRR   D) Profitability index, NPV, IRR

31) Internal rate of return (IRR) can reliably be used to choose between mutually exclusive projects.
    A) True   B) False

32) Which of the following decision rules is best defined as the amount of time it takes to pay back the initial investment?
    A) profitability index   B) payback period
    C) net present value (NPV)   D) internal rate of return (IRR)

33) How does the capital budgeting process begin?
    A) by analyzing alternate projects
    B) by forecasting the future consequences for the firm of each potential project
    C) by evaluating the net present value (NPV) of each project's cash flows
    D) by compiling a list of potential projects

34) Cameron Industries is purchasing a new chemical vapor depositor in order to make silicon chips. It will cost $6 million to buy the machine and $10,000 to have it delivered and installed. Building a clean room in the plant for the machine will cost an additional $3 million. The machine is expected to have a working life of six years. If straight-line depreciation is used, what are the yearly depreciation expenses in this case?
    A) $1,000,000   B) $1,501,667   C) $1,001,667   D) $1,500,000

35) Which of the following statements is FALSE?
    A) Many projects use a resource that the company already owns.
    B) As a practical matter, to derive the forecasted cash flows of a project, financial managers often begin by forecasting earnings.
    C) Only include as incremental expenses in your capital budgeting analysis the additional overhead expenses that arise because of the decision to take on the project.
    D) When evaluating a capital budgeting decision, we generally include interest expense.

36) Which of the following adjustments should NOT be made when computing free cash flow from incremental earnings?
    A) subtracting increases in Net Working Capital
    B) adding depreciation
    C) subtracting all non-cash expenses
    D) subtracting depreciation expenses from taxable earnings

37) Which of the following statements is FALSE?
    A) When evaluating a capital budgeting project, financial managers should make the decision that maximizes net present value (NPV).
    B) Sensitivity analysis reveals which aspects of the project are most critical when we are actually managing the project.
    C) The break-even level of an input is the level for which the investment has an internal rate of return (IRR) of zero.
    D) The most difficult part of capital budgeting is deciding how to estimate the cash flows and the cost of capital.

38) Historically, stocks have delivered a _____ return on average compared to Treasury bills but have experienced _____ fluctuations in values.
    A) higher, lower   B) lower, higher   C) higher, higher   D) lower, lower

39) You own shares in Yahoo that were purchased at a price of $21 per share. Microsoft has offered to purchase Yahoo and buy your shares at a price of $31 per share. What will be your return if you tender your shares to Microsoft and the deal is completed?
    A) 43.34%   B) 49.65%   C) 47.62%   D) 33.45%

40) Which of the following statements is FALSE?
   A) Riskier investments must offer investors higher average returns to compensate them for the extra risk they are taking on.
   B) Volatility seems to be a reasonable measure of risk when evaluating returns on large portfolios and the returns of individual securities.
   C) Investments with higher volatility have rewarded investors with higher average returns.
   D) Investments with higher volatility should have a higher risk premium and, therefore, higher returns.

41) The risk that inflation rates are likely to increase in the next year is an example of common risk.
   A) True   B) False

42) In general, it is possible to eliminate _____ risk by holding a large portfolio of assets.
   A) systematic   B) unsystematic and systematic
   C) unsystematic   D) none of the above

43) When we combine stocks in a portfolio, the amount of risk that is eliminated depends on the degree to which the stocks face common risks and move together.
   A) True   B) False

44) You expect General Motors (GM) to have a beta of 1.3 over the next year and the beta of Exxon Mobil (XOM) to be 0.9 over the next year. Also, you expect the volatility of General Motors to be 40% and that of Exxon Mobil to be 30% over the next year. Which stock has more systematic risk? Which stock has more total risk?
   A) XOM, GM   B) XOM, XOM   C) GM, GM   D) GM, XOM

45) Your estimate of the market risk premium is 7%. The risk-free rate of return is 3.5% and General Motors has a beta of 1.3. According to the Capital Asset Pricing Model (CAPM), what is its expected return?
   A) 12.6%   B) 11.3%   C) 12.9%   D) 12.1%

46) The relative proportion of debt, equity, and other securities that a firm has outstanding constitute its
   A) current ratio.   B) capital structure.   C) asset ratio.   D) none of the above

47) The fact that the interest paid on debt is a tax-deductible expense increases the cost of debt financing.
   A) True   B) False

48) Ford Motor Company is discussing new ways to recapitalize the firm and raise additional capital. Its current capital structure has a 20% weight in equity, 10% in preferred stock, and 70% in debt. The cost of equity capital is 14%, the cost of preferred stock is 10%, and the pretax cost of debt is 9%. What is the weighted average cost of capital for Ford if its marginal tax rate is 30%?
   A) 8.21%   B) 7.87%   C) 9.21%   D) 8.89%

49) Divisional costs of capital are more appropriate when evaluating a project for a line of business when the types of business in a firm are
   A) different.   B) similar.   C) mature businesses.   D) new businesses.

50) Internal financing is more costly than external financing because of issuance costs.
   A) True   B) False

1) B
2) D
3) D
4) C
5) A
6) FALSE
7) A
8) C
9) B
10) C
11) A
12) B
13) FALSE
14) C
15) B
16) B
17) C
18) A
19) D
20) D
21) D
22) C
23) B
24) A
25) B
26) B
27) FALSE
28) A
29) A
30) A
31) FALSE
32) B
33) D
34) C
35) D
36) D
37) C
38) C
39) C
40) B
41) TRUE
42) C
43) TRUE
44) C
45) A
46) B
47) FALSE
48) A
49) A
50) FALSE

Index

Note to reader: **Bold** page numbers refer to key topics, page numbers followed by *f* refer to figures, numbers followed by *t* refer to tables, and numbers followed by *b* refer to boxes. Numbers preceded by n. refer to content in footnotes.